The Translator

PETER CONSTANTINE is the translator of *The Complete Works of Isaac Babel*, which received the Koret Jewish Literature Award and a National Jewish Book Award citation. His numerous translations include *Six Stories* by Thomas Mann, which was awarded the PEN Translation Prize, and *The Undiscovered Chekhov: Forty-Three New Stories*, which received the National Translation Award. He has also translated works by Gogol, Tolstoy, and Dostoevsky. He is currently co-editing an anthology of Greek poetry from Homer to the present.

The Editor

GREGORY FREIDIN is Professor of Slavic Languages and Literatures at Stanford University. He is the author of a critical biography, *A Coat of Many Colors: Osip Mandelstam and His Mythologies of Self-Presentation*, and has published widely on modern Russian literature, culture, and current affairs. After writing and lecturing on Babel for many years, he is completing a book on Babel's life and legacy.

D1551567

W. W. NORTON & COMPANY, INC.
Also Publishes

A NORTON CRITICAL EDITION

ISAAC BABEL'S
SELECTED WRITINGS

AUTHORITATIVE TEXTS

SELECTED LETTERS, 1926–1939

ISAAC BABEL THROUGH THE EYES
OF HIS CONTEMPORARIES

ISAAC BABEL IN CRITICISM AND SCHOLARSHIP

Translated by
PETER CONSTANTINE

Selected and Edited by
GREGORY FREIDIN
STANFORD UNIVERSITY

W. W. NORTON & COMPANY • *New York* • *London*

W. W. Norton & Company has been independent since its founding in 1923, when William Warder Norton and Mary D. Herter Norton first published lectures delivered at the People's Institute, the adult education division of New York City's Cooper Union. The firm soon expanded its program beyond the Institute, publishing books by celebrated academics from America and abroad. By mid-century, the two major pillars of Norton's publishing program—trade books and college texts—were firmly established. In the 1950s, the Norton family transferred control of the company to its employees, and today—with a staff of four hundred and a comparable number of trade, college, and professional titles published each year—W. W. Norton & Company stands as the largest and oldest publishing house owned wholly by its employees.

Copyright © 2010 by W. W. Norton & Company, Inc.

All rights reserved.
Printed in the United States of America.
First Edition.

Every effort has been made to contact the copyright holders of each selection. Rights holders of selections not credited should contact W. W. Norton & Company at the address below for a correction to be made.

The text of this book is composed in Fairfield Medium
with the display set in Bernhard Modern.
Composition by Binghamton Valley Composition.
Manufacturing by the Maple-Vail Book Group.
Book design by Antonina Krass.
Production manager: Eric Pier-Hocking.

Library of Congress Cataloging-in-Publication Data

Babel', I. (Isaak), 1894–1941.
[Selections. English. 2006]
Issac Babel's selected writings / Isaac Babel ; translated by
Peter Constantine ; selected and edited by Gregory Freidin.
p. cm.—(Norton critical edition)
Includes bibliographical references.

ISBN: 978-0-393-92703-0 (pbk.)

1. Babel', I. (Isaak), 1894–1941—Translations into English.
2. Babel', I. (Isaak), 1894–1941—Correspondence.   3. Babel', I. (Isaak),
1894–1941—Criticism and interpretation.   I. Constantine, Peter, 1963–
II. Freidin, Gregory.   III. Title.   IV. Title: Selected writings.
PG3476.B2A2 2006
891.73'42—dc22
2006047243

W. W. Norton & Company, Inc., 500 Fifth Avenue
New York, N.Y. 10110-0017
wwnorton.com

W. W. Norton & Company Ltd., Castle House
75/76 Wells Street, London W1T 3QT

1 2 3 4 5 6 7 8 9 0

Contents

Selected Letters of Isaac Babel to His Sister and Mother, 1926–1939

Isaac Babel Through the Eyes of His Contemporaries

Criticism

Introduction

There are writers with a personal myth and writers without one. Ivan Turgenev and Henry James led interesting lives, but they did not cultivate their biographies in their fiction. It was otherwise for their contemporary, Leo Tolstoy. Having made his name with an eyewitness war story and the thinly veiled autobiographical *Childhood*, he went on to shape his long career in letters—from *The Cossacks* to *Confession*—as an increasingly personal moral and religious quest. A count turned peasant, an agnostic novelist turned religious prophet, a conservative turned radical visionary— Tolstoy became part of Tolstoy's writings, both in form and subject. Maxim Gorky, Tolstoy's celebrated young contemporary, radiated a mythic aura throughout much of his career. His public quest was even more personal. He ascended, or, better, pulled himself up by his bootstraps from the lower depths, to the summit of literary Olympus—an outcast and an exemplar of redemption through art who had crisscrossed on foot the length and breadth of provincial Russia. For his readers, Gorky's life lent a special authenticity to his fiction, and his fiction to his life.

Isaac Babel grew up in the shadow of Tolstoy's celebrity and entered the world of letters in 1916 as a protégé of Gorky. He was to become a worthy heir to their cultural legacy, but, as often happens in such cases, he did not inherit it entirely by choice. For his readers, however, his fiction and non-fiction, related documents and historical events naturally arrange themselves around their magnet—Isaac Babel, the author, the narrator, the man—all of them real and all of them imagined. After his meteoric rise to acclaim in the mid-1920s, Isaac Babel became inseparable from the Babel myth.

This is why the present volume brings together, along with his writings in the award-winning translation of Peter Constantine, a selection of letters, key documents and reminiscences of his contemporaries, a small set of critical views from the early 1920s to the present, and a chronology of his life and works. The aim is to allow the English-speaking reader to re-create the ambient space in which Babel's distinct voice first rang out and has been resonating to this day.

Little in his background could have suggested such a distinguished career. He was born in 1894 to a middle-class Jewish family in the port city of Odessa on the southwestern border of a tottering imperial colossus— modern Europe's last *ancien régime*. Despite the official restrictions on Jews in Russia, Babel's parents threw in their lot with the country and its modernization. Unschooled formally, they made sure that their two children received a good secular Russian education, replete with foreign languages and music lessons. In the manner of the time and place, they exposed Isaac and his sister Maria to some traditional Jewish instruction, but in moderate amounts (whatever Babel may have later claimed). Their firstborn, Isaac, was to make a successful career in business or law, or both. He graduated from a practical and progressive high school in Odessa (the so-called Commercial School), went on to get a business degree at the Commercial Institute in Kiev, and after graduation pursued a law degree at the Petrograd Free Public University (formerly the Psycho-Neurological Institute, founded by liberal Russian psychiatrist Vladimir Bekhterev).

But events in Petrograd took a surprising albeit not entirely unexpected turn. The heart of an aspiring author was beating under the uniform of the young *Bekhterevka* law student, and on an ordinary day in early November 1916, fortune smiled on him. He was, all of a sudden, lifted out of obscurity by Maxim Gorky's caring hand. By the end of the month, his name and that of Gorky, then Russia's most famous living author, were listed in the table of contents of *Letopis* (Chronicle), Gorky's journal of "literary and public affairs." Soon after came the Russian Revolution, and the rest . . . well, the rest is Babel's and Russia's history, both obscured and illuminated by Babel's compact and brilliant oeuvre.

Babel's early writings do not lend themselves readily to a "biography." He owed his later fame to the civil war and the revolution that triggered it. What sealed his fate was a cycle of stories ostensibly resembling entries in a personal diary—*Red Cavalry*—his unrivaled civil-war masterpiece. Published over a period of four years and collected into a book in 1926, these stories transformed a promising young author into a figure for whom the boundaries between his art and life were permeable, and whom readers perceived from then on in the glow of the Babel myth. When he stepped out onto the Russian and then international stage as the author of *Red Cavalry*, he came in the guise of his fictional legend: the proverbial bespectacled Jewish intellectual, transfixed, like his narrator and alter ego Lyutov, between a passionate commitment to a Marxist dream and the means—brutal, bloody, and base—required for its realization.

There was a need for such a proverbial character type in the twentieth century, as there was in the nineteenth for Balzac's Rastignac, Stendhal's Julien Sorel, Dostoevsky's Raskolnikov, or Tolstoy's Pierre Bezukhov. It fell to Babel's character Lyutov or Lyutov's creator Babel (often thought of as one and the same in myth) to fill this outstanding "social command"—the phrase Marxist critics invoked when they encountered writers or characters who seemed to be summoned up by history itself. Indeed, the twentieth century would be much duller without the figure of a politically engaged Jewish intellectual—"with glasses on his nose and autumn in his heart," at once an activist and *littérateur*, and one whose "ancient body" could "barely harness the storms" of his imagination ("How Things Were Done in Odessa" and "The Rabbi's Son"). We owe this prototypical figure to Isaac Babel. Creator and protagonist of the Babel myth, he both embodied and reenacted the deep and pervasive ironies of the century known for its world wars and one "world revolution."

Parallel to the character of a wimpy "four-eyed" war reporter and propagandist embedded amid Red Cossack brutes, Babel was developing the myth of his native city. *The Odessa Stories* were written and published at the same time as the *Red Cavalry* tales, and they transformed Babel's provincial birthplace into Russia's mythic Marseille by the Black Sea. Verily, the fabled author of *Red Cavalry* could not have been born anywhere other than in a fabled city. In Babel's fiction, the actual declining Odessa of his youth was outrigged as a giant stage on which larger-than-life operatic characters—the Jewish gangster Benya Krik and Lyubka the Cossack—could strut their outsized passions and instincts in full-dress Rabelaisian fashion. A mirror of the tragic world of revolution and civil war, Babel's Odessa was a comic, parodic parallel universe where colorful life overflowed with pleasures and men of violence preferred to shoot in the air "because if you don't shoot into the air you might kill someone" ("The King"). This personal myth turned out to be a great find, a true gold vein, and Babel mined it with gusto and imagination.

Next came the invention of Babel's mythic childhood, what Babel himself once offhandedly referred to as his "fictional autobiography." The result was another cycle, named after the first of its novellas, *The Story of My Dovecote*. Written between 1925 and 1937, these stories illuminated decisive moments, enchanting and cruel, in the narrator's early years. As a totality, they added up to an archetypal twentieth-century Jewish boyhood. There are only five novellas in this cycle, but they form a strong and prolific literary tree. Its roots go back to the fictionalized childhoods of Tolstoy and Gorky, while its branches, cross-bred with psychoanalysis, stretch all the way to the United States, where they bore fruit in the first-person cyclical narrative fiction of Grace Paley, Philip Roth, and others.

Even before the publication of *Red Cavalry* as a book in 1926, Babel began to chafe under the burden of the myth that he and the Revolution had created. In his film script for *Benya Krik*, he put a bullet through the head of the famous gangster, his mythic outlaw other. Babel may not have taken his film work seriously, but this was nevertheless a fateful gesture. He paraded Benya Krik for the last time in his 1928 play *Sunset*, in which Krik figures as a greedy mobster willing to risk killing his father for the sake of bourgeois respectability and cash.

"Make way for time" is a phrase repeated throughout the play, and in the late 1920s, Babel tried to heed it. Although the imaginary universe of his myth had an infinite potential for expression, the kind of expression it could generate fit poorly with the rhythms and colors of a country undergoing another—this time *Stalinist*—revolution. Irony, absence of a clearly articulated authoritative tone, and a deliberately elusive authorial intent—the very timbre of Babel's voice—were out of tune with the bravura music of the Five-Year Plans' cultural regimentation and repression. Babel looked for ways to adjust to the new realities.

He tried his hand at longer, third-person narrative fiction (*The Jewess*), but for whatever reason—lacking the instinct for this genre, discouraged by censorship, or both—he could not sustain it. Later on, in the manner of the day, when writers and artists were urged by the party-state to bear witness to the great feats of socialist construction, he traveled widely to collect material and impressions for what he thought would be his new fiction. Two of his stories about the collectivization of agriculture have survived, and one "Gapa Guzhva" (1931), was published. It is a tale about a village whore who, after days of rustic revelry, decides to join the collective farm because "under socialism whores will have a different, better life." In the sole surviving "industrial" story, oil refineries and production goals commingle with the personal drama of a young pregnant Russian woman, who has been abandoned by her Jewish lover, an engineering luminary, and is deciding whether to abort or not ("Petroleum," 1934). Although not disloyal, the stories were uncompromising in tone, pungent, vintage Babel, and—out of place.

Babel imagined he would be able to respond to the new challenge by resurrecting his operatic Jewish gangster type as the semi-reformed Soviet criminal Kolya Topuz. Nothing came of it. Babel either did not like the results or may have decided to drop the concept, realizing Topuz had been eclipsed by Ostap Bender, the sly operator protagonist of *The Twelve Chairs* and *The Little Golden Calf*, picaresque satires co-authored by young Odessans Ilya Ilf and Evgeny Petrov that were enormously popular in the early 1930s. All that has survived of Babel's experiments with Kolya Topuz are the memories of Babel's associates, who recall laughing heartily as he regaled them with anecdotes about Kolya's trials and tribulations.

A similar fate awaited another attempt to march in step with the times. Babel projected a book or a set of stories about Betal Kalmykov, the party boss of the small, poor, and backward Caucasus republic of Kabardino-Balkaria, then making remarkable progress. Kalmykov and Babel became friends: one, a "native," provincial viceroy with a heavy hand and a good heart, the other, the empire's literary celebrity, mesmerized by power. What drew Babel to Kalmykov was the contrast between the primitive and the visionary—a contrast that electrified his civil war stories. But there were problems. By the mid-1930s, the Soviet Union was already laying claim to great power status while projecting a more conventional, civilized image of itself abroad. Any emphasis on backwardness or primitivism was, on Stalin's orders, invariably suppressed. Babel learned this the hard way. The film *Bezhin Meadow*, on which he collaborated with director Sergei Eisenstein in 1936, was banned the following year, its entire stock destroyed, because the film, loyal in every other respect, dwelled on the contrast between the traditional forms of village culture and the new "content" of Soviet rural life. The Kalmykov project was no longer worth pursuing, except in table talk with good friends.

There was little chance for the realization of Babel's other much rumored project, a book about the Cheka, the Soviet secret police. As repression mounted, stories about the all-powerful "organs" became unfit even for oral transmission. In this atmosphere, Babel had ample reason to be practicing what he himself called in 1934 "the genre of literary silence." But there were significant pauses in this silence, too.

Stalinist cultural policies greatly narrowed the range of themes that could explore ambiguities of any sort, limiting it to the days of the old regime and to some extent the period of the Revolution and civil war. Given these constraints, Babel had no choice for expression except through the medium of the story lines he had established in the 1920s, which formed the core of his personal mythology. In the early 1930s he turned to rewriting his early Petersburg stories, using them also as a setting for the play *Maria*—all part of a strategy to safeguard his integrity as an artist and his reputation as an active author, even if this forced him into reviving his old myths.

Red Cavalry too was "recycled," receiving a new ending, the story "Argamak" (1932). In it, Lyutov, whom the Cossacks mock for his horsemanship, becomes an expert at riding a submissive mount. Pegasus has been tamed, its wings clipped. *The Odessa Stories* evolved in a like manner. Some of the more colorful figures were forcibly relocated to a new Soviet old-age home, and the good gangster Froim Grach was unceremoniously executed in the backyard of the Odessa Cheka ("The End of the Almshouse," 1932, and "Froim Grach," 1933).

The last known "childhood" story, "Di Grasso" offers a glimpse into the way Babel may have intended to develop his autobiographical fiction. The irreverent, adventuresome boy of *The Story of My Dovecote* is now seen scalping tickets for the primitive but powerful Sicilian tragedian on tour in Odessa. The boy has pawned his father's watch and is contemplating an escape abroad, unless he can make enough money to redeem the timepiece. Knowing Babel's biography, one reads the story as an allegory of Babel's career as an author—from *The Odessa Stories* and *Red Cavalry* to his failure to write a new Soviet masterpiece about the Five-Year Plan. To appreciate the allegory, one need only substitute Babel's *Red Cavalry* and *The Odessa Stories* for Di Grasso's primitive art (a distillation of circus and Italian opera); Babel's unredeemed publishers' advances for the pawning of a watch; Babel's lucrative moonlighting as a writer of film scripts and dialogue for the boy's ticket scalping; and Babel's thoughts about emigration (he contemplated it more than once) for the boy's escape plans. As to the father whose wrath was almost enough to drive the boy out of the country, one can easily draw an analogy with the "father of all people," Joseph Stalin; he haunted the thoughts of Babel's contemporaries, especially if they owed Stalin a debt, as Babel did. The story has a happy ending. The wife of the gangster who had pocketed the boy's watch is so moved by Di Grasso's great performance that she forces her husband to make restitution. A beneficiary of Di Grasso's artistry, the boy, the future writer, is now free to experience his final epiphany. The story ends with him standing alone under the moonlit statue of Alexander Pushkin, transfixed by the world's "serenity and ineffable beauty."

"Di Grasso" was published during the centenary of Pushkin's death in 1937, the year that also marked the peak of Stalin's mass terror. Babel's friends, the friends of his friends, as well as their friends had been disappearing at an alarming rate. Against this background, "Di Grasso" reads like a magic spell, a wish, a prayer for a deliverance. But what happened later unfolded according to a script very different from the one in the story. The "silent" Babel owed a debt to the Revolution that had once exalted him, and the debt kept compounding. Stalin inquired about Babel's progress on "his book" and soon after gave the sanction to arrest him. On May 15, 1939, at a time when the Great Terror was actually waning, the gates of the Lubyanka prison closed behind Babel and his entire personal archive. Neither was to be seen again.

In his 1932 story "Guy de Maupassant," a young writer learns that success in belles lettres exacts a price, but the story ends before he has to pay it. During his first interrogation in the Lubyanka prison, before he was formally charged, Babel was asked to give the reason for his arrest. In response, he cited his recent failure to write and publish. He was doubly a prisoner of the Gulag *and* of his own myth of the revolutionary writer, to which he owed his celebrity. On January 26, 1940, in a Kafkaesque parody of a trial, Babel was convicted of the preposterous charge of espionage for France and Austria as well as membership in an anti-Soviet Trotskyist

organization. The next day he was shot in the back of his head by one of
the chief executioners. He was forty-five years old. His body was cremated
and buried in the same unmarked grave as his friend, Betal Kalmykov and
his accuser, Nikolay Ezhov, former head of the NKVD.

"You don't know what you love, Gedali! I am going to shoot you, and
then you'll know, and I cannot *not* shoot, because I am the Revolution!" he
wrote in his 1924 story "Gedali." The writer's tragic end authenticated his
fiction.

The "social command" of history that once summoned Babel to write
Red Cavalry, The Odessa Stories, and *The Story of My Dovecote* emerged in
another place and another time. In the United States of the 1940s and
1950s, a pleiad of young American writers began to narrate stories of their
own emergence from a more traditional, marginal Jewish-American milieu
into the world of full-throated cosmopolitan American citizenship. The
transition was paid for in the blood spilled by their fathers, uncles, and
older brothers in World War II. To paraphrase Philip Roth, Babel's *ghost*
could still be seen bending over the desk of more than one American
writer.

A Note on the Translations
and Annotations

The writings of Isaac Babel published here are in Peter Constantine's translation, first published in *The Complete Works of Isaac Babel* (New York: W. W. Norton & Company, 2002). Some of the annotations to Babel's works that appear in this Norton Critical Edition are his; others—marked "*Ed.*"—are by its editor, Gregory Freidin. Isaac Babel's letters are translated by Andrew R. MacAndrew and Max Hayward; unless otherwise indicated, reminiscences of his contemporaries, and contemporary views are translated and annotated by the editor of this Norton Critical Edition.

A Note on the Organization
of the Collection

With the exception of *Red Cavalry* there is no accepted standard order to the publication of Babel's works. As a rule, editors respect the boundaries of his more or less complete cycles (*Red Cavalry*, *The Odessa Stories*, and *The Story of My Dovecote* or the "childhood cycle"), divide his works by genre (for example, stories, journalism, plays, essays), and wherever possible pay homage to the chronological order and Babel's editions published in his lifetime. Babel himself worked in "cycles," conceiving his stories as parts of a larger set, its meaning different from and exceeding the sum of its parts. In this regard, Babel followed the path well-trodden by Russian modernist poets, especially Alexander Blok. For reasons that may have had little or nothing to do with the author's will and everything with the times and the author's violent death, some of the cycles remained barely sketched out, some reached us woefully incomplete, and others, like the *Hershele* cycle and a planned "industrial" set, are represented by only one story. I have chosen to downplay the genre distinctions and to structure this volume according to key themes: geographic locations so important to Babel (Petersburg, the Polish Campaign, the Caucasus, Odessa, Paris) and subject (childhood, collectivization, and industrialization). Within each section, I tried to observe chronological order, making the 1933 play *Maria* part of the Petersburg section and the 1926 *Sunset* part of Odessa. This form of organization, I hope, will give the reader a better sense of what Babel's complete oeuvre might have looked like.

Throughout his career, Babel continued to revise his writings for aesthetic reasons and when forced by political circumstances or personal considerations. Wherever possible the translations in this edition are based on the last published version to appear in Babel's lifetime. In exceptional cases, differences between the earlier and later versions are indicated in the annotations. In those cases where Babel's revisions were clearly forced by the censor, the translation follows the earlier, uncensored publication.

Acknowledgments

This edition would have been impossible without the work of the Isaac Babel editors and scholars—Antonina Pirozhkova and the late Nathalie Babel foremost among them—who have kept his legacy alive and his writings accessible to the public. I am especially indebted to Nathalie Babel, a friend of many years, who proposed this edition and helped me along as the volume was taking shape. The three English-language collections of her father's writings she edited and introduced over the last four decades have been invaluable. I am equally grateful to Antonina Nikolayevna Pirozhkova and Lydia Isaakovna Babel who have always been generous with their knowledge and advice. I have repeatedly relied on the two-volume edition of Isaac Babel that Pirozhkova edited and compiled, with annotations by Sergey Povartsov: *Sochineniya v dvukh tomakh* (Moscow: Khudozhestvennaya literature, 1990). Among many Russian-language editions of Babel, I would also like to single out the two that were edited and annotated by Efraim Sicher: *Petersburg 1918* (Ann Arbor: Ardis, 1989) and *Detstvo I drugie rasskazy* (Jerusalem: Biblioteka Aliya, 1979). Another volume of distinction is *Izbrannoe*, edited and annotated by Elena Krasnoshchekova (Moscow: Khudozhestvennaya literature, 1966). I have consulted these editions on a regular basis.

During the many stages of manuscript preparation, I have been assisted by Stanford University's graduate students who share with me a keen interest in Isaac Babel and modern Russian literature. I wish to express my special gratitude to Elif Batuman, Martha Kelly, and Ilja Gruen for their help with editing and translations. I want to thank Philipp Dziadko, who rendered valuable assistance with archival collections in Moscow. I am also grateful to my colleagues Evgeny Dobrenko, Lazar Fleishman, Joseph Frank, Monika Greenleaf, Gabriella Safran, Eric Naiman, Yuri Slezkine, William Mills Todd III, Carl Weber, Victor Zhivov, and Steven Zipperstein for their comments and suggestions regarding my own contributions to this volume. I want to thank Tatyana Litvinova and the late Ilya Slonim for sharing with me their memories of Babel and his circle; their recollections breathed life into more than one scholarly annotation. I have also benefited from the unfailing sense of style and phrasing of Anna Bonnell-Freidin, my daughter, who has given me many hours of editorial assistance and advice. When I agreed to undertake this Norton Critical Edition, I had only a vague idea of its scope and complexity; what made it possible for me to keep to the publication schedule while enjoying the intellectual challenge was the encouragement, support, and, most important, expert editorial assistance offered generously by my wife, Victoria E. Bonnell, to whom I owe my deepest gratitude.

ISAAC BABEL'S
SELECTED WRITINGS

Unacknowledged Beginning

When he published "Old Shloyme" in 1913, the year of the Beilis trial, Isaac Babel was in his second year studying economics and business at the Kiev Commercial Institute. The weekly *Ogni*, which he had chosen as his venue, was known for its left-wing politics, and as a student Babel took some risk in associating himself with it. The earliest known publication by Babel, this story may have been Babel's debut as a writer, but he never referred to it in print. —*Ed.*

Old Shloyme[1]

Although our town is small, its inhabitants few in number, and although Shloyme had not left this town once in sixty years, you'd be hard-pressed to find a single person who was able to tell you exactly who Shloyme was or what he was all about. The reason for this, plain and simple, is that he was forgotten, the way you forget an unnecessary thing that doesn't jump out and grab you. Old Shloyme was precisely that kind of thing. He was eighty-six years old. His eyes were watery. His face—his small, dirty, wrinkled face—was overgrown with a yellowish beard that had never been combed, and his head was covered with a thick, tangled mane. Shloyme almost never washed, seldom changed his clothes, and gave off a foul stench. His son and daughter-in-law, with whom he lived, had stopped bothering about him—they kept him in a warm corner and forgot about him. His warm corner and his food were all that Shloyme had left, and it seemed that this was all he needed. For him, warming his old broken bones and eating a nice, fat, juicy piece of meat were the purest bliss. He was the first to come to the table, and greedily watched every bite with unflinching eyes, convulsively cramming food into his mouth with his long bony fingers, and he ate, ate, ate till they refused to give him any more, even a tiny little piece. Watching Shloyme eat was disgusting: his whole puny body quivered, his fingers covered with grease, his face so pitiful, filled with the dread that someone might harm him, that he might be forgotten. Sometimes his daughter-in-law would play a little trick on Shloyme. She would serve the food, and then act as if she had overlooked him. The old man would begin to get agitated, look around helplessly, and try to smile with his twisted, toothless mouth. He wanted to show that food was not important to him, that he could perfectly well make do without it, but there was so much pleading in the depths of his eyes, in the crease of his mouth, in his outstretched, imploring arms,

---

1. First published in the Kiev weekly *Ogni* (no. 6, February 9, 1913).

3

and his smile, wrenched with such difficulty, was so pitiful, that all jokes were dropped, and Shloyme received his portion.

And thus he lived in his corner—he ate and slept, and in the summer he also lay baking in the sun. It seemed that he had long ago lost all ability to comprehend anything. Neither his son's business nor household matters interested him. He looked blankly at everything that took place around him, and the only fear that would flutter up in him was that his grandson might catch on that he had hidden a dried-up piece of honey cake under his pillow. Nobody ever spoke to Shloyme, asked his advice about anything, or asked him for help. And Shloyme was quite happy, until one day his son came over to him after dinner and shouted loudly into his ear, "Papa, they're going to evict us from here! Are you listening? Evict us, kick us out!" His son's voice was shaking, his face twisted as if he were in pain. Shloyme slowly raised his faded eyes, looked around, vaguely comprehending something, wrapped himself tighter in his greasy frock coat, didn't say a word, and shuffled off to sleep.

From that day on Shloyme began noticing that something strange was going on in the house. His son was crestfallen, wasn't taking care of his business, and at times would burst into tears and look furtively at his chewing father. His grandson stopped going to high school. His daughter-in-law yelled shrilly, wrung her hands, pressed her son close to her, and cried bitterly and profusely.

Shloyme now had an occupation, he watched and tried to comprehend. Muffled thoughts stirred in his long-torpid brain. "They're being kicked out of here!" Shloyme knew why they were being kicked out. "But Shloyme can't leave! He's eighty-six years old! He wants to stay warm! It's cold outside, damp. . . . No! Shloyme isn't going anywhere! He has nowhere to go, nowhere!" Shloyme hid in his corner and wanted to clasp the rickety wooden bed in his arms, caress the stove, the sweet, warm stove that was as old as he was. "He grew up here, spent his poor, bleak life here, and wants his old bones to be buried in the small local cemetery!" At moments when such thoughts came to him, Shloyme became unnaturally animated, walked up to his son, wanted to talk to him with passion and at great length, to give him advice on a couple of things, but . . . it had been such a long time since he had spoken to anyone, or given anyone advice. And the words froze in his toothless mouth, his raised arm dropped weakly. Shloyme, all huddled up as if ashamed at his outburst, sullenly went back to his corner and listened to what his son was saying to his daughter-in-law. His hearing was bad, but with fear and dread he sensed something terrifying. At such moments his son felt the heavy crazed look of the old man, who was being driven insane, focused on him. The old man's two small eyes with their accursed probing, seemed incessantly to sense something, to question something. On one occasion words were said too loudly—it had slipped the daughter-in-law's mind that Shloyme was still alive. And right after her words were spoken, there was a quiet, almost smothered wail. It was old Shloyme. With tottering steps, dirty and disheveled, he slowly hobbled over to his son, grabbed his hands, caressed them, kissed them, and, not taking his inflamed eyes off his son, shook his head several times, and for the first time in many, many years, tears flowed from his eyes. He didn't say anything. With difficulty he got up from his knees, his bony hand wiping away the tears; for some reason he shook the dust off his frock coat and shuffled back to his corner, to where the warm stove stood. Shloyme wanted to warm himself. He felt cold.

From that time on, Shloyme thought of nothing else. He knew one thing for certain: his son wanted to leave his people for a new God. The old, forgotten faith was kindled within him. Shloyme had never been religious, had rarely ever prayed, and in his younger days had even had the reputation of being godless. But to leave, to leave one's God completely and forever, the God of an oppressed and suffering people—that he could not understand. Thoughts rolled heavily inside his head, he comprehended things with difficulty, but these words remained unchanged, hard, and terrible before him: "This mustn't happen, it mustn't!" And when Shloyme realized that disaster was inevitable, that his son couldn't hold out, he said to himself, "Shloyme, old Shloyme! What are you going to do now?" The old man looked around helplessly, mournfully puckered his lips like a child, and wanted to burst into the bitter tears of an old man. But there were no relieving tears. And then, at the moment his heart began aching, when his mind grasped the boundlessness of the disaster, it was then that Shloyme looked at his warm corner one last time and decided that no one was going to kick him out of here, they would never kick him out. "They will not let old Shloyme eat the dried-up piece of honey cake lying under his pillow! So what! Shloyme will tell God how he was wronged! After all, there is a God, God will take him in!" Shloyme was sure of this.

In the middle of the night, trembling with cold, he got up from his bed. Quietly, so as not to wake anyone, he lit a small kerosene lamp. Slowly, with an old man's groaning and shivering, he started pulling on his dirty clothes. Then he took the stool and the rope he had prepared the night before, and, tottering with weakness, steadying himself on the walls, went out into the street. Suddenly it was so cold. His whole body shivered. Shloyme quickly fastened the rope onto a hook, stood up next to the door, put the stool in place, clambered up onto it, wound the rope around his thin, quivering neck, kicked away the stool with his last strength, managing with his dimming eyes to glance at the town he had not left once in sixty years, and hung.

There was a strong wind, and soon old Shloyme's frail body began swaying before the door of his house in which he had left his warm stove and the greasy Torah of his forefathers.

Conquering Petersburg

DEBUT IN FICTION

"Elya Isaakovich and Margarita Prokofievna" and "Mama, Rimma, and Alla" appeared in the November 1916 issue of Maxim Gorky's monthly *Letopis* (Chronicle), right next to Gorky's own memoirs, which were then being serialized and read avidly by the Russian public. The publication of Babel's stories had Gorky's personal blessing and launched Babel's career as a writer. Although in 1916 Babel had more short fiction than the "two or three" stories he recalled bringing to Gorky, only three pieces have survived intact. The third one, "The Bathroom Window," included here, was published early in 1917. The existence of others is attested to by an occasional incomplete draft and recollections of his friends and contemporaries —*Ed.*

Elya Isaakovich and Margarita Prokofievna

Gershkovich came out of the police chief's office with a heavy heart. He had been informed that if he didn't leave Oryol on the first train, he would have to leave town in a chain gang.[1] And leaving meant he would lose business.

With briefcase in hand, gaunt, unhurried, he walked down the dark street. At the corner, a tall female figure called out to him, "Will you come with me, sweetie?"

Gershkovich raised his head, looked at her through his shimmering spectacles, thought it over, and guardedly said, "I'll come."

The woman took him by the arm. They walked around the corner.

"So where will we go? To a hotel?"

"I want something for the whole night," Gershkovich answered. "How about your place?"

"That'll cost you three rubles, Papa."

"Two," Gershkovich said.

"Not worth my while, Papa!"

He managed to haggle her down to two-and-a-half rubles. They began walking.

---

1. Imperial Russia maintained numerous restrictions on Jews, including ones on their residences. With some exceptions—merchants of the First Guild and various professions—Jews were restricted to parts of the southwest and west of the empire, the Pale of Settlement. In the twilight years of the old regime from 1905–17, these restrictions began to erode. —*Ed.*

The prostitute's room was small, nice, and clean, with frayed curtains and a pink lamp.

When they entered, the woman took off her coat, unbuttoned her blouse, and winked at him.

"Hey!" Gershkovich said, knitting his brow. "Stop messing around!"

"You're in a bad mood, Papa."

She came over and sat on his knee.

"Well, I'll be damned!" Gershkovich said. "You must weigh at least five *pood*!"[2]

"Four-point-three *pood*!"

She gave him a long kiss on his graying cheek.

"Hey!" Gershkovich said, knitting his brow again. "I'm tired, I want to go to sleep."

The prostitute stood up. Her face had become hard.

"You a Jew?"

He looked at her through his spectacles and answered, "No."

"Papa," the prostitute said slowly, "that'll be ten rubles."

He got up and walked to the door.

"Five," the woman said.

Gershkovich came back.

"Make up the bed for me," the Jew said wearily, then took off his jacket and looked for a place to hang it. "What's your name?"

"Margarita."

"Change the sheets, Margarita."

The bed was wide and covered with a soft eiderdown.

Gershkovich slowly started undressing. He took off his white socks, stretched his sweaty toes, locked the door with the key, put the key under his pillow, and lay down. Margarita yawned, and slowly took off her dress, squinted, squeezed out a pimple on her shoulder, and began plaiting a thin braid for the night.

"Papa, what's your name?"

"Eli. Elya Isaakovich."

"A tradesman?"

"Well, if you want to call it a trade . . ." Gershkovich answered vaguely.

Margarita blew out the night-light and lay down. . . .

"Well, I'll be damned!" Gershkovich said. "That's a whole lot of woman here."

Soon they were asleep.

Next morning the sun's bright light filled the room. Gershkovich woke up, dressed, and walked to the window.

"We have sea, and you have fields," he said. "Great."

"Where you from?" Margarita asked.

"Odessa," Gershkovich answered. "The number-one town, a good town." And he smiled slyly.

---

2. Equal to 36.11 pounds, the *pood* was part of the old Russian system of measurement, replaced by the metric system in 1924. Margarita weighs about 155 pounds. —*Ed.*

"It looks like you pretty much feel nice and fine everywhere," Margarita said.

"You can say that again," Gershkovich said. "Wherever there's people it's nice and fine."

"You're such a fool!" Margarita said, propping herself up on the bed. "People are evil."

"No," Gershkovich said. "People are good. They've been taught to think that they're evil, and they ended up believing it."

Margarita thought for a while, and then smiled.

"You're funny," she said slowly, and she ran her eyes carefully over him. "Turn around, I'm going to get dressed."

Then they ate breakfast, drank tea with hard rolls. Gershkovich taught Margarita how to spread butter on a roll in a special way and to put the sausage on top.

"Try it! Though I have to be on my way now.

"Here are three rubles for you, Margarita," he said on his way out. "Believe me, rubles don't come easy nowadays."

Margarita smiled.

"You skinflint, you! So give me three. You coming back this evening?"

"Yes, I am."

That evening Gershkovich brought dinner with him—a herring, a bottle of beer, sausages, apples. Margarita was wearing a dark, high-buttoned dress. They talked as they ate.

"Nowadays you can't get by on fifty rubles a month," Margarita said. "And what with this job, if you don't dress up, you don't get no cabbage soup. You have to take into account that I have to pay fifteen for this room."

"Back in Odessa," Gershkovich said pensively, straining to cut the herring into equal parts, "for ten rubles you can get a room in the Moldavanka fit for a Czar."

"You have to take into account that people tumble all over the place in my room, what with the drunks and everything."

"Every man must bear his burden," Gershkovich said, and started talking about his family, his faltering business dealings, his son who had been called up by the army.

Margarita listened, resting her head on the table, and her face was attentive, quiet, and thoughtful.

After supper, he took off his jacket, painstakingly wiped his spectacles with a piece of cloth, and sat down at the table to write some business letters. Margarita washed her hair.

Gershkovich wrote unhurriedly, carefully, raising his eyebrows, stopping to think, and when he dipped his pen into the inkwell, he never once forgot to shake off the extra ink.

After he finishing writing he had Margarita sit down on his notebook.

"Well, I'll be damned, but you sure are a lady with bulk![3] Do me a favor and keep sitting there, Margarita Prokofievna."

Gershkovich smiled, his spectacles shimmered, and his eyes became small, more sparkling, full of laughter.

The next day he left town. As he paced up and down the platform, a few minutes before the train was to leave, Gershkovich noticed Margarita

---

3. Gershkovich uses a Ukrainian idiom for corpulence, *nivroko*, meaning literally "not being exposed to an evil eye." —*Ed.*

walking quickly toward him with a small parcel in her hands. There were pies in the parcel, and oily blotches had seeped through the paper.

Margarita's face was red, pitiful, her chest agitated from walking so quickly.

"Greetings to Odessa!" she said. "Greetings. . . ."

"Thank you," Gershkovich answered. He took the pies, raised his eyebrows, thought about something for a moment, and bent forward.

The third bell rang. They stretched their hands out to each other.

"Good-bye, Margarita Prokofievna."

"Good-bye, Elya Isaakovich."

Gershkovich went inside the railway car. The train began moving.

Mama, Rimma, and Alla

From early in the morning the day had been going badly.

The day before, the maid had begun putting on airs and walked out. Barbara Stepanovna ended up having to do everything herself. Then the electric bill came first thing in the morning. And then the student boarders, the Rastokhin brothers, came up with a completely unexpected demand. They had allegedly received a telegram from Kaluga[1] in the middle of the night informing them that their father had been taken ill, and that they had to come to him at all costs. They were therefore vacating the room, and could they have the sixty rubles back that they had given Barbara Stepanovna "on loan."

To this Barbara Stepanovna answered that it was quite irregular to vacate a room in April, when there is no one to rent it to, and that it was difficult for her to return the money, as it was given to her not on loan but as a payment for the room, regardless of the fact that the payment had been made in advance.

The Rastokhin brothers disagreed with Barbara Stepanovna. The discussion became drawn-out and unfriendly. The students were stubborn, infuriating louts in long, clean frock coats. When they realized that getting their money back was a lost cause, the older brother suggested that Barbara Stepanovna give them her sideboard and pier glass[2] as collateral.

Barbara Stepanovna turned purple, and retorted that she would not tolerate being spoken to in such a tone, that the Rastokhins' suggestion was utter rubbish, that she knew the law, her husband being a member of the district court in Kamchatka, and so on. The younger Rastokhin flared up and told her that he didn't give a hoot that her husband was a member of the district court in Kamchatka, that it was quite obvious that once she got her hands on a kopeck there was no prying it loose, that they would remember their stay at Barbara Stepanovna's—with all that clutter, dirt, and mess—to their dying day, and that although the district court in Kamchatka was quite far away, the Moscow Justice of the Peace was just around the corner.

And that was how the discussion ended. The Rastokhins marched out haughtily and in silent fury, and Barbara Stepanovna went to the kitchen

1. An old Russian town, some 120 miles southwest of Moscow; at the time of the story, an epitome of small-town, provincial Russia. —*Ed.*
2. A large mirror hung between two windows. —*Ed.*

to make some coffee for her other boarder, a student by the name of Stanislaw Marchotski. There had been loud and insistent ringing from his room for quite a few minutes.

Barbara Stepanovna stood in front of the spirit stove in the kitchen. A nickel pince-nez, rickety with age, sat on her fat nose; her graying hair was disheveled, her pink morning coat full of stains. She made the coffee, and thought how these louts would never have spoken to her in such a tone if there hadn't been that eternal shortage of money, that unfortunate need to constantly snatch, hide, cheat.

When Marchotski's coffee and fried eggs were ready, she brought his breakfast to his room.

Marchotski was a Pole—tall, bony, light blond, with long legs and well-groomed fingernails. That morning he was wearing a foppish gray dressing gown with ornamental military clasps.

He faced Barbara Stepanovna with resentment.

"I've had enough of there never being a maid around!" he said. "I have to ring for a whole hour, and then I'm late for my classes."

It was true that all too often the maid wasn't there, and that Marchotski had to ring and ring, but this time he had a different reason for his resentment.

The evening before, he had been sitting on the living room sofa with Rimma, Barbara Stepanovna's oldest daughter. Barbara Stepanovna had seen them kissing two or three times and hugging in the darkness. They sat there till eleven, then till midnight, then Stanislaw laid his head on Rimma's breast and fell asleep. After all, who in his youth has not dozed off on the edge of a sofa with his head propped on the breast of a high school girl, met by chance on life's winding path? It is not necessarily such a bad thing, and more often than not there are no consequences, but one does have to show a little consideration for others, not to mention that the girl might well have to go to school the next day.

It wasn't until one-thirty in the morning that Barbara Stepanovna declared quite sourly that it was time to show some consideration. Marchotski, brimming with Polish pride, pursed his lips and took umbrage. Rimma cast an indignant look at her mother.

The matter had ended there. But the following morning it was quite clear that Stanislaw hadn't forgotten the incident. Barbara Stepanovna gave him his breakfast, salted the fried eggs, and left.

It was eleven in the morning. Barbara Stepanovna opened the drapes in her daughters' room. The gentle rays of the weak sun gleamed on the dirty floor, on the clothes scattered throughout the room, on the dusty bookshelf.

The girls were already awake. The eldest, Rimma, was thin, small, quick-eyed, black-haired. Alla was a year younger—she was seventeen—larger than her sister, pale, sluggish in her movements, with delicate, pudgy skin, and a sweetly pensive expression in her blue eyes.

When her mother left the room, she started speaking. Her heavy bare arm lay on the blanket, her little white fingers hardly moving.

"I had a dream, Rimma," she said. "Imagine—a strange little town, small, Russian, mysterious. . . . The light gray sky is hanging very low, and the horizon is very close. The dust in the streets is also gray, smooth, calm. Everything is dead. Not a single sound can be heard, not a single person can be seen. And suddenly I feel like I'm walking down some side streets I don't know, past quiet little wooden houses. I wander into blind alleys, then I find my way out into the streets again, but I can only see ten paces ahead, and I keep walking on and on. Somewhere in front of me is a light cloud of whirling dust. I approach it and see wedding carriages. Mikhail and his bride are in one of them. His bride is wearing a veil, and her face is happy. I walk up to the carriages, I seem to be taller than everyone else, and my heart aches a little. Then they all notice me. The carriages stop. Mikhail comes up to me, takes me by the arm, and slowly leads me into a side street. 'Alla, my friend,' he says in a flat voice, 'all this is very sad, I know. But there's nothing I can do, because I don't love you.' I walk next to him, my heart shudders, and more gray streets keep opening up before us."

Alla fell silent.

"A bad dream," she added. "But, who knows? Maybe because it's bad, everything will turn out well and he'll send me a letter."

"Like hell he will!" Rimma answered. "You should have been a little more clever and not run off to see him. By the way, I intend to have a word or two with Mama today!" she said suddenly.

Rimma got up, dressed, and went over to the window.

Spring lay over Moscow. The long somber fence outside their window, which stretched almost the whole length of the side street, glistened with warm dampness.

Outside the church, in its front yard, the grass was damp, green. The sun softly gilded the lackluster chasubles, and twinkled over the dark face of the icon standing on the slanting column by the entrance to the churchyard.

The girls went into the dining room. Barbara Stepanovna was sitting there, carefully eating large portions of food, intently studying the rolls, the coffee, the ham, through her spectacles. She drank the coffee with loud short gulps, and ate the rolls quickly, greedily, almost furtively.

"Mama!" Rimma said to her severely, proudly raising her pretty little face. "I'd like to have a little chat with you. You needn't blow up. We can settle this quietly, once and for all. I can no longer live with you. Set me free."

"Fine," Barbara Stepanovna answered calmly, raising her colorless eyes to look at Rimma. "Is this because of yesterday?"

"Not because of yesterday, but it has to do with yesterday. I'm suffocating here."

"And what do you intend to do?"

"I'll take some classes, learn stenography, right now the demand—"

"Right now stenographers are crawling out of the woodwork! You think the jobs will come running—"

"I won't come to you for help, Mama!" Rimma said shrilly. "I won't come to you for help. Set me free!"

"Fine," Barbara Stepanovna said again. "I'm not holding you back."

"I want you to give me my passport."

"I'm not giving you your passport."

The conversation had been unexpectedly restrained. Now Rimma felt that the passport matter gave her a reason to start yelling.

"Well, that's marvelous!" she shouted, with a sarcastic laugh. "I can't go anywhere without my passport!"

"I'm not giving you your passport!"

"I'll go turn myself into a kept woman!" Rimma yelled hysterically. "I shall give myself to a policeman!"

"Who do you think will want you?" Barbara Stepanovna answered, critically eyeing her daughter's shivering little body and flushed face. "You think a policeman can't find a better—"

"I'll go to Tverskaya Street!" Rimma shouted. "I'll find myself some old man—I don't want to live with her, with this stupid, stupid, stupid—"

"Ah, so this is how you speak to your mother," Barbara Stepanovna said, standing up with dignity. "We can't make ends meet, everything is falling apart around us, we're short of everything, all I ask is for a few minutes of peace and quiet, but you . . . Wait till your father hears about this!"

"I'm going to write him myself, to Kamchatka!" Rimma shouted in a frenzy. "I'll get my passport from him!"

Barbara Stepanovna walked out of the room. Rimma, small and disheveled, paced excitedly up and down the room. Angry, isolated phrases from her future letter to her father tore through her brain.

"Dear Papa!" she would write. "You are busy, I know, but I have to tell you everything. May the allegation that Stanny dozed on my breast lie heavy on Mama's conscience! It was an embroidered cushion that he was dozing on, but the center of gravity lies elsewhere. As Mama is your wife, you will doubtless side with her, but I can't stay here any longer, she is a difficult person! If you want, Papa, I can come to you in Kamchatka, but I will need my passport!"

Rimma paced up and down, while Alla sat on the sofa and watched her. Quiet and mournful thoughts lay heavily on her soul.

"Rimma is fussing about," she thought, "while I am completely desolate! Everything is painful, nothing makes sense!"

She went to her room and lay down. Barbara Stepanovna came in wearing a corset. She was thickly and naively powdered, flushed, perplexed, and pitiful.

"I just remembered that the Rastokhins are leaving today. I have to give them back their sixty rubles. They threatened to take me to court. There are some eggs in the cupboard. Make some for yourself—I'm going down to the pawnbroker."

When Marchotski came home from his classes at around six in the evening, he found the entrance hall filled with packed suitcases. There was noise coming from the Rastokhins' rooms—they were obviously arguing. Right there in the entrance hall Barbara Stepanovna, somehow, with lightning speed and desperate resolution, managed to borrow ten rubles from Marchotski. It was only when he got back to his room that he realized how stupid he had been.

His room was different from all the other rooms in Barbara Stepanovna's apartment. It was neat, filled with bibelots, and covered with carpets. Drawing utensils, foppish pipes, English tobacco, ivory paper knives were carefully laid out on the tables.

Before Stanislaw even managed to change into his dressing gown, Rimma quietly slipped into his room. He gave her a chilly reception.

"Are you angry, Stanny?" the girl asked.

"I am not angry," the Pole answered. "It is just that in the future I would prefer not to be encumbered with having to bear witness to your mother's excesses."

"It'll all be over very soon," Rimma said. "Stanny, I'm going to be free!" She sat down next to him on the sofa and embraced him.

"I am a man," Stanny began. "This platonic business is not for me, I have a career before me."

He gruffly told her the things that men more or less say to certain women when they've had enough. There's nothing to talk to them about, and flirting with them is pointless, as it is quite obvious they are not prepared to get down to business.

Stanny said that he was consumed by desire; it was hampering his work, making him nervous. The matter had to be settled one way or the other—he didn't care in the least which, as long as it was settled.

"Why are you saying such things to me?" Rimma asked him pensively. "What is all this 'I am a man' about, and what do you mean by 'the matter has to be settled'? Why is your face so cold and nasty? And why can we talk about nothing else but that one thing? This is so sad, Stanny! Spring is in the streets, it's so beautiful, and we are in such an ugly mood."

Stanny didn't answer. They both remained silent.

A fiery sunset was sinking over the horizon, flooding the distant sky with a scarlet glow. On the opposite horizon a volatile, slowly thickening darkness was descending. The room was illuminated by the last glowing light. On the sofa, Rimma leaned more and more tenderly toward the student. They were doing what they always did at this exquisite hour of the day.

Stanislaw kissed the girl. She rested her head on the pillow and closed her eyes. They both burst into flame. Within a few minutes, Stanislaw was kissing her incessantly, and in a fit of malicious, unquenchable passion began shoving her thin, burning body about the room. He tore her blouse and her bodice. Rimma, with parched mouth and rings under her eyes, offered her lips to be kissed, while with a distorted, mournful grin she defended her virginity. Suddenly there was a knock at the door. Rimma began rushing about the room, clutching the hanging strips of her torn blouse to her breast.

They eventually opened the door. It turned out to be a friend of Stanislaw's. He eyed Rimma with ill-concealed derision as she rushed past him. She slipped into her room furtively, changed into another blouse, and went to stand by the chilly windowpane to cool down.

The pawnbroker gave Barbara Stepanovna only forty rubles for the family silver. Ten rubles she had borrowed from Marchotski, and the rest of the money she got from the Tikhonovs, walking all the way from Strastny Boulevard to Pokrovka. In her dismay, she forgot that she could have taken a tram.

At home, besides the raging Rastokhins, she found Mirlits, a barrister's assistant, waiting for her. He was a tall young man with decaying stumps for teeth, and foolish, moist gray eyes.

Not too long ago, the shortage of money had driven Barbara Stepanovna to consider mortgaging a cottage her husband owned in Kolomna. Mirlits had brought over a draft of the mortgage. Barbara

Stepanovna felt that something was wrong with the draft, and that she ought to get some more advice before signing. But she told herself that she was being beset by altogether too many problems of every kind. To hell with everything—boarders, daughters, rudeness.

After the business discussion, Mirlits uncorked a bottle of Crimean Muscat-Lunelle that he had brought with him—he knew Barbara Stepanovna's weakness. They drank a glass each and right away had another. Their voices rang louder, Barbara Stepanovna's fleshy nose grew red, and the stays of her corset expanded and bulged out. Mirlits was telling a jovial story and burst out laughing. Rimma sat silently in the corner, wearing the blouse into which she had changed.

After Barbara Stepanovna and Mirlits finished the Muscat-Lunelle, they went for a walk. Barbara Stepanovna felt that she was just a tiny bit tipsy. She was a little ashamed about this, but at the same time couldn't care less because there was simply too much hardship in life, so everything could go to hell.

Barbara Stepanovna came back earlier than she had anticipated, because the Boikos, whom she had intended to visit, had not been home. She was taken aback by the silence that lay over the apartment. Usually at this time of the day the girls were always fooling around with the students, giggling, running about. The only noise came from the bathroom. Barbara Stepanovna went to the kitchen. There was a little window there from which one could see what was going on in the bathroom.

She went to the little window and saw a strange and most unusual scene.

The stove for boiling the bathwater was red-hot. The bath was filled with steaming water. Rimma was kneeling next to the stove. In her hands she held a pair of curling irons. She was heating them over the fire. Alla was standing naked next to the bath. Her long braids were undone. Tears were rolling down her cheeks.

"Come here," Alla told Rimma. "Listen, can you maybe hear its heart beating?"

Rimma laid her head on Alla's soft, slightly swollen belly.

"It's not beating," she answered. "Anyway there's no doubt about it."

"I'm going to die," Alla whispered. "I'm going to get scalded by the water! I won't be able to bear it! Not the curling irons! You don't know how to do it!"

"Everyone does it this way," Rimma told her. "Stop whimpering, Alla. You can't have that baby."

Alla was about to climb into the tub, but she didn't manage to, because at that very moment she heard the unforgettable, quiet, wheezing voice of her mother call out. "What are you doing in there, girls?"

Two or three hours later, Alla was lying on Barbara Stepanovna's wide bed, tucked in, caressed, and wept over. She had told her mother everything. She felt relieved. She felt like a little girl who had overcome a silly childish fear.

Rimma moved about the bedroom carefully and silently, tidying up, making tea for her mother, forcing her to eat something, seeing to it that the room would be clean. Then she lit the icon lamp in which the oil had not been refilled for at least two weeks, undressed, trying hard not to make any noise, and lay down next to her sister.

Barbara Stepanovna sat at the table. She could see the icon lamp, its even, darkish red flame dimly illuminating the Virgin Mary. Her tipsiness, somehow strange and light, still bubbled in her head. The girls quickly fell asleep. Alla's face was broad, white, and peaceful. Rimma nestled up against her, sighed in her sleep, and shuddered.

Around one in the morning, Barbara Stepanovna lit a candle, placed a sheet of paper in front of her, and wrote a letter to her husband:

Dear Nikolai,

Mirlits came by today, a very decent Jew, and tomorrow I'm expecting a gentleman who will give me money for the house. I think I'm doing things right, but I'm getting more and more worried, because I lack confidence.

I know you have your own troubles, your work, and I shouldn't be bothering you with this, but things at home, Nikolai, are somehow not going all too well. The children are growing up, life nowadays is more demanding—courses, stenography—girls want more freedom. They need their father, they need someone to maybe yell at them, but I simply don't seem to be able to. I can't help thinking that your leaving for Kamchatka was a mistake. If you were here, we would have moved to Starokolenny Street, where there is a very bright little apartment available.

Rimma has lost weight and looks rather bad. For a whole month we were ordering cream from the dairy across the street, and the girls started looking much better, but now we have stopped ordering it. At times my liver acts up a little, and at times it doesn't. Write me more often. After your letters I am a bit more careful, I don't eat herring and my liver doesn't bother me. Come and see us, Kolya, we could all unwind. The children send you their greetings. With loving kisses,

Your Barbara.

The Bathroom Window[1]

I have an acquaintance, a Madam Kebchik. In her day, Madam Kebchik assures me, "nothing in the world" would have induced her to take less than five rubles.

Now she has a nice, family apartment, and in this apartment she has two girls, Marusya and Tamara. There are more requests for Marusya than for Tamara. One of the windows of the girls' room has a view of the street, the other window, just an air vent near the ceiling, has a view of the bathroom. When I realized this, I said to Fanya Osipovna Kebchik, "How about putting a ladder by the little window in the bathroom in the evenings, so I can climb up and peek into Marusya's room? I'll give you five rubles."

---

1. The title is "*V shchelochku*," literally "through a crack." The story was first published in the Petersburg weekly *Zhurnal zhurnalov* 16 (1917). In a subsequent publication the story had a date "1915" and was designated as part of the cycle "Oforty" (Etchings), which Babel may have planned as a book. Babel asserted that it was to be published with the preceding two stories in *Letopis*, but it was excised by the imperial censor. This translation is based on a later, somewhat tighter version of the story, published in the almanac *Pereval*, vol. 6 (Moscow-Leningrad, 1928). —*Ed.*

"You rogue, you!" Fanya Osipovna said, and agreed.

She got her five rubles quite often. I made use of the little window when Marusya had clients.

Everything went without a hitch, but one time an extremely foolish thing happened. I was standing on the ladder. Luckily, Marusya hadn't turned off the light. Her guest was a pleasant, unassuming fellow with one of those large, harmless mustaches. He undressed in a prim and proper fashion: he took off his collar, looked in the mirror, noticed a pimple under his mustache, studied it, and pressed it out with a handkerchief. He took off a boot and examined it too—was there a scratch on the sole?

They kissed, undressed, and smoked a cigarette. I got ready to climb down. At that moment I felt the ladder sliding away under me. I tried to grab hold of the window, but it gave way. The ladder fell with a crash and there I was, dangling in the air.

Suddenly the whole apartment exploded with alarm. Everyone came running, Fanya Osipovna, Tamara, and an official I didn't know in a Ministry of Finance uniform. They helped me down. My situation was pitiful. Marusya and her lanky client came into the bathroom.

The girl looked at me, froze, and said quietly, "What a bastard, oh, what a bastard!"

She fell silent, stared at us foolishly, went over to the lanky man, and for some reason kissed his hand and started crying.

"My dear, O God, my dear!" she said, between kisses and sobs.

The lanky man stood there like a total idiot. My heart was pounding wildly. I dug my nails into my palms and went over to Madam Kebchik.

Within a few minutes, Marusya knew everything. All was forgiven and forgotten. But I was still wondering why she had kissed the lanky fellow.

"Madam Kebchik," I said. "Put up the ladder one last time, and you can have ten rubles."

"Your mind's even more unsteady than that ladder of yours!" the landlady answered, and agreed.

So there I was again, standing by the little window. I looked through it and saw Marusya, her thin arms wrapped around her client, kissing him with slow kisses, tears flowing from her eyes.

"My darling!" she whispered. "O God, my sweet darling!" And she gave herself to him with all the passion of a woman in love. She looked at him as if he, this lanky fellow, were the only man in the world.

And the lanky fellow wallowed in businesslike bliss.

MAN ABOUT TOWN

Babel rarely mentioned that after his debut in the November 1916 issue of *Letopis,* he was in demand as a roving city reporter—one with a fresh point of view on the capital, thanks in part to his Odessan eyes, as he explains to his Petrograd audience in the essay "Odessa." In a 1937 memoir piece, "Nachalo," he recalled producing in those months "a story a day"—an impossible pace for a prose writer, but not unthinkable for a newspaper man. —*Ed.*

The Public Library[1]

One feels right away that this is the kingdom of books. People working at the library commune with books, with the life reflected in them, and so become almost reflections of real-life human beings.

Even the cloakroom attendants—not brown-haired, not blond, but something in between—are mysteriously quiet, filled with contemplative composure.

At home on Saturday evenings they might well drink methylated spirits and give their wives long, drawn-out beatings, but at the library their comportment is staid, circumspect, and hazily somber.

And then there is the cloakroom attendant who draws. In his eyes there is a gentle melancholy. Once every two weeks, as he helps a fat man in a black vest out of his coat, he mumbles, "Nikolai Sergeyevich approves of my drawings, and Konstantin Vasilevich also approves of them. . . . In the first thing I was originating . . . but I have no idea, no idea where to go!"

The fat man listens. He is a reporter, a married man, gluttonous and overworked. Once every two weeks he goes to the library to rest. He reads about court cases, painstakingly copies out onto a piece of paper the plan of the house where the murder took place, is very pleased, and forgets that he is married and overworked.

The reporter listens to the attendant with fearful bewilderment, and wonders how to handle such a man. Do you give him a ten-kopeck coin on your way out? He might be offended—he's an artist. Then again, if you don't he might also be offended—after all, he's a cloakroom attendant.

In the reading room are the more elevated staff members, the librarians. Some, the "conspicuous ones," possess some starkly pronounced physical defect. One has twisted fingers, another has a head that lolled to the side and stayed there. They are badly dressed, and emaciated in the extreme. They look as if they are fanatically possessed by an idea unknown to the world.

Gogol would have described them well![2]

The "inconspicuous" librarians show the beginnings of bald patches, wear clean gray suits, have a certain candor in their eyes, and a painful slowness in their movements. They are forever chewing something, moving

1. First published in *Zhurnal zhurnalov* 48 (1916), subheaded "My Notes" and signed "Bab-El." In the early years of his career, Babel often reserved this comical, macaronic pen name for his journalism. —*Ed.*
2. Nikolay Gogol (1809–1852), author of the classic *Dead Souls* (1842) and stories about Ukraine and St. Petersburg. —*Ed.*

their jaws, even though they have nothing in their mouths. They talk in a practiced whisper. In short, they have been ruined by books, by being forbidden from enjoying a throaty yawn.

Now that our country is at war, the public has changed. There are fewer students. There are very few students. Once in a blue moon you might see a student painlessly perishing in a corner. He's a "white-ticketer," exempt from service. He wears a pince-nez and has a delicate limp. But then there is also the student on state scholarship. This student is pudgy, with a drooping mustache, tired of life, a man prone to contemplation: he reads a bit, thinks about something a bit, studies the patterns on the lampshades, and nods off over a book. He has to finish his studies, join the army, but—why hurry? Everything in good time.

A former student returns to the library in the figure of a wounded officer with a black sling. His wound is healing. He is young and rosy. He has dined and taken a walk along the Nevsky Prospekt. The Nevsky Prospekt is already lit. The late edition of the *Stock Exchange News* has already set off on its triumphal march around town. Grapes lying on millet are displayed in the store window at Eliseyev's. It is still too early to make the social rounds. The officer goes to the public library for old times' sake, stretches out his long legs beneath the table where he is sitting, and reads *Apollon*. It's somewhat boring. A female student is sitting opposite him. She is studying anatomy, and is copying a picture of a stomach into her notebook. It looks like she might be of Kalugan origin—large-faced, large-boned, rosy, dedicated, and robust. If she has a lover, that would be perfect—she's good material for love.

Beside her is a picturesque tableau, an immutable feature of every public library in the Russian Empire: a sleeping Jew. He is worn out. His hair is a fiery black. His cheeks are sunken. There are bumps on his forehead. His mouth is half open. He is wheezing. Where he is from, nobody knows. Whether he has a residence permit or not, nobody knows. He reads every day. He also sleeps every day. There is a terrible, ineradicable weariness in his face, almost madness. A martyr to books—a distinct, indomitable Jewish martyr.

Near the librarians' desk sits a large, broad-chested woman in a gray blouse reading with rapturous interest. She is one of those people who suddenly speaks with unexpected loudness in the library, candidly and ecstatically overwhelmed by a passage in the book, and who, filled with delight, begins discussing it with her neighbors. She is reading because she is trying to find out how to make soap at home. She is about forty-five years old. Is she sane? Quite a few people have asked themselves that.

There is one more typical library habitué: the thin little colonel in a loose jacket, wide pants, and extremely well-polished boots. He has tiny feet. His whiskers are the color of cigar ash. He smears them with a wax that gives them a whole spectrum of dark gray shades. In his day he was so devoid of talent that he didn't manage to work his way up to the rank of colonel so that he could retire a major general. Since his retirement he ceaselessly pesters the gardener, the maid, and his grandson. At the age of seventy-three he has taken it into his head to write a history of his regiment.

He writes. He is surrounded by piles of books. He is the librarians' favorite. He greets them with exquisite civility. He no longer gets on his family's nerves. The maid gladly polishes his boots to a maximal shine.

Many more people of every kind come to the public library. More than one could describe. There is also the tattered reader who does nothing but write a luxuriant monograph on ballet. His face: a tragic edition of Hauptmann's. His body: insignificant.

There are, of course, also bureaucrats riffling through piles of *The Russian Invalid* and the *Government Herald*. There are the young provincials, ablaze as they read.

It is evening. The reading room grows dark. The immobile figures sitting at the tables are a mix of fatigue, thirst for knowledge, ambition.

Outside the wide windows soft snow is drifting. Nearby, on the Nevsky Prospekt, life is blossoming. Far away, in the Carpathian Mountains, blood is flowing.

C'est la vie.

Nine[1]

There are nine people. All waiting to see the editor. The first to enter the editor's office is a broad-shouldered young man with a loud voice and a bright tie. He introduces himself. His name: Sardarov. His occupation: rhymester. His request: to have his rhymes published. He has a preface written by a well-known poet. And if need be, an epilogue, too.

The editor listens. He is an unruffled, pensive man, who has seen a thing or two. He is in no rush. The upcoming issue has gone to press. He reads through the rhymes:

> *O, dolefully the Austrian Kaiser groans,*
> *And I too emit impatient moans.*

The editor says that, unfortunately, for this reason and that, and so on. The magazine is currently looking for articles on cooperatives or foreign affairs.

Sardarov juts out his chest, excuses himself with exquisite politeness bordering on the caustic, and noisily marches out.

The second person to enter the editor's office is a young lady—slim, shy, very beautiful. She is there for the third time. Her poems are not intended for publication. All she wants to know, and absolutely nothing more, is if there's any point in her continuing to write. The editor is extremely pleasant to her. He sometimes sees her walking along the Nevsky Prospekt with a tall gentleman who, from time to time, gravely buys her half a dozen apples. His gravity is ominous. Her poems testify to this. They are a guileless chronicle of her life.

"You want my body," the girl writes. "So take it, my enemy, my friend! But where will my soul find its dream?"

"He'll be getting his hands on your body any day now, that's pretty clear!" the editor thinks. "Your eyes look so lost, weak, and beautiful. I doubt your soul will be finding its dream anytime soon, but you'll definitely make quite a spicy woman!"

In her poems the girl describes life as "madly frightening" or "madly

1. First published in *Zhurnal zhurnalov* 49 (1916), subheaded "My Notes" and signed "Bab-El." —*Ed.*

marvelous," in all its little aggravations: "Those sounds, sounds, sounds that me enfold, those sounds eternal, so drunken and so bold."

One thing is certain: once the grave gentleman's enterprise comes to fruition, the girl will stop writing poetry and start visiting midwives.

After the girl, Lunev, a small and nervous man of letters, enters the editor's office. Here things get complicated. On a former occasion Lunev had blown up at the editor. He is a talented, perplexed, hapless family man. In his fluster and scramble for rubles he is unable to discriminate who he can afford to shout at and who not. First he blew up at the editor, and then, to his own and the editor's amazement, handed over the manuscript, suddenly realizing how foolish all this was, how hard life was, and how unlucky he was, oh, how very unlucky! He had already begun having palpitations in the waiting room, and now the editor informed him that his "little daubs" weren't all that bad, but, *au fond*,[2] you couldn't really classify them as literature, they were, well . . . Lunev feverishly agreed, unexpectedly muttering, "Oh, Alexander Stepanovich! You are such a good man! And all the while I was so horrible to you! But it can all be seen from another perspective! Absolutely! That is all I want to elucidate, there is more to it than meets the eye, I give you my word of honor!" Lunev turns a deep crimson, scrapes together the pages of his manuscript with quaking fingers, endeavoring to be debonair, ironic, and God knows what else.

After Lunev, two stock figures found in every editorial office come in. The first is a lively, rosy, fair-haired lady. She emits a warm wave of perfume. Her eyes are naive and bright. She has a nine-year-old son, and this son of hers, "you wouldn't believe it, but he simply writes and writes, day and night, at first we didn't pay any attention, but then all our friends and acquaintances were so impressed, and my husband, you know, he works in the Department of Agricultural Betterment, a very practical man, you know, he will have nothing to do with modern literature, not Andreyev, not Nagrodskaya,[3] but even he couldn't stop laughing—I have brought along three notebooks. . . ."

The second stock figure is Bykhovsky. He is from Simferopol. He is a very nice, lively man. He has nothing to do with literature, he doesn't really have any business with the editor, he doesn't really have anything to say to him, but he is a subscriber, and has dropped by for a little chat and to exchange ideas, to immerse himself in the hurly-burly of Petrograd life. And he *is* immersing himself. The editor mumbles something about politics and cadets, and Bykhovsky blossoms, convinced that he is taking an active part in the nation's public life.

The most doleful of the visitors is Korb. He is a Jew, a true Ahasuerus.[4] He was born in Lithuania, and had been wounded in a pogrom in one of the southern towns. From that day on his head has been hurting very badly. He went to America. During the War he somehow turned up in Antwerp and, at the age of forty-four, joined the French Foreign Legion. He was hit on the head in Maubeuge. Now it won't stop shaking. Korb was somehow evacuated to Russia, to Petrograd. He gets a pension from somewhere, rents a ramshackle little place in a stinking basement in Peski, and

---

2. French idiom meaning "basically" or "by its very nature." —*Ed.*
3. Leonid Andreyev (1871–1919), Russian playwright; Yevdokiya Nagrodskaya (1866–1930), Russian novelist. —*Ed.*
4. A reference to the Christian folktale of the Wandering Jew, who roams the earth until Jesus' second coming. —*Ed.*

is writing a play called *The Czar of Israel*. Korb has terrible headaches, he cannot sleep at night, and paces up and down in his basement, deep in thought. His landlord, a plump, condescending man who smokes black four-kopeck cigars, was angry at first, but then was won over by Korb's gentleness and his diligence at writing hundreds of pages, and finally came to like him. Korb wears an old, faded Antwerp frock coat. He doesn't shave his chin, and there is a tiredness and fanatical determination in his eyes. Korb has headaches, but he keeps on writing his play, and the play's opening line is: "Ring the bells, for Judah hath perished!"

After Korb, three remain. One is a young man from the provinces. He is unhurried, lost in thought, takes a long time to settle into a chair, and stays settled there for a long time. His sluggish attention comes to rest on the pictures on the wall, the newspaper clippings on the table, the portraits of the staff. What is it exactly that he wants?—It is not that he really wants anything . . . He worked for a newspaper—What newspaper?—A newspaper in the provinces . . . Well, all he really wants to know is what the circulation of this magazine is and how much it pays. The young man is told that such information is not handed out to just anybody. If he were a writer, that would be another matter, if not, well then . . . The young man says that he isn't really a writer or anything, and that he hasn't really done this kind of work before, but he could take to, well, working as an editor, for instance.

The young "editor" exits, and Smursky enters. He too is a man with a background. He worked as an agriculturist in the district of Kashin in the province of Tver. A tranquil district, a wonderful province! But Smursky was drawn to Petrograd. He applied for a position as an agriculturist, and also submitted twenty manuscripts to an editor. Two had been accepted, and Smursky had come to the conclusion that his future lay in literature. Now he is no longer applying for a position as an agriculturist. He walks about town in a morning coat with his briefcase in hand. He writes a lot, and every day, but little is ever published.

The ninth visitor is none other than Stepan Drako, "the man who walked around the world on foot, bon vivant extraordinare, and public speaker."

Odessa[1]

Odessa is a horrible town. It's common knowledge. Instead of saying "a great difference," people there say "two great differences," and *"tuda i syuda,"*[2] they pronounce *"tudoyu i syudoyu"*! And yet I feel that there are quite a few good things one can say about this important town, the most charming city of the Russian Empire. If you think about it, it is a town in which you can live free and easy. Half the population is made up of Jews, and Jews are a people who have learned a few simple truths along the way. Jews get married so as not to be alone, love so as to live through the centuries, hoard money so they can buy houses and give their wives astrakhan jackets, love children because, let's face it, it is good and important to love one's children. The poor Odessa Jews get very confused when it comes to officials and regulations, but it isn't all that easy to get them to budge in

---

1. First published in *Zhurnal zhurnalov* 51 (1916), subheaded "My Notes" and signed "Bab-El."
     Seen in retrospect, this essay contains an outline of Babel's lifelong literary project. —*Ed.*
2. "Here and there."

their opinions, their very antiquated opinions. You might not be able to budge these Jews, but there's a whole lot you can learn from them. To a large extent it is because of them that Odessa has this light and easy atmosphere.

The typical Odessan is the exact opposite of the typical Petrogradian. Nowadays it is a cliché how well Odessans do for themselves in Petrograd. They make money. Because they are dark-haired, limpid blondes fall in love with them. And then, Odessans have a tendency to settle on the Kamenno-Ostrovsky Prospect. People will claim that what I am saying smacks of tall tales. Well, I assure you that these are not tall tales! There is much more to this than meets the eye. Dark-haired Odessans simply bring with them a little lightness and sunshine.

But I have a strong hunch that Odessa is about to provide us with much more than gentlemen who bring with them a little sunshine and a lot of sardines packed in their original cans. Any day now, we will fully experience the fecund, revivifying influence of the Russian south, Russian Odessa—perhaps, *qui sait*,[3] the only Russian town where there is a good chance that our very own, sorely needed, homegrown Maupassant might be born. I can even see a small, a very small sign, heralding Odessa's great future: Odessa's chanteuses (I am referring to Iza Kremer[4]). These chanteuses might not have much in the way of a voice, but they have a joy, an expressive joy, mixed with passion, lightness, and a touching, charming, sad feeling for life. A life that is good, terrible, and, *quand même et malgré tout*,[5] exceedingly interesting.

I saw Utochkin,[6] a *pur sang*[7] Odessan, lighthearted and profound, reckless and thoughtful, elegant and gangly, brilliant and stuttering. He has been ruined by cocaine or morphine—ruined, word has it, since the day he fell out of an airplane somewhere in the marshes of Novgorod. Poor Utochkin, he has lost his mind. But of one thing I am certain: any day now the province of Novgorod will come crawling down to Odessa.

The bottom line is: this town has the material conditions needed to nurture, say, a Maupassantesque talent. In the summer, the bronze, muscular bodies of youths who play sports glisten on beaches, as do the powerful bodies of fishermen who do not play sports, the fat, potbellied, good-natured bodies of the "businessmen," and the skinny, pimply dreamers, inventors, and brokers. And a little distance from the sea, smoke billows from the factories, and Karl Marx plies his familiar trade.

In Odessa there is an impoverished, overcrowded, suffering Jewish ghetto, an extremely self-satisfied bourgeoisie, and a very Black Hundred[8] city council.

---

3. French: Who knows? —*Ed.*
4. Iza (Isabelle) Kremer (1885–1956), an Odessa opera singer turned chanteuse, known for her own compositions and her own lyrics. Her career as a popular singer took off after a famous performance in Odessa in 1915, after which she toured Petrograd and Moscow. She and her husband, the editor of the Odessa daily, *Odesskiya novosti*, Israel Moiseyevich Kheifets, left Russia in 1919. Kremer had a long and successful touring career in emigration, and Babel was elated to be present at her Paris concert in July 1935. Her repertoire included songs in Russian, Yiddish, and German. —*Ed.*
5. French: Nevertheless and despite everything. —*Ed.*
6. Sergey Isayevich Utochkin (1874–1916), aviation pioneer, the first to fly from Moscow to St. Petersburg, in 1911.
7. French: Pure-blooded. —*Ed.*
8. The name of an extreme right-wing, anti-Semitic organization that emerged in 1905 and whose members, mostly urban lower-middle class, instigated and took part in anti-Jewish violence. Black Hundred became synonymous with extreme, lowbrow, right-wing attitudes; this is how Babel uses it here. —*Ed.*

In Odessa there are sweet and oppressive spring evenings, the spicy aroma of acacias, and a moon filled with an unwavering, irresistible light shining over a dark sea.

In Odessa the fat and funny bourgeois lie in the evenings in their white socks on couches in front of their funny, philistine dachas, digesting their meals beneath a dark and velvety sky, while their powdered wives, plump with idleness and naively corseted, are passionately squeezed behind bushes by fervent students of medicine or law.

In Odessa the destitute *"luftmenshen"*[9] roam through coffeehouses trying to make a ruble or two to feed their families, but there is no money to be made, and why should anyone give work to a useless person—a *"luftmensh"*?

In Odessa there is a port, and in the port there are ships that have come from Newcastle, Cardiff, Marseilles, and Port Said; Negroes, Englishmen, Frenchmen, and Americans. Odessa had its moment in the sun, but now it is fading—a poetic, slow, lighthearted, helpless fading.

"But Odessa is just a town like any other," the reader will argue. "The problem is that you are extremely biased, that's all."

Well, fine. So I am biased, I admit it. Maybe I'm even extremely biased, but *parole d'honneur,*[1] there is something to this place! And this something can be sensed by a person with mettle who agrees that life is sad, monotonous—this is all very true—but still, *quand même et malgré tout,* it is exceedingly, exceedingly interesting.

And now my thoughts move on from my Odessan discourse to higher matters. If you think about it, doesn't it strike you that in Russian literature there haven't been so far any real, clear, cheerful descriptions of the sun?

Turgenev poeticized the dewy morning, the calm night. With Dostoyevsky you feel the uneven, gray high road along which Karamazov walks to the tavern, the mysterious and heavy fog of Petersburg. The gray roads and the shrouds of fog that stifle people and, stifling them, distorts them in the most amusing and terrible way, giving birth to the fumes and stench of passions, making people rush around frenetically in the hectic humdrum pace. Do you remember the life-giving, bright sun in Gogol, a man who, by the way, was from the Ukraine? But such descriptions are few and far between. What you always get is "The Nose," "The Overcoat," "The Portrait," and "Notes of a Madman." Petersburg defeated Poltava. Akaki Akakiyevich, modestly enough but with terrible competence, finished off Gritsko, and Father Matvei finished off what Taras began.[2] The first person to talk about the sun in a Russian book, to talk about it with excitement and passion, was Gorky. But precisely because he talks about it with excitement and passion, it still isn't quite the real thing.

---

9. Yiddish: Literally "men of the air," referring to men who could not find a job and who relied on handouts to survive. —*Ed.*
1. French: On my word of honor. —*Ed.*
2. Babel implies that a cold, northern Petersburg frame of mind overpowered Gogol's earlier brighter southern "Poltavan" style, and that Akaki Akakiyevich, the somber and tragic protagonist of "The Overcoat," superseded Gritsko, the lively and witty protagonist of "Evenings on a Farm near Dikanka." Father Matvey Konstantinovsky was a fanatical ascetic priest who influenced Gogol's later writing. Taras is the protagonist of Gogol's novel *Taras Bulba* (1835). —*Ed.*

Gorky is a forerunner, and the most powerful forerunner of our times. Yet he is not a minstrel of the sun, but a herald of the truth. If anything is worth singing the praises of, then you know what it is: the sun! There is something cerebral in Gorky's love for the sun. It is only by way of his enormous talent that he manages to overcome this obstacle.

He loves the sun because Russia is rotten and twisted, because in Nizhny, Pskov, and Kazan, the people are pudgy, heavy, at times incomprehensible, at times touching, at times excessive, and at times boring to the point of distraction. Gorky knows why he loves the sun, why the sun must be loved. It is this very awareness that hides the reason why Gorky is a forerunner, often magnificent and powerful, but still a forerunner.

And on this point Maupassant is perhaps off the mark, or right on the mark. A stagecoach rumbles along a road scorched by the heat, and in it, in this stagecoach, sits a fat, crafty young man by the name of Polyte, and a coarse, healthy peasant girl. What they are doing there and why, is their business. The sky is hot, the earth is hot. Polyte and the girl are dripping with sweat, and the stagecoach rumbles along the road scorched by the bright heat. And that's all there is to it.

In recent times there has been a growing trend of writing about how people live, love, kill, and how representatives are elected in the provinces of Olonetsk, or Vologodsk, not to mention Arkhangelsk. All this is written with total authenticity, verbatim, the way people speak in Olonetsk and Vologodsk. Life there, as it turns out, is cold, extremely wild. It is an old story. And the time is approaching where we will have had more than enough of this old story. In fact, we have already had enough. And I think to myself: the Russians will finally be drawn to the south, to the sea, to the sun! "Will be drawn," by the way, is wrong. They already *have* been drawn, for many centuries. Russia's most important path has been her inexhaustible striving toward the southern steppes, perhaps even her striving for "the Cross of Hagia Sophia."[3]

It is high time for new blood. We are being stifled. Literature's Messiah, so long awaited, will issue from there—from the sun-drenched steppes washed by the sea.

Doudou[1]

Back in those days I was a medical orderly in the hospital in the town of N. One morning General S., the hospital administrator, brought in a young girl and suggested she be taken on as a nurse. Needless to say, she was hired.

3. The Hagia Sophia Cathedral of Constantinople (now Istanbul) was transformed into a mosque by the Ottoman Turks, who seized Constantinople in 1453. An architectural landmark of Orthodox Christianity and symbol of its struggle with Islam, the Hagia Sophia was associated with Russia's imperial ambitions in the south and its control over the Dardanelles Strait, the only navigable passage between the Black Sea and the Mediterranean. Babel presents the "Odessa style" as integral to Russia's imperial mission. —Ed.

1. First published in the Petrograd newspaper *Svobodnye mysli* (March 13, 1917), subheaded "My Notes." "Doudou" may have been based on a French story about World War I, not unlike Babel's other experiments in war literature (see his "On the Field of Honor" in *The Complete Works of Isaac Babel*, pp. 95–103). —Ed.

The new nurse was called *la petite Doudou*. She was kept by the general, and in the evenings danced at the café chantant.

She had a lithe, springy gait, the exquisite, almost angular gait of a dancer. In order to see her, I went to the café chantant. She danced an amazing *tango acrobatique,* with what I'd call chastity mixed with a vague, tender passion.

At the hospital she worshiped all the soldiers, and looked after them like a servant. Once, when the chief surgeon was walking through the halls, he saw Doudou on her knees trying to button up the underpants of a pockmarked, apathetic little man called Dyba.

"Dyba! Aren't you ashamed of yourself?" the surgeon called out. "You should have gotten one of the men to do that!"

Doudou raised her calm, tender face and said: "Oh, *mon docteur,* do you think I have never seen a man in his underpants before?"

I remember on the third day of Passover they brought us a badly injured French airman, a Monsieur Drouot. Both his legs had been smashed to bits. He was a Breton—strong, dark, and taciturn. His hard cheeks had a slight bluish tint. It was so strange to see his powerful torso, his strong, chiseled neck, and his broken, helpless legs.

They put him in a small, private room. Doudou would sit with him for hours. They spoke warmly and quietly. Drouot talked about his flights and how he was all alone, none of his family was here, and how sad it all was. He fell in love with her (it was clear to all), and looked at her as was to be expected: tenderly, passionately, pensively. And Doudou, pressing her hands to her breast, told Sister Kirdetsova in the corridor with quiet amazement: "*Il m'aime, ma soeur, il m'aime.*"[2]

That Saturday night she was on duty and was sitting with Drouot. I was in a neighboring room and saw them. When Doudou arrived, he said: "*Doudou, ma bien aimée!*"[3] He rested his head on her breast and slowly started kissing her dark blue silk blouse. Doudou stood there without moving. Her fingers quivered and picked at the buttons of her blouse.

"What is it you want?" Doudou asked him.

He answered something.

Doudou looked at him carefully and pensively, and slowly undid her lace collar. Her soft, white breast appeared. Drouot sighed, winced, and clung to her. Doudou closed her eyes in pain. But still, she noticed that he was uncomfortable, and so she unhooked her bodice. He clasped Doudou close, but moved sharply and moaned.

"You're in pain!" Doudou said. "You must stop. You mustn't—"

"Doudou!" he said. "I'll die if you leave!"

I left the window. But I still saw Doudou's pale, pitiful face. I saw her try desperately not to hurt him, I heard the moan of passion and pain.

The story got out. Doudou was dismissed—in short, she was fired. The last I saw of her she was standing in the hall, bidding me farewell. Heavy, bright tears fell from her eyes, but she was smiling so as not to upset me.

---

2. French: He loves me, Sister, he loves me.
3. French: Doudou, my lovely. —*Ed.*

"Good-bye!" Doudou said, stretching out her slim, white-gloved hand
to me. "*Adieu, mon ami!*" She fell silent and then added, looking me
straight in the eye: "*Il géle, il meurt, il est seul, il me prie, dirai-je non?*"[4]

At that moment, Dyba, filthy and small, hobbled in at the end of the
hall. "I swear to you," Doudou said to me in a soft, shaking voice. "I
swear to you, if Dyba had asked me to, I would have done the same for
him."

JEWISH FOLKLORE

Despite its subtitle, "Shabos-Nakhamu" is the only known story by Babel to
belong to the *Hershele* cycle. It shows that Babel shared a growing interest in
Jewish folklore, evident among the educated public, both Russian and Jewish,
on the eve of and during World War I. This culture had begun to disappear under the pressures of modernization in the late 1800s, but after August 1914 it
was threatened with physical destruction by the war in the western regions of
the Russian empire, where traditional Jewish life had been nurtured for centuries. Babel makes several references to his planned *Hershele* cycle in *Red
Cavalry* ("The Rabbi") and his *1920 Diary* (July 23, page 206). Apparently, he
continued working on the cycle during the Polish Campaign.—*Ed.*

Shabos-Nakhamu[1]

Morning came, evening came—it was the fifth day of the week. Morning
came, evening came—the sixth day of the week. On the sixth day, on
Friday evening, one prays. Having prayed, one puts one's best hat on and
goes for a stroll through the shtetl and then hurries home for dinner. At
home a Jew will empty a glass of vodka—and neither God nor the Talmud forbid him to empty two—he will eat gefilte fish and raisin cake.
After dinner he feels quite jovial. He talks to his wife and then dozes off,
one eye shut, his mouth hanging open. He dozes, but in the kitchen
Gapka, his wife, hears music—as if a blind fiddler had come from the
shtetl and was playing beneath the window.

This is how things go with your average Jew. But Hershele is not your
average Jew. It wasn't by chance that he was famous in all of Ostropol, in
all of Berdichev, and in all of Vilyuisk.

Hershele celebrated only one Friday evening in six. On other Fridays he
sat in the cold darkness with his family. His children cried. His wife hurled
reproaches at him, each as heavy as a cobblestone. Hershele answered her
with poetry.

Once, word has it, Hershele decided to act with foresight. He set off
on a Wednesday to go to a fair to make some money by Friday. Where
there's a fair there's a goyish gentleman, where there's a goyish gentle-

---

4. French: Good-bye, my love! . . . He is cold, he is dying, he is alone, he begs me to, would I say no?
1. First published in the Petrograd newspaper *Vechernyaya Zvezda* (March 16,1917), subtitled "From
the *Hershele* Cycle." —*Ed.*

man there are sure to be ten Jews hovering about. But you'll be lucky to squeeze three *groschen* out of ten Jews. They all listened to Hershele's routine, but quickly disappeared into thin air when the time came to pay up.

His stomach empty as a wind instrument, Hershele shuffled back home.

"What did you earn?" his wife asked him.

"Everlasting life," he answered. "Both the rich and the poor promised it to me."

Hershele's wife had only ten fingers, but she had many more curses. Her voice boomed like mountain thunder.

"Other women have husbands who are like husbands! All my husband knows how to do is feed his wife jokes! Come New Year, may God rip out his tongue, his arms, and his legs!"

"Amen!" Hershele said.

"Candles burn in every window as if people were burning oak trees in their houses. My candles are thin as matchsticks, and they give off so much smoke that it rises all the way to heaven! Everyone has made their white bread already, but my husband brings me firewood as wet as newly washed hair!"

Hershele did not say a word. First, why throw kindling on a fire when it is blazing brightly? Second, what can one say to a ranting wife when she is absolutely right?

The time came when his wife got tired of shouting. Hershele went to lie down on his bed and think.

"Why don't I go see Rabbi Boruchl?" he thought.

(As is common knowledge, Rabbi Boruchl had a tendency to fall into a black melancholia, and there was no better cure for him than Hershele's jokes.)

"Why don't I go see Rabbi Boruchl? It's true that the *tsaddik's*[2] helpers keep the meat and only give me bones. Meat is better than bones, but bones are better than air. Let's go to Rabbi Boruchl!"

Hershele got up and went to harness his mare. She looked at him severely and morosely.

"This is great, Hershele!" her eyes said. "Yesterday you didn't give me any oats, the day before yesterday you didn't give me any oats, and I didn't get anything today either. If I don't get any oats by tomorrow, I'm going to have to give my life some serious thought."

Hershele could not bear her penetrating stare. He lowered his eyes and patted her soft lips. Then he sighed so loudly that the horse understood. Hershele decided to go to Rabbi Boruchl on foot.

When Hershele set out, the sun stood high in the sky. The hot road ran on ahead. White oxen slowly pulled carts piled high with fragrant hay. Muzhiks sat on these piles, their legs dangling, and waved their long whips. The sky was blue and the whips were black.

About five versts[3] down the road, Hershele came to a forest. The sun was beginning to set. Soft fires raged in the sky. Barefoot girls chased cows from the pastures. The cows' pink udders swung heavily with milk.

---

2. A spiritual leader in a Hasidic community. According to tradition, Hershele served as a jester at the court of Rabbi Boruch (1753–1811), grandson of Hasidism's founder, Baal Shem Tov. —*Ed.*
3. Part of the old Russian measurement system, a verst is about 3,500 feet. —*Ed.*

In the forest, Hershele was met by a cool, quiet twilight. Green leaves bent toward one another, caressed each other with their flat hands, and, softly whispering high in the trees, returned to their places, rustling and quivering.

Hershele did not notice their whispering. An orchestra as large as the ones at Count Potocki's feasts was playing in his belly. The road before him was long. An airy darkness drifted from the edges of the earth, closed over Hershele's head, and scattered over the world. Unmoving lamps lit up in the sky. The world fell silent.

It was night when Hershele came to the inn. A light flickered through the small window by which Zelda the landlady was sitting, sewing swaddling clothes in the warm room. Her belly was so large it looked as if she were about to give birth to triplets. Hershele looked at her small red face and blue eyes and greeted her.

"May I rest here awhile, mistress?"

"You may."

Hershele sat down. His nostrils flared like a blacksmith's bellows. Hot flames were burning in the stove. In a large cauldron water was boiling, pouring steam over the waiting, snow-white dumplings. A plump chicken was bobbing up and down in a golden soup. The aroma of raisin pie wafted from the oven.

Hershele sat on the bench writhing like a woman in labor. His mind was hatching more plots in a minute than King Solomon had wives.

It was quiet in the room; the water was boiling, and the chicken bobbing in the golden soup.

"Where is your husband?"

"My husband went to the goyish gentleman to pay the money for the rent." The landlady fell silent. Her childish eyes widened. Suddenly she said, "I am sitting here at the window, thinking. And I would like to ask you a question, Mr. Jew. I am sure you wander about the world quite a bit, and that you've studied with a rabbi and know about our Jewish ways. Me, I never studied with anyone. Tell me, Mr. Jew, will Shabos-Nakhamu come to us soon?"

"Aha!" Hershele thought. "Not a bad little question! In God's garden all kinds of potatoes grow!"

"I am asking this because my husband promised that when Shabos-Nakhamu comes to us, we will go visit my mother, and he said I'll buy you a new dress, and a new wig, and we'll go to Rabbi Motalemi to ask that a son be born to us, and not a daughter, all of this when Shabos-Nakhamu comes. I think he's someone from the other world."

"You are not mistaken!" Hershele answered. "God placed these words in your mouth. You will have a son and a daughter. I am Shabos-Nakhamu, mistress!"[4]

The swaddling clothes slipped from Zelda's knees. She rose and banged her small head against a beam, for Zelda was tall and plump, flushed and young. Her breasts jutted up like two taut sacks filled with seed. Her blue eyes opened wide, like those of a child.

---

4. Shabbat Nachamu, Sabbath of Consolation, the first of the seven Sabbath of Consolation that follow the commemoration of the destruction of the Temple (Tish b' Ab, the Ninth of Av). —Ed.

"I am Shabos-Nakhamu, mistress!" Hershele said again. "This is the second month that I am walking the earth helping people. It is a long path from heaven down to earth. My shoes are falling apart. I have brought you greetings from all your loved ones."

"From Auntie Pesya?" the woman shouted. "And from Papa, and Auntie Golda? You know them?"

"Who doesn't?" Hershele answered. "I was speaking to them just the way I'm speaking to you now!"

"How are they doing up there?" the woman asked, clutching her belly with trembling fingers.

"They are doing badly," Hershele said dolefully. "How should a dead person be doing? There are no feasts up there!"

The woman's eyes filled with tears.

"It is cold up there," Hershele continued. "They are cold and hungry. They eat just what angels eat, nobody in that world is allowed to eat more than angels. And what do angels need? All they need is a swig of water—up there, you won't see a glass of vodka in a hundred years!"

"Poor Papa!" the devastated woman whispered.

"At Passover he gets one *latke*. And a blin has to last him a day and a night!"

"Poor Auntie Pesya!" the woman stammered.

"I myself have to go hungry!" Hershele said, turning his head away as a tear rolled down his nose and fell into his beard. "And I'm not allowed to complain, as they think of me as one of them."

Hershele didn't get any further.

With fat feet slapping over the floor, the woman ran to get plates, bowls, glasses, and bottles. When Hershele started eating, the woman was completely convinced that he was a man from the other world.

To start with, Hershele ate chopped liver with finely diced onions doused in fat. Then he had a glass of the best vodka (orange peels floated in it). Then he had fish, mashing soft potatoes into the aromatic broth, and he poured on the side of his plate half a jar of red horseradish—a horseradish that would have driven five fully decked-out counts to tears of envy.

After the fish, Hershele busied himself with the chicken, and spooned down the soup in which droplets of fat swam. The dumplings, dipped in melted butter, fled into Hershele's mouth like hares fleeing a hunter. I need not dwell on what happened to the pies—what else could have happened to them if one takes into account that at times a whole year would pass without Hershele ever seeing a pie?

After the meal, the woman collected all the things she wanted to send with Hershele to the other world for Papa, Auntie Golda, and Auntie Pesya. For her father she packed a new prayer shawl, a bottle of cherry liqueur, a jar of raspberry jam, and a pouch of tobacco. For Auntie Pesya she brought out some warm gray stockings. For Auntie Golda she packed an old wig, a large comb, and a prayerbook. She also gave Hershele some shoes for himself, a loaf of bread, fat cracklings, and a silver coin.

"Greet everyone from me, Mr. Shabos-Nakhamu! Greet everyone from me!" she called after Hershele as he left, carrying the heavy bundle. "Or why don't you stay a little longer, until my husband comes back?"

"No," Hershele said. "I must hurry! Do you think you are the only one I have to see?"

In the dark forest the trees were sleeping, the birds were sleeping, the green leaves were sleeping. The stars that stand watch over us had gone pale and began flickering.

After about a verst, Hershele stopped to catch his breath, heaved the bundle off his shoulder, sat on it, and thought things through.

"One thing I must tell you, Hershele!" he said to himself. "There's no lack of fools in this world! The mistress of the inn is a fool, but her husband might well be a clever man with big fists and fat cheeks—and a long whip! What if he comes home and then hunts you down in the forest?"

Hershele did not waste time weighing the odds. He immediately buried his bundle and marked the place so that he could find it again.

Then he ran off toward the opposite side of the forest, took off all his clothes, threw his arms around the trunk of a tree, and waited. He did not have to wait long. As dawn approached he heard the lashes of a whip, the smacking lips of a horse, and the clattering of hooves. It was the innkeeper in full pursuit of Mr. Shabos-Nakhamu.

The innkeeper pulled his cart up to Hershele, who stood naked, hugging the tree. He reined in his horse and looked at Hershele with an expression as foolish as that of a monk coming face-to-face with the devil.

"What are you doing?" the innkeeper asked him in a cracked voice.

"I am a man from the other world," Hershele told him dolefully. "I was robbed—they took some important papers which I was taking to Rabbi Boruchl."

"I know who robbed you!" the innkeeper shouted. "I myself have some accounts to settle with him! Which way did he go?"

"I cannot tell you which way he went!" Hershele whispered bitterly. "But give me your horse, and I shall catch him in an instant! Just wait for me here. Undress, stand by the tree, hug it, and don't move an inch until I return! This tree is a holy tree! Many things in our world depend on it!"

Hershele had been quick to size this man up. One glance had been enough to tell him that husband and wife were not all that far apart. And, sure enough, the innkeeper took off his clothes, went over to the tree, and stood by it. Hershele jumped into the cart and rode off. He dug up his things, put them in the cart, and rode to the edge of the forest.

Hershele left the horse, slung the bundle over his shoulder, and continued along the road that led to Rabbi Boruchl's house.

The sun had already risen. The birds sang, closing their eyes. The innkeeper's mare, her head hanging low, pulled the empty cart back to where she had left her master.

The innkeeper, naked beneath the rays of the rising sun, stood waiting for her huddled against the tree. He felt cold. He was shifting from one foot to the other.

A CULTURAL AND SOCIAL CRITIC
OF THE REVOLUTION

Nothing is known of Babel's whereabouts at the time of the October Revolution or the subsequent months, until in he resurfaced in Petrograd March 1918 and became a staff contributor for Gorky's newspaper *Novaya zhizn*. Gorky used his "Social-Democratic" paper as a vehicle for criticizing the new regime both for encouraging barbarism and for pandering to the barbarity of people ravaged by war and revolution. In later public pronouncements, Babel kept silent about his association with *Novaya zhizn*, which was shut down by the Bolsheviks in July 1918; he claimed instead that he was working as an interpreter for the Petrograd Cheka, the early precursor of the KGB, at the time a less sinister institution than its later incarnations. Such odd combinations of employment were not unheard of in those uncertain days of privation and hardship. Nevertheless, one wonders if Babel actually worked for the Cheka or simply invented this legend as proof of his pro-Bolshevik loyalties after his *Red Cavalry* stories triggered controversy in the Soviet press. —*Ed.*

Mosaic[1]

On Sunday, a day of springtime celebration, Comrade Shpitsberg gives a speech in the grand hall of the Winter Palace.

The title of his speech is "The All-forgiving Persona of Christ and the Vomiting Up of the Anathema of Christianity."

Comrade Shpitsberg calls God "Mr. God," the priests "clerics," "damn clericalists," and, more often than not, "paunchists" (a term he has coined from the word "paunch").

He defines all religions as the "market stalls of charlatans and quacks," denounces the Pope, bishops, archbishops, Jewish rabbis, and even the Tibetan Dalai Lama, "whose excrement the foolish Tibetan democracy considers a medicinal balm."

An attendant is sitting in a niche away from the hall. He is quiet, thin, and clean-shaven. He is surrounded by a horde of people: women, contented workers, unemployed soldiers. The attendant is telling them about Kerensky,[2] bombs exploding beneath the floors, ministers thrown against the smooth walls of dark, echoing corridors, of the feathers bursting from the pillows of Czar Alexander and Czarina Maria Fyodorovna.[3]

A little old woman interrupts his tale. "Where are they giving the lecture, dearie?" she asked him.

1. This is the seventh column Babel published in *Novaya zhizn* (April 21, 1918), Maxim Gorky's anti-Bolshevik "Social-Democratic" Petrograd Newspaper. The first column appeared on March 16, 1918, and the last on July 2, 1918, when the paper was closed by Bolshevik authorities. —*Ed.*
2. Alexander Fyodorovich Kerensky (1881–1970), served as Minister of Justice, Minister of War, and Prime Minister of the Provisional Government, which took over after the abdication of Nicholas II on March 15, 1917. The Provisional Government shared power with the Soviets of Workers' and Soldiers' Deputies, dominated by the Bolsheviks, until the Bolsheviks seized power on November 7, 1917. Kerensky was famous for the highly emotional style of his oratory. —*Ed.*
3. Czar Alexander III (1845–1894) and his wife, Czarina Maria Fyodorovna, then Dowager Empress (1847–1928), *née* Princess Dagmar of Denmark and the mother of Nicholas II (1868–1918).

"The Antichrist is in the Nikolayevsky Hall," the attendant answers indifferently.

A soldier standing nearby laughs. "The Antichrist is in the hall, and you're chattering away here?"

"I'm not frightened," the attendant says with the same indifference as before. "I live with him day and night."

"So you're living it up, ha—"

"No," the attendant says, fixing the soldier with his colorless eyes. "I'm not living it up. Life with him is boring."

And the old man despondently tells the smiling crowd that his devil is short and bashful, walks about in galoshes, and ruins schoolgirls when no one is looking.

The old man doesn't get to finish his tale. Two of his colleagues come and lead him away, saying that since October[4] he has "lost a few of his marbles."

I walk off deep in thought. This old man had seen the Czar, the Revolt, blood, death, the feathers of the Imperial pillows. And the Antichrist had come to him—the Devil had nothing better to do on earth than to dream of schoolgirls and dodge the guards of the Admiralty Subdistrict.[5]

Our devils are a humdrum bunch.

Shpitsberg's sermon on the killing off of Mr. God does not seem to be going all that well. The crowd listens sluggishly, applauds feebly. Things were very different a week before at a similar discussion, which contained "a few short words, but anti-religious ones." Four people were noteworthy: a church warden, a frail psalm reader, a retired colonel in a fez, and a stout storekeeper from the Gostiny Dvor Market. They marched up to the platform. Before them stood a crowd of women and taciturn, menacing shopkeepers.

The psalm reader began in an oily voice: "My friends, let us pray." And ended in a little whisper: "Not everyone is asleep, my friends. Some of us have taken a solemn oath at the tomb of Father Ioann.[6] Set up your parishes once more, my friends!"

The psalm reader left the platform and, squinting with rage, his scrawny body quaking, added: "The whole thing stinks of rotten fish, my friends. The rabbis—they've come out of this scot-free!"

Then the voice of the church warden thundered: "They slaughtered the spirit of the Russian army!" The colonel with the fez shouted: "We will not let them!" And the storekeeper gave a blunt and deafening roar: "Swindlers!"

Bareheaded women thronged around the meekly smiling priests and chased the speaker off the podium, jamming two workers, Red Guardsmen who had been wounded at Pskov, against the wall. One of them started yelling, shaking his fist: "We know your little tricks! In Kolpino[7]

---

4. According to the Julian Calendar, used in Russia until January 31, 1918, the Bolshevik seizure of power fell on October 25, 1917 (November 7, 1917, on the Gregorian Calendar). "October" became a shorthand reference to the Bolshevik October Revolution.
5. Area surrounding the Winter Palace.
6. St. Ioann of Kronstadt (1829–1908), a major figure in the Russian Orthodox Church, was an educator and a popular, charismatic priest associated with the revival of Orthodox Christianity at the turn of the twentieth century. Famous for his clear and simple sermons, he was also known for putting his parishioners into a state of religious ecstasy during his liturgical services. —Ed.
7. A small town outside Petrograd.

they hold evening masses till two in the morning now! They've come up with a new service—a rally in a church! We'll make those cupolas shake!"

"You won't shake nothing, you cursed wretch," a woman said in a muffled voice, turning away from him and crossing herself.

At Easter, the crowds stand with burning candles in the Cathedral of our Lady of Kazan. The people's breath makes the small yellow flames flutter. The immense cathedral is packed from wall to wall. The service is unusually long. Priests in sparkling miters proceed though the halls. There is an artful arrangement of electric lights behind the crucifix. It is as if Christ were stretched out across the starry dark blue sky.

In his sermon the priest speaks of the Holy Countenance that is once more averted in unbearable pain. He speaks of everything holy being spat upon, slapped, and of sacrileges committed by ignorant men "who know not what they do." The words of the sermon are mournful, vague, and portentous. "Flock to the church, our last stronghold! The church will not betray you!"

A little old woman is praying by the portal of the cathedral. "How nicely the chorus is chanting," she says to me tenderly. "What nice services these are! Last week the Metropolitan himself conducted the service—never before has there been such holy goodness! The workers from our factory, they too come to the services. The people are tired, they're all crumpled up with worry, and in the church there's quiet and there's singing, you can get away from everything."

An Incident on the Nevsky Prospekt[1]

I turn from the Liteiny Prospekt onto the Nevsky Prospekt. In front of me walks a young, one-armed man, swaying. He is in uniform. His empty sleeve is pinned to the black cloth of his jacket.

The young man sways. He looks cheerful to me. It is three in the afternoon. Soldiers are selling lilies of the valley, and generals are selling chocolate. It is spring, warm, bright.

I had been mistaken, the one-armed man is not cheerful. He walks up to the wooden fence, which is brightly decorated with posters, and sits down on the hot asphalt of the sidewalk. His body slides down, saliva dribbles out of his distorted mouth, his head, narrow and yellow, lolls to the side.

Slowly people start gathering. They have gathered. We stand there sluggish, whispering, eyeing each other with dull, dumbfounded eyes.

A golden-haired lady is quicker than the rest. She is wearing a wig, has light-blue eyes, bluish cheeks, a powdered nose, and bouncing false teeth. She has fully grasped the situation: the poor invalid has fainted from hunger after returning from a German prison camp.

Her blue cheeks bob up and down. "Ladies and gentlemen!" she says. "The Germans are filling the streets of our capital with their cigar smoke while our poor martyrs . . ."

1. First published in *Novaya zhizn* (Petrograd, June 27, 1918), subheaded "Diary." —*Ed.*

We all gather around the outstretched body in an unhurried but attentive herd. We are all touched by the lady's words.

Prostitutes drop little sugar cubes into the soldier's cap with anxious haste, a Jew buys potato pancakes from a stand, a foreigner throws a bright stream of new ten-kopeck coins, a young lady from one of the stores brings out a cup of coffee.

The invalid writhes on the asphalt, drinks the coffee from the Chinese cup, and chews sweet pies.

"Like a beggar on a church porch!" he mutters, hiccuping, his cheeks flooding with bright tears. "Just like a beggar, just like they've all come to a circus, my God!"

The lady asks us to go on our way. She asks us to show some tact. The invalid rolls onto his side. His stretched-out leg pops up into the air like the leg of a toy clown.

At that moment a carriage pulls up at the curb. A sailor climbs out, followed by a blue-eyed girl with white stockings and suede shoes. She is pressing an armful of flowers to her breast.

The sailor stands in front of the wooden fence, his legs apart. The invalid raises his limp neck and peers timidly at the sailor's bare neck, his carefully curled hair, and his drunk and joyful face covered with specks of powder.

The sailor slowly takes out his wallet and throws a forty-ruble note into the hat. The young man scrapes it up with his rigid, black fingers and raises his watery, canine eyes to the sailor.

The sailor sways on his long legs, takes a step backward, and winks slyly and tenderly at the soldier on the ground.

Stripes of flame light up the sky. An idiot's smile stretches the soldier's lips, we hear a wheezing, yowling laugh, and a stifling stench of alcohol pours from his mouth.

"Lie where you are, Comrade," the sailor tells him, "lie where you are!"

It is spring on the Nevsky Prospekt, warm, bright. The sailor's wide back slowly recedes. The blue-eyed girl, leaning against his round shoulder, smiles quietly. The cripple, wriggling on the asphalt, is overcome by an abrupt, joyous, and nonsensical fit of laughter.

At the Station:
A Sketch from Life[1]

This happened about two years ago at a godforsaken railway station not far from Penza. In the corner of the station a group had gathered. I joined them. It turned out that they were sending a soldier off to war. Someone, drunk, was playing a concertina, raising his face to the sky. A hiccuping youth, a factory hand by the look of him, his thin body quak-

---

1. First published in the short-lived Petrograd newspaper *Era* (July 17, 1918), this piece may have been intended for *Novaya zhizn*, which had just been shut down. —*Ed.*

ing, reached out his hand to the man with the concertina and whispered, "Come, make our souls weep, Vanya!"

Then the youth walked away and, turning his back to the crowd, slyly and carefully poured some eau de cologne into a glass of Khanzha liquor.

A bottle of lusterless liquid was passed from hand to hand. Everyone drank from it. The soldier's father was sitting pale and silent on the ground nearby. The soldier's brother was vomiting incessantly. He keeled over, his face lolling into the vomit, and passed out.

The train pulled in. They began saying their good-byes. The soldier's father kept trying to stand up—he couldn't open his eyes, let alone get on his feet.

"Get up, Semyonich," the factory hand said. "Give your son your blessing!"

The old man didn't answer. The others started shaking him. A button on his fur hat hung loose. A constable came up to them.

"How disgusting!" he muttered. "The man is dead and they're shaking him."

It turned out to be true. The old man had passed out and died. The soldier looked around in dismay. His concertina trembled in his hands and emitted some sounds.

"Just look at you!" the soldier said. "Just look at you!"

"The concertina is for Petka," he added, holding out the concertina.

The stationmaster came out onto the platform.

"Damn loafers!" he muttered. "Some place they've picked to gather! Prokhor, you son of a bitch, ring the second bell!"

The constable hit the bell twice with the large iron key to the station toilet. (The bell's tongue had been ripped out long ago.)

"You should be bidding your father farewell," they told the soldier, "and you're just standing around like an idiot!"

The soldier bent down, kissed his father's dead hand, crossed himself, and dully walked over to the railway car. His brother was still lying in his own vomit.

They took the old man away. The crowd began to disperse.

"That's sobriety for you," an old merchant standing next to me said. "They die like flies, those sons of bitches!"

"Well, brother, don't talk to me about sobriety!" a bearded muzhik said roughly. "Our people is a people that drinks. Our eyes need to be all fuzzy."

"What did you say?" the merchant asked him.

"Take a look," the muzhik said, pointing at the field. "It's black and endless."

"So?"

"Well, nothing, really. You see the murk? The people's eyes have to be like that too—murky."

PETERSBURG TALES

Babel the Petrograd journalist had a parallel life as Babel the author of short stories, which he hoped to organize into a cycle or a book—the promise held out by his subtitles, ("From a Petersburg Diary" "From Oforty, or Etchings," and "From the book *Petersburg 1918*"). Soon after the beginning of World War I, the German-sounding name of St. Petersburg was changed to the Russian-sounding Petrograd, but Babel preferred to use the old name, perhaps as a means of emphasizing both continuities and discontinuities with the Petersburg tradition of Russian letters (see his "Odessa" on page 21.) —*Ed.*

An Evening with the Empress[1]

Siberian salmon caviar and a pound of bread in my pocket. Nowhere to go. I am standing on Anichkov Bridge, huddling against Klodt's horses. A heavy evening is descending from Morskaya. Orange lights wrapped in gauze roam along the Nevsky Prospekt. I need shelter. Hunger is plucking at me the way a clumsy brat plucks at the strings of a violin. My mind skims over all the apartments abandoned by the bourgeoisie. The Anichkov Palace[2] shimmers into view in all its squat splendor. There's my shelter!

It isn't hard to slip into the entrance hall unnoticed. The palace is empty. An unhurried mouse is scratching away in one of the chambers. I am in the library of the Dowager Empress Fyodorovna. An old German is standing in the middle of the room, stuffing cotton wool in his ears. He is about to leave. Luck kisses me on the lips! I know this German! I once typed a report for him, free of charge, about the loss of his passport. This German belongs to me, from his puffy head to his good-natured toes. We decide that I have an appointment with Lunacharsky[3] in the library, and that I am waiting for him.

The melodic ticking of the clock erases the German from the room. I am alone. Balls of crystal blaze above me in the silky yellow light. A warmth beyond description rises from the steam pipes of the central heating. The deep divans wrap my frozen body in calm.

A quick inspection yields results. I discover a potato pie in the fireplace, a saucepan, a pinch of tea and sugar. And behold! The spirit stove just stuck its bluish little tongue out.

That evening I ate like a human being. I spread the most delicate of napkins on an ornate little Chinese table glittering with ancient lacquer. I washed down each piece of my brown ration bread with a sip of sweet, steaming tea, its coral stars dancing on the faceted sides of the glass. The bulging velvet palms of the cushion beneath me caressed my bony hips. Outside the windows, fluffy snow crystals fell on the Petersburg granite deadened by the hard frost.

---

1. First published in the Odessa journal *Siluety* 1 (1922), subheaded "From a Petersburg Diary." Babel reworked it later in his story "The Road" (see page 50). —*Ed.*
2. The main residence of the Dowager Empress Maria Fyodorovna. See note 3, p. 31. —*Ed.*
3. Anatoly Vasilyevich Lunacharsky (1875–1933), leading Bolshevik figure, poet, playwright, critic, and at the time of the story, People's Commissar of Enlightenment. —*Ed.*

Light streamed down the warm walls in glittering lemon torrents, touching book spines that responded with a bluish gold twinkle.

The books, their pages molding and fragrant, carried me to faraway Denmark. Over half a century ago they had been given to the young princess as she left her small, chaste country for savage Russia. On the austere title pages, the ladies of the court who had raised her bade her farewell in three slanting lines, in fading ink, as did her friends from Copenhagen, the daughters of state councilors, her tutors, parchment professors from the Lycée, and her father, the King, and her mother, the Queen, her weeping mother. Long shelves of small plump books with blackened gilt edges, children's Bibles speckled with timid ink splotches, clumsy little prayers written to Lord Jesus, morocco-leather volumes of Lamartine and Chénier[4] containing dried flowers crumbling to dust. I leaf through the gossamer pages that have survived oblivion, and the image of a mysterious country, a thread of exotic days, unfurls before me: low walls encircling the royal gardens, dew on the trimmed lawns, the drowsy emerald canals, the tall King with chocolate sideburns, the calm ringing of the bell above the palace cathedral and, maybe, love—a young girl's love, a fleeting whisper in the heavy halls. Empress Maria Fyodorovna, a small woman with a tightly powdered face, a consummate schemer with an indefatigable passion for power, a fierce female among the Preobrazhensky Grenadiers,[5] a ruthless but attentive mother, crushed by the German woman,[6] unfurls the scroll of her long, somber life before me.

It was very late that night when I tore myself from this sorrowful and touching chronicle, from the specters with their blood-drenched skulls. The balls of crystal covered in swirls of dust were still blazing peacefully above me on the ornate brown ceiling. Next to my tattered shoes, leaden rivulets had crystallized on the blue carpet. Exhausted by my thoughts and the silent heat, I fell asleep.

In the depths of the night I made my way toward the exit over the dully glinting parquet of the corridors. Alexander III's study was a high-ceilinged box with boarded-up windows facing the Nevsky Prospekt. Mikhail Alexandrovich's[7] rooms were the lively apartment of a cultivated

---

4. Alphonse de Lamartine (1790–1869), French Romantic poet. A passionate spokesman for social justice, he was active in the French Revolution of 1848. André de Chénier (1762–1794) was a French poet and journalist. Not unsympathetic to the Revolution, he was a critic of its excesses, and died at the guillotine only to become posthumously one of the most celebrated poets of the romantic age. —*Ed.*

5. Founded by Peter the Great and quartered in St. Petersburg, with one battalion right next to the Winter Palace, the Preobrazhensky Regiment of the Royal Guard figured prominently in palace coups and revolts. Its grenadiers, selected for their exceptional height, served as the royal guard and performed sentry duty at court functions. —*Ed.*

6. Empress Alexandra (1872–1918), the wife of Nicholas II and granddaughter of queen Victoria, was born Princess Alix of Hesse. During World War I, her German origins, made worse by her involvement with the healer monk Grigory Rasputin, became a liability for the royal family. In the popular imagination of 1916–17, Alexandra became the *German woman*, calling into question the royal family's loyalty to the Russian cause and feeding rumors about a German conspiracy in the Winter Palace. She was often contrasted with the "good" czarina, her mother-in-law Maria Fyodorovna. —*Ed.*

7. Grand Duke Mikhail Alexandrovich (1878–1918), the younger brother of Nicholas II. He fell into disfavor after his unsanctioned marriage to a divorcée but restored his reputation after the beginning of World War I as a military commander. In 1917, after Nicholas II abdicated in his favor, Mikhail held consultations with the Duma leadership and the Provisional Government and likewise decided to abdicate. Exiled to Perm by the Bolsheviks in March 1918, he was assassinated by agents of the Cheka on June 12, 1918. —*Ed.*

officer who likes his exercise. The walls were decorated with bright, pink-patterned wallpaper. Little porcelain bibelots, of the naive and redundantly fleshy genre of the seventeenth century, lined the low mantelpieces.

Pressed against a column, I waited for a long time for the last court lackey to fall asleep. He dropped his wrinkled jowls, clean-shaven out of age-old habit, the lantern weakly gilding his high, lolling forehead.

At one in the morning I was out in the street. The Nevsky Prospekt welcomed me into its sleepless womb. I went to the Nikolayevsky Station to sleep. Let those who have fled this city know that there is still a place in Petersburg where a homeless poet can spend the night.

Chink[1]

A vicious night. Slashing wind. A dead man's fingers pluck at the frozen entrails of Petersburg. The crimson pharmacies on street corners freeze over. A pharmacist's prim head lolls to the side. The frost grips the pharmacy by its purple heart. And the pharmacy's heart dies.

The Nevsky Prospekt is empty. Ink vials shatter in the sky. It is two in the morning. The end. A vicious night.

A young girl and a gentleman are sitting by the railing of the Café Bristol. Two whimpering backs. Two freezing ravens by a leafless bush.

"If, with the help of Satan, you manage to succeed the deceased Czar, then see if the masses will follow you, you mother-killers! Just you try! The Latvians will back them, and those Latvians are Mongols, Glafira!"

The man's jowls hang on both sides of his face like a rag peddler's sacks. In the man's reddish brown pupils wounded cats prowl.

"I beg you, for the love of Christ, Aristarkh Terentich! Please go to Nadezhinskaya Street! Who will walk up to me if I'm sitting with a man?"

A Chinese in a leather jacket walks past. He lifts a loaf of bread above his head. With his blue fingernail he draws a line across the crust. One pound. Glafira raises two fingers. Two pounds.

A thousand saws moan in the ossified snow of the side streets. A star twinkles in the hard, inky firmament.

The Chinese man stops and mumbles to her through clenched teeth, "You a dirty one? Huh?"

"I'm a nice clean girl, comrade!"

"Pound."

On Nadezhinskaya Street, Aristarkh looks back with sparks in his eyes.

"Darling," the girl says to the Chinese man in a hoarse voice, "I've got my godfather with me. Will you let him sleep in a corner?"

---

1. The original title, "Khodya," is pejorative slang for a Chinese man. First published in the Odessa journal *Siluety* 6–7 (1923) it was subheaded "From the book *Petersburg, 1918*." Babel was planning a whole cycle of stories linked together by this setting and bringing together short fiction and his "Petrograd Diary" accounts in a form similar to *Red Cavalry*. This cycle never materialized. (See Victor Shklovsky's essay on p. 464.) Chinese guest workers, stranded in Russia by the revolutions, were not uncommon in Petrograd. —*Ed.*

The Chinese man slowly nods his head. O great wisdom of the East!

"Aristarkh Terentich," the girl yells casually, leaning against the smooth leather shoulder. "My acquaintance is inviting you to join us for company!"

Aristarkh Terentich immediately livens up.

"For reasons beyond the control of management, he is currently not employed," she whispers, wriggling her shoulders. "But he had a past with meat and potatoes in it!"

"Definitely. I am pleased to make your acquaintance. Aristarkh Terentich Sheremetsev."

At the hotel they were served Chinese liquor and weren't even asked to pay.

Late at night, the Chinese man slipped out of bed into the darkness of the room.

"Where are you going?" Glafira asked gruffly, twisting her legs.

There was a large sweat stain under her back.

The Chinese man went over to Aristarkh, who was sleeping on the floor by the washstand. He shook the old man's shoulders and pointed to Glafira.

"Oh, yes, yes, pal!" Aristarkh prattled from the floor, "A definite yes!" And with quick little steps he hobbled over to the bed.

"Get away from me, you dog!" Glafira shouted. "Your Chinaman's finished me off already!"

"She won't do it, pal!" Aristarkh hissed quickly. "You ordered her to, but she isn't obeying!"

"He friend!" the Chinese man said. "He do! Big harlot!"

"You are an elderly gentleman, Aristarkh Terentich," the girl whispered, letting the old man climb into bed with her. "What's got into your head?"

Period.

The Sin of Jesus[1]

Arina had a little room by the grand stairway near the guest rooms, and Sergey, the janitor's assistant, had a room near the service entrance. They had done a shameful deed together. Arina bore Sergey twins on Easter Sunday. Water flows, stars shine, muzhiks[2] feel lust, and Arina again found herself in a delicate condition. She is in her sixth month, the months just roll by when a woman is pregnant, and Sergey ends up being drafted into the army—a fine mess! So Arina goes to him and says, "Listen, Sergunya, there's no point in me sitting around waiting for you. We won't see each other for four years, and I wouldn't be surprised if I had another brood of three or four by the time you come back. Working in a hotel, your skirt is

---

1. First published in the one-day newspaper *Na khleb* (To Buy Bread), issued August 29, 1921 to raise money for the victims of the famine that had struck the Volga region. The translation here is based on the 1936 edition of Babel's stories. —*Ed.*
2. Russian: male peasants, here used colloquially for men. —*Ed.*

hitched up more often than not. Whoever takes a room here gets to be your lord and master, Jews or whatever. When you come back from the army my womb will be worn out, I'll be washed up as a woman, I don't think I'll be of any use to you."

"True enough," Sergey said, nodding his head.

"The men who want to marry me right now are Trofimich the contractor, he's a rude roughneck, Isai Abramich, a little old man, and then there's the warden of Nilolo-Svyatskoi Church, he's very feeble, but your vigor has rattled my soul to pieces! As the Lord is my witness, I'm all chewed up! In three months I'll be rid of my burden, I'll leave the baby at the orphanage, and I'll go marry them."

When Sergey heard this he took off his belt and gave Arina a heroic beating, aiming for her belly.

"Hey!" the woman says to him. "Don't beat me on the gut, remember it's your stuffing in there, not no one else's!"

She received many savage wallops, he shed many a bitter tear, the woman's blood flowed, but that's neither here nor there. The woman went to Jesus Christ and said:

"This and that, Lord Jesus. Me, I'm Arina, the maid from the Hotel Madrid & Louvre on Tverskaya Street. Working in a hotel, your skirt is hitched up more often than not. Whoever takes a room there gets to be your lord and master, Jews or whatever. Here on earth walks a humble servant of Yours, Sergey the janitor's assistant. I bore him twins last year on Easter Sunday."

And she told him everything.

"And what if Sergey didn't go to the army?" the Savior pondered.

"The constable would drag him off."

"Ah, the constable," the Savior said, his head drooping. "I'd forgotten all about him. Ah!—and how about if you led a pure life?"

"For four years!" the woman gasped. "Do you mean to say that everyone should stop living a life? You're still singing the same old tune! How are we supposed to go forth and multiply? Do me a favor and spare me such advice!"

Here the Savior's cheeks flushed crimson. The woman had stung him to the quick, but he said nothing. You cannot kiss your own ear, even the Savior knew that.

"This is what you need to do, humble servant of the Lord, glorious maidenly sinner Arina!" the Savior proclaimed in all his glory. "I have a little angel prancing about up in heaven, his name is Alfred, and he's gotten completely out of hand. He keeps moaning, 'Why, O Lord, did you make me an angel at twenty, a fresh lad like me?' I'll give you, Arina, servant of God, Alfred the angel as a husband for four years. He'll be your prayer, your salvation, and your pretty-boy, too. And there's no way you'll get a child from him, not even a duckling, because there's a lot of fun in him, but no substance."

"That's just what I need!" maid Arina cried. "It's their substance that has driven me to the brink of the grave three times in two years!"

"This will be a sweet respite for you, child of God, a light prayer, like a song. Amen."

And thus it was decided. Alfred, a frail, tender youth, was sent down, and fluttering on his pale blue shoulders were two wings, rippling in a rosy glow like doves frolicking in the heavens. Arina hugged him, sobbing with emotion and female tenderness.

"My little Alfredushka, my comfort and joy, my one-and-only!"

The Savior gave her instructions that, before going to bed, she had to take off the angel's wings, which were mounted on hinges, just like door hinges, and she had to take them off and wrap them in a clean sheet for the night, because at the slightest frolic the wings could break, as they were made of infants' sighs and nothing more.

The Savior blessed the union one last time, and called over a choir of abbots for the occasion, their voices thundering in song. There was nothing to eat, not even a hint of food—that wouldn't have been proper—and Arina and Alfred, embracing, descended to earth on a silken rope ladder. They went to Petrovka, that's were the woman dragged him to, she bought him lacquered shoes, checkered tricot trousers (by the way, not only was he not wearing pants, he was completely in the altogether), a hunting frock, and a vest of electric-blue velvet.

"As for the rest, sweetie," she said, "we'll find that at home."

That day Arina did not work in the hotel, she took the day off. Sergey came and made a big to-do outside her room, but she wouldn't open, and called out from behind her door, "Sergey Nifantich, I'm busy washing my feet right now and would be obliged if you would distance yourself without all that to-do!"

He left without saying a word. The angelic power was already taking effect.

Arina cooked a meal fit for a merchant—ha, she was devilishly proud, she was! A quart of vodka, and even some wine, Danube herring with potatoes, a samovar filled with tea. No sooner had Alfred eaten this earthly abundance than he keeled over into a deep sleep. Arina managed to snatch his wings off their hinges just in time. She wrapped them up, and then carried Alfred to her bed.

Lying on her fluffy eiderdown, on her frayed, sin-ridden bed, is a snow-white wonder, an otherworldly brilliance radiating from him. Shafts of moonlight mix with red rays and dart about the room, trippling over their feet. And Arina weeps, rejoices, sings, and prays. The unheard of, O Arina, has befallen you in this shattered world, blessed art thou among women!

They had drunk down the whole quart of vodka. And it was pretty obvious, too. As they fell asleep, Arina rolled over onto Alfred with the hot, six-month gut that Sergey had saddled her with. You can imagine the weight! It wasn't enough that she was sleeping next to an angel, it wasn't enough that the man next to her wasn't spitting on the wall, or snoring, or snorting—no it wasn't enough for this lusty, crazed wench! She had to warm her bloated, combustible belly even more. And so she crushed the Lord's angel, crushed him in her drunken bliss, crushed him in her rapture like a week-old infant, mangled him beneath her, and he came to a fatal end, and from his wings, wrapped in the sheet, pale tears flowed.

Dawn came, the trees bowed down low. In the distant northern woods, every fir tree turned into a priest, every fir tree genuflected.

The woman comes again before the throne of the Savior. She is strong, her shoulders wide, her red hands carrying the young corpse.

"Behold, Lord!"

This was too much for Jesus' gentle soul, and he cursed the woman from the bottom of his heart.

"As it is in the world, Arina, so it shall be with you!"

"But Lord!" the woman said to him in a low voice. "Was it I who made my body heavy, who brewed the vodka, who made a woman's soul lonely and stupid?"

"I do not wish to have anything further to do with you," Lord Jesus exclaimed. "You have crushed my angel, you trollop, you!" And Arina was hurled back down to earth on a purulent wind, to Tverskaya Street, to her sentence at the Madrid & Louvre. There all caution had been thrown to the winds. Sergey was carousing away the last few days before he had to report as a recruit. Trofimich, the contractor, who had just come back from Kolomna, saw how healthy and red-cheeked she was.

"Ooh what a nice little gut!" he said, among other things.

Isai Abramich, the little old man, came wheezing over when he heard about the little gut.

"After all that has happened," he said, "I cannot settle down with you lawfully, but I can definitely still lie with you."

Six feet under, that's where he should be lying, and not spitting into her soul like everyone else! It was as if they had all broken loose from their chains—dishwashers, peddlers, foreigners. A tradesman likes to have some fun.

And here ends my tale.

Before she gave birth—the remaining three months flew by quickly— Arina went out into the backyard behind the janitor's room, raised her horribly large belly to the silken skies, and idiotically uttered, "Here you are, Lord, here is my gut! They bang on it as if it were a drum. Why, I don't know! And then, Lord, I end up like this again! I've had enough!"

Jesus drenched Arina with his tears. The Savior fell to his knees.

"Forgive me, my Arinushka, sinful God that I am, that I have done this to you!"

"I will not forgive you, Jesus Christ!" Arina replied. "I will not!"

Line and Color[1]

I first met Alexander Fyodorovich Kerensky[2] on December 20, 1916, in the dining room of the Ollila Spa. We were introduced by Zatsareni, a barrister from Turkestan. I had heard that Zatsareni had had himself circumcised at the age of forty. That disgraced imbecile Grand Duke Peter Nikolayevich, who was banished to Tashkent, prized Zatsareni's friendship very highly. The Grand Duke used to walk about Tashkent stark naked, married a Cossack woman, lit candles before a portrait of Voltaire[3]

---

1. First published in the Moscow journal *Krasnaya nov* 7 (1923). —*Ed.*
2. See note 2, p. 31. —*Ed.*
3. The pen name of François-Marie Arouet (1694–1778), Enlightenment philosopher and a free thinker. —*Ed.*

as if it were an icon of Jesus Christ, and had the boundless flatlands of Amu-Dari drained. Zatsareni was a good friend to him.

So, there we were at the Ollila Spa. Ten kilometers away shimmered the blue granite walls of Helsingfors.[4] O Helsingfors, love of my heart! O sky, pouring down onto the esplanades and soaring high like a bird!

So, there we were at the Ollila Spa. Northern flowers were withering in vases. Antlers spread across the murky ceilings. The air of the dining room was filled with the fragrance of pine trees, the cool breasts of Countess Tyszkiewicz, and the British officers' silk underwear.

At the table, a courteous converted Jew from the police department was sitting next to Kerensky. To his right, a Norwegian by the name of Nickelsen, the owner of a whaling vessel. To his left, Countess Tyszkiewicz, as beautiful as Marie Antoinette.

Kerensky ate three pieces of cake and went with me for a walk in the forest. Fröken[5] Kirsti hurried past us on skis.

"Who was that?" Kerensky asked me.

"That was Nickelsen's daughter, Fröken Kirsti," I said. "She's beautiful, isn't she?"

Then we saw old Johannes's sledge.

"Who was that?" Kerensky asked.

"That was old Johannes," I said. "He brings cognac and fruit from Helsingfors. Can it be that you don't know old Johannes the coachman?"

"I know everyone here," Kerensky replied, "but I can't see anyone."

"Are you nearsighted, Alexander Fyodorovich?"

"Yes, I'm nearsighted."

"You need glasses, Alexander Fyodorovich."

"Never!"

"If you think about it," I said to him with the brashness of youth, "you are not merely blind, you are as good as dead. The line—that divine trait, that queen of the world—has escaped you forever. You and I are walking through this enchanted garden, this marvelous Finnish forest. To our dying day we will not encounter anything better, and you, you cannot even see the rosy, ice-crusted edges of the waterfall, over there, on the river. The weeping willow, leaning over the waterfall—you cannot see its Japanese delicacy. The red trunks of the pine trees heaped with snow! The granular sparkle that scintillates over the snows! It begins as a frozen line above the tree's wavy surface, like Leonardo's line, crowned by the reflection of the blazing clouds. And what about Fröken Kirsti's silk stockings, and the line of her maturing legs? I beg of you, Alexander Fyodorovich, buy some spectacles!"

"My dear boy," he answered, "don't waste your gunpowder! That half-ruble coin you want me to squander on a pair of spectacles is the one coin that will never leave my pocket! You can keep that line of yours with its repulsive reality. You are living the sordid life of a trigonometry teacher, while I am enveloped by wonders, even in a hole like Klyazma! Why do I need the freckles on Fröken Kirsti's face when I, who can

---

4. A former name (Swedish) for Helsinki, which until Finland's declaration of independence in 1917 was Russian.
5. Swedish: Miss, similar to the German *Fraulein.* —*Ed.*

barely make her out, can imagine everything I want to imagine about her? Why do I need these clouds in the Finnish sky, when I can see a dreamy ocean above my head? Why do I need lines when I have colors? For me the whole world is a gigantic theater in which I am the only spectator without opera glasses. The orchestra plays the prelude to the third act, the stage is far away as in a dream, my heart swells with delight, I see Juliet's crimson velvet, Romeo's violet silk, and not a single false beard—and you want to blind me with a pair of half-ruble spectacles?"

That evening I left for town. O Helsingfors, refuge of my dreams!

I saw Alexander Fyodorovich again half a year later, in June of 1917, after he had become Supreme Commander of the Russian army and master of our fate.[6]

That day[7] the Troitsky drawbridge had been lifted. The Putilov workers were heading for the arsenal. Burning tramcars lay in the streets like dead horses.

The mass rally had gathered at the House of the People.[8] Alexander Fyodorovich gave a speech on Russia, our mother and our wife. The crowd smothered him with its sheepskin-coat passion. Could he, the only spectator without opera glasses, even see the bristling passion of the sheepskin coats? I have no idea. But after him, Trotsky came to the podium, twisted his lips, and, in a voice that chased away one's last hopes, said:

"My Comrades and Brothers!"

Guy de Maupassant[1]

In the winter of 1916 I found myself in Petersburg with forged papers and without a kopeck to my name. Aleksei Kazantsev, a teacher of Russian philology, gave me shelter.

He lived on a frozen, reeking, yellow street in Peski.[2] To increase his meager income, he did Spanish translations—in those days the fame of Blasco Ibáñez[3] was on the rise.

Kazantsev had never been to Spain, not even once, but his whole being was flooded with love for the country—he knew every Spanish castle, park, and river. Besides myself, a large number of men and women who had

6. On June 18, on Kerensky's orders, the Russian army went on the offensive on the Western front, a move that came to be known as the Brusilov breakthrough. —Ed.

7. Babel recalls the massive demonstration of workers and soldiers on June 18, 1917, organized by the Soviets, but dominated by the Socialist Revolutionaries and Mensheviks. Intended to show solidarity with the Provisional Government, the demonstration instead displayed the growing influence of the Bolsheviks among the Soviets' constituency of workers and soldiers. —Ed.

8. The so-called House of the People, formerly the residence of the Emir of Bukhara, housed the pro-Bolshevik First Reserve Machine Gun Regiment, which played a leading role in the demonstration of June 18. Babel must have conflated the dates of the oratorical duel of Kerensky and Trotsky—on June 18, 1917, Kerensky was visiting the city of Kazan on the Volga. —Ed.

1. First published in the Moscow illustrated journal 30 dney 6 (1932), with a dateline at the end of the story, "1920–1922," indicating perhaps the time when the story was drafted. Guy de Maupassant (1850–1893), French short-story writer, was admired by Babel. —Ed.

2. A largely working-class neighborhood in St. Petersburg, notorious for street crime, hooliganism, and dilapidated tenements. —Ed.

3. Vicente Blasco Ibáñez (1867–1928), Spanish novelist and antimonarchist politician. His novels, with their themes of war and social injustice, were particularly popular in Soviet Russia.

fallen through the cracks of life flocked to him. We lived in dire poverty. From time to time our pieces on current events appeared in small print in the popular press.

In the mornings I lounged about in morgues and police stations.

But the happiest of us all was Kazantsev. He had a motherland—Spain.

In November I was offered the position of clerk at the Obukhovsky Factory,[4] not a bad job, bringing with it an exemption from conscription. I refused to become a clerk.

Even in those days, at the age of twenty, I said to myself: Better to suffer hunger, prison, and homelessness than to sit at a clerk's desk ten hours a day. There is no particular daring in making such a pledge, but I haven't broken it to this day, nor will I. The wisdom of my forefathers was ingrained in me: we have been born to delight in labor, fighting, and love. That is what we have been born for, and nothing else.

Kazantsev patted the short yellow down on his head as he listened to my sermon. The horror in his eyes was mixed with rapture.

At Christmas, fortune smiled upon us. Bendersky, a lawyer who owned the Halcyon Publishing House,[5] had decided to bring out a new edition of Maupassant's works. His wife, Raisa, was going to do the translation. But nothing had yet come of the grand enterprise.

Kazantsev, as a Spanish translator, was asked if he knew anyone who might be able to help Raisa Mikhailovna. Kazantsev suggested me.

The following day, donning another man's jacket, I set out to the Benderskys'. They lived at the corner of the Nevsky Prospekt by the Moika River, in a house built of Finnish granite trimmed with pink columns, embrasures, and stone coats of arms. Before the war, bankers without family or breeding—Jewish converts to Christianity who grew rich through trade—had built a large number of such spuriously majestic, vulgar castles in Petersburg.

A red carpet ran up the stairs. Stuffed bears on their hind legs stood on the landings. Crystal lamps shone in their wide-open jaws.

The Benderskys lived on the third floor. The door was opened by a maid in a white cap and pointed breasts. She led me into a living room, decorated in old Slavic style. Blue paintings by Roerich,[6] prehistoric rocks and monsters, hung on the walls. Ancient icons stood on little stands in the corners. The maid with the pointed breasts moved ceremoniously about the room. She was well built, nearsighted, haughty. Debauchery had congealed in her gray, wide-open eyes. Her movements were indolent. I thought how she must thrash about with savage agility when she made love. The brocade curtain that hung over the door swayed. A black-haired, pink-eyed woman, bearing her large breasts before her, came into the living room. It took me no more than a moment to see that Benderskaya was one of those ravishing breed of Jewesses from Kiev or Poltava, from the sated towns of the steppes that abounded

---

4. Steelworks founded in 1863. Its almost twelve thousand workers were to play an important role in the Revolution.

5. The Moscow publishing house "Altsiona" (Halcyon), whose list of authors included some of the best known names of Russian modernism, was active in the 1910s and early 1920s. —*Ed.*

6. Nikolay Konstantinovich Roerich (1874–1947), Russian painter and popular mystic. Many of his works depicted primitive, prehistoric Russia, a subject that was then in vogue. —*Ed.*

with acacias and chestnut trees. These women transmute the money of
their resourceful husbands into the lush pink fat on their bellies, napes,
and round shoulders. Their sleepy smiles, delicate and sly, drive garrison
officers out of their minds.

"Maupassant is the one passion of my life," Raisa told me.

Struggling to restrain the swaying of her large hips, she left the room
and came back with her translation of "Miss Harriet." The translation
had no trace of Maupassant's free-flowing prose with its powerful breath
of passion. Benderskaya wrote with laborious and inert correctness and
lack of style—the way Jews in the past used to write Russian.

I took the manuscript home with me to Kazantsev's attic, where all
night, among his sleeping friends, I cut swaths through Benderskaya's
translation. This work isn't as bad as it might seem. When a phrase is
born, it is both good and bad at the same time. The secret of its success
rests in a crux that is barely discernible. One's fingertips must grasp the
key, gently warming it. And then the key must be turned once, not twice.

The following morning I brought back the corrected manuscript. Raisa
had not lied in speaking of her passion for Maupassant. She sat transfixed as I read to her, her hands clasped together. Her satin arms flowed
down toward the ground, her forehead grew pale, and the lace between
her struggling breasts swerved and trembled.

"How did you do this?"

I spoke to her of style, of an army of words, an army in which every
type of weapon is deployed. No iron spike can pierce a human heart as
icily as a period in the right place. She listened with her head inclined
and her painted lips apart. A black gleam shone in her lacquered hair,
parted and pulled smoothly back. Her stockinged legs, with their strong,
delicate calves, were planted apart on the carpet.

The maid, turning away her eyes in which debauchery had congealed,
brought in breakfast on a tray.

The glass sun of Petersburg reclined on the uneven, faded carpet.
Twenty-nine books by Maupassant stood on a shelf above the table. The
sun, with its melting fingers, touched the books' morocco leather
bindings—the magnificent crypt of the human heart.

We were served coffee in little blue cups, and we began to translate
"Idyll." Who can forget the tale of the hungry young carpenter sucking
milk from the overflowing breasts of the fat wet-nurse. This took place
on a train going from Nice to Marseilles, on a sultry midday in the land
of roses, the motherland of roses where flower plantations stretch down
to the shores of the sea.

I left the Benderskys' with a twenty-five-ruble advance. That evening
our commune in Peski got as drunk as a flock of inebriated geese. We
scooped up the finest caviar and chased it down with liverwurst. Heated
by liquor, I began ranting against Tolstoy.

"He got frightened, our count did! He lacked courage! It was fear that
made him turn to religion! Frightened of the cold, of old age, the count
knitted himself a jersey out of faith!"

"Go on," Kazantsev said, wagging his birdlike head.

We fell asleep on the floor next to our beds. I dreamt of Katya, the
forty-year-old washerwoman who lived on the floor beneath us. In the

---

mornings we would go and get boiling water from her. I'd never had a good look at her face, but in my dream Katya and I did God only knows what. We consumed each other with kisses. The following morning I could not resist going down to her for boiling water.

I came face-to-face with a wilted woman, a shawl tied across her chest, with disheveled ash-gray curls and sodden hands.

From then on I breakfasted every day at the Benderskys'. In our attic we now had a new stove, herring, and chocolate. Twice Raisa drove me out to the islands.[7] I couldn't resist telling her about my childhood. To my own surprise, my tale sounded doleful. Her frightened sparkling eyes peered at me from under her fur hat. The reddish hairs of her eyelashes quivered mournfully.

I met Raisa's husband, a yellow-faced Jew with a bald head and a lean, powerful body that always seemed poised to surge up into the air. There were rumors that he was close to Rasputin. The profits he had made from military supplies had given him the look of a madman. His eyes wandered—the fabric of his reality had been rent. Raisa was embarrassed introducing her husband to new people. Because of my youth, it took me a week longer than it should have to realize this.

After the New Year, Raisa's two sisters came up from Kiev. One day I went to her house with the manuscript of "The Confession," and, not finding her there, dropped by again in the evening. They were in the dining room at the dinner table. I heard silvery neighing and the thunder of excessively jubilant men's voices. Dining is invariably boisterous in wealthy houses that lack pedigree. Their boisterousness was Jewish, with peals of thunder and melodious flourishes. Raisa came out to me in a ball gown, her back bare. Her feet tottered in wavering patent leather shoes.

"Oh, how drunk I am!" And she stretched out her arms draped in platinum chains and emerald stars.

Her body swayed like the body of a snake rising to music toward the ceiling. She shook her curly head, her rings tinkled, and suddenly she fell into an armchair with ancient Russian carving. Scars shimmered on her powdered back.

There was another explosion of women's laughter in the room next door. Out of the dining room came her sisters with their little mustaches, just as big-breasted and tall as Raisa. Their breasts were thrust forward, their black hair flowed free. Both were married to Benderskys of their own. The room filled with rambling female vivacity, the vivacity of mature women. The husbands wrapped the sisters in sealskin coats, in Orenburg shawls,[8] and shod them in black boots. Peering out from the snowy shields of their shawls were their burning, rouged cheeks, their marble noses, and eyes with a nearsighted Semitic sparkle. After some lively commotion, they left for the theater, where Chaliapin was appearing in *Judith*.[9]

7. Islands of the Neva River and the Bay of Finland, on which St. Petersburg was built.
8. Delicate lace shawls, fashionable in Russia at the time, knitted from goat's wool by Orenburg Tatars.
9. Fyodor Chaliapin (1873–1938), the great Russian bass, famous for, among other things, the role of Holofernes in *Judith* (1861–63), an opera by Alexander Nikolayevich Serov (1820–1871). He performed this role in Petrograd in January 1915 and in Moscow from November to December of that year. —Ed.

"I want to work," Raisa jabbered, stretching out her bare arms. "We've lost a whole week."

She brought a bottle and two glasses from the dining room. Her breasts lay loose in the silken sack of her dress. Her nipples stiffened, the silk impeding them.

"A cherished vintage," Raisa said, pouring the wine. "A Muscatel '83. My husband will kill me when he finds out!"

I had never had any dealings with a Muscatel '83 before, and did not hesitate to empty three glasses one after the other. I was immediately wafted off to a little side street where orange flames flickered and music played.

"Oh, how drunk I am. . . . What are we going to do today?"

"Today we're doing 'L'aveu.'"[1]

In other words, "The Confession." The hero of this tale is the sun, *le soleil de France*. Incandescent drops of sun, falling on red-haired Céleste, turned into freckles. Wine, apple cider, and the sun with its steep rays had burnished the face of Polyte, the coachman. Twice a week, Céleste drove into town to sell cream, eggs, and chickens. She paid Polyte ten sous for the ride and four to carry her basket. And on every ride Polyte winked at her and asked, "When are we going to have a bit of fun, *ma belle?*"[2]

"What do you mean by that, Monsieur Polyte?"

"Having fun means having fun, damn it!" Polyte explained, bouncing on the seat. "A man and a woman, no need for music!"

"I don't like such jokes, Monsieur Polyte," Céleste answered, and swept her skirts, which hung over her powerful, red-stockinged calves, away from the young man.

But Polyte, the devil, kept guffawing and coughing. "We'll have fun someday, *ma belle!*" And tears of mirth trickled down his face, which was the color of rust-red blood and wine.

I drank another glass of the cherished Muscatel. Raisa clinked glasses with me.

The maid with the congealed eyes walked through the room and disappeared.

Ce diable de Polyte[3] . . . Over a period of two years Céleste paid him forty-eight francs. Two francs short of fifty! One day at the end of the second year, when they were alone together in the buggy, Polyte, who had drunk some cider before they set out, asked her as usual, "How about having some fun today, Ma'mselle Céleste?"

"I'm at your service, M'sieur Polyte."

Raisa laughed out loud, slumping over the table. *Ce diable de Polyte!*

The buggy was harnessed to a white nag. The white nag, its lips pink with age, walked a slow walk. The joyful sun of France embraced the buggy, shut off from the world by a faded brown cover. The young man and the girl—they needed no music.

---

1. Short story by Guy de Maupassant, from his *Tales of Day and Night* (1885). —*Ed.*
2. French: My pretty one. —*Ed.*
3. French: That devil Polyte.

Raisa handed me a glass. It was the fifth.

"To Maupassant, *mon vieux!*"[4]

"Aren't we going to have some fun today, *ma belle?*"

I reached over to Raisa and kissed her on the lips. They trembled and bulged.

"You're so funny," Raisa muttered through her teeth, tottering backward.

She pressed herself against the wall, spreading her bare arms. Blotches flared up on her arms and shoulders. Of all the gods ever crucified, she was the most captivating.

"Be so kind as to seat yourself, M'sieur Polyte."

She pointed to the reclining blue Slavic armchair. Its back was made of interlaced carved wood on which tails were painted. I stumbled toward it.

Night obstructed my youth with a bottle of Muscatel '83 and twenty-nine books, twenty-nine petards crammed with pity, genius, and passion. I jumped up, knocking over the armchair and bumping into the shelf. Twenty-nine volumes came tumbling onto the carpet, falling onto their spines, their pages flying wild . . . and the white nag of my fate walked a slow walk.

"You're so funny," Raisa growled.

I left the granite house on the Moika Canal after eleven, just before her husband and sisters came back from the theater. I was sober and could have walked a thin plank, but stumbling was far better, and I swayed from side to side, singing in a language I had just invented. Mists of fog rolled in waves through the tunnels of streets girded with a chain of street lamps. Monsters roared behind seething walls. The carriageways cut the legs that walked over them.

Back at home Kazantsev was asleep. He slept sitting up, his haggard legs stretched out in felt boots. The canary down was fluffed up on his head. He had fallen asleep by the stove, hunched over a 1624 edition of *Don Quixote*. There was a dedication on the title page to the Duke de Broglio. I lay down quietly so as not to wake Kazantsev, pulled the lamp toward me, and began to read Édouard de Maynial's book *The Life and Works of Guy de Maupassant*.[5]

Kazantsev's lips moved, his head lolled forward.

That night I learned from Édouard de Maynial that Maupassant was born in 1850 to a Norman nobleman and Laure Le Poittevin, Flaubert's cousin. At twenty-five, he had his first attack of congenital syphilis. He fought the disease with all the potency and vitality he had. In the beginning, he suffered from headaches and bouts of hypochondria. Then the phantom of blindness loomed before him. His eyesight grew weaker. Paranoia, unsociability, and belligerence developed. He struggled with passion, rushed about the Mediterranean on his yacht, fled to Tunis, Morocco, and central Africa, and wrote unceasingly. Having achieved fame, he cut his throat at the age of forty, bled profusely, but lived. They locked him in a madhouse. He crawled about on all fours and ate his

---

4. French: My old friend. —*Ed.*
5. *La vie et l'oeuvre de Guy de Maupassant* was published by Société du Mercure de France in 1906.

own excrement. The last entry in his sorrowful medical report announces: "*Monsieur de Maupassant va s'animaliser.*" (Monsieur de Maupassant is degenerating to an animal state.) He died at the age of forty-two. His mother outlived him.

I read the book through to the end and got up from my bed. The fog had come to the window, hiding the universe. My heart constricted. I was touched by a premonition of truth.

The Road[1]

I left the crumbling front in November 1917. At home my mother packed underwear and dried bread for me. I arrived in Kiev the day before Muravyov began shelling the city.[2] I was trying to get to Petersburg. For twelve days and nights I hid with Chaim Tsiryulnik in the basement of his hotel in Bessarabka.[3] The commander of Soviet Kiev issued me a pass to leave the city.

In all the world there is no more cheerless sight than the Kiev train station. For many years makeshift wooden barracks have defaced the town outskirts. Lice crackled on wet planks. Deserters, smugglers, and gypsies were all crowded together in the station. Old Galician women urinated standing on the platform. The low sky was furrowed with clouds full of rain and gloom.

Three days went by before the first train left. At first it stopped every verst; then it gathered speed, its wheels rattling faster, singing a powerful song. This filled everyone in our transport car with joy. Fast travel filled people with joy in 1918. At night, the train gave a jolt and stopped. The door of our car opened, and we saw the green glimmer of snow before us. A station telegrapher in soft Caucasian boots and a fur coat tied with a strap climbed aboard. The telegrapher stretched out his hand and tapped his finger on his open palm. "Put all travel permits here!"

Right by the door an old woman lay quietly curled up on some bundles. She was heading for Lyuban to her son, who was a railroad worker. Dozing next to me was a schoolmaster, Yehuda Veynberg, and his wife. The schoolmaster had married a few days earlier, and was taking his young wife to Petersburg. They had been whispering throughout the journey about new structured methods in teaching, and then dozed off. Their hands were clasped even in sleep.

The telegrapher read their permit signed by Lunacharsky,[4] pulled a Mauser with a thin, dirty muzzle from under his coat, and shot the schoolmaster in the face.

---

1. First published in the Moscow illustrated journal *30 dney* 3 (1930). Babel datelined the story "1920–1930" in part to highlight its autobiographical character and also to affirm his loyalty to the regime after he came under suspicion in 1930. See also "An Evening with the Empress."—*Ed.*
2. Kiev was then the capital of the Ukraine, which declared its independence from Russia on January 22, 1918. The Red forces, under the command of Mikhail Artemiyevich Muravyov (1880–1918), began shelling Kiev on January 27 and had complete control of the city by February 9, 1918. —*Ed.*
3. A poor district on the outskirts of Kiev. —*Ed.*
4. See note 3, p. 36.

A big, hunchbacked muzhik in a fur cap with dangling earflaps was standing behind the telegrapher. The telegrapher winked at him, and the muzhik put his lamp on the floor, unbuttoned the dead man's trousers, sliced off his sexual organs with a pocketknife, and stuffed them into the wife's mouth.

"*Tref*[5] wasn't good enough for you!" the muzhik said. "So now eat something kosher!"

The woman's soft throat swelled. She remained silent. The train was standing on the steppes. The furrowed snows swarmed with polar brilliance. Jews were being thrown out of the cars onto the rails. Shots rang out unevenly, like shouts. The muzhik in the fur cap with the dangling earflaps took me behind a pile of logs and began to search me. The darkened moon shone down on us. Smoke rose from the forest's lilac wall. Frozen wooden fingers crept stiffly over my body.

"A Yid or a Russian?" the telegrapher yelled from the car platform.

"Yeah, a Russian! So much so, he'd make a first-rate rabbi!" the muzhik muttered as he searched me.

He brought his wrinkled, anxious face close to mine, ripped out the four golden ten-ruble coins which my mother had sewn into my underwear for the journey, took my boots and my coat, and then, turning me around, hit me on the back of my neck with the edge of his palm and said in Yiddish, "*Ankloyf, Chaim!*"[6]

I ran, my bare feet sinking in the snow. I felt him mark a target on my back, the nip of his aim cutting through my ribs. But the muzhik did not shoot. A light was quavering within a garland of smoke among the columns of pine trees, within the covered cellar of the forest. I ran toward the hut. The smoke of burning dung patties rose from it. The forester groaned when I burst into his hut. Huddled in strips cut from furs and coats, he was sitting on a finely wrought bamboo armchair with velvet cushions, crumbling tobacco on his knees. Enveloped in smoke, the forester groaned again, got up, and bowed deeply.

"You mustn't come in here, my dearest friend! You mustn't come in here, dearest Citizen!"

He led me to a path and gave me some rags to wrap my feet in. By late next morning I had reached a shtetl. There was no doctor at the hospital to amputate my frostbitten feet. The medical orderly was running the ward. Every morning he came galloping over to the hospital on his short black stallion, tied it to the hitching post, and came over to us full of fire, sparks burning in his eyes.

"Friedrich Engels teaches us that there should be no nations," the medical orderly said, bending over the head of my bed, his pupils fiery coals. "And yet we say the opposite—nations have to exist."[7]

Ripping the bandages off my feet, he straightened his back, and, gnashing his teeth asked me in a low voice, "So where is it taking you,

5. The dietary laws, *kashruth*, observed by Orthodox Jews, distinguish between *tref* (or *treif*, improper food) and *kosher* (proper or fit for consumption). —*Ed.*
6. Yiddish: Run away, Chaim.
7. The orderly is a Ukrainian nationalist, opposed to the Marxist internationalist vision that animated Bolshevik expansionism after the revolution. His invocation of Engels is a garbled reference to the *Communist Manifesto* of Karl Marx and Friedrich Engels, the founding document of the world communist movement. Identification of Jews with the communists was a commonplace prejudice during the Civil War. —*Ed.*

this nation of yours? Where? Why doesn't it stay in one place? Why is it stirring up trouble, making waves?"

The Soviets moved us out on a cart in the night: patients who had not seen eye to eye with the medical orderly and old Jewesses in wigs, the mothers of the shtetl commissars.

My feet healed. I continued along the destitute road to Zhlobin, Orsha, and Vitebsk. The muzzle of a howitzer acted as my shelter from Novosokolniki to Loknya.[8] We were riding on the uncovered cannon platform. Fedyukha, my chance traveling companion, a storyteller and witty jokester, was undertaking the great journey of the deserters. We slept beneath the powerful, short, upward-pointing muzzle, and warmed each other in the canvas pit, covered with hay like the den of an animal. After Loknya, Fedyukha stole my suitcase and disappeared. The shtetl soviet had issued me the suitcase along with two pairs of soldier's underwear, dried bread, and some money. Two days went by without food as we approached Petersburg. At the station in Tsarskoe Selo[9] I witnessed the last of the shooting. The defense detachment fired shots into the air as our train pulled in. The smugglers were led out onto the platform and their clothes were ripped off, and rubber suits filled with vodka came tumbling off of them onto the asphalt.

Shortly after eight in the evening, the Petersburg station hurled me from its howling bedlam onto the Zagorodny Boulevard. A thermometer on the wall of a boarded-up pharmacy across the street showed −24 degrees Celsius. The wind roared through the tunnel of Gorokhovaya Street; jets of gaslight faded over the canals. This frozen, basalt Venice stood transfixed. I entered Gorokhovaya Street, which lay there like a field of ice cluttered with rocks.

The Cheka[1] had installed itself at number 2, the former office of the governor. Two machine guns, iron dogs with raised muzzles, stood in the entrance hall. I showed the commandant the letter from Vanya Kalugin, my sergeant in the Shuysky Regiment. Kalugin had become an investigator in the Cheka, and had sent me a letter to come see him.

"Go to Anichkov Palace," the commandant told me. "He's there now."

"I'll never make it," I thought, and smiled at him.

The Nevsky Prospekt flowed into the distance like the Milky Way. Dead horses lay along it like milestones. Their legs, pointing upward, supported the descending sky. Their bare bellies were clean and shiny. An old man who resembled an Imperial guardsman trudged past me, dragging a wooden toy sledge behind him, driving his boots with difficulty into the ice. A Tyrolean hat was perched on his head, and he had tied his beard with a piece of string and stuck it into his shawl.

"I'll never make it," I said to the old man.

---

8. Zhlobin, Orsha, and Vitebsk are towns, today in Belarus, that the narrator passed through on his way north from Kiev to Petersburg. Novosokolniki and Loknya are Russian towns on the other side of the Belarus border.
9. The summer residence of the royal family outside St. Petersburg, now Pushkin.
1. Cheka, the All-Russian Extraordinary Commission for the Struggle Against Counter-Revolution and Sabotage, was founded in Petrograd on December 20, 1917. Unlike the regular police, who dealt with more ordinary and minor criminal offences, Cheka was run by the Party and dealt with political crimes, espionage, corruption, the black market, and other forms of economic activity outlawed by the Bolsheviks. It grew into the secret police, the most powerful Soviet institution known variously as GPU, NKVD, MGB, and KGB. —Ed.

He stopped. His furrowed leonine face was filled with calm. He hesitated for a moment, but then continued dragging the sledge along the street.

"Thus falls away the need to conquer Petersburg," I said to myself, and tried to remember the name of the man who had been crushed by the hooves of Arab stallions at the very end of his journey. It was Yehuda Halevi.[2]

Two Chinese men in bowler hats stood on the corner of Sadovaya Street with loaves of bread under their arms. They showed them to passing prostitutes, and with frozen fingernails drew lines across the crust. The women walked past them in a silent parade.

At Anichkov Bridge I sat on the base of the statue by Klodt's horses.[3]

I lay down on the polished flagstone, my elbow under my head, but the freezing granite blistered me, and drove, pushed, propelled me forward to the palace.

The portal of the raspberry-red side wing stood open. Blue gaslight shone above a lackey, who had fallen asleep in an armchair. His lower lip was hanging from an inky, moribund face filled with wrinkles, and his military tunic, flooded with light, hung beltless over livery trousers trimmed with gold lace. A splotchy arrow, drawn in ink, pointed the way to the commandant. I went up the stairs and passed through low, empty chambers. Women painted in somber black danced rounds on ceilings and walls. Iron grates covered the windows, their broken latches hung on the frames. At the end of the suite of chambers Kalugin was sitting at a table, lit as if on stage, his head framed by straw-colored muzhik hair. On the table in front of him was a heap of toys, colorful rags, and torn picture books.

"So here you are!" Kalugin said, raising his head. "Great! We need you here."

I brushed aside the toys piled on the table, lay down on the shining tabletop, and . . . woke up on a low sofa—perhaps a few minutes, perhaps a few hours later. The lights of a chandelier danced above me in a waterfall of glass. The wet rags that had been cut off me lay on the floor in a puddle.

"You need a bath," Kalugin told me, standing above the sofa. He lifted me up and carried me to a bathtub. It was an old-fashioned tub, with low sides. The water didn't flow from taps. Kalugin poured water over me with a bucket. Clothes were laid out on yellowish satin pouffes, on wicker stools—a robe with buckles, a shirt and socks of double woven silk. The long underpants went all the way up to my head, the robe had been tailored for a giant, the sleeves were so long I tripped over them.

"So you're making fun of old Alexander Alexandrovich?" Kalugin said as he rolled up my sleeves. "The old boy weighed a good nine *pood*!"[4]

We somehow managed to tie Czar Alexander III's robe, and went back to the room we had been in before. It was the library of Maria

2. Yehuda Halevi (1075–1141), Jewish poet and religious philosopher from Toledo, who embarked on a pilgrimage to Palestine at the end of his life. According to legend, he died within sight of Jerusalem, killed by an Arab horseman. —Ed.
3. A sculpture of a group of horses by Peter Karlovich Klodt (1805–1867).
4. Czar Alexander III (1845–1894) lived in the Anichkov Palace. Nine *pood* is 325 pounds.

Fyodorovna,[5] a perfumed box, its walls lined with gilded bookcases filled with crimson spines.

I told Kalugin which of our men in the Shuysky Regiment had been killed, who had become a commissar, who had gone to Kuban. We drank tea, and stars streamed over the crystal walls of our glasses. We chased our tea down with horsemeat sausages, which were black and somewhat raw. The thick, airy silk of a curtain separated us from the world. The sun, fixed to the ceiling, reflected and shone, and the steam pipes from the central heating gave off a stifling heat.

"You only live once," he said, after we had finished our horsemeat. He left the room and came back with two boxes—a gift from Sultan Abdul Hamid[6] to the Russian sovereign. One was made of zinc, the other was a cigar box sealed with tape and paper emblems. *"A sa majesté, l'Empereur de toutes les Russies,"*[7] was engraved on the zinc lid, "from his well-wishing cousin."

Maria Fyodorovna's library was flooded with an aroma she had known a quarter of a century ago. Cigars twenty centimeters long and thick as a finger were wrapped in pink paper. I do not know if anyone besides the autocrat of all the Russias had ever smoked such cigars, but nevertheless I chose one. Kalugin looked at me and smiled.

"You only live once," he said. "Let's hope they've not been counted. The lackeys told me that Alexander III was an inveterate smoker. He loved tobacco, kvass, and champagne. But on his table—take a look!—there are five-kopeck clay ashtrays, and there are patches on his trousers!"

And sure enough, the robe I had been arrayed in was stained, shiny, and had been mended many times.

We passed the rest of the night going through Nicholas II's toys, his drums and locomotives, his christening shirt, and his notebooks with their childish scribbles. Pictures of grand dukes who had died in infancy, locks of their hair, the diaries of the Danish Princess Dagmar,[8] the letters of her sister, the Queen of England,[9] breathing perfume and decay, crumbling in our fingers. On the title pages of the Bible and Lamartine,[1] her friends and governesses—the daughters of burgomasters and state councilors—bade farewell in laborious slanting lines to the princess leaving for Russia. Her mother, Louisa, queen of a small kingdom, had put much effort into seeing her children well settled. She gave one of her daughters to Edward VII, the Emperor of India and King of England, and the other to a Romanov. Her son George was made King of Greece. Princess Dagmar turned into Maria in Russia. The canals of Copenhagen and the chocolate sideburns of King Christian faded in the distance. Bearing the last of the sovereigns, Maria, a tiny woman with the fierceness of a fox, hurried through the palisades of the Preobrazhensky

5. See note 3, p. 31. —*Ed.*
6. Abdul Hamid II (1842–1918), Sultan of the Ottoman Empire.
7. French: To your majesty, the emperor of all of the Russias. —*Ed.*
8. Empress Maria Fyodorovna.
9. Queen Alexandra (1844–1925), Queen Consort of Edward II of England.
1. See note 4, p. 37.

Grenadiers.[2] But her maternal blood was to spill on Russia's implacable, unforgiving granite earth.[3]

We could not tear ourselves from the dull, fatal chronicle till dawn. I had finished smoking Abdul-Hamid's cigar. In the morning, Kalugin took me to the Cheka, to Gorokhovaya Street, number two. He had a word with Uritsky.[4] I stood behind a heavy curtain that hung to the ground in cloth waves. Fragments of words made their way through to me.

"He's one of us," Kalugin said. "His father is a storekeeper, a merchant, but he's washed his hands of them. . . . He knows languages."

Uritsky came out of his office with a tottering gait. His swollen eyelids, burned by sleeplessness, bulged behind the glass of his pince-nez.

They made me a translator in the Foreign Division. I was issued a military uniform and food coupons. In a corner of the Petersburg City Hall that was allocated to me I set about translating depositions of diplomats, agents provocateurs, and spies.

Within a single day I had everything: clothes, food, work, and comrades true in friendship and death, comrades the likes of which you will not find anywhere in the world, except in our country.

That is how, thirteen years ago, a wonderful life filled with thought and joy began for me.[5]

The *Ivan and Maria*[1]

In the summer of 1918 Sergey Vasilevich Malishev,[2] who was to become the chairman of the Nizhny-Novgorod Fair Committee, organized our nation's first produce expedition. With Lenin's approval, he loaded a series of trains with goods useful to peasants, and sent these trains to the Volga region to exchange the goods for wheat.

I ended up in the clerical department of this expedition. We chose the Novo-Nikolayev district in the province of Samara as our field of operation. According to the specialists, this province, if properly cultivated, was capable of feeding the whole Moscow region.

2. The Romanovs' royal guard, selected for their height. See note 5, p. 37.
3. Babel refers to the death of Maria Fyodorovna's sons, including Nicholas II and his family, at the hands of the Bolsheviks in 1918. —*Ed.*
4. Mikhail (Moisey) Solomonovich Uritsky (1873–1918), People's Commissar of Internal Affairs for the Northern Region (formerly St. Petersburg Gubernia) and chairman of the Petrograd Cheka. He was assassinated on August 30, 1918. A sharp increase in Red Terror followed the assassination, and Uritsky's image became fixed in the pantheon of Bolshevik martyrs. —*Ed.*
5. Scholars and members of Babel's family are skeptical about Babel's service in the Cheka in 1918. Babel scholar Vadim Kovsky queried the St. Petersburg branch of the agency after the fall of communism and was told officially that there were no records indicating that Babel (or Ivan Kalugin) ever worked for the agency ("Sudba tekstov v kontekste sudby," *Voprosy literatury* 1 [1995]). Vitaly Shentalinsky, the first to examine Babel's secret police dossier, also drew a blank (*Arrested Voices*, 1996). Babel may have done occasional translating or interpreting for the Cheka, which would not have left any records in 1918. He may have later stressed this work when it suited him, as it did in 1932 when he was trying to get permission to visit his family in France. —*Ed.*
1. First published in the Moscow monthly *30 dney* 4 (1932) with the dateline 1920–1928. The Russian title of this novella, *Ivan-da-Marya* (Ivan-and-Maria), also the name of the steamer in the story, is a common Russian name for a field plant (*Melampyrum nemorosum*, a type of salvia) that combines violet and yellow flowers. It often appears in Russian folklore as a symbol of contrasting but interrelated pairs. —*Ed.*
2. Sergey Vasilyevich Malyshev (1877–1938), nicknamed "The Red Merchant," one of the chief trade administrators during the early years of Soviet rule.

Near Saratov,[3] the goods were reloaded onto a barge at the river docks of Uvek. The hold of this barge became a makeshift department store. We pinned up portraits of Lenin and Marx between the curved ribs of our floating warehouse and framed the portraits with ears of corn, and we arranged bales of calico, scythes, nails, and leather goods on the shelves, even concertinas and balalaikas.

At Uvek we had been given a tugboat, the *Ivan Tupitsin*, named after a Volga merchant who had been its previous owner.[4] The "staff," Malishev with his assistants and cashiers, made themselves at home on the tugboat, while the guards and sales clerks slept on the barge, under the counters.

It took a week to load the goods onto the barge. On a July morning[5] the *Ivan Tupitsin*, gushing fat puffs of smoke, began to pull us up the Volga to Baronsk.[6] The local German settlers call it Katarinenstadt. It is now the capital of the Volga German Province, a wonderful region settled by hardy, taciturn folk.

The steppes outside Baronsk are covered with heavy, golden wheat, such as you can only find in Canada. They are filled with sunflower and black oily clumps of earth. We had traveled from a Petersburg licked clean by granite flames to a California that was Russian through and through, and therefore even more outlandish. In our own California a pound of grain cost sixty kopecks, and not ten rubles as it did back in the north. We threw ourselves onto the loaves of bread with a savagery that nowadays is impossible to understand. We plunged our canine teeth, sharpened by hunger, into the bread's gossamer core. For two weeks we languished in a blissful drunkenness of indigestion. To me, the blood flowing through our veins had the taste and color of raspberry jam.

Malishev's calculations had been right: sales went well. Slow streams of carts flowed to the riverbank from all corners of the steppes. The sun crept over the backs of well-fed horses. The sun shone on the tops of the wheat-covered hills. Carts in a thousand dots descended to the Volga. Giants in woolen jerseys, descendants of the Dutch farmers who had settled in the Volga regions in the days of Catherine, strode beside the horses. Their faces looked just as they had back in Zaandam[7] and Haarlem. Drops of sparkling turquoise shone from within a mesh of leathery wrinkles beneath patriarchal mossy eyebrows. Smoke from tobacco pipes melted into the bluish lightning that flashed over the steppes. The settlers slowly climbed the gangplank onto the barge. Their wooden shoes clanged like bells heralding strength and peace. The goods were chosen by old women in starched bonnets and brown bodices. Their purchases were carried to the carts. Village painters had strewn armfuls of wildflowers and pink bull muzzles along the sides of the carts—the outer sides were usually painted a

3. Saratov, the capital of Saratov Gubernia, situated to the south and east of Moscow in the Volga basin, close to the border of Europe and Asia. Founded in the sixteenth century, it was settled by German colonists in the eighteenth century by the invitation of Catherine the Great. —*Ed.*
4. The tugboat steamer *Ivan Tupitsyn* did indeed ply the waters of the Volga at the time of this story. —*Ed.*
5. There are no known publications by Babel in the Petrograd press between July 17 and November 11, 1918. —*Ed.*
6. Baronsk, named after the founder Baron Beauregard, a town of German settlers some fifty kilometers northeast of Saratov. It was variously referred to as Katarinenstadt, Ekaterinstadt, or Katarinstadt, and was renamed Marxstadt under the Soviets. —*Ed.*
7. Today Zaanstad.

deep blue, within which waxen apples and plums gleamed, touched by the rays of the sun.

People from far away rode in on camels. These animals lay on the river-bank, their collapsed humps cutting into the horizon. Our trading always ended toward evening. We locked our store. The guards—war invalids—and the sales clerks undressed and jumped off the barges into the Volga burning in the sunset. On the distant steppes the wheat rolled in red waves. The walls of the sunset were collapsing in the sky. The swimming workers of the Samara Province Produce Expedition (that is what we were called in official documents) were an unusual spectacle. The cripples spouted silty pink streams from the river. Some of the guards were one-legged, others were missing an arm or an eye. They hooked themselves up in twos so they could swim. Two men would then have two legs, thrashing the water with their stumps, silty streams rushing in whirls between their bodies. Growling and snorting, the cripples rolled out onto the riverbank, frolicking, shaking their stumps at the flowing skies, covering themselves with sand, and wrestling, grabbing hold of each other's chopped extremities. After swimming, we went to the tavern of Karl Biedermayer. Our day was crowned by supper there. Two girls with brick-red hands, Augusta and Anna, served us meat patties—red flagstones quivering under whorls of seething butter and heaped with haystacks of fried potatoes. They spiced this mountain of village fare with onions and garlic. They placed jars of sour pickles in front of us. The smoke of the sunset wafted in from the marketplace through little round windows high up near the ceiling. The pickles smoldered in the crimson smoke and smelled of the seashore. We washed down the meat with cider. Every evening we, the residents of Peski and Okhta, men of the Petersburg suburbs that were frozen over with yellow urine, once again felt like conquerors. The little windows, cut into black walls centuries old, resembled portholes. Through them shone a courtyard, blissfully clean, a little German courtyard with rosebushes and wisteria, and the violet precipice of an open stable. Old women in bodices sat on stoops, knitting stockings for Gulliver. Herds were coming back from the pastures. Augusta and Anna sat down on stools beside the cows. Radiant bovine eyes glittered in the twilight. It was as if there had never been war on earth. And yet the front of the Ural Cossacks was only twenty versts from Baronsk.[8] Karl Biedermayer had no idea that the Civil War was rolling toward his home.

At night I returned to our hold in the barge with Seletsky, who was a clerk, just as I was. He sang as we walked. Heads in nightcaps peered out of lancet windows. The moonlight flowed down the roof tiles' red canals. The muffled barking of dogs rose above this Russian Zaandam. Riveted Augustas and Annas listened to Seletsky's song. His deep bass carried us to the steppes, to the gothic enclosure of the wheat barns. Crossbeams of moonlight flickered on the river, and the breezy darkness swept over the sand of the riverbanks. Iridescent worms writhed in a torn sweep net.

Seletsky's voice was unnaturally powerful. He was an enormous fellow who belonged to that race of provincial Chaliapins,[9] of which so many, to our great fortune, have arisen throughout Russia. He even had the same

---

8. The Red Army was fighting the White counterrevolutionary troops made up of Ural Cossacks and Czech divisions.
9. See note 9, p. 47.

kind of face as Chaliapin, part Scottish coachman, part grandee from
the era of Catherine the Great. Seletsky was a simple man, unlike his
divine prototype, but his voice resounded boundlessly, fatally, filled one's
soul with the sweetness of self-destruction and gypsy oblivion. Seletsky
preferred the songs of convicts to Italian arias. It was from him that I
first heard Grechaninov's[1] song "Death." It resounded, menacing, relentless, passionate, over the dark water through the night.

> She will not forget, she will come to you,
> Caress, embrace, and love you for all eternity.
> But a bridal wreath of thorns shall crown her head.[2]

This song flows within man's ephemeral shell like the waters of eternity. It washes away everything, it gives birth to everything.

The front was twenty versts away. The Ural Cossacks, joined by Major
Vozenilek's Czech battalion,[3] were trying to drive the dispersed Red
detachments out of Nikolayevsk. Farther north, the troops of Komuch—
the Committee of the Members of the Constituent Assembly—were advancing from Samara.[4] Our scattered, untrained units regrouped on the
left bank. Muravyov had just betrayed us. Vatsetis was appointed the Soviet commander in chief.[5]

Weapons for the front were brought from Saratov. Once or twice a
week the pink and white paddle steamer Ivan and Maria docked at
Baronsk. It carried rifles and shells. Its deck was full of boxes with skulls
stenciled on them, under which the word "lethal" was written.

The ship's captain, Korostelyov, was a man ravished by drink, with lifeless flaxen hair. He was an adventurer, a restless soul, and a vagabond.
He had traveled the White Sea on sailing vessels, walked the length and
breadth of Russia, had done time in jail and penance in a monastery.

We always dropped by to see him on our way back from Biedermayer's
if there were still lights on board the Ivan and Maria. One night, as we
passed the wheat barns with their enchanted blue and brown castle sil-
houettes, we saw a torch blazing high in the sky. Seletsky and I were
heading back to our barge in that warm, passionate state of mind that
can only be spawned by this wondrous land, youth, night, and the melting rings of fire on the river.

1. Alexander Grechaninov (1864–1956), Russian composer and author of some two hundred lieder. —Ed.
2. The Russian Orthodox marriage rite is referred to in Russian as venchanie or crowning. In the song, it is Death (feminine in Russian) who bestows her heavy crown (tiazhelyi venets) on her "beloved."—Ed.
3. The Czechoslovak Corps, prisoners of war at the time of the Revolution and stationed in the Urals region, staged a revolt against the Bolshevik authorities in May 1918 and for the next four months held large swaths of territory east of the Volga. —Ed.
4. Samara, a major commercial and industrial center on the Volga north of Saratov, was then in the hands of the anti-Bolshevik Committee of the Members of the Constituent Assembly (Komuch). —Ed.
5. Mikhail Artemyevich Muravyov (1880–1918), a czarist officer and a Socialist Revolutionary who offered his military services to the Bolsheviks in 1917 and was put in charge of the defense of Petrograd. In the spring and summer of 1918, he commanded the Eastern Front but mutinied after learning of the Socialist Revolutionary uprising in Moscow. He was defeated and shot by the Latvian detachments commanded by Ioakim Ioakimovich Vatsetis (1873–1938), a Baltic German or Latvian, like the Larson character in the story. Vatsetis was an officer in the czar's army and switched to the Bolsheviks in 1917. He commanded the crack "Latvian" infantry division in 1918. After suppressing Muravyov's mutiny in July 1918, he was promoted to Commander of the Eastern Front. From September 1, 1918, to July 1919 he served as the Supreme Commander of the Soviet armed forces. He perished in the Great Terror. —Ed.

The Volga was rolling on silently. There were no lights on the *Ivan and Maria,* and the hulk of the ship lay dark and dead, with only the torch burning above it. The flame was flaring and fuming above the mast. Seletsky was singing, his face pale, his head thrown back. He stopped when we came to the edge of the river. We walked up the unguarded gangplank. Boxes and gun wheels lay about the deck. I knocked on the door of the captain's cabin, and it fell open. A tin lamp without a glass cover was burning on the table, which was covered with spilled liquor. The metallic ring around the wick was melting. The windows had been boarded up with crooked planks. The sulfuric aroma of home-brewed vodka rose from cans under the table. Captain Korostelyov was sitting on the floor in a canvas shirt among green streams of vomit. His clotted, monastic hair stood around his head. He was staring fixedly up at Larson, his Latvian[6] commissar, who was sitting, holding a *Pravda* in a yellowish cardboard folder open in front of him, reading it in the light of the melting kerosene flicker.

"You're showing your true colors!" Captain Korostelyov said from the floor. "Go on with what you were saying . . . go on torturing us if you have to."

"Why should I do the talking?" Larson answered, turning his back and fencing himself off with his *Pravda.* "I'd rather listen to you."

A redheaded muzhik, his legs dangling, was sitting on a velvet sofa.

"Lisyei! Vodka!" the captain said to him.

"None left," Lisyei said. "And nowhere to get none."

Larson put down his paper and burst out laughing, as if he were pounding a drum.

"A Russian man needs his drink, the Russian man's soul wants to carouse, but there's not a drop to be found anywhere around here!" the Latvian said in his thick accent. "And it still calls itself the Volga!"

Captain Korostelyov stretched out his thin, boyish neck, and his legs in their canvas trousers sprawled out across the floor. There was pitiful bewilderment in his eyes, and then they flashed. "Torture us," he said to the Latvian, barely audibly, stretching out his neck. "Torture us, Karl."

Lisyei clasped his plump hands together and peered at the Latvian. "Ha! He's trumping the Volga! No, Comrade, you will not trump our Volga, you will not bad-mouth her! Don't you know the song we sing: Mother Volga, Czarina of all rivers?"

Seletsky and I were still standing by the door. I kept thinking of retreating.

"Well, this is simply beyond my grasp!" Larson said, turning to us, but clearly continuing the argument. "Maybe these comrades here can explain to me why reinforced concrete is worse than birches and aspens, and airships worse than Kaluga dung?"[7]

Lisyei's head twisted in his quilted collar. His legs didn't reach the floor. His plump fingers, pressed to his stomach, were knotting an invisible net.

---

6. Latvian soldiers formed a particularly loyal, efficient, and disciplined core of the Bolshevik regime. They were for the most part literate, urbanized, trained military personnel, raised in a Protestant milieu heavily influenced by German culture. They contrasted sharply with the majority of Red Army soldiers who were often illiterate Russian peasants. —*Ed.*

7. An old Russian town, some 120 miles southwest of Moscow, used here as the epitome of small-town, semi-rural provincial Russia.

"Ha! And what is it you know about Kaluga, my friend?" Lisyei asked in a pacifying tone. "I'll have you know there's famous folk that lives in Kaluga! Yes, fabulous folk!"

"Some vodka," Captain Korostelyov muttered from the floor.

Larson again threw back his piggish head and laughed out loud. "You win some, you lose some," he muttered, pulling the *Pravda* closer. "Yes, you win some, you lose some."

Sweat was seething on his forehead, and oily streams of fire were dancing in his clotted, dirt-crusted hair.

"You win some, you lose some," Larson snorted again. "Yes, you win some, you lose some."

Captain Korostelyov patted the floor around him with his fingers. He began crawling forward, hauling himself along with his hands, dragging his skeletal body in its sackcloth shirt behind him.

"Don't you dare bait Russia, Karl," he whispered, crawling toward the Latvian, hitting him in the face with his clenched fist, and then, with a sudden shriek, beginning to flail at him. The Latvian puffed himself up and looked at us over his skewed glasses. Then he wound a silken rivulet of Korostelyov's hair around his finger and banged Korostelyov's head on the floor. He yanked his head up and banged it down again.

"There!" Larson said curtly, flinging the bony body to the side. "And there's more where that came from!"

The captain propped himself up on his hands and got on all fours like a dog. Blood was flowing from his nostrils, and his eyes were crossed, darting about. Suddenly he flung himself up and hurled himself with a howl under the table.

"Russia!" he mumbled from under the table, and started kicking and flailing. "Russia!"

The shovels of his bare feet thrashed about. Only one whistling, moaning word could be heard in his screeching.

"Russia!" he moaned, stretching out his hands, beating his head against the floor.

Redheaded Lisyei was still sitting on the velvet sofa.

"This has been going on since noon," he said, turning to Seletsky and me. "Fighting for Russia, feeling sorry for Russia."

"Vodka!" Korostelyov said harshly from under the table. He crawled out and stood up. His hair, dripping with blood, hung down on his cheeks.

"Where's the vodka, Lisyei?"

"The vodka, my friend, is forty versts away, in Voznesenskoe—forty versts by water or by land. There's a church there now, so there must be home brew to be had. Whatever you do, the Germans don't have none!"[8]

Captain Korostelyov turned around and walked out on rigid heron's legs.

"We're Kalugans!" Larson yelled out unexpectedly.

"He has no respect for Kaluga," Lisyei sighed, "whichever way you look at it. But me, I've been there in Kaluga! Proper folk live there, famous—"

---

8. The German settlers in the area were mostly Mennonites and did not distill spirits. Lisyei assumes that inhabitants of a Russian Orthodox village, one with a church, should have some vodka. —*Ed.*

Outside, someone yelled an order, and the clanking of the anchor was heard—the anchor was being weighed. Lisyei raised his eyebrows.

"We're not off to Voznesenskoe, are we?"

Larson burst out laughing, throwing his head back. I ran out of the cabin. Korostelyov stood barefoot on the bridge. The copper rays of the moon lay on his gashed face. The gangplanks fell onto the riverbank. Whirling sailors unwound the moorings.

"Dimitri Alekseyevich," Seletsky shouted up to Korostelyov. "At least let us get off! What do you need us along for?"

The engines erupted into erratic hammering. The paddlewheel dug into the river. A rotten plank on the pier creaked softly. The *Ivan and Maria* swung its bow around.

"So we're off," Lisyei said, coming out of the cabin. "So we're off to Voznesenskoe to get some home brew."

The *Ivan and Maria*'s uncoiling paddlewheel was gaining speed. The engine's oily clanking, rustling, and whistling grew. We flew through the darkness, forging straight ahead, plowing through buoys, beacons, and red signals. The water foamed beneath the paddles and went flashing back like the golden wings of a bird. The moon plunged into swirls of black water. "The Volga's waterway is full of bends" was a phrase I remembered from a schoolbook. "It abounds in sandbanks." Captain Korostelyov was shuffling about on the bridge. Blue shining skin stretched over his cheekbones.

"Full steam ahead!" he said into the tube.

"Full steam ahead it is!" a muffled invisible voice answered.

"I want even more steam!"

There was silence from the engine room.

"The engine will blow," the voice said, after a moment of silence. The signal torch toppled off the mast and streamed over the rolling waves. The steamer rocked. An explosion shuddered through the hull. We flew through the darkness, straight ahead. A rocket went soaring up from the riverbank, a three-inch gun started pounding us. A shell went whistling between the masts. The galley boy, dragging a samovar across the deck, raised his head. The samovar went skidding out of his hands and rolled down the stairs, split open, and a glittering stream poured down the dirty steps. The galley boy snarled, tottered over to the stairs, and fell asleep. The deadly aroma of home-brewed vodka came pouring from his mouth. Belowdecks, among the oily cylinders, the stokers, stripped to the waist, were roaring, waving their arms, and rolling on the floor. Their twisted faces shone in the pearly gleam of the pistons. The crew of the *Ivan and Maria* was drunk. Only the helmsman stood firmly at his wheel. He turned and looked at me.

"Hey, Yid!" he called out to me. "What's going to become of the children?"

"What children?"

"The children aren't going to school," the helmsman shouted, turning the wheel. "The children will turn into thieves!"

He brought his leaden, blue cheekbones close to my face and gnashed his teeth. His jaws grated like millstones. It was as if his teeth were being ground to sand.

"I'll rip you to pieces!"

I edged away from him. Lisyei came walking across the deck.

"What's going on here, Lisyei!"

"I guess he'll get us there," the redheaded muzhik said, and sat down on a bench.

When we got to Voznesenskoe, we sent him ashore. There was no "church" to be found, no lights, no carousel. The sloping riverbank was dark, covered by a low-hanging sky. Lisyei sank into darkness. He had been away for more than an hour when he resurfaced right by the water, hauling some large cans. A pockmarked woman, as well built as a horse, was following him. The child's blouse she was wearing was much too small and stretched tightly over her breasts. A dwarf in a pointed hat and tiny little boots was standing nearby, openmouthed, watching us haul the cans on deck.

"Plum liquor," Lisyei said, putting the cans on the table. "The plummiest home brew!"

And the race of our spectral ship began once more. We arrived in Baronsk toward daybreak. The river spread out boundlessly. Water trickled off the riverbanks, leaving a blue satin shadow. A pink ray struck the mist hanging on the ragged bushes. The bleak, painted walls of the barns and their thin steeples slowly turned and floated toward us. We steamed toward Baronsk among peals of song. Seletsky had cleared his throat with a bottle of the plummiest home brew, and was singing his heart out. Mussorgsky's *Flea* was in his song, Mephistopheles' booming laughter, and the aria of the crazed miller, "I am a raven, no miller am I."

The barefoot captain lay slumped over the railing of the bridge. His head was lolling, his eyelids shut tight, and his gashed face, a vague childish smile wandering over it, was flung up toward the sky. He regained consciousness when the boat began slowing down.

"Alyosha!" he shouted into the tube. "Full steam ahead!"

And we went charging toward the pier at full steam ahead. The gangplank we had mangled as we pulled out the night before went flying into the air. The engines stopped just in time.

"You see, he brought us back," Lisyei said, turning up beside me. "And there you were, all worried."

Chapayev's machine gun carts were already lining up on the riverbank.[9] Rainbow stripes darkened and cooled on the bank from which the tidewaters had just ebbed. In a heap next to the pier were boxes of cartridges left by boats that had come and gone. Makeyev, the commander of one of Chapayev's squadrons, was sitting beltless on a box in a peasant shirt and a tall fur hat. Captain Korostelyov went up to him with outspread arms.

"I was a real idiot again, Kostya," he said with his childlike smile. "I used up all the fuel!"

Makeyev was sitting sideways on the box, scraps of his fur hat hanging over the yellow, browless arches of his eyes. A Mauser with an unpainted butt was lying on his knees. Without turning around, he fired at Korostelyov, but missed.

---

9. Vasily Ivanovich Chapayev (1887–1919), a hero of World War I and a legendary Red Army commander of an infantry division. —*Ed.*

"What can I say?" Korostelyov whispered, with wide, shining eyes. "So you're angry with me?" He spread out his thin arms farther. "What can I say?"

Makeyev jumped up, turned around, and fired all the bullets in his Mauser. The shots rang out rapidly. There was something more Korostelyov had wanted to say, but he didn't manage to. He sighed and fell to his knees. He tumbled forward onto the rim of the spoked wheel of a machine gun cart, his face shattering, milky strips of brain bespattering the wheel. Makeyev, bending forward, was trying to yank out the last bullet which was jammed in the cartridge clip.

"They thought it was a good joke!" he said, eyeing the crowd of Red Army men and the rest of us who had gathered by the gangplank.

Lisyei crouched and went sidling over to Korostelyov with a horse blanket in his hands, and covered him as he lay there like a felled tree. Random shots rang from the steamer. Chapayev's soldiers were running over the deck, arresting the crew. The pockmarked woman, her hand pressed to her cheek, stood at the railing, peering at the shore with narrow, unseeing eyes.

"I'll show you too!" Makeyev yelled up at her. "I'll teach you to waste fuel!"

The sailors were led down one by one. German settlers, trickling from their houses, came out from behind their barns. Karl Biedermayer was standing among his people. The war had come to his doorstep.

We had much work to do that day. The large village of Friedental had come to trade. A chain of camels was lying by the water. In the far distance, windmills were turning on the colorless, metallic horizon.

We loaded the Friedental grain onto our barge until suppertime, and toward evening Malishev sent for me. He was washing on the deck of the *Ivan Tupitsin*. An invalid with a pinned-up sleeve was pouring water over him from a pitcher. Malishev snorted and chuckled, holding his cheeks under the stream of water. He toweled himself off and said to his assistant, obviously continuing a conversation, "And rightly so! You can be the nicest fellow in the world, have locked yourself up in monasteries, sailed the White Sea, been a desperado—but, please, whatever you do, don't waste fuel!"

Malishev and I went into the cabin. I laid out the financial records in front of me, and Malishev started dictating to me a telegram to be sent to Ilyich.

"Moscow. The Kremlin. To Comrade Lenin."

In the telegram we reported the dispatching of the first shipments of wheat to the proletariat of Petersburg and Moscow: two trainloads, each twenty thousand *poods* of grain.

Maria

A Play in Eight Scenes

[Babel completed the first draft of *Maria*, his second known play, in 1933 while visiting Maxim Gorky in Sorrento, Italy. After returning to the Soviet Union in August, he offered the play to the Vakhtangov Theater and the State Jewish Theater, where it was to be performed in Yiddish translation. Both theaters began rehearsals but the productions were cancelled because the play was deemed ideologically flawed. The text of *Maria* appeared in the April 1935 issue of *Teatr i Dramaturga* and soon after as a book. Set in civil war Petrograd during the harsh winter and spring of 1920, the play is Babel's last work to explore the theme of St. Petersburg. —*Ed.*]

CHARACTERS

Nikolai Vasilevich Mukovnin—quartermaster general in the Czar's army.

Ludmila Nikolayevna Mukovnina—his daughter.

Katerina Vyacheslavovna Felsen (Katya).

Isaac Markovich Dimshits.

Sergey Hilarionovich Golitsyn—a former prince.

Nefedovna—the Mukovnins' nanny.

Yevstigneyich—invalid.

Bishonkov—invalid.

Filip—invalid.

Viskovsky—a former captain of the Guards.

Yasha Kravchenko.

Madame Dora.

A police inspector.

Kalmikova—a maid in the hotel at Nevsky Prospekt, 86.

Agasha—a female janitor.

Andrei—a floor polisher.

Kuzma—a floor polisher.

Sushkin.

Safonov—a worker.

Elena—his wife.

Nyushka.

A policeman.

A drunk man—at the police station.

A Red Army fighter—just in from the front.

The action takes place in Petrograd during the first years of the Revolution.

Scene One

A hotel on Nevsky Propekt. ISAAC MARKOVICH DIMSHITS's *hotel room: dirty and piled high with sacks, boxes, furniture. Two invalids,* BISHONKOV *and* YEVSTIGNEYICH, *are unwrapping packets of food.* YEVSTIGNEYICH, *a stout man with a large red face, has had both legs amputated above the knee.* BISHONKOV *has an empty, pinned-up sleeve. Both invalids are wearing medals and a St. George Cross on their chests.* DIMSHITS *is calculating profits on an abacus.*

YEVSTIGNEYICH   They hassled us the whole way. Back when Zanberg was running the checkpoint at Viritsa[1] he used to let us do our thing, but they sent him packing.

BISHONKOV   We're being hassled too much, Isaac Markovich.

DIMSHITS   Is Korolev still there?

YEVSTIGNEYICH   What d'you mean, still there? They finished him off. No wonder we're being hassled, what with all the checkpoint guards being new.

BISHONKOV   Getting our hands on produce is getting tougher, Isaac Markovich. The moment you get to know a checkpoint guard, he gets replaced by a new one. If they just snatched your stuff that would be one thing, but you never know when they're going to hold a gun to your head.

YEVSTIGNEYICH   And you can't keep up with them. Every day they come up with new tricks. Last night we pulled in at Tsarskoye Selo Station[2] and they started shooting. We say, "Hey! What's going on?" We thought the government was being overthrown again, and that they were overthrowing it by shooting everyone in sight.

BISHONKOV   Today they grabbed a lot of produce from us! For the street kids, they said. There's a whole colony of them at Tsarskoye Selo.

YEVSTIGNEYICH   Yeah, right! Kids with beards on their faces!

BISHONKOV   If a man's hungry, he'll grab whatever food he can for himself! Yes, if he's hungry, for himself!

DIMSHITS   Where's Filip? I've been worried about him—why did you drop him and run?

BISHONKOV   We didn't drop him and run, Isaac Markovich. He got cold feet.

YEVSTIGNEYICH   Someone's been talking to him.

BISHONKOV   It's tyranny, that's what it is!

YEVSTIGNEYICH   Well, take Filip himself: he's a big, strong man, you notice him right away, but he's got no guts, his insides are weak. We drive up to the station—they're shooting, everyone's screaming, falling—I tell him, "Filip," I tell him, "we'll get over to Zagorodny Boulevard with no hassle—all the guards are friends!" But Filip's falling apart right before my eyes. "I'm afraid to go," he tells me. "Well, if you're afraid," I tell him, "then stay right where you are! Vodka smuggling is no big deal, you'll just get a kick in the pants, so what are you worried about? All you've got is one load of alcohol." But he was already lying there flat on his belly. A strong man, strong as a horse, but no guts.

---

1. A small town outside Petrograd (St. Petersburg). —*Ed.*
2. Now Pushkin, Tsarskoye Selo station, Czar's Village, was the summer residence of the czars.

BISHONKOV   We're all hoping he'll turn up. We haven't seen hide nor hair of him.

DIMSHITS   How much did you pay for the sausage?

BISHONKOV   We got sausage for eighteen thousand, Isaac Markovich, and it tastes awful. Nowadays you can be in Petrograd or out in Vitebsk, it's the same deal.

YEVSTIGNEYICH [*Opens a secret cubbyhole in the wall and stashes the food there.*]   They're ruining Russia!

DIMSHITS   How much was the grain?

BISHONKOV   The grain was nine thousand. There's nothing you can do about it. They're not interested in selling. They're just waiting for you to open your mouth. I can't tell you how greedy these dealers have gotten.

YEVSTIGNEYICH [*Hides loaves of bread in the wall.*]   My wife toiled over the oven to bake these. She sends her regards.

DIMSHITS   How're the kids? Doing well?

BISHONKOV   The kids are doing well. Very well indeed. They're all wearing fur coats, they're rich. . . . The wife asks if you'll come and visit.

DIMSHITS   Like I have nothing else to do. [*He flips the beads on the abacus.*] Bishonkov!

BISHONKOV   Yes?

DIMSHITS   I don't see no profits.

BISHONKOV   Getting our hands on food is getting tougher.

DIMSHITS   I don't see no profits.

BISHONKOV   You won't see no profits. Me and Yevstigneyich, we've been thinking that we should start handling some other product. There's a lot of bulk to this merchandise here: flour is bulky, grain is bulky, leg of veal is also bulky. We've got to move over to something else, saccharine, or gems. Diamonds are great. You pop them in your mouth and they're gone!

DIMSHITS   Filip's disappeared. . . . I'm worried about him.

YEVSTIGNEYICH   I guess they must have broken all his bones by now.

BISHONKOV   Before the Revolution you could live quite well as a crippled veteran, but now . . .

YEVSTIGNEYICH   Now you can forget it—it's all about education! In the past, soldiers got a hell of a lot of respect—now it's zilch. "How come you're an invalid?" this fellow asks me. "A shell blew both my legs off," I tell him. "What's so special about that?" he asks me. "Your legs got blown off right away without no suffering. You didn't have no suffering." So I ask him, "What d'you mean, no suffering?" "Well," he says, "it's common knowledge: you were chloroformed when they took your legs off, you didn't feel nothing. It's just that you can't come to grips with your toes—your toes kind of act up, itch, even though they've been chopped off, that's the only problem." "And how," I ask him, "do you happen to know all this?" "It's easy enough," he tells me, "everyone's educated now, thanks to those sons-of-bitches in charge." "Ha! I can tell how educated everyone is now, the way they kick crippled veterans off trains. . . . What do you want to kick me off the train for? I'm a cripple!" "We're throwing you off because goddamn Russia's sick and tired of all the cripples!" And he throws me off the train like a bundle of rags. I'm really upset at what our people have turned into.

[VISKOVSKY *enters in riding breeches and a jacket. His shirt is unbuttoned.*]

DIMSHITS   Is that you?

VISKOVSKY   It's me.

DIMSHITS   So you forgot how to say hello?

VISKOVSKY   Did Ludmila Nikolayevna come to see you, Dimshits?

DIMSHITS   Did the dog grab your "hello" and run away with it? So what's it to you if she came to see me?

VISKOVSKY   I know you've got Mukovnin's ring, and her sister, Maria Nikolayevna, couldn't have given it to you—

DIMSHITS   Who says it had to be people who gave it me?

VISKOVSKY   How d'you get that ring, Dimshits?

DIMSHITS   I was given it to sell.

VISKOVSKY   So sell it to me.

DIMSHITS   Why should I sell it to you?

VISKOVSKY   Ever tried your hand at being a gentleman, Dimshits?

DIMSHITS   I'm always a gentleman.

VISKOVSKY   Gentlemen don't ask questions.

DIMSHITS   Those people want hard currency for the ring.

VISKOVSKY   You owe me fifty pounds sterling.

DIMSHITS   What for, if I may ask?

VISKOVSKY   For the thread deal.

DIMSHITS   You mean the deal you messed up?

VISKOVSKY   In the Cavalry Guard they didn't teach us the ins and outs of the thread trade.

DIMSHITS   You messed up the deal because you're hotheaded.

VISKOVSKY   So give me forty, Maestro, and I'll mend my ways.

DIMSHITS   How are you going to mend your ways if you never listen? You're told to do one thing, and you go do something completely different. In the war you were a captain or a count, whatever you were— maybe it's good to be hotheaded in war, but when pulling off a deal, a merchant has to watch where he puts his foot.

VISKOVSKY   Yessir!

DIMSHITS   And there's something else I'm pissed off about, Viskovsky! What was that trick you pulled with bringing me that princess?

VISKOVSKY   I thought the more refined, the better.

DIMSHITS   Didn't you know Ludmila Nikolayevna was a virgin?

VISKOVSKY   The best *tsimmes* you can get your hands on.[3]

DIMSHITS   Thank you, I don't need that kind of *tsimmes*. I am a humble man, Captain Viskovsky, and I wouldn't want the princess to come to me like the Mother of God from an icon and look at me with eyes like silver spoons. Remember what we'd agreed on? Yes or no? I don't mind if it's a woman pushing thirty, that's what we agreed on, or thirty-five, a housewife who's having a hard time making ends meet and who'd take the grain and the bread I'd give her, along with the pound of cocoa for her kids, without yelling, "You goddamn bootlegger, you dirtied me, you used me!"

VISKOVSKY   There's still the younger Mukovnina.

DIMSHITS   That one's a liar. I don't like women who are liars. . . . Why don't you introduce me to the older one?

VISKOVSKY   Maria Nikolayevna has joined the army.

---

3. *Tsimmes*, a traditional Jewish sweetened vegetable stew, is the high point of a meal. It also denotes a complex and laborious process of preparation. Viskovsky seems to be aware only of the first meaning, while Dimshits knows both. —*Ed.*

DIMSHITS   Now, Maria Nikolayevna, that's some woman! A feast for the
     eyes, a person you can talk to. . . . Why did you wait till she was gone?
VISKOVSKY   It's a tough call with her, Dimshits. Very tough.
YEVSTIGNEYICH   "You got blown up without even getting shook up!" he said
     to me. "No suffering for you!" That's the kind of crap he was saying to me.
          [*A shot is heard far away, then nearer. The shots become more
          frequent.* DIMSHITS *turns out the light and locks the doors.
          Light shining through the windows, green glass, frost.*]
YEVSTIGNEYICH   [*In a whisper.*]   You call this a life?
BISHONKOV   Goddamn it!
YEVSTIGNEYICH   The damn sailors are on the loose again.
BISHONKOV   This is no life, Isaac Markovich.
          [*There is a knock at the door. Silence.* VISKOVSKY *takes a revolver
          out of his pocket and releases the safety catch. A second knock.*]
BISHONKOV   Who's there?
FILIP   [*From outside.*]   It's me.
YEVSTIGNEYICH   Me who? Your name!
FILIP   Open up!
DIMSHITS   It's Filip.
          [BISHONKOV *opens the door. An enormous, shapeless man enters the
          room and slumps wordlessly against the wall. A light flares up.
          Half of* FILIP's *face is scarred with burned flesh. His head has lolled
          onto his chest, his eyes are closed.*]
DIMSHITS   You been shot?
FILIP   No.
YEVSTIGNEYICH   You look wasted, Filip.
          [YEVSTIGNEYICH *and* BISHONKOV *help* FILIP *out of his sheepskin coat
          and his outer clothes, and then take off his rubber suit filled with
          bootlegged vodka and throw it on the floor. The armless rubber
          dummy—a second* FILIP—*is lying on the floor.* FILIP's *fingers are
          lacerated, covered in blood.*]
YEVSTIGNEYICH   They've really worked him over! And they call them-
     selves human beings!
FILIP   [*His head still lolling on his chest.*]   A man was following me . . .
     following me . . .
YEVSTIGNEYICH   Following you?
FILIP   Yeah.
YEVSTIGNEYICH   A man wearing leggings?
FILIP   Yeah.
YEVSTIGNEYICH   We're done for. . . .
DIMSHITS   What, you brought him all the way here?
FILIP   No I didn't bring him all the way here. There was shooting, so he
     ran off to see what was up.
          [BISHONKOV *and* YEVSTIGNEYICH *lift up the wounded man
          and lay him on the bed.*]
YEVSTIGNEYICH   I told you we'd have got through with no hassle.
          [FILIP *is groaning. Faraway shots, machine gun fire, then silence.*]
YEVSTIGNEYICH   You call this a life?
BISHONKOV   Goddamn it!
VISKOVSKY   Where's the ring, Maestro?
DIMSHITS   That ring's got you all fired up!

Scene Two

A room in the apartment of Mukovnin, a former aristocrat and quarter-master general in the Czar's army. The room serves as bedroom, dining room, and office—a typical room of the 1920s. Elegant antique furniture, but next to it a little makeshift tin stove, its pipes extending through the whole room. A pile of thinly chopped logs are stashed beneath the stove. Behind a screen, LUDMILA, *his daughter, is dressing for the theater. Curling tongs are heating over an oil lamp.* KATYA (KATERINA VYACHESLAVOVNA), *also a former aristocrat, is ironing a dress.*

LUDMILA   Darling, you are behind the times! Nowadays the audience at the Mariinsky Theater is extremely elegant. The Krimov sisters and Varya Meindorf look as if they've just stepped out of a fashion magazine, and I can assure you that they live in the lap of luxury.

KATYA   No one is living well nowadays. No one.

LUDMILA   There you are wrong. You are behind the times, Katya, darling. The gentlemen of the proletariat are acquiring a taste for style. They want a woman to be elegant. Why, do you think Redko likes it when you run around dressed like a fishwife? You can bet your life he doesn't! No, Katya, darling, the gentlemen of the proletariat are definitely acquiring a taste for style!

KATYA   I wouldn't overdo the mascara if I were you, and I'm not at all sure about that sleeveless dress.

LUDMILA   You seem to be forgetting that I am being escorted by a gentleman.

KATYA   Well, your gentleman friend wouldn't know the difference.

LUDMILA   There you are wrong. He does have taste, and he is passionate too!

KATYA   Redheaded fellows are hot-blooded, everyone knows that.

LUDMILA   What do you mean, redheaded! My Dimshits's hair is chocolate brown.

KATYA   Does he really have that much money? I think Viskovsky is mistaken.

LUDMILA   Dimshits has six thousand pounds sterling to his name.

KATYA   What? He's conned all that from the cripples?

LUDMILA   He has conned nothing from the cripples! That is merely hearsay. They have formed a cooperative association, and all the profits are shared. Until recently, no crippled veteran was ever searched, so it was easier for them to carry things.

KATYA   Only a Jew could come up with a scheme like that!

LUDMILA   Oh, Katya, darling. Better a Jew than a cocaine addict, like most of the men of our set. This one is a cocaine addict, another has gotten himself shot, another has ended up as a coachman standing outside the Europa waiting for fares. *Par le temps qui court,*[4] Jews have become the safest bet.

KATYA   I suppose you will not find a safer bet than Dimshits.

LUDMILA   Do not forget we are women, *ma chère.* We are just women, tired of "trolloping around," as the janitor's wife downstairs always

---

4. French: The way things are now.

says. We cannot just sit here twiddling our thumbs, can we? We can't—

KATYA   Are you thinking of having children?

LUDMILA   I shall have two little redheads.

KATYA   So we are talking marriage?

LUDMILA   You have to with these Jews, Katya, darling. They are obsessed with family—they lean on their wives, and their children are everything to them. Not to mention that a Jew is always grateful to the woman who has given herself to him. It's a really noble trait, this respect they have for women.

KATYA   How is it that you know the Jews so well?

LUDMILLA   Well, you know—from back then. When Papa commanded the troops back in Vilna, the whole place was full of Jews. Papa had a rabbi as a friend. They are all philosophers, these rabbis of theirs.

KATYA   [*Hands her the ironed dress over the screen.*]   You'll be dining after the theater?

LUDMILA   I wouldn't be surprised.

KATYA   I'm sure you'll have a drink or two, Ludmila Nikolayevna, passions will be excited, and the mists will engulf you.

LUDMILA   No mists will engulf me, *ma chère*. I shall let him call on me for a month, maybe two—that is how one handles Jews. I have not come to a decision yet as to whether I shall allow myself to be kissed.

[GENERAL MUKOVNIN *enters, wearing felt boots. His greatcoat with a red lining has been refashioned into a dressing gown. He is wearing two pairs of spectacles.*]

MUKOVNIN [*Reads.*]   "On the sixteenth day of October, in the year 1820, in the reign of our blessed Czar Alexander, a company of Life Guards from the Semyonovsky Regiment, forgetting their oath of allegiance and the military obedience they owed their commanders, had the effrontery to gather together without authorization at an advanced nocturnal hour. "[*He raises his head.*] And how did they forget their oath of allegiance? They forgot it by going out into the corridors after roll call with the intention of asking the company commander to call off the upcoming routine inspections of all the barracks. The regimental commander sometimes ordered these strict inspections. For this so-called mutiny, they were punished. And do you know how? [*He reads.*] "The men of lower rank, the ones considered ringleaders, were deprived of their lives, and the men of the first and second companies were sentenced to hang for setting a bad example, and the private soldiers that were specified in paragraph three had to run the gauntlet through the battalion six times, as an example to their peers."

LUDMILA   Oh, that's awful!

KATYA   We all know that there was much cruelty in the old days.

LUDMILA   If you ask me, the Bolsheviks would love Papa's book. They can use it most effectively to rant against the old army.

KATYA   All the Bolsheviks care about is the here and now.

MUKOVNIN   I am dividing the Semyonovsky tragedy into two chapters: the first is an analysis of the reasons for the mutiny, and the second a description of the insurrection, the torture, and banishment to the mines. My book will be a history of the barracks. It won't be a history of nations, but a history of all the Ivans and Sergeys that were handed over to Arakcheyev[5] and sent off for twenty years of hard labor in military camps.

LUDMILA   Papa, you must read Katya the chapter on Czar Paul. If Tolstoy were alive today, he'd be impressed. I am sure of it.

KATYA   All the newspapers care about is the here and now.

MUKOVNIN   Without knowledge of the past there is no road to the future. The Bolsheviks are continuing the work of Grand Prince Ivan Kalita,[6] unifying the Russian lands. They need skilled officers like myself, even if only to inform them of the mistakes we made.

[*The doorbell rings. There is bustling in the front hall.* DIMSHITS *enters in a fur coat, carrying packages.*]

DIMSHITS   Greetings, General! Greetings, Katerina Vyacheslavovna! Is Ludmila Nikolayevna at home?

KATYA   She is expecting you.

LUDMILA   [*From behind the screen.*]   I am dressing. . . .

DIMSHITS   Greetings, Ludmila Nikolayevna! The weather outside is so bad that no man would send his dog out in it. Hypolite drove me here, he talked my ears off, nothing but jabbering—what a strange bird! Isn't it getting late, Ludmila Nikolayevna?

MUKOVNIN   It's broad daylight, and they're off to the theater?

KATYA   Theaters start now at five in the afternoon.

MUKOVNIN   Saving on electricity, are they?

KATYA   Yes, they're saving on electricity. And then, if people go home late they're likely to get robbed.

DIMSHITS   [*Unwrapping his packages.*]   Here is a nice leg of ham, General. It's not my specialty, but they told me it was corn-fed. Now, whether they fed it with corn or something else, it's not like I was there or anything.

[KATYA *goes to a corner and smokes a cigarette.*]

MUKOVNIN   I must say, Isaac Markovich, you are being too good to us.

DIMSHITS   Some cracklings?

MUKOVNIN   [*Not understanding.*]   Begging your pardon?

DIMSHITS   I'm sure they didn't serve no cracklings at your papa's table, but back in Minsk, in Vilyuysk, in Chernobyl,[7] cracklings are held in the highest esteem. They are bits of goose. Have some and give me your opinion. . . . How is your book doing, General?

MUKOVNIN   The book is moving ahead. I have reached the reign of Czar Alexander I.

LUDMILA   It reads just like a novel, Isaac Markovich. In my opinion, it is reminiscent of *War and Peace*—the part where Tolstoy talks about the soldiers.

DIMSHITS   That's very nice to hear. Let them shoot in the streets, General, let them bang their heads against the walls—just keep on working.

---

5. Count Alexei Andreyevich Arakcheyev (1769–1834), a trusted advisor of Alexander I (1801–25) and a powerful figure in his government from 1815 to 1825. He is chiefly remembered for the establishment of the notoriously cruel military-agricultural colonies. Because of his conservatism, ruthless efficiency, and brutality, Arakcheyev's name became synonymous with autocratic regimentation and oppression. He retired in 1826 soon after Nicholas I (1825–55) ascended the throne. —Ed.

6. Ivan I, also known as Ivan Kalita (Ivan the Moneybag), the grand prince of Moscow from 1328 to 1340. He is credited with establishing Moscow as the preeminent political and commercial center of medieval Russia. —Ed.

7. Minsk and Chernobyl were centers of traditional Jewish life in the Pale. Vilyuysk, a town in Siberia, was a proverbial "end of the earth" and a place of forced exile. —Ed.

Finish the book and I'll throw you a feast, and I'll buy up the first hundred copies! How about some nice jellied pork head? A German gave it to me—

MUKOVNIN   Isaac Markovich, you mustn't! I will become angry!

DIMSHITS   It would be a great honor if General Mukovnin were to get angry at me. It is an exquisite jellied pork head! This German was quite a renowned professor, now he specializes in sausages. . . . Ludmila Nikolayevna, I have a strong feeling we'll be late.

LUDMILA [*From behind the screen.*]   I am ready.

MUKOVNIN   How much do I owe you, Isaac Markovich?

DIMSHITS   You don't owe me the horseshoe of the horse that dropped dead on Nevsky Prospekt earlier today.

MUKOVNIN   No, I am being serious, how much?

DIMSHITS   You are being serious? Fine—then let's make it two horseshoes from two horses.

[LUDMILA *appears from behind the screen. She is dazzlingly beautiful, well built, with rosy cheeks. She is wearing diamond earrings and a sleeveless black velvet dress.*]

MUKOVNIN   Isn't my daughter beautiful, Isaac Markovich?

DIMSHITS   I wouldn't say she isn't.

KATYA   She is a real Russian beauty, that's what she is, Isaac Markovich.

DIMSHITS   It's not my specialty, but I can see the quality.

MUKOVNIN   I also want to introduce you to my older daughter, Maria.

LUDMILA   I must warn you, Maria is the favorite here, and yet, believe it or not, our favorite went off to join the army.

MUKOVNIN   What are you talking about, Ludmila, darling? She joined the army's Political Department.[8]

DIMSHITS   Your Excellency—anything you want to know about the Political Department, you ask me! They are soldiers too.

KATYA [*Taking* LUDMILA *to the side.*]   I would not wear those earrings if I were you.

LUDMILA   You think so?

KATYA   Of course not. Don't forget there's that dinner afterward. . . .

LUDMILA   Have no fear, *ma chère*. No need to teach a Viennese how to waltz. [*She kisses* KATYA.] Katyusha, you sweet, silly girl. [*To* DIMSHITS.] My boots. [*She turns away and takes off her earrings.*]

DIMSHITS [*Rushing to help her.*]   At your service!

[*She puts on her boots, fur coat, and knitted wool kerchief.* DIMSHITS *eagerly bustles about, helping her.*]

LUDMILA   I still can't believe that we haven't sold all these things yet. Papa, don't forget to take your medicine. And Katya, don't let him do any work.

MUKOVNIN   Katya and I are going to spend a cozy evening at home.

LUDMILA [*Kisses her father on the forehead.*]   How do you like my papa, Isaac Markovich? Isn't he precious?

DIMSHITS   The general is not a mere man, he is a jewel!

8. The Red Army's political departments were staffed by ideologically reliable and disciplined cadres who supervised the military command on behalf of the Bolshevik party. Along with creating and distributing propaganda, their functions included vetting the military personnel for political loyalty and purging the undesirables. All major military decisions were made with the consent of the head of the political department. Dimshits is well aware that the political departments were directly involved in life-and-death decisions. —Ed.

LUDMILA   We are the only ones who truly appreciate him. Where did you leave Prince Hypolite?

DIMSHITS   I left him outside the door. I ordered him to wait there, it's a question of discipline. We'll be there in a minute. So long, Nikolai Vasilevich!

KATYA   Don't drink too much.

DIMSHITS   We won't—there's not much chance of that nowadays.

LUDMILA   Good-bye, Papa, darling.

[GENERAL MUKOVNIN *escorts* DIMSHITS *and his daughter to the front hall; voices and laughter are heard.* MUKOVNIN *returns.*]

MUKOVNIN   What a charming and virtuous Jew.

KATYA   [*Curled up at the edge of the sofa, smoking.*]   They all seem to be somewhat lacking in tact.

MUKOVNIN   Katya, darling! Where do you expect them to have picked up tact? They were only allowed to live on one side of the street, and if they ever crossed over to the other side, the police would immediately chase them back. That is how it used to be in Kiev on Bibikovsky Boulevard. So where do you expect them to have picked up tact? What is really surprising is their energy, their vitality, their resilience!

KATYA   That energy has poured into Russian life. But we, after all, are different. It's all so foreign to us.

MUKOVNIN   One thing that isn't foreign to us is fatalism. Another, that Rasputin and the German Czarina destroyed the Romanov dynasty. And yet nothing but good has come from that wonderful Jewish race, which has given us Heine, Spinoza, and Christ.

KATYA   You used to praise the Japanese too, Nikolai Vasilevich.

MUKOVNIN   The Japanese? They are a great nation, there is much we can learn from them!

KATYA   It is clear enough who Maria takes after. You are a Bolshevik, Nikolai Vasilevich.

MUKOVNIN   I am a Russian officer, Katya, and I ask the simple question: gentlemen, please tell me when it was that the rules of war became foreign to you? We tormented and humiliated these people, is what I tell them, they defended themselves, they attacked, fighting with resourcefulness, circumspection, desperation—they are fighting in the name of an ideal,[9] Katya!

KATYA   An ideal? I'm not so sure about that. We're unhappy, and it doesn't look like that will change. We've been sacrificed, Nikolai Vasilevich.

MUKOVNIN   So let them shake up Russia's Vanyas and Petrushkas. That would be wonderful. Time is running out, Katya. Peter the Great, the only true Russian Czar, once said, "Delay is death!"[1] What a maxim. And if this is so, my dear fellow officers, shouldn't you have the courage to look at your field maps and figure out which of your flanks faltered, and where and why you were defeated? I have a right to look the truth in the eye, and I shall not renounce that right.

9. Mukovnin seems to conflate the resourceful, practical Jewish businessmen and the idealistic Jewish revolutionaries, who provided some of the most loyal and visible cadres in the Bolshevik party. —*Ed.*
1. This maxim, attributed to Peter the Great, was used by Lenin on the eve of the October revolution to persuade his Bolshevik comrades to seize power. Invoking it here, Mukovnin draws a parallel between Peter's reforms and the Bolshevik revolution. —*Ed.*

KATYA   You have to take your medicine.

MUKOVNIN   What I tell my comrades in arms, the men I fought shoulder
to shoulder with is, *"Tirez vos conclusions*[2]—delay is death!"

> [*He exits. Next door a Bach fugue is being played coldly and with
> precision on a cello.* KATYA *listens, then gets up and walks over to
> the telephone.*]

KATYA   Could you connect me with the District Headquarters? . . .
Redko, please. . . . Is that you, Redko? . . . I just wanted to tell you . . .
Don't forget you're not the only man fighting for the Revolution, and
yet you're the only one who never has time to see a person . . . a per-
son at whose house you spend the night whenever you need to. . . .
[*Pause.*] Take me out, Redko. Come and pick me up in your car. . . .
Well, if you're busy . . . No, I'm not angry. Why should I be angry?

> [*She hangs up. The music stops.* GOLITSYN, *a lanky man in a soldier's
> jacket and leg wrappings, enters, carrying a cello.*]

KATYA   What did they tell you in the tavern—"Don't play weepy tunes"?

GOLITSYN   "Don't play weepy tunes, don't pull at our heartstrings."

KATYA   They need something cheerful, Sergey Hilarionovich. People want
to forget their worries, they want to rest. . . .

GOLITSYN   Not all of them. Some ask for plaintive tunes.

KATYA [*Seats herself at the piano.*]   What kind of audience do you have?

GOLITSYN   Dockworkers from the Obvodny Canal.

KATYA   I suppose you go to their trade union. . . . They give you some
supper there, don't they?

GOLITSYN   Yes, they do.

> KATYA [*Plays "Yablochko," singing softly.*][3]
> *"Through wind and wave our ship sails free,*
>   *As we throw the damn Whites to the fish in the sea."*

Try playing this. It should go down well at that tavern of yours.

> [GOLITSYN *tries to play the tune, misses a few notes, then gets it
> right.*]

KATYA   Would it be worth me learning stenography, *mon prince?*

GOLITSYN   Stenography? I have no idea.

KATYA   *"I sit on a barrel crying tears of dismay,*
>   *The boys don't want marriage,*
>   *Just a roll in the hay."*

They need stenographers right now.

GOLITSYN   I wouldn't know. [*He tries to follow her tune.*]

KATYA   Maria is the only true woman of all of us. She is strong, gutsy, a
real woman. We sit around here sighing, while she's happy in her Political Propaganda Division. . . . What have people come up with to replace
happiness? There isn't anything.

GOLITSYN   Maria Nikolayevna has always made sharp turns.[4] That's always
been her strong point.

---

2. French: Draw your own conclusions.
3. "Yablochko," a catchy tune popularized by the revolutionary sailors but sung by both the Reds and
   the Whites. The first line of the song was fixed: "My little apple, where are you rolling?" The second line was open to improvisation, depending on one's political allegiences: "The Bolsheviks [or
   the Whites] will get you, and you won't come back." —*Ed.*
4. Babel obliquely quotes the expression Stalin used in explaining party purges: "passengers" fall off
   the Party "cart" as it makes sharp turns. —*Ed.*

KATYA   And right she is.
> *"Oh sweet little apple, whither did you roll?"*

And then, she is involved with Akim Ivanich.

GOLITSYN   [*Stops playing.*]   Who is this Akim Ivanich?

KATYA   Their division commander, a former blacksmith. She mentions him in every letter.

GOLITSYN   How do you know she's involved with him?

KATYA   I have read it between the lines, I'm certain of it. . . . Or should I maybe move to my family in Borisoglebsk? At least it's home. You, for instance, you go to that monastery to see that monk—what was his name?

GOLITSYN   Sioni.

KATYA   Yes, to Father Sioni. What does he teach you?

GOLITSYN   You just mentioned happiness. Well, he teaches me that there is no happiness in having power over people, or in this neverending greed—this unquenchable greed.

KATYA   Let's play, Sergey Hilarionovich!
> *"I sit on my barrel,*
> *While the market hags bicker,*
> *Not a kopeck in my pocket*
> *But I'm thirsty for liquor."*

Sioni is a beautiful name.

Scene Three

LUDMILA *and* DIMSHITS *in his hotel room. Bottles and the remains of their meal stand on the table. Part of an adjacent room is visible in which* BIS-HONKOV, FILIP, *and* YEVSTIGNEYICH *are playing cards.* YEVSTIGNEYICH's *little invalid cart has been placed on a chair; his legs, amputated above the knee, are jutting out.*

LUDMILA   Felix Yusupov[5] was as beautiful as a god—a tennis player, a Russian champion. Though his beauty was not really masculine enough . . . there was something doll-like about it. Well, I met Vladimir Bagalei[6] at Felix's. Right to the very end the Czar simply could not understand what a gallant nature that man had. We used to call him the "Teutonic Knight." Fredriks[7] was a friend of Prince Sergey, you know Prince Sergey—he's the one who plays the cello. That evening there was another surprise *hors programme:*[8] Archbishop Ambrosii. The old man started flirting with me, can you imagine? He kept topping up my glass and peering at me with such a crafty, pious twinkle in his eye! At first Vladimir was not particularly impressed with me. "In my eyes you were only a snubnosed little girl," he admitted, *"si démesurement russe,*[9] with flushed cheeks." At dawn we drove out to the Czar's palace

---

5. Feliks Feliksovich Yusupov (1887–1967), young aristocrat and courtier who organized and led the assassination of Grigory Rasputin in 1916. —*Ed.*
6. A famous courtier and aristocrat. —*Ed.*
7. Vladimir Borisovich Frederiks (1838–1927), Minister of the Imperial Court of Nicholas II (1894–1917). —*Ed.*
8. French: In musical performance, this idiom refers to an encore or an unexpected addition to a concert. —*Ed.*
9. French: so incredibly Russian. —*Ed.*

at Tsarskoye Selo, left the car in the park, and rode on in a buggy.
Vladimir drove it himself. "I could not take my eyes off of you all evening, Ludmila Nikolayevna." "Of which Nina Buturlina is well aware,
mon prince." I knew they were having a liaison—more probably a flir-
tation. "Buturlina, *c'est le passé!*"[1] "*On revient toujours à ses premiers
amours, mon prince.*"[2] Vladimir had never been accorded the title of
Grand Duke, as he was the offspring of a morganatic marriage, and the
Czarina refused to meet his family. Vladimir always called her "an evil
genius." Furthermore, he was a poet, naive, and had no head for politics. We arrived at Tsarskoye Selo. It was dawn. Somewhere, right over
the pond, a nightingale was singing. Vladimir told me again: "*Mademoiselle Boutourline c'est le passé.*" "The past, *mon prince*, has a tendency to return at times, and when it does, it does so with a
vengeance."

> [DIMSHITS *turns out the light, pushes* LUDMILA *back onto the sofa,
> and throws himself on her. There is a struggle. She frees herself,
> straightens her hair, her dress.*]

BISHONKOV [*Throws down a card.*]   Try beating this!

FILIP   Nope, no one can beat that!

YEVSTIGNEYICH   Well, they lead him up to the fence, his hands tied. "So,
my friend," they tell him. "Turn around!" And he tells them, "There's
no need for me to turn around. I'm a fighting man, finish me off as I
am." Their fence is just a tiny wattle fence, really, about hip high. It's
night, they're at the edge of the village, beyond the village are the
steppes, at the edge of the steppes is a forest—

BISHONKOV [*Throws down another card.*]   That's it! You're out!

FILIP   Not so fast!

YEVSTIGNEYICH   So they lead him out there and take aim. He is standing
by the fence, and suddenly it's as if he'd been snatched up from the
earth, his hands still tied! It was as if God Almighty whisked him away.
He jumped over the wattle fence and off he scampered! They fired,
but it was night, darkness everywhere, and he was running and dodg-
ing, so he got away.

FILIP [*Puts down his cards.*]   What a hero!

YEVSTIGNEYICH   A real hero! A great horseman. I knew him as well as I
know you. He was on the run for half a year before they finally caught him.

FILIP   So they finished him off?

YEVSTIGNEYICH   They did. It's unfair, if you ask me. When a man manages to crawl out of the grave after coming face-to-face with his
maker, it goes against the grain to kill him.

FILIP   No one gives a damn nowadays.

YEVSTIGNEYICH   It's unfair, if you ask me. It's the law in every country in
the world: if a firing squad misses you, then fortune has smiled on you
and they set you free.

FILIP   Not here they don't! Give them half a chance and they'll finish
you off!

BISHONKOV   Yeah, give them half a chance—

1. French: Bouturline is a thing of the past. —*Ed.*
2. French: One always returns to one's first loves, my prince. —*Ed.*

LUDMILA   Turn on the light!

[DIMSHITS *switches it on.*]

LUDMILA   I am leaving. [*She turns around, looks at* DIMSHITS, *and bursts out laughing.*] Don't pout. Come here. You have to understand—I must get used to you first.

DIMSHITS   I'm not a boot one has to get used to.

LUDMILA   I will admit that you have awakened within me feelings of warmth toward you. But these feelings need time to develop. Maria is about to come back on leave, and you will meet her. Nothing in our family is ever done without her. . . . Papa is well disposed toward you, but, as you yourself saw, he is helpless. . . . And then, there is much that still remains unresolved. Your wife, for instance.

DIMSHITS   What's my wife got to do with all this?

LUDMILA   I am aware that Jews are attached to their children.

DIMSHITS   What are you bringing that up for?

LUDMILA   And that is why for the time being you must sit next to me quietly, and be patient.

DIMSHITS   Since the day the Jews began waiting for the Messiah, they have been patient. Have another glass.

LUDMILA   I've already had too much.

DIMSHITS   They brought me this wine from a battleship. The grand duke had a case on board. . . .

LUDMILA   How do you manage to get all these things?

DIMSHITS   I can get stuff where no one else can. Drink up.

LUDMILA   Gladly—that is, if you sit there nice and quiet.

DIMSHITS   Is this some synagogue, for me to sit nice and quiet or something?

LUDMILA   I must say, this frock coat you are wearing is the kind I imagine one would wear to a synagogue. Frock coats, Isaac, darling, are worn by headmasters at graduation ceremonies, and by merchants at memorial dinners.

DIMSHITS   I'll stop wearing frock coats.

LUDMILA   And then those tickets. Never buy front-row tickets. It's the mark of a social climber, a parvenu.

DIMSHITS   I *am* a social climber.

LUDMILA   But you have an inner nobility, and that makes all the difference. However, your name is unfitting.[3] When we put our announcement in the papers, the *Izvestia*, for instance . . . you could, you know, change Isaac to Alexei. Do you like Alexei?

DIMSHITS   I like it. [*He turns out the light again, and throws himself on* LUDMILA.]

YEVSTIGNEYICH   The two of them are at it.

FILIP [*Listens.*]   It looks like she's finally . . .

BISHONKOV   I like Ludmila Nikolayevna best of all. She treats you like a person, which is more than I can say for some of those other trollops around here . . . She even remembers my name.

[VISKOVSKY *enters the room, stands behind* YEVSTIGNEYICH's *back, and watches the cards being played.*]

LUDMILA [*Tearing free.*]   Call me a cab!

DIMSHITS   Yeah, right away! Like I got nothing better to do!

---

3. In Russian, Isaac is generally a Jewish name. —*Ed.*

LUDMILA   Call me a cab this minute!

DIMSHITS   It's thirty below zero outside—you wouldn't send a rabid dog out in such weather.

LUDMILA   All my clothes are torn! How can I show myself at home like this?

DIMSHITS   You made your bed, now lie in it!

LUDMILA   How vulgar! You're knocking on the wrong door.

DIMSHITS   Just my luck.

LUDMILA   I told you I have a toothache, an unbearable toothache!

DIMSHITS   That's apples and oranges. What's teeth got to do with things?

LUDMILA   Will you find me some drops for my toothache? I am suffering!

[DIMSHITS *exits. He bumps into* VISKOVSKY *in the adjacent room.*]

VISKOVSKY   Congratulations.

DIMSHITS   Her teeth's hurting her.

VISKOVSKY   That can happen.

DIMSHITS   What can happen is that they don't hurt.

VISKOVSKY   It's all an act, Isaac Markovich. It's definitely all an act.

FILIP   The toothache is an invention of hers, Isaac Markovich, and not a real toothache at all.

LUDMILA   [*Fixes her hair in front of the mirror. Singing a song, she walks about the room, regal, cheerful, flushed.*]

"My sweetheart is a man who is tall and brash,
My sweetheart is a man both gentle and cruel,
He thrashes and whips me with a silken lash . . ."[4]

DIMSHITS   I'm not a boy—a lot of time has passed since I last was a boy!

VISKOVSKY   Yessir!

LUDMILA [*Picks up the telephone.*]   3-75-02. Papa, darling, is that you? . . . I'm very well. . . . Nadia Johanson was at the theater with her husband. Isaac Markovich and I are having dinner. . . . You must see Spessivtseva,[5] she's far better than Pavlova! . . . Did you take your medicine? You must go to bed. . . . No, your daughter knows exactly what she is doing. . . . Katya, darling, is that you? . . . I am following your instructions, *ma chère. Le manège continue, j'ai mal aux dents ce soir.*[6] [*She walks about the room, singing, and patting her hair into place.*]

DIMSHITS   She shouldn't be surprised if I'm not home next time she comes around!

VISKOVSKY   Well, it's up to you, after all.

DIMSHITS   Because, though I don't mind other people asking about my wife and children, I won't take that sort of thing from her!

VISKOVSKY   Yessir!

DIMSHITS   For your information, these people don't deserve to tie my wife's shoelace! Not even her shoelace!

---

4. Lyudmila sings a Gypsy ballad, a "cruel romance" of a sadomasochistic variety, that tells of a woman testifying at an inquest for the suicide of her former lover. The previous evening she had left him for another man, but when she returned from a tryst, she found her former beloved hanging from the ceiling on the same "silken cord" with which he used to "whip" her. —Ed.

5. Olga Spessivtseva (1895–1991), ballerina at the Mariinsky Theater (1913–21) and Paris Opera and Ballet (1924–1932). She also danced for Diaghilev's Ballets Russes, including during its tour of the United States in 1916. She returned to Petrograd in 1917 and was welcomed back to the Mariinsky. In 1919, she premiered there as Giselle, a role hitherto identified with the great Anna Pavlova (1881–1931). She left Russia in 1924 and, though she contemplated coming back, never returned. —Ed.

6. French: The horse training is continuing, I have a toothache tonight —Ed.

Scene Four

In VISKOVSKY's *room. He is wearing riding breeches and boots, but no jacket. His shirt collar is undone. There are bottles on the table—there has been much drinking.* KRAVCHENKO, *a tiny, flushed man in a military uniform, is lounging on the sofa with* MADAME DORA, *a gaunt woman dressed in black wearing large dangling earrings and with a Spanish comb in her hair.*

VISKOVSKY   Just for one deal, that's all, Yasha!
> *"I was possessed by one power alone,*
> *A single passion, a passion that consumes."*[7]
KRAVCHENKO   How much d'you need?
VISKOVSKY   Ten thousand pounds sterling. For one deal. You ever seen sterling pounds, Yasha?
KRAVCHENKO   All that cash just for thread?
VISKOVSKY   Forget the thread! We're talking diamonds. Three carat, blue water diamonds, clean, no sand. That's all they take in Paris.
KRAVCHENKO   There's none like that left here.
VISKOVSKY   There's diamonds in every house. You just have to know how to get at them. The Rimsky-Korsakovs have them, the Shakhovskys have them. No, there's still enough diamonds in imperial St. Petersburg!
KRAVCHENKO   You'll never make a Red merchant.
VISKOVSKY   Just you wait and see. My father used to trade—he traded estates against horses. . . . The horse guards may surrender, but they do not die.
KRAVCHENKO   Go and bring in Ludmila Nikolayevna. She's at the end of her rope in the corridor.
VISKOVSKY   I will arrive in Paris like a count.
KRAVCHENKO   Where the hell did Dimshits disappear to?
VISKOVSKY   He's hanging out in the outhouse, or playing cards with Shapiro and the Finn. [*He opens the door.*] Hey, miss, come warm yourself at our fire. [*He goes out into the corridor.*]
DORA [*Kisses* KRAVCHENKO's *hands.*]   My sunshine! My everything!
> [VISKOVSKY *enters with* LUDMILA, *who is wearing her fur coat.*]
LUDMILA   This is beyond comprehension. We had an agreement.
VISKOVSKY   And an agreement is more precious than money.
LUDMILA   We agreed that I would be here at eight. It's quarter to ten now . . . and he didn't even leave me a key . . . where could he be?
VISKOVSKY   A bit of speculating and he'll be back.
LUDMILA   Be that as it may, these people are no gentlemen.
VISKOVSKY   Have a vodka, sweetheart.
LUDMILA   Yes, I will have one, I'm frozen through . . . still, all this is simply beyond comprehension!

---

7. A garbled quotation from *Mtsyri*, a romantic poem by Lermontov. It comes from the monologue of the protagonist expressing his desire for freedom, and should read: "There was one thought that had complete power over me, Mikhail / One passion all-consuming . . ." —*Ed.*

VISKOVSKY   Allow me, Ludmila Nikolayevna, to introduce you to Madame
     Dora, a citizen of the republic of France—*Liberté, Égalité, Fraternité.*[8]
     Among her other good qualities, she is also the owner of a foreign
     passport.
LUDMILA   [*Extends her hand.*]   Mukovnina.
VISKOVSKY   You know Yasha Kravchenko. He was an ensign in the Czar's
     army, now he's a Red Artillerist. He's with the ten-inch gun detach-
     ment at Kronstadt, and you can turn those guns every which way.
KRAVCHENKO   Viskovsky has been on a roll all evening.
VISKOVSKY   Every which way! Who knows what can happen, Yasha. They
     might ask you to blow up the street you were born on, and you would
     blow it up, or to blast an orphanage to bits, and you'd say, "A two-zero-
     eight fuse!" and blast that orphanage to bits. That's what you'd do,
     Yasha, as long as they let you live your life, strum your guitar, and sleep
     with thin women. You're fat but you like them thin. You'll do anything,
     and if they tell you to renounce your mother three times, you would
     renounce her three times. But that's not the point, Yasha! The point is
     they will want more: they won't let you drink vodka with the people you
     like, they'll make you read boring books, and the songs they'll teach you
     will be boring too! Then you'll be mad, my dear Red Artillerist! You'll be
     furious, your eyes will start rolling! Then two citizens will come visiting:
     "Let's go, Comrade Kravchenko." "Should I take any personal effects
     with me, or not?" you'll ask them. "No, you needn't take any personal
     effects with you. It'll be a quick interrogation, over in a minute." And
     that will be the end of you, my dear Red Artillerist. It'll cost them four
     kopecks. It's been calculated that a Colt bullet costs four kopecks and
     not a centime more."
DORA   [*In broken Russian.*]   Jacques, take me to home.
VISKOVSKY   To your health, Yasha! To victorious France, Madame Dora!
LUDMILA   [*Her glass has already been topped up a few times.*]   I'll quickly
     go see if he's back yet.
VISKOVSKY   A bit of speculating and he'll be back. Hey, Countess, did
     you think up that trick with the teeth yourself?
LUDMILA   Yes, I did . . . good, wasn't it? [*She laughs.*]   I had no choice.
     Those Jews don't know how to respect a woman they want to be close to.
VISKOVSKY   When I look at you, Ludmila, I think of a little tomtit. Let's
     have a drink, my little tomtit!
LUDMILA   Are you trying to corner me? You've put something in this
     vodka, Viskovsky, haven't you?
VISKOVSKY   My little tomtit. All the strength of the Mukovnins went to
     Maria. All you were left with was a row of delicate teeth.
LUDMILA   That's cheap, Viskovsky.
VISKOVSKY   And I don't like your small breasts. A woman's breasts should
     be beautiful, large, helpless, like those of a ewe.
KRAVCHENKO   We'll be going, Viskovsky.
VISKOVSKY   No, you're not. . . . Why don't you marry me, my little tomtit?
LUDMILA   No, I'd be better off marrying Dimshits. I know exactly how
     things would turn out if I married you: you'd be drunk the first day,

---

8. French: Liberty, equality, fraternity—slogan of the French Revolution (1789–94) and later of the
   French Republic. —*Ed.*

have a hangover the second, then you'd go off to God knows where, and then you'd end up shooting yourself. No, I think I'll stick to Dimshits.

KRAVCHENKO We want to go, Viskovsky. Please!

VISKOVSKY You're not going anywhere! A toast! A toast to all women! [*To* DORA.] This here is Ludmila . . . her sister's name is Maria.

KRAVCHENKO I think Maria Nikolayevna has joined the army.

LUDMILA She's at the Polish border right now.

VISKOVSKY At the front! At the front, Kravchenko! They've got a waiter for a division commander.

LUDMILA That is not true, Viskovsky! He's a metalworker.

VISKOVSKY The waiter's name is Akim. Let's have a drink in honor of women, Madame Dora! Women love ensigns, waiters, petty officials, Chinamen. . . . [9] A woman's business is love—the police will sort out what's what. [*He raises his glass.*] To all sweet women, wonderful women, who love us, even if only for an hour! Not even an hour, if you think about it. A veil of gossamer. Then the gossamer is torn. . . . Her sister is called Maria. . . . Imagine, Yasha, that you fall in love with the Czarina. "You're scum!" the Czarina says. "Go away!"

LUDMILA [*Laughs.*] That sounds just like Maria.

VISKOVSKY "You're scum! Go away!" She spurned the horse guardsman and decided to go to Furshtadskaya Street, 16, apartment 4.

LUDMILA Don't you dare, Viskovsky!

VISKOVSKY Let's drink to the Kronstadt Artillery, Yasha! . . . That's when she decided to go to Furshtadskaya Street. Maria Nikolayevna went out in a gray tailored dress suit. She had bought some violets by Troitsky Bridge, and pinned them to the lapel of her jacket . . . The prince—the one who plays the cello—the prince got his bachelor pad all nice and tidy, crammed his dirty clothes under the sideboard, put all the dirty dishes on a top shelf. . . . Then coffee and petit fours were served at Furshtadskaya Street. They drank their coffee. She had brought violets and spring with her, and curled her legs up on the sofa. He took a shawl, covered those strong, tender legs, and was met by a dazzling smile—a heartening, humble, sad, but still encouraging smile . . . she embraced his graying head. . . . "Prince! What is the matter, my Prince?" And his voice issued like that of a Papal choirboy. "*Passe, rien ne va plus.*"[1]

LUDMILA You're such a bastard!

VISKOVSKY Imagine, Yasha, right before your eyes the Czarina is removing her corset, her stockings, and her bloomers. . . . Even you, Yasha, might well blush and not know where to look.

[LUDMILA *laughs out loud, throwing her head back.*]

VISKOVSKY She left 16 Furshtadskaya Street. . . . Where were her footprints for me to kiss? Where were they? But let us hope that Akim's voice rings deeper than that of a papal choirboy. . . . What do you think, Ludmila Nikolayevna?

9. An oblique reference to stories about "two Chinamen" with which Babel used to regale his friends in Petrograd. See the essay by Viktor Shklovsky, p. 464, and Babel's story "Chink." —*Ed.*
1. French: That's it, no more—the croupier's call when bets are closed at the roulette table.

LUDMILA   You put something in this vodka, Viskovsky! My head is spin-
ning. . . .
VISKOVSKY   Come here, girly. [*He grabs her shoulders and pulls her toward
him.*] How much did Dimshits pay you for that ring?
LUDMILA   What are you talking about?
VISKOVSKY   It's not your ring, it's your sister's. You sold a ring that wasn't
yours.
LUDMILA   Let me go!
VISKOVSKY [*Pushes her through a side door.*]   Come with me, girly!
     [DORA *and* KRAVCHENKO *remain alone in the room. In the window,
     the slow beam of a searchlight.* DORA, *puffy and disheveled, leans
     over to* KRAVCHENKO *and kisses his hands, babbling and moaning.*
     FILIP, *with his scarred face, comes tiptoeing in unhurriedly on his
     bare feet, and quietly takes the wine, sausage, and bread from the
     table.*]
FILIP [*In a low voice, his head bent to the side.*]   You don't mind, do you,
Yasha?
[KRAVCHENKO *shakes his head, and* FILIP *carefully tiptoes out.*]
DORA   You are my sunshine! My life! My everything!
[KRAVCHENKO *remains silent. He hears steps outside.* VISKOVSKY *enters,
smoking a cigarette, his hands shaking. The door to the adjacent room is
open.* LUDMILA *is lying on the sofa, crying.*]
VISKOVSKY   Calm down, Ludmila Nikolayevna. You'll get over it.
DORA [*In broken Russian.*]   Jacques, I want our room. . . . Take me to
home, Jacques!
KRAVCHENKO   In a minute, Dora.
VISKOVSKY   One for the road, Comrades?
KRAVCHENKO   In a minute, Dora.
VISKOVSKY   One for the road—to all the l-ladies . . .
KRAVCHENKO   This is very bad, Captain.
VISKOVSKY   To all the ladies, Yasha!
KRAVCHENKO   This is very bad, Captain.
VISKOVSKY   What is very bad, if I may ask?
KRAVCHENKO   Men with the clap should not sleep with women, Mr.
Viskovsky.
VISKOVSKY [*In a military tone.*]   Would you care to repeat that?
[*Pause.* LUDMILA *stops sobbing.*]
KRAVCHENKO   What I said was: men infected with gonorrhea—
VISKOVSKY   Remove your glasses this instant, Kravchenko! I am going to
punch your ugly mug.
     [KRAVCHENKO *pulls out his revolver.*]
VISKOVSKY   Fine, if that's the way you want it!
     [KRAVCHENKO *fires. Curtain. Behind the curtain: shots, falling
     bodies, a woman's scream.*]

Scene Five

At the MUKOVNINS' *apartment. The* OLD NANNY *is lying curled up on a
trunk in the corner. She is asleep. A lamp casts a pool of light onto the
table.* KATYA *is reading a letter from* MARIA *to* MUKOVNIN.

KATYA   "At dawn the bugle from squadron headquarters wakes me. By eight I have to be in the Political Propaganda Division, I'm in charge there—I edit the articles of the divisional newspaper, I run the literacy classes. Our reinforcements are all Ukrainians. They remind me of Italians, the way they talk and act. Russia has been suppressing and destroying their culture for centuries. In our house in Petersburg, opposite the Hermitage and the Winter Palace, we might as well have been living in Polynesia for all we knew anything at all about our people! Yesterday I read aloud in class the chapter in Papa's book about the murder of Czar Paul. It was so clear that the Czar deserved his fate that nobody in class questioned it. What they asked me instead— in their typically forthright way—was about the disposition of the regiment, the rooms in the palace, which regimental guard it had been that had stood watch that night, who were the conspirators, and in what way the Czar had wronged them. I keep hoping that Papa will come out here in the summer, as long as the Poles don't start acting up again. You will see a new army, Papa, new barracks, quite the opposite of what you are describing. In summer our garden here will be green and blossoming, the horses will regain their strength in the pastures, and their saddles will have been mended. I have already spoken to Akim Ivanovich, and he has agreed that you should come. Let's hope that you'll be well enough. It's night now. I came off duty late and climbed the worn, four-hundred-year-old stairs to my room. I live up in the tower, in a vaulted hall that was once Count Krasnicki's armory. The castle was built on a ledge below which a river flows. Meadows stretch into infinity, with a misty forest wall in the distance. There are lookout niches on every floor of the castle from which the approaching Tatars and Russians were observed, and from which boiling oil was poured onto the heads of the besiegers. Old Hedwig, the housekeeper of the last Krasnicki, cooked me some dinner and lit the fireplace, deep and black as a dungeon. The horses are stomping and dozing in the park below. Kuban Cossacks are sitting around a fire, eating and singing. The trees are covered with snow, the oak and chestnut branches hang heavy, and an uneven, silver blanket is lying over the snowy walks and statues. The statues are still unscathed—youths throwing javelins, and nude, frozen goddesses, their arms curved, their hair flying in waves, their eyes blind. Hedwig is dozing, her head shaking, the logs in the fireplace flare up and crumble. The centuries have made the bricks of this building resonant as glass, and they sparkle with gold as I sit here writing to you. I have Alyosha's photograph beside me on the table. My comrades here are the very people who didn't think twice about killing him. I was with them just a few minutes ago, working to set them free. Am I doing the right thing, Alyosha? Am I fulfilling your command to live a life of courage? The immortal essence of Alyosha keeps egging me on. It is late, but I cannot sleep. An inexplicable fear for you and a dread of my dreams keep me awake. I see pursuit, torture, and death. I live a strange dichotomy: closeness to nature and anxiety for you. Why does Ludmila write so rarely? A few days ago I sent her a paper signed by Akim Ivanovich, stating that as I am on active duty the authorities have no right to requisition my room at home. Furthermore, we must see to the official document allowing

Papa to keep his library. If the document has expired, it has to be renewed at the People's Commissariat for Education at Chernishev Bridge, room 40. I would be so happy if Ludmila were to settle down and start a family, but the man should be a frequent guest at our house so that Papa can get to know him; Papa's heart won't deceive him. And Nanny should meet him too. Katya keeps complaining about Nanny, saying that she isn't doing any work. Katya, Nanny is old. She has raised two generations of Mukovnins. She has her own opinions and feelings about things, and she's no simpleton. I always felt that she did not have much of a peasant's soul in her, though if you think about it, what did we, tucked away in our Polynesia as we were, know about the peasantry? I hear that finding provisions in Petersburg has become even harder, and that the rooms and linen of everybody who is not working are being requisitioned. I am ashamed that we here at the front are living so well. Akim Ivanovich has taken me hunting twice, and I have a horse, a Don Cossack horse. . . ." [KATYA *raises her head.*] So you see how well things stand, Nikolai Vasilevich? [MUKOVNIN *covers his eyes with his palms.*] Don't cry. . . .

MUKOVNIN I am asking God—we all have a God of our souls—why he gave me, egotistical, foolish man that I am, such wonderful children as Maria and Ludmila.

KATYA But that is good, Nikolai Vasilevich. There is no need to cry.

Scene Six

A police station at night. A DRUNK *lies huddled under a bench. He is waving his fingers in front of his face and holding a conversation with himself. A thickset* OLD MAN *is dozing on the bench. He is wearing an expensive raccoon coat and a tall fur hat. The coat is open wide, revealing the old man's bare, gray chest. A* POLICE INSPECTOR *is cross-examining* LUDMILA. *Her fur hat is askew, her hair disheveled, and her coat has been tugged off one of her shoulders.*

INSPECTOR Name?

LUDMILA I want to go home.

INSPECTOR Name?

LUDMILA Barbara.

INSPECTOR Father's name?

LUDMILA Ivan.

INSPECTOR Where do you work?

LUDMILA At Laferme, the tobacco factory.

INSPECTOR Your union card.

LUDMILA I don't have it on me.

INSPECTOR Why are you dealing in smuggled goods?

LUDMILA I'm a married woman. . . . I want to go home!

INSPECTOR What makes you want to deal in smuggled goods? Have you known Brilyov for a long time?

LUDMILA I do not know any Brilyov. I have never heard of him.

INSPECTOR Brilyov signed for the shipment of thread that passed through you to Gutman. Where did you stash the thread?

LUDMILA   What are you talking about? What do you mean, stash?

INSPECTOR   I'll tell you right away what I mean by stash! [*To a policeman.*] Call in Kalmikova!

[*The policeman brings in* SHURA KALMIKOVA, *the maid in the hotel at Nevsky Prospekt, 86, where* DIMSHITS *and his men are staying.*]

INSPECTOR   Are you a hotel maid?

KALMIKOVA   I am just standing in for someone else.

INSPECTOR   Do you recognize this woman?

KALMIKOVA   I most certainly do.

INSPECTOR   What can you tell me?

KALMIKOVA   I can answer your questions—her father's a general.

INSPECTOR   Does she work?

KALMIKOVA   She steams up men, that's her job.

INSPECTOR   Does she have a husband?

KALMIKOVA   Yeah, she got married in the bushes—she's got quite a few husbands. One of them spent a whole night in the outhouse because of her teeth.

INSPECTOR   What teeth? What are you going on about?

KALMIKOVA   She knows perfectly well what teeth.

INSPECTOR [*To* LUDMILA.]   You been arrested before? How many times?

LUDMILA   I have been infected. . . . I am ill.

INSPECTOR [*To* KALMIKOVA.]   We need to ascertain how many times she's been arrested before.

KALMIKOVA   That I don't know. I can't tell you that. I can't tell you what I don't know.

LUDMILA   I am exhausted. . . . Let me go home!

INSPECTOR   Calm down! Look at me!

LUDMILA   My head is spinning. . . . I'm going to faint.

INSPECTOR   Look at me!

LUDMILA   My God, why do I have to look at you?

INSPECTOR [*Furious.*]   Because I haven't had any sleep for five nights, that's why! Do you understand?

LUDMILA   Yes, I understand.

INSPECTOR [*Moves closer to her, grabs her by the shoulders, and looks into her eyes.*]   How many times have you been arrested?

Scene Seven

At the MUKOVNINS' *apartment. There are shadows on the walls.* GOLITSYN *is praying in front of an illuminated icon. The* NANNY *is sleeping on the trunk.*

GOLITSYN   Verily, verily, I say unto you, except a corn of wheat fall into the ground and die, it abideth alone: but if it die, it bringeth forth much fruit. He that loveth his life shall lose it; and he that hateth his life in this world shall keep it unto life eternal. If any man serve me, let him follow me; and where I am, there shall also my servant be: if any man serve me, him will my Father honor. Now is my soul troubled;

and what shall I say? Father, save me from this hour: but for this cause came I unto this hour.[2]

KATYA [*Comes up to him silently, stands next to him, and rests her head on his shoulder.*] I always meet Redko at the headquarters in what used to be an antechamber. There's an oilskin sofa there. I go in, Redko locks the door, and afterward he unlocks it.

GOLITSYN   I see.

KATYA   I am going home to Borisoglebsk, *mon prince*.

GOLITSYN   That would be for the best.

KATYA   Redko keeps lecturing me on whom to love, whom to hate. He says that the law of big numbers is now in effect. But I, you see, am a small number. What do I matter?

GOLITSYN   But you do matter.

KATYA   Yes, I do matter! I should count! I am free now, Nanny. . . . Wake up. Please wake up. You'd sleep right through the Second Coming!

NEFEDOVNA [*Raises her head.*]   Where's Ludmila?

KATYA   Ludmila will be back soon, and I'm leaving town, so there'll be nobody to give you a hard time.

NEFEDOVNA   Why give me a hard time? What is there for me to do? I was born to be a nanny, hired to raise children, but there are no children here. The house is full of women, but there's not a single child in sight. One's gone off to fight a war, as if there's no one else who can do the fighting, the other one is roaming around lost. What kind of a house is this to be without children?

KATYA   We'll have some children by Immaculate Conception.

NEFEDOVNA   You're trolloping around, girls. You think I can't see what you're up to? But it's not like you've got anything to show for it!

GOLITSYN   Go to Borisoglebsk,[3] they need you. It's a wasteland there, with beasts devouring each other.

NEFEDOVNA   Look at the Molostovs—two-bit merchants, but they saw to it that their nanny was given a pension. Fifty rubles a month! Prince, why don't you see to it that I get a pension too?

GOLITSYN [*Lights the makeshift tin stove.*]   No one would listen to me now, Nanny. I have no connections these days.

NEFEDOVNA   But they were just two-bit merchants!

[MUKOVNIN *enters. The front door opens, and* MUKOVNIN *staggers back at the sight of* FILIP, *large and shapeless, hooded and wrapped in rags. Half of* FILIP's *face is covered in raw scar tissue. He is wearing felt boots.*]

MUKOVNIN   Who are you?

FILIP [*Moves closer.*]   One of Ludmila Nikolayevna's acquaintances.

MUKOVNIN   How may I help you?

FILIP   There has been a small disaster, your Excellency.

KATYA   Did Mr. Dimshits send you?

FILIP   Yes, he sent me. The whole thing started from nothing.

---

2. John 12:24–27. Dostoevsky used this verse as an epigraph to *The Brothers Karamazov* (1879–80).
3. Most likely, the characters are referring not to the southern Borisoglebsk near Voronezh but to the old northern Russian town of Borisogleb. Located near Yaroslavl, it is famous for its monastery and its old tradition of Orthodox sages. Situated in a forested area, it invokes the primitive, native Russia that Prince Golitsyn has in mind. —*Ed.*

KATYA   What about Ludmila Nikolayevna?

FILIP   They were all there together. . . . They were having a little fun, your Excellency, but things got out of hand. Captain Viskovsky and, well, Kravchenko . . . they went at each other, both were a little tipsy—

GOLITSYN   General Mukovnin, let me have a word with our Comrade here.

FILIP   It's not like anything special happened. It was a misunderstanding. Both were a little tipsy, both had weapons—

MUKOVNIN   Where is my daughter?

FILIP   We are not sure, your Excellency.

MUKOVNIN   Tell me where my daughter is! You need not hold anything back from me!

FILIP   [Barely audibly.]   She's been nabbed.

MUKOVNIN   I have looked death in the eye. I am a soldier!

FILIP   [Louder.]   They've nabbed her, your Excellency.

MUKOVNIN   You mean they've arrested her? What for?

FILIP   Some illness or something got them going. Kravchenko says, "You gave her that illness, Captain Viskovsky, so I'll shoot you!" And they had weapons on them, so she—

MUKOVNIN   The Cheka[4] came for her?

FILIP   Some men came and took her away, who knows who they were. . . . nowadays no one wears no uniform, your Excellency. You can't tell who's who.

MUKOVNIN   Katya, I must go to Smolny![5]

KATYA   You're not going anywhere, Nikolai Vasilevich! You mustn't!

MUKOVNIN   I must go to Smolny immediately!

KATYA   Please, Nikolai Vasilevich—

MUKOVNIN   The thing is, Katya, that my daughter must be returned to me immediately. [He goes to the telephone.] Would you please connect me to Military Headquarters!

KATYA   You mustn't!

MUKOVNIN   I would like to speak to Comrade Redko. . . . This is Mukovnin. . . . All I can tell you, Comrade, is that in former days I was quartermaster general of the Sixth Army. . . . Hello, is that you, Comrade Redko? Hello, Comrade Redko! This is Mukovnin speaking. I hope you are well. . . . I am very sorry to disturb you. . . . The thing is that yesterday evening some armed men came and arrested my daughter Ludmila at a hotel on Nevsky Prospekt, number 86. I am not asking you to pull strings, Comrade Redko, I know that that sort of thing is frowned upon in your organization, I simply wish to announce that it is vital I see my oldest daughter, Maria Nikolayevna. You see, I have been somewhat unwell recently, and I feel it essential that I consult with her. We have sent telegrams and express letters to her—I know Katya has asked for your help in that—but we've received no answer. I would like to request to speak to her directly. . . . I should add that

---

4. See note 1 on p. 52.
5. The Smolny Institute for Noble Girls was taken over by the Bolsheviks in 1917 and became Lenin's revolutionary headquarters. It remained the party center for the city after the government relocated to Moscow in 1918. —Ed.

General Brusilov[6] has invited me to come to Moscow to discuss my return to active duty. . . . Oh, you say our letters were delivered? On the eighth? Well, I am very grateful to you! The best of luck, Comrade Redko! [*He hangs up.*] Everything is fine. They have found Maria and our telegram was delivered to her on the eighth! She'll be in Petersburg tomorrow, or the day after tomorrow at the latest. Nanny, we must tidy up Maria's room—tomorrow you will have to get up at the crack of dawn and tidy it up! Katya is right—this apartment is a mess. We really have let it go, there's dust everywhere! We have to put covers on all the furniture. . . . Do we have covers, Katya?

KATYA　We have some, but not for all the furniture.

MUKOVNIN [*Rushing around the room.*]　We must cover the furniture at all cost! It will be nice for Maria to find everything just as she left it. Why not make things comfortable, if one is able to? Not to mention, at our place there's no chance to at least *s'amuser* a little. You have no penchant whatsoever for *amusement*, Katya, darling, you'll lag behind the times if you don't go to the theater.

KATYA　When Maria comes back, I shall go to the theater.

MUKOVNIN [*To* FILIP.]　I'm sorry, what is your name?

FILIP　Filip Andreyevich.

MUKOVNIN　Why don't you take a seat, Filip Andreyevich? We didn't even thank you for all your trouble. We must offer Filip Andreyevich something to eat. Nanny, do we have anything we can offer him? We always like having guests, Filip Andreyevich, though you must forgive our simple hospitality. Please, make yourself comfortable. We must introduce you to Maria Nikolayevna—

KATYA　You must get some rest, Nikolai Vasilevich. You must go and lie down.

MUKOVNIN　And for your information, I'm not in the least bit worried about Ludmila. It will be a lesson for her, a lesson because of her childishness, her lack of experience. . . . For your information, I'm even glad. . . . [*He shudders, stops, collapses into a chair.* KATYA *rushes over to him.*] Don't worry, Katya, don't worry. . . .

KATYA　Are you all right?

MUKOVNIN　It's nothing, it's just my heart. . . .

[KATYA *and* GOLITSYN *help him up and lead him out.*]

FILIP　He looks a bit rattled.

NEFEDOVNA [*Laying out plates on the table.*]　Were you there when they arrested our young lady?

FILIP　Yes, I was.

NEFEDOVNA　Did she fight back?

FILIP　At first she did, but then she just went with them.

NEFEDOVNA　I'll give you some potatoes and some fruit pudding too.

FILIP　Believe it or not, Grandma, we had a whole tubful of meat noo-

---

6. General Alexey Alexeyevich Brusilov (1853–1926), a leading commander of Russian armed forces during World War I, served as Supreme Commander of the Russian forces under the Provisional Government in May and June 1917. After the Bolshevik revolution, Brusilov refused to join the Whites. In May 1920, after the beginning of Polish hostilities against Soviet Russia, Brusilov was appointed head of a Special Advisory Council that included several generals from the imperial army. The Council called on the members of the old officer corps to join the Red Army in the Polish campaign. Babel presents General Mukovnin as someone who was summoned by Brusilov to join the Special Council. —Ed.

dles back at our place, and then with all these troubles, we looked away for a second and they'd disappeared into thin air.

NEFEDOVNA [*She puts the potatoes in front of him.*]   They boiled off your face during the civil war?

FILIP   No, it got boiled off a while back, during the civil peace.

NEFEDOVNA   So, you think there'll be another war? What do your people say?

FILIP [*Eating.*]   There'll be war in August.

NEFEDOVNA   What, with the Poles?

FILIP   With the Poles.

NEFEDOVNA   Haven't we already given them all the land they want?

FILIP   What they want is for their country to stretch from sea to sea. They want it to be like it was in old times again.[7]

NEFEDOVNA   What idiots!

[KATYA *enters.*]

KATYA   The general is in very bad shape. We must call the doctor.

FILIP   Doctors, miss, don't come at such an hour.

KATYA   He is dying, Nanny! His nose has turned blue. . . . He already has the look of death on him!

FILIP   The doctors have all bolted their doors. You couldn't get them to come out at night even at gunpoint.

KATYA   We must go and get some oxygen from a pharmacy!

FILIP   Is His Excellency a union member?

KATYA   I don't know. We don't know anything about such things here.

FILIP   If he's not a union member, then they won't give him any.

[*The doorbell rings sharply.* FILIP *goes to open the door, and then returns.*]

FILIP   It's . . . it's . . . Maria Nikolayevna. . . .

KATYA   Maria?

[KATYA *goes toward the door with outstretched arms, bursts into tears, stops, covers her face with her hands, and then drops them. In front of her stands a* RED ARMY FIGHTER, *about nineteen years old, with long legs. He is dragging a sack behind him.* GOLITSYN *enters and stops by the door.*]

RED ARMY FIGHTER   Greetings!

KATYA   My God! What happened to Maria!

RED ARMY FIGHTER   Maria Nikolayevna has sent you some supplies.

KATYA   Where is she? Is she with you?

RED ARMY FIGHTER   Maria Nikolayevna is with the division—everyone's at their positions now. I've got something here for you—some boots—

KATYA   She didn't come with you?

RED ARMY FIGHTER   No, of course not. We're in the middle of a battle, Comrade.

KATYA   We've sent her letters, telegrams. . . .

RED ARMY FIGHTER   You can send what you want, it makes no difference. The units are on the move night and day.

KATYA   Are you going to see her?

---

7. Filip is referring to the proposal, championed by Josef Pilsudski, to create a Federation of Poland, Lithuania, Belarus, and Ukraine that essentially replicated the borders of the Polish-Lithuanian Commonwealth before the first partition of Poland. The proposal was known as Międzymorze, or "Intersea," and was meant to cover the territory from the Baltic to the Black seas. —*Ed.*

RED ARMY FIGHTER   Sure I am. Do you want me to tell her something?

KATYA   Yes, please tell her . . . tell her that her father is dying—that there is no hope of saving him. Tell her that he called out to her on his deathbed . . . and that her sister, Ludmila, is no longer living with us, as she's been arrested. Tell Maria Nikolayevna that we wish her all the best, and that she mustn't feel remorse about not being here with us in our hour of need. . . .

> [*The* RED ARMY FIGHTER *looks around, and steps back*—MUKOVNIN *comes staggering out of his room. His eyes are wandering, his hair disheveled, there is a smile on his face.*]

MUKOVNIN   You see, Maria, all the time you were away I wasn't in the least bit sick! On best behavior! [*He sees the* RED ARMY FIGHTER.] Who is this? [*He repeats his question louder.*] Who is this? Who is this? [*He collapses.*]

NEFEDOVNA   [*Sinks to her knees beside* MUKOVNIN.]   Are you leaving me, my little Kolya? Aren't you going to wait for your poor old Nanny?

> [MUKOVNIN *wheezes. Death throes.*]

Scene Eight

Noon. Blinding light. Outside the window, the sun-drenched columns of the Hermitage and a corner of the Winter Palace. The empty apartment of the MUKOVNINS. ANDREI *and his apprentice* KUZMA, *a fat-faced young man, are polishing the floor upstage.* AGASHA *is shouting out of the window.*

AGASHA   Damn you, Nyushka, don't let the child get all dirty down there! Where are your eyes, you sitting on them or something? A grown wench and still a fool! Tikhon! Hey, Tikhon! Why did you leave the shed door open? Lock the shed! Hello, Yegorovna! Is there any way I can get some salt from you till the first? I'll have my coupons by then and you'll get it back. I'll send my girl over to you with a little jar, and you can put the salt in it. . . . Tikhon! Hey, Tikhon! Have you been by the Novoseltsevs? When are they moving out?

TIKHON'S VOICE   They say they have nowhere to go!

AGASHA   They knew how to live nice and grand, now let them move out nice and grand! Tell them they've got till Sunday. Tell them that if they're still there after Sunday, things will get ugly! Nyushka! Damn you! Open your eyes! The child is stuffing dirt up its nose! Bring the child up here this instant, and come and wash windows instead! [*To the floor polisher.*] So, how are things moving along?

ANDREI   We're putting some muscle into it.

AGASHA   Then how about putting some muscle into those corners too? You haven't done them!

ANDREI   What corners?

AGASHA   All four corners. And you've turned the whole floor rusty brown. Is it supposed to be like that? The color's off!

ANDREI   We don't have the right materials to work with nowadays.

AGASHA   You think I was born yesterday? If there was money in it, you'd come up with the right materials in a second.

ANDREI   If it was up to me, I wouldn't ask my worst enemy to clean floors after the Revolution! During the Revolution the dirt grew to three inches thick on these floors—you couldn't shave it off with a plane! I should get a medal for cleaning floors after the Revolution, and all you do is bark.

[KATYA, *wearing mourning, enters upstage with* SUSHKIN.]

SUSHKIN The only reason I'm buying all this stuff is because I'm a furniture fanatic. I'm nuts about furniture! I simply can't walk past an antique piece and resist it. Antiques make me crazy. But as we all know, buying anything large nowadays is like hanging a millstone around your neck and jumping into a lake, you get dragged right to the bottom. So you buy something, you're full of enthusiasm, and then the next morning, in the cold light of day, you don't know what to do with all the stuff.

KATYA You forget that everything here is of exquisite quality. The Stroganoffs had this furniture brought from Paris a hundred years ago.

SUSHKIN And that is why I'm giving you a billion two hundred rubles for it.

KATYA How many loaves of bread does that buy?

SUSHKIN Well, but you can't count these things in loaves of bread—you have to take into consideration the fact that I'm buying these pieces as a madman, as an enthusiast. I'm sure you know well enough what a risk I'm taking, owning grand pieces of furniture—I'll be the first in line to get carted off. [*Changes his tone.*] I've brought some young men with me. [*Shouts downstairs.*] Okay, everyone, you can come up now! And bring some ropes!

AGASHA [*Steps forward.*] And where d'you think you're going to drag this off to?

SUSHKIN I don't believe I have had the pleasure . . .

KATYA This is our caretaker.

AGASHA I'm the janitor here.

SUSHKIN Pleased to meet you. How about this: you help us carry down the furniture, and we'll take care of you.

AGASHA That will not be possible, Comrade.

SUSHKIN What do you mean, not possible?

AGASHA There's people moving in here from the basement.

SUSHKIN [*Dismissively.*] Really? Fascinating!

AGASHA And where are they going to get furniture from, if I may ask?

SUSHKIN That is of no concern to us, Comrade.

KATYA Agasha, Maria Nikolayevna has authorized me to sell all the furniture.

SUSHKIN [*To* AGASHA.] Excuse me, Comrade, but does this furniture belong to you?

AGASHA The furniture isn't mine, just as it isn't yours.

SUSHKIN Listen, lady, first of all, you and I haven't shat in the same hole, okay? Secondly, your attitude is going to get you into trouble.

AGASHA You bring a warrant, and I'll let you cart off the furniture.

KATYA Agasha, this furniture belongs to Maria Nikolayevna, and as you know—

AGASHA Everything I knew, madame, I have forgotten—I've had to relearn everything.

SUSHKIN Careful, you're getting into deep waters!

AGASHA You raise your voice to me and you're out of here!

KATYA   Let us go, Mr. Sushkin.

SUSHKIN [*To* AGASHA.] You're a bit above yourself.

AGASHA   Bring me a warrant, and then you can cart everything out.

SUSHKIN   We'll be discussing this elsewhere.

AGASHA   Yes, down at the police station.

KATYA   Let us go, Mr. Sushkin.

SUSHKIN   I will go, but of one thing you can be sure: when I come back, I won't be alone.

AGASHA   Madame, what you're doing isn't right.

[*They leave.* ANDREI *and* KUZMA *finish polishing the floor. They gather their equipment.*]

KUZMA   She sure gave it to him.

ANDREI   That little lady knows how to throw punches.

KUZMA   Was she here when the general was around?

ANDREI   Back then she kept her head low and her mouth shut.

KUZMA   I'm sure the general was a nasty customer!

ANDREI   No, he wasn't! He never was! Whenever you went up to him, he'd say hello, shake hands with you. We all loved him.

KUZMA   What are you saying? How could you all love a general?

ANDREI   Because we're a bunch of fools! He didn't do any more harm than was to be expected. He chopped his own firewood.

KUZMA   Was he old?

ANDREI   Not really.

KUZMA   Then why did he die?

ANDREI   *"Man doesn't die because he's infirm*
                  He dies because he's served his term."
And the general had served his term.

[*Enter* AGASHA, SAFONOV—*a bony, young, taciturn worker—and his pregnant wife* ELENA, *a tall woman, not more than twenty, with a small, bright face. She is in the final stages of her pregnancy. They are loaded with household goods: stools, mattresses, a little paraffin stove.*]

ANDREI   Wait a second, wait a second—let me spread something on the floor!

AGASHA   Come in, Safonov, don't be afraid! This is where you are going to live!

ELENA   This is so fancy, couldn't we get a place that's less . . .

AGASHA   It's time you got used to better things.

ANDREI   You'll be surprised how fast you'll get used to better things.

AGASHA   The kitchen's to the left, and the bath where you can wash is over there. Come on, young man, let's go get the rest of the stuff. You stay here, Elena, and don't walk around—you'll lose your baby.

[AGASHA *and* SAFONOV *exit.* ANDREI *is gathering up his things— brushes, buckets.* ELENA *sits down on a stool.*]

ANDREI   Well, good luck in your new home.

ELENA   It doesn't really look all that comfortable—it's so big.

ANDREI   When is it due?

ELENA   I'm going in tomorrow.

ANDREI   It'll be easy enough for you. You'll be going to the palace on the Moika Canal, right?

ELENA   That's right, the Moika Canal.

ANDREI   That palace is now called "Mother and Child"—a Czarina had it built for a shepherd, now women go there to have kids. Everything's nicely fixed up, it'll be no hassle.[7]

ELENA   I have to go in tomorrow. One minute I'm frightened, the next I'm not.

ANDREI   What's there to be frightened of—you're going in to give birth, one hiccup and it'll be out. You squeeze all your insides, you give birth, then you'll be as good as new.

ELENA   It's just that I have such narrow hips.

ANDREI   When push comes to shove, they'll widen. You should see some of those pretty little women, tiny, with lots of nice hair, the prettiest little hands and feet, and they give birth to large roughnecks who can drink vodka by the bucket and fell a bull with a single punch. Giving birth is a woman's specialty. [*He swings his sack onto his shoulder.*] You want a girl or a boy?

ELENA   I don't mind either way.

ANDREI   You're right, both are fine. What I say is that all kids born today have a good life to look forward to. That's a sure thing nowadays! [*He picks up the rest of his tools.*] Let's go, Kuzma! [*To* ELENA.] One hiccup and it'll be out. Every trade has its specialty. Let's go, Cossack boy!

   [*The floor polishers exit.* ELENA *opens the windows, and the sun and the noise of the street come pouring in. Sticking out her belly, she carefully walks along the walls, touching them, peeks into adjacent rooms, turns on the chandelier, and turns it off again.* NYUSHKA, *an enormous crimson-faced girl, comes in carrying a bucket and a rag to wash the windows. She climbs up onto the windowsill and tucks in her skirt above her knees. She is bathed in sunlight. She stands against the background of the springtime sky like a statue holding up an arch.*]

ELENA   Will you come to our housewarming party, Nyushka?

NYUSHKA   [*In a bass voice.*]   You ask me—I'll come. What're you going to serve?

ELENA   Not much, whatever I can get my hands on.

NYUSHKA   What I want is some red wine, nice and sweet. [*She suddenly bursts into song with a loud, piercing voice.*]

   "*A Cossack galloped through valleys unseen*
   Into cold and distant Manchurian lands,
   He galloped through gardens and orchards green,
   A precious ring clasped in his powerful hands.
   The precious ring was from his sweetheart true:
   'Think of me as you ride through those distant lands,
   And in a year forever I shall belong to you.'

   Alas, a year had come and gone . . ."[8]

[*Curtain*]

---

7. Babel makes an oblique reference to a piece he wrote for Gorky's *Novaya zhizn*, "Palace of Motherhood" (1918). —*Ed.*

8. This popular Cossack ballad, dating from the Russo-Japanese War (1904–05), was familiar to Babel's contemporaries. The rest of the story goes as follows (in a literal translation): "Like an arrow, the Cossack galloped to his native village. He saw a hut in the foothills, and his heart began to pound. An old woman approached him and gently spoke: 'Your Cossack girl betrayed you. She made another man happy.' The Cossack turned his horse to the right and rode into a clear field. He took his rifle off his shoulder and ended his life forever. And that young Cossack girl—she is still waiting and waiting for her Cossack. And that old woman—an evil witch—she had been bribed with money [to deceive the Cossack]." —*Ed.*

The Polish Campaign:
Civil War or World Revolution

RED CAVALRY

The Polish Campaign of April–September 1920 is the setting for Babel's most famous work, *Red Cavalry* (in Russian, *Konarmiya*—Cavalry Army). Dismembered by the neighboring powers of Russia, Austria, and Prussia in the eighteenth century, Poland reestablished itself as a nation-state in the wake of World War I. Despite the blessing of the victorious Allies, it took diplomacy, politics, and force to set the boundaries of the new Polish state. In April 1920, the Polish army, aided by the Ukrainian nationalists, moved east and occupied Kiev. The Reds counterattacked successfully, and the Poles began to retreat. Lenin saw an opportunity for exporting communism to the rest of Europe, and the world revolution was treated as an objective fact at the Second Congress of the Communist International held in Petrograd and Moscow in July–August 1920. By August, the Red Army reached the outskirts of Warsaw and Lwów (now Lviv in Ukraine), but the offensive soon failed and by the end of the month the Reds were retreating in disarray. Leon Trotsky, the founder of the Red Army and the People's Commissar of War in 1917–24, blamed Stalin and his ambition to seize Lwów for delaying Semyon Budyonny's First Cavalry Army, which was desperately needed to support the assault on Warsaw. In October, the two sides signed a truce, confirmed by the treaty of Riga (1922) fixing the new border that remained in force until 1939, the beginning of World War II.

In April 1920, Babel was in Odessa. With the help of friends, he got himself dispatched as a war correspondent to Budyonny's Cavalry. Babel's reports were issued under the pen name of the ostensibly Russian Kiril Vasilievich Lyutov, to afford Babel protection from the Cossacks, notorious for their anti-Semitism. Babel joined Budyonny's corps in April or May and stayed with them until some time in September 1920. His duties varied from writing propaganda copy for the *Red Cavalryman* to doing odd jobs for the staff headquarters, including interrogating an American airman, a volunteer for the Polish side who was shot down by Red Army snipers.

The diary Babel kept during the campaign (see *The 1920 Diary*, beginning on page 184) became the basis for a series of stories published in newspapers and journals in 1923–26 with the subtitle "From the Book *Red Cavalry*" ("iz knigi 'Konarmiya' "). Thirty-four were included in the book, released on June 1, 1926; it sold out in six weeks. In all of the eight *Red Cavalry* editions printed in Russia in Babel's lifetime (the last one in 1936) the stories, some datelined, are arranged in one particular order. The only change was the addition of a new story, "Argamak" (1932), as the final novella of the cycle in the 1933 and 1936 edition.

Despite its enormous popularity, not everyone was a fan of *Red Cavalry*. Among those associated with the Polish campaign, Semyon Budyonny was the one who denounced it in public. Kliment Voroshilov, since 1925 the People's Commissar of Defense, and, most important, the supremo himself, Joseph Stalin, preferred to grumble from the shadows and to bide their time. —*Ed.*

Crossing the River Zbrucz[1]

The commander of the Sixth Division reported that Novograd-Volynsk was taken at dawn today. The staff is now withdrawing from Krapivno, and our cavalry transport stretches in a noisy rear guard along the high road that goes from Brest to Warsaw, a high road built on the bones of muzhiks by Czar Nicholas I.

Fields of purple poppies are blossoming around us, a noon breeze is frolicking in the yellowing rye, virginal buckwheat is standing on the horizon like the wall of a faraway monastery. Silent Volhynia is turning away, Volhynia is leaving, heading into the pearly white fog of the birch groves, creeping through the flowery hillocks, and with weakened arms entangling itself in the underbrush of hops. The orange sun is rolling across the sky like a severed head, gentle light glimmers in the ravines among the clouds, the banners of the sunset are fluttering above our heads. The stench of yesterday's blood and slaughtered horses drips into the evening chill. The blackened Zbrucz roars and twists the foaming knots of its rapids. The bridges are destroyed, and we wade across the river. The majestic moon lies on the waves. The water comes up to the horses' backs, purling streams trickle between hundreds of horses' legs. Someone sinks, and loudly curses the Mother of God. The river is littered with the black squares of the carts and filled with humming, whistling, and singing that thunders above the glistening hollows and the snaking moon.

Late at night we arrive in Novograd. In the quarters to which I am assigned I find a pregnant woman and two red-haired Jews with thin necks, and a third Jew who is sleeping with his face to the wall and a blanket pulled over his head. In my room I find ransacked closets, torn pieces of women's fur coats on the floor, human excrement, and fragments of the holy Seder plate that the Jews use once a year for Passover. "Clean up this mess!" I tell the woman. "How can you live like this?"

The two Jews get up from their chairs. They hop around on their felt soles and pick up the broken pieces of porcelain from the floor. They hop around in silence, like monkeys, like Japanese acrobats in a circus, their necks swelling and twisting. They spread a ripped eiderdown on the floor for me, and I lie down by the wall, next to the third, sleeping Jew. Timorous poverty descends over my bed.

Everything has been killed by the silence, and only the moon, clasping its round, shining, carefree head in its blue hands, loiters beneath my window.

I rub my numb feet, lie back on the ripped eiderdown, and fall asleep. I dream about the commander of the Sixth Division. He is chasing the

---

1. First published in the newspaper *Pravda* (Moscow), August 3, 1924. The actual crossing into Poland took place over the river Slucz, not Zbrucz.—*Ed.*

brigade commander on his heavy stallion, and shoots two bullets into his eyes. The bullets pierce the brigade commander's head, and his eyes fall to the ground. "Why did you turn back the brigade?" Savitsky, the commander of the Sixth Division, shouts at the wounded man, and I wake up because the pregnant woman is tapping me on the face.

"*Pan*,"[2] she says to me, "you are shouting in your sleep, and tossing and turning. I'll put your bed in another corner, because you are kicking my papa."

She raises her thin legs and round belly from the floor and pulls the blanket off the sleeping man. An old man is lying there on his back, dead. His gullet has been ripped out, his face hacked in two, and dark blood is clinging to his beard like a clump of lead.

"*Pan*," the Jewess says, shaking out the eiderdown, "the Poles were hacking him to death and he kept begging them, 'Kill me in the backyard so my daughter won't see me die!' But they wouldn't inconvenience themselves. He died in this room, thinking of me. . . . And now I want you to tell me," the woman suddenly said with terrible force, "I want you to tell me where one could find another father like my father in all the world!"

The Church in Novograd[1]

Yesterday I took a report over to the military commissar who had been billeted to the house of a Catholic priest who had fled. In the kitchen I was met by *Pani*[2] Eliza, the Jesuit's housekeeper. She gave me a cup of amber tea and some sponge cake. Her sponge cakes had the aroma of crucifixion. Within them was the sap of slyness and the fragrant frenzy of the Vatican.

In the church next to the house the bells were howling, tolled by the crazed bell ringer. It was an evening filled with the stars of July. *Pani* Eliza, shaking her attentive gray hair, kept on heaping cookies on my plate, and I delighted in the Jesuitical fare.

The old Polish woman addressed me as "*Pan*," gray old men with ossified ears stood to attention near the door, and somewhere in the serpentine darkness slithered a monk's soutane. The *Pater* had fled, but he had left behind his curate, *Pan* Romuald.

Romuald was a eunuch with a nasal voice and the body of a giant, who addressed us as "Comrade." He ran his yellow finger along the map, circling the areas where the Poles had been defeated. He counted the wounds of his fatherland with rasping ecstasy. May gentle oblivion engulf the memory of Romuald, who betrayed us without pity and was then shot without so much as a second thought. But that evening his tight soutane rustled at all the portieres and swept through all the corridors in a frenzy, as he smiled at everyone who wanted a drink of vodka. That evening the monk's shadow crept behind me wherever I went. *Pan* Romuald could have become a bishop if he had not been a spy.

---

2. Polish for "Sir" or "Mr." Babel uses the correct Polish form, *pane*. —Ed.
1. First published in the Odessa newspaper *Izvestia*, February 18, 1923. —Ed.
2. Polish: "Miss" or "Mrs." —Ed.

I drank rum with him. The breath of an alien way of life flickered beneath the ruins of the priest's house, and *Pan* Romuald's ingratiating seduction debilitated me. O crucifixes, tiny as the talismans of a courtesan! O parchment of the Papal Bull and satin of women's love letters moldering in blue silken waistcoats!

I can see you now, you deceptive monk with your purple habit, your puffy, swollen hands, and your soul, tender and merciless like a cat's! I can see the wounds of your God, oozing with the seed, the fragrant poison that intoxicates young maidens.

We drank rum, waiting for the military commissar, but he still hadn't come back from headquarters. Romuald had collapsed in a corner and fallen asleep. He slept and quivered, while beyond the window an alley seeped into the garden beneath the black passion of the sky. Thirsting roses swayed in the darkness. Green lightning bolts blazed over the cupolas. A naked corpse lay on the embankment. And the rays of the moon streamed through the dead legs that are pointing upward.

So this is Poland, this is the arrogant grief of the Rzeczpospolita Polska![3] A violent intruder, I unroll a louse-ridden straw mattress in this church abandoned by its clergymen, lay under my head a folio in which a Hosanna has been printed for Jozef Pilsudski,[4] the illustrious leader of the Polish nobility.

Hordes of beggars are converging on your ancient towns, O Poland! The song of all the enslaved is thundering above them, and woe unto you, Rzeczpospolita Polska, and woe unto you, Prince Radziwill, and you Prince Sapieha,[5] who have risen for an hour.

My military commissar has still not returned. I go look for him at the headquarters, the garden, the church. The doors of the church are wide open, I enter, and suddenly come face-to-face with two silver skulls flashing up from the lid of a shattered coffin. Aghast, I stumble back and fall down into the cellar. The oak staircase leads up to the altar from here, and I see a large number of lights flitting high up, right under the cupola. I see the military commissar, the commander of the special unit, and Cossacks carrying candles. They hear my weak cry and come down to haul me out from the basement.

The skulls turn out to have been carved into the church catafalque and no longer frighten me. I join the others on their search of the premises, because it turned out that *that* was what they were doing in the church, conducting a search, as a large pile of military uniforms had been found in the priest's apartment.

With wax dripping from our hands, the embroidered gold horse heads on our cuffs glittering, we whisper to one another as we circle with clinking spurs through the echoing building. Virgin Marys, covered with precious stones, watch us with their rosy, mouselike eyes, the flames flicker in our fingers, and rectangular shadows twist over the statues of Saint Peter,

---

3. Literally the Polish Republic, Poland's name before the partitions in the eighteenth century, restored in 1918. —*Ed.*
4. Jozef Klemens Pilsudski (1867–1935), the first Chief of State of Poland after its independence from Russia in 1918 and commander in chief of the Polish army.
5. Prince Janusz Radziwill (1880–1969), scion of one of the most important and oldest Polish-Lithuanian noble families and leader of the Polish Conservatives; Prince Eustachy Sapieha (1881–1963), Polish Foreign Minister. —*Ed.*

Saint Francis, Saint Vincent, and over their crimson cheeks and curly, carmine-painted beards.

We continue circling and searching. We run our fingers over ivory buttons and suddenly icons split open, revealing vaults and caverns blossoming with mold. This church is ancient and filled with secrets. Its lustrous walls hide clandestine passages, niches, and noiseless trapdoors.

You foolish priest, hanging the brassieres of your female parishioners on the nails of the Savior's cross! Behind the holy gates we found a suitcase of gold coins, a morocco-leather sackful of banknotes, and Parisian jewelers' cases filled with emerald rings.

We went and counted the money in the military commissar's room. Columns of gold, carpets of paper money, wind gusts blowing on our candle flames, the raven madness in the eyes of *Pani* Eliza, the thundering laughter of Romuald, and the endless roar of the bells tolled by *Pan* Robacki, the crazed bell ringer.

"I have to get away from here," I said to myself, "away from these winking Madonnas conned by soldiers."

A Letter[1]

Here is a letter home dictated to me by Kurdyukov, a boy in our regiment. This letter deserves to be remembered. I wrote it down without embellishing it, and am recording it here word for word as he said it.

> Dearest Mama, Evdokiya Fyodorovna,
> I hasten in these first lines of my letter to set your mind at rest and to inform you that by the grace of the Lord I am alive and well, and that I hope to hear the same from you. I bow most deepest before you, touching the moist earth with my white forehead. (There follows a list of relatives, godfathers, and godmothers. I am omitting this. Let us proceed to the second paragraph.)
> Dearest Mama, Evdokiya Fyodorovna Kurdyukova, I hasten to inform you that I am in Comrade Budyonny's Red Cavalry Regiment,[2] and that my godfather Nikon Vasilich is also here and is at the present time a Red Hero. He took me and put me in his special detachment of the Polit-otdel[3] in which we hand out books and newspapers to the various positions: the Moscow TsIK *Izvestia*,[4] the Moscow *Pravda*, and our own merciless newspaper the *Krasny Kavalerist*,[5] which every fighter on the front wants to read and then go and hero-

1. The first story of *Red Cavalry* to appear in print, "A Letter" was published in *Izvestia* (Odessa) on February 11, 1923, with the dateline "Novograd-Volynsk, June 1920." —*Ed.*
2. Semyon Mikhailovich Budenny (1883–1973), legendary cavalry commander, a noncommissioned officer in the Russo-Japanese War and World War I, who founded, along with Kliment Voroshilov, the First Cavalry Army in 1919. The Army's spectacular victories and Budenny's loyalty to Stalin, along with his talent for self-promotion and his cultivated trademark giant mustachios, help account for his advancement in the 1920s and 1930s and his mythic stature in Soviet popular culture, resonating to this day. —*Ed.*
3. Political department. See note 8, page 72. —*Ed.*
4. *Izvestia of the Central Executive Committee (TsIK)*, the newspaper of the highest Soviet executive organ. —*Ed.*
5. *The Red Cavalryman*, the newspaper distributed to the Red Cavalry forces and for which Babel also wrote pieces. See Babel's articles for it in this volume, beginning on page 251.

ically hack the damn Poles to pieces, and I am living real marvelous at Nikon Vasilich's.

Dearest Mama, Evdokiya Fyodorovna, send me anything that you possibly in any way can. I beg you to butcher our speckled pig and make a food packet for me, to be sent to Comrade Budyonny's Polit-otdel unit, addressed to Vasily Kurdyukov. All evenings I go to sleep hungry and bitterly cold without any clothes at all. Write to me a letter about my Stepan—is he alive or not, I beg you to look after him and to write to me about him, is he still scratching himself or has he stopped, but also about the scabs on his forelegs, have you had him shod, or not? I beg you dearest Mama, Evdokiya Fyodor-ovna, to wash without fail his forelegs with the soap I hid behind the icons, and if Papa has swiped it all then buy some in Krasnodar, and the Lord will smile upon you. I must also describe that the country here is very poor, the muzhiks with their horses hide in the woods from our Red eagles, there's hardly no wheat to be seen, it's all scrawny and we laugh and laugh at it. The people sow rye and they sow oats too. Hops grow on sticks here so they come out very well. They brew home brew with them.

In these second lines of this letter I hasten to write you about Papa, that he hacked my brother Fyodor Timofeyich Kurdyukov to pieces a year ago now. Our Comrade Pavlichenko's Red Brigade attacked the town of Rostov, when there was a betrayal in our ranks. And Papa was with the Whites back then as commander of one of Denikin's companies. All the folks that saw Papa says he was cov-ered in medals like with the old regime. And as we were betrayed, the Whites captured us and threw us all in irons, and Papa caught sight of my brother Fyodor Timofeyich. And Papa began hacking away at Fyodor, saying: you filth you, red dog, son of a bitch, and other things, and hacked away at him until sundown until my brother Fy-odor Timofeyich died. I had started writing you a letter then, about how your Fyodor is lying buried without a cross, but Papa caught me and said: you are your mother's bastards, the roots of that whore, I've plowed your mother and I'll keep on plowing her my whole damn life till I don't have a drop of juice left in me, and other things. I had to bear suffering like our Savior Jesus Christ. I man-aged to run away from Papa in the nick of time and join up with the Reds again, Comrade Pavlichenko's company. And our brigade got the order to go to the town of Voronezh to get more men, and we got more men and horses too, bags, revolvers, and everything we needed. About Voronezh, beloved Mama Evdokiya Fyodorovna, I can describe that it is indeed a marvelous town, a bit larger I think than Krasnodar, the people in it are very beautiful, the river is bril-liant to the point of being able to swim. We were given two pounds of bread a day each, half a pound of meat, and sugar enough so that when you got up you drank sweet tea, and the same in the evenings, forgetting hunger, and for dinner I went to my brother Semyon Tim-ofeyich for blini or goose meat and then lay down to rest. At the time, the whole regiment wanted to have Semyon Timofeyich for a commander because he is a wild one, and that order came from Comrade Budyonny, and Semyon Timofeyich was given two horses, good clothes, a cart specially for rags he's looted, and a Red Flag Medal, and they really looked up to me as I am his brother. Now when some neighbor offends you, then Semyon Timofeyich can completely slash him to pieces. Then we started chasing General Denikin, slashed them down by the thousand and chased them to the Black Sea, but Papa was nowhere to be seen, and Semyon Timofeyich looked for him in all the positions, because he mourned for our brother Fyodor. But only, dearest Mama, since you know Papa and his stubborn character, do you know what he did? He impudently painted his red beard black and was in the town of Maykop in civilian clothes, so that nobody there knew that he is he himself, that very same police constable in the old regime. But truth will always show its head—my godfather Nikon Vasilich saw him by chance in the hut of a townsman, and wrote my brother Semyon Timofeyich a letter. We got on horses and galloped two hundred versts—me, my brother Semyon, and boys which wants to come along from the Cossack village.

And what is it we saw in the town of Maykop? We saw that people away from the front, they don't give a damn about the front, and it's all full of betrayal and Yids like in the old regime. And my brother Semyon Timofeyich in the town of Maykop had a good row with the Yids who would not give Papa up and had thrown him in jail under lock and key, saying that a decree had come not to hack to pieces prisoners, we'll try him ourselves, don't be angry, he'll get what he deserves. But then Semyon Timofeyich spoke and proved that he was the commander of a regiment, and had been given all the medals of the Red Flag by Comrade Budyonny, and threatened to hack to pieces everyone who argued over Papa's person without handing him over, and the boys from the Cossack villages threatened them too. But then, the moment Semyon got hold of Papa, Semyon began whipping him, and lined up all the fighters in the yard as befits military order. And then Semyon splashed water all over Papa's beard and the color flowed from the beard. And Semyon asked our Papa, Timofey Rodyonich, "So, Papa, are you feeling good now that you're in my hands?"

"No," Papa said, "I'm feeling bad."

Then Semyon asked him, "And my brother Fyodor, when you were hacking him to pieces, did he feel good in your hands?"

"No," Papa said, "Fyodor was feeling bad."

Then Semyon asked him, "And did you think, Papa, that someday you might be feeling bad?"

"No," Papa said, "I didn't think that I might be feeling bad."

Then Semyon turned to the people and said, "And I believe, Papa, that if I fell into your hands, I would find no mercy. So now, Papa, we will finish you off!"

Timofey Rodyonich began impudently cursing Semyon, by Mama and the Mother of God, and slapping Semyon in the face, and Semyon sent me out of the yard, so that I cannot, dearest Mama, Evdokiya Fyodorovna, describe to you how they finished off Papa, because I had been sent out of the yard.

After that we stopped at the town of Novorossisk. About that town one can say that there isn't a single bit dry anywhere anymore, just water, the Black Sea, and we stayed there right until May, and then we set off for the Polish Front where we are slapping the Polish masters about in full swing.

I remain your loving son, Vasily Timofeyich Kurdyukov. Mama, look in on Stepan, and the Lord will smile upon you.

This is Kurdyukov's letter, without a single word changed. When I had finished, he took the letter and hid it against the naked flesh of his chest.

"Kurdyukov," I asked the boy, "was your father a bad man?"

"My father was a dog," he answered sullenly.

"And your mother?"

"My mother's good enough. Here's my family, if you want to take a look." He held out a tattered photograph. In it was Timofey Kurdyukov, a wide-shouldered police constable in a policeman's cap, his beard neatly combed. He was stiff, with wide cheekbones and sparkling, colorless, vacant eyes. Next to him, in a bamboo chair, sat a tiny peasant woman in a loose blouse, with small, bright, timid features. And against this provincial photographer's pitiful backdrop, with its flowers and doves, towered two boys, amazingly big, blunt, broad-faced, goggle-eyed, and frozen as if standing at attention: the Kurdyukov brothers, Fyodor and Semyon.

The Reserve Cavalry Commander[1]

A wail spreads over the village. The cavalry is trampling the grain and trading in horses. The cavalrymen are exchanging their worn-out nags for the peasants' workhorses. One can't argue with what the cavalrymen are doing—without horses there can be no army.

But this isn't much of a comfort to the peasants. They are stubbornly gathering outside the headquarters, dragging behind them struggling old nags tottering with weakness. The muzhiks' breadwinners have been taken away from them, and with a surge of bitter valor, aware that this valor will not last long, they hurry to rant despairingly at the authorities, at God, and at their bitter lot.

Chief of Staff Z.[2] is standing on the front porch in full uniform. His inflamed eyelids half closed, he listens to the muzhiks' complaints with evident attention. But his attention is only a ploy. Like all disciplined and weary bureaucrats, he has a knack for shutting down all cerebral activity during empty moments of existence. During these moments of blissful empty-headedness our chief of staff recharges his worn-out instrument.

And this is what he is doing this time too, with the muzhiks.

To the soothing accompaniment of their desperate and disjointed clamor, Chief of Staff Z. cautiously follows his brain's soft wisps, those precursors of clear and energetic thought. He waits for the necessary pause, grasps the final muzhik sob, yells in a commanderial fashion, and returns to his office to work.

But on this particular occasion even yelling would not have been necessary. Galloping up to the porch on an Anglo-Arabian steed came Dyakov,[3] a former circus rider and now commander of the Reserve Cavalry—red-faced with a gray mustache, a black cape, and wide red Tatar trousers with silver stripes.

1. The Russian title is "Nachal' nik konzapasa" (remount officer); first published in *LEF* (Moscow) 4 (1923; printed in 1924) as "Dyakov," datelined "Beliow, July 1920." —*Ed.*
2. Konstantin Karlovich Zholnarkevich, the staff commander in the *1920 Diary*.
3. For Dyakov, see *1920 Diary*, entries for July 13, 1920 and July 16, 1920.

"The Father Superior's blessing on all the honest filth of the earth!" he shouted, reining in his horse in front of the porch, and at that very instant a shabby little horse that had been given in exchange by the Cossacks collapsed in front of him.

"There, you see, Comrade Commander!" a muzhik shouted, slapping his thighs in despair. "There you have what your people are giving our people! Did you see what they've given us? And we're supposed to farm with that?"

"For this horse," Dyakov proclaimed distinctly and momentously, "for this horse, my highly esteemed friend, you have every right to request fifteen thousand rubles from the Reserve Cavalry, and if this horse were a trifle livelier, you, my dearest of friends, would be entitled to twenty thousand rubles. Just because a horse falls does not mean it's *factual!* If a horse falls but then gets up—that is a horse. If, to invert what I am saying, the horse does not get up—then that is not a horse. But I do believe I can make this lively little mare spring to her feet again!"

"Lord in Heaven and Mother of God!" the muzhik cried, throwing his hands up in the air. "How is this poor thing supposed to get up? It's on its last legs!"

"You are insulting this horse, my dear fellow!" Dyakov answered with fierce conviction. "Pure blasphemy, my dear fellow!" And he deftly swung his athlete's body out of his saddle. Splendid and deft as if in the circus ring, he stretched his magnificent legs, his trousers girded by cords around the knees, and walked up to the dying animal. She peered at him dolefully with a severe, penetrating eye, licked some invisible command from his crimson palm, and immediately the feeble mare felt bracing power flow from this sprightly, gray, blossoming Romeo. Her muzzle lolling, her legs skidding under her, feeling the whip tickling her stomach with imperious impatience, the mare slowly and deliberately rose onto her legs. And then we all saw Dyakov's slender hand with its fluttering sleeve run through her dirty mane, and his whining whip swatting her bleeding flanks. Her whole body shivering, the mare stood on all four legs without moving her timid, doglike, lovestruck eyes from Dyakov.

"So you see—this is a horse," Dyakov said to the muzhik, and added softly, "and you were complaining, my dearest of friends!"

Throwing his reins to his orderly, the commander of the Reserve Cavalry jumped the four stairs in a single leap and, swirling off his operatic cloak, disappeared into the headquarters.

Pan Apolek[1]

The wise and wonderful life of *Pan* Apolek went straight to my head, like an old wine. Among the huddling ruins of Novograd-Volynsk, a town crushed in haste, fate threw at my feet a gospel that had remained hidden from the world. There, surrounded by the guileless shine of halos, I

1. First published in *Krasnaya nov* 7 (1923).

took a solemn oath to follow the example of *Pan* Apolek. The sweetness of dreamy malice, the bitter contempt for the swine and dogs among men, the flame of silent and intoxicating revenge—I sacrificed them all to this oath.

An icon was hanging high on the wall in the home of the Novograd priest, who had fled. It bore the inscription: "The Death of John the Baptist." There was no doubt about it: in the portrayal of John I saw a man I had seen somewhere before.

I remember the gossamer stillness of a summer morning hung on the bright, straight walls. The sun had cast a ray straight on the foot of the icon. Sparkling dust swarmed in it. The tall figure of John came straight at me from the blue depths of the niche. A black cape hung triumphantly on that inexorable, repulsively thin body. Droplets of blood shone in the cape's round buckles. His head had been hacked diagonally off the flayed neck. It lay on an earthen platter that was held by the large yellow fingers of a warrior. The face of the dead man seemed familiar. I was touched by a mysterious premonition. The hacked-off head on the earthen platter was modeled after *Pan* Romuald, the curate of the priest who had fled. Out of his snarling mouth curled the tiny body of a snake, its scales shining brightly. Its head, a tender pink, was bristling with life, and stood out powerfully against the deep background of the cape.

I was amazed at the painter's artistry, his dark inventiveness. I was even more amazed the following day when I saw the red-cheeked Virgin Mary hanging above the matrimonial bed of *Pani* Eliza, the old priest's housekeeper. Both paintings bore the marks of the same brush. The meaty face of the Virgin Mary was a portrait of *Pani* Eliza. And this is where I found the key to the mystery of the Novograd icons. And the key led me to *Pani* Eliza's kitchen, where on fragrant evenings the shadows of old servile Poland gather, with the holy fool of a painter at their center. But was *Pan* Apolek a holy fool, peopling the local villages with angels, and elevating lame Janek, the Jewish convert, to sainthood?

Pan Apolek had come here thirty years ago on a summer day like any other with blind Gottfried. The two friends, Apolek and Gottfried, had gone to Shmerel's tavern on the Rovno high road, two versts from the edge of the town. In his right hand Apolek was holding a box of paints, and with his left hand leading the blind concertina player. The melodious tread of their reinforced German boots echoed with calmness and hope. A canary-yellow scarf hung from Apolek's thin neck, and three chocolate-brown feathers swung on the blind man's Tyrolean hat.

The newcomers had placed the paints and the concertina on a windowsill in the tavern. The artist unwound his scarf, which was neverending, like a fairground magician's ribbon. Then he went out into the yard, took off all his clothes, and poured freezing water over his thin, feeble, pink body. Shmerel's wife brought them raisin vodka and a bowl of meat cutlets stuffed with rice. Gottfried ate his fill, and then placed his concertina on his bony knees. He sighed, threw his head back, and flexed his thin fingers. The chords of the Heidelberg songs echoed against the walls of the Jewish tavern. With his scratchy voice Apolek accompanied the blind man. It was as if the organ had been brought from the Church of Saint Indegilda to Shmerel's tavern and the muses, with their quilted

scarves and reinforced German boots, had seated themselves in a row
upon this organ.

The two men sang till sunset, then they put the concertina and the
paints into canvas sacks. *Pan* Apolek bowed deeply and gave Brayna, the
taverner's wife, a sheet of paper.

"My dear *Pani* Brayna," he said. "Please accept from the hands of a
wandering artist, upon whom the Christian name of Apollinarius has
been bestowed, this portrait as a sign of our most humble gratitude for
your sumptuous hospitality. If the Lord Jesus Christ sees fit to lengthen
my days and give strength to my art, I will come back and add color to
this portrait. There shall be pearls in your hair and a necklace of emeralds upon your breast."

Drawn on a small sheet of paper with a red pencil, a pencil red and
soft like clay, was *Pani* Brayna's laughing face, surrounded by a mass of
copper curls.

"My money!" Shmerel shouted when he saw his wife's portrait. He
grabbed a stick and started running after the two men. But as he ran,
Shmerel remembered Apolek's pink body with water splashing all over it,
the sun in his little courtyard, and the soft sound of the concertina. The
taverner's soul drooped, and, putting the stick down, he went back
home.

The following morning, Apolek showed the priest of Novograd his
diploma from the Munich Academy, and laid out before him twelve
paintings with biblical motifs. They had been painted with oil on boards
of thin cypress wood. On his table the *Pater* saw the burning purple of
cloaks, the emerald sparkle of fields, and blossoming blankets of flowers
flung over the plains of Palestine.

Pan Apolek's saints, a multitude of simple, jubilating elders with gray
beards and red faces, were encircled by streams of silk and potent evening skies.

That same day, *Pan* Apolek was commissioned to do paintings for the
new church. And over Benedictine wine, the *Pater* said to the artist:
"Sancta Maria! My dear *Pan* Apollinarius, from what wondrous realms
has your joyous grace descended upon us?"

Apolek worked with great zeal, and within a month the new church
was filled with the bleating of herds, the dusty gold of setting suns, and
straw-colored cow udders. Buffaloes with worn hides struggled under
their yokes, dogs with pink muzzles trotted in front of the large flocks of
sheep, and plump infants rocked in cradles that hung from the trunks of
tall palm trees. The tattered brown habits of Franciscan monks crowded
around a cradle. The group of wise men stood out with their shining bald
heads and their wrinkles red like wounds. The small, wrinkled old face
of Pope Leo XIII twinkled with its fox-like smile from the group of wise
men, and even the priest of Novograd was there, running the fingers of
one hand through the carved beads of a Chinese rosary while with his
other, free hand, he blessed the infant Jesus.

For five months Apolek inched along the walls, the cupola, and the
choir stalls, fastened to the wooden scaffolding.

"You have a predilection for familiar faces, my dear *Pan* Apolek," the
priest once said, recognizing himself among the wise men and *Pan*
Romuald in the severed head of John the Baptist. The old *Pater* smiled,

and sent a tumbler of cognac up to the artist working beneath the cupola.

Apolek finished the Last Supper and the Stoning of Mary Magdalene. Then one Sunday he unveiled the walls. The distinguished citizens the priest had invited recognized Janek the lame convert in the Apostle Paul, and in Mary Magdalene Elka, a Jewish girl of unknown parentage and mother of many of the urchins roaming the streets. The distinguished citizens demanded that the blasphemous images be painted over. The priest showered threats over the blasphemer, but Apolek refused to paint over the walls.

And so an unprecedented war broke out, with the powerful body of the Catholic Church on one side, and the unconcerned icon painter on the other. The war lasted for three decades. The situation almost turned the gentle idler into the founder of a new heresy; in which case he would have been the most whimsical and ludicrous fighter among the many in the slippery and stormy history of the Church of Rome, a fighter roaming the earth in blessed tipsiness with two white mice under his shirt and with a collection of the finest little brushes in his pocket.

"Fifteen zloty for the Virgin Mary, twenty-five zloty for the Holy Family, and fifty zloty for the Last Supper portraying all the client's family. The client's enemy can be portrayed as Judas Iscariot, for which an extra ten zloty will be added to the bill," *Pan* Apolek informed the peasants after he had been thrown out of the Novograd church.

There was no shortage of commissions. And when a year later the archbishop of Zhitomir sent a delegation in response to the frenzied epistles of the Novograd priest, they found the monstrous family portraits, sacrilegious, naive, and flamboyant, in the most impoverished, foul-smelling hovels. Josephs with gray hair neatly parted in the middle, pomaded Jesuses, many-childed village Marys with parted knees. The pictures hung in the icon corners, wreathed with garlands of paper flowers.

"He has bestowed sainthood upon you people during your lifetime!" the bishop of Dubno and Novokonstantinov shouted at the crowd that had come to defend Apolek. "He has endowed you with the ineffable attributes of the saints, you, thrice fallen into the sin of disobedience, furtive moonshiners, ruthless moneylenders, makers of counterfeit weights, and sellers of your daughters' innocence!"

"Your holiness!" lame-footed Witold, the town's cemetery watchman and procurer of stolen goods, then said to the bishop. "Where does our all-forgiving Lord God see truth, and who will explain it to these ignorant villagers? Is there not more truth in the paintings of *Pan* Apolek, who raises our pride, than in your words that are filled with abuse and tyrannical anger?"

The shouts of the crowd sent the bishop running. The agitation in the villages threatened the safety of the clerics. The painter who had taken Apolek's place could not work up the courage to paint over Elka and lame Janek. They can still be seen today above a side altar of the Novograd church: Janek, as Saint Paul, a timorous cripple with the shaggy black beard of a village apostate, and Elka as the whore from Magdala, decrepit and crazed, with dancing body and fallen cheeks.

The battle with the priest lasted three decades. Then the Cossack flood chased the old monk out of his aromatic stone nest, and Apolek—

O fickle fortune!—settled into *Pani* Eliza's kitchen. And here I am, a passing guest, imbibing the wine of his conversation in the evenings.

What do we converse about? About the romantic days of the Polish nobility, the fanatical frenzy of women, the art of Luca della Robbia,[2] and the family of the Bethlehem carpenter.

"There is something I have to tell you, Mr. Clerk,"[3] Apolek tells me secretively before supper.

"Yes," I answer. "Go ahead, Apolek, I'm listening."

But *Pan* Robacki, the lay brother of the church—stern, gray, bony, and with large ears—is sitting too close. He unfolds a faded screen of silence and animosity before us.

"I have to tell you, *Pan*," Apolek whispers, taking me aside, "that Jesus Christ, the son of Mary, was married to Deborah, a Jerusalem girl of low birth—"

"O, *ten czlowiek!*"[4] *Pan* Robacki shouts in despair. "This man not dies in his bed! This man the peoples will be killing!"

"After supper," Apolek murmurs in a gloomy voice. "After supper, if that will suit you, Mr. Clerk."

It suits me. Inflamed by the beginning of Apolek's story, I pace up and down the kitchen waiting for the appointed time. And outside the window night stands like a black column. Outside the window the bristling, dark garden has fallen still. The road to the church flows beneath the moon in a sparkling, milky stream. The earth is covered with a dismal sheen, a necklace of shining berries is draped over the bushes. The aroma of lilacs is clean and strong as alcohol. The seething oily breath of the stove drinks in this fresh poison, killing the stuffy resinous heat of the spruce wood lying about the kitchen floor.

Apolek is wearing a pink bow tie and threadbare pink trousers, and is puttering about in his corner like a friendly graceful animal. His table is smeared with glue and paint. He is working in quick small movements. A hushed, melodic drumming comes drifting from his corner: it is old Gottfried tapping with his trembling fingers. The blind man is sitting rigidly in the greasy yellow lamplight. His bald head is drooping as he listens to the incessant music of his blindness and the muttering of Apolek, his eternal friend.

". . . And what the priests and the Evangelist Mark and the Evangelist Matthew are telling you, *Pan* Clerk, is not truth. But truth can be revealed to you, *Pan*, for I am prepared for fifty marks to paint your portrait in the form of Saint Francis on a background of green and sky. He was a very simple saint, *Pan* Francis was. And if you have a bride in Russia, *Pan* Clerk, women love Saint Francis, although not all women, *Pan*."

And from his spruce-wood-scented corner he began telling me the tale of the marriage of Jesus to Deborah. According to Apolek, Deborah already had a bridegroom, a young Israelite who traded in ivory. But Deborah's wedding night ended in bewilderment and tears. The woman was grabbed by fear when she saw her husband approach her bed. Hiccups bulged in her throat and she vomited all the food she had eaten at the

---

2. Luca della Robbia (1399–1482), Florentine sculptor known primarily for his works in enameled terra cotta. —*Ed.*
3. Apolek uses the Polish *pisarz*, which may be rendered as "clerk" or "writer." —*Ed.*
4. Polish: Oh, this man!

wedding table. Shame fell upon Deborah, on her father, her mother, and on all her kin. The bridegroom abandoned her with words of ridicule, and called all the guests together. And Jesus, filled with pity at seeing the anguish of the woman who was thirsting for her husband but also fearing him, donned the robes of the newlywed man and united himself with Deborah as she lay in her vomit. Afterward she went out to the wedding guests, loudly exulting like a woman proud of her fall. And only Jesus stood to the side. His body was drenched with mortal sweat, for the bee of sorrow had stung his heart. He left the banquet hall unnoticed, and went into the desert east of Judea, where John the Baptist awaited him. And Deborah gave birth to her first son. . . ."

"So where is that son?" I yelled.

"The priests have hidden him," Apolek said with gravity, raising his thin, cold finger to his drunkard's nose.

"*Pan* Artist!" Robacki suddenly shouted, stepping out of the shadows, his gray ears quaking. "What you saying? But this is outrage!"

"*Tak, tak,*" Apolek said, cringing and grabbing hold of Gottfried. "*Tak, tak, panie.*"[5]

Apolek pulled the blind man toward the door, but stopped by the doorpost and beckoned me with his finger.

"Saint Francis with a bird on your sleeve," he whispered, winking at me. "A dove or a goldfinch, you can choose, *Pan* Clerk!"

And he disappeared with his blind eternal friend.

"Oh, what foolishness!" Robacki, the church lay brother, said. "This man not dies in his bed!"

Pan Robacki opened his mouth wide and yawned like a cat. I wished him a good night, and went home, to my plundered Jews, to sleep.

The vagrant moon trailed through the town and I tagged along, nurturing within me unfulfillable dreams and dissonant songs.

Italian Sun[1]

Yesterday I was sitting once more under a heated garland of green spruce twigs in *Pani* Eliza's servants' quarters. I sat by the warm, lively, crackling stove, and then returned to my lodgings late at night. Below, in the ravine, the silent Zbrucz rolled its glassy, dark waves.

The burned-out town—broken columns and the hooks of evil old women's fingers dug into the earth—seemed to me raised into the air, comfortable and unreal like a dream. The naked shine of the moon poured over the town with unquenchable strength. The damp mold of the ruins blossomed like a marble bench on the opera stage. And I waited with anxious soul for Romeo to descend from the clouds, a satin Romeo singing of love, while backstage a dejected electrician waits with his finger on the button to turn off the moon.

Blue roads flowed past me like rivulets of milk trickling from many breasts. On my way back, I had been dreading running into Sidorov, with

5. Polish: Yes, yes, sir. —*Ed.*
1. First published in *Krasnaya nov* 3 (1924) under the title "Sidorov." —*Ed.*

whom I shared my room, and who at night brought his hairy paw of dejection down upon me. That night, luckily, harrowed by the milk of the moon, Sidorov did not say a single word to me. I found him writing, surrounded by books. On the table a hunchbacked candle was smoking—the sinister bonfire of dreamers. I sat to the side, dozed, dreams pouncing around me like kittens. And it wasn't until late that night that I was awakened by an orderly who had come to take Sidorov to headquarters. They left together. I immediately hurried over to the table where Sidorov had been writing, and leafed through his books. There was an Italian primer, a print of the Roman Forum, and a street map of Rome. The map was completely marked up with crosses. I leaned over the sheet of paper covered with writing and, with clenched fingers and an expiring heart, read another man's letter. Sidorov, the dejected murderer, tore the pink cotton wool of my imagination to shreds and dragged me into the halls of his judicious insanity. I began reading on the second page, as I did not dare look for the first one:

> . . . shot through the lungs, and am a little off my head, or, as Sergey always says, flying mad. Well, when you go mad, idiotically mad, you don't go, you fly. Anyway, let's put the horsetail to one side and the jokes to the other. Back to the events of the day, Victoria, my dear friend.
>
> I took part in a three-month Makhno campaign[2]—the whole thing a grueling swindle, nothing more! Only Volin[3] is still there. Volin is wearing apostolic raiment and clamoring to be the Lenin of anarchism. Terrible. And Makhno listens to him, runs his fingers through his dusty wire curls, and lets the snake of his peasant grin slither across his rotten teeth. And I'm not all that sure anymore if there isn't a seed of anarchy in all this, and if we won't wipe your prosperous noses for you, you self-proclaimed Tsekists from your self-proclaimed Tsekhs,[4] "made in Kharkov," your self-proclaimed capital.[5] Your strapping heroes prefer not to remember the sins of their anarchist youth, and now laugh at them from the heights of their governmental wisdom! To hell with them!
>
> Then I ended up in Moscow. How did I end up in Moscow? The boys had treated someone unjustly, something to do with requisitions or something. Well, fool that I am, I defended him. So they let me have it, and rightly so. My wound was not even worth mentioning, but in Moscow, O Victoria, in Moscow I was struck dumb by the misery all around. Every day the hospital nurses would bring me a nibble of kasha. Bridled with reverence, they brought it in on a large tray, and I despised this shock-brigade kasha, this unregimented treatment in regimented Moscow. Then, in the Soviet Council, I ran into a handful of anarchists. All fops and dithering old men! I managed to get all the way to the Kremlin with my plan for some real work. But they patted me on the back and promised to

---

2. Nestor Ivanovich Makhno (1889–1934), leader and commander of the anarchist forces in the Ukraine, which temporarily sided with the Bolsheviks in the civil war. —Ed.
3. Vsevolod Mikhailovich Volin (Eikhenbaum, 1882–1945), well-known anarchist, leading figure during the revolution, and in 1919 the chief ideologist of the Makhno movement. He was exiled from Russia in 1922 along with other members of the anarchist movement. His brother, Boris Eikhenbaum, was a leading Formalist critic and literary scholar. —Ed.
4. A pun: the Tsekists are members of the Tseka, the Central Committee of the Bolshevik Party. A "tsekh," however, is a simple guild.
5. Today Kharkiv, a city in northeastern Ukraine. The "self-proclaimed" capital in the sense that Kharkiv replaced Kiev as the capital of the Ukraine from 1917 until 1934.

give me a nice deputy position if I changed my ways. I did not change my ways. And what came next? Next came the front, the Red Cavalry, and the damn soldiers stinking of blood and corpses.

Save me, Victoria! Governmental wisdom is driving me insane, boredom is inebriating me. If you won't help me I will die like a dog without a five-year plan! And who wants a worker to die unplanned? Surely not you, Victoria, my bride who will never be my wife. See, I'm becoming maudlin again, damn it to hell!

But let's get to the point now. The army bores me. I cannot ride because of my wound, which means I cannot fight. Use your connections, Victoria, have them send me to Italy! I am studying the language, and I'll be speaking it within two months. The land down there is smoldering, things there are almost ready. All they need is a few shots. One of these shots I shall fire. It is high time that their King be sent to join his ancestors. That is very important. He is a nice old fellow who plays for popularity and has himself photographed with the tamer socialists for family magazines.

But don't say anything about shots or kings at the Tseka or the People's Commissariat for Foreign Affairs. They will pat you on the head and coo: "What a romantic he is!" Just tell them plain and simple: "He's sick, he's angry, he's drunk with depression, he wants some Italian sun and he wants some bananas! Does he deserve it, or doesn't he? He'll recuperate, and *basta!*[6] And if not, then send him to the Odessa Cheka.[7] They're very sensible there!"

The things I am writing you are so foolish, so unfairly foolish, Victoria, my dear friend.

Italy has seeped into my heart like an obsession. Thinking about that country that I have never seen is as sweet to me as a woman's name, as your name, Victoria. . . .

I read the letter through and then went to lie down on my dirty, crumpled bed, but sleep would not come. On the other side of the wall the pregnant Jewess was crying heartfelt tears, her lanky husband answering with mumbling groans. They were lamenting the things that had been stolen, and blaming each other for their bad luck. Then, before daybreak, Sidorov came back. The dwindling candle was expiring on the table. He pulled another candle end out of his boot and pressed it with unusual pensiveness onto the drowned wick. Our room was dark, gloomy, everything in it breathed a damp, nocturnal stench, and only the window, lit up by the fire of the moon, shone like salvation.

He came over, my agonizing neighbor, and hid the letter. Bending forward, he sat down at the table and opened the picture album of Rome. The magnificent book with its gilt-edged pages stood opposite his expressionless, olive-green face. The jagged ruins of the Capitol and the Coliseum, lit by the setting sun, glittered over his hunched back. The photograph of the royal family was also there. He had inserted it between the large, glossy pages. On a piece of paper torn from a calendar was the picture of the pleasant, frail King Victor Emmanuel with his black-haired wife, Crown Prince Umberto, and a whole brood of princesses.

6. Italian: Enough! —*Ed.*
7. The Odessa Cheka had a reputation for exceptional brutality. —*Ed.*

It is night, a night full of distant and painful sounds, with a square of light in the damp darkness, and in this square is Sidorov's deathly face, a lifeless mask hovering over the yellow flame of the candle.

Gedali[1]

On the eve of the Sabbath I am always tormented by the dense sorrow of memory. In the past on these evenings, my grandfather's yellow beard caressed the volumes of Ibn Ezra.[2] My old grandmother, in her lace bonnet, waved spells over the Sabbath candle with her gnarled fingers, and sobbed sweetly. On those evenings my child's heart was gently rocked, like a little boat on enchanted waves.

I wander through Zhitomir looking for the timid star.[3] Beside the ancient synagogue, beside its indifferent yellow walls, old Jews, Jews with the beards of prophets, passionate rags hanging from their sunken chests, are selling chalk, bluing, and candle wicks.

Here before me lies the bazaar, and the death of the bazaar. Slaughtered is the fat soul of abundance. Mute padlocks hang on the stores, and the granite of the streets is as clean as a corpse's bald head. The timid star blinks and expires.

Success came to me later, I found the star just before the setting of the sun. Gedali's store lay hidden among the tightly shut market stalls. Dickens, where was your shadow that evening?[4] In this old junk store you would have found gilded slippers and ship's ropes, an antique compass and a stuffed eagle, a Winchester hunting rifle with the date "1810" engraved on it, and a broken stewpot.

Old Gedali is circling around his treasures in the rosy emptiness of the evening, a small shopkeeper with smoky spectacles and a green coat that reaches all the way to the ground. He rubs his small white hands, tugs at his gray beard, lowers his head, and listens to invisible voices that come wafting to him.

This store is like the box of an intent and inquisitive little boy who will one day become a professor of botany. This store has everything from buttons to dead butterflies, and its little owner is called Gedali. Everyone has left the bazaar, but Gedali has remained. He roams through his labyrinth of globes, skulls, and dead flowers, waving his cockerel-feather duster, swishing away the dust from the dead flowers.

We sit down on some empty beer barrels. Gedali winds and unwinds his narrow beard. His top hat rocks above us like a little black tower. Warm air flows past us. The sky changes color—tender blood pouring from an overturned bottle—and a gentle aroma of decay envelops me.

"So let's say we say 'yes' to the Revolution. But does that mean that we're supposed to say 'no' to the Sabbath?" Gedali begins, enmeshing me in the silken cords of his smoky eyes. "Yes to the Revolution! Yes! But the

---

1. First published in *Krasnaya nov* 4 (1924). —Ed.
2. Ibn Ezra, aka Abraham ben Meir (1092–1167), Jewish poet and philosopher known for his commentaries on Scripture, a foremost representative of the Golden Age of Spanish Judaism. —Ed.
3. The star that signals nightfall and the beginning of evening prayers for the Sabbath.
4. A reference to Charles Dickens's novel *The Old Curiosity Shop* (1840–41).

Revolution keeps hiding from Gedali and sending gunfire ahead of itself."

"The sun cannot enter eyes that are squeezed shut," I say to the old man, "but we shall rip open those closed eyes!"

"The Pole has closed my eyes," the old man whispers almost inaudibly. "The Pole, that evil dog! He grabs the Jew and rips out his beard, *oy,* the hound! But now they are beating him, the evil dog! This is marvelous, this is the Revolution! But then the same man who beat the Pole says to me, 'Gedali, we are requisitioning your gramophone!' 'But gentlemen,' I tell the Revolution, 'I love music!' And what does the Revolution answer me? 'You don't know what you love, Gedali! I am going to shoot you, and then you'll know, and I cannot *not* shoot, because I am the Revolution!'"

"The Revolution cannot *not* shoot, Gedali," I tell the old man, "because it is the Revolution."

"But my dear *Pan!* The Pole did shoot, because he is the counterrevolution. And you shoot because you are the Revolution. But Revolution is happiness. And happiness does not like orphans in its house. A good man does good deeds. The Revolution is the good deed done by good men. But good men do not kill. Hence the Revolution is done by bad men. But the Poles are also bad men. Who is going to tell Gedali which is the Revolution and which the counterrevolution? I have studied the Talmud. I love the commentaries of Rashi[5] and the books of Maimonides.[6] And there are also other people in Zhitomir who understand. And so all of us learned men fall to the floor and shout with a single voice, 'Woe unto us, where is the sweet Revolution?'"

The old man fell silent. And we saw the first star breaking through and meandering along the Milky Way.

"The Sabbath is beginning," Gedali pronounced solemnly. "Jews must go to the synagogue."

"*Pan* Comrade," he said, getting up, his top hat swaying on his head like a little black tower. "Bring a few good men to Zhitomir. Oy, they are lacking in our town, *oy,* how they are lacking! Bring good men and we shall give them all our gramophones. We are not simpletons. The International,[7] we know what the International is. And I want the International of good people, I want every soul to be accounted for and given first-class rations. Here, soul, eat, go ahead, go and find happiness in your life. The International, *Pan* Comrade, you have no idea how to swallow it!"

"With gunpowder," I tell the old man, "and seasoned with the best blood."

And then from the blue darkness young Sabbath climbed onto her throne.

"Gedali," I say to him, "today is Friday, and night has already fallen. Where can I find some Jewish biscuits, a Jewish glass of tea, and a piece of that retired God in the glass of tea?"

---

5. Rabbi Shlomo Yitzhaqi (1040–1105), known by his acronym Rashi, renowned French rabbi and exegete of the Bible and Talmud. —*Ed.*
6. Moses ben Maimon or Maimonides (1135–1204), the most famous Jewish philosopher of medieval Spain.
7. The Third Communist International (1919–43), an organization founded in Moscow by the delegates of twelve countries to promote communism worldwide.

"You can't," Gedali answers, hanging a lock on his box, "you can't find any. There's a tavern next door, and good people used to run it, but people don't eat there anymore, they weep."

He fastened the three bone buttons of his green coat. He dusted himself with the cockerel feathers, sprinkled a little water on the soft palms of his hands, and walked off, tiny, lonely, dreamy, with his black top hat, and a large prayer book under his arm.

The Sabbath begins. Gedali, the founder of an unattainable International, went to the synagogue to pray.

My First Goose[1]

Savitsky, the commander of the Sixth Division, rose when he saw me, and I was taken aback by the beauty of his gigantic body. He rose—his breeches purple, his crimson cap cocked to the side, his medals pinned to his chest—splitting the hut in two like a banner splitting the sky. He smelled of perfume and the nauseating coolness of soap. His long legs looked like two girls wedged to their shoulders in riding boots.

He smiled at me, smacked the table with his whip, and picked up the order which the chief of staff had just dictated. It was an order for Ivan Chesnokov to advance to Chugunov-Dobryvodka with the regiment he had been entrusted with, and, on encountering the enemy, to proceed immediately with its destruction.

". . . the destruction of which," Savitsky began writing, filling the whole sheet, "I hold the selfsame Chesnokov completely responsible for. Noncompliance will incur the severest punitive measures, in other words I will gun him down on the spot, a fact that I am sure that you, Comrade Chesnokov, will not doubt, as it's been quite a while now that you have worked with me on the front. . . ."

The commander of the Sixth Division signed the order with a flourish, threw it at the orderlies, and turned his gray eyes, dancing with merriment, toward me.

I handed him the document concerning my assignment to the divisional staff.

"See to the paperwork!" the division commander said. "See to the paperwork, and have this man sign up for all the amusements except for those of the frontal kind.[2] Can you read and write?"

"Yes, I can," I answered, bristling with envy at the steel and bloom of his youth. "I graduated in law from the University of Petersburg."

"So you're one of those little powder puffs!" he yelled, laughing. "With spectacles on your nose! Ha, you lousy little fellow, you![3] They send you to us, no one even asks us if we want you here! Here you get hacked to pieces just for wearing glasses! So, you think you can live with us, huh?"

1. First published in *Izvestia* (Odessa), May 4, 1924, datelined July 1920.
2. The division commander is punning, substituting the word *udovolstvie*, "amusement" or "pleasure," for *dovolstvie*, rations. —*Ed.*
3. Savitsky uses the word *parkhatyi*, or scabby, a modifier commonly accompanying an insult hurled at a shtetl Jew—*zhid parkhatyi*, a scabby Yid—and sometimes used alone. Speaking in code transparent to Babel's readers, Savitsky is in fact asking, Why are they sending us Jews when they know our Cossacks kill Jews? —*Ed.*

"Yes, I do," I answered, and went to the village with the quartermaster to look for a place to stay.

The quartermaster carried my little suitcase on his shoulder. The village street lay before us, and the dying sun in the sky, round and yellow as a pumpkin, breathed its last rosy breath.

We came to a hut with garlands painted on it. The quartermaster stopped, and suddenly, smiling guiltily, said, "You see we have a thing about spectacles here, there ain't nothing you can do! A man of high distinguishings they'll chew up and spit out—but ruin a lady, yes, the most cleanest lady, and you're the darling of the fighters!"

He hesitated for a moment, my suitcase still on his shoulder, came up very close to me, but suddenly lunged away in despair, rushing into the nearest courtyard. Cossacks were sitting there on bundles of hay, shaving each other.

"Fighters!" the quartermaster began, putting my suitcase on the ground. "According to an order issued by Comrade Savitsky, you are required to accept this man to lodge among you. And no funny business, please, because this man has suffered on the fields of learning!"

The quartermaster flushed and marched off without looking back. I lifted my hand to my cap and saluted the Cossacks. A young fellow with long, flaxen hair and a wonderful Ryazan face walked up to my suitcase and threw it out into the street. Then he turned his backside toward me, and with uncommon dexterity began emitting shameless sounds.

"That was a zero-zero caliber!" an older Cossack yelled, laughing out loud. "Rapid-fire!"

The young man walked off, having exhausted the limited resources of his artistry. I went down on my hands and knees and gathered up the manuscripts and the old, tattered clothes that had fallen out of my suitcase. I took them and carried them to the other end of the yard. A large pot of boiling pork stood on some bricks in front of the hut. Smoke rose from it as distant smoke rises from the village hut of one's childhood, mixing hunger with intense loneliness inside me. I covered my broken little suitcase with hay, turning it into a pillow, and lay down on the ground to read Lenin's speech at the Second Congress of the Comintern,[4] which *Pravda* had printed. The sun fell on me through the jagged hills, the Cossacks kept stepping over my legs, the young fellow incessantly made fun of me, the beloved sentences struggled toward me over thorny paths, but could not reach me. I put away the newspaper and went to the mistress of the house, who was spinning yarn on the porch.

"Mistress," I said, "I need some grub!"

---

4. The Communist International, Comintern, or The Third International (1919–43), an international communist organization established on Vladimir Lenin's initiative with the aim of fomenting world revolution. While the First Congress in 1919 included only nineteen countries (their delegates happened to be in Moscow at the time), the Second Congress (July 19–August 7, 1920) brought together representatives from thirty-seven countries, indicating the growing support for the Bolshevik cause. Here Babel refers to Lenin's opening speech at the Congress, "Report on the International Situation and the Chief Goals of the Communist International" (*Pravda*, 20 July 1920). A large map was on display in the main hall of the Congress showing delegates the daily progress of the Red Army's march on Warsaw. Following the Red Army's defeat in Poland in the wake of the Second Congress, the Comintern evolved into an organ of Soviet foreign policy—among its various activities was illicitly bankrolling the communist parties abroad.—*Ed.*

The old woman raised the dripping whites of her half-blind eyes to me and lowered them again.

"Comrade," she said, after a short silence. "All of this makes me want to hang myself!"

"Goddammit!"[5] I muttered in frustration, shoving her back with my hand. "I'm in no mood to start debating with you!"

And, turning around, I saw someone's saber lying nearby. A haughty goose was waddling through the yard, placidly grooming its feathers. I caught the goose and forced it to the ground, its head cracking beneath my boot, cracking and bleeding. Its white neck lay stretched out in the dung, and the wings folded down over the slaughtered bird.

"Goddammit!" I said, poking at the goose with the saber. "Roast it for me, mistress!"

The old woman, her blindness and her spectacles flashing, picked up the bird, wrapped it in her apron, and hauled it to the kitchen.

"Comrade," she said after a short silence. "This makes me want to hang myself." And she pulled the door shut behind her.

In the yard the Cossacks were already sitting around their pot. They sat motionless, straight-backed like heathen priests, not once having looked at the goose.

"This fellow'll fit in here well enough," one of them said, winked, and scooped up some cabbage soup with his spoon.

The Cossacks began eating with the restrained grace of muzhiks who respect one another. I cleaned the saber with sand, went out of the courtyard, and came back again, feeling anguished. The moon hung over the yard like a cheap earring.

"Hey, brother!" Surovkov, the oldest of the Cossacks, suddenly said to me. "Sit with us and have some of this till your goose is ready!"

He fished an extra spoon out of his boot and handed it to me. We slurped the cabbage soup and ate the pork.

"So, what are they writing in the newspaper?" the young fellow with the flaxen hair asked me, and moved aside to make room for me.

"In the newspaper, Lenin writes," I said, picking up my *Pravda*, "Lenin writes that right now there is a shortage of everything."

And in a loud voice, like a triumphant deaf man, I read Lenin's speech to the Cossacks.

The evening wrapped me in the soothing dampness of her twilight sheets, the evening placed her motherly palms on my burning brow.

I read, and rejoiced, waiting for the effect, rejoicing in the mysterious curve of Lenin's straight line.

"Truth tickles all and sundry in the nose,"[6] Surovkov said when I had finished. "It isn't all that easy to wheedle it out of the pile of rubbish, but Lenin picks it up right away, like a hen pecks up a grain of corn."

That is what Surovkov, the squadron commander, said about Lenin, and then we went to sleep in the hayloft. Six of us slept there warming each other, our legs tangled, under the holes in the roof which let in the stars.

I dreamed and saw women in my dreams, and only my heart, crimson with murder, screeched and bled.

---

5. The Russian hints at a far more profane Cossack expression mentioning God, the Holy Virgin, and the Holy Ghost. —*Ed.*

6. A pun on "truth," *Pravda*, also the name of the Communist Party daily that the narrator is reading to the Cossacks.

The Rabbi[1]

"All things are mortal. Only a mother is accorded eternal life. And when a mother is not among the living, she leaves behind a memory that no one has yet dared to defile. The memory of a mother nourishes compassion within us, just as the ocean, the boundless ocean, nourishes the rivers that cut through the universe."

These were Gedali's words. He uttered them gravely. The dying evening wrapped him in the rosy haze of its sadness.

"In the ardent house of Hasidism," the old man said, "the windows and doors have been torn out, but it is as immortal as a mother's soul. Even with blinded eyes, Hasidism still stands at the crossroads of the winds of history."

That is what Gedali said, and, after having prayed in the synagogue, he took me to Rabbi Motale, the last rabbi of the Chernobyl dynasty.

Gedali and I walked up the main street. White churches glittered in the distance like fields of buckwheat. A gun cart moaned around the corner. Two pregnant Ukrainian women came out through the gates of a house, their coin necklaces jingling, and sat down on a bench. A timid star flashed in the orange battles of the sunset, and peace, a Sabbath peace, descended on the slanted roofs of the Zhitomir ghetto.

"Here," Gedali whispered, pointing at a long house with a shattered facade.

We went into a room, a stone room, empty as a morgue. Rabbi Motale sat at a table surrounded by liars and men possessed. He was wearing a sable hat and a white robe, with a rope for a belt. The rabbi was sitting, his eyes closed, his thin fingers digging through the yellow fluff of his beard.

"Where have you come from, Jew?" he asked me, lifting his eyelids.

"From Odessa," I answered.

"A devout town,"[2] the rabbi said. "The star of our exile, the reluctant well of our afflictions! What is the Jew's trade?"

"I am putting the adventures of Hershele of Ostropol[3] into verse."

"A great task," the rabbi whispered, and closed his eyelids. "The jackal moans when it is hungry, every fool has foolishness enough for despondency, and only the sage shreds the veil of existence with laughter . . . What did the Jew study?"

"The Bible."

"What is the Jew looking for?"

"Merriment."

"Reb Mordkhe," the rabbi said, and shook his beard. "Let the young man seat himself at the table, let him eat on the Sabbath evening with other Jews, let him rejoice that he is alive and not dead, let him clap his hands as his neighbors dance, let him drink wine if he is given wine!"

And Reb Mordkhe came bouncing toward me, an ancient fool with inflamed eyelids, a hunchbacked little old man, no bigger than a ten-year-old boy.

---

1. First published in *Krasnaya nov* 1 (1924). —Ed.
2. The Hasidic rabbi is joking, testing his interlocutor's capacity for mirth. Among the devout, Odessa had the reputation of Sin City, as in the old Yiddish saying "Ten miles around Odessa burn the fires of hell." —Ed.
3. In Yiddish folklore, a trickster. See "Shabos-Nakhamu," p. 26.

"Oy, my dear and so very young man!" ragged Reb Mordkhe said, winking at me. "Oy, how many rich fools have I known in Odessa, how many wise paupers have I known in Odessa! Sit down at the table, young man, and drink the wine that you will not be given!"

We all sat down, one next to the other—the possessed, the liars, the unhinged. In the corner, broad-shouldered Jews who looked like fishermen and apostles were moaning over prayer books. Gedali in his green coat dozed by the wall like a bright bird. And suddenly I saw a youth behind Gedali, a youth with the face of Spinoza, with the powerful forehead of Spinoza, with the sickly face of a nun. He was smoking and twitching like an escaped convict who has been tracked down and brought back to his jail. Ragged Reb Mordkhe sneaked up on him from behind, snatched the cigarette from his mouth, and came running over to me.

"That is Ilya, the rabbi's son," Mordkhe wheezed, turning the bloody flesh of his inflamed eyelids to me, "the damned son, the worst son, the disobedient son!"

And Mordkhe threatened the youth with his little fist and spat in his face.

"Blessed is the Lord," the voice of Rabbi Motale Bratslavsky rang out, and he broke the bread with his monastic fingers. "Blessed is the God of Israel, who has chosen us among all the peoples of the world."

The rabbi blessed the food, and we sat down at the table. Outside the window horses neighed and Cossacks shouted. The wasteland of war yawned outside. The rabbi's son smoked one cigarette after another during the silent prayer. When the dinner was over, I was the first to rise.

"My dear and so very young man," Mordkhe muttered behind me, tugging at my belt. "If there was no one in the world except for evil rich men and destitute tramps, how would holy men live?"

I gave the old man some money and went out into the street. Gedali and I parted, and I went back to the railroad station. There at the station, on the propaganda train of the First Cavalry, I was greeted by the sparkle of hundreds of lights, the enchanted glitter of the radio transmitter, the stubborn rolling of the printing presses, and my unfinished article for the *Krasny Kavalerist*.[4]

The Road to Brody[1]

I mourn for the bees. They have been destroyed by warring armies. There are no longer any bees in Volhynia.

We desecrated the hives. We fumigated them with sulfur and detonated them with gunpowder. Smoldering rags have spread a foul stench over the holy republics of the bees. Dying, they flew slowly, their buzzing barely audible. Deprived of bread, we procured honey with our sabers. There are no longer any bees in Volhynia.

The chronicle of our everyday crimes oppresses me as relentlessly as a bad heart. Yesterday was the first day of the battle for Brody. Lost on the

4. The newspaper *The Red Cavalryman*.
1. First published in a supplement to *Izvestia* (Odessa), June 17, 1923, with the dateline "Brody, August 1920." —*Ed.*

blue earth, we suspected nothing—neither I, nor my friend Afonka Bida. The horses had been fed grain in the morning. The rye stood tall, the sun was beautiful, and our souls, which did not deserve these shining, soaring skies, thirsted for lingering pain.

"In our Cossack villages the womenfolk tell tales of the bee and its kind nature," my friend began. "The womenfolk tell all sorts of things. If men wronged Christ, or if no wrong was done, other people will have to figure out for themselves. But if you listen to what the womenfolk of the Cossack villages tell, Christ is hanging tormented on the cross, when suddenly all kinds of gnats come flying over to plague him! And he takes a good look at the gnats and his spirits fall. But the thousands of little gnats can't see his eyes. At that moment a bee flies around Christ. 'Sting him!' a gnat yells at the bee. 'Sting him for us!'—'That I cannot do,' the bee says, covering Christ with her wings. 'That I cannot do, he belongs to the carpenter class.' One has to understand the bees," Afonka, my platoon commander, concluded. "I hope the bees hold out. We're fighting for them too!"

Afonka waved dismissively and started to sing. It was a song about a light bay stallion. Eight Cossacks in Afonka's platoon joined in the song.

The light bay stallion, Dzhigit was his name, belonged to a junior Cossack captain who got drunk on vodka the day of his beheading,[1] sang Afonka sleepily, his voice taut like a string. Dzhigit had been a loyal horse, but on feast days the Cossack's carousing knew no bounds. He had five jugs of vodka on the day of his beheading. After the fourth jug, the junior Cossack captain mounted his steed and rode up to heaven. The climb was long, but Dzhigit was a true horse. They rode into heaven, and the Cossack reached for his fifth jug. But the last jug had been left back on earth. He broke down and wept, for all his efforts had been in vain. He wept, and Dzhigit pointed his ears, and turned to look at his master. Afonka sang, clinking and dozing.

The song drifted like smoke. We rode toward the sunset, its boiling rivers pouring over the embroidered napkins of the peasants' fields. The silence turned rosy. The earth lay like a cat's back, covered with a thick, gleaming coat of grain. The mud hamlet of Klekotov crouched on a little hill. Beyond the pass, the vision of deadly, craggy Brody awaited us. But in Klekotov a loud shot exploded in our faces. Two Polish soldiers peered out from behind a hut. Their horses were tied to a post. A light enemy battery came riding up the hill. Bullets unfurled like string along the road.

"Run for it!" Afonka yelled.

And we fled.

Brody! The mummies of your trampled passions have breathed their irresistible poison upon me. I had felt the fatal chill of your eye sockets filled with frozen tears. And now, in a tumbling gallop, I am being carried away from the smashed stones of your synagogues. . . .

---

1. In the original, the day of the beheading (*den' useknoveniya glavy*) refers to the Russian Orthodox holiday commemorating the beheading of St. John the Baptist. Celebrated on September 11 and coinciding with the end of the harvest, it is an occasion for excess and revelry in some agricultural communities.—*Ed.*

The *Tachanka* Theory[1]

Headquarters sent me a coachman, or, as we generally say here, a vehicular driver. His name is Grishchuk. He is thirty-nine years old.

He had spent five years in a German prison camp, escaped a few months ago, walked across Lithuania and northwest Russia, reached Volhynia, only, in Byelov, to fall into the hands of what must be the world's most brainless draft commission, which reconscripted him into active service. He had been a mere fifty versts from his home in the Kremenec District. He has a wife and children in the Kremenec District. He hasn't been home for five years and two months. The Draft Commission made him my vehicular driver, and now I am no longer a pariah among the Cossacks.

I have a *tachanka*[2] and a driver for it. *Tachanka!* That word has become the base of the triangle on which our way of fighting rests: hack to pieces—*tachanka*—blood.

The simplest little open carriage, the *britzka*, the kind you would see some cleric or petty official riding in, has, through a whim of all the civil strife, become a terrible and fast-moving war machine, creating new strategies and tactics, twisting the traditional face of war, spawning *tachanka* heroes and geniuses. Such was Makhno,[3] who had made the *tachanka* the crux of his secretive and cunning strategy, abolishing infantry, artillery, even cavalry, and replaced that clumsy hodgepodge by mounting three hundred machine guns onto *britzkas*. Such was Makhno, as innovative as nature: hay carts lined up in military formation to conquer towns. A wedding procession rolls up to the headquarters of a provincial executive committee, opens fire, and a frail little cleric, waving the black flag of anarchy, demands that the authorities immediately hand over the bourgeois, hand over the proletariat, hand over music and wine.

An army of *tachankas* is capable of unprecedented mobility.

Budyonny was just as adept at demonstrating this as Makhno was. To hack away at such an army is difficult, to corner it impossible. A machine gun buried under a stack of hay, a *tachanka* hidden in a peasant's shed, cease to be military targets. These hidden specks—the hypothetically existing but imperceptible components of a whole—when added up result in the new essence of the Ukrainian village: savage, rebellious, and self-seeking. Makhno can bring an army like this, its ammunition concealed in all its nooks and crannies, into military readiness within an hour, and can demobilize it even faster.

Here, in Budyonny's Red Cavalry, the *tachanka* does not rule so exclusively. But all our machine gun detachments travel only in *britzkas*. Cossack fantasy distinguishes two kinds of *tachanka*, "German settler" and "petty official," which is not fantasy but a real distinction.

The petty official *britzkas*, those rickety little carts built without love or imagination, had rattled through the wheat steppes of Kuban carrying

---

1. First published in *Izvestia* (Odessa), February 23, 1923. —*Ed.*
2. An open carriage or buggy with a machine gun mounted on the back.
3. See note 2 on p. 108. —*Ed.*

the wretched, red-nosed civil servants, a sleep-starved herd of men hurrying to autopsies and inquests, while the settler *tachankas* came to us from the fat German settlements of the Volga regions of Samara and the Urals. The broad oaken seat backs of the settler *tachankas* are covered with simple paintings, plump garlands of rosy German flowers. The sturdy cart decks are reinforced with steel. The frame rests on soft, unforgettable springs. I can feel the ardor of many generations in these springs, now bouncing over the torn-up high roads of Volhynia.

I am experiencing the delight of first possession. Every day after we eat, we put on the harnesses. Grishchuk leads the horses out of the stable. They are becoming stronger with every passing day. With proud joy I notice a dull sheen on their groomed flanks. We rub the horses' swollen legs, trim their manes, throw Cossack harnesses—a tangled, withered mesh of thin straps—over their backs, and drive out of the yard at a fast trot. Grishchuk is sitting sideways on the box. My seat is covered with a bright sackcloth and hay smelling of perfume and tranquillity. The high wheels creak in the white, granular sand. Patches of blooming poppies color the earth, ruined churches glow on the hills. High above the road, in a niche wrecked by shells, stands the brown statue of Saint Ursula with bare round arms. And narrow, ancient letters form an uneven chain on the blackened gold of her pediment: "Glory be to Jesus and the Mother of God."

Lifeless Jewish shtetls cluster around the foot of the Polish nobles' estates. The prophetic peacock, a passionless apparition in the blue vastness, glitters on brick walls. The synagogue, enmeshed in a tangle of huts, crouches eyeless and battered, round as a Hasidic hat, on the barren earth. Narrow-shouldered Jews hover sadly at crossroads. And the image of southern Jews flares up in my memory—jovial, potbellied, sparkling like cheap wine. There is no comparison between them and the bitter aloofness of these long bony backs, these tragic yellow beards. In their fervent features, carved by torture, there is no fat or warm pulse of blood. The movements of the Galician and the Volhynian Jew are abrupt, brusque, and offensive to good taste, but the power of their grief is filled with dark grandeur, and their secret contempt for the Polish masters is boundless. Looking at them, I understood the fiery history of these faraway hinterlands, the stories of talmudists who leased out taverns, of rabbis who dabbled in moneylending, of girls who were raped by Polish mercenaries and for whom Polish magnates dueled.

Dolgushov's Death[1]

The veils of battle swept toward the town. At midday, Korotchayev, the disgraced commander of the Fourth Division, who fought alone and rode out seeking death, flew past us in his black Caucasian cloak. As he came galloping by, he shouted over to me, "Our communications have been cut, Radzivillov and Brody are in flames!"

And off he charged—fluttering, black, with eyes of coal.

---

1. First published in *Izvestia* (Odessa), May 1, 1923, with the dateline "Brody, August 1920." —*Ed.*

On the plain, flat as a board, the brigades were regrouping. The sun rolled through the crimson dust. Wounded men sat in ditches, eating. Nurses lay on the grass and sang in hushed voices. Afonka's scouts roamed over the field, looking for dead soldiers and ammunition. Afonka rode by two paces from me and, without turning his head, said, "We got a real kick in the teeth! Big time! They're saying things about our division commander—it looks like he's out. Our fighters don't know what's what!"

The Poles had advanced to the forest about three versts away from us, and set up their machine guns somewhere nearby. Flying bullets whimper and yelp; their lament has reached an unbearable pitch. The bullets plunge into the earth and writhe, quaking with impatience. Vytyagaichenko, the commander of the regiment, snoring in the hot sun, cried out in his sleep and woke up. He mounted his horse and rode over to the lead squadron. His face was creased with red stripes from his uncomfortable sleep, and his pockets were filled with plums.

"Son of a bitch!" he said angrily, spitting out a plum stone. "A damn waste of time! Timoshka, hoist the flag!"

"Oh, so we're going for it?" Timoshka asked, pulling the flagpole out of the stirrup, and unrolling the flag on which a star had been painted, along with something about the Third International.

"We'll see what happens," Vytyagaichenko said, and suddenly shouted wildly, "Come on, girls, onto your horses! Gather your men, squadron leaders!"

The buglers sounded the alarm. The squadrons lined up in a column. A wounded man crawled out of a ditch and, shading his eyes with his hand, said to Vytyagaichenko, "Taras Grigorevich, I represent the others here. It looks like you're leaving us behind."

"Don't worry, you'll manage to fight them off," Vytyagaichenko muttered, and reared his horse.

"We sort of think we won't be able to fight them off, Taras Grigorevich," the wounded man called after Vytyagaichenko as he rode off.

Vytyagaichenko turned back his horse. "Stop whimpering! Of course I won't leave you!" And he ordered the carts to be harnessed.

At that very moment the whining, high-pitched voice of my friend Afonka Bida burst out, "Let's not set off at full trot, Taras Grigorevich! It's five versts. How are we supposed to hack them down if our horses are worn out? Why the rush? You'll be there in time for the pear pruning on St. Mary's Day!"

"Slow trot!" Vytyagaichenko ordered, without raising his eyes.

The regiment rode off.

"If what they're saying about the division commander is true," Afonka whispered, reining in his horse, "and they're getting rid of him, well then thank you very much—we might as well kill off the cattle and burn down the barn!"

Tears flowed from his eyes. I looked at him in amazement. He spun like a top, held his cap down, wheezed, and then charged off with a loud whoop.

Grishchuk, with his ridiculous *tachanka*,[2] and I stayed behind, rushing back and forth among walls of fire until the evening. Our divisional staff

2. See note 2 on p. 118.

had disappeared. Other units wouldn't take us in. The regiments pushed forward into Brody but were repelled. We rode to the town cemetery. A Polish patrol jumped up from behind the graves, put their rifles to their shoulders, and started firing at us. Grishchuk spun his *tachanka* around. It shrieked with all its four wheels.

"Grishchuk!" I yelled through the whistling and the wind.

"What damn stupidity!" he shouted back morosely.

"We're done for!" I hollered, seized by the exhilaration of disaster. "We're finished!"

"All the trouble our womenfolk go to!" he said even more morosely. "What's the point of all the matchmaking, marrying, and in-laws dancing at weddings?"

A rosy tail lit up in the sky and expired. The Milky Way surfaced from under the stars.

"It makes me want to laugh!" Grishchuk said sadly, and pointed his whip at a man sitting at the side of the road. "It makes me want to laugh that women go to such trouble!"

The man sitting by the roadside was Dolgushov, one of the telephonists. He stared at us, his legs stretched out in front of him.

"Here, look," Dolgushov said, as we pulled up to him. "I'm finished . . . know what I mean?"

"I know," Grishchuk answered, reining in the horses.

"You'll have to waste a bullet on me," Dolgushov said.

He was sitting propped up against a tree. He lay with his legs splayed far apart, his boots pointing in opposite directions. Without lowering his eyes from me, he carefully lifted his shirt. His stomach was torn open, his intestines spilling to his knees, and we could see his heart beating.

"When the Poles turn up, they'll have fun kicking me around. Here's my papers. Write my mother where, what, why."

"No," I replied, and spurred my horse.

Dolgushov placed his blue palms on the ground and looked at his hands in disbelief.

"Running away?" he muttered, slumping down. "Then run, you bastard!"

Sweat slithered over my body. The machine guns hammered faster and faster with hysterical tenacity. Afonka Bida came galloping toward us, encircled by the halo of the sunset.

"We're kicking their asses!" he shouted merrily. "What're you up to here, fun and games?"

I pointed at Dolgushov and moved my horse to the side.

They spoke a few words, I couldn't hear what they said. Dolgushov held out his papers. Afonka slipped them into his boot and shot Dolgushov in the mouth.

"Afonka," I said, riding up to him with a pitiful smile. "*I* couldn't have done that."

"Get lost, or I'll shoot you!" he said to me, his face turning white. "You spectacled idiots have as much pity for us as a cat has for a mouse!"

And he cocked his trigger.

I rode off slowly, without looking back, a feeling of cold and death in my spine.

"Hey! Hey!" Grishchuk shouted behind me, and grabbed Afonka's hand. "Cut the crap!"

"You damn lackey bastard!" Afonka yelled at Grishchuk. "Wait till I get my hands on him!"

Grishchuk caught up with me at the bend in the road. Afonka was not with him. He had ridden off in the opposite direction.

"Well, there you have it, Grishchuk," I said to him. "Today I lost Afonka, my first real friend."

Grishchuk took out a wrinkled apple from under the cart seat.

"Eat it," he told me, "please, eat it."

The Commander of the Second Brigade[1]

General Budyonny, in his red trousers with the silver stripes, stood by a tree. The commander of the Second Brigade had just been killed. The general had appointed Kolesnikov to replace him.

Only an hour ago, Kolesnikov had been a regimental captain. A week ago Kolesnikov had been a squadron leader.

The new brigade commander was summoned to General Budyonny. The general waited for him, standing by the tree. Kolesnikov came with Almazov, his commissar.

"The bastards are closing in on us," the general said with his dazzling grin. "We win, or we die like dogs. No other options. Understood?"

"Understood," Kolesnikov answered, his eyes bulging from their sockets.

"You run for it, I'll have you shot," the general said with a smile, and he turned and looked at the commander of the special unit.

"Yes, General!" the commander of the special unit said.

"So start rolling, Koleso!"[2] one of the Cossacks standing nearby shouted cheerfully.

Budyonny swiftly turned on his heel and saluted his new brigade commander. The latter lifted five young red fingers to his cap, broke into a sweat, and walked along the plowed field. The horses were waiting for him fifty yards away. He hung his head, placing one long and crooked leg in front of the other with agonizing slowness. The fire of the sunset swept over him, as crimson and implausible as impending doom.

And suddenly, on the outstretched earth, on the yellow, harrowed nakedness of the fields, we saw nothing but Kolesnikov's narrow back, his dangling arms, and his hanging head with its gray cap.

His orderly brought him his horse.

He jumped into the saddle and galloped to his brigade without looking back. The squadrons were waiting for him on the main road, the high road to Brody.

A moaning hurrah, shredded by the wind, drifted over to us.

1. First published in *LEF* (Moscow) 4 (1923; actually issued in 1924), with the dateline "Brody, August 1920." The title of the original publication was "Kolesnikov." —*Ed.*
2. A pun: *Koleso*, short for Kolesnikov, means "wheel."

Aiming my binoculars, I saw the brigade commander on his horse cir-
cling through columns of thick dust. "Kolesnikov has taken over the brigade," said our lookout, who was sitting in a tree above our heads.
"So he has," Budyonny answered, lighting a cigarette and closing his eyes.
The hurrahs faded. The cannonade died down. Pointless shrapnel
burst above the forest. And we heard the great, silent skirmish.
"He's a good boy," Budyonny said, getting up. "Wants honors. Looks
like he'll make it." And Budyonny had the horses brought over, and rode
off to the battlefield. His Staff followed him.
As it happened, I was to see Kolesnikov again that very night, about an
hour after the Poles had been finished off. He was riding in front of his
brigade, alone, on a brown stallion, dozing. His right arm was hanging in
a sling. A cavalry Cossack was carrying the unfurled flag about ten paces
behind him. The men at the head of the squadron lazily sang bawdy dit-
ties. The brigade stretched dusty and endless, like peasant carts heading
to a market fair. At the rear, tired bands were gasping.
That evening, as Kolesnikov rode, I saw in his bearing the despotic indifference of a Tatar khan and saw in him a devotee of the glorified
Kniga, the willful Pavlichenko, and the captivating Savitsky.

Sashka Christ[1]

Sashka, that was his real name, and Christ is what we called him because
he was so gentle. He had been one of the shepherds of his Cossack village and had not done any heavy work since he was fourteen, when he
had caught the evil disease.
This is what had happened. Tarakanich,[2] Sashka's stepfather, had gone
to the town of Grozny for the winter, and had joined a guild there. The
guild was working well—it was made up of Ryazan muzhiks. Tarakanich
did carpentry for them, and his income increased. When he realized that
he could not manage the work alone anymore, he sent home for the boy to
come and be his assistant—the village could survive the winter well
enough without him. Sashka worked with his stepfather for a week. Then
Saturday came, and they put their tools away and sat down to drink some
tea. Outside it was October, but the air was mild. They opened the window, and put on a second samovar. A beggar woman was loitering near the
windows. She knocked on the frame and said, "A good day to you! I see
you're not from these parts. You can see what state I'm in, no?"
"What is it about your state?" Tarakanich said. "Come in, you old cripple!"
The beggar woman scrambled up and clambered into the room. She
came over to the table and bowed deeply. Tarakanich grabbed her by her
kerchief, pulled it off, and ruffled her hair. The beggar woman's hair was
gray, ashy, and hanging in dusty tatters.
"Ooh, will you stop that, you naughty handsome man you!" she said.
"You're a joke a minute, you are! But please, don't be disgusted by me

---

1. Frist published in *Krasnaya nov* 1 (1924). —Ed.
2. *Tarakan* is Russian for cockroach. —Ed.

just because I'm a little old woman," she quickly whispered, scampering onto the bench.

Tarakanich lay with her. The beggar woman turned her head to the side and laughed.

"Ooh, luck is raining on this little old woman's field!" she laughed. "I'll be harvesting two hundred *pood* of grain an acre!"

And she suddenly noticed Sashka, who was drinking his tea at the table, not looking up as if his life depended on it.

"Your boy?" she asked Tarakanich.

"More or less mine," Tarakanich answered. "My wife's."

"Ooh, look at him staring at us," the old woman said. "Hey, come over here!"

Sashka went over to her—and he caught the evil disease. But the evil disease had been the last thing on their minds. Tarakanich gave the beggar woman some leftover bones and a silver fiver, a very shiny one.

"Polish the fiver nicely with sand, holy sister," Tarakanich said to her, "and it'll look even better. If you lend it to the Almighty on a dark night, it will shine instead of the moon."

The old cripple tied her kerchief, took the bones, and left. And within two weeks the muzhiks realized what had happened. The evil disease made them suffer. They tried to cure themselves all winter long, dousing themselves with herbs. And in spring they returned to the Cossack village and their peasant work.

The village was about nine versts from the railroad. Tarakanich and Sashka crossed the fields. The earth lay in its April wetness. Emeralds glittered in the black ditches. Green shoots hemmed the soil with cunning stitches. A sour odor rose from the ground, as from a soldier's wife at dawn. The first herds trickled down from the hills, the foals played in the blue expanse of the horizon.

Tarakanich and Sashka walked along barely visible paths.

"Let me be one of the shepherds, Tarakanich," Sashka said.

"What for?"

"I can't bear that the shepherds have such a wonderful life."

"I won't allow it."

"Let me be one, Tarakanich, for the love of God!" Sashka repeated. "All the saints came from shepherds."

"Sashka the Saint!" the stepfather laughed. "He caught syphilis from the Mother of God!"

They passed the bend in the road by Red Bridge, then the grove and the pasture, and saw the cross on the village church.

The women were still puttering around in their vegetable gardens, and Cossacks were sitting among the lilacs, drinking vodka and singing. It was another half verst to Tarakanich's hut.

"Let us pray that everything is fine," Tarakanich said, crossing himself.

They walked over to the hut and peeked in the little window. Nobody was there. Sashka's mother was in the shed milking the cow. They crept over to her silently. Tarakanich came up behind her and laughed out loud.

"Motya, your excellency," he shouted, "how about some food for your guests!"

The woman turned around, began to shake, and rushed out of the shed and ran circling around the yard. Then she came back into the shed and, trembling, pressed her head on Tarakanich's chest.

"How silly and ugly you look," Tarakanich said, gently pushing her away. "Where are the children?"

"The children have left the yard," the woman said, her face ashen, and ran out again, throwing herself onto the ground.

"Oh, Aleshonka!" she shrieked wildly. "Our babies have gone, feet first!"

Tarakanich waved at her dismissively and went over to the neighbors. The neighbors told him that a week ago the Lord had taken the boy and the girl with typhus. Motya had written him a letter, but he probably hadn't gotten it. Tarakanich went back to the hut. The woman was stoking the oven.

"You got rid of them quite nicely, Motya," Tarakanich said. "Rip you to pieces, that's what I should do!"

He sat down at the table and fell into deep grief—and grieved till he fell asleep. He ate meat and drank vodka, and did not see to his work around the farm. He snored at the table, woke up, and snored again. Motya prepared a bed for herself and her husband, and another for Sashka to the side. She blew out the light, and lay down next to her husband. Sashka tossed and turned on the hay in his corner. His eyes were open, he did not sleep, but saw, as if in a dream, the hut, a star shining through the window, the edge of the table, and the horse collars under his mother's bed. A violent vision took hold of him; he surrendered to it and rejoiced in his waking dream. It was as if two silver strings hung from the sky, entwined into a thick rope to which a cradle was fastened, a rosewood cradle with carvings. It swung high above the earth but far from the sky, and the silver rope swayed and glittered. Sashka was lying in this cradle, fanned by the air. The air, loud as music, rose from the fields, and the rainbow blossomed above the unripe wheat.

Sashka rejoiced in his waking sleep, and closed his eyes so as not to see the horse collars under his mother's bed. Then he heard panting from the bed, and thought that Tarakanich must be pawing his mother.

"Tarakanich," he said loudly. "There's something I need to talk to you about."

"In the middle of the night?" Tarakanich yelled angrily. "Sleep, you fleabag!"

"I swear by the Holy Cross that there's something I need to talk to you about," Sashka said. "Come out into the yard!"

And in the yard, beneath the unfading stars, Sashka said to his stepfather, "Don't wrong my mother, Tarakanich, you're tainted."

"You should know better than to cross me, boy!" Tarakanich said.

"I know, but have you seen my mother's body? She has legs that are clean, and a breast that is clean. Don't wrong her, Tarakanich. We're tainted."

"Boy!" his stepfather said. "Avoid my blood and my wrath! Here are twenty kopeks, go to sleep and your head will be clearer in the morning."

"I don't need the twenty kopeks," Sashka muttered. "Let me go join the shepherds."

"I won't allow that," Tarakanich said.

"Let me join the shepherds," Sashka muttered, "or I'll tell mother what we are. Why should she suffer with such a body?"

Tarakanich turned around and went into the shed to get an axe.

"Saint Sashka," he said in a whisper, "you wait and see, I'll hack you to pieces!"

"You'd hack me to pieces on account of a woman?" the boy said, barely audibly, and leaned closer to his stepfather. "Take pity on me and let me join the shepherds."

"Damn you!" Tarakanich said, and threw away the axe. "So go join the shepherds!"

And Tarakanich went back into the hut and slept with his wife.

That same morning Sashka went to the Cossacks to be hired, and from that day on he lived as a village shepherd. He became known throughout the whole area for his simple heart, and the people of the village gave him the nickname Sashka Christ, and he lived as a shepherd until he was drafted. The old men, who had nothing better to do, came out to the pasture to chat with him, and the women came running to Sashka for respite from their husbands' rough ways, and were not put off by Sashka's love for them or by his illness. Sashka's draft call came in the first year of the war. He fought for four years, and then returned to the village, where the Whites were running the show. Sashka was urged to go to the village of Platovskaya, where a detachment was being formed to fight the Whites. A former cavalry sergeant-major—Semyon Mikhailovich Budyonny—was running things in that detachment, and he had his three brothers with him: Emelian, Lukian, and Denis. Sashka went to Platovskaya, and there his fate was sealed. He joined Budyonny's regiment, his brigade, his division, and finally his First Cavalry Army. He rode to the aid of heroic Tsaritsyn,[3] joined with Voroshilov's Tenth Army, and fought at Voronezh, Kastornaya, and at the Generalsky Bridge on the Donets. In the Polish Campaign, Sashka joined the cavalry transport unit, because he had been wounded and was considered an invalid.

So that's how everything had come about. I had recently met Sashka Christ, and took my little suitcase and moved over to his cart. Many times we watched the sunrise and rode into the sunset. And whenever the obdurate will of war brought us together, we sat in the evenings on a sparkling earth mound,[4] or boiled tea in our sooty kettle in the woods, or slept next to each other on harvested fields, our hungry horses tied to our legs.

The Life of Matvey
Rodionovich Pavlichenko[1]

Dear comrades, brothers, fellow countrymen! Hear in the name of mankind the life story of Red General Matvey Pavlichenko. This general

---

3. Renamed Stalingrad in 1925 in honor of Joseph Stalin, who had played a major role in the defense of the city against General Denikin's White Russian Army. Today Volgograd.
4. Zavalinka: a mound of earth around a Russian peasant hut that protects it from the weather and is often used for sitting outside.
1. First published in the Odessa journal *Shkval* 8 (1924), with a dedication to D. A. Shmidt (Gutman). A close friend of Babel's, renowned Red Cossack commander Shmidt (1895–1937) began

had been a mere swineherd, a swineherd on the estate of Lidino of which Nikitinsky was master, and, until life gave him battle stripes, this swineherd tended his master's pigs, and then with those battle stripes our little Matvey was given cattle to herd. Who knows—had he been born in Australia, my friends, our Matvey, son of Rodion, might well have worked his way up to elephants, yes, our Matyushka would have herded elephants, but unfortunately there are no elephants to be found in our district of Stavropol. To be perfectly honest, there is no animal larger than a buffalo in all the lands of Stavropol. And the poor fellow would not have had any fun with buffaloes—Russians don't enjoy taunting buffaloes. Give us poor orphans a mare on Judgment Day, and I guarantee you we will know how to taunt her till her soul goes tearing out of her sides.

So here I am, herding my cattle, cows crowding me from all sides, I'm doused in milk, I stink like a slit udder, all around me calves and mouse-gray bullocks roam. Freedom lies all around me in the fields, the grass of all the world rustles, the skies above me open up like a many-buttoned concertina, and the skies, my brothers, the skies we have in the district of Stavropol, can be very blue. So there I am, herding the beasts and playing my flute to the winds with nothing better to do, when an old man comes up to me and tells me, "Go, Matvey," he says to me, "go to Nastya."

"What for?" I ask him. "Or are you maybe pulling my leg, old man?"

"Go to her," he says. "She wants you."

So I go to her.

"Nastya!" I say to her, and all my blood runs dark. "Nastya," I say to her, "or are you making fun of me?"

But she does not speak a word, runs straight past me, running as fast as her legs can carry her, and she and I run together until we're out on the meadow, dead tired, flushed, and out of breath.

"Matvey," Nastya says to me at this point. "On the third Sunday before this one, when the spring fishing season began and the fishermen came back to shore, you were walking with them, and you let your head hang. Why did you let your head hang, or is it that a thought is squeezing down on your heart? Answer me!"

And I answer her.

"Nastya," I say to her. "I have nothing to tell you, my head is not a gun, it has neither a fore-sight nor back-sight, and you know my heart full well, Nastya, it is empty, completely empty, except perhaps for being doused in milk—it's a terrible thing how I stink of milk!"

And I can see that Nastya is about to burst into laughter at my words.

"I swear by the Holy Cross," she says, bursting into laughter, laughing loudly, laughing with all her might, her laughter booming across the steppes as if she were pounding a drum, "I swear by the Holy Cross, you sure know how to sweet-talk a girl!"

---

his revolutionary career as an anarchist but joined the Bolsheviks in 1915. A noncommissioned cavalry officer and a Jew, he received three St. George Crosses for gallantry in World War I before distinguishing himself in the Red Army. In the 1920s, Shmidt was a loyal Trotskyist and was even rumored to have threatened Stalin with his saber in 1927 for expelling Trotsky from the party. The incident, whether true or not, did not slow down Shmidt's advancement. He went on to command a tank division in the all-important Kiev Military District until his arrest in July 1936. He resisted his interrogator despite torture and was executed a year later.—*Ed.*

So we exchange a few foolish words, and soon enough we're married. Nastya and me began living together as best we could, and we did our best. We felt hot all night, we felt hot all winter, all night we went naked and tore the hide off each other. We lived it up like devils, until the day the old man came to me again.

"Matvey," he says. "The other day the master touched your wife in all those places, and the master is going to have her."

And I say to him, "No," I say to him, "it cannot be, and please excuse me, old man, or I shall kill you right here and now."

The old man rushed off without another word, and I must have marched a good twenty versts over land that day, yes, that day a good chunk of earth passed beneath my feet, and by evening I sprouted up in the estate of Lidino, in the house of my merry master Nikitinsky. The old man was sitting in his drawing room busy taking apart three saddles, an English, a dragoon, and a Cossack saddle, and I stood rooted by his door like a burdock, I stood rooted there for a good hour. Then he finally clapped eyes on me.

"What do you want?"

"I want to quit."

"You have a grudge against me?"

"I don't have a grudge, but I want to quit."

At this point he turned his eyes away, leaving the high road for the field path, put the red saddlecloths on the floor—they were redder than the Czar's banners, his saddlecloths were—and old Nikitinsky stepped on them, puffing himself up.

"Freedom to the free," he tells me, all puffed up. "Your mothers, all Orthodox Christian women, I gave the lot of them a good plowing! You can quit, my dear little Matvey, but isn't there one tiny little thing you owe me first?"

"Ho, ho!" I answer. "What a joker! May the Lord strike me dead if you're not a joker! It is *you* who still owes *me* my wage!"

"Your wage!" my master thunders, shoving me down onto my knees, kicking me and yelling in my ear, cursing the Father, the Son, and the Holy Ghost. "You want your wage, but the bull's yoke you ruined seems to have slipped your mind! Where is my bull's yoke? Give me back my bull's yoke!"

"I will give you back your bull's yoke," I tell my master, raising my foolish eyes up at him as I kneel there, lower than the lowest of living creatures. "I'll give you back your bull's yoke, but don't strangle me with debts, master, just wait awhile!"

So, my dear friends, my Stavropol compatriots, fellow countrymen, my comrades, my very own brothers: for five years the master waited with my debts, five years I lost, until, lost soul that I was, finally the year '18 came![2] It rode in on merry stallions, on Kabardinian steeds! It brought big armies with it and many songs. O, my sweet year '18! O, for us to dance in each other's arms just one more time, my sweet darling year '18! We sang your songs, drank your wine, proclaimed your truth, but all that's left of you now is a few scribblers! Yet, ah, my love, it was not the scribblers back then who came flying through Kuban, shooting the souls of generals to Kingdom

2. 1918, the beginning of the civil war and massive, unrestrained violence. —Ed.

Come! No! It was me, Matvey Rodionovich, who lay outside Prikumsk in a pool of my own blood, and from where I, Matvey Rodionovich, lay to the estate of Lidino was a mere five versts. And I rode to Lidino alone, without my regiment, and as I entered the drawing room, I entered peacefully. People from the local authorities were sitting there in the drawing room, Nikitinsky was serving them tea, groveling all over them. When he saw me his face tumbled to pieces, but I lifted my fur hat to him.

"Greetings," I said to the people there. "Greetings. May I come in, your lordship, or how shall we handle this?"

"Let's handle this nicely, correctly," one of the men says, who, judging by the way he speaks, must be a land surveyor. "Let us handle things nicely, correctly, but from what I see, Comrade Pavlichenko, it seems you have ridden quite a distance, and dirt has crossed your face from side to side. We, the local authorities, are frightened of such faces. Why is your face like that?"

"Because you are the local cold-blooded authorities," I answer. "Because in my face one cheek has been burning for five years now, burning when I'm in a trench, burning when I'm with a woman, and it will be burning at my final judgment! At my final judgment!" I tell him, and look at Nikitinsky with fake cheerfulness. But he no longer has any eyes—there are now two cannonballs in the middle of his face, ready and in position under his forehead, and with these crystal balls he winks at me, also with fake cheerfulness, but so abominably.

"My dear Matyusha," he says to me, "we've known each other so long now, and my wife Nadyezhda Vasilevna, whose mind has come unhinged on account of the times we're living in, she was always kind to you, Nadyezhda Vasilevna was, and you, my dear Matyusha, always looked up to her above all others! Wouldn't you like to at least see her, even though her mind has come unhinged?"

"Fine," I tell him, and follow him into another room, and there he started clasping my hands, the right one, then the left.

"Matyusha!" he says. "Are you my fate or are you not?"

"No," I tell him. "And stop using such words! God has dropped us lackeys and run. Our fate is a chicken with its head cut off, our life is not worth a kopeck! Stop using such words and let me read you Lenin's letter!"

"Lenin wrote me, Nikitinsky, a letter?"

"Yes, he wrote you a letter," I tell him, and take out the book of decrees, open it to an empty page, and read—though I'm illiterate to the bottom of my soul. "In the name of the people," I read, "for the establishment of a future radiant life, I order Pavlichenko—Matvey Rodionovich—to deprive, at his discretion, various persons of their lives."

"There we are," I tell him. "That is Lenin's letter to you!"

And he says to me, "No!"

"No," he says, "my dear Matyusha, even if life has gone tumbling to the devil, and blood has become cheap in Holy Mother Russia! But regardless of how much blood you want, you'll get it anyway, and you'll even forget my last dying look, so wouldn't it be better if I just show you my secret hideaway?"

"Show me," I tell him. "Maybe it'll be for the better."

And again we went through the rooms, climbed down into the wine cellar, where he pulled out a brick, and behind this brick lay a little case.

In it, in this case, were rings, necklaces, medals, and a pearl-studded icon. He threw the case over to me and stood there rigidly.

"Take it!" he says. "Take what is most holy to the Nikitinskys, and go off to your den in Prikumsk!"

And here I grabbed him by the neck, by the hair.

"And what about my cheek?" I tell Nikitinsky. "How am I supposed to live with my cheek this way?"

And he burst out laughing for all he was worth, and stopped struggling to get away.

"A jackal's conscience," he says, and does not struggle. "I speak to you as to an officer of the Russian Empire, and you, you scum, were suckled by a she-wolf. Shoot me, you son of a bitch!"

But shoot him I did not—I did not owe him a shot. I just dragged him up to the sitting room. There in the sitting room Nadyezhda Vasilevna was wandering about completely mad, with a drawn saber in her hand, looking at herself in the mirror. And when I dragged Nikitinsky into the sitting room, Nadyezhda Vasilevna runs to sit in the chair, and she is wearing a velvet crown and feathers on her head. She sat in the chair and saluted me with the saber. Then I started kicking Nikitinsky, my master, I kicked him for an hour, maybe even more than an hour, and I really understood what life actually is. With one shot, let me tell you, you can only get rid of a person. A shot would have been a pardon for him and too horribly easy for me, with a shot you cannot get to a man's soul, to where the soul hides and what it looks like. But there are times when I don't spare myself and spend a good hour, maybe even more than an hour, kicking the enemy. I want to understand life, to see what it actually is.

The Cemetery in Kozin[1]

The cemetery in a shtetl. Assyria and the mysterious decay of the East on the overgrown, weed-covered fields of Volhynia.

Gray, abraded stones with letters three hundred years old. The rough contours of the reliefs cut into the granite. The image of a fish and a sheep above a dead man's head. Images of rabbis wearing fur hats. Rabbis, their narrow hips girded with belts. Beneath their eyeless faces the wavy stone ripple of curly beards. To one side, below an oak tree cleft in two by lightning, stands the vault of Rabbi Asriil, slaughtered by Bogdan Khmelnitsky's Cossacks.[2] Four generations lie in this sepulcher, as poor

---

1. First published in *Izvestia* (Odessa), February 23, 1923. —*Ed.*
2. Bogdan Khmelnitsky (Bohdan Khmelnystki, 1595–1697), leader of the Zaporozhian Cossacks during their rebellion against Polish dominion over Ukraine in mid-seventeenth century. Lasting for almost a decade, the rebellion ultimately led to the transfer of Ukrainian lands east of the Dnieper to Russian suzerainty (1648–53). Khmelnitsky's forces, as well as Khmelnitsky personally, were notorious for their brutality in fighting the Polish nobility and the largely defenseless Jewish population inhabiting the borderlands between what are now Poland and Ukraine. They perpetrated numerous massacres throughout the region, including towns that are now part of Moldova and Belarus. The decade of the Khmelnitsky rebellion, genocidal in its anti-Jewish animus, has been fixed in the memory of East European Jews as a calamity on the scale of the destruction of First and Second Temple (586 B.C.E. and 70 C.E.), commemorated as Tishah b'Ab (Tisha B'Av). Babel draws an implicit parallel between this calamity and the fate of the region in his own day. See the entry in Babel's *1920 Diary* for 24 July 1920, the day, Saturday, directly preceding Tishah b'Ab. —*Ed.*

as the hovel of a water carrier, and tablets, moss-green tablets, sing of them in Bedouin prayer:

"Azriil, son of Anania, mouth of Jehovah.
Elijah, son of Azriil, mind that fought oblivion hand to hand.
Wolf, son of Elijah, prince taken from his Torah in his nineteenth
*   spring.*
Judah, son of Wolf, Rabbi of Krakow and Prague.
O death, O mercenary, O covetous thief, why did you not, albeit one
*   single time, have mercy upon us?"*

Prishchepa[1]

I'm making my way to Leshniov, where the divisional staff has set up quarters. My traveling companion, as usual, is Prishchepa, a young Cossack from Kuban, a tireless roughneck, a Communist whom the party kicked out, a future rag looter, a devil-may-care syphilitic, an unflappable liar. He wears a crimson Circassian jacket made of fine cloth, with a ruffled hood trailing down his back. As we rode, he told me about himself.

A year ago Prishchepa had run away from the Whites. As a reprisal, they took his parents hostage and killed them at the interrogation. The neighbors ransacked everything they had. When the Whites were driven out of Kuban, Prishchepa returned to his Cossack village.

It was morning, daybreak, peasant sleep sighed in the rancid stuffiness. Prishchepa hired a communal cart and went through the village picking up his gramophone, kvas jugs, and the napkins that his mother had embroidered. He went down the street in his black cloak, his curved dagger in his belt. The cart rattled behind him. Prishchepa went from one neighbor's house to the next, the bloody prints of his boots trailing behind him. In huts where he found his mother's things or his father's pipe, he left hacked-up old women, dogs hung over wells, icons soiled with dung. The people of the village smoked their pipes and followed him sullenly with their eyes. Young Cossacks had gathered on the steppes outside the village and were keeping count. The count rose and the village fell silent. When he had finished, Prishchepa returned to his ransacked home. He arranged his reclaimed furniture the way he remembered it from his childhood, and ordered vodka to be brought to him. He locked himself in the hut and for two days drank, sang, cried, and hacked tables to pieces with his saber.

On the third night, the village saw smoke rising above Prishchepa's hut. Seared and gashed, he came staggering out of the shed pulling the cow behind him, stuck his revolver in her mouth, and shot her. The earth smoked beneath his feet, a blue ring of flame flew out of the chimney and melted away, the abandoned calf began wailing. The fire was as bright as a holy day. Prishchepa untied his horse, jumped into the saddle, threw a lock of his hair into the flames, and vanished.

---

1. First published in a supplement to *Izvestia* (Odessa), June 17, 1923. —*Ed.*

The Story of a Horse[1]

One day Savitsky, our division commander, took for himself a white stallion belonging to Khlebnikov, the commander of the First Squadron. It was a horse of imposing stature, but with a somewhat raw build, which always seemed a little heavy to me. Khlebnikov was given a black mare of pretty good stock and good trot. But he mistreated the mare, hankered for revenge, waited for an opportunity, and when it came, pounced on it.

After the unsuccessful battles of July, when Savitsky was dismissed from his duties and sent to the command personnel reserves, Khlebnikov wrote to army headquarters requesting that his horse be returned to him. On the letter, the chief of staff penned the decision: "Aforementioned stallion is to be returned to primordial owner." And Khlebnikov, rejoicing, rode a hundred versts to find Savitsky, who was living at the time in Radzivillov, a mangled little town that looked like a tattered old whore. The dismissed division commander was living alone, the fawning lackeys at headquarters no longer knew him. The fawning lackeys at headquarters were busy angling for roasted chickens in the army commander's smiles, and, vying to outgrovel each other, had turned their backs on the glorious division commander.

Drenched in perfume, looking like Peter the Great, he had fallen out of favor. He lived with a Cossack woman by the name of Pavla, whom he had snatched away from a Jewish quartermaster, and twenty thoroughbreds which, word had it, were his own. In his yard, the sun was tense and tortured with the blindness of its rays. The foals were wildly suckling on their mothers, and stableboys with drenched backs were sifting oats on faded winnowing floors. Khlebnikov, wounded by the injustice and fired by revenge, marched straight over to the barricaded yard.

"Are you familiar with my person?" he asked Savitsky, who was lying on some hay.

"Something tells me I've seen you somewhere before," Savitsky said to him with a yawn.

"In that case, here is the chief of staff's decision," Khlebnikov said gruffly. "And I would be obliged, Comrade of the reserve, if you would look at me with an official eye!"

"Why not?" Savitsky mumbled appeasingly. He took the document and began reading it for an unusually long time. He suddenly called over the Cossack woman, who was combing her hair in the coolness under the awning.

"Pavla!" he yelled. "As the Lord's my witness, you've been combing your hair since this morning! How about heating a samovar for us!"

The Cossack woman put down her comb, took her hair in both hands, and flung it behind her back.

---

1. First published in *Izvestia* (Odessa), April 13, 1923, under the title "Timoshenko and Melnikov" and the dateline: "Radziwillów, July 1920." After the story was republished in Moscow in *Krasnaya nov* 3 (1924) and attacked in the journal *Oktyabr* 3 (1924), Babel had to retract the original title and apologize for what he called his absentmindedness. Timoshenko was enraged and threatened to kill Babel; their mutual friend Yakov Okhotnikov reconciled the two. In all subsequent publications the actual Semyon Timoshenko (1895–1970), the future People's Commissar of Defense and Marshal, was replaced with the fictional Savitsky. Melnikov, who in his reminiscences (*Krasnaya niva* 6) published in 1930 denied ever resigning from the Party, was replaced with the fictional Khlebnikov. —*Ed.*

"You've done nothing but bicker all day, Konstantin Vasilevich," she said with a lazy, condescending smile. "First you want this, then you want that!" And she came over to Savitsky; her breasts, bobbing on her high heels, squirmed like an animal in a sack.

"You've done nothing but bicker all day," the woman repeated, beaming, and she buttoned up the division commander's shirt.

"First I want this, then I want that," the division commander said, laughing, and he got up, clasped Pavla's acquiescing shoulders, and suddenly turned his face, deathly white, to Khlebnikov.

"I am still alive, Khlebnikov," he said, embracing the Cossack woman tighter. "My legs can still walk, my horses can still gallop, my hands can still get hold of you, and my gun is warming next to my skin."

He drew his revolver, which had lain against his bare stomach, and stepped closer to the commander of the First Squadron.

The commander turned on his heels, his spurs yelped, he left the yard like an orderly who has received an urgent dispatch, and once again rode a hundred versts to find the chief of staff—but the chief of staff sent him packing.

"I have already dealt with your matter, Commander!" the chief of staff said. "I ordered that your stallion be returned to you, and I have quite a few other things to deal with!"

The chief of staff refused to listen, and finally ordered the errant commander back to his squadron. Khlebnikov had been away a whole week. During that time we had been transferred to the Dubno forest to set up camp. We had pitched our tents and were living it up. Khlebnikov, from what I remember, returned on the twelfth, a Sunday morning. He asked me for some paper, a good thirty sheets, and for some ink. The Cossacks planed a tree stump smooth for him, he placed his revolver and the paper on it, and wrote till sundown, filling many sheets with his smudgy scrawl.

"You're a real Karl Marx, you are!" the squadron's military commissar said to him in the evening. "What the hell are you writing there?"

"I am describing various thoughts in accordance with the oath I have taken," Khlebnikov answered, and handed the military commissar his petition to withdraw from the Communist Party of the Bolsheviks.

"The Communist Party," his petition went, "was, it is my belief, founded for the promotioning of happiness and true justice with no restrictings, and thus must also keep an eye out for the rights of the little man. Here I would like to touch on the matter of the white stallion who I seized from some indescribably counterrevolutionary peasants, and who was in a horrifying condition, and many comrades laughed brazenly at that condition, but I was strong enough to withstand that laughing of theirs, and gritting my teeth for the Common Cause, I nursed the stallion back to the desired shape, because, let it be said, Comrades, I am a white-stallion enthusiast and have dedicated to white stallions the little energy that the Imperial War and the Civil War have left me with, and all these stallions respond to my touch as I respond to his silent wants and needs! But that unjust black mare I can neither respond to, nor do I need her, nor can I stand her, and, as all my comrades will testify, there's bound to be trouble! And yet the Party is unable to return to me, according to the chief of staff's decision, that which is my very own, handing me no option but to write this here petition with tears that do not befit a fighter, but which flow endlessly, ripping my blood-drenched heart to pieces!"

This and much more was written in Khlebnikov's petition. He spent the whole day writing it, and it was very long. It took me and the military commissar more than an hour to struggle through it.

"What a fool you are!" the military commissar said to him, and tore it up. "Come back after dinner and you and I will have a little talk."

"I don't need your little talk!" Khlebnikov answered, trembling. "You and I are finished!"

He stood at attention, shivering, not moving, his eyes darting from one side to the other as if he were desperately trying to decide which way to run. The military commissar came up to him but couldn't grab hold of him in time. Khlebnikov lunged forward and ran with all his might.

"We're finished!" he yelled wildly, jumped onto the tree stump, and began ripping his jacket and tearing at his chest.

"Go on, Savitsky!" he shouted, throwing himself onto the ground. "Kill me!"

We dragged him to a tent, the Cossacks helped us. We boiled some tea for him, and rolled him some cigarettes. He smoked, his whole body shivering. And it was only late in the evening that our commander calmed down. He no longer spoke about his deranged petition, but within a week he went to Rovno, presented himself for an examination by the Medical Commission, and was discharged from the army as an invalid on account of having six wounds.

That's how we lost Khlebnikov. I was very upset about this because Khlebnikov had been a quiet man, very similar to me in character. He was the only one in the squadron who owned a samovar. On days when there was a break in the fighting, the two of us drank hot tea. We were rattled by the same passions. Both of us looked upon the world as a meadow in May over which women and horses wander.

Konkin[1]

So there we were making mincemeat of the Poles at Belaya Tserkov. So much so that the trees were rattling. I'd been hit in the morning, but managed to keep on buzzing, more or less. The day, from what I remember, was toppling toward evening. I got cut off from the brigade commander, and was left with only a bunch of five proletarian Cossacks tagging along after me. All around me everyone's hugging each other with hatchets, like priests from two villages, the sap's slowly trickling out of me, my horse is bloody all over. Need I say more?

Me and Spirka Zabuty ended up riding off a ways from the forest. We look—and yes, two and two does make four!—no less than a hundred and fifty paces away, we see a dust cloud which is either the staff or the cavalry transport. If it's the staff—that's great, if it's the cavalry transport—that's even better! The boys' tattered clothes hung in rags, their shirts barely covering their manhood.

1. First published in *Krasnaya nov* 3 (1924) with the dateline "Dubno, August 1924."

"Zabuty!" I yell over to Spirka, telling him he's a son of a whore, that his mother is a you-know-what, or whatever (I leave this part up to you, as you're the official orator here). "Isn't that *their* staff that's riding off there?" "You can bet your life it's their staff!" Spirka yells back. "The only thing is, we're two and they're eight!"

"Let's go for it, Spirka!" I shout. "Either way, I'm going to hurl some mud at their chasubles! Let's go die for a pickle and World Revolution!"

And off we rode. They were eight sabers. Two of them we felled with our rifles. I spot Spirka dragging a third to Dukhonin's headquarters to get his papers checked. And me, I take aim at the big King of Aces. Yes, brothers, a big, red-faced King of Aces, with a chain and a gold pocket watch. I squeezed him back toward a farm. The farm was full of apple and cherry trees. The horse that the Big Ace was riding was nice and plump like a merchant's daughter, but it was tired. So the general drops his reins, aims his Mauser at me, and puts a hole in my leg.

"Ha, fine, sweetheart!" I think to myself. "I'll have you on your back with your legs spread wide in no time!"

I got my wheels rolling and put two bullets in his horse. I felt bad about the horse. What a Bolshevik of a stallion, a true Bolshevik! Copper-brown like a coin, tail like a bullet, leg like a bowstring. I wanted to present him alive to Lenin, but nothing came of it. I liquidated that sweet little horse. It tumbled like a bride, and my King of Aces fell out of his saddle. He dashed to one side, then turned back again and put another little loophole in my body. So, in other words, I had already gotten myself three decorations for fighting the enemy.

"Jesus!" I think to myself. "Just watch him finish me off by mistake!"

I went galloping toward him, he'd already pulled his saber, and tears are running down his cheeks, white tears, the milk of man.

"You'll get me a Red Flag medal!" I yell. "Give yourself up while I'm still alive, Your Excellency!"

"I can't do that, *Pan*!" the old man answers. "Kill me!"

And suddenly Spirka is standing before me like a leaf before a blade of grass.[2] His face all lathered up with sweat, his eyes as if they're dangling on strings from his ugly mug.

"Konkin!" he yells at me. "God knows how many I've finished off! But you have a general here, he's got embroidery on him, I'd like to finish him off myself!"

"Go to the Turk!" I tell Zabuty, and get furious. "It's my blood that's on his embroidery!"

And with my mare I edge the general into the barn, where there was hay or something. It was silent in there, dark, cool.

"*Pan*, think of your old age!" I tell him. "Give yourself up to me, for God's sake, and we can both have a rest."

And he's against the wall, panting with his whole chest, rubbing his forehead with a red finger.

"I can't," he says. "Kill me, I will only hand my saber to Budyonny!"

He wants me to bring him Budyonny! O, Lord in Heaven! And I can tell the old man's on his last legs.

---

2. From the popular Russian tale, "The Little Humpbacked Horse" by Peter Ershov, in which the hero summons his magic horse with "Appear before me like a leaf before a blade of grass!"

"Pan!" I shout at him, sobbing and gnashing my teeth. "On my proletarian honor, I myself am the commander-in-chief. Don't go looking for embroidery on me, but the title's mine. You want my title? I am the musical eccentric and salon ventriloquist of Nizhny . . . Nizhny, a town on the Volga!"

Then the devil got into me. The general's eyes were blinking like lanterns in front of me. The Red Sea parted before me. His snub enters my wound like salt, because I see that the old man doesn't believe me. So, my friends, what I did is, I closed my mouth, pulled in my stomach, took a deep breath, and demonstrated, in the proper way, our way, the fighter's way, the Nizhny way—demonstrated to this Polish nobleman my ventriloquy.

The old man went white in the face, clutched his heart, and sat on the ground.

"Do you now believe Konkin the Eccentric, commissar of the Third Invincible Cavalry Brigade?"

"A commissar?" he shouts.

"A commissar," I tell him.

"A Communist?" he shouts.

"A Communist," I tell him.

"At my hour of death," he shouts, "at my last breath, tell me, my dear Cossack friend, are you a Communist, or are you lying to me?"

"I am a Communist," I tell him.

So there's grandpa, sitting on the ground, kissing some kind of amulet or something, breaks his saber in half, and in his eyes two sparks flare up, two lanterns above the dark steppes.

"Forgive me," he says, "but I cannot give myself up to a Communist." And he shakes my hand. "Forgive me," he says, "and finish me off like a soldier."

Konkin, the political commissar of the N. Cavalry Brigade and three-time Knight of the Order of the Red Flag, told us this story with his typical antics during a rest stop one day.

"So, Konkin, did you and the *Pan* come to some sort of an agreement in the end?"

"Can you come to an agreement with someone like that? He was too proud. I begged him again, but he wouldn't give in. So we took his papers, those he had with him, we took his Mauser, and the old fool's saddle, the one I'm sitting on right now. Then I see all my life flowing out of me in drops, a terrible tiredness grabs hold of me, my boots are full of blood, I lost interest in him."

"So you put the old man out of his misery?"

"Well, I guess I did."

Berestechko[1]

We were advancing from Khotin to Berestechko. Our fighters were dozing in their saddles. A song rustled like a stream running dry. Horrifying corpses lay on thousand-year-old burial mounds. Muzhiks in white shirts raised their caps and bowed as we passed. The cloak of Division Commander Pavlichenko was fluttering ahead of the staff officers like a

---

1. First published in *Krasnaya nov* 3 (1924), with the dateline "Berestechko, August 1920."

gloomy banner. His ruffled hood hung over his cloak, his curved saber at his side.

We rode past the Cossack burial mounds and the tomb of Bogdan Khmelnitsky.[2] An old man with a mandolin came creeping out from behind a gravestone and with a child's voice sang of past Cossack glory. We listened to the song in silence, then unfurled the standards, and burst into Berestechko to the beat of a thundering march. The inhabitants had put iron bars over their shutters, and silence, a despotic silence, had ascended to the shtetl throne.

I happened to be billeted in the house of a redheaded widow, who was doused with the scent of widow's grief. I washed off the dirt of the road and went out into the street. An announcement was already nailed up on telegraph poles that Divisional Military Commissar Vinogradov would be giving a speech on the Second Congress of the Comintern.[3] Right outside the house a couple of Cossacks were getting ready to shoot an old silver-bearded Jew for espionage. The old man was screeching, and tried to break free. Kudrya from the machine gun detachment grabbed his head and held it wedged under his arm. The Jew fell silent and spread his legs. Kudrya pulled out his dagger with his right hand and carefully slit the old man's throat without spattering himself. Then he knocked on one of the closed windows.

"If anyone's interested," he said, "they can come get him. It's no problem."

And the Cossacks disappeared around the corner. I followed them, and then wandered through Berestechko. Most of the people here are Jewish, and only on the outskirts have a few Russian townspeople, mainly tanners, settled. The Russians live cleanly, in little white houses behind green shutters. Instead of vodka, they drink beer or mead, and in their front gardens grow tobacco which, like Galician peasants, they smoke in long curved pipes. That they are three diligent and entrepreneurial races living next to each other awakened in all of them an obstinate industriousness that is sometimes inherent in a Russian man, if he hasn't become louse-ridden, desperate, and besotted with drink.

Everyday life, which once flourished, has blown away. Little sprouts that had survived for three centuries still managed to blossom in Volhynia's sultry hotbed of ancient times. Here, with the ropes of profit, the Jews had bound the Russian muzhiks to the Polish *Pans* and the Czech settlers to the factory in Lodz.[4] These were smugglers, the best on the frontier, and almost always warriors of the faith. Hasidism kept this lively population of taverners, peddlers, and brokers in a stifling grip. Boys in long coats still trod the ancient path to the Hasidic cheder, and old women still brought daughters-in-law to the *tsaddik* with impassioned prayers for fertility.

The Jews live here in large houses painted white or a watery blue. The traditional austerity of this architecture goes back centuries. Behind the houses are sheds that are two, sometimes three stories high. The sun never enters these sheds. They are indescribably gloomy and replace our yards. Secret passages lead to cellars and stables. In times of war, people

---

2. See note 2, p. 130.
3. See note 4, p. 113.
4. The original Russian conveys a value-neutral, not to say positive, view of the Berestechko Jews. According to Babel (he was, after all, a trained economist), the local economy prospered thanks to the profit motive ("threads of gain") introduced by the Jews who, as middlemen, joined the productive forces of the area into a total that was greater than the sum of its parts. —Ed.

hide in these catacombs from bullets and plunder. Over many days, human refuse and animal dung pile up. Despair and dismay fill the catacombs with an acrid stench and the rotting sourness of excrement.

Berestechko stinks inviolably to this day. The smell of rotten herring emanates from everyone. The shtetl reeks in expectation of a new era, and, instead of people, fading reflections of frontier misfortune wander through it. I had had enough of them by the end of the day, went beyond the edge of the town, climbed the mountain, and reached the abandoned castle of the Counts Raciborski, the recent owners of Berestechko.

The silence of the sunset turned the grass around the castle blue. The moon rose green as a lizard above the pond. Looking out the window, I could see the estate of the Raciborskis—meadows and fields of hops hidden beneath the crepe ribbons of dusk.

A ninety-year-old countess and her son had lived in the castle. She had tormented him for not having given the dying clan any heirs, and—the muzhiks told me this—she used to beat him with the coachman's whip.

A rally was gathering on the square below. Peasants, Jews, and tanners from the outlying areas had come together. Above them flared Vinogradov's ecstatic voice and the clanking of his spurs. He gave a speech about the Second Congress of the Comintern,[5] and I roamed along the walls where nymphs with gouged eyes danced their ancient round dance. Then on the trampled floor, in a corner, I found the torn fragment of a yellowed letter. On it was written in faded ink:

> *Berestechko, 1820, Paul, mon bien aimé, on dit que l'empereur Napoléon est mort, est-ce vrai? Moi, je me sens bien, les couches ont été faciles, notre petit héros achève sept semaines. . . .* [6]

Below me, the voice of the divisional military commissar is droning on. He is passionately haranguing the bewildered townspeople and the plundered Jews: "You are the power. Everything here belongs to you. There are no masters. I shall now conduct an election for the Revolutionary Committee."

Salt[1]

Dear Comrade Editor,
   I want to tell you of some ignorant women who are harmful to us. I set my hopes on you, that you who travel around our nation's fronts, have not overlooked the far-flung station of Fastov, lying afar beyond the mountains grand, in a distant province of a distant land, where many a jug of home-brewed beer we drank with merriment and cheer. About this aforementioned station, there is much you can write about, but as we say back home: you can shovel till the cows come home, but the master's dung heap never gets no smaller. So I will only describe what my eyes have seen in person.
   It was a quiet, glorious night seven days ago when our well-deserved Red Cavalry transport train, loaded with fighters, stopped at that station.

5. See note 4, p. 113
6. French: Berestechko, 1820, my beloved Paul, I hear that Emperor Napoleon is dead. Is it true? I
    feel well; it was an easy birth, our little hero is already seven weeks old.
1. First published in a supplement to *Izvestia* (Odessa), November 25, 1923.

We were all burning to promote the Common Cause and were heading to Berdichev. Only, we notice that our train isn't moving in any way at all, our Gavrilka is not beginning to roll, and the fighters begin mistrusting and asking each other: "Why are we stopping here?" And truly, the stop turned out to be mighty for the Common Cause, because the peddlers, those evil fiends among whom there was a countless force of the female species, were all behaving very impertinently with the railroad authorities. Recklessly they grabbed the handrails, those evil fiends, they scampered over the steel roofs, frolicked, made trouble, clutching in each hand sacks of contraband salt, up to five *pood* in a sack. But the triumph of the capitalist peddlers did not last long. The initiative showed by the fighters who jumped out of the train made it possible for the struggling railroad authorities to emit sighs from their breasts. Only the female species with their bags of salt stayed around. Taking pity, the soldiers let some of the women come into the railroad cars, but others they didn't. In our own railroad car of the Second Platoon two girls popped up, and after the first bell there comes an imposing woman with a baby in her arms: "Let me in, my dear Cossacks," she says. "I have been suffering through the whole war at train stations with a suckling baby in my arms, and now I want to meet my husband, but the way the railroad is, it is impossible to get through! Don't I deserve some help from you Cossacks?"

"By the way, woman," I tell her, "whichever way the platoon decides will be your fate." And, turning to the platoon, I tell them that here we have a woman who is requesting to travel to her husband at an appointed place and that she does, in fact, have a child with her, so what will your decision be? Let her in or not?

"Let her in," the boys yell. "Once we're done with her, she won't be wanting that husband of hers no more!"

"No," I tell the boys quite politely, "I bow to your words, platoon, but I am astonished to hear such horse talk. Recall, platoon, your lives and how you yourselves were children with your mothers, and therefore, as a result, you should not talk that way!"

And the Cossacks said, "How persuasive he is, this Balmashov!" And they let the woman into the railroad car, and she climbs aboard thankfully. And each of the fighters, saying how right I am, tumble all over each other telling her, "Sit down, woman, there in the corner, rock your child the way mothers do, no one will touch you in the corner, so you can travel untouched to your husband, as you want, and we depend upon your conscience to raise a new change of guard for us, because what is old grows older, and when you need youth, it's never around! We saw our share of sorrow, woman, both when we were drafted and then later in the extra service, we were crushed by hunger, burned by cold. So just sit here, woman, and don't be frightened!"

The third bell rang and the train pulled out of the station. The glorious night pitched its tent. And in that tent hung star lanterns. And the fighters remembered the nights of Kuban and the green star of Kuban. And thoughts flew like birds. And the wheels clattered and clattered.

With the passing of time, when night was relieved of its watch and the red drummers drummed in the dawn on their red drums, then the Cossacks came to me, seeing that I am sitting sleepless and am unhappy to the fullest.

"Balmashov," the Cossacks say to me, "why are you so horribly unhappy and sitting sleepless?"

"I bow to you deeply, O fighters, and would like to ask you the small favor of letting me speak a few words with this citizen."

And trembling from head to toe, I rise from my bunk from which sleep had run like a wolf from a pack of depraved dogs, and walk up to her, take the baby from her arms, rip off the rags it's swaddled in and its diaper, and out from the diaper comes a nice fat forty-pound sack of salt.

"What an interesting little baby, Comrades! It does not ask mommy for titty, doesn't peepee on mommy's skirty, and doesn't wake people from their sleep!"

"Forgive me, my dear Cossacks," the woman cut into our conversation very coolly, "it wasn't me who tricked you, it was my hard life."

"I, Balmashov, forgive your hard life," I tell the woman. "It doesn't cost Balmashov much. What Balmashov pays for something, that is the price he sells it for! But address yourself to the Cossacks, woman, who elevated you as a toiling mother of the republic. Address yourself to these two girls, who are now crying for having suffered under us last night. Address yourself to our women on the wheat fields of Kuban, who are wearing out their womanly strength without husbands, and to their husbands, who are lonely too, and so are forced against their will to rape girls who cross their paths! And you they didn't touch, you improper woman, although you should have been the first to be touched! Address yourself to Russia, crushed by pain!"

And she says to me, "As it is I've lost my salt, so I'm not afraid of calling things by their real name! Don't give me that about saving Russia—all you care about is saving those Yids, Lenin and Trotsky!"

"Right now our topic of conversation is not the Yids, you evil citizen! And by the way, about Lenin I don't really know, but Trotsky is the dashing son of the Governor of Tambov who, turning his back on his high social rank, joined the working classes. Like prisoners sentenced to hard labor, Lenin and Trotsky are dragging us to life's road of freedom, while you, foul citizen, are a worse counterrevolutionary than that White general waving his sharp saber at us from his thousand-ruble horse. You can see him, that general, from every road, and the worker has only one dream—to kill him! While you, you dishonest citizen, with your bogus children who don't ask for bread and don't run out into the wind, you one doesn't see. You're just like a flea, you bite and bite and bite!"

And I truthfully admit that I threw that citizen off the moving train and onto the embankment, but she, being brawny as she was, sat up, shook out her skirts, and went on her deceitful way. Seeing this uninjured woman and Russia all around her, the peasant fields without an ear of corn, the raped girls, and the comrades, many of whom were heading for the front but few of whom would ever return, I wanted to jump from the train and either kill myself or kill her. But the Cossacks took pity on me and said, "Just shoot her with that rifle."

And I took the loyal rifle from the wall and wiped that blot off the face of the working land and the republic.

And we, the fighters of the Second Platoon, swear before you, dear Comrade Editor, and before you, dear Comrades of the editorial office, that we will deal relentlessly with all the traitors who pull us into the pit and want to turn back the stream and cover Russia with corpses and dead grass.

In the name of all the fighters of the Second Platoon,

Nikita Balmashov, Fighter of the Revolution.

Evening[1]

O statutes of the RCP![2] You have laid impetuous rails across the rancid dough of Russian prose. You have transformed three bachelors, their hearts filled with the passion of Ryazan Jesuses, into editors of the *Krasny Kavalerist*.[3] You have transformed them so that day after day they can churn out a rambunctious newspaper filled with courage and rough-and-ready mirth.

Galin with his cataract, consumptive Slinkin, and Sychev with his withered intestines shuffle through the barren soil of the rear lines, spreading the revolt and fire of their news sheet through the ranks of dashing, pensioned-off Cossacks, reserve cheats who have registered as Polish translators, and girls sent out to our Polit-otdel train[4] from Moscow for recuperation.

By evening the newspaper is ready—a dynamite fuse placed under the cavalry. The cross-eyed lantern of the provincial sun expires in the sky, the lights of the printing press scatter in all directions and burn uncontrollably like the passion of a machine. And then, toward midnight, Galin comes out of the railroad car shuddering from the bite of his unrequited love for Irina, our train's washerwoman.

"Last time," Galin says, pale and blind, his shoulders narrow, "last time, Irina, we discussed the shooting of Nicholas the Bloody, executed by the proletariat of Ekaterinburg.[5] Now we will proceed to the other tyrants who died like dogs. Peter III was strangled by Orlov, his wife's lover. Paul was torn to pieces by his courtiers and his own son. Nikolai Palkin poisoned himself, his son perished March first, his grandson drank himself to death. It is important for you to know all this, Irina!"

And raising his blank eye, filled with adoration, to the washerwoman, Galin rummages relentlessly through the crypts of murdered emperors. He is standing stoop-shouldered, bathed in the rays of the moon hovering high above like a nagging splinter, the printing presses are hammering somewhere nearby, and the radio station is shining with clear light. Irina nestles against the shoulder of Vasily the cook as she stands listening to Galin's dull and nonsensical mutterings of love. Above her, the stars are dragging themselves through the black seaweed of the sky. The washerwoman yawns, makes the sign of the cross over her puffy lips, and stares wide-eyed at Galin.

Next to Irina, rough-faced Vasily yawns. Like all cooks he scorns mankind. Cooks: they constantly have to handle the meat of dead animals and the greed of the living, which is why, when it comes to politics, a cook always seeks things that have nothing to do with him. This goes for Vasily too. Hiking his pants up to his nipples, he asks Galin about the civil lists

1. First published in *Krasnaya nov* 1 (1925), titled "Galin" with the dateline "Kovel, 1920."
2. The Russian Communist Party.
3. *The Red Cavalryman.*
4. The propaganda train belonging to Polit-otdel for Polit-otdel see note 8, p. 72.
5. Nicholas II, the last czar, earned the title "bloody" for the shooting of petitioners on January 9, 1905. He was killed on orders from the Bolshevik leadership, along with the royal family, in Ekaterinburg on July 17, 1918. —*Ed.*

of various kings, the dowries of czars' daughters. Then he yawns and says, "It's night, Irina, another day will be rolling in tomorrow. Let's go crush some fleas."

They closed the kitchen door, leaving Galin alone, with the moon hovering high above like a nagging splinter. I sat opposite the moon on the embankment by the sleeping pond, wearing my spectacles, with boils on my neck, my legs bandaged. My confused poetic brain was digesting the class struggle when Galin came up to me with his twinkling cataracts.

"Galin," I said, overcome with self-pity and loneliness, "I am sick, my end is near, I am tired of life in the Red Cavalry!"

"You're a wimp!" Galin said, and the watch on his bony wrist showed one in the morning. "You're a wimp, and we end up having to put up with wimps like you! We're cracking the nut for you, and soon enough you will be able to see the meat inside, at which point you'll take your thumb out of your mouth and sing the glories of the new life in striking prose—but for the time being, just sit where you are, nice and quiet, you wimp, and stop getting in the way with all your whimpering!"

He came closer to me, fixed the bandages which had slipped off my itching sores, and let his head loll onto his pigeon breast. The night comforted us in our anguish; a light breeze rustled over us like a mother's skirt, and the weeds below us glittered with freshness and moisture.

The roaring machines of the train's printing press screeched and fell silent. Dawn drew a line across the edge of the earth, the kitchen door creaked and opened a crack. Four feet with fat heels came thrusting out into the coolness, and we saw Irina's loving calves and Vasily's big toe with its crooked black nail.

"Vasilyok," the woman whispered in a throaty, expiring voice. "Get out of my bed, you troublemaker!"

But Vasily only jerked his heel and moved closer to her.

"The Red Cavalry," Galin said to me, "the Red Cavalry is a public conjuring trick pulled off by our Party's Central Committee. The curve of the Revolution has thrown the Cossack marauders, saddled with all kinds of prejudices, into the forefront, but the Central Committee is going to weed them out with its iron rake."

Then Galin began talking about the political education of the First Cavalry. He spoke long, in a dull voice, with complete clarity. His eyelid fluttered over his cataract.

Afonka Bida[1]

We were fighting by Leshniov. A wall of enemy cavalry rose all around us. The new Polish strategy was uncoiling like a spring, with an ominous whistle. We were being pushed back. It was the first time in our campaign that we felt on our own backs the devilish sharpness of flank attacks and breaches in the rear lines—slashes from the very weapons that had served us so well.

The front at Leshniov was being held by the infantry. Blond and barefoot, Volhynian muzhiks shuffled along crooked trenches. This infantry

1. First published in *Krasnaya nov* 1 (1924). —*Ed.*

had been plucked from behind its plows the day before to form the Red Cavalry's infantry reserve. The peasants had come along eagerly. They fought with the greatest zeal. Their hoarse peasant ferocity amazed even the Budyonny fighters. Their hatred for the Polish landowners was built of invisible but sturdy material.

In the second phase of the war, when our whooping had lost its effect on the enemy's imagination, and cavalry attacks on our opponents, burrowed in their trenches, had become impossible, this ragtag infantry could have proved extremely useful to the Red Cavalry. But our poverty got the upper hand: there were three muzhiks to every rifle, and the cartridges that were issued didn't fit. The venture had to be dropped, and this true peasant home guard was sent back to its villages.

But back to the fighting at Leshniov. Our foot soldiers had dug themselves in three versts from the shtetl. A hunched youth with spectacles was walking up and down in front of them, a saber dangling at his side. He moved along in little hops, with a piqued look on his face, as if his boots were pinching him. This peasant *ataman*,[2] chosen and cherished by the muzhiks, was a Jew, a half-blind Jewish youth, with the sickly, intent face of a talmudist. In battle, he showed circumspect and cool-headed courage that reflected the absentmindedness of a dreamer.

It was after two o'clock on a crystalline July day. A gossamer rainbow of heat glittered in the air. A festive stripe of uniforms and horse manes braided with ribbons came sparkling from behind the hills. The youth gave the signal for the men to take their positions. The muzhiks, shuffling in their bast sandals, ran to their posts and took aim. But it turned out to be a false alarm. It was Maslak's[3] colorful squadrons that came riding up the Leshniov high road, their emaciated but spirited horses trotting at a steady pace. In fiery pillars of dust, magnificent banners were fluttering on gilded poles weighed down by velvet tassels. The horsemen rode with majestic and insolent haughtiness. The tattered foot soldiers came crawling out of their trenches and, their mouths hanging open, watched the light-footed elegance of the unruffled stream.

In front of the regiment, riding a bowlegged steppe horse, was Brigade Commander Maslak, filled with drunken blood and the putridness of his fatty juices. His stomach lay like a big cat on the silver-studded pommel of his saddle. When Maslak saw the muzhik foot soldiers, his face turned a merry purple, and he beckoned Platoon Commander Afonka Bida to come over. We had given the platoon commander the nickname "Makhno"[4] because he looked so much like him. Maslak and Bida whispered for about a minute. Then Bida turned toward the First Squadron, leaned forward, and in a low voice ordered, "Charge!" The Cossacks, one platoon after another, broke into a trot. They spurred their horses and went galloping toward the trenches from which the muzhik foot soldiers were peering, dazzled by the sight.

"Prepare to engage!" sang Afonka's voice, dismal and as if he were calling from far away.

Maslak, wheezing and coughing, relishing the spectacle, rode off to

---

2. Term for Cossack leader.
3. Maslakov, commander of the First Brigade of the Fourth Division, a relentless partisan who was soon to betray the Soviet regime. [Babel's footnote.] An anarchist, Maslak (G.S. Maslakov) staged a mutiny and joined Makhno's army. He was assassinated by Cheka agents in 1921. —*Ed.*
4. See note 2 on p. 108.

the side, and the Cossacks charged. The poor muzhik foot soldiers ran, but it was too late. The Cossack lashes were already cutting across their tattered jackets as the horsemen circled the field, twirling their whips with exquisite artistry.

"What's all this nonsense about?" I shouted over to Afonka.

"Just a bit of fun," he shouted back, fidgeting in his saddle, and he dragged a young man out of the bushes in which he was hiding.

"Just a bit of fun!" he yelled, clobbering away at the terrified young man. The fun ended when Maslak, tired and majestic, waved his plump hand.

"Foot soldiers! Stop gawking!" Afonka yelled, haughtily straightening his frail body. "Go catch some fleas!"

The Cossacks grinned at each other and gathered into formation. The foot soldiers vanished without a trace. The trenches were empty. And only the hunched Jewish youth stood in the same spot as before, eyeing the Cossacks haughtily through his spectacles.

The gunfire from the direction of Leshniov did not let up. The Poles were encircling us. We could see the single figures of their mounted scouts through our binoculars. They came galloping from the shtetl and disappeared again like jack-in-the-boxes. Maslak gathered together a squadron and divided it on either side of the high road. A sparkling sky hung above Leshniov, indescribably void as always in hours of danger. The Jew threw his head back and blew mournfully and loud on his metallic pipe. And the foot soldiers, the battered foot soldiers, returned to their positions.

Bullets flew thickly in our direction. Our brigade staff came under machine gun fire. We rushed into the forest and fought our way through the bushes on the right side of the high road. Branches, hit, cracked heavily above us. By the time we had managed to cut our way through the bushes, the Cossacks were no longer positioned where they had been. The division commander had ordered them to retreat toward Brody. Only the muzhiks sent a few snarling shots out of their trenches, and Afonka, trailing behind, went chasing after his platoon.

He was riding on the outermost edge of the road, looking around him and sniffing at the air. The shooting died down for a few moments. Afonka decided to take advantage of the lapse and began galloping at full speed. At that moment a bullet plunged into his horse's neck. Afonka galloped on another hundred paces or so, and then, right in front of our line, his horse abruptly bent its forelegs and sank to the ground.

Afonka casually pulled his wedged foot out of the stirrup. He sat on his haunches and poked about in the wound with his copper-brown finger. Then he stood up again and ran his agonized eyes over the glittering horizon.

"Farewell, Stepan," he said in a wooden voice, and, taking a step away from the dying horse, bowed deeply to it. "How will I return to my quiet village without you? Who am I to throw your embroidered saddle on? Farewell, Stepan!" he repeated more loudly, then choked, squeaked like a mouse in a trap, and began wailing. His gurgling howls reached our ears, and we saw Afonka frantically bowing like a possessed woman in a church. "But you'll see! I won't give in to goddamn fate!" he yelled, lifting his hands from his ashen face. "You'll see! From now on I'm going to hack those cursed Poles to pieces with no mercy at all! Right down to their gasping hearts, right down to their very last gasp, and the Mother of God's blood! I swear this to you, Stepan, before my dear brothers back home!"

Afonka lay down with his face on the horse's wound and fell silent. The horse turned its deep, sparkling, violet eye to its master, and listened to his convulsive wheezing. In tender oblivion it dragged its fallen muzzle over the ground, and streams of blood, like two ruby-red harness straps, trickled over its chest covered in white muscles.

Afonka lay there without moving. Maslak walked over to the horse, treading daintily on his fat legs, slid his revolver into its ear, and fired. Afonka jumped up and swung his pockmarked face to Maslak.

"Take the harness off, Afanasi, and go back to your unit," Maslak said to him gently.

And from our slope we saw Afonka, bent under the weight of the saddle, his face raw and red like sliced meat, tottering toward his squadron, boundlessly alone in the dusty, blazing desert of the fields.

Late that evening I saw him at the cavalry transport. He was sleeping on a cart which held all his "possessions"—sabers, uniform jackets, and pierced gold coins. His blood-caked head with its wrenched, dead mouth, lay as if crucified on the saddle's bow. Next to him lay the harness of the dead horse, the inventive and whimsical raiment of a Cossack racer: breastplates with black tassels, pliant tail cruppers studded with colored stones, and the bridle embossed with silver.

Darkness thickened around us. The cavalry transport crawled heavily along the Brody high road. Simple stars rolled through Milky Ways in the sky, and distant villages burned in the cool depths of the night. Orlov, the squadron subcommander, and big-mustached Bitsenko were sitting right there on Afonka's cart discussing his grief.

"He brought the horse all the way from home," long-mustached Bitsenko said. "Where's one to find another horse like that?"

"A horse—that's a friend," Orlov answered.

"A horse—that's a father," Bitsenko sighed. "The horse saves your life more times than you can count. Bida is finished without his horse."

In the morning Afonka was gone. The skirmishes near Brody began and ended. Defeat was replaced by fleeting victory, we had a change of division commander, but Afonka was still nowhere to be seen. And only a terrible rumbling from the villages, the evil and rapacious trail of Afonka's marauding, showed us his difficult path.

"He's off somewhere getting a horse," the men of the squadron said about him, and on the endless evenings of our wanderings I heard quite a few tales of this grim, savage pillaging.

Fighters from other units ran into Afonka about ten versts from our position. He lay in wait for Polish cavalrymen who had fallen behind, or scoured the forests looking for herds hidden by the peasants. He set villages on fire and shot Polish elders for hiding horses. Echoes of the frenzied one-man battle, the furtive ransacking robbery of a lone wolf attacking a herd, reached our ears.

Another week passed. The bitter events of the day crowded out the tales of Afonka's sinister bravado, and we began to forget our "Makhno." Then the rumor went round that Galician peasants had slaughtered him somewhere in the woods. And on the day we entered Berestechko, Yemelyan Budyak from the First Squadron went to the division commander to ask if he could have Afonka's saddle and the yellow saddlecloths. Yemelyan wanted to ride in the parade on a new saddle, but it was not to be.

We entered Berestechko on August 6. Fluttering in front of our division was our new division commander's Asiatic quilted jacket and his red Cossack coat. Lyovka, the division commander's brutal lackey, walked behind him leading his stud mare. A military march filled with protracted menace resounded through the pretentious, destitute streets. The town was a colorful forest of dead-end alleys and decrepit and convulsive planks and boards. The shtetl's heart, corroded by time, breathed its despondent decay upon us. Smugglers and philistines hid in their large, shadowy huts. Only *Pan* Ludomirski, a bell ringer in a green frock coat, met us at the church.

We crossed the river and entered deeper into the petit-bourgeois settlement. We were nearing the priest's house when Afonka suddenly came riding around the corner on a large stallion.

"Greetings," he called out in a barking voice, and, pushing the fighters apart, took his old position in the ranks.

Maslak stared into the colorless distance.

"Where did you get that horse?" he wheezed, without turning around.

"It's my own," Afonka answered, and rolled himself a cigarette, wetting the paper with a quick dart of his tongue.

One after the other, the Cossacks rode up to greet him. A monstrous pink pustule shone repugnantly in his charred face where his left eye had been.

The following morning Bida went carousing. He smashed Saint Valentine's shrine in the church and tried to play the organ. He was wearing a jacket that had been cut from a blue carpet and had an embroidered lily on its back, and he had combed his sweat-drenched forelock[5] over his gouged-out eye.

After lunch he saddled his horse and fired his rifle at the knocked-out windows of the castle of the Count Raciborski. Cossacks stood around him in a semicircle. They tugged at the stallion's tail, prodded its legs, and counted its teeth.

"A fine figure of a horse!" Orlov, the squadron subcommander, said.

"An exemplary horse," big-mustached Bitsenko confirmed.

At Saint Valentine's[1]

Our division occupied Berestechko yesterday evening. The headquarters have been set up in the house of Father Tuzynkiewicz. Dressed as a woman, Tuzynkiewicz had fled Berestechko before our troops entered the town. All I know about him is that he had dealt with God in Berestechko for forty-five years, and that he had been a good priest. The townspeople make a point of this, telling us he was even loved by the Jews. Under Tuzynkiewicz, the old church had been renovated. The renovations had been completed on the day of the church's three-hundredth anniversary, and the bishop had come from Zhitomir. Prelates in silk cassocks had held a service in front of the church. Potbellied and

5. Ukrainian Cossacks shaved their heads, leaving only a forelock known as a *chub*.
1. First published in *Krasnaya nov* 3 (1924) with the dateline "Berestechko, August 1920." —*Ed.*

beatific, they stood like bells on the dewy grass. Faithful streams flowed in from the surrounding villages. The muzhiks bent their knees, kissed priestly hands, and on that day clouds never before seen flamed in the sky. Heavenly banners fluttered in honor of the church. The bishop himself kissed Tuzynkiewicz on the forehead and called him the Father of Berestechko, *Pater Berestechkae.*

I heard this tale in the morning at the headquarters, where I was checking over the report of our scout column that was on a reconnaissance mission near Lvov in the district of Radziekhov. I read the documents. The snoring of the orderlies behind me bespoke our never-ending homelessness. The clerks, sodden with sleeplessness, wrote orders to the division, ate pickles, and sneezed. It wasn't until midday that I got away, went to the window, and saw the church of Berestechko, powerful and white. It shone in the mild sun like a porcelain tower. Flashes of midday lightning sparkled on its shining flanks. The lightning's arcs began at the ancient green cupolas and ran lightly downward. Pink veins glimmered in the white stone of the portal, and above it were columns as thin as candles.

Then organ music came pouring into my ears, and that instant an old woman with disheveled yellow hair appeared outside the doors of the headquarters. She moved like a dog with a broken paw, hobbling in circles, her legs tottering. The pupils of her eyes, filled with the white liquid of blindness, oozed tears. The sounds of the organ, now drawn-out, now rapid, came fluttering over to us. Their flight was difficult, their wake reverberated plaintive and long. The old woman wiped her eyes with her yellow hair, sat on the floor, and began kissing the tops of my boots. The organ fell silent and then burst into a laughter of bass notes. I took the old woman by the arm and looked around. The clerks were pounding their typewriters and the orderlies snored ever louder, the spurs on their boots ripping the felt under the velvet upholstery of the sofas. The old woman kissed my boots tenderly, hugging them as she would an infant. I led her to the door and locked it behind me. The church towered strikingly before us, like a stage set. Its side doors were open, and on the graves of Polish officers lay horses' skulls.

We hurried into the churchyard, went through a dark corridor, and arrived in a square-shaped room, which had been built as an extension to the chancel. Sashka, the nurse of the Thirty-first Regiment, was puttering about in there, rummaging through a pile of silk that somebody had thrown on the floor. The cadaverous aroma of brocade, scattered flowers, and fragrant decay seeped into her nostrils, tickling and poisonous. Then Cossacks entered the room. They burst into guffaws, grabbed Sashka by the arms, and flung her with gusto onto a pile of cloth and books. Sashka's body, blossoming and reeking like the meat of a freshly slaughtered cow, was laid bare, her raised skirts revealing the legs of a squadron woman, slim, cast-iron legs, and dim-witted Kurdyukov, the silly fool, sat on top of Sashka, bouncing as if he were in a saddle, pretending to be in the grip of passion. She pushed him off and rushed out the door. We passed the altar, and only then did we enter the nave of the church.

The church was filled with light, filled with dancing rays, columns of air, and an almost cool exultation. How can I ever forget Apolek's painting, hanging over the right side-altar? In this painting twelve rosy *Paters* are rocking a cradle girdled with ribbons, with a plump infant Jesus in it. His toes are stretched out, his body lacquered with hot morning sweat. The child is writhing on his fat, wrinkly back, and twelve apostles in cardinals' miters are bending over the cradle. Their faces are meticulously shaven, flaming cloaks are billowing over their bellies. The eyes of the Apostles sparkle with wisdom, resolution, and cheer. Faint grins flit over the corners of their mouths, and fiery warts have been planted on their double chins—crimson warts, like radishes in May.

This church of Berestechko had its private and beguiling approach to the death agonies of the sons of man. In this church the saints marched to their deaths with the flair of Italian opera singers, and the black hair of the executioners shone like the beard of Holofernes.[2] Here, above the altar, I saw the sacrilegious painting of John the Baptist, which had also sprung from Apolek's heretical, intoxicating brush. In this painting the Baptist was beautiful in the ambiguous and reticent way that drives the concubines of kings to shed their half-lost honor and their blossoming lives.

At first I did not notice the signs of destruction in the church, or didn't think they looked too bad. Only the shrine of Saint Valentine had been smashed. Lying around it were shreds of decayed wadding and the saint's ridiculous bones, which, if they resembled anything, looked like chicken bones. And Afonka Bida was still playing the organ. Afonka was drunk, wild, his body was lacerated. He had come back to us only yesterday with the horse he had seized from local farmers. Afonka was obstinately trying to play a march, and someone was badgering him in a sleepy voice, "Enough, Afonka, enough, let's go eat!" But Afonka wouldn't give up. Many more of Afonka's songs followed. Each sound was a song, and one sound was torn from the other. The song's dense tune lasted for a moment and then crossed over into another. I listened, looked around—the signs of destruction didn't look too bad. But *Pan* Ludomirski, the bell ringer of the Church of Saint Valentine and husband of the old blind woman, thought otherwise.

Ludomirsky had suddenly appeared out of nowhere. He walked through the church with measured steps, his head lowered. The old man could not bring himself to cover the scattered relics because a simple man, a lay person, may not touch what is holy. The bell ringer threw himself on the blue slabs of the floor, lifted his head, his blue nose jutting up above him like a flag above a corpse. His blue nose quivered above him and at that moment a velvet curtain by the altar swayed, rustled, and fell open. In the depths of the niche, against the backdrop of a sky furrowed with clouds, ran a bearded little figure wearing an orange Polish caftan—barefoot, his mouth lacerated and bleeding. A hoarse wail assailed our ears. The man in the orange caftan was being pursued by hatred, and his pursuer had caught up with him. The man lifted his arm to ward off the blow, and blood poured from it in a purple stream. The young Cossack standing next to me yelled out and, ducking, started to run, even though there was nothing to run from, because the figure in the niche was only Jesus Christ—the most unusual portrayal of the Son of God I have ever seen in my life.

2. Assyrian general in the Book of Judith, whose brutal murder is famously depicted in Artemisia Gentileschi's 1612–21 painting *Judith Beheading Holofernes*. See note 9, p. 47. —*Ed.*

Pan Ludomirski's Savior was a curly-headed Jew with a scraggly little beard and a low, wrinkled forehead. His sunken cheeks were tinted with carmine, and thin, red-brown eyebrows curved over eyes that were closed in pain.

His mouth was wrenched open, like a horse's mouth, his Polish caftan fastened with a precious girdle, and from under the caftan jutted crooked little porcelain feet, painted, bare, pierced by silver nails.

Pan Ludomirski stood under the statue in his green frock coat. He stretched his withered arm toward us and cursed us. The Cossacks stared at him with wide eyes and let their straw-colored forelocks hang. In a thundering voice, the bell ringer of the Church of Saint Valentine cursed us in the purest Latin. Then he turned away, fell to his knees, and clasped the feet of the Savior.

Back at the headquarters, I wrote a report to the division commander about the insult to the religious feelings of the local population. A decree was issued that the church be closed, and the guilty parties were charged with a breach of discipline and sent before the military tribunal.

Squadron Commander Trunov[1]

At noon we brought the bullet-ridden body of Trunov, our squadron commander, back to Sokal. He had been killed that morning in a battle with enemy airplanes. All the hits had caught Trunov in the face; his cheeks were riddled with wounds, his tongue torn out. We washed the dead man's face as best we could so that he would look less horrifying, placed his Caucasian saddle at the head of his coffin, and dug him a grave in a stately spot—in the public park in the middle of the town, right by the fence. Our squadron rode there on horseback. The regimental staff and the divisional military commissar were also present. And at two in the afternoon, by the cathedral clock, our rickety little cannon fired the first shot. The cannon saluted Squadron Commander Trunov with its time-worn three-inch bore, did a full salute, and we carried the coffin to the open pit. The coffin was open, the clean midday sun lit the lanky corpse, lit his mouth filled with smashed teeth and his carefully polished boots, their heels placed together as at a drill.

"Fighters!" Regimental Captain Pugachov said, as he eyed the dead man and walked up to the edge of the pit. "Fighters!" he said, standing at attention, shaking with emotion. "We are burying Pashka Trunov, an international hero! We are according Pashka the final honor!"

Pugachov raised his eyes, burning with sleeplessness, to the sky and shouted out his speech about the dead fighters of the First Cavalry, that proud phalanx which pounds the anvil of future centuries with the hammer of history. Pugachov shouted out his speech loudly, clenched the hilt of his curved Chechen saber, and scuffed the earth with his tattered boots and their silver spurs. After his speech the orchestra played the "Internationale," and the Cossacks took leave of Pashka Trunov. The

1. First published in *Krasnaya nov* 2 (1925). See also Babel's article "What We Need Is More Men Like Trunov" on p. 251.

whole squadron leaped onto their horses and fired a volley into the air, our three-inch cannon hissed toothlessly a second time, and we sent three Cossacks to find a wreath. They whirled off at full gallop, firing as they rode and plunging from their saddles in a display of acrobatics, and brought back armfuls of red flowers. Pugachov scattered the flowers around the grave, and we stepped up to Trunov for the last kiss. I touched my lips on an unblemished patch of forehead crowned by his saddle, and then left to go for a walk through the town, through gothic Sokal, which lay in its blue dust and in Galicia's dejection.

A large square stretched to the left of the park, a square surrounded by ancient synagogues. Jews in long, torn coats were cursing and shoving each other on this square. Some of them, the Orthodox, were extolling the teachings of Adassia, the Rabbi of Belz, which led the Hasidim of the moderate school, students of Rabbi Iuda of Husyatyn, to attack them. The Jews were arguing about the Kabbala, and in their quarrel shouted the name of Elijah, Gaon of Vilna, the persecutor of the Hasidim.

Ignoring war and gunfire, the Hasidim were cursing the name of Elijah, the Grand Rabbi of Vilna,[2] and I, immersed in my sorrow over Trunov, joined in the jostling and yelled along with them to ease my pain, until I suddenly saw a Galician before me, sepulchral and gaunt as Don Quixote.

This Galician was wearing a white linen garment that reached down to his ankles. He was dressed as for burial or as for the Eucharist, and led a bedraggled little cow tied to a rope. Over its wide back darted the tiny wriggling head of a snake. On the snake's head was a teetering wide-brimmed hat made of village straw.[3] The pitiful little cow tagged along behind the Galician. He led her with importance, and his lanky body cut into the hot brilliance of the sky like a gallows.

He crossed the square with a stately stride and went into a crooked little alley seasoned with sickeningly thick smoke. In the charred little hovels, in beggarly kitchens, were Jewesses who looked like old Negro women, Jewesses with boundless breasts. The Galician walked past them and stopped at the end of the alley before the pediment of a shattered building.

There by the pediment, near a crooked white column, sat a gypsy blacksmith shoeing horses. The gypsy was pounding the horses' hooves with a hammer, shaking his greasy hair, whistling, and smiling. A few Cossacks with horses were standing around him. My Galician walked up to the blacksmith, gave him a dozen or so baked potatoes without a word, and turned and walked off, not looking up at anyone. I was about to follow him, but one of the Cossacks, waiting for his horse to be shod, stopped me. This Cossack's name was Seliverstov. He had left Makhno[4] some time ago and was serving in the Thirty-third Cavalry Regiment.

"Lyutov," he said, shaking my hand, "you can't keep from picking quarrels with everyone! You've got the devil in you! Why did you finish off Trunov this morning?"

And from the scraps of gossip he had heard, Seliverstov yelled foolish gibberish at me, about how that very morning I had given Trunov, my squadron

2. In the original: the High Priest (*pervosviashchennik*). —Ed.
3. In the original, marred by a typo (*probitaya*, stamped, rather than the correct *probritaya*, shaved), it is the Galician man whose grotesquely small head—"the wriggling tiny shaved head of a snake"—sits atop his "giant trunk" and is covered with an enormous peasant straw hat.—Ed.
4. See note 2 on p. 108.

commander, a good beating. Seliverstov hurled all kinds of reproaches at me, reproached me in front of all the Cossacks, but there wasn't a grain of truth in what he said. It was true that Trunov and I had argued that morning, because Trunov wasted so much time dawdling with the prisoners. He and I had argued, but Pashka Trunov is dead, he will no longer be judged in this world, and I would be the last to do so. I will tell you why we quarreled.

We had taken some men prisoner at dawn today near the train station. There were ten of them. They were in their underwear when we took them. A pile of clothes lay next to the Poles—it was a trick, so that we couldn't tell the officers from the regular men by their uniforms. They had taken off their clothes themselves, but this time Trunov decided to find out the truth.

"All officers, step forward!" he commanded, walking up to the prisoners and pulling out his revolver.

Trunov had already been wounded in the head that morning. His head was bandaged with a rag, and blood trickled from it like rain from a haystack.

"Officers! Own up!" he repeated, and began prodding the Poles with the butt of his revolver.

Suddenly a thin old man with yellow cheekbones, a drooping mustache, and a large, bare bony back, came forward.

"End of this war!" the old man said with incomprehensible delight. "All officers run away, end of this war!"

And the Pole held out his blue hands to Trunov.

"Five fingers," he said, sobbing, twisting his large, wilted hands from side to side. "I raising with these five fingers my family!"

The old man gasped, swayed, and broke into tears of delight. He fell on his knees before Trunov, but Trunov pushed him back with his saber.

"Your officers are dogs!" Trunov said. "Your officers threw their uniforms here, but I'm going to finish off whoever they fit! We're going to have a little fitting!"

And Trunov picked out an officer's cap from the pile of rags and put it on the old man's head.

"It fits," Trunov murmured, stepping up closer to him, "it fits." And he plunged his saber into the prisoner's gullet.

The old man fell, his legs twitching, and a foamy, coral-red stream poured from his neck. Then Andryushka Vosmiletov, with his sparkling earring and his round villager's neck, sidled up to the dying man. Andryushka unbuttoned the dying Pole's trousers, shook him lightly, and pulled the trousers off. He flung them onto his saddle, grabbed another two uniforms from the pile, and then trotted off, brandishing his whip. At that moment the sun came out from behind the clouds. It nimbly enveloped Andryushka's horse, its cheerful trot, the carefree swish of its docked tail. Andryushka rode along the path to the forest—our cavalry transport was in the forest, the carters of the transport yelling and whistling, and making signs to Vosmiletov like to a deaf man.

The Cossack was already halfway there when Trunov, suddenly falling to his knees, hoarsely yelled after him.

"Andrei!" he shouted, lowering his eyes to the ground. "Andrei!" he repeated without looking up. "Our Soviet Republic is still alive, it's too early to be dealing out her property! Bring back those rags, Andrei!"

But Vosmiletov didn't even turn around. He rode at his amazing Cossack trot, his horse pertly swatting its tail, as if to shoo us away.

"Treason!" Trunov mumbled in disbelief. "Treason!" he said, quickly shouldering his gun and shooting, missing in his haste. This time Andrei stopped. He turned his horse toward us, bouncing on his saddle like a woman, his face red and angry, his legs jerking.

"Listen, countryman!" he yelled, riding closer, and immediately calming down at the sound of his own deep and powerful voice. "I should knock you to Kingdom Come to where your you-know-what mother is! Here you've caught a dozen Poles, and make a big song-and-dance of it! We've taken hundreds and didn't come running for your help! If you're a worker, then do your job!"

Andryushka threw the trousers and the two uniforms off his saddle, snorted, turned away from the squadron commander, and came over to help me draw up a list of the remaining prisoners. He loafed about and snorted unusually loudly. The prisoners howled and ran away from him. He ran after them and gathered them under his arms, the way a hunter grips an armful of reeds and pushes them back to see a flock of birds flying to the river at dawn.

Dealing with the prisoners, I exhausted my repertoire of curses, and somehow managed to write up eight of the men, the numbers of their units, the type of gun they carried, and moved on to the ninth prisoner. The ninth was a young man who looked like a German acrobat from a good circus, a young man with a white, German chest, sideburns, a tricot undershirt, and a pair of long woolen drawers. He turned the nipples on his high chest toward me, threw back his sweaty blond hair, and told me the number of his unit. Andryushka grabbed him by his drawers and sternly asked him, "Where did you get those?"

"My mama knitted them," the prisoner answered, suddenly tottering.

"She's a great knitter, that mama of yours," Andryushka said, looking more closely at the drawers, and ran his fingertips over the Pole's neat nails. "Yes, a great knitter—us, we never got to wear nothing like that."

He felt the woolen drawers again and took the ninth man by the hand in order to take him over to the other prisoners who were already on my list. But at that moment I saw Trunov creeping out from behind a mound. Blood was trickling from his head like rain from a haystack and the dirty rag had come undone and was hanging down. He crawled on his stomach holding his carbine in his hands. It was a Japanese carbine, lacquered and with a powerful shot. From a distance of twenty paces, Pashka shot the young Pole's skull to pieces and his brains spattered onto my hands. Trunov ejected the empty cartridges from his carbine and came over to me.

"Cross that one off," he said, pointing at my list.

"I'm not crossing him off," I answered, quaking. "From what I see, Trotsky's orders don't apply to you!"

"Cross that one off the list!" Trunov repeated, pressing his black finger down onto the paper.

"I'm not crossing him off!" I yelled with all my might. "There were ten of them, now there are eight—back at headquarters, Trunov, they're not going to let you get away with this!"

"At headquarters they'll chalk it up to the rotten life we live," Trunov said, coming up to me, all tattered, hoarse, and covered in soot. But then he stopped, raised his blood-drenched face to the sky, and said with bitter reproach, "Buzz, buzz! And there comes another one buzzing!"

And Trunov pointed to four dots in the sky, four bombers that came floating out from behind the shining, swanlike clouds. These were machines from the air squadron of Major Fauntleroy,[3] large, armored machines.

"To horse!" the platoon commanders yelled when they saw the airplanes, and took the squadron at a fast trot into the woods. But Trunov did not ride with his squadron. He stayed back at the station building, huddled silently against the wall. Andryushka Vosmiletov and two machine-gunners, two barefoot fellows in crimson breeches, stood next to him, increasingly anxious.

"Run for it, boys!" Trunov said to them, and the blood began to drain from his face. "Here's a message to Pugachov from me."

And Trunov scrawled gigantic peasant letters on a crookedly torn piece of paper.

"As I have to perish today," he wrote, "I see it my duty to add two dead toward my possible shooting down of the enemy, and at the same time I am handing over my command to Platoon Commander Semyon Golov."

He sealed the letter, sat down on the ground, and took off his boots with great difficulty.

"For you," he said, handing the machine-gunners the message and his boots. "These boots are new."

"Good luck to you, Commander," the machine-gunners muttered back to him, shifting from one foot to the other, hesitating to leave.

"And good luck to you too," Trunov said, "whatever happens." And he went over to the machine guns that stood on a mound by the station hut. Andryushka Vosmiletov, the rag looter, was waiting for him there.

"Yes, whatever happens," Trunov said to him, and aimed his machine gun. "So you're staying with me, Andryushka?"

"Jesus Christ!" Andryushka answered, terrified, started sobbing, went white, and burst out laughing. "Damned Mother of Lord Jesus Christ!"

And he aimed the second machine gun at the airplanes.

The airplanes came flying over the station in tighter circles, rattled fussily high in the air, plunged, drew arcs, and the sun rested its pink rays on the sparkle of their wings.

In the meantime we, the Fourth Squadron, sat in the forest. There, in the forest, we awaited the outcome of the unequal battle between Pashka Trunov and Major Reginald Fauntleroy of the American forces. The major and three of his bombers proved their ability in this battle. They descended to three hundred meters, and first shot Andryushka and then Trunov. None of the rounds our men fired did the Americans any harm. The airplanes turned and flew away without even noticing our squadron hidden in the forest. And that was why, after waiting for half an hour, we were able to go pick up the bodies. Andryushka Vosmiletov's body was taken by two of his kinsmen who were serving in our squadron, and we took Trunov, our deceased squadron commander, to the gothic

---

3. Cedric E. Fauntleroy, also known as Cedric Earl Faunt Le Roy, World War I combat pilot who commanded the Kosciuszko Squadron of American volunteer pilots, who fought on the Polish side in the Polish-Soviet War. —Ed.

town of Sokal and buried him there in a stately spot—in a flower bed, in the public park in the middle of the town.

Ivan and Ivan[1]

Deacon Aggeyev had deserted from the front twice. For this he had been sent to Moscow's "regiment of the branded." Sergey Sergeyevich Kamenev,[2] the commander in chief, had inspected this regiment at Mozhaysk before it was to be sent to the front.

"I have no use for them," the commander in chief had said. "Send them back to Moscow to clean latrines."

In Moscow the branded regiment was somehow absorbed into an infantry company. The deacon also ended up in it. He arrived at the Polish front, where he claimed to be deaf. Barsutsky, the medical assistant from the first-aid detachment, after going back and forth with him for a week, was amazed at the deacon's obstinacy.

"To hell with that deaf man!" Barsutsky said to Soychenko, the medical orderly. "Go see if you can get a cart from the cavalry transport, we'll send the deacon to Rovno for a checkup."

Soychenko went to the transport and got three carts. Akinfiev was the driver of the first cart.

"Ivan," Soychenko said to him, "you're going to take the deaf man to Rovno."

"Take him I can," Akinfiev answered.

"Be sure to get me a receipt."

"Will do," Akinfiev said. "And what was it that caused it, this deafness of his?"

"To save his own goods and chattels a man will gladly set fire to another man's hide," Soychenko, the medical orderly, said. "That's what caused it. He's a damn freemason, that's what he is, not deaf!"

"Take him I can," Akinfiev repeated, and drove off after the other carts.

Three carts pulled up in front of the first-aid station. In the first cart sat a nurse who was being transferred to the rear lines, the second cart had been brought for a Cossack with an inflamed kidney, and in the third cart sat Ivan Aggeyev, the deacon.

Having arranged everything, Soychenko called the medical assistant.

"There goes that damn freemason," he said. "I'm putting him on the Revolutionary Tribunal cart[3] against receipt. They'll be off any minute now."

Barsutsky looked out the window, saw the carts, and went running out of the house, red-faced and hatless.

"Hey, I know you're going to cut his throat!" he yelled to Ivan Akinfiev. "I want the deacon in another cart!"

"Wherever you put him," the Cossacks standing nearby said, laughing, "our Ivan's going to get him."

---

1. First published in *Russky sovremennik* 1 (1924) under the title "Ivany" (Ivans). —*Ed.*
2. Sergey Sergeyevich Kamenev (1881–1936), commander in chief of the Eastern Front.
3. The Revolutionary Tribunals were the Red Army's courts martial.

Ivan Akinfiev, whip in hand, was also standing there next to his horses. "Greetings, Comrade Medical Assistant," he said politely, taking off his cap.

"Greetings, my friend," Barsutsky answered. "You're going to have to put the deacon in another cart, you wild beast!"

"It would interest me to know," Akinfiev began in a whiny voice, and his upper lip shivered, slid up, and began quivering over his dazzling teeth, "it would interest me to know, if this is right behavior or behavior that is not right, that when the enemy is tormenting us unbelievably, when the enemy is pounding our last breath out of us, when the enemy is clinging to our legs like a lead weight and tying our hands with snakes, is it correct behavior for us to clog our ears at such a deadly hour?"

"Our Ivan thinks like a commissar!" Korotkov, the driver of the first cart, shouted.

"So what if he thinks like a commissar!" Barsutsky muttered, and turned away. "We all do. But we have to stick to the rules."

"But our deaf friend, he can hear perfectly well!" Akinfiev suddenly interrupted. He twirled his whip with his fat fingers, laughed, and winked at the deacon. The deacon sat on the cart, his large shoulders drooping, his head trembling.

"Well then, go with God!" the medical assistant yelled in desperation. "I hold you responsible, Ivan!"

"I'll gladly be held responsible," Ivan Akinfiev said slowly, and lowered his head. "Make yourself comfortable," he said to the deacon, without looking back at him. "Make yourself even more comfortable," he repeated, and took the reins in his hands.

The carts formed a line and hurried off one after the other along the high road. Korotkov drove in front and Akinfiev at the back, whistling a tune and waving the reins. They rode this way some fifteen versts, but as evening fell they came up against a sudden enemy attack.

On that day, July 22, the Poles in a swift maneuver had mangled the rear lines of our army, stormed the shtetl of Kozin, and had taken prisoner many of our fighters of the Eleventh Division. The squadrons of the Sixth Division rushed off to Kozin to counterattack the enemy. The lightning maneuvers of the units threw the cavalry transport into turmoil, and the Revolutionary Tribunal carts rolled through the raging throes of battle for two days and nights, and it was only on the third night that they came out onto the road along which the rearguard staff was retreating. It was on this road at midnight where I ran into the three carts.

Numb with despair, I ran into them after the battle at Khotin. In the battle at Khotin my horse had been killed. After I lost him, I climbed onto an ambulance cart, and gathered up wounded men until evening. Then all the able-bodied men were kicked off the ambulance cart, and I was left behind near a destroyed hut. Night came galloping toward me on swift steeds. The wailing of the transport carts deafened the universe; on the earth enveloped by screams the roads faded away. Stars slithered out of the cool gut of the sky, and on the horizon abandoned villages flared up. With my saddle on my shoulders I walked along a torn-up field path, stopping by a bend to answer the call of nature. Relieved, I buttoned myself up, but suddenly felt droplets falling on my hand. I switched on my flashlight, turned around, and saw lying on the ground the body of a Pole, drenched in my urine. A notebook and scraps of Pilsudski's proclamation[4] lay next to the corpse. The Pole's notebook had a list of his expenses, a schedule of performances at the Krakow Dramatic Theater, and an entry indicating the birthday of a woman by the name of Marie-Louisa. I picked up Pilsudski's proclamation, wiped the stinking liquid from my unknown brother's skull, and walked on, bent under the weight of my saddle.

At that moment, there was a groaning of wheels close by.

"Halt!" I yelled. "Who goes there?"

Night came galloping toward me on swift steeds, flames danced on the horizon.

"We're from the Revolutionary Tribunal," a voice smothered by darkness called back.

I rushed forward and ran right into the cart.

"They killed my horse!" I said loudly. "His name was Lavrik."

No one answered. I climbed onto the cart, put the saddle under my head, fell asleep, and slept till dawn, warmed by the rotting hay and the body of Ivan Akinfiev, my chance neighbor. In the morning, the Cossack woke up later than I did.

"Thank God it's light enough to see again," he said, took his revolver out from under his little trunk, and fired a shot next to the deacon's ear. The deacon was sitting right in front of us, driving the horses. Airy gray hair fluttered over his large, balding skull. Akinfiev fired another shot next to the deacon's other ear, and slipped the revolver back into its holster.

"Good day to you, Ivan!" he said to the deacon, grunting as he pulled on his boots. "So we'll grab a bite, huh?"

"Hey!" I yelled. "What the hell d'you think you're doing?"

"Not enough, that's what I'm doing!" Akinfiev answered, unpacking the food. "It's the third day now he's been pretending."

Then Korotkov, who I knew from the Thirty-first Regiment, yelled back from the first cart, telling me the whole story of the deacon from the beginning. Akinfiev listened carefully, cupping his ear, and then from under his saddle pulled out a roasted leg of ox. It was wrapped in a sackcloth and had straw all over it.

The deacon climbed over to us from the box, carved off a slice of green meat with his knife, and gave everyone a piece. After breakfast, Akinfiev wrapped the leg of ox in the sackcloth and slid it into the hay.

"Ivan," he said to Deacon Aggeyev, "let's drive out the devil. We have to stop anyway, since the horses need water."

He took a medicine bottle out of his pocket and a Tarnovsky syringe,[5] and gave them to the deacon. They climbed off the cart and walked about twenty paces into the field.

"Nurse!" Korotkov yelled from the first cart. "Adjust your eyes for distance, and you'll be dazzled by Akinfiev's endowment!"

"I you-know-what you and your endowments," the woman muttered, and turned away.

4. See note 4 on p. 97.
5. A device for treating syphilis.

Akinfiev pulled up his shirt. The deacon knelt in front of him and gave him his injection. Then he wiped the syringe with a rag and held it up to the light. Akinfiev pulled his trousers up. He waited a moment, went behind the deacon, and fired another shot right next to his ear.

"My humblest thanks, Ivan," he said, buttoning up his trousers.

The deacon laid the medicine bottle on the grass and got up from his knees. His airy hair flew up.

"I will answer to a higher judge," he said dully. "You are not above me, Ivan."

"Nowadays everyone judges everyone else," the driver of the second cart, who looked like a boisterous little hunchback, interrupted. "They even sentence you to death, just like that!"

"Or even better," Deacon Aggeyev said, straightening up, "kill me, Ivan."

"Don't talk nonsense, Deacon!" Korotkov, whom I knew from before, said, coming up to him. "You should realize what kind of man you're riding with here. A lesser man would have shot you down like a duck, you wouldn't have had time to quack, yet he's trying to fish the truth out of you, and teach you a thing or two, you defrocked cleric!"

"Or even better," the deacon repeated obstinately, stepping forward, "kill me, Ivan."

"As it is, you'll kill yourself, you bastard," Akinfiev answered, going white and breaking into a lisp. "You're digging your own pit and burying yourself in it!"

Akinfiev waved his arms, tore his collar open, and fell down on the ground in a fit.

"O my dear little sweetheart!" he yelled wildly, and threw sand into his face. "O my bittersweet darling, my sweet darling Soviet power!"

"Ivan," Korotkov said, coming up to him, tenderly laying his hand on his shoulder. "Don't beat yourself, my dear friend, don't be sad. Come, we have to go now."

Korotkov filled his mouth with water and spat it into Akinfiev's face, and then carried him over to the cart. The deacon sat on the box again, and we drove off.

There were no more than two versts left to the shtetl of Verba. Countless transport carts had crowded into the town that morning. They were from the Eleventh, the Fourteenth, and the Fourth Divisions. Jews in waistcoats, with raised shoulders, stood in their doorways like bedraggled birds. Cossacks went from yard to yard collecting rags and eating unripe plums. The moment we arrived, Akinfiev curled up on the hay and fell asleep, and I took a blanket from his cart and went to look for some shade to lie down in. But the fields on both sides of the road were covered with excrement. A bearded muzhik in copper-rimmed spectacles and a Tyrolean hat was sitting by the wayside reading a newspaper. He waved to me and said, "We call ourselves human, but we make more filth than the jackals! One is ashamed to face the earth!"

And he turned away and went back to reading his newspaper through his large spectacles.

I headed for the forest to the left, and saw the deacon approaching me.

"Where are you off to, countryman?" Korotkov yelled to him from the first cart.

"To relieve myself," the deacon mumbled. He grabbed my hand, and kissed it. "You are a fine gentleman," he whispered with a grimace, shuddering and gasping for air. "I beg you, whenever you have a free moment, to write a letter to the town of Kasimov, so my wife can mourn for me."

"Are you deaf, Father Deacon, or not?" I shouted into his face.

"Excuse me?" he said. "Excuse me?" And he cupped his ear.

"Are you deaf, Aggeyev, or not?"

"That's exactly it, deaf!" he quickly said. "Three days ago I could hear perfectly well, but Comrade Akinfiev crippled my hearing with a shot. He was supposed to deliver me to Rovno, Comrade Akinfiev was, but I really doubt he'll deliver me there."

And the deacon fell to his knees and crawled headfirst between the carts, completely entangled in his disheveled, priestly hair. Then he got up from his knees, pulled himself free from in between the carts, and went over to Korotkov, who gave him some tobacco. They rolled cigarettes and lit them for each other.

"That's better," Korotkov said, and made some space next to him.

The deacon sat down, and both were silent.

Then Akinfiev woke up. He rolled the leg of ox out of the sackcloth, carved off a slice of green meat with his knife, and gave everyone a piece. At the sight of the festering meat I felt overcome by weakness and desperation, and gave my piece back.

"Farewell, boys!" I said. "Good luck to you all!"

"Farewell," Korotkov said.

I took my saddle from the cart and left. As I walked off, I heard the endless muttering of Akinfiev.

"Ivan, you made a big mistake, my friend," he was saying to the deacon. "You should have trembled at my name, but you just got into my cart without a second thought. You could still have escaped before you ran into me, but now I'm going to hurt you, Ivan, you can bet on it, I'm really going to hurt you!"

The Continuation of
the Story of a Horse[1]

Four months ago, Savitsky, our former division commander, took away the white stallion belonging to Khlebnikov, commander of the First Squadron. Khlebnikov had left the army shortly after, and today Savitsky received a letter from him.

Khlebnikov to Savitsky

And no anger upon the Budyonny army can I have longer, my sufferings in that army I understand and keep within my heart purer than anything holy. But to you, Comrade Savitsky, as an international hero, the working masses of Vitebsk, where I am the chairman of the District Revolutionary Committee, send the proletarian cry: "Give us

---

1. First published in *Krasnaya nov* 3 (1924) with the title "Timoshenko and Melnikov" and the dateline "Galicia, September 1920." —*Ed.*

World Revolution!'" And we hope that that white stallion will trot beneath you on soft paths for many a year to come in aid of Freedom so beloved by all, and the Brother Republics in which we must keep a sharp eye out for the provincial authorities and the district units in an adminis- trative respect. . . .

Savitsky to Khlebnikov

My true and dear Comrade Khlebnikov,

Which letter you wrote me is very commendable for the Common Cause, all the more after your foolishness when the good of your own hide made your eyes blind and you de-joined our Communist Party of the Bolsheviks. Our Communist Party, Comrade Khlebnikov, is an iron column of fighters sacrificing their blood in the front lines, and when blood flows from iron, then it is no joke, Comrade, but victory or death. The same goes for the Common Cause, the dawn of which I do not expect to see because the fighting is heavy and I have to change commanding officers every two weeks. Thirty days I have been fighting in the rear guard, covering the retreat of the invincible First Red Cav- alry, and finding myself facing powerful gunfire from airplanes and artillery. Tardy was killed, Likhmanikov was killed, Gulevoy was killed, Trunov was killed, and the white stallion is no longer under me, so with the change in our fortunes of war, Comrade Khlebnikov, do not expect to see your beloved Division Commander Savitsky ever again. To tell you the truth, we shall meet again in the Kingdom of Heaven, although, from what people say, the old man up there in heaven isn't running a kingdom, but an all-out whorehouse, and as it is we have enough clap down here on earth—so, who knows, we might not get to see each other after all. Farewell, Comrade Khlebnikov.

The Widow[1]

Shevelyov, the regimental captain, is dying in an ambulance cart. A woman is sitting at his feet. Night, pierced by the flashes of the cannon- ade, is stooping over the dying man. Lyovka, the division commander's driver, is warming up food in a pot. Lyovka's forelock is hanging over the fire, the hobbled horses are crackling in the bushes. Lyovka is stirring the pot with a twig and talking to Shevelyov, who is stretched out in the ambulance cart.

"I worked in the town of Temryuk, Comrade, as a circus rider and also as a lightweight wrestler. The women in a small town like that get very bored, so when the little ladies saw me, all the walls came tumbling down. 'Lev Gavrilich,' they'd say to me, 'surely you won't turn down a lit- tle à la carte appetizer—you won't find it a waste of your time.' So I went with one of them to a tavern. We order two portions of veal, we order a jug of vodka, we sit there nice and quiet, we drink, I look, and what do I see? Some sort of gentleman bustling over toward me, nicely dressed,

---

1. First published in the supplement to *Izvestia* (Odessa), July 15, 1923, with the title "Shevelyov" and the dateline "Galicia, August 1920." —*Ed.*

clean, but I notice that he is full of himself, not to mention that he was two sheets to the wind.

"'If you will pardon me,' he says to me, 'what, if I may ask, is your nationality?'

"'For what reason are you touching me about my nationality when I am in the company of a lady?' I ask him.

"And he: 'You? You are an athlete?' he says. 'In French wrestling they'd finish you off in the twinkle of an eye. Show me your nationali—' Yet I, believe it or not, still don't catch what's going on.

"So I ask him, 'Why do you—I don't even know your name—why do you try to provoke the kind of misunderstanding where one man or the other will have to lose his life, in other words, lie flat on his back awaiting his last breath?'"

"Lie flat on his back awaiting his last breath!" Lyovka repeats enthusiastically, stretching his arms up to the sky, letting the night envelop him like an aura. The tireless wind, the clean wind of the night, sings, fills itself with sound, and gently rocks the soul. The stars, blazing in the darkness like wedding rings, fall on Lyovka, become entangled in his hair, and expire on his tousled head.

"Lyovka, come here," Shevelyov suddenly whispers to him with blue lips. "The gold I have is for Sashka," the wounded man whispers. "The rings, the harness—everything's hers. We did our best to get by, I want to reward her. My clothes, my underwear, my medal for selfless heroism, are for my mother on the Terek. Send them to her with a letter and write in the letter: The regimental captain sends his regards, and don't cry. The house is yours, old woman, enjoy it. If anyone lays a finger on you, go straight to Budyonny and tell him, 'I'm Shevelyov's mama!' My horse, Abramka, I offer to the regiment, I am offering the horse in memory of my soul."

"Don't worry, I'll see to the horse," Lyovka mumbles. "Sashka!" he yells to the woman, waving to her. "You heard what he said? Swear before him—will you be sure to give the old woman what's hers or won't you?"

"I you-know-what the old woman!" Sashka says, and walks off into the bushes, holding her head high like a blind woman.

"Will you give her her miserable share?" Lyovka asks, catching up with her and grabbing her by the throat. "Say it here in front of him!"

"I'll give it to her, let me go!"

And then, having forced the declaration out of her, Lyovka grabbed the pot from the fire and began pouring soup into the dying man's rigid mouth. Cabbage soup trickled down Shevelyov's face, the spoon clanked against his sparkling, dead teeth, and bullets sang with growing mournfulness and force through the dense expanses of the night.

"They're shooting with rifles, the bastards," Lyovka said.

"The damn lackeys!" Shevelyov answered. "They're ripping open our right flank with their machine guns."

And Shevelyov, closing his eyes, stately as a corpse on a slab, listened to the battle with his large, waxen ears. Next to him, Lyovka was chewing meat, crunching and panting. When he had finished, Lyovka licked his lips and pulled Sashka into a ditch.

"Sash," he said, trembling, burping, his hands fidgeting. "Sash, as the Lord is my witness, we're covered in vice like yard dogs with lice. You only live once and then you die! Let me have you, Sash—I'll serve you, even if it's with my blood! His time's up, Sash, but the Lord has plenty more days in store for us!"

They sat down in the tall grass. The wavering moon crept from behind the clouds and stopped over Sashka's bare knee.

"You're warming each other," Shevelyov mumbled, "but it looks like the Fourteenth Division has been routed."

Lyovka crunched and panted in the bushes. The misty moon loitered in the sky like a beggar woman. Distant gunfire floated in the air. Feather grass rustled on the troubled earth onto which August stars fell.

Then Sashka returned to her previous place. She changed the wounded man's bandages and raised the flashlight over the festering wound.

"By tomorrow you'll be gone," Sashka said, wiping the cold sweat off Shevelyov. "By tomorrow you'll be gone. Death's already in your guts."

At that moment a heavy, many-voiced blast hit the earth. Four fresh enemy brigades, sent into battle under a unified command, had fired their first shell at Busk, lighting up the Bug watershed and severing our communications. Obedient blazes rose on the horizon, and heavy birds of cannon fire soared up from the flames. Busk was burning and Lyovka sped through the forest with the rattling cart of the commander of Division Six. He gripped the red reins tightly; the lacquered wheels banged against tree stumps. Shevelyov's ambulance cart came flying behind, Sashka checking the horses, which were straining at their harnesses.

They came to a clearing in the forest where there was a first-aid station. Lyovka unharnessed the horses and set out for the medical officer to ask for a horse blanket. He walked through the forest, which was filled with carts. Nurses' bodies jutted out from under their carts, timid dawn trudged over the soldiers' sheepskins. The sleeping men's boots lolled in a jumble, their pupils pointed to the sky, the black pits of their mouths askew.

The medical officer did have a horse blanket. Lyovka returned to Shevelyov, kissed his forehead, and pulled the blanket over his head. Then Sashka came up to the cart. She had knotted her kerchief under her chin and shaken the straw out of her dress.

"Pavlik," she said. "Jesus Christ in Heaven." And she lay herself against the dead man, covering him with her massive body.

"Her grief's killing her," Lyovka said. "Say what you want, she had it good with him. Now she'll have to take on the whole squadron again. It's tough."

And he drove off to Busk, where the headquarters of the Sixth Cavalry Division had been set up.

There, about ten versts from town, the battle against the Savinkov Cossacks was raging. The traitors were fighting us under the command of Cossack Captain Yakovlev, who had gone over to the Poles. They fought with courage. It was the second day our division commander was out with the troops, and as Lyovka did not find him at the headquarters, he went back to his hut, cleaned his horses, poured water over the wheels of his cart, and lay down to sleep on the threshing floor in the shed. The shed was filled with fresh hay, as arousing as perfume. Lyovka slept himself out, and then sat down to eat. His landlady boiled him some potatoes, which she doused in buttermilk. Lyovka was still sitting at the table when the funereal wail of trumpets and the clatter of many hooves resounded in the street. A squadron with bugles and banners rode along the winding Galician street. Shevelyov's body, covered with flags, was lying on a gun carriage. Sashka was riding behind the coffin on Shevelyov's stallion. A Cossack song came drifting from the back rows.

The squadron marched along the main street and turned toward the river. Lyovka, barefoot and without a cap, ran after the marching detachment and grabbed the reins of the squadron commander's horse.

Neither the division commander, who had stopped by the crossroads to salute the dead commander, nor his staff could hear what Lyovka was saying to the squadron commander.

"Drawers . . . mother on the Terek . . ." came wafting over to us in fragments on the breeze. Lyovka was shouting incoherently.

The squadron commander, without listening any further, freed his reins and pointed at Sashka. The woman shook her head and rode on. Lyovka jumped onto her horse behind her, grabbed her by the hair, pulled her head back, and slammed his fist into her face. Sashka wiped the blood away with the hem of her skirt and rode on. Lyovka slipped off her saddle, shook his forelock out of his face, and tied his red scarf around his hips. And the howling bugles led the squadron to the sparkling shore of the River Bug.

Lyovka came back to us later that day, his eyes glittering, and shouted, "I gave it to her! 'When the time comes,' she says, 'I'll send it to his mother. I won't forget him,' she says, 'I'll remember him.' 'You'd better remember him, you evil snake! If you forget, we'll come around and remind you! And if you forget a second time, we'll come around and remind you a second time!' "

Zamosc[1]

The division commander and his staff were lying on a harvested field about three versts from Zamosc. The troops were going to attack the town that evening. Our orders were that we were to spend the night in Zamosc, and the division commander was waiting for a report of victory.

It was raining. Wind and darkness blew over the sodden earth. Stars were extinguished in the swelling ink of the clouds. Exhausted horses sighed and stamped their hooves in the darkness. We had nothing to give them to eat. I tied my horse's reins to my foot, wrapped myself in my cloak, and lay down in a waterlogged pit. The wet earth wrapped me in its comforting sepulchral embrace. The mare tugged at her reins, pulling at my leg. She found a tuft of grass and began nibbling at it. I fell asleep and dreamed of a threshing floor covered with hay. The dusty gold of threshed corn droned over it. Sheaves of wheat flew into the sky, the July day turned into evening, and the thickets of the sunset arched back over the village.

1. First published in *Krasnaya nov* 3 (1924) with the dateline "Sokal, September 1920." —*Ed.*

I lay stretched out on my silent bed of hay, and the hay caressing the nape of my neck drove me out of my mind. Then the barn doors opened with a whistle. A woman in a ball gown came up to me. She released one of her breasts from the black lace of her bodice and carefully offered it to me, like a wet nurse about to suckle an infant. She laid her breast on mine. An agonizing warmth shook the foundations of my soul, and drops of sweat—living, flowing sweat—seethed between our nipples.

"Margot!" I wanted to shout. "The earth is dragging me away with the rope of its wretchedness like a stubborn dog, and yet I have managed to see you again!"

I wanted to shout these words, but my jaws, clamped shut by a sudden frost, would not unclench.

Then the woman moved away from me and fell to her knees.

"Lord Jesus," she said, "take unto Thee the soul of Thy departed slave!" She pressed two worn five-kopeck coins onto my lids and stuffed fragrant hay into the opening of my mouth. A moan tried in vain to flutter through my clenched jaws; my expiring pupils slowly rolled beneath the copper coins; I could not unclasp my hands, and . . . I awoke.

A muzhik with a tangled beard was lying in front of me. He held a rifle in his hands. My horse's back cut the sky like a black crossbeam. The reins gripped my foot in a tight noose, pulling it upward.

"You fell asleep, countryman," the muzhik said, and smiled with nocturnal, sleepless eyes. "That horse has dragged you a good half verst!"

I untied the reins and got up. Blood was trickling down my face, slashed by thistles.

Right there, not two paces away from me, lay the front line. I could see the chimneys of Zamosc, the thievish lights in the ravines of its ghetto, and the watchtower with its shattered lantern. The damp sunrise poured down on us like waves of chloroform. Green rockets soared over the Polish camp. They flashed in the air, came showering down like roses beneath the moon, and expired.

And in the silence I heard the distant breath of a moan. The smoke of a furtive murder encircled us.

"They're killing someone," I said. "Who is it they're killing?"

"The Pole's on a rampage," the muzhik told me. "The Pole is slashing the Yids' throats."

The muzhik moved the rifle from his right hand to his left. His beard had slid completely to one side. He looked at me fondly. "These nights on the front line are long," he said. "There's no end to these nights. One itches all over to talk to someone, but where d'you find this someone?"

The muzhik passed me his cigarette for me to light mine.

"It's all the fault of those Yids," he said. "They try to please everybody. After the war there'll be hardly any of them left. How many Yids you reckon there's in the world?"

"Around ten million," I answered, and began to bridle my horse.

"There'll be two hundred thousand of them left!" the muzhik yelled, grabbing me by the arm, afraid that I was about to leave. But I climbed onto my saddle and galloped off in the direction of our headquarters.

The division commander was preparing to ride off. The orderlies were standing at attention before him, dozing on their feet. Squadrons of dismounted horsemen crept over wet hillocks.

"They've turned the screws on us," the division commander whispered, and rode off.

We followed him along the road to Sitaniec.

It began raining again. Dead mice floated down the roads. Autumn surrounded our hearts with traps. Trees, upright naked corpses, stood swaying at crossroads.

We arrived in Sitaniec in the morning. I was with Volkov, the staff quartermaster. He found us a hut at the edge of the village.

"Wine," I told the mistress of the house. "Wine, meat, and bread!"

The old woman sat down on the floor and fed the calf she had hidden under her bed.

"*Nic niema*,"[2] she answered indifferently, "and I don't remember a time when there ever was anything."

I sat at the table, took off my revolver, and fell asleep. A quarter of an hour later I opened my eyes and saw Volkov hunched over the windowsill. He was writing a letter to his bride.

"Highly esteemed Valya," he wrote. "Do you remember me?"

I read the first line, and then took some matches out of my pocket and lit a pile of straw lying on the floor. Unfettered flames flashed up and came moving toward me. The old woman hurled herself chest-first onto the fire and extinguished it.

"What you doing, *Pan*?" the old woman gasped, staggering back in horror.

Volkov turned around and stared at her with his empty eyes, and went back to writing his letter.

"I'm going to burn you, old woman," I muttered, drowsily. "I'm going to burn you and that stolen calf of yours."

"*Czekaj!*"[3] she shouted in a high-pitched voice. She ran out into the hall and came back with a jug of milk and some bread.

We had barely eaten half the bread when we heard shots rattling outside in the yard. There were many shots. They went on rattling and got on our nerves. We finished the milk, and Volkov went out into the yard to see what was going on.

"I've saddled your horse," he called through the window. "They've shot mine full of holes. The Poles have set up their machine guns less than a hundred paces from here!"

So the two of us ended up with one horse. She barely managed to take us out of Sitaniec. I sat in the saddle, and Volkov climbed on behind.

Transport carts rolled, roared, and sank in the mud. The morning seeped out of us like chloroform seeping over a hospital table.

"You married, Lyutov?" Volkov suddenly said, sitting behind me.

"My wife left me," I answered, dozing off for a few seconds, and I dreamed that I was sleeping in a bed.

Silence.

Our horse totters.

"Two more versts and this mare will be finished," Volkov says, sitting behind me.

Silence.

"We've lost the campaign," Volkov mutters, and begins to snore.

"Yes," I say.

2. Polish: There is nothing.
3. Polish: Wait!

Treason[1]

Comrade Investigator Burdenko. Answering your question, my Party Membership Number is twenty-four zero-zero, issued to Nikita Balmashov by the Krasnodar Party Committee. My life history I would describe as domestic until 1914, as I worked on my father's fields, and I went from the fields into the ranks of the imperialists to defend Citizen Poincaré and the butchers of the German Revolution Ebert-Noske,[2] who, it looks like, were fast asleep one day and in their dreams saw how they could help St. Ivan, my Cossack village in the District of Kuban. And so the string kept unraveling all the way until Comrade Lenin, together with Comrade Trotsky, turned my beast of a bayonet to point it at new and better guts and paunches. From that time on I've been carrying number twenty-four zero-zero on the watchful tip of my bayonet, and I find it shameful and laughable to hear your words, Comrade Investigator Burdenko, this impossible sham about some unknown hospital in N. I neither fired at this hospital nor attacked it—I couldn't have. We were wounded, the three of us, in other words, Fighter Golovitsyn, Fighter Kustov, and me, not to mention that we had a fever in our bones and so didn't attack, but were crying, standing there in our hospital shirts out on the square among the free people of Jewish nationality! And as for the destruction of the three windowpanes, which we destroyed with an officer's revolver, I declare from the bottom of my heart that these windowpanes did not correspond to their purpose, as they were in the storeroom, which did not need them. And Dr. Yaveyn, seeing our bitter gunshot, only laughed with lots of chuckles, standing by the window of his hospital, and this too can be corroborated by the aforementioned free Jews of the shtetl of Kozin. As to Dr. Yaveyn, I also submit the following material, Comrade Investigator, that he laughed when we, the three wounded men, in other words Fighter Golovitsyn, Fighter Kustov, and me, initially presented ourselves for cure, and from his very first words, he informed us far too roughly, 'You, fighters, will each take a bath in the tub, and this very instant remove your weapons and clothes, as I'm worried they might be infectious—I want them out of here and dropped off at the storeroom!' And as Fighter Kustov saw a beast before him and not a man, he stepped forward with his broken leg and expressed himself, that the only people who need fear an infection from his sharp Kuban saber are the enemies of our Revolution, and Fighter Kustov also expressed an interest in knowing if at the storeroom one would find among the things there a Party Fighter or, on the contrary, someone from the partyless masses. And here Dr. Yaveyn obviously saw that we were well able to recognize treason. He turned his back and without another word and—again with lots of chuckles—sent us to the ward where we also went, limping with broken legs, waving our crippled arms, holding each other up, as the three of us are from the same Cossack village of St.

1. First published in *Izvestia* (Odessa), March 20, 1923. —*Ed.*
2. Raymond Poincaré (1860–1932), president of France, supported the Whites forces against the Bolsheviks in the Russian civil war. Friedrich Ebert (1871–1925), president of the Weimar Republic, and Gustav Noske (1868–1948), the Weimar Republic's Minister of Defense (1919–20), both Social Democrats, were instrumental in suppressing the Communist rebellion (Spartacist League) in Berlin in January 1919. Conflating the names of the two leaders into one Ebert-Noske was typical of Red Army soldiers exposed to primitive political propaganda. —*Ed.*

Ivan, in other words Fighter Golovitsyn, Fighter Kustov, and me, we have the selfsame fate, and he who has a ripped-off leg, he holds on to his comrade's arm, and he who is missing an arm, he leans on his comrade's shoulder! Following the order issued, we went to the ward where we expected to encounter Cultural and Educational Work and devotion to the Cause, but what did we see in the ward? We saw Red Army soldiers, only infantrymen, sitting on neat beds, playing checkers, and with them nurses of tall build, smooth, standing by the windows, fluttering their eyelashes. When we saw this, we stood there as if lightning had struck us.

"You're done with fighting, boys?" I shout to the wounded.

"We're done with fighting," the wounded answer, and they move their checkers made of bread pellets.

"Too soon," I tell the wounded, "too soon have you finished fighting, infantry, when the enemy walks on soft paws not fifteen versts from this town, and when you can read of our international situation in the *Krasny Kavalerist* newspaper, that it's one big disaster and that the horizon is full of black clouds!" But my words bounced off the heroic infantry like sheep dung from a regimental drum, and instead of a discussion the sisters of mercy led us off to some bunks and started all that drivel again about how we should hand in our weapons as if we had already been defeated! They agitated Kustov beyond words, and he began tearing at the wound on his left shoulder above his bleeding heart of a fighter and proletarian. Seeing his struggle, the nurses were quiet, but they only were quiet for the shortest time, and then again the partyless masses began making fun, and in the night the nurses sent volunteers ready to rip our clothes off us as we slept, or force us for Cultural and Educational Work to play theater roles in women's clothes, which is unseemly.

Unmerciful sisters! They tried more than once to trick us out of our clothes with sleeping powders, so that we started sleeping in shifts with one eye open, and we even went to the latrine in full uniform and with our revolvers. And suffering like this for a week and a day, so that we were already ranting and seeing visions, finally, waking on the accused morning of August 4, we noted on ourselves the following change: that we are lying there in shirts with numbers on them, like prisoners, without weapons and without the clothes sewn by our mothers, poor doddering old women from Kuban. And the sun, we see, is shining nice and bright, but the trench infantry, among who we three Red Cavalrymen are suffering, is hooliganizing us! And along with them the unmerciful sisters, who the night before gave us sleeping powders and now are wiggling their fresh breasts, bringing us trays with cococoa to drink, and milk enough in this cococoa to drown in! This whole frolicking merry-go-round makes the infantry bang their crutches on the ground so loud it's dreadful, and they pinch our bottoms like we're buyable females, yelling that Budyonny's First Cavalry has also finished fighting. But no, my curly-headed Comrades, you who have stuffed yourselves with such splendid paunches that rattle like machine guns in the night! Budyonny's First Cavalry has not yet finished fighting! So what we did was we excused ourselves as if we had to go answer a call of nature. Then the three of us went down into the courtyard and from the courtyard we went with our fevers and blue boils to Citizen Boyderman, the chairman of the Revolutionary Committee, without whom, Comrade Investigator Burdenko, it would never have come to this misunderstanding with the shooting—in other words, if it hadn't been for him, I mean if it hadn't been for the chairman of the Revolutionary Committee, who made us lose our senses completely. And even though we cannot present hard evidence about Citizen Boyderman, when we came in to the office of the chairman of the Revolutionary Committee, we noticed that he was a citizen of advanced years in a sheepskin coat, of Jewish nationality, sitting at the table, and the table is so full of papers that it is a terrible sight to see. And Citizen Boyderman's eyes dart first to one side, then to the other, and it is clear he has no idea what these papers are. These papers are a misery to him, even more so when unknown but deserving fighters come threatening, demanding rations, while one after the other local workers interrupt, informing him of the counterrevolution in the surrounding villages. And also regular workers suddenly appear who wish to get married at the Revolutionary Committee as soon as possible and without red tape. And we too announced with loud voices the incidents of treason at the hospital, but Citizen Boyderman only stared at us and his eyes darted again first to one side and then to the other, and he patted us on the shoulder, which already is not an Authority, and unworthy of an Authority! He didn't issue any resolution at all, and only announced, "Comrade Fighters, if you have compassion for the Soviet State, then leave these premises!" But we would not agree to do this, in other words, leave the premises, but demanded a full verification of his person, which, when he would not do that, we lost consciousness. And having lost consciousness, we went out onto the square in front of the hospital, where we disarmed the militia which was made up of one cavalry individual, and with tears in our eyes destroyed the three poor-quality windowpanes in the aforementioned storeroom. Dr. Yaveyn, during this unallowable action, made faces and chuckled, and all that at the very moment when four days later Comrade Kustov was to die of his illness!

In his short Red life, Comrade Kustov was endlessly distressed about treason, which one moment is winking at us from the window, the next is making fun of the coarse proletariat. But the proletariat, Comrades, knows full well how coarse treason is, and we are pained by that, our soul is burning, and its fire tears our bodily prison to pieces.

Treason, I tell you, Comrade Investigator Burdenko, grins at us from the window, treason creeps in its socks through our house, treason has flung its boots over its shoulders, so that the floorboards of the house it is about to ransack will not creak.

Czesniki[1]

The Sixth Division had gathered in the forest near the village of Czesniki and waited for the signal to attack. But Pavlichenko, commander of the

1. First published in *Krasnaya nov* 3 (1924). The Battle of Czesniki (or the Battle of Komarów) was the last large-scale battle fought by cavalries with cold steel. Although it suffered a major defeat, Budyonny's Cavalry Army was able to retreat while intact. Before the battle, Babel's Sixth Cavalry Division was stationed outside Zamosc, between Zamosc and Czesniki. —*Ed.*

Sixth Division, was waiting for the Second Brigade, and would not give the signal. So Voroshilov[2] rode up to the division commander and prodded his chest with the muzzle of his horse.

"We're dawdling, Division Commander," he said, "we're dawdling!"

"The Second Brigade is proceeding as you ordered at full trot to the place of engagement," Pavlichenko answered in a hollow voice.

"We're dawdling, Division Commander, we're dawdling!" Voroshilov repeated, tugging at his reins.

Pavlichenko took a step back.

"In the name of conscience," he shouted, wringing his clammy fingers, "in the name of conscience, do not rush me, Comrade Voroshilov."

"Do not rush me?" hissed Klim Voroshilov, the political representative of the Revolutionary War Council, closing his eyes. He sat on his horse, silent, his eyes closed, his lips moving. A Cossack wearing bast sandals and a bowler hat stared at him in amazement. The galloping squadrons went crashing through branches, roaring through the forest like the wind. Voroshilov combed his horse's mane with his Mauser.

"Army Commander!" he yelled, turning to Budyonny. "Say a few words to your troops before we ride! There he is, the Pole, standing on top of the hill like a pretty picture, laughing at you!"

As a matter of fact, we could see the Poles through our binoculars. The army staff jumped onto their horses and the Cossacks streamed toward Budyonny from all sides.

Ivan Akinfiev, the former vehicular driver of the Revolutionary Tribunal, rode past sitting sidesaddle, and prodded me with his stirrup.

"What? You're with the troops now, Ivan?" I called out to him. "You've got no ribs left!"

"I you-know-what these ribs," Akinfiev called back. "Let's hear what the man has to say!"

He rode on and pushed his way through right up to Budyonny.

Budyonny shuddered, and said in a quiet voice: "Men! Our situations . . . well, it's . . . bad. A bit more liveliness, men!"

"To Warsaw!" the Cossack in the bast sandals and the bowler hat yelled, his eyes wild, and he slashed the air with his saber.

"To Warsaw!" Voroshilov shouted, rearing his horse and vaulting into the center of the squadrons.

"Fighters and Commanders!" he shouted passionately. "In Moscow, our ancient capital, there rages a power never before seen! A government of workers and peasants, the first in the world, orders you, fighters and commanders, to attack the enemy and bring back victory!"

"Draw your sabers!" Pavlichenko sang out from far behind the army commander, and his fat crimson lips glistened foam-speckled through the ranks. Pavlichenko's red Cossack coat hung in tatters, his repulsive, meaty face was twisted. He saluted Voroshilov with the blade of his precious saber.

"In accordance with my duty to the revolutionary pledge," said the commander of division six, wheezing, his eyes darting around, "I hereby report to the Revolutionary War Council that the Second Invincible Cavalry Brigade is at the present time moving at a fast trot to the place of engagement!"

---

2. Kliment Yefremovich Voroshilov (1881–1969), a close associate of Stalin, cofounder with Budyonny of the First Cavalry Army and People's Commissar of Defense (1925–41). —Ed.

"Well, get on with it," Voroshilov answered, waving him away. He tugged at his reins and rode off, with Budyonny at his side. On their long-limbed chestnut mares they rode next to each other in identical military jackets and glittering silver-embroidered trousers. The fighters, whooping, flocked after them, and pale steel gleamed in the purulence of the autumn sun. But I did not hear solidarity in the howls of the Cossacks, and, waiting for the attack, I went into the forest, into its heart, to our provision station.

A wounded Red Army soldier lay there in a delirium, and Styopka Duplishchev, a young, dim-witted Cossack, was rubbing down Hurricane, the division commander's thoroughbred stallion, which was descended from Lyulyusha, the Rostov record holder. The wounded man was rambling, reminiscing about Shuya, about a heifer and some sort of flax strands. Duplishchev, to drown out the pitiful muttering, was singing a song about an orderly and a fat general's wife. He sang louder and louder, waving his currycomb and patting the horse. But he was interrupted by Sashka, puffy Sashka, the lady of all the squadrons. She rode up to Duplishchev and jumped off her horse.

"So we'll do it, or what?" Sashka said to him.

"Get out of here," the young Cossack answered, turning his back to her, and began plaiting ribbons into Hurricane's mane.

"You stick to your word, Styopka!" Sashka told him. "Or are you just a lump of boot wax?"

"Get out of here!" Styopka answered. "I stick to my word."

He plaited all the ribbons into the horse's mane, and suddenly turned to me in despair. "Just look at that! See how she tortures me, Kiril Vasilich? For a whole month already you wouldn't believe what I've had to put up with! Wherever I turn to, she's there, wherever I run to, she blocks my path, always wanting me to let the stallion have a go. But the division commander tells me every day, 'Styopka,' he tells me, 'with a stallion like this one, many will be coming to ask you to let the stallion have a go, but don't let him, not before he's four!' "

"I bet you you won't be letting anyone before he's fifteen," Sashka muttered, and turned away. "And when he's fifteen, you'll be drooling bubbles, for all I know!"[1]

She went over to her mare, tightened the saddle strap, and was about to ride off.

The spurs on her boots clattered, her lace stockings were full of straw and spattered with dirt, her monstrous breasts went swinging toward her back.

"And to think I brought a ruble with me," Sashka said to herself, shoving her spurred boot into the stirrup. "I brought it with me but now I'll have to take it away again."

She took out two fifty-kopeck coins, jingled them in her palm, and hid them again in her cleavage.

"So we'll do it, or what?" Duplishchev said, his eyes fixed on the silver, and he brought over the stallion.

Sashka went to a sloping place in the clearing and had her mare stand there.

---

1. In the original, Sashka's soliloquy conveys the sense that since she had allowed fifteen-year-old virgins to have sex with her, the fifteen-year-old Styopka, out of reciprocity, must allow her to mate her mare with his virginal stallion. —*Ed.*

"You'd be amazed, but you're the only one in these mudfields who's got a stallion," she said to Styopka, pushing Hurricane into position. "My mare's a frontline war horse, two years now she hasn't been humped, so I says to myself—why not get her some good blood?"

Sashka finished with the stallion, and then led her horse to the side.

"So, sweetie, we got our stuffing now," she whispered, kissing her mare's wet, skewbald lips from which slobbering strands of spittle hung. She rubbed her cheek against the mare's muzzle, and suddenly noticed the noise thudding through the forest.

"The Second Brigade's coming back," Sashka said sternly, turning to me. "We must go, Lyutov!"

"Coming back, not coming back, I don't give a damn!" Duplishchev shouted, the words getting stuck in his throat. "You've had your feast, now pay the priest!"

"My money's nice and fine where it is!" Sashka muttered, and leaped onto her mare.

I dashed after her, and we rode off in full gallop. Duplishchev's howl and the light thud of a gunshot rang out behind us.

"Just look at that!" the Cossack boy yelled as loudly as he could, running through the forest.

The wind hopped through the branches like a crazed rabbit, the Second Brigade went flying through the Galician oak trees, the placid dust of the cannonade rose above the earth as above a peaceful hut. And at a sign from the division commander, we launched our attack, the unforgettable attack on Czesniki.

After the Battle[1]

The story of my fight with Akinfiev is as follows:

On the thirty-first came the attack on Czesniki. The squadrons had gathered in the forest next to the village, and hurled themselves at the enemy at six in the evening. The enemy was waiting for us on a hill three versts away. We galloped the three versts on our totally exhausted horses, and when we got to the hill we saw a deadly wall of black uniforms and pale faces. They were Cossacks who had betrayed us at the beginning of the Polish Campaign and had been rounded up into a brigade by Cossack Captain Yakovlev. The Cossack captain formed his horsemen into a square formation, and waited with his saber unsheathed. A gold tooth flashed in his mouth and his black beard lay on his chest like an icon on the chest of a corpse. The enemy's machine guns fired at twenty paces; wounded men fell in our lines. We went trampling over them and hurled ourselves at the enemy, but his square formation did not waver, and we turned and ran.

So the Savinkov Cossacks gained a short-lived victory over the Sixth Division. They gained the victory because they did not turn their faces from the lava flow of our oncoming squadrons. The Cossack captain

1. First published in the illustrated weekly *Prozhektor* 20 (1924) with the dateline "Galicia, September 1920." —*Ed.*

stood firm that time, and we ran without reddening our sabers with the traitors' contemptible blood.

Five thousand men, our whole division, poured down the slope with no one in pursuit. The enemy stayed on the hill, unable to believe their illogical victory and muster their wits to set out in pursuit after us. That is why we survived and went bounding into the valley unharmed, where we were met by Vinogradov, our military commissar. Vinogradov was dashing about on his crazed horse trying to send the fleeing Cossacks back into battle.

"Lyutov!" he yelled when he saw me. "Get those fighters to turn around or I'll rip your soul out!"

Vinogradov pounded his tottering stallion with the butt of his Mauser, howled, and tried rounding up the men. I got away from him and rode up to Gulimov, a Kirghiz, who was galloping past.

"Gulimov! Get back up there!" I yelled to him. "Turn back your horse!"

"Turn back your own damn horse!" Gulimov yelled back. His eyes darted about thievishly and he fired a shot, singeing the hair above my ear.

"Turn your own horse back," Gulimov hissed, grabbed my shoulder with one hand, and tried unsheathing his saber with the other. The saber was jammed in its sheath, the Kirghiz shuddered and looked around. He held my shoulder tightly and brought his head closer and closer.

"Yours first," he whispered almost inaudibly, "and mine will follow." And he tapped me lightly on the chest with the blade of his saber, which he had managed to unsheathe.

I felt a wave of nausea from death's closeness and its tight grip. With the palm of my hand I pushed away the Kirghiz's face, hot as a stone in the sun, and scratched it with all my might. Warm blood rippled under my nails, tickling them. I rode away from Gulimov, out of breath as after a long journey. My horse, my tormented friend, trotted slowly. I rode without looking where I was going, I rode without turning around, until I came across Vorobyov, the commander of the First Squadron. Vorobyov was looking for his quartermasters and couldn't find them. He and I made our way to Czesniki and sat down on a bench along with Akinfiev, the former vehicular driver of the Revolutionary Tribunal. Sashka, the nurse of the Thirty-first Cavalry Regiment, came by, and two commanders sat down on the bench with us. The commanders sat there in silence, dozing. One of them was shell-shocked, shaking his head uncontrollably and winking with one bloated eye. Sashka went to tell the people at the field hospital about him, and then came back to us, dragging her horse behind her by the reins. Her mare resisted, her hooves skidding in the wet mud.

"So where are you sailing off to?" Vorobyov asked the nurse. "Sit down here with us, Sash!"

"I'm not sitting with you!" Sashka answered, and slapped her mare on the belly. "No way!"

"What d'you mean?" Vorobyov shouted, laughing. "Or have you had second thoughts about drinking tea with men?"

"It's you that I've had second thoughts about!" she told the commander, hurling away the reins. "Yes, I've had second thoughts about drinking tea with you, after I saw you all today and saw what heroes you all are, and how disgusting you are, Commander!"

"So when you saw it," Vorobyov muttered, "how come you didn't join in the shooting?"

"Join in the shooting?" Sashka shouted in desperation, tearing off her nurse's band. "What am I supposed to shoot with? This?"

Here Akinfiev, the former vehicular driver of the Revolutionary Tribunal, with whom I still had some unfinished business to settle, came up to us.

"You've got nothing to shoot with, Sash," he said soothingly. "No one's blaming you for that! I blame those who get all mixed up in battle and forget to load cartridges in their revolvers!" A spasm suddenly shot over his face. "You rode in the attack!" he shouted at me. "You rode but didn't put any cartridges in! Why?"

"Back off, Ivan," I said to Akinfiev. But he wouldn't back off, and kept coming closer to me, an epileptic with a twisted spine and no ribs.

"The Pole shot at you, yes, but you didn't shoot at him!" he muttered, twisting and turning with his shattered hip. "Why?"

"The Pole did shoot at me," I told him brusquely, "but I didn't shoot at the Pole!"

"So you're a Molokan, right?"[2] Akinfiev whispered, stepping back.

"So I'm a Molokan!" I said, louder than before. "What do you want?"

"What I want is for you to be aware," Akinfiev yelled in wild triumph, "aware that you're a Molokan, because in my books all Molokans should be shot dead, they believe in God!"

A crowd gathered, and Akinfiev yelled on about Molokans without stopping. I wanted to walk away, but he ran after me, and caught up with me, and punched me in the back with his fist.

"You didn't put any cartridges in!" Akinfiev whispered in a breathless voice right next to my ear, and with his large thumbs began trying to wrench my mouth open. "You believe in God, you traitor!"

He tugged and tore at my mouth. I pushed the epileptic back and hit him in the face. He keeled over onto his side, hit the ground, and began to bleed.

Sashka went over to him with her dangling breasts. She poured water over him, and pulled out of his mouth a long tooth which was swaying in the blackness like a birch tree on a bare country road.

"These bantams know just one thing," Sashka said, "and that's how to belt each other in the mouth. With a day like this and everything, I just want to shut my eyes!"

There was anguish in her voice, and she took wounded Akinfiev with her, while I staggered off into the village of Czesniki, which was sliding around in the relentless Galician rain.

The village floated and bulged, crimson clay oozing from its gloomy wounds. The first star flashed above me and tumbled into the clouds. The rain whipped the willow trees and dwindled. The evening soared into the sky like a flock of birds and darkness laid its wet garland upon me. I was exhausted, and, crouching beneath the crown of death, walked on, begging fate for the simplest ability—the ability to kill a man.

---

2. A member of a pacifist Protestant sect that emerged in Russia in the seventeenth century. —Ed.

The Song[1]

When we were quartered in the village of Budziatycze, it was my lot to end up with an evil landlady. She was a widow, she was poor. I broke many locks on her storerooms, but found no provisions.

All I could do was to try and outsmart her, and one fine day, coming home early before dusk, I caught her closing the door of the stove, which was still warm. The hut smelled of cabbage soup, and there might well have been some meat in that soup. I did smell meat in her soup and laid my revolver on the table, but the old woman denied everything. Her face and black fingers were gripped by spasms, she glowered at me with fear and extraordinary hatred. Nothing would have saved her—I would have made her own up with my revolver if Sashka Konyayev, in other words Sashka Christ, hadn't suddenly turned up.

He came into the hut with his concertina under his arm, his exquisite legs shuffling in battered boots.

"How about a song?" Sashka said, looking at me, his eyes filled with blue and dreamy ice crystals. "How about a song?" he said, and sat down on the bench and played a prelude.

The pensive prelude came as if from far away. He stopped, and his blue eyes filled with longing. He turned away, and, knowing what I liked, started off on a song from Kuban.

"Star of the fields," he sang, "star of the fields over my native hut, and my mother's hand, so sorrowful. . . ."

I loved that song. Sashka knew this, because both of us, both he and I, had first heard this song back in '19 in the shallows of the Don in the Cossack village of Kagalnitskaya.

A hunter who poached in the protected waters there had taught it to us. There, in the protected waters, fish spawn and countless flocks of birds nest. The fish multiply in the shallows in incredible numbers, you can scoop them up with a ladle or even with your bare hands, and if you dip your oar in the water, it just stands there upright—a fish will have grabbed it and will carry it away. We saw this with our own eyes, we will never forget the protected waters of Kagalnitskaya. Every government has banned hunting there—a good ban—but back in '19 a war was raging in the shallows, and Yakov the hunter, who plied his forbidden trade right before our eyes, gave Sashka Christ, our squadron singer, a concertina as a present so that we would look the other way. He taught Sashka his songs. Many of them were soulful, old songs. So we forgave the roguish hunter, for we needed his songs: back then, no one could see the war ever ending, and Sashka covered our arduous paths with melody and tears. A bloody trail followed our paths. The songs soared over this trail. That is how it was in Kuban and on our campaigns against the Greens,[2] and that is how it was in the Urals and in the Caucasian

1. First published in *Krasnaya nov* 3 (1925) with the title "Evening" and the dateline "Sokal, August 1920." —*Ed.*
2. Defectors from the Imperial army and later also from the new Soviet army, who banded together in guerrilla groups. They were called "Greens" because they hid in forests. Both the Whites and the Reds tried to organize them under their influence, creating bands of Red Greens and White Greens.

foothills, and that is how it is to this very day. We need these songs, no one can see this war ever ending, and Sashka Christ, our squadron singer, is too young to die.

And this evening too, cheated of my landlady's cabbage soup, Sashka calmed me with his soft, wavering voice.

"Star of the fields," he sang, "star of the fields over my native hut, and my mother's hand, so sorrowful. . . ."

And I listened, stretched out in a corner on my rotting bedding. A dream broke my bones, the dream shook the putrid hay beneath me, and through the dream's burning torrent I could barely make out the old woman, who was standing by the wall, her withered cheek propped on her hand. She hung her ravaged head and stood fixed by the wall, not moving even after Sashka had finished playing. Sashka finished and put down his concertina, yawned, and burst out laughing as after a long sleep, and then, noticing the chaos in the widow's hut, he wiped the debris from the bench and brought in a bucket of water.

"You see, deary, what your boss is up to?" the landlady said to him, pointing at me and rubbing her back against the door. "Your boss came in here, yelled at me, stamped his foot, broke all the locks in my house, and shoved his gun at me. It is a sin before the Lord to shove a gun at me—I'm a woman, after all!"

She rubbed her back against the door again and threw a sheepskin coat over her son. Her son lay snoring beneath an icon on a large bed covered with rags. He was a deaf-mute boy with a white, water-swollen head and gigantic feet, like those of a grown muzhik. His mother wiped the snot from his nose and came back to the table.

"Mistress," Sashka said to her, caressing her shoulder, "if you wish, I could be really nice to you."

But it was as if the woman hadn't heard what he had said.

"I didn't see no cabbage soup at all," she said, her cheek propped on her hand. "It ran away, my cabbage soup, and people shove their guns at me, so that even when a nice man comes along and I get a chance to tumble a little, I've ended up feeling so drab, I can't even enjoy sinning!"

She dragged out her mournful lament and, mumbling, rolled her deaf-mute son to the wall. Sashka lay with her on the rag-covered bed while I tried to sleep, conjuring up dreams so that I would doze off with pleasant thoughts.

The Rabbi's Son[1]

Do you remember Zhitomir, Vasily? Do you remember the River Teterev, Vasily, and that night in which the Sabbath, the young Sabbath, crept along the sunset crushing the stars with the heel of her red slipper?

The thin horn of the moon dipped its arrows in the black waters of the

---

1. First published in *Krasnaya nov* 1 (1924), this story was the coda of the cycle until the publication of the eighth edition in 1932, which concluded with the new story "Argamak." —*Ed.*

Teterev. Little, funny Gedali, the founder of the Fourth International,[2] who took us to Rabbi Motale Bratslavsky for evening prayer. Little, funny Gedali, shaking the cockerel feathers of his top hat in the red smoke of the evening. The candles' predatory pupils twinkled in the rabbi's room. Broad-shouldered Jews crouched moaning over prayer books, and the old jester of the Chernobyl line of *tsaddiks* jingled copper coins in his frayed pocket.

You remember that night, Vasily? Outside the window horses neighed and Cossacks shouted. The wasteland of war yawned outside and Rabbi Motale Bratslavsky, clutching his tallith with his withered fingers, prayed at the eastern wall. Then the curtains of the cabinet fell open, and in the funerary shine of the candles we saw the torah scrolls wrapped in coverings of purple velvet and blue silk, and above the torah scrolls hovered the humble, beautiful, lifeless face of Ilya, the rabbi's son, the last prince of the dynasty.

And then, Vasily, two days ago the regiments of the Twelfth Army opened the front at Kovel. The victors' haughty cannonade thundered through the town. Our troops were shaken and thrown into disarray. The Polit-otdel train[3] crept along the dead spine of the fields. The typhoid-ridden muzhik horde rolled the gigantic ball of rampant soldier death before it. The horde scampered onto the steps of our train and fell off again, beaten back by rifle butts. It panted, scrambled, ran, was silent. And after twelve versts, when I no longer had any potatoes to throw to them, I threw a bundle of Trotsky leaflets at them. But only one of them stretched out a dirty, dead hand to grab a leaflet. And I recognized Ilya, the son of the Zhitomir rabbi. I recognized him straightaway, Vasily! It was so painful to see the prince, who had lost his trousers, his back snapped in two by the weight of his soldier's rucksack, that we broke the rules and dragged him up into the railroad car. His naked knees, clumsy like the knees of an old woman, knocked against the rusty iron of the steps. Two fat-breasted typists in sailor blouses dragged the dying man's timid, lanky body along the floor. We laid him out in the corner of the train's editorial compartment. Cossacks in red Tatar trousers fixed his slipped clothing. The girls, their bandy bovine legs firmly planted on the floor, stared coolly at his sexual organs, the withered, curly manhood of the emaciated Semite. And I, who had met him during one of my nights of wandering, packed the scattered belongings of Red Army soldier Ilya Bratslavsky into my suitcase.

I threw everything together in a jumble, the mandates of the political agitator and the mementos of a Jewish poet. Portraits of Lenin and Maimonides lay side by side—the gnarled steel of Lenin's skull and the listless silk of the Maimonides portrait. A lock of woman's hair lay in a book of the resolutions of the Sixth Party Congress, and crooked lines of Ancient Hebrew verse huddled in the margins of Communist pamphlets. Pages of *The Song of Songs* and revolver cartridges drizzled on me in a sad, sparse

2. See the story "Gedali" in which Gedali envisions an ideal International that would supplant the Third Communist International founded in Moscow in 1919 to promote Communism worldwide.
3. The train sent out by the Polit-otdel. See note 8, p. 72. —*Ed.*

rain. The sad rain of the sunset washed the dust from my hair, and I said to the young man, who was dying on a ripped mattress in the corner, "Four months ago, on a Friday evening, Gedali the junk dealer took me to your father, Rabbi Motale, but back then, Bratslavsky, you were not in the Party."

"I was in the Party back then," the young man answered, scratching his chest and twisting in his fever. "But I couldn't leave my mother behind."

"What about now, Ilya?"

"My mother is just an episode of the Revolution," he whispered, his voice becoming fainter. "Then my letter came up, the letter 'B,' and the organization sent me off to the front. . . ."

"So you ended up in Kovel?"

"I ended up in Kovel!" he shouted in despair. "The damn kulaks opened the front. I took over a mixed regiment, but it was too late. I didn't have enough artillery."

He died before we reached Rovno. He died, the last prince, amid poems, phylacteries, and foot bindings. We buried him at a desolate train station. And I, who can barely harness the storms of fantasy raging through my ancient body, I received my brother's last breath.

RED CAVALRY: ALTERNATE ENDINGS

Argamak[1]

I decided to join the ranks at the front. The division commander grimaced when he heard this.

"Why the hell d'you want to go there? If you let your mouth hang open for a second, they shoot you point-blank!"

I held my ground. And that wasn't all. My choice fell on the most active division, the Sixth. I was assigned to the Fourth Squadron of the Twenty-third Cavalry Regiment. The squadron was commanded by Baulin, a Bryansk factory metalworker, who was a mere boy. He had grown a beard to inspire respect. Ash-blond tufts covered his chin. In his twenty-two years, Baulin had let nothing ruffle him. This quality, found in thousands of Baulins, proved an important element in the victory of the Revolution. Baulin was hard, taciturn, and headstrong. The path of his life had been decided. He had no doubts about the rightness of this path. Deprivation came easy to him. He could sleep sitting up. He slept pressing one arm against the other, and when he woke, his path from oblivion to full alertness was seamless.

One could expect no mercy under Baulin's command. My service started with an unusual omen of success—I was given a horse. There weren't any horses in the reserve stables or with the peasants. Chance helped. The Cossack Tikhomolov had killed two captured officers with-

---

1. First published in *Novy mir* 3 (1932), "Argamak" became the concluding story of the cycle beginning with the 1932 edition of *Red Cavalry*. —Ed.

out authorization. He had been instructed to take them to the brigade headquarters, as enemy officers could give important information. Tikhomolov did not take them there. It was decided that he would be tried before the Revolutionary Tribunal,[2] but then they changed their minds. Squadron Commander Baulin came up with a punishment much harsher than anything the tribunal could have inflicted—he took Tikhomolov's stallion Argamak away from him, and sent Tikhomolov off to the transport carts.

The agony I had to suffer with Argamak was beyond what a man can endure. Tikhomolov had brought his horse from the Terek, where he was from. The stallion had been trained in the Cossack trot, that specific Cossack hard trot—dry, violent, sudden. Argamak's stride was long, extended, obstinate. With this devilish stride he carried me off, out of the lines, separating me from the squadron. I lost my sense of direction, roamed for days on end looking for my unit, ended up in enemy territory, slept in ravines, tried to tag along with other regiments but was chased away by them. My horsemanship was limited to the fact that in the Great War I had served with an artillery unit in the Fifteenth Infantry Division. Most of the time we had spent sitting on ammunition carts; we rarely rode out on raids. I didn't have an opportunity to get used to Argamak's cruel, bounding trot. Tikhomolov had bestowed on his horse all the devils of his downfall. I shook like a sack on the stallion's long, dry spine. I rode his back to pieces. Sores appeared on it. Metallic flies preyed upon these sores. Hoops of baked black blood girded the horse's flanks. Bad shoeing made Argamak trip, his hind legs became swollen at the breeching strap and turned elephantine. Argamak grew thin. His eyes filled with the fire one sees in tortured horses, the fire of hysteria and obstinacy. He no longer let me saddle him.

"You've liquidated that horse, four-eyes!" my platoon commander said.

The Cossacks said nothing in my presence, but behind my back plotted like plunderers in drowsy treachery. They didn't even ask me to write letters for them anymore.

The cavalry took Novograd-Volynsk. In a single day we had to cover seventy, eighty versts. We were getting close to Rovno. Rest days were annulled. Night after night I had the same dream: I am riding Argamak at full trot. Campfires are burning by the roadside. The Cossacks are cooking food. I ride past them, they don't even look up. A few call out a greeting, others don't even turn around, they're not interested in me. What does this mean? Their indifference indicates that there is nothing unusual in my horsemanship, I ride like everyone else, there's no reason for them to look at me. I gallop off and am happy. My thirst for peace and happiness was never quenched in my waking hours, which is why I dreamed these dreams.

There was no sign of Pashka Tikhomolov. He was watching me from somewhere on the fringes of the march, in the bumbling tail of carts crammed full with looted rags.

"Pashka keeps asking what's with you," my platoon commander said to me one day.

2. Court martial. —Ed.

"Why, he has a problem with me?"

"It looks like he does."

"I reckon he feels I've done him wrong."

"Why, you reckon you didn't do him wrong?"

Pashka's hatred followed me through forests and over rivers. I felt it on my hide and shuddered. He nailed his bloodshot eyes on my path.

"Why did you saddle me with an enemy?" I asked Baulin.

Baulin rode past, yawning.

"Not my problem," he answered without looking back. "It's your problem."

Argamak's back healed a little, then his wounds opened up again. I put three saddlecloths under his saddle, but I could not really ride him, the wounds weren't healing. The knowledge that I was sitting on an open wound made me cringe.

A Cossack from our platoon, his name was Bizyukov, was Tikhomolov's countryman from the Terek, and he knew Pashka's father.

"His father, Pashka's father, he breeds horses for fun," Bizyukov told me one day. "A rough rider, sturdy. He comes to a herd, he picks out a horse on the spot, and they bring it to him. He stands face-to-face with the horse, his legs planted firm, glares at it. What does he want? This is what he wants: he waves his fist and punches the horse right between the eyes—the horse is dead. 'Why did you finish off the horse, Kalistrat?'—'I had a terrible desire for this horse, but I wasn't fated to ride it. The horse didn't take to me, but my desire for this horse was deadly!' He's a rough rider, let me tell you!"

And then Argamak, who had survived Pashka's father, who had been chosen by him, fell into my hands. How was this to end? I weighed many plans in my mind. The war had released me from other worries. The cavalry attacked Rovno. The town was taken. We stayed there for two days. The following night the Poles pushed us out. They engaged us in a skirmish to get their retreating units through. Their maneuver worked. The Poles were covered by a storm, lashing rain, a violent summer storm that tumbled onto the world in floods of black water. We cleared out of Rovno for a day. During the nocturnal battle we lost Dundic, the Serb, one of our bravest men. Pashka Tikhomolov also fought in this battle. The Poles attacked his transport carts. The area there was flat, without any cover. Pashka lined up his carts in a battle formation known only to him. It was, doubtless, how the Romans lined up their chariots. Pashka had a machine gun. He had probably stolen it and hidden it, for an emergency. With this machine gun he repelled the attack, saved his possessions, and led the whole transport to safety, except for two carts whose horses had been shot.

"What do you intend to do with your best fighters, marinate them?" they asked Baulin at headquarters a few days after the battle.

"If I'm letting them marinate, there must be a reason, right?"

"Careful, you'll run into trouble."

No amnesty was proclaimed for Pashka, but we knew that he was coming back. He came wearing galoshes on his bare feet. His toes had been hacked off, ribbons of black gauze hung from them. The ribbons dragged behind him like a train. In the village of Budziatycze, Pashka appeared at the square in front of the church where our horses stood tied to the hitching post. Squadron Commander Baulin was sitting on the church, steps, his feet soaking in a steaming bucket. His toes were rotting. They were pink, the way steel is pink before it is forged. Tufts of young straw-blond hair tumbled over Baulin's forehead. The sun burned on the bricks and tiles of the church. Bizyukov, standing next to Baulin, popped a cigarette into Baulin's mouth and lit it. Tikhomolov, dragging his tattered train behind him, went up to the hitching post. His galoshes shuffled. Argamak stretched his long neck and neighed to his master in greeting, a quiet, rasping neigh, like that of a horse in a desert. Pus coiled like lace between the strips of torn flesh on the horse's back. Pashka stood next to the horse. The dirty ribbons lay still on the ground.

"So that's how things stand," the Cossack said, barely audibly.

I stepped forward.

"Let's make peace, Pashka. I'm glad the horse is going back to you. I can't handle him. Let's make peace?"

"It's not Easter yet, for people to make peace," the platoon commander said from behind me, rolling a cigarette. His Tatar trousers loose, his shirt open over his copper chest, he was resting on the church steps.

"Kiss him three times, Pashka,"[3] mumbled Bizyukov, Tikhomolov's countryman, who knew Kalistrat, Pashka's father. "He wants to kiss three times."

I was alone among these men whose friendship I had not managed to win.

Pashka stood in front of the horse as if rooted there. Argamak, breathing strong and free, stretched his muzzle to him.

"So that's how things stand," the Cossack repeated. He turned to me sharply, and said emphatically, "I will not make peace with you."

He walked away, dragging his galoshes down the chalk-white, heat-baked street, his bandages sweeping the dust of the village square. Argamak walked behind him like a dog. The reins swung beneath his muzzle, his long neck hung low. Baulin continued soaking the reddish steel of his feet's rotting flesh in the tub.

"Why did you saddle me with an enemy?" I said to him. "None of this is my fault."

The squadron commander raised his head.

"I can see right through you!" he said. "Right through you! What you want is to live without enemies, you'll do anything not to have enemies."

"Kiss him three times," Bizyukov muttered, turning away.

A fiery spot burned on Baulin's forehead. His cheek twitched.

"You know what you end up with like that?" he said in a gasping voice. "You end up being bored! To goddamn hell with you!"

It was obvious I had to leave. I got myself transferred to the Sixth Squadron. Things went better there. The long and the short of it was that Argamak had taught me some of Tikhomolov's horsemanship. Months passed. My dream had become a reality. The Cossacks' eyes stopped following me and my horse.

3. A ritual triple kiss honoring the Resurrection of Christ and implying reconciliation (*pokhristosyvatsya*). In colloquial Russian, to reconcile, to make up. —*Ed.*

The Kiss[1]

At the beginning of August, headquarters sent us to Budziatycze to regroup. The Poles had occupied it at the beginning of the war, but we had been quick to win it back. Our brigade entered the shtetl at dawn. I arrived later in the day. The best billets had already been taken, and I ended up at the schoolmaster's house. He was a paralyzed old man sitting in an armchair in a low-ceilinged room, among buckets with fruit-bearing lemon trees. On his head was a Tyrolean hat with a feather. His gray beard lay on his chest, which was covered with cigarette ash. Babbling, his eyes fluttering, he seemed to be asking me for something. I washed, went to the headquarters, and didn't come back until night. My orderly, Mishka Surovtsev,[2] a cunning Cossack from Orenburg, gave me a full report: besides the paralyzed old man, there was also a daughter present, Elizaveta Alekseyevna Tomilina,[3] and her five-year-old son who was also called Mishka, like Surovtsev. The daughter, the widow of an officer who had fallen in the Great War, was a respectable woman but, according to Surovtsev's information, would be willing to make herself available to a proper gentleman.

"I can arrange things," he told me, and went off to the kitchen, where he began clattering about with plates. The schoolmaster's daughter helped him. As they cooked, Surovtsev told her of my brave feats, how I had knocked two Polish officers out of their saddles in a battle, and how much the Soviet authorities respected me. He was answered by the restrained, soft voice of Tomilina.

"Where d'you sleep?" Surovtsev asked her as he left the kitchen. "You should come sleep closer to us, we're living, breathing people."

He brought me some fried eggs in a gigantic frying pan, and put it on the table.

"She's up for it," he said, sitting down. "She just hasn't come out and said it yet."

At that very instant we heard whispering, rattling, and heavy, careful steps. We didn't have time to finish eating our war meal, when some old men on crutches and old women with kerchiefs on their heads came hobbling through the house. They dragged little Mishka's bed into the dining room, into the lemon-tree forest, next to his grandfather's armchair. The feeble guests, readying themselves to defend Elizaveta Alekseyevna's honor, huddled together in a flock, like sheep in a storm, and, barricading the door, spent the whole night silently playing cards, whispering, "My trick," and falling silent at every sound. I was so mortified, so embarrassed, that I simply could not fall asleep behind that door, and could barely wait for the sun to rise.

"For your information," I told Tomilina when I ran into her in the

---

1. First published in *Krasnaya nov* 7 (1937). According to A. N. Pirozhkova, Babel intended to include "The Kiss" in the new edition of *Red Cavalry*, part of his planned collected works, perhaps as the new concluding story of the cycle. —*Ed.*
2. The name is based on the Russian stem *surov-*, meaning "rough" or "stern." —*Ed.*
3. The name is based on the Russian stem *tomi-*, as in *tomit*—to weary someone with desire or expectation. Babel pointedly sets this story in a Russian milieu. The Russian *mestechko* can be translated as either a shtetl or a small town. —*Ed.*

hall, "for your information, I have a law degree and am a member of the so-called intelligentsia!"

Rigid, her arms dangling, she stood there in her old-fashioned house-dress, which clung tightly to her slim body. Without blinking, she looked straight at me with widening blue eyes sparkling with tears. Within two days we were friends. The schoolmaster's family, a family of kind, weak people, lived in boundless fear and uncertainty. Polish officials had convinced them that Russia had fallen in fire and barbarity, like Rome. They were overcome with a childlike, fearful joy when I told them of Lenin, the Moscow Arts Theater, of a Moscow in which the future was raging. In the evenings, twenty-two-year-old Bolshevik generals with scraggly red beards came to visit us. We smoked Moscow cigarettes, we ate meals that Elizaveta Alekseyevna prepared with army provisions, and sang student songs. Leaning forward in his armchair, the paralyzed old man listened avidly, his Tyrolean hat bobbing to the rhythm of our songs. Through all these days the old man was in the clutches of a sudden, stormy, vague hope, and, in order not to let anything darken his happiness, he did his best to overlook the foppish bloodthirstiness and loudmouthed simplicity with which in those days we solved all the problems of the world.

After our victory over the Poles—the family counsel decided—the Tomilins would move to Moscow. We would have a celebrated professor cure the old man, Elizaveta Alekseyevna would take classes, and we would put Mishka in the selfsame school that his mother had once gone to at Patriarshy Prudy. The future seemed incontestably ours, and war was merely a stormy prelude to happiness, happiness, the core of our being. The only things that remained unresolved were the specific details, and nights passed in discussing these details, mighty nights, in which the candle end was mirrored in the dull bottle of our home-brewed vodka. Elizaveta Alekseyevna, blossoming, was our silent listener. I have never met a more impulsive, free, or timorous being. In the evenings, cunning Surovtsev, in the wicker cart he had requisitioned back in Kuban, drove us up the hill to where the abandoned house of the Counts Gąsiorowski shone in the flames of the sunset. The horses, thin but long-bodied and thoroughbred, were running in step in their red reins. A carefree earring swayed on Surovtsev's ear. Round towers rose up from a pit that was overgrown with a yellow tablecloth of flowers. The ruined walls drew a crooked line flooded with ruby-red blood across the sky. A dog-rose bush hid its berries, and blue steps, the remains of the flight of stairs that Polish kings had once mounted, shone in the thickets. Once, as I sat there, I pulled Elizaveta Alekseyevna's head toward me and kissed her. She slowly pulled away, got up, and leaned against the wall, holding on to it with both hands. She stood there motionless, and around her, around her dazzled head, swirled a fiery dusty ray. Shuddering, as if she had just heard something, Tomilina raised her head and let go of the wall. She ran down the hill, her uncertain steps becoming faster. I called out to her, she didn't answer. Below, red-cheeked Surovtsev lay sprawled out in his wicker cart.

At night, when everyone was asleep, I crept to Elizaveta Alekseyevna's room. She sat reading, holding her book at arm's length. Her hand, lying on the table, seemed lifeless. She turned when I knocked, and rose.

"No," she said, looking me in the eyes, "please, dearest, no." And, embracing my head with her long, bare arms, she gave me an increasingly violent, never-ending, silent kiss.

The shrill ring of the telephone in the next room pushed us apart. An orderly was calling from headquarters.

"We're pulling out!" he said over the phone. "You are to report to the brigade commander now!"

I rushed out of the house without even putting on my hat, stuffing my papers into my bag as I ran. Horses were being brought out of yards, horsemen galloped yelling through the darkness. The brigade commander, tying his cloak, told us that the Poles had broken through our lines near Lublin, and that we had been ordered to execute a bypass maneuver. Both regiments pulled out an hour later. The old man, awoken from his sleep, anxiously followed me with his eyes through the leaves of a lemon tree.

"Promise me you will return," he kept saying, his head wagging.

Elizaveta Alekseyevna, a fur jacket over her batiste nightdress, accompanied us out onto the street. An invisible squadron raced past violently. At the curve in the road by the field I turned to look back—Elizaveta Alekseyevna was bending down to fix the jacket of little Mishka, who was standing in front of her, and the erratic light of the lamp burning on the windowsill streamed over the tender bones of her nape.

After riding a hundred kilometers without rest, we joined forces with the Fourteenth Cavalry Division and, fighting, we began our retreat. We slept in our saddles. At rest stops, we fell to the ground overwhelmed with exhaustion, and our horses, pulling at their reins, dragged us fast asleep through the harvested fields. It was the beginning of autumn and the soundless, drizzling Galician rain. Huddled together in a bristling silent herd, we dodged and circled, fell into the Poles' waiting net, but managed to slip out again just before they could close it. We lost all sense of time. When we were quartered in the church in Hoshcha, it did not even occur to me that we were only nine versts from Budziatycze. Surovtsev reminded me, we exchanged glances.

"The problem is that the horses are exhausted," he said cheerfully. "Otherwise we could go."

"We couldn't anyway," I replied. "They'd notice if we left in the middle of the night."

And we went. We tied gifts to our saddles—a clump of sugar, a fox-fur wrap, and a live, two-week-old goat kid. The road went through a swaying wet forest, a metallic star strayed through the crowns of the oaks. In less than an hour we arrived at the shtetl, its burned-out center filled with trucks, pale with flour dust, and with machine-gun-cart harnesses and broken shafts. Without dismounting, I knocked on the familiar window. A white cloud flitted through the room. Wearing the same batiste nightdress with its hanging lace, Tomilina came rushing out onto the porch. She took my hand in her hot hand and led me into the house. Men's underclothes were hanging out to dry on the broken branches of the lemon trees, and unknown men were sleeping in camp beds lined up in tight rows like in a field hospital. With crooked, hardened mouths they yelled out hoarsely in their sleep, breathing greedily and loud, their dirty feet jutting out. The house was occupied by our War Spoils Commission, and the Tomilins had been bundled off into a single room.

"When will you take us away from here?" Elizaveta Alekseyevna asked, clasping my hand.

The old man woke, his head wagging. Little Mishka cuddled the goat kid, and brimmed over with happy, soundless laughter. Above him stood Surovtsev, puffing himself up. Out of the pockets of his Cossack trousers he shook spurs, shot-through coins, and a whistle hanging on a yellow string. In this house occupied by the War Spoils Commission there was nowhere to hide, and Tomilina and I went to the wooden shed where the potatoes and beehive frames were kept in winter. There, in the shed, I saw what an inevitably pernicious path that kiss had been, the path that had begun by the castle of the Counts Gąsiorowski.

Surovtsev came knocking shortly before dawn.

"When will you take us from here?" Elizaveta Alekseyevna asked, turning her head away.

I stood there silently, and then walked over to the house to say goodbye to the old man.

"The problem is we're running out of time," Surovtsev said, blocking my way. "Get on your horse, we've got to go!"

He jostled me out onto the street and brought me my horse. Elizaveta Alekseyevna gave me her chilled hand. As always, she held her head high. The horses, well rested overnight, carried us off at a brisk trot. The flaming sun rose through the black tangle of the oak trees. The rejoicing morning filled my whole being.

A glade in the forest opened up before us. I directed my horse toward it, and, turning back to Surovtsev, called out to him, "We could have stayed a bit longer. You came for me too early!"

"Too early?" he said, riding up closer to me, pushing away the wet branches that dropped their sparkling raindrops. "If it wasn't for the old man, I'd have come for you even earlier. He was trying to tell me something and suddenly was all nerves, started squawking, and keeled over. I rush to him, I look, he's dead, dead as a doornail!"

The forest came to an end. We rode over a plowed field without paths. Standing up in his stirrups, looking all around, whistling, Surovtsev sniffed out the right direction and, breathing it in with the air, hunched forward and went galloping toward it.

We arrived in time. The men of the squadron were just being awakened. The sun shone warmly, promising a hot day. That morning our brigade crossed the former border of the Kingdom of Poland.

1920 DIARY

In April or May 1920, the Political Department of the Sixth Division; First Cavalry Army was joined by a new staff member: Kiril Lyutov, sent by the Odessa Gubernia Party Committee as a reporter for the Army's newspaper *The Red Cavalryman*. His real name was Isaac Babel.

Babel took weeks to catch up with Budyonny's Army, which was then on its legendary 750-mile march, soon to engage the Polish forces. Hostilities started on May 29; Budyonny won his first major victory on June 5; at the end of August, fortunes were reversed; and by mid-September, the Red Army, supposed to bring world revolution to Western Europe, had been defeated by the Polish national army under the command of General Josef Pilsudski, the new Poland's head of state.

During this time, Babel kept a diary. Almost a century later, this unique document conveys what it was like for someone who belonged to the cultural elite of the backward, war-ravaged Russia to be a propagandist among the Red Cossacks, recasting for them their violent discontent (and greed) into the abstraction of the world socialist revolution. Like the narrator of the *Red Cavalry* stories, the war reporter Lyutov was committed to Bolshevik ideals. But the author of the *Diary* had a far more ironic, at times sarcastic, attitude to what he saw in the course of the campaign. Like other left-leaning intellectuals, he hoped that the revolution would help to modernize old-regime Russia. But such limited identification with the cause hardly explains his decision to risk his life by joining the Cavalry Army. And risk he did: he was a target both for the enemy and his own Red Cossacks, known for their violent anti-Semitism.

What drove Babel, a pacifist, to take this risk was the need to see and experience war firsthand. World War I and the Civil War had shaped his generation, and Babel, an aspiring writer with a draft deferment, had to immerse himself in the life of war to claim the attention of his future readers. The diary then is also and perhaps primarily the writer's precious, intimate sketchbook, a storehouse of ideas and impressions. We know how invaluable it proved to be for his *Red Cavalry*. Read side by side, the stories and the *Diary* acquire new depth, and the reader is, as Babel wrote in "Guy de Maupassant," "touched by a premonition of truth"—for Babel, the precious moment when life miraculously turns into art and allows one to glimpse its secrets.

In a rare public appearance in the late 1930s, Babel claimed that the *Diary* had been lost. In fact, he had given the *Diary* to his Kiev friend for safekeeping. She passed it on to Babel's old Odessa friends, the Stakhs, who courageously preserved it during the years of terror. The notebook begins on page fifty-five; the first fifty-four pages as well as pages 69–89 were torn out and are missing. We can only wonder what they contained. The extant sixty-six entries cover almost the entire time Babel served with Budyonny's Cavalry Army and practically the whole of the Polish campaign. The *Diary* was published in its entirety for the first time in 1989 in the two-volume edition of Babel's writings, edited by Antonina Nikolaevna Pirozhkova. The geographical names in *Diary* entries appear in both Russian and Polish spellings, reflecting the fluid history of this borderland in the twentieth century. —*Ed.*

June 3, 1920. Zhitomir

Morning in the train,[1] came here to get my tunic and boots. I sleep with Zhukov, Topolnik,[2] it's dirty, in the morning the sun shines in my eyes, railroad car dirt. Lanky Zhukov, voracious Topolnik, the whole editorial crew unbelievably dirty people.

Bad tea in borrowed mess tins. Letters home, packages off to Yugrosta,[3] interview with Pollak, operation to seize Novograd, discipline is weakening in the Polish army, Polish White Guard literature, packets of cigarette paper, matches, former (Ukrainian) Yids, commissars—the whole thing stupid, malicious, feeble, talentless, and surprisingly unconvincing. Mikhailov copying out Polish articles word for word.

The train's kitchen, fat soldiers with flushed faces, gray souls, stifling heat in the kitchen, kasha, noon, sweat, fat-legged washerwomen, apathetic women—printing presses—describe the soldiers and women, fat, fed, sleepy.

Love in the kitchen.[4]

Off to Zhitomir after lunch. A town that is white, not sleepy, yet battered and silent. I look for traces of Polish culture. Women well dressed, white stockings. The Catholic church.

Bathe at Nuski in the Teterev, a horrible little river, old Jews in the bathing boxes with long, emaciated legs covered with gray hairs. Young Jews. Women are washing clothes in the Teterev. A family, beautiful woman, husband holds the child.

The bazaar in Zhitomir, old cobbler, bluing, chalk, laces.

The synagogue buildings, old architecture—how all this touches my soul. Watch crystal, 1,200 rubles. Market. A small Jewish philosopher. An indescribable store: Dickens, brooms, and golden slippers.[5] His philosophy: they all say they're fighting for truth yet they all plunder. If only one government at least were good! Wonderful words, his scant beard, we talk, tea and three apple turnovers—750 rubles. An interesting old woman, malicious, practical, unhurried. How greedy for money they all are. Describe the bazaar, the baskets of cherries, the inside of a tavern. A conversation with a Russian woman who came over to borrow a tub. Sweat, watery tea, I'm sinking my teeth into life again, farewell to you, dead men.

Podolsky, the son-in-law, a half-starved intellectual, something about trade unions and service with Budyonny,[6] I, needless to say, am Russian, my mother a Jewess, what for?

The Zhitomir pogrom carried out by the Poles, and then, of course, by the Cossacks.

After our vanguard units appeared, the Poles entered the town for three days, Jewish pogrom, cut off beards, they always do, rounded up forty-five Jews in the market, took them to the slaughterhouses, torture, they cut out tongues, wailing over the whole town square. They torched six houses, the

1. The propaganda train of the political department. See note 8, p. 72.
2. Babel's colleagues, reporters for the *Krasny Kavalerist* (*The Red Cavalryman*).
3. The Ukrainian division of ROSTA, the Soviet news service agency from 1918 to 1935.
4. See the story "Evening." —*Ed.*
5. See the story "Gedali." —*Ed.*
6. Semyon Mikhailovich Budyonny, the commander of the First Cavalry. See note 9, p. 98.

Konyukhovsky house, I went to take a look, those who tried to save them were machine-gunned down, they butchered the janitor into whose arms a mother had thrown an infant out of a burning window, the priest put a ladder against the back wall, and so they managed to escape.

The Sabbath is drawing to a close, we leave the father-in-law and go to the *tsaddik*.[7] Didn't get his name. A stunning picture for me, though the decline and decadence are plain to see. Even the *tsaddik*—his broad-shouldered, gaunt body. His son, a refined boy in a long overcoat, I can see petit bourgeois but spacious rooms. Everything nice and proper, his wife a typical Jewess, one could even call her of the modern type.

The faces of the old Jews.

Conversations in the corner about rising prices.

I can't find the right page in the prayer book. Podolsky shows me.

Instead of candles—an oil lamp.

I am happy, large faces, hooked noses, black, gray-streaked beards, I have many thoughts, farewell to you, dead men. The face of the *tsaddik*, a nickel-rimmed pince-nez.

"Where are you from, young man?"

"From Odessa."

"How is life there?"

"People are alive."

"Here it's terrible."

A short conversation.

I leave shattered.

Podolsky, pale and sad, gives me his address, a marvelous evening. I walk, think about everything, quiet, strange streets. Kondratyev with a dark-haired Jewess, the poor commandant with his tall sheepskin hat, he doesn't succeed.

And then nightfall, the train, painted Communist slogans (the contrast with what I saw at the old Jews').

The hammering of the presses, our own electrical generator, our own newspapers, a movie is being shown, the train flashes, rumbles, fat-faced soldiers stand in line for the washerwomen (for two days).

June 4, 1920. Zhitomir

Morning—packages off to Yugrosta, report on the Zhitomir pogrom, home, to Oreshnikov, to Narbut.

I'm reading Hamsun.[8] Sobelman tells me his novel's plot.

A new story of Job, an old man who has lived centuries, his students carried him off to feign a resurrection, a glutted foreigner, the Russian Revolution.

Schulz, what's most important, voluptuousness, Communism, how we are filching apples from the masters, Schulz is chatting away, his bald patch, apples hidden under his shirt, Communism, a Dostoyevskyan figure, there is something interesting there, must give it some thought, that inexhaustible overindulgence of his, Schulz in the streets of Berdichev.

---

7. A Hasidic holy man. See stories "The Rabbi" and "The Rabbi's Son." —Ed.
8. Knut Hamsun (1859–1952), Norwegian novelist, awarded the Nobel Prize for Literature in 1920. —Ed.

Khelemskaya, she's had pleurisy, diarrhea, has turned yellow, dirty overcoat, applesauce. What're you doing here, Khelemskaya? You've got to get married, a husband, an engineer in a technical office, abortion or first child, that was what your life has been about, your mother, you took a bath once a week, your romance, Khelemskaya, that's how you should live, and you'll adapt to the Revolution.

The opening of a Communist club in the editorial office. That's the proletariat for you: incredibly feeble Jews and Jewesses from the underground. March forward, you pitiful, terrible tribe! Then describe the concert, women singing Ukrainian songs.

Bathing in the Teterev. Kiperman, and how we search for food. What kind of man is Kiperman? What a fool I am, he never paid me back. He sways like a reed, he has a large nose, and he is nervous, possibly insane, yet he managed to trick me, the way he puts off repaying me, runs the club. Describe his trousers, nose, and unruffled speech, torture in prison, Kiperman is a terrible person.

Night on the boulevard. The hunt for women. Four streets, four stages: acquaintance, conversation, awakening of desire, gratification of desire. The Teterev below, an old medical orderly who says that the commissars have everything, wine too, but he is nice about it.

Me and the Ukrainian editors.

Guzhin, whom Khelemskaya complained about today, they're looking for something better. I'm tired. And suddenly loneliness, life flows before me, but what is its significance?

June 5, 1920. Zhitomir

Received boots, tunic on the train. Going to Novograd at sunrise. The automobile is a Thornicroft. Everything seized from Denikin. Sunrise in the monastery yard or the schoolyard. Slept in the automobile. Arrived in Novograd at 11. Travel farther in another Thornicroft. Detour bridge. The town is livelier, the ruins appear normal. I take my suitcase. The staff left for Korets. One of the Jewesses gave birth, in a hospital, of course. A gangly hook-nosed man asks me for a job, runs behind me with my suitcase. He promised to come again tomorrow. Novograd is Zvyagel.

A man from the supplies division in a white sheepskin hat, a Jew, and stoop-shouldered Morgan are on the truck. We wait for Morgan, he's at the pharmacy, our little friend has the clap. The automobile has come from Fastov. Two fat drivers. We're flying, a true Russian driver, all our insides thoroughly shook up. The rye is ripening, orderlies gallop by, miserable, enormous, dusty trucks, half-naked, plump, light-blond Polish boys, prisoners, Polish noses.

Korets: describe, the Jews outside the large house, a *yeshiva bokher*[9] in spectacles, what are they talking about, these old men with their yellow beards, stoop-shouldered merchants, feeble, lonely. I want to stay, but the telephone operators roll up the wires. Of course the staff has left. We pick apples and cherries. Moved on at a wild pace. Then the driver, red sash, eats bread with his motor-oil-stained fingers. Six versts short of our goal the

9. Yiddish: student in a Jewish religious school, colloquial for a bookish, unworldly young man. —Ed.

magneto floods with oil. Repairs beneath the scorching sun, sweat and drivers. I get there on a hay cart (I forgot: Artillery Inspector Timoshenko (?) [sic] is inspecting the cannons in Korets. Our generals.) Evening. Night. The park in Hoshcha. Zotov[1] and the staff rush on, transport carts go galloping by, the staff left for Rovno, damn it, what bad luck. The Jews, I decide to stay at Duvid Uchenik's, the soldiers try to talk me out of it, the Jews beg me to stay. I wash myself, bliss, many Jews. Are Uchenik's brothers twins? The wounded want to meet me. Healthy bastards, just flesh wounds on their legs, they get about on their own. Real tea, I eat supper. Uchenik's children, a small but shrewd girl with squinting eyes, a shivering six-year-old girl, a fat wife with gold teeth. They sit around me, there's anxiety in the air. Uchenik tells me the Poles were out plundering, then others raided, whooping and hollering, they carried off everything, his wife's things.

The girl: Aren't you a Jew? Uchenik sits watching me eat, the girl sits shivering on his lap. "She is frightened, the cellar and the shooting and your people." I tell them everything will be fine, what the Revolution means, I talk profusely. "Things are bad, we're going to be plundered, don't go to bed."

Night, a lantern in front of the window, a Hebrew grammar, my soul aches, my hair is clean, clean is my sorrow. Sweating from the tea. As backup: Tsukerman with a rifle. A radio-telegrapher. Soldiers in the yard, they chase everyone off to sleep, they chuckle. I eavesdrop on them, they hear something: Halt, who goes there? We'll mow you down!

The hunt for the woman prisoner. Stars, night over the shtetl. A tall Cossack with an earring and a cap with a white top. They had arrested mad Stasova, a mattress, she beckoned with her finger: Let's go, I'll let you have some, I can keep it working all night writhing, hopping, not running away! The soldiers chase everyone off to sleep. They eat supper—fried eggs, tea, stew—indescribable coarseness, sprawled all over the table, Mistress, more! Uchenik in front of his house, he's on sentry duty, what a laugh, "Go off to sleep!" "I'm guarding my house!" A terrible situation with the fugitive madwoman. If they catch her, they'll kill her.

I can't sleep. I meddled, now they say everything's lost.

A difficult night, an idiot with a piglet's body—the radio-telegrapher. Dirty nails and refined manners. Discussion about the Jewish question. A wounded man in a black shirt, a milksop and lout, the old Jews are running, the women have been sent off. Nobody is asleep. Some girls or other on the porch, some soldier asleep on the sofa.

I write in my diary. There is a lamp. The park in front of the window, transport carts roll by. No one's going off to sleep. An automobile has arrived. Morgan is looking for a priest, I take him to the Jews.

Goryn, Jews and old women on the porches. Hoshcha has been ransacked, Hoshcha is clean, Hoshcha is silent. A clean job. In a whisper: Everything's been taken and they don't even weep, they're experts. The Horyn, a network of lakes and tributaries, evening light, here the battle for Rovno took place. Discussions with Jews, my people, they think I'm Russian, and my soul opens up to them. We sit on the high embank-

---

1. S. A. Zotov, Commander of the Cavalry Field Headquarters.

ment. Peace and soft sighs behind me. I leave to defend Uchenik. I told them my mother is a Jewess, the story, Belaya Tserkov, the rabbi.[2]

June 6, 1920. Rovno

Slept anxiously, just a few hours. I wake up, sun, flies, a good bed, pink Jewish pillows, feathers. The soldiers are banging their crutches. Again: Mistress, we want more! Roasted meat, sugar from a cut-glass chalice, they sit sprawled out, their forelocks[3] hanging down, dressed in riding gear, red trousers, sheepskin hats, leg stumps swinging boisterously. The women have brick-red faces, they run around, none of them slept. Duvid Uchenik is pale, in a vest. He tells me, Don't leave as long as they're still here. A cart comes by to pick them up. Sun, the cart is waiting across from the park, they're gone. Salvation.

The automobile arrived yesterday evening. At 1 P.M. we leave Hoshcha for Rovno. The River Horyn is sparkling in the sun. I go for a morning walk. It turns out the mistress of the house hadn't spent the night at home. The maid and her friends were sitting with the soldiers who wanted to rape her, all night till dawn the maid kept feeding them apples, quiet conversations: we've had enough of war, want to get married, go to sleep. The cross-eyed girl became talkative, Duvid puts on his vest, his *tallith*, prays solemnly, offers thanks, flour in the kitchen, dough is being kneaded, they're getting things under way, the maid is a fat, barefoot, thick-legged Jewess with soft breasts, tidying up, talking endlessly. The landlady's speech—what she wants is for everything to end well. The house comes to life.

I travel to Rovno in the Thornicroft. Two fallen horses. Smashed bridges, the automobile on wooden planks, everything creaks, endless line of transport carts, traffic jam, cursing, describe the transport carts in front of the broken bridge at noon, horsemen, trucks, two-wheelers with ammunition. Our truck drives with crazed speed, even though it is completely falling to pieces, dust.

Eight versts short of our goal, it breaks down. Cherries, I sleep, sweat in the sun. Kuzitsky, an amusing fellow, can immediately tell you your future, lays out cards, a from Borodyanitsy, in exchange for treatment women offered him their services, roasted chicken, and themselves, he is constantly worried that the chief of the medical division won't let him go, shows me his genuine wounds, when he walks he limps, left a girl on the road forty versts from Zhitomir, go, she told him, because the divisional chief of staff was courting her. Loses his whip, sits half naked, babbles, lies without restraint, photograph of his brother, a former staff cavalry captain, now a division commander married to a Polish countess, Denikin's men shot him.

I'm a medical man.

Dust in Rovno, dusty molten gold flows over the dreary little houses.

The brigade rides past, Zotov at the window, the people of Rovno, the Cossacks' appearance, a remarkably peaceful, self-confident army. Jewish youths and maidens watch them with admiration, the old Jews look

2. See Babel's "The Story of My Dovecote" on p. 349. —Ed.
3. Ukrainian Cossacks shaved their heads, leaving only a forelock, known as a *chub*.

on indifferently. Describe the air in Rovno, something agitated and unstable about it, and there are Polish store signs and life.

Describe the evening.

The Khast family. A sly, black-haired girl from Warsaw takes us there. The medical orderly, malicious verbal stench, coquetry, You'll eat with us! I wash up in the hallway, everything is uncomfortable, bliss, I'm dirty and sweat-drenched, then hot tea with my sugar.

Describe this Khast, a complex fury of a man, unbearable voice, they think I don't understand Yiddish, they argue incessantly, animal fear, the father quite inscrutable, a smiling medical orderly, treats the clap (?) [sic], smiles, lies low, but seems hotheaded, the mother: We're intellectuals, we own nothing, he's a medical orderly, a worker, we don't mind having them here as long as they're quiet, we're exhausted! A stunning apparition: their rotund son with his cunning and idiotic smile behind the glass of his round spectacles, the fawning conversation, they scrape and bow to me, a gaggle of sisters, all vixens (?) [sic]. The dentist, some sort of grandson to whom they all talk with the same whining hysteria as to the old folk, young Jews come over, people from Rovno with faces that are flat and yellow with fear and fish eyes, they talk of Polish taunts, show their passports, there was a solemn decree of Poland annexing Volhynia as well, I recall Polish culture, Sienkiewicz, the women, the empire, they were born too late, now there is class consciousness.

I give my clothes to be laundered. I drink tea incessantly and sweat like a beast and watch the Khasts carefully, intently. Night on the sofa. Undressed for the first time since the day I set out. All the shutters are closed, the electric light burns, the stuffiness is unbearable, many people sleep there, stories of pillaging by Budyonny's men, shivering and terror, horses snort outside the window, transport carts roll down Shkolnaya Street, night.

The following twenty-one pages of the diary are missing.

July 11, 1920. Belyov

Spent the night with the soldiers of the staff squadron, in the hay. Slept badly, thinking about the manuscripts. Dejection, loss of energy, I know I'll get over it, but when will that be? I think of the Khasts, those worms, I remember everything, those reeking souls, and the cow eyes, and the sudden, high, screeching voices, and the smiling father. The main thing: his smile and he is hotheaded, and many secrets, reeking memories of scandals. The mother, a gigantic figure—she is malicious, cowardly, gluttonous, repugnant, her fixed, expectant stare. The daughter's repulsive and detailed lies, the son's eyes laughing behind his spectacles.

I roam about the village. I ride to Klevan, the shtetl was taken yesterday by the Third Cavalry Brigade of the Sixth Division. Our mounted patrols appeared on the Rovno-Lutsk high road, Lutsk is being evacuated.

8th–12th heavy fighting, Dundic[4] killed, Shadilov, commander of the Thirty-sixth Regiment, killed, many horses fell, tomorrow we'll have the details.

---

4. Oleko Dundich (1893–1920), civil war hero and commander of the Thirty-Sixth Regiment of the Sixth Division. —*Ed.*

Budyonny's orders concerning our loss of Rovno, the unbelievable exhaustion of the units, the frenzied attacks of our brigades which don't have the same results as before, incessant battles since May 27, if the army isn't given a breather, it will become unfit for battle.

Isn't it premature to issue such orders? No, they make sense: their objective is to rouse the rear lines—Klevan. Burial of six or seven Red Army fighters. I rode behind a *tachanka*. The funeral march, on the way back from the cemetery, a bravura infantry march, no sign of the funeral procession. A carpenter—a bearded Jew—is rushing around the shtetl, he's banging some coffins together. The main street is also Shossova.

My first requisition is a notebook. Menashe, the synagogue *shamas*, goes with me. I have lunch at Mudrik's, the same old story, the Jews have been plundered, their perplexity, they looked to the Soviet regime as saviors, then suddenly yells, whips, Yids. I am surrounded by a whole circle, I tell them about Wilson's note,[5] about the armies of labor, the Jews listen, sly and commiserating smiles, a Jew in white trousers had come to the pine forests to recuperate, wants to go home. The Jews sit on earth mounds,[6] girls and old men, stillness, stifling, dusty, a peasant (Parfenty Melnik, the one who did his military service at Elizavetopol) complains that his horse has swollen up with milk, they took her foal away, sadness, the manuscripts, the manuscripts—that's what is clouding my soul.

Colonel Gorov, elected by the people, village headman—sixty years old—a pre-reform rat of a nobleman. We talk about the army, about Brusilov,[7] if Brusilov set off, why shouldn't we? Gray whiskers, sputters, a man of the past, smokes homegrown tobacco, lives in the government building, I feel sorry for the old man.

The clerk of the district government, a handsome Ukrainian. Flawless order. Has relearned everything in Polish, shows me the books, the district statistics: 18,600 people, 800 of whom are Poles, wanted to be united with Poland, a solemn petition of unification with the Polish state.

The clerk is also a pre-reform figure in velvet trousers, with Ukrainian speech, touched by the new times, a little mustache.

Klevan, its roads, streets, peasants, and Communism are far from one another.

Hops-growing, many nurseries, rectangular green walls, sophisticated cultivation.

The colonel has blue eyes, the clerk a silken mustache.

Night, headquarters work at Belyov. What kind of man is Zholnarkevich? A Pole? His feelings? The touching friendship of two brothers.[8]

---

5. Babel refers here to the Note of Soviet Commissar of Foreign Affairs Chicherin to President Woodrow Wilson, dated 24 October 1918, protesting the intervention by the United States and its Allies on the side of the forces opposed to the Soviet regime. The Note also contained a threat that unless the Allies curtailed their intervention, the Soviet regime would rouse to its cause the "toiling masses of all countries." The "armies of labor" were a institution introduced by the Bolsheviks in the civil war that allowed the regime to use elements of the Red Army sometimes as labor, sometimes as a fighting force. The Ukrainian Labor Army was based on the units of the Southwestern Front but was returned to active fighting duty early in 1920 with the beginning of hostilities on the Polish Front and in the Crimea. —Ed.

6. *Zavalinka*: a mound of earth around a hut that protects it from the weather and is often used for sitting on outside.

7. General Alexey Alexeyevich Brusilov (1853–1926), Supreme Commander of the Russian forces under the Provisional Government (May–June 1917), refused to join the Whites in the civil war and headed the Special Advisory Council of old army generals who appealed to members of the old officer corps to join the Reds in the Polish campaign. —Ed.

8. Konstantin Karlovich Zholnarkevich was the chief of staff of the Sixth Cavalry Division, and his brother, Mikhail, was a staff officer. —Ed.

Konstantin and Mikhail. Zholnarkevich is an old hand, exact, hardworking without overexerting himself, energetic without kicking up a fuss, Polish mustache, slim Polish legs. The headquarters staff is made up of Zholnarkevich and three other clerks toiling away till nightfall.

A colossal job, the positioning of the brigades, no provisions, the main thing: the operational itineraries are handled unobtrusively. The orderlies at the headquarters sleep on the ground. Thin candles burn, the divisional chief of staff in his hat wipes his forehead and dictates, ceaselessly dictates operational reports, orders to the artillery division, we are continuing our advance on Lutsk.

Night, I sleep on the hay next to Lepin,[9] a Latvian, horses that have broken from their tethers roam about, snatch away the hay from under my head.

July 12, 1920. Belyov

This morning I began my journal of military operations, analyzing the operational reports. The journal is going to be an interesting piece of work.

After lunch I go riding on the horse of Sokolov, the orderly. (He is ill with a relapse of typhus, he lies next to me on the ground in a leather jacket, thin, a man of breeding, a whip in his emaciated hand, he left the hospital, they didn't feed him, and he was bored, he lay there sick on that terrible night of our retreat from Rovno, he had been totally soaked in water, lanky, totters, talks to the people of the house with curiosity but also imperiously, as if all muzhiks were his enemy). Shpakovo, a Czech settlement. A rich region, lots of oats and wheat, I ride through the villages: Peresopnitsa, Milostovo, Ploski, Shpakovo. There is flax, they make sunflower oil, and a lot of buckwheat.

Rich villages, hot noon, dusty roads, transparent sky without clouds, my horse lazy, when I whip it it moves. My first mounted ride. In Milostovo—I take a cart from Shpakovo—I'm going to get a *tachanka* and horses with an order from divisional headquarters.

I'm too softhearted. I look admiringly at the clean, hearty, un-Russian life of the Czechs. A good village elder, horsemen galloping in all directions, constantly new demands, forty cartloads of hay, ten pigs, the agents of the Requisitions Committee—grain, the elder is given a receipt—oats have been received, thank you. Reconnaissance commander of the Thirty-fourth Regiment.

The sturdy huts glitter in the sun, roof tiles, iron, stone, apples, the stone schoolhouse, a demi-urban type of woman, bright aprons. We go to Yuripov, the miller, the richest and best-educated man around here, a typical tall, handsome Czech with a Western European mustache. A wonderful courtyard, a dovecote—I'm touched by that—new mill machinery, former affluence, white walls, an extensive farm, a bright, spacious, single-story house and a nice room, and this Czech most probably has a good family, his father—a poor sinewy old man—all of them good people, a robust son with gold teeth, trim and broad-shouldered. A good wife, probably young, and his children.

9. A staff officer in the Sixth Cavalry Division.

The mill has, of course, been modernized.

The Czech has been stuffed full of receipts. They took four of his horses and gave him a note for the Rovno District Commissariat, they took a phaeton and gave him a broken *tachanka* in exchange, and three receipts for flour and oats.

The brigade arrives, red flags, a powerful, unified body, self-assured commanders, experienced, calm eyes of the forelocked Cossacks, dust, silence, order, marching band, they are swallowed into their billets, the brigade commander shouts over to me: We mustn't take anything from here, this is our territory. With worried eyes the Czech watches the dashing young brigade commander bustling about in the distance, chats politely with me, returns the broken *tachanka*, but it falls apart. I don't waste any energy. We go to a second, a third house. The village elder lets us know where there are things to be had. An old man actually does have a phaeton, his son keeps jabbering that it is broken, the front part is damaged—you have a bride, I think to myself, or you ride in it to church on Sundays—it's hot, I feel lazy and sorry for them, the horse-men scavenging through everything, this is what freedom initially looks like. I didn't take anything, even though I could have, I'll never be a true Budyonny fighter.

I'm back, it's evening, a Pole was caught in the rye, they hunted him down like an animal, wide fields, scarlet sun, golden fog, swaying grain, in the village they're driving cattle home, rosy, dusty streets, surprisingly tender forms, flaming tongues, orange flames shoot from the borders of the pearly clouds, the carts raise dust.

I work at the headquarters (my horse galloped nicely), I sleep next to Lepin. He is Latvian, his snout blunt, piglety, spectacles, he seems kind. A general staff man.

Cracks sudden, dull jokes. Hey, woman, when're you going to drop dead? And he grabs hold of her.

There's no kerosene at the headquarters. He says: We're striving toward enlightenment, but we have no light, I'm going to play with the village girls. Stretched out his arm, won't let go, his snout strained, his piggy lips quiver, his glasses shake.

July 13, 1920. Belyov

My birthday. Twenty-six years old. I think of home, of my work, my life is flying past. No manuscripts. Dull misery, I will surmount it. I'm keeping my diary, it will be an interesting piece of work.

The clerks are handsome young men, the young Russians from head-quarters sing arias from operettas, they are a little corrupted by the work there. Describe the orderlies, the divisional chief of staff and the others—Cherkashin, Tarasov—rag-looters, lickspittles, fawners, glut-tons, loafers, products of the past, they know who their master is.

The work at the headquarters in Belyov. A well-oiled machine, a bril-liant chief of staff, routine work, a lively man. They discovered that he is a Pole, relieved him of his duties, and then reinstated him on the order of the division commander. He is loved by all, gets on well with the divi-sion commander, what does he feel? He's not a Communist, he's a Pole, yet he is as loyal as a guard dog—try figuring that out!

About our operations.

The position of our units.

Our march on Lutsk.

The makeup of the division, the brigade commanders.

The work flow at headquarters: the directive, then the order, then the operational report, then the intelligence report, we drag the Polit-otdel along, the Revolutionary Tribunal,[1] the reserve horses.

I ride over to Yasinevichi to exchange my carriage for a *tachanka* and horses. Unbelievable dust, heat. We ride through Peresopnitsa, delight in the fields, my twenty-seventh year, I think the rye and barley are ripe, here and there the oats look very good, the poppies are past their bloom, there are no cherries, the apples aren't ripe, a lot of flax, buckwheat, many trampled fields, hops.

A rich land, but within bounds.

Dyakov, commander of the Reserve Cavalry: a fantastical apparition, red trousers with silver stripes, an embossed belt, a Stavropol Cossack, the body of an Apollo, a cropped gray mustache, forty-five years old, has a son and a nephew, outlandish cursing, things were sent over to him from the Supply Department, he had smashed a table to pieces there, but finally got what he wanted. Dyakov, his men love him: our commander is a hero. He was an athlete, can barely read and write, he says: I'm a cavalry inspector now, a general. Dyakov is a Communist, a daring old Budyonny fighter. He met a millionaire with a lady on his arm: "I say, Mr. Dyakov, did we not meet at my club?"—"I have been in eight countries, when I come out on stage, I need only wink."

Dancer, concertina player, trickster, liar, a most picturesque figure. Has a hard time reading documents, he keeps losing them—all this paperwork, he says, has finished me off, if I walk out, what will they do without me?—cursing, chats with the muzhiks, their mouths hang open.

The *tachanka* and two emaciated horses, describe the horses.

People go to Dyakov with requests, phew, I'm being worn down to the bone, distribute underwear, one thing after the other, fatherly relationship, you (to one of the patients) will end up being the head cattle driver here. I go home. Night. Headquarters work.

We have been billeted in the house of the village elder's mother. The merry mistress of the house keeps up an endless babble, hitches up her skirts and works like a bee for her family and then seven people on top of that.

Cherkashin (Lepin's orderly) is rude and tiresome, won't leave her in peace, we're always asking for something or other, children are loafing about the house, we requisition hay, the hut is full of flies, some children, old people, a bride, soldiers jostle and holler. The old woman is sick. The old people drop by to visit her and are mournfully silent, the lamp.

Night, headquarters, the pompous telephone operator, K. Karlovich writes reports, orderlies, the clerks on duty are sleeping, the village pitch-black, a sleepy clerk is typing an order, K. Karlovich is precise as clockwork, the orderlies arrive silently.

---

1. The *polit-otdel*, or political department, provided political education and Bolshevik party control over the military. The Revolutionary Tribunals, present in each army division and brigade, were the organs of military justice that investigated crimes committed by military personnel and dealt with prisoners of war. —*Ed.*

The march on Lutsk. The Second Brigade is leading it, they still haven't managed to take it. Where are our advance units?

July 14, 1920. Belyov

Sokolov has been billeted with us. He is lying on the hay, lanky, Russian, in leather boots. Misha is a nice, red-cheeked fellow from Oryol. Lepin plays with the maid when no one is watching, he has a blunt, tense face, our landlady keeps up an endless babble, tells tales, works tirelessly, her old mother-in-law—a shriveled-up little old woman—loves her, Cherkashin, Lepin's orderly, eggs her on, she prattles on without stopping to catch her breath.

Lepin fell asleep at the headquarters, a completely idiotic face, he simply can't wake up. A wail over the village, the cavalrymen are trading in their horses, giving the villagers their worn-out nags, trampling the grain, taking their cattle, complaints to the chief of staff, Cherkashin is arrested for whipping a muzhik. Lepin spends three hours writing a letter to the tribunal, Cherkashin, he writes, had been influenced by the scandalously provocative behavior of the Red Officer Sokolov. My advice: don't put seven men in one hut.

Gaunt, angry Sokolov tells me: We're destroying everything, I hate the war.

Why are they all here in this war—Zholnarkevich, Sokolov? All this is subconscious, inert, unthinking. A nice system.

Frank Mosher.[2] A shot-down American pilot, barefoot but elegant, neck like a column, dazzlingly white teeth, his uniform covered with oil and dirt. He asks me worriedly: Did I maybe commit a crime by fighting against Soviet Russia? Our position is strong. O the scent of Europe, coffee, civilization, strength, ancient culture, many thoughts, I watch him, can't let him go. A letter from Major Fountleroy: things in Poland are bad, there's no constitution, the Bolsheviks are strong, the socialists the center of attention but not in power. One has to learn the new methods of warfare. What are they telling Western European soldiers? Russian imperialism is out to destroy the nationalities, customs, that's the main thing, to take over all the Slavic lands, what old and tired words these are! An endless conversation with Mosher, I sink into the past, they'll shake you up, Mosher, ha, Mr. Conan Doyle, letters to New York. Is Mosher being sly or not—he keeps asking frantically what Bolshevism is. A sad, heart-warming impression.

I'm getting used to the headquarters, I have what they call a vehicular driver, thirty-nine-year-old Grishchuk, a prisoner in Germany for six years, fifty versts from his home (he is from the Kremenets district), the army won't let him go, he says nothing.[3]

Division Commander Timoshenko[4] is at headquarters. A colorful figure. A colossus, red half-leather trousers, a red cap, slender, a former platoon

---

2. The assumed name of Captain Merian Caldwell Cooper, the American pilot whom Babel interrogated in Belyov, who later achieved fame as the creator and producer of the motion picture *King Kong* (1933). See "Squadron Commander Trunov," p. 149. —*Ed.*
3. See the story "The *Tachanka* Theory," p. 118.
4. Semyon Konstantinovich Timoshenko (1895–1970), the prototype of the *Red Cavalry* Savitsky ("My First Goose" and elsewhere), joined the Russian cavalry as a private in 1915, went over to the Bolsheviks in 1917, and rose through the ranks during the civil war: Commander of the Sixth Division of the First Cavalry Army (November 1919–August 1920), to which Babel had been

commander, a machine-gunner, an artillery warrant officer in the past. Legendary tales. The commissar of the First Brigade had been frightened by the fire—Boys, on your horses!—and Timoshenko had begun lashing at all his commanders with his whip: Kniga,[5] the regimental commanders, he shoots the commissar—On your horses, you sons of bitches!—goes charging after them, five shots—Comrades, help!—I'll show you!—Help!—a shot through the hand, in the eye, the revolver misfires, and I bawl out the commissar. He fires up the Cossacks, a Budyonny man, when you ride with him into battle, if the Poles don't kill you, he'll kill you.

The Second Brigade attacks Lutsk and withdraws toward evening, the enemy counterattacks, heavy forces, wants to break through to Dubno. We occupy Dubno.

Report: Minsk, Bobruisk, Molodechno, Proskurov, Sventsyany, Sarny, Staro-Konstantinov have been taken, they are entering Galicia where there will be a cav. maneuver—by the River Styr or the Bug. Kovel is being evacuated, heavy forces at Lvov, Mosher's deposition. There will be an assault.

The division commander's gratitude for the battle at Rovno. Issue a statement.

The village silent, a light at the headquarters, arrested Jews. The Budyonny fighters bring Communism, a little old woman weeps. Ha, what a gloomy life these Russians lead! Where is that Ukrainian mirth? The harvest is beginning. The poppies are ripening, I wonder where I can get some grain for the horses and cherry dumplings.

Which divisions are to our left?

Mosher barefoot, noon, dull Lepin.

July 15, 1920. Belyov

Interrogation of defectors. They show us our leaflets. Their power is great, the leaflets help the Cossacks.

We have an interesting military commissar: Bakhturov,[6] a fighter, fat, foul-mouthed, always in the front lines.

Describe the job of a war correspondent, what exactly is a war correspondent?

I have to get the operational reports from Lepin, it's torture. The headquarters have been set up in the house of a converted Jew.

At night the orderlies stand in front of the headquarters building.

The harvest has begun. I am learning to tell the plants apart. Tomorrow is my sister's birthday.

A description of Volhynia. The muzhiks live revoltingly, dirty, we eat, poetic Matyash, a womanizer, even when he's talking to an old woman he is still mellifluous.

Lepin is courting the maid.

Our units are one-and-a-half versts from Lutsk. The army is preparing

assigned, and later, the Fourth Cavalry Division. He advanced steadily in the 1920s and 1930s, and in 1939 led Soviet forces that occupied eastern Poland in accordance with the Molotov-Ribbentrop Pact. Awarded the rank of marshall for winning the Soviet-Finnish War he replaced Kliment Voroshilov as the People's Commissar of Defense (1940–1941), and continued to play a major role in the Soviet armed forces in World War II and for the rest of his career. —Ed.

5. Vasily Ivanovich Kniga (1883–1961) was the commander of the Fourth Brigade of the Sixth Cavalry Division. —Ed.

6. Pavel Vasilevich Bakhturov, the military commissar of the Sixth Cavalry Division from February to August 1920. He had just been decorated with the Order of the Red Banner, at that time the highest military decoration of Revolutionary Russia. —Ed.

a cavalry attack, is concentrating its forces in Lvov, moving them up to Lutsk.

We've found a Pilsudski[7] proclamation: Warriors of the Rzecz Pospolita. A touching proclamation. Our graves are white with the bones of five generations of fighters, our ideals, our Poland, our happy home, your Motherland is relying on you, our young freedom is shuddering, one last stand, we will remember you, everything will be for you, Soldiers of the Rzecz Pospolita!

Touching, sad, without the steel of Bolshevik slogans, no promises and words like *order*, *ideals*, and *living in freedom*.

Victory will be ours!

July 16, 1920. Novoselki

Received an army order: seize the crossings over the River Styr in the Rozhishche-Yalovichi sector.

The headquarters move to Novoselki, twenty-five versts. I ride with the division commander, the staff squadron, the horses gallop, forests, oak trees, forest paths, the division commander's red cap, his powerful frame, buglers, beauty, the new army, the division commander and the squadron—one body.

Our billet, our landlord and his wife, young and quite wealthy, they have pigs, a cow, all they ever say: *nemae*.[8]

Zholnarkevich's tale of the sly medical orderly. Two women, he had to deal with them. He gave one of them castor oil—when it got to her, he dashed off to the other one.

A terrible incident, soldiers' love, two sturdy Cossacks came to an agreement with a woman—Can you hold out with two of us?—Yes, I can. One of them did it three times, the other one climbed onto her, she went running around the room dirtying the whole floor, they threw her out, didn't give her any money, she had been too hardworking.

About the Budyonny commanders: are they soldiers of fortune or future usurpers? They are of Cossack background, that's the main thing, describe the provenance of these detachments, all these Timoshenkos and Budyonnys had set up these detachments themselves, mainly with neighbors from their Cossack villages, now the detachments have been organized by the Soviet government.

The division is carrying out the order it was given, a powerful column is moving from Lutsk to Dubno, the evacuation of Lutsk has obviously been called off, troops and equipment are arriving there.

Our young landlord and his wife: she is tall with traces of village beauty, bustling about among her five children, who are rolling about on the bench. Interesting—each child looks after the next, Mama, give him titty. The mother, well built and flushed, lies sternly among her swarming brood of children. The husband is a good man. Sokolov: these pups should be shot, why keep breeding? The husband: out of little ones big ones grow.

Describe our soldiers: Cherkashin (today he came back from the tribunal a little browbeaten), insolent, lanky, depraved, what an inhabitant of Communist Russia, Matyash, a Ukrainian, boundlessly lazy, keen on women,

7. See note 4, page 97. See also the story "Ivan and Ivan." —*Ed.*
8. Ukrainian: there isn't any.

always torpid, his boots unlaced, lazy movements, Misha, Sokolov's orderly, has been to Italy, handsome, messy.

Describe: the ride with the division commander, a small squadron, the division commander's retinue, Bakhturov, old Budyonny fighters, a march plays as we set off.

The divisional chief of staff is sitting on a bench, a peasant is choking with fury, points at a mare on her last legs that he has been given in exchange for a good horse. Dyakov comes riding in, the conversation is short, for a horse like this you can get fifteen thousand, for a horse like this, even twenty thousand. If it gets up, then it's a horse.

They are taking away the pigs, the chickens, the village wails. Describe our provisions. I sleep in the hut. The horror of their lives. Flies. Research on flies, myriads of them. Five hollering, unhappy little children.

They hide provisions from us.

July 17, 1920. Novoselki

I am beginning my war journal from 7/16. I go to Pozha [Pelcha]. The Polit-otdel,[9] they eat cucumbers there, sun, they sleep barefoot behind the haystacks. Yakovlev[1] promises to help. The day passes with work. Lepin's lip is swollen. He has round shoulders. He's tough to get along with. A new page: I am studying the science of military operations.

Next to one of the huts lies a slaughtered cow that has only recently calved. Her bluish teats lying on the ground, just skin. An indescribable pity! A murdered young mother.

July 18, 1920. Novoselki—Mali Dorogostai

The Polish army is gathering in the region of Dubno-Kremenets for a decisive attack. We are paralyzing their maneuver, we are a step ahead of them. The army launches an attack on the southern sector, our division is being held in reserve. Our task: to seize the crossings over the River Styr around Lutsk.

In the morning we arrive in Mali Dorogostai (north of Mlynov), we leave the transport carts behind, also the sick and the administrative staff, it is obvious that an operation is ahead.

We receive an order from the Southwestern Front,[2] when we cross into Galicia—it will be the first time that Soviet troops will cross the border—we are to treat the population well. We are not entering a conquered nation, the nation belongs to the workers and peasants of Galicia, and to them alone, we are only there to help them set up a soviet power. The order is important and sensible—will the rag-looters stick to it? No.

We set out. Buglers. The division commander's cap glitters. A discussion with the division commander about the fact that I need a horse. We ride, forests, the fields are being harvested, but the harvest is poor, scanty, here and there two women and two old men. The centuries-old

9. See note 8, p. 72. —Ed.
1. The political commissar of the Sixth Cavalry Division.
2. The Southwestern Front was formed on January 10, 1920, to fight the Polish Army and the White forces. —Ed.

Volhynian forests, majestic green oaks and hornbeams, it is clear why the oak is king.

We ride along forest paths with two staff squadrons, they are always with the division commander, they are handpicked. Describe their horses' garb, sabers in red velvet, curved sabers, vests, carpets over their saddles. Dressed poorly, though each of them has ten service jackets—it's doubtless a matter of chic.

Fields, roads, sun, the wheat is ripening, we are trampling the fields, the harvest is weak, the grain stunted, there are many Czech, German, and Polish settlements. Different people, prosperity, cleanliness, marvelous gardens, we eat unripe apples and pears, everyone wants to be quartered with the foreigners, I also catch myself wishing for that, the foreigners are frightened.

The Jewish cemetery outside Malin, centuries old, the stones have toppled, almost all the same shape, oval at the top, the cemetery is overgrown with weeds, it saw Khmelnitsky,[3] now Budyonny, the unfortunate Jewish population, everything repeats itself, once again the same story of Poles, Cossacks, Jews is repeating itself with striking exactness, what is new is Communism.

More and more often we come across trenches from the last war, barbed wire everywhere, enough for fences for the next ten years, destroyed villages, they are being rebuilt again everywhere, but slowly, there's nothing, no materials of any kind, no cement.

With the Cossacks at the rest stops, hay for the horses, they all have long stories to tell: Denikin, their farms, their leaders, Budyonnys and Knigas, campaigns with two hundred men, plundering raids, the rich, free life of a Cossack, how many officers' heads they have chopped off. They read the newspaper, but the names just don't sink in, how easily they twist everything.

Wonderful camaraderie, unity, love of horses, a horse takes up a quarter of a day, incessant bartering and chatting. A horse's role and life.

Completely wayward attitude toward the leaders—they address them with the familiar "you."

M[ali] Dorogostai was completely destroyed, is being rebuilt.

We ride into the priest's garden. We take hay, eat fruit. A shady, sunny, wonderful garden, a little white church, there had been cows, horses, a priest with a little braid is wandering around in a daze collecting receipts. Bakhturov is lying on his stomach eating yogurt with cherries, I'll give you a receipt, really, I will!

We've eaten enough of the priest's food to last us a whole year. Word has it he's ruined, is trying to get a position, do you have any openings for a regimental clergyman?

Evening at my quarters. Again *nemae*[4]—they're all lying, I write in my journal, they give us potatoes with butter. Night in the village, an enormous, crimson fiery circle before my eyes, yellow fields flee from the ravaged village. Night. Lights at the headquarters. There are always lights

3. See note 2, p. 130.
4. Ukrainian: there isn't any.

at headquarters, Karl Karlovich dictates an order from memory, he never forgets anything, the telephone operators sit with hanging heads. Karl Karlovich served in Warsaw.

July 19, 1920. M[ali] Dorogostai—Smordva—Berezhtsy

Slept badly last night. Cramps in my stomach. We ate green pears yesterday. I feel dreadful. We're setting off at dawn.

The enemy is attacking us in the sector of Mlynov-Dubno. We pushed forward all the way to Radzivillov.

Today at dawn, the decisive attack by all the divisions—from Lutsk to Kremenets. The Fifth, the Sixth Division are concentrated in Smordva, we have reached Kozino.

In other words, we're heading south.

We're pulling out of M. Dorogostai. The division commander is greeting the squadrons, his horse is trembling. Music. We are stretched out along the road. The road is unbearable. We are going via Mlynov to Berezhtsy. A pity we can't enter Mlynov, it's a Jewish shtetl. We get to Berezhtsy, cannonade, the staff heads back, there's a smell of fuel oil, cavalry units are crawling over the slopes. Smordva, the priest's house, young provincial ladies in white stockings, their eyes red from weeping, it has been a long time since I have seen anything like it, the priest's wounded wife, limping, the sinewy cleric, a solid house, the divisional staff and the commander of Division Fourteen, we are waiting for the arrival of the brigades, our staff is on a hill, a truly Bolshevik staff: the division commander, Bakhturov, the military commissars. We're under gunfire, the division commander knows his stuff: he's clever, a go-getter, somewhat of a dandy, self-assured, the bypass movement toward Bokunin was his idea, the attack is held up, orders issued to the brigades. Kolesov and Kniga[5] came galloping over (the famous Kniga, why is he famous?). Kolesov's superb horse, Kniga has the face of a bakery sales clerk, a diligent Ukrainian. Swift orders, everyone confers, the gunfire gets stronger, shells are falling a hundred paces from us.

The commander of Division Fourteen is of a weaker mettle, a fool, talkative, an intellectual, wants to pass for a Budyonny fighter, curses incessantly—I've been fighting all night—likes to brag a bit. The brigades are winding in long ribbons along the opposite bank, the transport carts are under fire, columns of dust. Budyonny's regiments with their transport carts, carpets across their saddles.

I feel worse and worse. I have a temperature of 39.8. Budyonny and Voroshilov[6] arrive.

There's a conference. The division commander goes flying past. The battle begins. I'm lying in the priest's garden. Grishchuk is completely impassive. What kind of a man is Grishchuk? Submissiveness, endless silence, boundless indolence. Fifty versts from home, hasn't been home in six years, doesn't run away.

5. Nikolay Petrovich Kolesov was commander of the Third Brigade, and Vasily Ivanovich Kniga was commander of the Fourth Brigade of the Sixth Cavalry Division.
6. The two founding members of the First Cavalry Army, Semyon Mikhailovich Budyonny, its commander, and Kliment Efremovich Voroshilov, its commissar. See also note 2, p. 98 and note 2, p. 168.

He knows the meaning of authority, the Germans taught him that. Wounded men start coming in, bandages, bare stomachs, forbearing, unbearable heat, incessant gunfire from both sides, can't doze off. Budyonny and Voroshilov on the porch. A picture of the battle, the cavalrymen return covered with dust, sweating, red, no traces of excitement, they've been slashing, they're professionals, everything done with the utmost calm, that's what sets them apart, self-assuredness, hard work, nurses go flying by on horses, a Zhguchy armored car. In front of us is Count Ledochowski's[7] mansion, a white building above the lake, not tall, not flamboyant, very noble, memories of my childhood, novels—many more memories. At the medical assistants': a pitiful, handsome young Jew, he might well have been on the count's payroll, gray with worry. If I may ask, what is the situation at the front? The Poles mocked and tormented, he thinks life is about to begin, but the Cossacks don't always behave well.

Echoes of battle—galloping horsemen, reports, the wounded, the dead.

I sleep in the churchyard. Some brigade commander or other is sleeping with his head resting on some young lady's stomach.

I have been sweating, I feel better. I ride to Berezhtsy, the headquarters office is there, a destroyed house, I drink cherry tea, lie down in the landlady's bed, sweat, aspirin powder. It would do me good to sleep a little. I remember—I have a fever, heat, some soldiers in the churchyard kicking up a fuss, others cool, they are coupling their stallions with mares.

Berezhtsy, Sienkiewicz, I drink cherry tea, I'm lying on a spring mattress, next to me lies a child gasping for breath. I dozed off for about two hours. They wake me. I'm drenched in sweat. At night we return to Smordva, from there we continue, a clearing in the forest. Night journey, moon, somewhere in front of us, the squadron.

A hut in the forest. The muzhiks and their womenfolk sleep along the walls. Konstantin Karlovich is dictating. A rare picture: the squadron is sleeping all around, everything is steeped in darkness, nothing can be seen, a chill flows in from the forest, I bump into the horses, at the headquarters everyone's eating, I feel sick and lie down on the ground next to a *tachanka*, I sleep for three hours covered with Barsukov's shawl and coat, it feels good.

July 20, 1920. The heights near Smordva. Pelcha.

We set out at five in the morning. Rain, damp, we stick to the forests. The operation is going very well, our division commander chose the right bypass maneuver, we're continuing to detour. We're soaked, forest paths. The bypass is taking us through Bokuika to Pelcha. Information: at 10 o'clock Dobryvodka was taken, at twelve o'clock, after negligible resistance, Kozin. We're pursuing the enemy, we go to Pelcha. Forests, forest paths, the squadrons are winding on ahead.

My health is better, for inexplicable reasons.

---

7. Ignacy Ledochowski, commander of the Polish Fourteenth Artillery Brigade.

I am studying the flora of the province of Volhynia, there has been much logging, the clearing in the forest with felled trees, remains of the war, barbed wire, white trenches. Majestic green oaks, hornbeams, many pines, the willow is a majestic and gentle tree, rain in the forest, washed-out roads in the forest, ash trees.

To Pelcha along forest paths. We arrive around ten o'clock. Another village, lanky landlady, boring—*nemae*, very clean, son had been a soldier, gives us eggs, there's no milk, in the hut it's unbearably stuffy, it's raining, washes out all the roads, black squelching mud, it's impossible to get to the headquarters. Sitting all day in the hut, it's warm, there, outside the window, the rain. How boring and banal this kind of life is for me—chicks, a hidden cow, dirt, idiocy. An indescribable sadness lies over the earth, everything is wet, black, autumn, whereas back in Odessa . . .

In Pelcha we captured the transport carts of the Forty-ninth Polish Infantry Regiment. The spoils are being divided outside my window, completely idiotic cursing, nonstop, other words are boring, they avoid them, as for the cursing: the Mother of Christ, the Goddamn Mother, the peasant women cringe, the Mother of God, the children ask questions—the soldiers curse. Mother of God. I'll shoot you, damn it!

I get a document bag and a saddlebag. Describe this dull life. The peasant doesn't go to work on the field. I sleep in the landlady's bed. We heard that England proposed that Sov. Russia and Poland make peace—is it possible this will end soon?

July 21, 1920. Pelcha—Boratin

We have taken Dubno. The resistance, regardless of what we say, has been insignificant. What is going on? The prisoners talk, and it is clear that it is the revolution of the little people. Much can be said about that, the beauty of the Polish pediments, there is something touching about it, Milady. Fate, slighted honor, Jews, Count Ledochowski. Proletarian Revolution. How I drink in the aroma of Europe that flows from over there.

We set out for Boratin by way of Dobryvodka, forests, fields, soft outlines, oak trees, again music and the division commander, and, nearby, the war. A rest stop in Zhabokriki, I eat white bread. Grishchuk sometimes seems dreadful to me—downtrodden. The Germans: that grinding jaw.

Describe Grishchuk.

In Boratin, a hardy, sunny village. Khmil, smiling at his daughter, he is a closemouthed but wealthy peasant, eggs fried in butter, milk, white bread, gluttony, sun, cleanliness, I am recuperating from my illness, to me all these peasants look alike, a young mother. Grishchuk is beaming, they gave him fried eggs with bacon, a wonderful, shadowy threshing shed, clover. Why doesn't Grishchuk run away?

A wonderful day. My interview with Konstantin Karlovich [Zholnarke-vich]. What kind of men are our Cossacks? Many-layered: rag-looting, bravado, professionalism, revolutionary ideals, savage cruelty. We are the vanguard, but of what? The population is waiting for liberators, the Jews for freedom—but who arrives? The Kuban Cossacks. . . .

The army commander summons the division commander for a meeting in Kozin. Seven versts. I ride. Sand. Every house remains in my heart. Clusters of Jews. Faces, ghetto, and we, an ancient people, tormented, we still have strength, a store, I drink excellent coffee, I pour balm on the storekeeper's soul as he listens to the rumpus in his store. The Cossacks are yelling, cursing, climbing up to the shelves, the poor store, the sweaty, red-bearded Jew. . . . I wander endlessly, I cannot tear myself away, the shtetl was destroyed, is being rebuilt, has existed for four hundred years, the ruins of a synagogue, a marvelous destroyed old temple, a former Catholic church, now Russian Orthodox, enchanting whiteness, three wings, visible from afar, now Russian Orthodox. An old Jew—I love talking with our people—they understand me. A cemetery, the destroyed house of Rabbi Azrail, three generations, the tombstone beneath the tree that has grown over it, these old stones, all of the same shape, the same contents, this exhausted Jew, my guide, some family of dim-witted, fat-legged Jews living in a wooden shed by the cemetery, the coffins of three Jewish soldiers killed in the Russian-German war.[8] The Abramoviches of Odessa, the mother had come to bury him, and I see this Jewess, who is burying her son who perished for a cause that to her is repulsive, incomprehensible, and criminal.

The old and the new cemetery, the shtetl is four hundred years old.

Evening, I walk among the buildings, Jews and Jewesses are reading the posters and proclamations: Poland is the dog of the bourgeoisie, and so on. Insects bring death, and don't remove heaters from the railroad cars.

These Jews are like paintings: lanky, silent, long-bearded, not like ours, fat and jovial. Tall old men hanging around with nothing to do. Most important: the store and the cemetery.

Seven versts back to Boratin, a marvelous evening, my soul is full, our landlord rich, sly girls, fried eggs, lard, our men are catching flies, the Russo-Ukrainian soul. All in all, uninteresting.

July 22, 1920. Boratin

Before lunch, a report to army field headquarters. Nice, sunny weather, rich, solid village, I go to the mill, describe what a water mill is like, Jewish workman, then I bathe in the cold, shallow stream beneath the weak sun of Volhynia. Two girls are playing in the water, a strange, almost irrepressible urge to talk dirty, rough slippery words.

Sokolov is doing badly. I give him horses to get him to the hospital. The staff leaves for Leshniov (Galicia, we cross the border for the first time). I wait for the horses. It is nice here in the village, bright, stomach full.

Two hours later I leave for Khotin. The road goes through the forest, anxiety. Grishchuk is dull-witted, frightening. I am on Sokolov's heavy horse. I am alone on the road. Bright, clear, not hot, a light warmth. A cart up ahead, five men who look like Poles. A game: we ride, we stop, where are you from? Mutual fear and anxiety. By Khotin we can see our troops, we ride off, gunfire. A wild gallop back, I yank the horse's reins. Bullets buzz,

8. World War I. —*Ed.*

howl. Artillery fire. At times Grishchuk gallops with dark and taciturn energy, and then at dangerous moments he is unfathomable, limp, black, a heavy growth of beard on his jaw. There's no longer anyone in Boratin. Our transport carts have passed beyond it, a mess begins. The transport-cart saga, aversion and vileness. Gusev is in charge. We wait outside Kozin half the night, gunfire. We send out a scout, nobody knows anything, horsemen ride about the place with an intent air, tall German fellow from the district commander's, night, want to sleep, the feeling of helplessness—you don't know where they're taking you, I think it's the twenty or thirty men we chased into the woods, an assault. But where did they get the artillery from? I sleep for half an hour, they say there was an exchange of fire, a line of our men advanced. We move farther. The horses are exhausted, a terrible night, we move in a colossal train of transport carts through the impenetrable darkness, we don't know which villages we're passing through, there's a great blaze to one side, other trains of transport carts cross our path. Has the front collapsed or is this just a transport-cart panic?

Night drags on endlessly, we fall into a ditch. Grishchuk drives strangely, we're rammed from behind by a shaft, there are yells from somewhere far away, we stop every half verst and stand around futilely and for an agonizingly long time.

A rein tears, our *tachanka* no longer responds, we drive off into a field, night, Grishchuk has an attack of savage, blunt, hopeless despair that infuriates me: O may these reins burn in hell, burn, burn! Grishchuk is blind, he admits it, at night he can't see a thing. The train of transport carts leaves us behind, the roads are harsh, black mud, Grishchuk, clutching the remnants of the reins, with his surprising jangling tenor: we're done for, the Poles are going to catch up with us, they're shelling us from all around, our cavalry transport is surrounded. We drive off at random with torn reins. Our *tachanka* screeches, in the distance a heavy gloomy dawn, wet fields. Violet streaks in the sky with black voids. At dawn the shtetl of Verba. Railroad tracks—dead, frail—the smell of Galicia. 4 o'clock in the morning.

July 23, 1920. In Verba

Jews, who have been up all night, stand pitiful, like birds, blue, disheveled, in vests and without socks. A wet and desolate dawn, all of Verba crammed with transport carts, thousands of them, all the drivers look alike, first-aid units, the staff of the Forty-fifth Division, depressing rumors and doubtless absurd, and these rumors are circulating despite our chain of victories. . . . Two brigades of the Eleventh Division have been taken prisoner, the Poles have captured Kozin, poor Kozin, I wonder what will happen there? The strategic position is interesting, the Sixth Division is at Leshniov, the Poles are at Kozin, at Boratin, at our rear lines, we are like squashed pies. We are waiting on the road from Verba. We stand there for two hours, Misha in a tall white cap with a red ribbon gallops over the field. Everyone eats bread with straw, green apples, with dirty fingers and reeking mouths. Dirty, disgusting food. We drive on. Amazing, we come to a standstill every five steps, an endless line of provision carts of the Forty-fifth and the Eleventh Divisions, at times we lose our transport unit, then we find it again. The fields, the trampled rye, villages stripped of food and others not yet completely stripped of food, a hilly region, where are we going? The road to Dubno. Forests, wonderful, ancient, shadowy forests. Heat, shade in the forest. Many trees have been felled for military purposes, a curse upon them, the bare forest clearings with their protruding stumps. The ancient Volhynian forests of Dubno—must find out where they get that fragrant black honey.

Describe the forests.

Krivikha: ruined Czechs, a tasty-looking woman. The horror that follows, she cooks for a hundred men, flies, the commissar's moist and rattled woman, Shurka, wild game with potatoes, they take all the hay, reap the oats, potatoes by the ton, the girl at the end of her tether, the vestiges of a prosperous farm. The pitiful, lanky, smiling Czech, the nice, fleshy foreign woman, his wife.

A bacchanalia. Gusev's tasty-looking Shurka with her retinue, the Red Army scum, cart drivers, everyone tramping about in the kitchen, grabbing potatoes, ham, pies are being baked for them. The heat is unbearable, you can't breathe, clouds of flies. The tortured Czechs. Shouting, coarseness, greed. And yet my meal is marvelous: roast pork with potatoes and marvelous coffee. After the meal I sleep under the trees—a quiet, shady slope, swings are swaying before my eyes. Before my eyes lie quiet green and yellow hills drenched in sunlight, and forests. The forests of Dubno. I sleep for about three hours. Then we're off to Dubno. I ride with Prishchepa, a new acquaintance, caftan, white hood, illiterate Communist, he takes me to see Zhenya. Her husband—a *grober mensh*[9]— rides on his little horse from village to village buying up produce from the peasants. The wife a tasty-looking, languorous, sly, sensual young Jewess, married five months, doesn't love her husband, and, by the way, she's flirting with Prishchepa. I'm the center of attention—*er ist ein* [illegible][1]—she keeps staring at me, asks me my surname, doesn't take her eyes off me, we drink tea, I'm in an idiotic bind, I am quiet, slack, polite, and thank her for every gesture. Before my eyes: the life of a Jewish family, the mother comes by, some young ladies or other, Prishchepa is quite the ladies' man. Dubno has changed hands quite a few times. Our side, it seems, didn't plunder it. So once again they are all shivering, once again degradation without end and hatred toward the Poles who tear out their beards. The husband: Will there be freedom to trade, to buy a few things and then sell them right away, no speculating? I tell him yes, there will, everything will be for the better—my usual system—in Russia wondrous things are happening: express trains, free food for children, theaters, the International.[2] They listen with delight and mistrust. I think to myself: a sky full of diamonds[3] will be yours, everything will be turned upside down, everyone will be uprooted yet again, I feel sorry for them.

The Dubno synagogues. Everything destroyed. Two small anterooms remain, centuries, two minute little rooms, everything filled with memo-

9. Yiddish: an uncouth individual.
1. German: he is a . . .
2. The Third Communist International, also known as the Comintern, a world-wide headquarters of national communist parties established by the Bolsheviks in Russia in 1919. Its Second Congress, held in Russia in July–August 1920, when a world revolution seemed imminent, was deemed a great success. See also note 4, p. 113. —Ed.
3. "A sky full of diamonds," the words from the final scene of Anton Chekhov's *Uncle Vanya*, became a proverbial expression for daydreaming and empty utopianism. —Ed.

ries, four synagogues in a row, and then the pasture, the fields, and the setting sun. The synagogues are pitiful, squat, ancient, green and blue little buildings, the Hasidic one, inside, no architecture whatsoever. I go into the Hasidic synagogue. It's Friday. What stunted little figures, what emaciated faces, for me everything that existed for the past 300 years has come alive, the old men bustle about the synagogue, there is no wailing, for some reason they all run back and forth, the praying is extremely informal. It seems that Dubno's most repulsive-looking Jews have gathered. I pray, rather, I almost pray, and think about Hershele,[4] this is how I should describe him. A quiet evening in the synagogue, this always has an irresistible effect on me, four synagogues in a row. Religion? No decoration at all in the building, everything is white and plain to the point of asceticism, everything is incorporeal and bloodless to a monstrous degree, to grasp it fully you have to have the soul of a Jew. But what does this soul consist of? Is it not bound to be our century in which they will perish?

A little nook in Dubno, four synagogues, Friday evening, Jews and Jewesses by the ruined stones—all etched in my memory. Then evening, herring, I am sad because there's no one to copulate with. Prishchepa and the teasing and exasperating Zhenya, her sparkling Jewish eyes, fat legs, and soft breasts. Prishchepa, his hands slip deeper, and her unyielding gaze, while her fool of a husband is out in the tiny shed feeding his commandeered horse.

We stay the night with other Jews, Prishchepa asks them to play some music, a fat boy with a hard, idiotic face, gasping with terror, says that he is not in the mood. The horse is nearby in the yard. Grishchuk is only fifty versts from home. He does not run away.

The Poles attack in the area of Kozin-Boratin, they are at our rear lines, the Sixth Division is in Leshniov, Galicia. We're marching to Brody, Radzivillov is in front and one brigade is in the rear. The Sixth Division is in hard fighting.

July 24, 1920

Morning at army headquarters. The Sixth Division is annihilating the enemy assaulting us in Khotin, the area of battle is Khotin-Kozin, and I think to myself, poor Kozin.

The cemetery, round stones.

Prishchepa and I ride from Krivikha to Leshniov by way of Demidovka. Prishchepa's soul—an illiterate fellow, a Communist, the Kadety[5] killed his parents, he tells me how he went about his Cossack village collecting his belongings. Colorful, wearing a hood, as simple as grass, will turn into a rag-looter, despises Grishchuk because he doesn't love or understand horses. We ride through Khorupan, Smordva, and Demidovka. Remember the picture: transport carts, horsemen, half-wrecked villages, fields and forests, oak trees, now and then wounded men and my *tachanka*.

We arrive in Demidovka toward evening. A Jewish shtetl, I am on guard. Jews in the steppes, everything is destroyed. We are in a house with a

---

4. See Editor's Note and Babel's story "Shabos-Nakhamu" on p. 26.
5. The Whites, a detachment of officer school cadets. —*Ed.*

horde of women. The Lyakhetskys and the Shvevels,[6] no, this isn't
Odessa. Dora Aronovna, a dentist, is reading Artsybashev,[7] a Cossack rab-
ble loitering about. She is proud, angry, says that the Poles destroyed all
sense of self-respect, despises the Communists for their plebianism, a
horde of daughters in white stockings, devout father and mother. Each
daughter distinctly individual: one is pitiful, black-haired, bowlegged, the
other fleshy, a third housewifely, and all, doubtless, old maids.

The main friction: today is the Sabbath. Prishchepa wants them to roast
potatoes, but tomorrow is a day of fasting, *Tishah b'Ab*,[8] and I say nothing
because I am Russian. The dentist, pale with pride and self-respect, announces that nobody will dig up potatoes because it is a holy day.

I manage to restrain Prishchepa for quite a while, but then he explodes:
Yids, sons-of-bitches, a whole arsenal of curses, all of them hate us and
me, dig up potatoes, frightened in the garden that isn't theirs, they
blame the Christians, Prishchepa is outraged. How painful it all is—
Artsybashev, the orphaned schoolgirl from Rovno, Prishchepa in his
hood. The mother wrings her hands: the stove has been lit on the Sabbath, curses fly. Budyonny was here and left again. An argument between
a Jewish youth and Prishchepa. A youth with spectacles, black-haired,
highly strung, scarlet, inflamed eyelids, inaccurate Russian speech. He
believes in God, God is the ideal we carry in our souls, every person has
their own God in their soul, if you act badly, God grieves, this nonsense
is proclaimed with rapture and pain. Prishchepa is offensively idiotic, he
talks of religion in ancient times, mixes Christianity and Paganism, his
main point, in ancient times there was the commune, needless to say
nothing but rubbish—you have no education whatsoever—and the Jew
with his six years of Rovno high-school education quotes Platonov[9]—
touching and comical—the clans, the elders, Perun, paganism.

We eat like oxen, fried potatoes, and five glasses of coffee each. We
sweat, they serve us everything, it's all terrible, I tell fairy tales about
Bolshevism, its blossoming, the express trains, the Moscow textile mills,
the universities, the free food, the Revel Delegation, and, to crown it all,
my tale about the Chinese, and I enthrall all these poor tortured people.
Tishah b'Ab. The old woman sobs sitting on the floor, her son, who wor-
ships her, says that he believes in God to make her happy, he sings in a
pleasant tenor and tells the story of the destruction of the Temple. The
terrible words of the prophets: they will eat dung, the maidens will be
defiled, the menfolk slaughtered, Israel crushed, angry and dejected
words. The lamp smokes, the old woman wails, the youth sings melodi-
ously, the girls in their white stockings, outside the window Demidovka,
night, Cossacks, everything just as it had been in the days when the
Temple was destroyed. I go to sleep in the wet, reeking yard.

It's a disaster with Grishchuk, he is in a daze, hovering around like a

6. Babel was related to the Shvekhvels through his mother, Faina Aronovna, née Shvekhvel, and her
sister, Katerina Aronovna Lyakhetsky, a dentist. The Shvekhvels came originally from Brody in
Poland. —*Ed.*
7. The novelist Mikhail Petrovich Artsybashev (1878–1927), notorious for his frank discussion of
sex. —*Ed.*
8. The ninth day of the month Ab, a Jewish day of mourning commemorating the destruction of the
First and Second Temples in Jerusalem.
9. Russian historian Sergey Fyodorovich Platonov (1860–1933), author of a standard high school
textbook on Russian history. —*Ed.*

sleepwalker, he is feeding the horses badly, informs me about problems *post factum*, favors the muzhiks and their children.

Machine-gunners have come in from the front lines, they come over to our yard, it is night, they are wrapped in their cloaks. Prishchepa is courting a Jewess from Kremenets, pretty, fleshy, in a smooth dress. She blushes tenderly, her one-eyed father-in-law is sitting nearby, she blossoms, it's nice talking with Prishchepa, she blossoms and acts coquettish—what are they talking about?—then, he wants to go to bed, spend some time with her, she is tormented, who understands her soul better than I? He: we will write to each other. I wonder with a heavy heart: surely she won't give in. Prishchepa tells me she agrees (with him they all agree). I suddenly remember that he seemed to have had syphilis, I wonder: was he fully cured?

The girl later on: I will scream. Describe their initial pussyfooting conversation—how dare you—she is an educated person, she served on the Revolutionary Committee.[1]

God almighty, I think, the women are hearing all these curses now, they live like soldiers, what happened to their tenderness?

At night rain and storm, we run over to the stable, dirty, dark, damp, cold, the machine-gunners will be sent back to the front lines at dawn, they assemble in the pouring rain, cloaks and freezing horses. Miserable Demidovka.

July 25, 1920

We pull out of Demidovka in the morning. A tortured two hours, they woke the Jewesses at four o'clock in the morning and had them boil Russian meat,[2] and that on *Tishah b'Ab*. Half-naked and disheveled girls run through wet gardens, Prishchepa is in the grip of lust, he throws himself on the bride of the one-eyed man's son while their cart is being requisitioned, an incredible bout of cursing, the soldiers are eating meat out of the pots, she, I will scream, her face, he pushes her against the wall, a shameless spectacle. Under no circumstances does she want to hand over the cart, they had hidden it in the loft, she will make a good Jewess. She wrangles with the commissar, who says that the Jews do not want to help the Red Army.

I lost my briefcase and then found it at the headquarters of the Fourteenth Division in Lishnya.

We head for Ostrov—fifteen versts, there is a road from there to Leshniov, it's dangerous there, Polish patrols. The priest, his daughter looks like Plevitskaya[3] or a merry skeleton. She is a Kiev student, everyone yearns for civility, I tell my fairy tales, she cannot tear herself away. Fifteen dangerous versts, sentries gallop past, we cross the border, wooden planks. Trenches everywhere.

We arrive at the headquarters. Leshniov. The little town half destroyed. The Russians have fouled up the place pretty badly. A Catholic church, a Uniate church, a synagogue, beautiful buildings, miserable life, a few spectral Jews, a revolting landlady, a Galician woman, flies and dirt, a lanky, shy blockhead, second-grade Slavs. Convey the spirit of destroyed Leshniov, its enfeeblement and its depressing, semi-foreign dirt.

1. Local organs of the Soviet government.
2. Nonkosher.
3. Nadezhda Plevitskaya (1882–1941), celebrated Russian folk singer and actress. —*Ed.*

I sleep in the threshing shed. A battle is raging at Brody and at the Tsurovitse crossing. Leaflets about Soviet Galicia. Pastors. Night in Leshniov. How unimaginably sad this all is, and these pitiful Galicians gone wild, and the destroyed synagogues, and trickles of life against a backdrop of horrifying events, of which only reflections come through to us.

July 26, 1920. Leshniov

The Ukraine in flames. Wrangel[4] has not been annihilated. Makhno[5] is launching raids in the districts of Ekaterinoslav and Poltava. New gangs have appeared, a rebellion near Kherson. Why are they rebelling? Is the Communist jacket too short for them?

What's going on in Odessa? Longing.

Much work, I'm remembering the past. This morning Brody was taken, again the surrounded enemy managed to get out, a sharp order from Budyonny, we've let them get away four times now, we are able to shake them loose but we don't have the strength to hold them.

A meeting in Kozin, Budyonny's speech: We've stopped all maneuvering, from now on frontal attacks, we are losing contact with the enemy, no reconnaissance, no defense, the division commanders show no initiative, lifeless operations.

I talk with Jews, for the first time uninteresting Jews. Nearby, the destroyed synagogue, a red-haired man from Brody, some countrymen of mine from Odessa.

I move in with a legless Jew, affluence, cleanliness, quiet, marvelous coffee, clean children, the father lost both legs on the Italian Front, new house, they're still building, the wife has an eye for profit but is decent, polite, a small shady room, I recover from the Galicians.

I am distressed, I must think things through: Galicia, the World War, and my own fate.

Life in our division. About Bakhturov,[6] about our division commander, the Cossacks, the marauding, the vanguard's vanguard. I don't belong.

In the evening panic: the enemy pushed us back out of Churovitse, they were a verst and a half away from Leshniov. The division commander went galloping off and came galloping back. And our wanderings begin again, another night without sleep, transport carts, enigmatic Grishchuk, the horses walk quietly; cursing, forests, stars, we stop somewhere. Brody at dawn, all this is horrifying: barbed wire everywhere, burned-out chimneys, a bloodless city, drab houses, word has it there are goods to be had, our men won't hold back, there were factories here, a Russian military cemetery, and, judging by the nameless lonely crosses on the graves, these were Russian soldiers.

The road is completely white, cut-down forests, everything disfigured, Galicians on the road, Austrian uniforms, barefoot with pipes in their mouths, what is in their faces, what mystery of insignificance, commonplaceness, submissiveness.

4. Baron Pyotr Nikolayevich Wrangel (1878–1928), commander of the anti-Bolshevik armies in southern Russia in 1920. —Ed.
5. See note 2 on p. 108. —Ed.
6. See note 5 on p. 196. See also "Evening," p. 141. —Ed.

Radzivillov is worse than Brody, barbed wire on poles, pretty buildings, dawn, pitiful figures, fruit trees plucked bare, bedraggled, yawning Jews, destroyed roads, defiled crucifixes, sterile earth, shattered Catholic churches, where are their priests, smugglers used to be here, and I can see how life used to be.

Khotin. July 27, 1920

After Radzivillov—endless villages, horsemen charging on, difficult after a sleepless night.

Khotin is the same village where we had been under fire. My quarters are horrifying: abject poverty, bathhouse, flies, an unruffled, gentle, well-built muzhik, a crafty woman, she won't give a thing, I get some lard, potatoes. They live absurdly, wild, the dingy room and the myriad flies, the terrible food, and they don't strive for anything better—and the greed, and the repulsive, immutable way their dwelling is set up, and the hides reeking in the sun, the limitless dirt, exasperate me.

There was a landowner here—Sveshnikov—the factory is destroyed, his manor is destroyed, the majestic skeleton of the factory, a red brick-building, cobbled paths, now no trace of them, the muzhiks indifferent.

Artillery supplies are lagging, I'm immersing myself in headquarters work: the vile work of murder. What is to Communism's credit: at least it doesn't advocate animosity toward the enemy, only toward Polish soldiers.

Prisoners were brought in, a Red Army fighter wounded a perfectly healthy man with two gunshots for no reason whatsoever. The Pole doubles over, moans, they put a pillow under his head.

Zinoviev was killed, a young Communist in red trousers, a rattle in his throat and blue eyelids.

Astonishing rumors are going around—on the 30th, discussions for an armistice will begin.

Night in a reeking hole they call a yard. I can't sleep, it's late, I go over to the headquarters, the situation with the crossings is not all that good.

Late night, red flag, silence, Red Army fighters thirsting for women.

July 28, 1920. Khotin

The skirmish for the crossing at Churovitse. The Second Brigade is bleeding to death in Budyonny's presence. The whole infantry battalion is wounded, almost completely destroyed. The Poles are in old reinforced trenches. Our men weren't successful. Is the Poles' resistance growing stronger?

There is no sign of slackening due to the prospect of peace.

I'm staying in a poor hut where a son with a big head plays the violin. I terrorize the mistress of the house, she won't give me anything. Grishchuk, sullen as a stone, does not take good care of the horses, it turns out he was schooled by hunger.

A ruined estate, Sveshnikov the landowner, the majestic, destroyed distillery (the symbol of the Russian landed gentry?), when the alcohol was handed out all the fighters drank themselves into a stupor.

I am exasperated, I can't contain my indignation: the dirt, the apathy, the hopelessness of Russian life are unbearable, the Revolution will do some good work here.

The mistress of the house hides the pigs and the cow, talks fast, sugary, and with impotent hatred, is lazy, and I have the impression she is running their household into the ground, her husband believes in a strong government, is charming, gentle, passive, resembles Stroyev.

The village is boring, living here is dreadful. I'm immersing myself in headquarters work. Describe the day, the reverberations of the battle raging only a few versts away from us, the orderlies, Lepin's[7] hand is swollen.

The Red Army fighters sleep with the women.

A story: How a Polish regiment had laid down its weapons four times, but then each time began defending itself again as we hacked them down.

Evening, quiet, a discussion with Matyazh, he is boundlessly lazy, indolent, snot-nosed, and somehow pleasantly, affectionately lustful. The terrible truth is that all the soldiers have syphilis. Matyazh is almost cured (with practically no treatment). He had syphilis, got treatment for two weeks, he and a fellow countryman were to pay ten silver kopecks in Stavropol, his fellow countryman died, Misha had it many times, Senechka and Gerasya have syphilis, and they all go with women, and back home they have brides. The soldier's curse. Russia's curse—it's - horrifying. They swallow ground crystal, at times they drink either carbolic acid or crushed glass. All our fighters: velvet caps, rapes, Cossack forelocks, battle, Revolution, and syphilis. The whole of Galicia is infected.

A letter to Zhenya,[8] I long for her and home.

Must keep an eye on the Osobotdel[9] and the Revolutionary Tribunal.[1]

Will there really be peace talks on the 30th?

An order from Budyonny. We've let the enemy escape a fourth time, we had completely surrounded them at Brody.

Describe Matyazh, Misha. The muzhiks, I want to fathom them. We have the power to maneuver, to surround the Poles, but, when it comes down to it, our grip is weak, they can break free, Budyonny is furious, reprimands the division commander. Write the biographies of the division commander, the military commissar, Kniga,[2] and so on.

July 29, 1920. Leshniov

In the morning we set out for Leshniov. Again the same landlord as before, black-bearded, legless Froim. During my absence he was robbed of four thousand guldens, they took his boots. His wife, a smooth-tongued bitch, is colder to me, now that she has realized she can't make any

7. A staff officer in the Sixth Cavalry Division.
8. Evgeniya Borisovna Babel (1897–1957), née Gronfain, Babel's wife.
9. Osoby Otdel ("Special Section") was formed in December 1918 to identify and eradicate counterrevolutionary elements in the Red Army.
1. The Revolutionary Tribunals were the organs of military justice representing the Revolutionary Military Council.
2. The commander of the First Brigade of the Sixth Cavalry Division who had been decorated with the Order of the Red Banner. —Ed.

money off me, how greedy they are. I talk with her in German. Bad weather begins.

Froim has lame children, there are many of them, I can't tell them apart, he has hidden his cow and his horse.

Galicia is unbearably gloomy, destroyed churches and crucifixes, overcast low-hanging sky, the battered, worthless, insignificant population. Pitiful, inured to the slaughter and the soldiers and the disarray, matronly Russian women in tears, the torn-up roads, stunted crops, no sun, Catholic priests with wide-brimmed hats, without churches. An oppressive anguish emanates from all who are struggling to survive.

Are the Slavs the manure of history?

The day passes full of anxiety. The Poles broke through the Fourteenth Division's position to the right of where we are, they've again occupied Berestechko. No information whatsoever, quite a quadrille, they are moving behind our rear lines.

The mood at headquarters. Konstantin Karlovich[3] is silent. The clerks, that band of gorged, impudent, venereal ruffians, are worried. After a hard, monotonous day, a rainy night, mud—I'm wearing low shoes. And now a really powerful rain is setting in, the real victor.

We trudge through the mud, a fine, penetrating rain.

Cannon and machine gun fire closer and closer. I have an unbearable urge to sleep. There's nothing to feed the horses with. I have a new coachman: a Pole, Gowinski, tall, adept, talkative, bustling, and, needless to say, impudent.

Grishchuk is going home, at times he explodes—"I'm worn out"—he did not manage to learn German because his master had been a severe man, all they did was quarrel, but they never talked.

It also turns out he had starved for seven months, and I didn't give him enough food.

The Pole: completely barefoot, with haggard lips, blue eyes. Talkative and happy-go-lucky, a defector, he disgusts me.

An insurmountable urge to sleep. It's dangerous to sleep. I lie there fully clothed. Froim's two legs are standing on a chair next to me. A little lamp is shining, his black beard, the children are lying on the floor.

I get up ten times—Gowinski and Grishchuk are asleep—anger. I fall asleep around four o'clock, a knock at the door: we must go. Panic, the enemy is right outside the shtetl, machine gun fire, the Poles are getting nearer. Pandemonium. They can't bring the horses out, they break down the gates, Grishchuk with his repulsive despair, there's four of us, the horses haven't been fed, we have to go get the nurse, Grishchuk and Gowinski want to leave her behind, I yell in a voice not my own—the nurse? I'm furious, the nurse is foolish, pretty. We fly up the high road to Brody, I rock and sleep. It's cold, penetrating wind and rain. We have to keep an eye on the horses, the harness is unreliable, the Pole is singing, I'm shivering with cold, the nurse is chattering away foolishly. I rock and sleep. A new sensation: I can't keep my eyelids open. Describe the inexpressible urge to sleep.

---

3. Zholnarkevich, the chief of staff of the Sixth Cavalry Division.

Again we are fleeing from the Pole. There you have it: the cavalry war. I wake up, we have stopped in front of some white buildings. A village? No, Brody.

July 30, 1920. Brody

A gloomy dawn. I've had enough of that nurse. We dropped Grishchuk off somewhere. I wish him good luck.

Where do we go from here? Tiredness is stifling me. It's six o'clock in the morning. We end up with some Galician. The wife is lying on the floor with a newborn baby. He is a quiet little old man, children are lying with his naked wife, there are three or four of them.

There's some other woman there too. Dust soaked down with rain. The cellar. A crucifix. A painting of the Holy Virgin. The Uniates are really neither one thing nor the other. A strong Catholic influence. Bliss—it is warm, some kind of hot stench from the children, from the women. Silence and dejection. The nurse is sleeping, but I can't, bedbugs. There is no hay, I yell at Gowinski. The landlord doesn't have any bread, milk.

The town is destroyed, looted. A town of great interest. Polish culture. An old, rich, distinctive, Jewish population. The terrible bazaars, the dwarves in long coats, long coats and *peyes*, ancient old men. Shkolnaya Street, nine synagogues, everything half destroyed, I take a look at the new synagogue, the architecture [one word illegible, the kondesh/kodesh], the *shamas*, a bearded, talkative Jew: If only there were peace, then we'd have trade. He talks about the Cossacks' looting of the town, of the humiliations inflicted by the Poles. A wonderful synagogue, how lucky we are that we at least have some old stones. This is a Jewish town, this is Galicia, describe. Trenches, destroyed factories, the Bristol, waitresses, "Western European" culture, and how greedily we hurl ourselves onto it. Pitiful mirrors, pale Austrian Jews—the owners. And the stories: there had been American dollars here, oranges, cloth.

The high road, barbed wire, cut-down forests, and dejection, boundless dejection. There's nothing to eat, there's nothing to hope for, war, everyone's as bad as the next, as strange as the next, hostile, wild, life had been quiet and, most important, full of tradition.

Budyonny fighters in the streets. In the shops nothing but lemon fizz, and also the barbershops have opened. At the bazaar the shrews are only selling carrots, constant rain, ceaseless, penetrating, smothering. Unbearable sorrow, the people and their souls have been killed.

At the headquarters: red trousers, self-assuredness, little souls puffing themselves up, a horde of young people, Jews also among them, they are at the personal disposal of the army commander and are in charge of food.

Mustn't forget Brody and the pitiful figures, and the barbershop, and the Jews from the world beyond, and the Cossacks in the streets.

It's a disaster with Gowinski, there's absolutely no fodder for the horses. The Odessan hotel Galpernia, there is hunger in town, nothing to eat, good tea in the evening, I comfort my landlord, pale and panicky as a mouse. Gowinski found some Poles, he took their army caps, someone helped Gowinski. He is unbearable, doesn't feed the horses, is wandering about somewhere, is constantly jabbering away, can't get his hands on anything, is frightened they might arrest him, and they've already tried to arrest him, they came to me.

Night in the hotel, next door a married couple and their conversation, and words and [blacked out] coming from the woman's lips. Oh, you Russians, how disgustingly you spend your nights, and what voices your women have now! I listen with bated breath and feel despondent.

A terrible night in tortured Brody. Must be on the alert. I haul hay for the horses at night. At the headquarters. I can sleep, the enemy is advancing. I went back to my billet, slept deeply with a deadened heart, Gowinski wakes me.

July 31, 1920. Brody, Leshniov

In the morning before we leave, my *tachanka* is waiting on Zolotaya Street, an hour in a bookstore, a German store. All marvelous uncut books, albums, the West, here it is, the West and chivalrous Poland, a chrestomathy, a history of all the Boleslaws,[4] and for some reason this seems to me so beautiful: Poland, glittering garments draped over a decrepit body. I rummage like a madman, leaf through books, it is dark, then a horde pours in and rampant pillaging of office supplies begins, repulsive young men from the War Spoils Commission with a super-military air. I tear myself away from the bookstore in despair.

Chrestomathies, Tetmajer,[5] new translations, a heap of new Polish national literature, textbooks.

The headquarters are in Stanislavchik or Koziuzkov. The nurse served with the Cheka, very Russian, tender and shattered beauty. She lived with all the commissars, that's my impression, and suddenly: her album from the Kostroma Gymnasium, the schoolmistresses, idealistic hearts, the Romanoff boarding school, Aunt Manya, skating.

Again Leshniov and my old landlord, terrible dirt, the thin veneer of hospitality and respect for the Russians. Despite my kindness there is an air of unfriendliness emanating from these ruined people.

The horses, there's nothing to feed them with, they are growing thin, the *tachanka* is falling apart because of stupid little things, I hate Gowinski, he is such a happy-go-lucky, gluttonous walking disaster. They're no longer giving me any coffee.

The enemy has circumvented us, pushed us back from the river crossings, ominous rumors about a breach of the Fourteenth Division's lines, orderlies gallop off. Toward evening—Grzhimalovka (north of Churovitse). A destroyed village, we got oats, ceaseless rain, my shoes can't make the shortcut to headquarters, a torturing journey, the front line is moving closer to us, I drank some marvelous tea, boiling hot, at first the mistress of the house pretended to be ill, the village has continually been within the range of the battles to secure the crossing. Darkness, anxiety, the Pole is stirring.

Toward evening the division commander came, a marvelous figure of a man, gloves, always out in the front lines, night at the headquarters, Konstantin Karlovich's work.

4. A dynasty of medieval Polish kings.
5. Kazimierz Przerwa Tetmajer (1865–1940), Polish poet and writer.

August 1, 1920. Grzhimalovka, Leshniov

God, it's August, soon we shall die, man's brutality is indestructible. The situation is getting worse at the front. Gunfire right outside the village. They are forcing us back from the crossing. Everyone's left, a few staff people have remained, my *tachanka* is standing by the headquarters, I am listening to the sounds of battle, for some reason I feel good, there are only a few of us, no transport carts, no administrative staff, it's peaceful, simple, Timoshenko's[6] tremendous sangfroid. Kniga is impassive, Timoshenko—if he doesn't kick them out I'll shoot him, tell him that from me!—and yet he smiles. In front of us the road bloated by rain, machine guns flare up here and there, the invisible presence of the enemy in this gray and airy sky. The enemy has advanced all the way to the village. We are losing the crossing over the Styr. How many times have we headed back to ill-fated Leshniov?

The division commander is off to the First Brigade. It is terrible in Leshniov, we are stopping for two hours, the administrative staff is fleeing, the enemy wall is rising all around.

The battle near Leshniov. Our infantry is in the trenches, this is amazing: barefoot, semi-idiotic Volhynian fellows—the Russian village, and they are actually fighting the Poles, the *Pans*[7] who oppressed them. Not enough weapons, the cartridges don't fit, the boys are moping about in the stifling hot trenches, they are moved from one clearing to another. A hut by the clearing, an obliging Galician makes some tea for me, the horses are standing in a little hollow.

I went over to a battery, precise, unhurried, technical work.

Under machine gun fire, bullets shriek, a dreadful sensation, we creep along through the trenches, some Red Army fighter is panicking, and, of course, we are surrounded. Gowinski had gone to the road, wanted to dump the horses, then drove off, I found him at the clearing, my *tachanka* destroyed, peripeteia, I look for somewhere to sit, the machine-gunners push me away, they are bandaging a wounded young man, his leg is up in the air, he is howling, a friend whose horse was killed is with him, we strap the *tachanka* together, we drive off, the *tachanka* is screeching, won't turn. I have the feeling that Gowinski will be the death of me, that's fate, his bare stomach, the holes in his shoes, his Jewish nose, and the endless excuses. I move to Mikhail Karlovich's[8] cart, what a relief, I doze, it's evening, my soul is shaken, transport carts, we come to a halt on the road to Bielavtsy, then go along a road bordered by the forest, evening, cool, high road, sunset, we are rolling toward the front lines, we bring Konstantin Karlovich [Zholnarkevich] some meat.

I am greedy and pitiful. The units in the forest have left, typical picture, the squadron, Bakhturov is reading a report on the Third International, about how people from all over the world came together, a nurse's white kerchief is flashing through the trees, what is she doing here? We drive back, what kind of man is Mikhail Karlovich? Gowinski's run off,

---

6. Commander of the Sixth Cavalry Division. See note 3, p. 196. —Ed.
7. Polish: Lords.
8. Mikhail Karlovich Zholnarkevich, staff officer and brother of Konstantin Karlovich, the divisional chief of staff.

no horses. Night, I sleep in the cart next to Mikhail Karlovich. We're outside Bielavtsy.

Describe the people, the air.

The day has passed, I saw death, white roads, horses between trees, sunrise and sunset. The main thing: Budyonny fighters, horses, troop movements, and war, through the wheat fields walk solemn, barefoot, spectral Galicians.

Night in the wagon.

I chatted with some clerks by their *tachanka* on the edge of the forest.

August 2, 1920. Bielavtsy

The problem with my *tachanka*. Gowinski drives toward the shtetl, needless to say he hasn't found a blacksmith. My shouting match with the blacksmith, he jostled a woman, shrieks and tears. The Galicians don't want to fix the *tachanka*. A whole arsenal of devices, persuasion, threats, begging, what proved most effective was the promise of sugar. A long story, one smith is ill, I drag him over to another one, tears, they drag him home. They don't want to wash my clothes, nothing will induce them to.

Finally they fix the *tachanka*.

I am tired. Alarm at the headquarters. We leave. The enemy is closing in, I run to warn Gowinski, heat, I'm afraid of being late, I run through sand, manage to warn him, catch up again with the headquarters staff outside the village, no one will take me, they leave, dejection, I ride for a while with Barsukov, we are rolling toward Brody.

I am given an ambulance *tachanka* from the Second Squadron, we drive to the forest, my driver Ivan and I wait there. Budyonny arrives, Voroshilov, it is going to be a decisive battle, no more retreating, all three brigades turn around, I speak with the staff commandant. The atmosphere at the start of a battle, a large field, airplanes, cavalry maneuvers on the field, our cavalry, explosions in the distance, the battle has begun, machine guns, the sun, somewhere the two armies clash, muffled shouts of "Hurrah!" Ivan and I move back, deadly danger, I do not feel fear, but passivity, he seems to be frightened, which way should we drive, Korotchayev's[9] group turns to the right, we, for some reason, go left, the battle is raging, wounded men on horses catch up with us, one of them, deathly pale—"Brother, take me with you!"—his trousers soaked with blood, he threatens to shoot us if we don't take him, we rein in our horses, he is in a terrible state, Ivan's jacket becomes soaked with blood, a Cossack, we stop, I will bandage him, his wound is light, in the stomach, a rib has been hit, we take another one whose horse has been killed. Describe the wounded man. For a long time we go roving through the fields under fire, we can't see a thing, these indifferent roads, the weeds, we send out horsemen, we come to a high road—which way should we go, Radzivillov or Brody?

The administrative staff is supposed to be at Radzivillov along with all the transport carts, but in my opinion, Brody would be more interesting, the battle is being fought for Brody. Ivan's opinion prevails, some of the

9. D. D. Korotchayev was the provisional commander of the Fourth Cavalry Division from May 1 to June 18, 1920.

cart drivers are saying the Poles are in Brody, the transport carts are fleeing, the army staff has left, we drive to Radzivillov. We arrive in the
night. All this time we've been eating carrots and peas, penetrating
hunger, we're covered in dirt, haven't slept. I took a hut on the outskirts
of Radzivillov. Good choice, my knack for this sort of thing is getting better. An old man, a girl. The buttermilk is marvelous, we had all of it,
they're making tea with milk, Ivan is going to get some sugar, machine
gun fire, the thunder of carts, we run out of the house, the horse is suddenly limping, that's how things are sometimes, we are running in panic,
we're being shot at, we have no idea what's going on, they'll catch us any
moment now, we make a dash for the bridge, pandemonium, we fall into
the marshes, wild panic, a dead man lying there, abandoned carts,
shells, *tachankas*. Traffic jam, night, terror, carts standing in an endless
line, we are moving, a field, we stop, we sleep, stars. What upsets me
most in all of this is the lost tea, I'm so upset, it's peculiar. I think about
it all night and hate the war.

 What a crazy life.

August 3, 1920

Night in the field, we are rolling toward Brody in a buggy. The town
keeps changing hands. The same horrifying picture, the town, half
destroyed, is waiting once more. The provision station, I run into Barsukov at the edge of town. I drive over to the headquarters. Deserted,
dead, dismal. Zotov[1] is sleeping stretched out on some chairs, like a
corpse. Borodulin and Pollak are also asleep. The building of the Bank
of Prague, ransacked and gutted, water closets, those bank cashier windows, mirror glass.

 Word has it that the division commander is in Klyokotovo, we spent
about two hours in devastated Brody with its ominous air, tea in a barbershop. Ivan is standing outside the headquarters. Should we leave,
shouldn't we leave. We leave for Klyokotovo, we turn off the Leshniov
high road, we don't know—is it ours or Polish, we drive on feeling our
way, the horses are exhausted, one of them is limping harder, we eat
potatoes in the village, brigades show up, indescribable beauty, a frightful force is moving, endless lines, a big farm, everything in ruins, a
thresher, a Clenton locomobile, a tractor, the locomobile is still working,
it's a hot day.

 The battlefield, I meet the division commander, where is the staff,
we've lost Zholnarkevich. The battle begins, artillery cover, explosions
nearby, a grim moment, the decisive battle over whether we will stem the
Polish offensive or not, Budyonny to Kolesnikov[2] and Grishin: "I'll shoot
you!" They leave on foot, pale.

 Before that, the terrible field sown with hacked-up men, an inhuman
cruelty, inconceivable wounds, crushed skulls, young, white, naked bodies are gleaming in the sun, notebooks lying around, single pages, military booklets, Bibles, bodies in the rye.

 I absorb these impressions mainly with my mind. The battle begins,
I'm given a horse. I see columns forming, chains, they attack, I feel sorry

---

1. See note 1, p. 188.
2. Actually Nikolay Petrovich Kolesov, commander of the Third Brigade.

for these poor men—they are not men, they are columns—the gunfire reaches maximum intensity, the carnage is carried out in silence. I ride on, rumors that the division commander is being recalled?

The beginning of my adventures, I ride with the transport carts toward the high road, the battle is growing fiercer, I find the provision station, we're being fired at on the high road, the whistling of shells, explosions a mere twenty paces away, the feeling of hopelessness, the transport carts are flying at full gallop, tag along with the Twentieth Regiment of the Fourth Division, wounded men, the querulous commander: No, he says, not wounded, just a little bang on the head. They're professionals. And everywhere fields, sun, bodies, I sit by the field kitchen, hunger, peas, nothing to feed my horse with.

Field kitchen, talking, we sit on the grass, the regiment suddenly pulls out, I have to go to Radzivillov, the regiment heads for Leshniov and I feel helpless, I am afraid of getting cut off from them. An endless journey, dusty roads, I move to a cart, a Quasimodo, two donkeys, a grim spectacle: the hunchbacked driver, silent, his face dark like the forests of Murom.

We drive, I have a terrible feeling—I am getting farther and farther from the division. Hope flutters up—then suddenly the opportunity to take a wounded man to Radzivillov, the wounded man has a pale, Jewish face.

We ride into the forest, we're fired at, shells a hundred paces away, endless rushing back and forth along the forest edge.

Thick sand, impassable. The ballad of the tortured horses.

An apiary, we search the hives, four huts in the forest—nothing there, everything ransacked, I ask a Red Army fighter for bread, he answers me, "I don't want anything to do with Jews." I'm an outsider, in long trousers, not one of them, I am lonely, we ride on, I am so tired I can barely stay on my mare, I have to look after her myself, we arrive at Konyushkovo, we steal some barley, they tell me: Go take whatever you want, take everything. I go through the village looking for a nurse, the womenfolk are hysterical, within five minutes of our arrival the looting begins, some women are beating their breasts, lamenting, sobbing unbearably, these never-ending horrors are hard to bear, I look for a nurse, insuperable sorrow, I swipe a jug of milk from the regimental commander, snatch a dough-bun out of the hands of a peasant woman's son.

Ten minutes later, we're off. Who'd have thought it! The Poles are somewhere nearby. Back we go again, I don't think I can bear this for much longer, and at a fast trot at that, at first I ride with the commander, then I tag along with the transport carts, I want to move over onto a cart, they all give me the same answer: The horses are tired. You want me to get off so you can sit here, huh? Well, so get yourself up here, just mind the corpses! I look at the sackcloth, corpses are lying under it.

We come to a field, there are many transport carts from the Fourth Division, a battery, again a field kitchen, I look for some nurses, a difficult night, I want to sleep, I have to feed my horse, I lie down, the horses are eating the excellent wheat, Red Army fighters in the wheat, ashen, at the end of their tether. My mare is tormenting me, I run after her, I join a nurse, we sleep on a *tachanka*, the nurse is old, bald, most probably a Jewess, a martyr, unbearable cursing, the vehicular driver keeps trying to push her off, the horses roam about, the vehicular driver won't wake up, he is rough and foul-mouthed, she says: Our heroes are terrible people. She covers him, they sleep in each other's arms, the poor old nurse, that driver should be shot, the foul language, the cursing, this is not the nurse's world—we fall asleep. I wake up two hours later—our bridle has been stolen. Despair. Dawn. We are seven versts away from Radzivillov. I ride off willy-nilly. The poor horse, all of us are poor, the regiment moves on. I get going.

For this day, the main thing is to describe the Red Army fighters and the air.

August 4, 1920

I am heading alone to Radzivillov. A difficult road, nobody on it, the horse is tired, with every step I'm afraid of running into Poles. Things turned out well, in the area around Radzivillov there are no units, in the shtetl uneasiness, they send me to the station, the townspeople devastated and completely used to change. Sheko[3] in the automobile. I'm in Budyonny's billet. A Jewish family, young ladies, a group from the Bukhteyev Gymnasium, Odessa, my heart skips a beat.

O joy, they give me cocoa and bread. The news: we have a new division commander, Apanasenko,[4] and a new divisional chief of staff, Sheko. Wonder of wonders.

Zholnarkevich arrives with his squadron, he is pitiable, Zotov informs him he has been replaced: I'll go sell buns on Sukharevka! Of course you're of the new school, he says, you know how to set up units, in the old days I could do that too, but now, without any reserves, I can't.

He has a high fever, he says things that would be better left unsaid, a shouting match with Sheko, he immediately raises his voice: "The general chief of staff ordered you to report to headquarters!"—"I don't have to pass any tests, I'm not some little boy who hangs out at headquarters!" He leaves the squadron and goes off. The old guard is leaving, everything is falling apart, now Konstantin Karlovich [Zholnarkevich] is gone too.

Another impression, both harsh and unforgettable, is the arrival of the division commander on his white horse, along with his orderlies. The whole ragtag from the headquarters comes running with chickens for the army commander, they are patronizing, loutish, Sheko, haughty, asks about the operations, the division commander tells him, smiles, a marvelous, statuesque figure of a man, and despair. Yesterday's battle—the Sixth Division's brilliant success—1,000 horses, three regiments chased back into the trenches, the enemy routed, pushed back, the division headquarters are in Khotin. Whose success is this, Timoshenko's or Apanasenko's? Comrade Khmelnitsky: a Jew,[5] a guzzler, a coward, insolent, but for the army commander a chicken, a piglet, corn on the cob.

3. Yakov Vasilevich Sheko, the new chief of staff of the Sixth Cavalry Division, who replaced Konstantin Karlovich Zholnarkevich.
4. Iosif Rodinovich Apanasenko (1890–1943), the prototype of Babel's Pavlichenko in Red Cavalry, a noncommissioned officer in World War I, a commander of a Cossack partisan regiment that joined the First Cavalry and later became the Sixth Division. Commander of the First Brigade, he replaced Timoshenko as commander of the Sixth Division in August and continued through October. Several of the division's regiments (Babel was attached to one of them) were disbanded, and eight hundred of its soldiers were court-martialed and many shot for their mutiny "against Communists and Jews" (killing their commissars and staging Jewish pogroms) during the army's hasty retreat from Poland. Both Apanasenko and Kniga were sentenced to death but were allowed to restore their honor by leading their units in the campaign against the Whites in the Crimea in November to December in 1920. Like many other commanders of the First Cavalry Army, Apanasenko rose through the ranks in the 1920s and 1930s; he died in battle in 1943 as General and Deputy Commander of the Voronezh Front. —Ed.
5. R. P. Khmelnitsky, Voroshilov's aide-de-camp, was a Jew who happened to have the same name as Bogdan Khmelnitsky, the legendary seventeenth-century Cossack leader.

The orderlies detest him, the insolent orderlies, their only interest: chickens, lard, they eat like pigs, they're fat, the chauffeurs stuff themselves with lard, all this on the porch in front of the house. My horse has nothing to eat.

The mood has changed completely, the Poles are retreating, even though they are still occupying Brody, we're beating them again, Budyonny's pulled us through.

I want to sleep, I can't. The changes in the life of the division will have a significant effect. Sheko in a cart. Me with the squadron. We are riding to Khotin, again at a trot, we've put fifteen versts behind us. I'm billeted with Bakhturov. He is devastated, the division commander is out and he feels he will be next.[6] The division is shaken, the fighters walk around in silence, what will come next? Finally I have had some supper: meat, honey. Describe Bakhturov, Ivan Ivanovich, and Petro. I sleep in the threshing shed, finally some peace.

August 5, 1920. Khotin

A day of rest. We eat, I wander through the sun-drenched village, we rest, I had some lunch, supper—there is honey, milk.

The main thing: internal changes, everything is topsy-turvy.

I feel so sorry for our division commander it hurts, the Cossacks are worried, a lot of hushed talk, an interesting sight, they gather in groups, whisper to one another, Bakhturov is crestfallen, our division commander was a hero, the new commander won't let him into the room, from 600–6,000, a harsh humiliation, they hurled it in his face, "You are a traitor!" Timoshenko laughed.[7] Apanasenko is a new and colorful figure of a man, ugly, pockmarked, passionate, haughty, ambitious, he sent an appeal to headquarters at Stavropol and the Don about the disorder in the rear lines, in order to let them know back home that he was a division commander. Timoshenko was more pleasant, cheerful, broad-minded, and, perhaps, worse. The two men—I suppose they didn't like each other. Sheko is showing his true colors, unbelievably heavy-handed orders, haughtiness. Work at headquarters now completely changed. There is no transport or administrative staff. Lepin is raising his head—he is hostile, idiotic, answers back to Sheko.[8]

In the evening music, and dance—Apanasenko trying to be popular— the circle widens, he chooses a horse for Bakhturov from the Polish ones, now everyone is riding Polish horses, they are marvelous, narrow-chested, tall, English, chestnut horses—I mustn't forget this. Apanasenko has the horses paraded.

All day long, talk of intrigues. A letter to the rear lines.

Longing for Odessa.

Remember the figure, face, cheerfulness of Apanasenko, his love of horses, chooses one for Bakhturov.

About the orderlies who throw their lot in with the "masters." What will Mikheyev, lame Sukhorukov, all the Grebushkos, Tarasovs, and Ivan Ivanoviches do with Bakhturov?[9] They all follow blindly.

---

6. Bakhturov was in fact to be relieved of his duties the following day.
7. Timoshenko's tenure as commander of the Sixth Cavalry Division ended with the battle near Brody. He was held responsible for the defeat.
8. Lepin, as a staff officer, now had to report to Sheko, the new chief of staff.
9. Now that Bakhturov, their former "master," has lost his tenure.

About the Polish horses, about the squadrons galloping through the dust on the tall, golden, narrow-chested, Polish horses. Forelocks, chains, suits tailored out of carpets.

Six hundred horses got stuck in the marshes, unlucky Poles.

August 6, 1920. Khotin

The exact same place. We get ourselves in order, shoe the horses, eat, there is a break in operations.

My landlady is a small, timorous, fragile woman with tortured, meek eyes. Lord, how the soldiers torment her, the endless cooking, we steal honey. Her husband came home, bombs from an airplane chased his horses away. The old man hasn't eaten for five days, now he is going off into the wide world to look for his horses, a saga. An ancient old man.

A sultry day, thick, white silence, my soul rejoices, the horses are standing, oats are being threshed for them, the Cossacks sleep next to them all day long, the horses are resting, that's our top priority.

From time to time Apanasenko flits by, unlike the reserved Timoshenko he is one of us, he is our fatherly commander.

In the morning Bakhturov leaves, his retinue follows, I watch the new military commissar's work, a dull but polished Moscow worker, this is where his strength lies: humdrum but grand visions, three military commissars, absolutely must describe limping Gubanov, the scourge of the regiment, a desperate fighter, a young, twenty-three-year-old youth, modest Shiryayev, cunning Grishin. They are sitting in the garden, the military commissar is asking them questions, they gossip, talk pompously about World Revolution, the mistress of the house is shaking apples from the trees because all her apples have been eaten, the military commissar's secretary, lanky, with a ringing voice, goes looking for food.

New trends at the headquarters: Sheko is issuing special orders, bombastic and highfalutin, but short and energetic, he gives the Revolutionary Council his opinion, he acts on his own initiative.

Everyone is pining for Timoshenko, there won't be a mutiny.

Why am I gripped by a longing that will not pass? Because I am far from home, because we are destroying, moving forward like a whirlwind, like lava, hated by all, life is being shattered to pieces, I am at a huge, never-ending service for the dead.

Ivan Ivanovich is sitting on a bench, talking of the days when he spent twenty thousand, thirty thousand. Everyone has gold, everyone ransacked Rostov, threw sacks of money over their saddles and rode off. Ivan Ivanovich dressed and kept women. Night, threshing shed, fragrant hay, but the air is heavy, I am smothered by something, by the sad senselessness of my life.

August 7, 1920. Berestechko

It is evening now, 8. The lamps in the shtetl have just been lit. There is a funeral service in the room next door. Many Jews, the doleful chants of home, they rock, sit on benches, two candles, the eternal light on the windowsill. The funeral service is for the landlady's granddaughter, who died of fright after their house was looted. The mother is crying, tells me the story as she prays, we stand at the table, I have been pounded by sorrow for two months now. The mother shows me a photograph tattered by teardrops, and they all say what an uncommon beauty she was, some commander ran amok, banging on the door in the night, they dragged them out of bed, the Poles ransacked the house, then the Cossacks, ceaseless vomiting, she wasted away. The main thing for the Jews—she was a beauty, no other like her in all the shtetl.

A memorable day. In the morning we went from Khotin to Berestechko. I ride with Ivanov, the military commissar's secretary, a lanky, voracious, spineless fellow, a lout—and, believe it or not, he is the husband of Komarova, the singer, "We used to do concerts, I'll write to her to come." A Russian maenad.

The corpse of a slaughtered Pole, a terrible corpse, naked and bloated, monstrous.

Berestechko has changed hands quite a few times. There are historic sites outside Berestechko, Cossack graves. And this is the main thing, everything is repeating itself: Cossack against Pole, or rather serf against *Pan.*

I won't forget this shtetl, covered courtyards, long, narrow, stinking, everything 100–200 years old, the townsfolk more robust than in other places, the main thing is the architecture, the white and watery blue little houses, the little backstreets, the synagogues, the peasant women. Life is almost back on track again. People had led a good life here—respected Jewry, rich Ukrainians, market fairs on Sundays, a specialized class of Russian artisans: tanners trading with Austria, contraband.

The Jews here are less fanatical, better dressed, heartier, they even seem more cheerful, the very old men in long coats, the old women, everything exudes the old days, tradition, the shtetl is saturated in the bloody history of the Polish Jewish ghetto. Hatred for the Poles is unanimous. They looted, tortured, scorched the pharmacist's body with white-hot iron pokers, needles under his nails, tore out his hair, all because a Polish officer had been shot at—sheer idiocy! The Poles have gone out of their minds, they are destroying themselves.

An ancient church, the graves of Polish officers in the churchyard, fresh burial mounds, ten days old, white birch crosses, all this is terrible, the house of the Catholic priest has been destroyed, I find ancient books, precious Latin manuscripts. The priest, Tuzynkiewicz, I find a photograph of him, he is short and fat, he worked here for forty-five years, he lived in one place, a scholar, the assortment of books, many of them in Latin, editions of 1860, that was when Tuzynkiewicz lived. His living quarters are old-fashioned, enormous, dark paintings, photographs of the prelate conventions at Zhitomir, portraits of Pope Pius X, a nice face, an exquisite portrait of Sienkiewicz[1]—here he is the essence of the nation. Blanketing all this is the stench of Sukhin's pitiful little soul. How new all this is for me, the books, the soul of the Catholic *Pater,* a Jesuit, I want to fathom the heart and soul of Tuzynkiewicz, and I have. Lepin suddenly plays the piano, touchingly. He sometimes sings in Latvian. Remember: his little bare feet, so droll you could die. What a funny creature.

1. Henryk Sienkiewicz (1846–1916), Polish novelist, author of *Quo Vadis?* (1896).

A terrible incident: the looting of the church, they've ripped down the chasubles, the precious, glittering material is torn and lying on the floor, a sister of mercy dragged off three bundles, they are tearing the linings, the candles have been taken, the receptacles smashed open, the papal bulls thrown out, the money taken—this magnificent church, what its eyes have seen these past 200 years (Tuzynkiewicz's manuscripts), how many counts and serfs, magnificent Italian art, rosy *Paters* rocking the infant Jesus, the magnificent dark Jesus, Rembrandt, a Madonna like that of Murillo, maybe even by Murillo, and the main thing: the pious, well-fed Jesuits, the eerie Chinese figurine behind a veil, Jesus, a little bearded Jew in crimson Polish raiment, a bench, the shattered shrine, the figure of St. Valentine. The beadle, shivering like a bird, squirms, speaks in a jumble of Russian and Polish, I mustn't touch these things, he sobs. These animals are only here to plunder. It's very clear, the old gods are being destroyed.

An evening in the town. The church has been closed. In the late afternoon I go to the castle of Count Raciborski. A seventy-year-old man, his mother ninety. It was just the two of them, they were mad, people say. Describe the two of them. An old, aristocratic Polish house, most probably over a hundred years old, antlers, old bright paintings on the ceilings, remains of antlers, small rooms for the servants upstairs, flagstones, corridors, excrement on the floors, little Jewish boys, a Steinway piano, sofas slashed down to the springs, remember the white, delicate oak doors, French letters dated 1820, *notre petit héros achève 7 semaines.*[2] My God, who wrote that, when, the letters have been trampled on, I took some relics, a century, the mother is a countess, Steinway piano, park, pond.

I cannot tear myself away—I think of Hauptmann, *Elga.*[3]

A rally in the castle park, the Jews of Berestechko, dull Vinokurov,[4] children running around, a Revolutionary Committee is being elected, the Jews twirl their beards, the Jewesses listen to words about the Russian paradise, the international situation, about the uprising in India.

A night filled with anxiety, someone said we should be on the alert, all alone with feeble *mishures,*[5] unexpected eloquence, what did he talk about?

August 8, 1920. Berestechko

I am settling down in the shtetl. There were fairs here. The peasants sell pears. They are paid with long-abolished banknotes. This place had been bubbling over with life, Jews had exported grain to Austria, human and commodity contraband, the closeness of the border.

Unusual barns, cellars.

I've been billeted with the proprietress of a coach inn, a gaunt, redheaded bitch. Ilchenko bought some cucumbers, reads the *Zhurnal dlya Vsekh,*[6] and is pontificating about economic policy, the Jews are to blame for everything, a blunt, Slavic creature who filled his pockets during the

---

2. French: our little hero is already seven weeks old.
3. Gerhart Hauptmann (1862–1946), German dramatist whose play *Elga* was first performed in 1905.
4. Aleksander Nikolayevich Vinokurov was the military commissar of the Sixth Cavalry Division. He replaced Bakhturov.
5. Yiddish: servants.
6. *Magazine for All*, a popular monthly magazine published before the October Revolution. —*Ed.*

plundering of Rostov. Some adopted children, the mother recently died. The tale of the pharmacist under whose nails the Poles stuck needles, people gone berserk.

A hot day, the townsfolk are roaming about, they are coming alive again, there will be trade.

Synagogue, Torahs, built thirty-six years ago by an artisan from Kremenets, they paid him fifty rubles a month, gold peacocks, crossed arms, ancient Torahs, the *shamases* show no enthusiasm whatever, wizened old men, the bridges of Berestechko, how they shook, the Poles gave all this a long-faded tint. The little old man at whose house Korotchayev, the demoted division commander,[7] and his Jewish subaltern, are billeted. Korotchayev was chairman of the Cheka somewhere in Astrakhan, rotten to the core. Friendship with the Jew. We drink tea at the old man's. Silence, placidity. I roam about the shtetl, there is pitiful, powerful, undying life inside the Jewish hovels, young ladies in white stockings, long coats, so few fat people.

We are sending out scouts to Lvov. Apanasenko[8] sends dispatches to the Stavropol Executive Committee, heads will roll on the home front, he is delighted. The battle outside Radzivillov, Apanasenko acts heroically—instantaneous disposition of the troops, he almost opened fire on the retreating Fourteenth Division. We're nearing Radzikhov. Moscow newspapers of July 29. The commencement of the Second Congress of the Third International, finally the unification of all peoples has been realized, everything is clear: two worlds, and a declaration of war. We will be fighting endlessly. Russia has thrown down a challenge. We will march to Europe to subjugate the world. The Red Army has become an international factor.

I have to take a closer look at Apanasenko. *Ataman*.[9]

The quiet old man's funeral service for his granddaughter.

Evening, performance in the count's garden, the theatergoers of Berestechko, an idiot of an orderly, the young ladies of Berestechko, silence descends, I would like to stay here awhile and get to know it.

August 9, 1920. Lashkov

The move from Berestechko to Lashkov. Galicia. The division commander's carriage, the division commander's orderly is Lyovka—the one who chases horses like a gypsy. The tale of how he whipped his neighbor Stepan, a former constable under Denikin who had harassed the people, when Stepan came back to the village. They wouldn't just "butcher" him, they beat him in prison, slashed his back, jumped up and down on him, danced, an epic exchange: "Are you feeling good, Stepan?" "I'm feeling bad." "And the people you harassed, did they feel good?" "No, they felt bad." "And did you think that someday you might be feeling bad?" "No, I didn't." "You should have thought about that, Stepan, because what we think is that if we'd fallen into your hands, you'd have butchered us, so f— it, now, Stepan, we will kill you." When they finally left him he was

7. See note 6, p. 216.
8. The new commander of the Sixth Cavalry Division.
9. Also *hetman,* a Cossack leader.

already getting cold. Another tale about Shurka the nurse. Night, battle, regiments form, Lyovka in the phaeton, Shurka's lover is heavily wounded, gives Lyovka his horse, they take away the wounded man and return to the battle. "Shurka, we only live once, and then we die!" "Well, okay, then." She went to a boarding school in Rostov, gallops with the regiment, she can do fifteen. "But now, Shurka, let's go, we're retreating." The horses got caught up in the barbed wire, he galloped four versts, a village, he sits down, cuts through the barbed wire, the regiment rides through, Shurka leaves the formation. Lyovka prepares supper, they want food, they ate, chatted, go on, Shurka, one more time. Well, okay. But where?

She went galloping after the regiment, he went to sleep. If your wife comes, I'll kill her.

Lashkov is a green, sunny, quiet, rich Galician village. I've been billeted at the deacon's house. His wife has just given birth. Downtrodden people. A clean, new hut, but there's nothing in the hut. Next door typical Galician Jews. They think—he must be Jewish, no? The story: they came plundering, one of them chopped off the heads of two chickens, found the things in the threshing shed, dug up things from the earth, herded everyone together in the hut, the usual story, remember the young man with sideburns. They tell me that the head rabbi lives in Belz, they finished off the rabbis.

We rest, the First Squadron is in my front garden. Night, a lamp is standing on my table, the horses snort quietly, everyone here is a Kuban Cossack, they eat, sleep, cook together, marvelous, silent camaraderie. They're all peasants, in the evenings they sing with rich voices songs that sound like hymns, devotion to horses, small bundles, saddle, bridle, ornate sabers, greatcoat, I sleep surrounded by them.

I sleep in the field during the day. No operations, rest—what a marvelous and necessary thing it is. The cavalry, the horses are recuperating after this inhuman work, people are recuperating from all the cruelty, living together, singing songs with quiet voices, they are telling each other things.

The headquarters are in the school. The division commander at the priest's.

August 10, 1920. Lashkov

Our rest continues. Scouts to Radzikhov, Sokolovka, Stoyanov, all in the direction of Lvov. News has come that Aleksandrovsk was taken, gigantic complications in the international situation, will we have to go to war against the whole world?

A fire in the village. The priest's threshing shed is burning. Two horses, thrashing around with all their might, burned. You can't lead a horse out of a fire. Two cows broke out, the hide of one of them split, blood is coming out of the crack, touching and pitiful.

The smoke envelops the entire village, bright flames, plump black billows of smoke, a mass of wood, hot in the face, everything carried out of the priest's house and the church, thrown into the front garden. Apanasenko in a red Cossack jacket, a black coat, clean-shaven face, a terrifying apparition, an ataman.

Our Cossacks, a sad sight, dragging loot out over the back porch, their eyes burning, all of them looking uneasy, ashamed, this so-called habit of theirs is ineradicable. All the church banners, ancient saints' books,[1] icons are being carried out, strange figures painted whitish pink, whitish blue, monstrous, flat-faced, Chinese or Buddhist, heaps of paper flowers, will the church catch fire, peasant women are wringing their hands in silence, the townspeople, frightened and silent, are running barefoot, everyone sits in front of their hut with a bucket. They are apathetic, cowed, remarkably numb, but they'd drop everything to put out their own fires. They've come to terms with the plundering—the soldiers are circling around the priest's trunks like rapacious, overwrought beasts, they say there's gold in there, one can take it away from a priest, a portrait of Count Andrzej Szceptycki, the Metropolitan of Galicia. A manly magnate with a black ring on his large, aristocratic hand. The lower lip of the old priest, who has served in Lashkov for thirty-five years, is constantly trembling. He tells me about Szceptycki, that he is not "educated" in the Polish spirit, comes from Ruthenian grandees, "The Counts of Szceptycki," then they went over to the Poles, his brother is commander in chief of the Polish forces, Andrzej returned to the Ruthenians. His ancient culture, quiet and solid. A good, educated priest who has laid in a supply of flour, chickens, wants to talk about the universities, Ruthenians, the poor man, Apanasenko with his red Cossack jacket is staying with him.

Night—an unusual sight, the high road is brilliantly lit, my room is bright, I'm working, the lamp is burning, calm, the Kuban Cossacks are singing with feeling, their thin figures by the campfires, the songs are totally Ukrainian, the horses lie down to sleep. I go to the division commander. Vinokurov tells me about him—a partisan, an ataman, a rebel, Cossack freedom, wild uprising, his ideal is Dumenko,[2] an open wound, one has to submit oneself to the organization, a deadly hatred for the aristocracy, clerics, and, most of all, for the intelligentsia, which he cannot stomach in the army. Apanasenko will graduate from a school—how is it different from the times of Bogdan Khmelnitsky?

Late at night. Four o'clock.

August 11, 1920. Lashkov

A day of work, sitting at the headquarters, I write to the point of exhaustion, a day of rest. Toward evening, rain. Kuban Cossacks are staying the night in my room, strange: peaceful and warlike, domestic, and peasants of obvious Ukrainian origin, not all that young.

About the Kuban Cossacks. Camaraderie, they always stick together, horses snort beneath the windows night and day, the marvelous smell of horse manure, of sun, of sleeping Cossacks, twice a day they boil large pails of soup and meat. At night Kuban Cossacks come to visit. Ceaseless rain, they dry themselves and eat their supper in my room. A religious Kuban Cossack in a soft hat, pale face, blond mustache. They are decent,

1. *Chetyi Minei*, anthologies of Old Church Slavonic writings about the lives of saints, organized by month and date.
2. Boris Mokiyevich Dumenko, the legendary commander of the Fourth Cavalry Division. Decorated in early 1920, he was charged with conspiracy and executed in May. His command passed to Semyon Budyonny. —*Ed.*

friendly, wild, but somehow more sympathetic, domestic, less foul-mouthed, more calm than the Cossacks from Stavropol and the Don.

The nurse came, how clear it all is, must describe that, she is worn out, wants to leave, everyone has had her—the commandant, at least that's what they say, Yakovlev,[3] and, O horror, Gusev. She's pitiful, wants to leave, sad, talks gibberish, wants to talk to me about something and looks at me with trusting eyes, she says I am her friend, the others, the others are scum. How quickly they have managed to destroy a person, debase her, make her ugly. She is naive, foolish, receptive even to revolutionary phrases, and the silly fool talks a lot about the Revolution, she worked in the Cheka's Culture and Education Division, how many male influences.

Interview with Apanasenko. This is very interesting. Must remember this. His blunt, terrible face, his hard body, like Utochkin's.[4]

His orderlies (Lyovka), magnificent golden horses, his hangers-on, carriages, Volodya, his adopted son—a small Cossack with an old man's face, curses like a grown man.

Apanasenko, hungry for fame, here we have it: a new class of man. Whatever the operational situation might be, he will always go off and come back again, an organizer of units, totally hostile to officers, four George Crosses, a career soldier, a noncommissioned officer, an ensign under Kerensky, chairman of the Regimental Committee, stripped officers of their stripes, long months on the Astrakhan steppes, indisputable authority, a professional soldier.

About the atamans, there had been many there, they got themselves machine guns, fought against Shkuro and Mamontov,[5] merged into the Red Army, a heroic epic. This is not a Marxist Revolution, it is a Cossack uprising that wants to win all and lose nothing. Apanasenko's hatred for the rich, an unquenchable hatred of the intelligentsia.

Night with the Kuban Cossacks, rain, it's stuffy, I have some sort of strange itch.

August 12, 1920. Lashkov

The fourth day in Lashkov. A completely downtrodden Galician village. They used to live better than the Russians, good houses, strong sense of decency, respect for priests, the people honest but blood-drained, my landlord's deformed child, how and why was he born, not a drop of blood left in the mother, they are continually hiding something somewhere, pigs are grunting somewhere, they have probably hidden cloth somewhere.

A day off, a good thing—my correspondence, mustn't neglect that.

Must write for the newspaper, and the life story of Apanasenko.

The division is resting, a kind of stillness in one's heart, and people are better, songs, campfires, fire in the night, jokes, happy, apathetic horses, someone reads the newspaper, they stroll around, shoe their horses. What all this looks like, Sokolov is going on leave, I give him a letter home.

---

3. The political commissar of the Sixth Cavalry Division.
4. Sergey Utochkin, a celebrated Russian aviation pioneer from Odessa.
5. Andrey Grigoryevich Shkuro and Konstantin Konstantinovich Mamontov were White Cossack generals.

I keep writing about pipes, about long-forgotten things, so much for the Revolution, that's what I should be concentrating on.

Don't forget the priest in Lashkov, badly shaven, kind, educated, possibly mercenary: a chicken, a duck, his house, lived well, droll etchings.

Friction between the military commissar and the division commander. He got up and left with Kniga[6] while Yakovlev, the divisional political commissar, was giving a report, Apanasenko went to the military commissar.

Vinokurov: a typical military commissar, always wants things done his way, wants to put the Sixth Division on track, struggle with the partisan attitude, dull-witted, bores me to death with his speeches, at times he's rude, uses the informal "you" with everyone.

August 13, 1920. Nivitsa

At night the order comes: head for Busk, thirty-five versts east of Lvov.

We set out in the morning. All three brigades are concentrated in one place. I'm on Misha's horse, it was taught to run and won't go at a walking pace, it goes at a trot. The whole day on horseback with the division commander. The farm at Porady. In the forest, four enemy airplanes, a volley of fire. Three brigade commanders: Kolesnikov, Korotchayev, Kniga. Vasily Ivanovich [Kniga]'s sly move, headed for Toporov (Chanyz) in a bypass maneuver, didn't run into the enemy anywhere. We are at the Porady farm, destroyed huts, I pull an old woman out of a hatch door, dovecotes. Together with the lookout on the battery. Our attack by the woods.

A disaster—swamps, canals, the cavalry can't be deployed anywhere, attacks in infantry formation, inertia, is our morale flagging? Persistent and yet light fighting near Toporov (in comparison to the Imperialist carnage), they're attacking on three sides, cannot overpower us, a hurricane of fire from our artillery, from two batteries.

Night. All the attacks failed. Overnight the headquarters move to Nivitsa. Thick fog, penetrating cold, horse, roads through forests, campfires and candles, nurses on *tachankas,* a harsh journey after a day of anxiety and ultimate failure.

All day long through fields and forests. Most interesting of all: the division commander, his grin, foul language, curt exclamations, snorting, shrugs his shoulders, is agitated, responsibility for everything, passion— if only he had been there everything would have been fine.

What can I remember? The night ride, the screams of the women in Porady when we began (I broke off writing here, two bombs thrown from an airplane exploded a hundred paces from us, we're at a clearing in the forest west of St[ary] Maidan) taking away their linen, our attack, something we can't quite make out, not frightening at a distance, some lines of men, horsemen riding over a meadow, at a distance this all looks like it is done haphazardly, it does not seem in the least bit frightening.

When we advanced close to the little town, things began to heat up, the moment of the attack, the moment when a town is taken, the feverish, frightening, mounting rattle of the machine guns driving one to

6. See note 4, p. 200.

hopelessness and despair, the ceaseless explosions and, high up over all of this, silence, and nothing can be seen.

The work of Apanasenko's headquarters, every hour there are reports to the army commander, he is trying to ingratiate himself.

We arrive frozen through, tired, at Nivitsa. A warm kitchen. A school.

The captivating wife of the schoolmaster, she's a nationalist, a sort of inner cheerfulness about her, asks all kinds of questions, makes us tea, defends her *mowa*,[7] your *mowa* is good and so is my *mowa*, and always laughter in her eyes. And this in Galicia, this is nice, it's been ages since I've heard anything like this. I sleep in the classroom, in the straw next to Vinokurov.[8]

I've got a cold.

August 14, 1920

The center of operations—the taking of Busk and the crossing of the Bug. All day long attacking Toporov, no, we've stopped. Another indecisive day. The forest clearing by St[ary] Maidan. The enemy has taken Lopatin.

Toward evening we throw them out. Once again Nivitsa. Spend the night at the house of an old woman, in the yard together with the staff.

August 15, 1920

Morning in Toporov. Fighting near Busk. Headquarters are in Busk. Force our way over the Bug. A blaze on the other side. Budyonny's in Busk.

Spend the night in Yablonovka with Vinokurov.

August 16, 1920

To Rakobuty, a brigade made it across.

I'm off to interrogate the prisoners.

Once again in Yablonovka. We're moving on to N[ovy] Milatin, St[ary] Milatin, panic, spend the night in an almshouse.

August 17, 1920

Fighting near the railroad tracks near Liski. The butchering of prisoners. Spend the night in Zadvurdze.

August 18, 1920

Haven't had time to write. We're moving on. We set out on August 13. From that time on we've been on the move, endless roads, squadron banners, Apanasenko's horses, skirmishes, farms, corpses. Frontal attack on Toporov, Kolesnikov[9] in the attack, swamps, I am at an observation point, toward evening a hurricane of fire from two batteries. The Polish infantry is waiting in the trenches, our fighters go, return, horse-holders are leading the

---

7. Ukrainian: language.
8. The military commissar of the Sixth Cavalry Division.
9. Kolesov, commander of the Third Brigade.

wounded, Cossacks don't like frontal attacks, the cursed trenches cloud with smoke. That was the 13th. On the 14th, the division moves to Busk, it has to get there at all cost, by evening we had advanced ten versts. That's where the main operation has to take place: the crossing of the Bug. At the same time they're searching for a ford.

A Czech farm at Adamy, breakfast in the farmhouse, potatoes with milk, Sukhorukov thrives under every regime, an ass-kisser, Suslov dances to his tune, as do all the Lyovkas. The main thing: dark forests, transport carts in the forests, candles above the nurses, rumbling, the tempos of troop movement. We're at a clearing in the forest, the horses are grazing, the airplanes are the heroes of the day, air operations are on the increase, airplane attacks, five-six planes circle endlessly, bombs at a hundred paces, I have an ash-gray gelding, a repulsive horse. In the forest. An intrigue with the nurse: Apanasenko made her a revolting proposition then and there, they say she spent the night with him, now she speaks of him with loathing. She likes Sheko, but the divisional military commissar likes her, cloaking his interest in her with the pretext that she is, as he says, without protection, has no means of transport, no protector. She talks of how Konstantin Karlovich courted her, fed her, forbade others to write her letters, but everyone kept on writing to her. She found Yakovlev extremely attractive, and the head of the Registration Department, a blond-haired boy in a red hood asked for her hand and her heart, sobbing like a child. There was also some other story but I couldn't find out anything about it. The saga of the nurse, and the main thing: they talk a lot about her and everyone looks down on her, her own coachman doesn't talk to her, her little boots, aprons, she does favors, Bebel brochures.

Woman and Socialism.[1]

One can write volumes about the women in the Red Army. The squadrons set off into battle—dust, rumbling, the baring of sabers, savage cursing—they gallop ahead with hitched-up skirts, dust-covered, fat-breasted, all of them whores, but comrades too, and whores because they are comrades, that's the most important thing, they serve in every way they can, these heroines, and then they're looked down upon, they give water to the horses, haul hay, mend harnesses, steal things from churches and from the townsfolk.

Apanasenko's agitation, his foul language, is it willpower?

Night again in Nivitsa, I sleep somewhere in the straw, because I can't remember anything, everything in me is lacerated, my body aches, a HUNDRED versts by horse.

I spend the night with Vinokurov. His attitude toward Ivanov.[2] What kind of man is this gluttonous, pitiful, tall youth with a soft voice, wilted soul, and sharp mind? The military commissar is unbearably rough with him, swears at him ceaselessly, finds fault with everything: What's up with you—curses fly—You didn't do it? Go pack your things, I'm kicking you out!

---

1. *Die Frau und der Sozialismus* (Woman and Socialism, 1879) by August Bebel (1840–1913), a founder of the Social Democratic Party of Germany. —*Ed.*
2. Vinokurov's secretary.

I have to fathom the soul of the fighter, I am managing, this is all terrible, they're animals with principles.

Overnight the Second Brigade took Toropov in a nocturnal attack. An unforgettable morning. We move at a fast trot. A terrible, uncanny shtetl, Jews stand at their doors like corpses, I wonder about them: what more are you going to have to go through? Black beards, bent backs, destroyed houses, here there's [illegible], remnants of German efficiency and comfort, some sort of inexpressible, commonplace, and burning Jewish sadness. There's a monastery here. Apanasenko is radiant. The Second Brigade rides past. Forelocks, jackets made out of carpets, red tobacco pouches, short carbines, commanders on majestic horses, a Budyonny brigade. Parade, marching bands, we greet you, Sons of the Revolution. Apanasenko is radiant.

We move on from Toporov—forests, roads, the staff on the road, orderlies, brigade commanders, we fly on to Busk at a fast trot, to its eastern part. What an enchanting place (on the 18th an airplane is flying, it will now drop bombs), clean Jewesses, gardens full of pears and plums, radiant noon, curtains, in the houses the remnants of the petite bourgeoisie, a clean and possibly honest simplicity, mirrors, we have been billeted at the house of a fat Galician woman, the widow of a schoolmaster, wide sofas, many plums, unbearable exhaustion from overstrained nerves (a shell came flying, didn't explode), couldn't fall asleep, lay by the wall next to the horses remembering the dust and the horrible jostle in the transport cart, dust—the majestic phenomenon of our war.

Fighting in Busk. It's on the other side of the bridge. Our wounded. Beauty—over there the shtetl is burning. I ride to the crossing, the sharp experience of battle, have to run part of the way because it's under fire, night, the blaze is shining, the horses stand by the huts, a meeting with Budyonny is under way, the members of the Revolutionary War Council[3] come out, a feeling of danger in the air, we didn't take Busk with our frontal attack, we say good-bye to the fat Galician woman and drive to Yablonovka deep in the night, the horses are barely moving ahead, we spend the night in a pit, on straw, the division commander has left, the military commissar and I have no strength left.

The First Brigade found a ford and crossed the Bug by Poborzhany. In the morning with Vinokurov at the crossing. So here is the Bug, a shallow little river, the staff is on a hill, the journey has worn me out, I'm sent back to Yablonovka to interrogate prisoners. Disaster. Describe what a horseman feels: exhaustion, the horse won't go on, the ride is long, no strength, the burned steppe, loneliness, no one there to help you, endless versts.

Interrogation of prisoners in Yablonovka. Men in their underwear, exhausted, there are Jews, light-blond Poles, an educated young fellow, blunt hatred toward them, the blood-drenched underwear of a wounded man, he's not given any water, a fat-faced fellow pushes his papers at me. You lucky fellows—I think—how did you get away. They crowd around me, they are happy at the sound of my benevolent voice, miserable dust, what a difference between the Cossacks and them, they're spineless.

---

3. *Revvoensoviet*, founded in 1918, were councils in which military commanders and political representatives of the Bolshevik government conferred on military tactics.

From Yablonovka I return by *tachanka* to the headquarters. Again the crossing, endless lines of transport carts crossing over (they don't wait even a minute, they are right on the heels of the advancing units), they sink in the river, trace-straps tear, the dust is suffocating, Galician villages, I'm given milk, lunch in a village, the Poles have just pulled out of here, everything is calm, the village dead, stifling heat, midday silence, there's no one in the village, it is astounding that there is such light, such absolute and unruffled silence, peace, as if the front were well over a hundred versts away. The churches in the villages.

Farther along the road is the enemy. Two naked, butchered Poles with small, slashed faces are glittering through the rye in the sun.

We return to Yablonovka, tea at Lepin's, dirt, Cherkashin[4] denigrates him and wants to get rid of him. If you look closely, Cherkashin's face is dreadful. In his body, tall as a stick, you can see the muzhik—he is a drunkard, a thief, and a cunning bastard.

Lepin is dirty, dim-witted, touchy, incomprehensible.

Handsome Bazkunov's long, endless tale, a father, Nizhny-Novgorod, head of a chemistry department, Red Army, prisoner under Denikin, the biography of a Russian youth, his father a merchant, an inventor, dealt with Moscow restaurants. Chatted with him during the whole trip. We are heading for Milatin, plums along the road. In St[ary] Milatin there is a church, the priest's house, the priest lives in a luxurious house, unforgettable, he keeps squeezing my hand, sets off to bury a dead Pole, sits down with us, asks whether our commander is a good man, a typical Jesuitical face, shaven, gray eyes dart around—a pleasure to behold—a crying Polish woman, his niece, begging that her heifer be returned to her, tears and a coquettish smile, all very Polish. Mustn't forget the house, knickknacks, pleasant darkness, Jesuitical, Catholic culture, clean women, and the most aromatic and agitated *Pater*, opposite him a monastery. I want to stay here. We wait for the order for where we are to stay—in Stary Milatin or in Novy Milatin. Night. Panic. Some transport carts, the Poles have broken through somewhere, pandemonium on the road, three rows of transport carts, I'm in the Milatin schoolhouse, two beautiful old maids, it's frightening how much they remind me of the Shapiro sisters from Nikolayev, two quiet, educated Galician women, patriots, their own culture, bedroom, possibly curlers, in thundering, war-torn Milatin, outside these walls transport carts, cannons, fatherly commanders telling tales of their heroic feats, clouds of orange dust, the monastery is enveloped by them. The sisters offer me cigarettes, they breathe in my words of how everything will be marvelous— it's like balm, they have blossomed out, and we speak elegantly about culture.

A knock at the door. The commandant wants me. A fright. We ride over to Novy Milatin. *N. Milatin.* With the military commissar in the almshouse, some sort of town house, sheds, night, vaults, the priest's maid, dark, dirty, myriads of flies, tiredness beyond compare, the tiredness of the front.

Daybreak, we depart, the railroad has to be breached (this all takes place on August 17), the Brody-Lvov railroad.

<hr>

4. Lepin's orderly.

My first battle, I saw the attack, they gather in the bushes, the brigade commanders ride up to Apanasenko—careful Kniga, all slyness, rides up, talks up a storm, they point to the hills, there beneath the forest, there over the hollow, they've spotted the enemy, the regiments ride to attack, sabers in the sun, pale commanders, Apanasenko's hard legs, hurrah.

What happened? A field, dust, the staff in the plains, Apanasenko curses in a frenzy, brigade commander—destroy those bastards, f—ing bandits.

The mood before the battle, hunger, heat, they gallop in attack, nurses.

A thunder of hurrahs, the Poles are crushed, we ride out onto the battlefield, a little Pole with polished nails is rubbing his pink, sparsely haired head, answers evasively, prevaricating, hemming and hawing, well, yes, Sheko, roused and pale, answer, who are you—I'm, he ducks the question, a sort of ensign, we ride off, they take him, a good-looking fellow behind him loads his gun, I shout—"Yakov Vasilevich [Sheko]!" He acts like he didn't hear, rides on, a shot, the little Pole in his underwear falls on his face and twitches. Life is disgusting, murderers, it's unbearable, baseness and crime.

They are rounding up the prisoners, undressing them, a strange picture—they undress incredibly fast, shake their heads, all this in the sun, mild embarrassment, all the command personnel is there, embarrassment, but who cares, so cover your eyes. I will never forget that "sort of" ensign who was treacherously murdered.

Ahead—terrible things. We crossed the railroad tracks by Zadvurdze. The Poles are fighting their way along the railroad tracks to Lvov. An attack in the evening at the farm. Carnage. The military commissar and I ride along the tracks, begging the men not to butcher the prisoners, Apanasenko washes his hands of it. Sheko's tongue ran away with him: "Butcher them all!" It played a horrifying role. I didn't look into their faces, they impaled them, shot them, corpses covered with bodies, one they undress, another they shoot, moans, yells, wheezing, our squadron led the attack, Apanasenko stands to the side, the squadron has dressed up, Matusevich's horse was killed, his face frightening, dirty, he is running, looking for a horse. This is hell. How we bring freedom—terrible. They search a farm, men are dragged out, Apanasenko: Don't waste bullets, butcher them. Apanasenko always says—butcher the nurse, butcher the Poles.

We spend the night in Zadvurdze, bad quarters, I'm with Sheko, good food, ceaseless skirmishes, I'm living a soldier's life, completely worn out, we are waiting in the forest, nothing to eat all day, Sheko's carriage arrives, brings something, I'm often at the observation point, the work of the batteries, the clearings, hollows, the machine guns are mowing, the Poles are mainly defending themselves with airplanes, they are becoming a menace, describe the air attacks, the faraway and seemingly slow hammering of the machine guns, panic in the transport carts, it's harrowing, they are incessantly gliding over us, we hide from them. A new use of aviation, I think of Mosher, Captain Fauntleroy in Lvov, our wanderings from one brigade to the next, Kniga only likes bypass maneuvers, Kolesnikov frontal attacks, I ride with Sheko on reconnaissance, endless forests, deadly danger, on the hills, bullets are buzzing all around before

the attack, the pitiful face of Sukhorukov with his saber, I tag along
behind the staff, we await reports, but they advancing, doing bypass
maneuvers. The battle for Barshchovitse. After a day of fluctuations, Polish columns
manage in the evening to break through to Lvov. When Apanasenko saw
this, he went mad, he is shaking, the brigades are going full force even
though they are dealing with a retreating enemy, and the brigades stretch
out in endless ribbons, three cavalry brigades are hurled into the attack,
Apanasenko is triumphant, snorts, sends out Litovchenko as the new commander of the Third Brigade to replace Kolesnikov, who's been wounded,
you see them, there they are, go finish them off, they're running. He med-
dles in the artillery action, interferes with the orders of the battery commanders, feverish, they were hoping to repeat what had happened at
Zadvurdze, but it wasn't to be. Swamps on one side, ruinous fire on the
other. March to Ostrov, the Sixth Cavalry Division is supposed to take
Lvov from the southeast.

Gigantic losses among the command personnel: Korotchayev, heavily
wounded, his adjutant, a Jew, was killed, the commander of the Thirty-
fourth Regiment wounded, all the commissars of the Thirty-first Regiment out of action, all the chiefs of staff wounded, above all Budyonny's
commanders.

The wounded crawl onto *tachankas*. This is how we're going to take
Lvov, the reports to the army commander are written in the grass,
brigades gallop, orders in the night, again forests, bullets buzz, artillery
fire chases us from one place to another, miserable fear of airplanes, get
down off your horse, a bomb's about to explode, there's a revolting sensation in your mouth. Nothing to feed the horses with.

I see now what a horse means to a Cossack and a cavalryman.

Unhorsed cavalrymen on the hot dusty roads, their saddles in their
arms, they sleep like corpses on other men's carts, horses are rotting
all around, all that's talked about is horses, the customs of barter, the
excitement, horses are martyrs, horses are sufferers—their saga, I
myself have been gripped by this feeling, every march is an agony for
the horse.

Apanasenko's visits to Budyonny with his retinue. Budyonny and
Voroshilov at a farm, they sit at a table. Apanasenko's report, standing at
attention. The failure of the special regiment: they had planned an
attack on Lvov, set out, the special regiment's sentry post was, as always,
asleep, it was taken down, the Poles rolled their machine guns within a
hundred paces, rounded up the horses, wounded half the regiment.

The Day of the Transfiguration of Our Savior Jesus Christ—19
August—in Barshchovitse, a butchered, but still breathing, village, peace,
a meadow, a flock of geese (we dealt with them later—Sidorenko or
Yegor chopped up the geese on a block with their sabers), we eat boiled
goose. That day, white as they were, they beautified the village, on the
green meadows the villagers, festive but feeble, spectral, barely able to
crawl out of their hovels, silent, strange, dazed, and completely cowed.

There is something quiet and oppressive about this holiday.

The Uniate priest in Barshchovitse. A ruined, defiled garden, Budyonny's headquarters had been here, and smashed, smoked-out beehives,

this is a terrible, barbaric custom—I remember the broken frames, thousands of bees buzzing and fighting by the destroyed hives, their panicking swarms.

The priest explains to me the difference between the Uniate and the Russian Orthodox faith.[5] Sheptitsky is a tall man, he wears a canvas cassock. A plump man, a dark, chubby face, shaved cheeks, sparkling little eyes with a sty.

The advance on Lvov. The batteries are drawing nearer and nearer. A rather unsuccessful skirmish by Ostrov, but still the Poles withdraw. Information on Lvov's defenses—schoolmasters, women, adolescents. Apanasenko will butcher them—he hates the intelligentsia, with him it's deep-rooted, he wants an aristocracy on his own terms, a muzhik and Cossack state.

August 21, a week of battle has passed, our units are four versts outside Lvov.

An order: the whole Red Cavalry is being put under the command of the Western Front.[6] They are moving us north to Lublin. There will be an attack there. They are withdrawing the army, now four versts from the town, even though it took so much time for them to get there. The Fourteenth Army will replace us. What is this? Madness, or the impossibility of a town being taken by the cavalry? I will remember the forty-five-verst ride from Barshchovitse to Adamy for the rest of my life. I on my little piebald horse, Sheko in his carriage, heat and dust, the dust of the Apocalypse, stifling clouds, endless lines of transport carts, all the brigades are on the move, clouds of dust from which there is no escape, one is afraid of suffocating, shouting all around, movement, I ride with a squadron over fields, we lose Sheko, the most horrendous part of it begins, the ride on my little horse which can't keep up, we ride endlessly and always at a trot, I am completely exhausted, the squadron wants to overtake the transport carts, we overtake them, I am afraid of being left behind, my horse is drifting along like a bit of fluff, to the point of inertia, all the brigades are on the move, all the artillery, they've each left one regiment behind as a covering force, and these regiments are to reunite with the division at the onset of darkness. In the night we ride through silent, dead Busk. What is special about Galician towns? The mixture of the dirty, ponderous East (Byzantium and the Jews) with the beer-drinking German West. Fifteen km. from Busk. I can't hold out anymore. I change my horse. It turns out that there is no covering on the saddle. Riding is torture. I keep constantly changing position. A rest stop in Kozlov. A dark hut, bread with milk. A peasant, a warm and pleasant person, was a prisoner of war in Odessa, I lie on the bench, mustn't fall asleep, I'm wearing another man's service jacket, the horses in the dark, it's stuffy in the hut, children on the floor. We arrived in Adamy at four in the morning. Sheko is asleep. I leave my horse somewhere, there is hay, and I lie down to sleep.

5. The Uniate church, also known as the Eastern Rite or Eastern Catholic Church, recognizes the primacy of the Pope while retaining the Orthodox liturgy, sacred art, and autonomous organizational structure that are in keeping with the Eastern Orthodox tradition. Among the Eastern Catholic churches in communion with Rome, the largest to this day is the Ukrainian Catholic Church.—Ed.

6. Zapfront (Zapadny Front), February 1919 to January 1921, was the central Red Army command of western and northwestern strategic points in Soviet Russia.

August 21, 1920. Adamy

Frightened Ruthenians. Sun. Nice. I'm ill. Rest. The whole day in the threshing shed. I sleep, feel better toward evening, my head pounds, aches. I'm billeted with Sheko. Yegor, the chief of staff's lackey. We eat well. How we get our food. Vorobyov took over the Second Squadron. The soldiers are pleased. In Poland, where we are heading, there's no need to hold back—with the Galicians, who are completely innocent, we had to be more careful. I'm resting, I'm not in the saddle.

Conversation with Artillery Division Commander Maksimov, our army is out to make some money, what we have is not revolution but an uprising of renegade Cossacks.

They are simply an instrument the party is not above using.

Two Odessans, Manuilov and Boguslavsky,[7] operational air force military commissar, Paris, London, a handsome Jew, a big talker, articles in a European magazine, the divisional chief of staff's adjutant, Jews in the Red Cavalry, I tell them what's what. Wearing a service jacket, the excesses of the Odessan bourgeoisie, painful news from Odessa. They're being smothered there. What about my father? Have they really taken everything away from him? I have to give some thought to the situation back home.

I'm turning into a sponger.

Apanasenko has written a letter to the officers of the Polish army: You bandits, stop fighting, surrender, you *Pans,* or we will butcher you all!

Apanasenko's letter to the Don headquarters, to Stavropol, there they are making things difficult for our fighters, for the Sons of the Revolution, we are heroes, we have no fear, we will march ahead.

A description of the squadron's rest, they steal hens, the squealing of pigs, agents, musical flourishes on the town square. They wash clothes, thresh oats, come galloping with sheaves. The horses, wiggling their ears, eat oats. The horse is everything. Horse names: Stepan, Misha, Little Brother, Old Girl. Your horse is your savior, you are aware of it every moment, even if you might beat it inhumanly. No one takes care of my horse. They barely take care of it.

August 22, 1920. Adamy

Manuilov, the divisional chief of staff's adjutant, has a stomachache. I'm not surprised. Served with Muravyov,[8] in the Cheka, something to do with military investigation, a bourgeois, women, Paris, air force, something to do with his reputation, and he's a Communist. Boguslavsky, the secretary, frightened, sits silently and eats.

A peaceful day. We march on northward.

I'm billeted with Sheko. I can't do anything. I'm tired, battered. I sleep and eat. How we eat. The system. The provisions depot men and the

---

7. Manuilov was the adjutant to Sheko, the divisional chief of staff, and Boguslavsky was staff secretary.
8. Mikhail Artemyevich Muravyov, a legendary figure who in 1918, during his tenure as commander of the Western Front, instigated the anti-Bolshevik Muravyov revolt, for which he was executed. See note 5, p. 58.

foragers won't give us anything. The arrival of the Red Army fighters in the village, they search through everything, cook, all night the stoves sputter, the household daughters suffer, the squealing of pigs, they come to the military commissar with receipts. The pitiful Galicians.

The saga of how we eat. We eat well: pigs, hens, geese.

Those who don't take part are "rag-looters" and "wimps."

August 23/24, 1920. Viktov

Ride on to Vitkov in a cart. System of using civilian carts, poor civilians, they are harassed for two, three weeks, are let go, given a pass, are snatched up by other soldiers, are harassed again. An episode: where we are billeted a boy comes back from the transport carts. Night. His mother's joy.

We march into the Krasnostav-Lublin district. We've overtaken the army, which is four versts from Lvov. The cavalry did not manage to take it.

The road to Vitkov. Sun. Galician roads, endless transport carts, factory horses, ravaged Galicia, Jews in shtetls, somewhere an unscathed farm, Czech we imagine, we attack the unripe apples, the beehives.

More details about the beehives another time.

On the road, in the cart, I think, I mourn the fate of the Revolution.

The shtetl is unusual, rebuilt on a single plan after its destruction, little white houses, tall wooden roofs, sadness.

We are billeted with the divisional chief of staff's aides, Manuilov knows nothing about staff work, the hassles of trying to get horses, no one will give us any, we ride on the civilians' carts, Boguslavsky wears lilac-colored drawers, a great success with the girls in Odessa.

The soldiers ask for a theatrical show. They're fed *His Orderly Let Him Down*.[9]

The divisional chief of staff's night: where's the Thirty-third Regiment, where did the Second Brigade go, telephone, orders from army headquarters to the brigade commander, 1, 2, 3!

The orderlies on duty. The setup of the squadrons—Matusevich and Vorobyov,[1] a former commandant, an unalterably cheerful and, from what I can see, a foolish man.

The divisional chief of staff's night: the division commander wants to see you.

August 25, 1920. Sokal

Finally, a town. We ride through the shtetl of Tartakuv, Jews, ruins, cleanliness of a Jewish kind, the Jewish race, little stores.

I am still ill, I've still not gotten back on my feet after the battles outside Lvov. What stuffy air these shtetls have. The infantry had been in Sokal, the town is untouched, the divisional chief of staff is billeted with some Jews. Books, I saw books. I'm billeted with a Galician woman, a rich one at that, we eat well, chicken in sour cream.

---

9. A stock comic farce of Russian amateur theatricals, *A Ukrainian Bumpkin Confused Him, Or, His Orderly Let Him Down* was made into a popular film in 1911, scripted and directed by Alexander Arbo (1882–1962). —*Ed.*

1. Now demoted to the rank of squadron commander.

I ride on my horse to the center of town, it's clean, pretty buildings, everything soiled by war, remnants of cleanliness and originality.

The Revolutionary Committee. Requisitions and confiscation. Interesting: they don't touch the peasantry, all the land has been left at its disposal. The peasantry is left alone.

The declarations of the Revolutionary Committee.

My landlord's son—a Zionist and *ein ausgesprochener Nationalist*.[2] Normal Jewish life, they look to Vienna, to Berlin, the nephew, a young man, is studying philosophy, wants to go to the university. We eat butter and chocolate. Sweets.

Friction between Manuilov and the divisional chief of staff.[3] Sheko tells him to go to—

"I have my pride," they won't give him a billet, no horse, there's the cavalry for you, this isn't a holiday resort. Books—*polnische, Juden*.[4]

In the evening, the division commander in his new jacket, well fed, wearing his multicolored trousers, red-faced and dim-witted, out to have some fun, music at night, the rain disperses us. It is raining, the tormenting Galician rain, it pours and pours, endlessly, hopelessly.

What are our soldiers up to in this town? Dark rumors.

Boguslavsky has betrayed Manuilov. Boguslavsky is a slave.

August 26, 1920. Sokal

A look around town with the young Zionist. The synagogues: the Hasidic one is a staggering sight, it recalls three hundred years ago, pale, handsome boys with *peyes*, the synagogue as it was two hundred years ago, the selfsame figures in long coats, rocking, waving their hands, howling. This is the Orthodox party, they support the Rabbi of Belz, the famous Rabbi of Belz, who's made off to Vienna. The moderates support the Rabbi of Husyatin. Their synagogue. The beauty of the altar made by some artisan, the magnificence of the greenish chandeliers, the worm-eaten little tables, the Belz synagogue—a vision of ancient times. The Jews ask me to use my influence so they won't be ruined, they're being robbed of food and goods.

The Yids hide everything. The cobbler, the Sokal cobbler, is a proletarian. His apprentice's appearance, a red-haired Hasid—a cobbler.

The cobbler has been waiting for Soviet rule—now he sees the Yid-killers and the looters, and that there'll be no earnings, he is shaken, and looks at us with distrust. A hullabaloo over money. In essence, we're not paying anything, 15–20 rubles. The Jewish quarter. Indescribable poverty, dirt, the boxed-in quality of the ghetto.

The little stores, all of them open, whiting and resin, soldiers ransacking, swearing at the Yids, drifting around aimlessly, entering homes, crawling under counters, greedy eyes, trembling hands, a strange army indeed.

The organized looting of the stationery store, the owner in tears, they tear up everything, they come up with all kinds of demands, the

---

2. German: a vehement nationalist.
3. Manuilov was the divisional chief of staff's adjutant, and Sheko, his boss, was the divisional chief of staff.
4. German: Polish ones, Jews.

daughter with Western European self-possession, but pitiful and red-faced, hands things over, is given some money or other, and with her storekeeper's politeness tries to act as if everything were as it should be, except that there are too many customers. The owner's wife is so full of despair that she cannot make head or tail of anything.

At night the town will be looted—everyone knows that.

Music in the evening—the division commander is out to have some fun. In the morning he wrote some letters to Stavropol and the Don. The front will not tolerate the disgraceful goings-on in the rear lines. The same old story.

The division commander's lackeys lead his magnificent horses with their breastplates and cruppers back and forth.

The military commissar and the nurse. A Russian man—a sly muzhik—coarse and sometimes insolent and confused. Has a high opinion of the nurse, sounds me out, asks me all kinds of questions, he is in love.

The nurse goes to say good-bye to the division commander, and this after everything that's happened. Everyone's slept with her. That boor Suslov is in the adjoining room—the division commander is busy, he's cleaning his revolver.

I'm given boots and underwear. Sukhorukov received them and dealt them out himself, he's a super-lackey, describe him.

A chat with the nephew who wants to go to university.

Sokal: brokers and artisans—Communism, they tell me, isn't likely to strike root here.

What battered, tormented people these are.

Poor Galicia, poor Jews.

My landlord has eight doves.

Manuilov has a sharp confrontation with Sheko, he has many sins in his past. A Kiev adventurer. He came to us demoted from having been chief of staff of the Third Brigade.

Lepin. A dark, terrifying soul.

The nurse—twenty-six men and one woman.[5]

August 27, 1920

Skirmishes near Znyatin, Dluzhnov. We ride northwest. Half the day with the transport carts. Heading to Laszczow, Komarow. In the morning we set off from Sokal. A regular day with the squadrons: we wander through forests and glades with the division commander, the brigade commanders come, sun, for five hours I haven't gotten off my horse, brigades ride past. Transport cart panic. I left the carts at a clearing in the forest, rode over to the division commander. The squadrons on a hill. Reports to the army commander, a cannonade, there are no airplanes, we ride from one place to another, a regular day. Heavy exhaustion toward evening, we spend the night in Wasylow. We didn't reach Laszczow, our target destination.

The Eleventh Division is in Wasylow or somewhere near there, pandemonium, Bakhturov[6]—a tiny division, he has lost some of his sparkle. The Fourth Division is mounting successful battles.

5. A reference to Maxim Gorky's story, "Twenty-Six Men and One Woman."
6. Pavel Vasilyevich Bakhturov, the former military commissar of the Sixth Cavalry Division, had become the military commissar of the Eleventh Division on August 8.

August 28, 1920. Komarow

I rode off from Wasylow ten minutes after the squadrons. I am riding with three horsemen. Earth mounds, glades, destroyed farms, somewhere in the greenery are the Red Columns, plums. Gunfire, we don't know where the enemy is, we can't see anybody, machine guns are hammering quite near and from different directions, my heart tenses, and so every day single horsemen are out looking for their field headquarters, they are carrying reports. Toward noon I found my squadron in a ravaged village with all the villagers hiding in their cellars, under trees covered in plums. I ride with the squadrons. I ride into Komarow with the division commander, red hood. A magnificent, unfinished, red church. Before we entered Komarow, after the gunfire (I was riding alone), silence, warm, a bright day, a somewhat strange and translucent calm, my soul ached, all alone, nobody getting on my nerves, fields, forests, undulating valleys, shady roads.

We stop opposite the church.

The arrival of Voroshilov and Budyonny. Voroshilov blows up in front of everyone: "Lack of energy!" He gets heated, a heated individual, the whole army restless, he rides and yells, Budyonny is silent, smiles, white teeth. Apanasenko defends himself: "Let's go inside"—"Why do we keep letting the enemy get away?" Voroshilov shouts. "Without contact you can't strike."

Is Apanasenko worthless?

The pharmacist who offers me a room. Rumors of atrocities. I go into the shtetl. Indescribable fear and desperation.

They tell me what happened. Hiding in a hut, they are frightened that the Poles will return. Last night Captain Yakovlev's[7] Cossacks were here. A pogrom. The family of David Zis, in their home, the old prophet, naked and barely breathing, the butchered old woman, a child with chopped-off fingers. Many of these people are still breathing, the stench of blood, everything turned topsy-turvy, chaos, a mother over her butchered son, an old woman curled up, four people in one hut, dirt, blood under a black beard, they're just lying there in their blood. Jews in the town square, the tormented Jew who shows me everything, a tall Jew takes his place. The rabbi has gone into hiding, everything has been smashed to pieces in his house, he doesn't leave his burrow until evening. Fifteen people have been killed: Hasid Itska Galer, 70 years old, David Zis, synagogue *shamas*, 45 years old, his wife and his daughter, 15 years old, David Trost, his wife, the butcher.

At the house of a raped woman.

Evening—at my landlord's, a conventional home, Sabbath evening, they didn't want to cook until the Sabbath was over.

I look for the nurses, Suslov laughs. A Jewish woman doctor.

We are in a strange, old-fashioned house, they used to have everything here—butter, milk.

At night, a walk through the shtetl.

The moon, their lives at night behind closed doors. Wailing inside. They will clean everything up. The fear and horror of the townsfolk. The

7. A Cossack captain fighting on the Polish side.

main thing: our men are going around indifferently, looting where they can, ripping the clothes off the butchered people.

The hatred for them is the same, they too are Cossacks, they too are savage, it's pure nonsense that our army is any different. The life of the shtetls. There is no escape. Everyone is out to destroy them, the Poles did not give them refuge. All the women and girls can scarcely walk. In the evening a talkative Jew with a little beard, he had a store, his daughter threw herself out of a second-floor window, she broke both arms, there are many like that.

What a powerful and magnificent life of a nation existed here. The fate of the Jewry. At our place in the evening, supper, tea, I sit drinking in the words of the Jew with the little beard who asks me plaintively if it will be possible to trade again.

An oppressive, restless night.

August 29, 1920. Komarow, Labunye, Pnevsk

We pull out of Komarow. During the night our men looted, in the synagogue they threw away the Torah scrolls and took the velvet coverings for their saddles. The military commissar's orderly eyes the phylacteries, wants to take the straps. The Jews smile obsequiously. That is religion.

Everyone is greedily looking at what hasn't yet been taken. They rummage through bones and ruins. They've come here to make some money.

My horse is limping, I take the divisional chief of staff's horse, want to trade, I am too soft, a talk with the village elder, nothing comes of it.

Labunye. A vodka distillery. A hundred thousand liters of spirits. Under guard. Rain, penetrating and incessant. Autumn, everything points to autumn. The Polish family of the bailiff. The horses under a canopy, the Red Army fighters drinking in spite of the prohibition. Labunye is a threatening peril for the army.

Everything is secretive and simple. The people are silent, as if nothing out of the ordinary were going on. Oh, you Russians! Everything breathes secrecy and menace. Sidorenko has calmed down.

The operation to take Zamosc. We are ten versts from Zamosc. There I will ask about R.Y.

The operation, as always, is uncomplicated. Bypass via the west and the north, and then take the town. Alarming news from the Western Front. The Poles have taken Bialystok.

We ride on. The looted estates of Kulaczkowski near Labunki. White columns. An enchanting, even if manorial, setup. The destruction is beyond belief. The real Poland: bailiffs, old women, white-blond children, rich, semi-European villages with elders, local headmen, all Catholic, beautiful women. Our men are dragging away oats on the estate. The horses stand in the drawing room, black horses. Well—after all, we do have to keep them out of the rain. Extremely precious books in a chest, they didn't have time to take them along: the constitution approved by the Sejm[8] at the beginning of the eighteenth century, old folios from the times of Nicholas I, the Polish code of laws, precious bindings, Polish

---

8. The Polish Parliament.

manuscripts of the sixteenth century, the writings of monks, old French novels.

There is no destruction upstairs, it was merely searched, all the chairs, walls, sofas have been slashed open, the floors ripped up—not destroyed, just searched. Delicate crystal, the bedroom, the oak beds, powder case, French novels on the tables, many French and Polish books about child care, smashed intimate feminine toiletries, remnants of butter in a butter dish, newlyweds?

A settled way of life, gymnastic equipment, good books, tables, bottles of medicine—everything sacrilegiously besmirched. An unbearable feeling of wanting to run away from the vandals, but they walk about, search, describe how they walk, their faces, hats, their cursing: Goddamn, f—ing Mother of God, the Holy Virgin. They drag sheaves of oats through the impassable mud.

We near Zamosc. A terrible day. The rain is the victor, not letting up even for a minute. The horses can barely pull the carts. Describe this unendurable rain. We wander deep into the night. We are soaked to the bone, tired, Apanasenko's red hood. We bypass Zamosc, the units are three to four versts away from it. The armored trains won't let us pass, they shower us with artillery fire. We stay in the fields, wait for reports, dull rivulets flow. Brigade Commander Kniga in a hut, a report. Our fatherly commander. We cannot do a thing against the armored train. It turns out we didn't know that there was a railroad here, it's not marked on the map, a mix-up, so much for our reconnaissance.

We roam around and keep waiting for them to take Zamosc. Damn it to hell. The Poles keep fighting better and better. Horses and men are shivering. We spend the night in Pnevsk. A fine Polish peasant family. The difference between Poles and Russians is striking. The Poles live more cleanly, cheerfully, play with their children, beautiful icons, beautiful women.

August 30, 1920

In the morning we leave Pnevsk. The operation to take Zamosc continues. The weather is as bad as before, rain, slush, impassible roads, we barely slept: on the floor, in the straw, wearing our boots—on constant alert.

Again roaming around. We go with Sheko to the Third Brigade. He goes with his revolver drawn to attack the Zavadi Train Station. Lepin and I stay in the forest. Lepin is squirming. The skirmish at the station. Sheko has a doomed look on his face. Describe the "rapid fire." The station has been taken. We ride along the railroad tracks. Ten prisoners, one of them we arrive too late to save.[9] A revolver wound? An officer. Blood is flowing out of his mouth. Thick, red, clotting blood is drenching his whole face, it looks terrible, red, covered in his thick blood. The prisoners are all undressed. Trousers have been slung over the squadron leader's saddle. Sheko makes him give them back. They try to make the prisoners put on their clothes, but they won't put anything on. An

---

9. See Babel's stories "And Then There Were Nine" and "And Then There Were Ten" (in *The Complete Works of Isaac Babel*), in which the Cossacks capture Polish prisoners at the Zavadi Station. Babel and Lepin arrive too late to stop the Cossacks from murdering one of the prisoners.

officer's cap. "And then there were nine." Foul words all around. They want to kill the prisoners. A bald, lame Jew in his drawers who can't keep up with the horse, a terrible face, an officer no doubt, gets on everyone's nerves, he can't walk, they are all in the grip of animal fear, pitiful, unfortunate people, Polish proletarians, one of the Poles is stately, calm, with sideburns, wearing a knitted jersey, he comports himself with dignity, everyone keeps asking if he's an officer. They want to butcher them. A dark cloud gathers over the Jew. A frenzied Putilov worker—They should all be butchered, the scum—the Jew is hopping after us, we always drag prisoners along, and then hand them over to the authorities of the military escort. What happens to them. The rage of the Putilov worker, foaming at the mouth, his saber: I will butcher the scum and won't have to answer for it.

We ride over to the division commander, he is with the First and Second Brigades. We are always within sight of Zamosc, we can see its chimneys, houses, we are trying to take it from all sides. A night attack is in preparation. We are three versts from Zamosc, are waiting for the town to be seized, will spend the night there. Field, night, rain, penetrating cold, we are lying on the wet earth, there's nothing to feed the horses with, it's dark, men ride with messages. The First and the Third Brigades will lead the attack. Kniga and Levda[1]—a semiliterate Ukrainian who is commander of the Third Brigade—arrive the way they always do. Tiredness, apathy, the unquenchable thirst for sleep, almost desperation. A line advances briskly in the dark, a whole brigade on foot. Next to us a cannon. An hour later the infantry advances. Our cannon is firing continuously, a soft, cracking sound, flames in the night, the Poles are firing rockets, crazed shooting from rifles and machine guns, this is hell, we wait, it's three in the morning. The battle ebbs. Nothing came of it. For us more and more often now things come to nothing. What does this mean? Is the army giving up?

We ride ten versts to Sitaniec to lodge for the night. The rain is getting stronger. An indescribable fatigue. My one and only dream—a billet. My dream becomes a reality. A dismayed old Pole with his wife. The soldiers, needless to say, clean him out. Extreme fear, they've all been hiding in cellars. Heaps of noodles, butter, milk, bliss. I keep unearthing more and more food. A tortured, nice old woman. Delightful melted butter. Suddenly gunfire, bullets whistling about the stables, about the horses' legs. We up and run. Despair. We ride to the other end of the village. Three hours of sleep interrupted by reports, debriefings, anxiety.

August 31, 1920. Czesniki

A meeting with the brigade commanders. A farm. A shady glade. The destruction total. Not even any clothes left. We clean out the last of the oats. An orchard, an apiary, the destruction of the hives, terrible, the bees buzz around in desperation, the hives are detonated with gunpowder, the men wrap themselves in their greatcoats and launch an attack on the hives, a bacchanalia, they drag out the frames with their sabers, the honey streams onto the ground, the bees sting, they are smoked out

1. Ya. A. Levda was commander of the Third Brigade of the Fourteenth Cavalry Division.

with tarred rags, burning rags. Cherkashin.[2] In the apiary there is chaos and complete destruction, smoke rises from the ruins.

I am writing in the garden, a glade, flowers, I feel sorrow for all this.

The military order to leave Zamosc, to go to the rescue of the Fourteenth Division, which is being forced back from Komarow. The shtetl has again been taken by the Poles. Poor Komarow. We ride along the flanks and the brigades. Before us, the enemy cavalry—nothing to hold us back, whom should we butcher if not the Cossacks of Captain Yakovlev.[3] An attack is imminent. The brigades are gathering in the forest—two versts from Czesniki.

Voroshilov and Budyonny are with us all the time. Voroshilov, short, graying, in red trousers with silver stripes, always goading, getting on everyone's nerves, keeps hounding Apanasenko about why the Second Brigade hasn't arrived. We are waiting for the arrival of the Second Brigade. Time is dragging with torturing slowness. Do not rush me, Comrade Voroshilov. Voroshilov: Everything is ruined, f— it to hell.

Budyonny is silent, at times he smiles, showing his dazzling white teeth. We must send the brigade first, and then the regiment. Voroshilov's patience snaps, he sends everyone he has into the attack. The regiment marches past Voroshilov and Budyonny. Voroshilov pulls out his enormous revolver, show the Polish *Pans* no mercy, his cry is met with joy. The regiment flies off helter-skelter, hurrah, go for it, some gallop off, others hold back, others again move in a trot, the horses balk, bowler hats and carpets.[4] Our squadron launches an attack. We gallop about four versts. They are waiting for us in columns on the hill. Amazing: none of them so much as move. Sangfroid, discipline. An officer with a black beard. I'm being shot at. My sensations. Flight. The military commissars turn. Nothing helps. Luckily, the enemy doesn't pursue us, otherwise we would have had a catastrophe on our hands. We try to gather a brigade together for a second attack, nothing comes of it. Manuilov is threatened with revolvers. The nurses are the heroines.

We ride back. Sheko's horse is wounded, Sheko has a concussion, his terrible, rigid face. He doesn't understand what is happening, he is crying, we lead his mare. She is bleeding.

The nurse's story: there are nurses who are only out for sympathy, we help the fighters, go through thick and thin with them, I would shoot, but what can I shoot with, a f—ing dick, I don't even have that.

The command staff is crushed, menacing signs of our army's disintegration. Cheerful, foolish Vorobyov recounts his heroic feats, he went galloping up, four shots point-blank. Apanasenko suddenly turns around: You ruined the attack, you bastard.

Apanasenko in a black mood, Sheko pitiful.

There is talk about how the army isn't in the shape it used to be, it's high time for a rest. What next? We spend the night in Czesniki, we are frozen through, tired, silent—impassable, all-engulfing mud, autumn, destroyed roads, dejection. Before us somber prospects.

2. An orderly at the Sixth Cavalry Division headquarters.
3. The Cossack captain fighting on the Polish side.
4. Babel is referring to the colorful attire of the Cossacks, some of whom are wearing bowler hats and clothes cut out of carpets, and have draped carpets looted from houses over their saddles.

September 1, 1920. Terebin

We set out from Czesniki in the night. We stopped there for two hours. Night, cold, on our horses. We are shivering. The military order to retreat, we are surrounded, we have lost contact with the Twelfth Army,[5] we don't have contact with anybody. Sheko is crying, his head shaking, his face that of a hurt child, he is pitiful, crushed. What bastards people are. Vinokurov[6] wouldn't give him the military order to read—he is not on active duty. Apanasenko gives him his carriage, but I'm not their driver.

Endless conversations about yesterday's attack, lies, sincere regrets, the fighters are silent. That idiot Vorobyov keeps shooting his mouth off. The division commander cuts him off.

The beginning of the end of the First Cavalry Army. Rumors of retreat. Sheko is a man deep in misfortune.

Manuilov has a temperature of 40°C, fever, everyone hates him, Sheko harasses him, why? He doesn't know how to comport himself. Borisov, the orderly, cunning, ingratiating, secretive, no one has any pity for him, that's what's dreadful. A Jew?

The Fourth Division saves the army. And that with Timoshenko—the traitor.[7]

We arrive in Terebin, a half-destroyed village, cold. It's autumn, during the day I sleep in the threshing shed, at night together with Sheko.

My talk with Arzam Slyagit. Riding next to me. We spoke about Tiflis, fruit, sun. I think about Odessa, my soul is torn.

We are dragging Sheko's bleeding horse behind us.

September 2, 1920. Terebin—Metelin

Pitiful villages. Unfinished huts. Half-naked villagers. We ruin them once and for all. The division commander is with the troops. The military order: delay the enemy's advance on the Bug, attack in the area of Wakijow-Hostyne. We fight but without success. Rumors about the weakening of the army's fighting efficiency are becoming more persistent. Desertion. Masses of reports of men going on leave, illness.

The main illness of the division is the absence of command staff, all the commanders are from the ranks, Apanasenko hates the democrats, they don't understand a thing, there's no one who can lead a regiment into an attack.

Squadron commanders are leading regiments.

Days of apathy, Sheko is recovering, he is depressed. Life is tough in the atmosphere of an army whose side has split open.

September 3, 4, 5, 1920. Malice

We have moved on to Malice.

Orlov is the new chief of staff's adjutant. A figure from Gogol. A pathological liar, his tongue always wagging, a Jewish face, the main

---

5. The infantry, the main force in the Russian-Polish campaign.
6. The military commissar of the Sixth Cavalry Division.
7. An ironic comment. After Timoshenko had been relieved of his command of the Sixth Cavalry Division on August 5, 1920, he became the division commander (August 25) of the Fourth Cavalry Division. He was awarded his second Order of the Red Banner for his leadership in the Battle for Zamosc.

thing: the terrifying ease, when you think about it, with which he talks, chatters, lies, he's in pain (he limps), a partisan, a Makhno[8] fighter, he went to high school, commanded a regiment. His ease frightens me, what is behind it.

Finally Manuilov has fled, and not without scandal—he was threatened with arrest, how addle-brained Sheko is, they had sent him to the First Brigade, sheer idiocy, Army headquarters sent him to the air force. Amen.

I'm billeted with Sheko. Dull, amiable if you know how to stay on his good side, inept, does not have a strong will. I grovel—and so I get to eat. Boguslavsky, languid, half Odessan, dreams of "Odessan girls," from time to time will ride out at night to collect an army order. Boguslavsky in a Cossack saddle.

The First Platoon of the First Squadron. Kuban Cossacks. They sing songs. Staid. They smile. They're not rowdy.

Levda reported sick. A cunning Ukrainian. "I have rheumatism. I am too weak to work." Three report sick from the brigades, they're in cahoots. If we're not given any leave, the division will go under, there's no ardor, the horses won't go on, the men are impassive, the Third Brigade, two days in the field, cold, rain.

A sad country, impassable mud, no muzhiks to be seen anywhere, they hide their horses in the forests, women sobbing quietly.

A report from Kniga: Unable to execute my duties without a command staff.

All the horses are in the forests, the Red Army fighters exchange them, a science, a sport.

Barsukov is falling apart. He wants to go to school.

There are skirmishes. Our side is trying to advance on Wakijow-Honiatycki. Nothing comes of it. A strange weakness.

The Pole is slowly but surely pushing us back. The division commander is useless, he has neither the initiative nor the necessary tenacity. His purulent ambition, philandering, gluttony, and probably feverish activity should it be needed.

Our way of life.

Kniga writes: The previous ardor no longer exists, the fighters are dragging their feet.

Dispiriting weather all the time, destroyed roads, terrible Russian village mud in which your boots get stuck, there is no sun, it is raining, gloomy, what a cursed land.

I am ill, angina, fever, I can barely move, terrible nights in stifling, smoke-filled huts in the straw, my whole body torn to pieces, flea-bitten, itching, bleeding, there's nothing I can do.

Our operations continue sluggishly, a period of equilibrium in which, however, the ascendancy is beginning to shift to the Poles.

The command staff is passive, doesn't even exist anymore.

I rush over to the nurse to pick up bandages, I have to go through kitchen gardens, impassable mud. The nurse is staying with a platoon. A heroine, even though she copulates with many. A hut, everyone smoking, cursing, changing foot wrappings, a soldier's life, and another person,

8. See note 2, p. 108.

the nurse. Anyone too squeamish to drink from the same mug as the rest gets thrown out.

The enemy advances. We took Lot, have to give it up again, the enemy pushes us back, not a single attack of ours has brought results, we send off the transport carts, I ride to Terebin on Barsukov's cart, from there on rain, slush, misery, we cross the Bug, Budyatichi. So—it has been decided to relinquish the Bug line.

September 6, 1920. Budyatichi

Budyatichi is occupied by the Forty-fourth Division. Clashes. They are startled by our division pouring in like a wild horde. Orlov:[9] Hand this place over to us and get out!

The nurse—a proud woman, pretty and somewhat dim-witted—is in tears, the doctor is outraged at the shouts of "Down with the Yids, save Russia!" They are stunned, the quartermaster was thrashed with a whip, the field hospital demolished, pigs are requisitioned and dragged off without receipts or anything, and before everything had been well ordered, all sorts of representatives go to see Sheko to complain. There you have the Budyonny fighters.

The proud nurse, a kind we've never seen before, in white shoes and stockings, a full, shapely leg, they have things nicely organized, respect for human dignity, quick, thorough work.

We are billeted with Jews.

My thoughts of home are becoming increasingly persistent. I see no way out.

September 7, 1920. Budyatichi

We are occupying two rooms. The kitchen is full of Jews. There are refugees from Krylow, a pitiful little bunch of people with the faces of prophets. They sleep side by side. All day long they are boiling and baking, the Jewess works like a slave, sewing, laundering. They pray there too. Children, young girls. The damn bastards, the lackeys, they are continually stuffing themselves, drinking vodka, guffawing, growing fat, hiccuping with lust for women.

We eat every two hours.

A unit is placed on the opposite shore of the Bug, a new phase in the operation.

It's been two weeks now that everyone's been saying more and more doggedly that the army has to be pulled out for a rest. A rest!—our new battle cry.

A delegation turns up, the division commander entertains them, they're constantly eating, his stories about Stavropol, Suslov is growing fatter, the bastard has gotten himself a good deal.

Terrible tactlessness: Sheko, Suslov, Sukhorukov have been put up for a Red Flag Medal.

The enemy is trying to cross over to our side of the Bug, the Fourteenth Division acted quickly and pushed them back.

---

9. The adjutant of the chief of staff of the Sixth Cavalry Division.

I am issuing certificates.

I've gone deaf in one ear. The result of my cold? My body is all scratched up, cuts everywhere, I don't feel well. Autumn, rain, everything is depressing, deep mud.

September 8, 1920. Vladimir-Volynsk

In the morning I head to the administrative headquarters on a civilian cart. I have to testify, some song and dance about money. Some demi-rearguard sordidness: Gusev, Nalyotov, money at the Revolutionary Tribunal. Lunch with Gorbunov.

Off to Vladimir with the same nags. An arduous ride, insurmountable mud, the roads impassable. We arrive at night. A squabble about the billet, a cold room in a widow's house. Jews—storekeepers. Mama and Papa are old.

Poor Grandma. The gentle, black-bearded husband. The redheaded, pregnant Jewess is washing her feet. The girl has diarrhea. It is cramped, but there is electricity, it's warm.

For supper there are dumplings with sunflower oil—pure bliss. There you have it: Jewish abundance. They think I don't understand Yiddish, they are as cunning as flies. The town is destitute.

Borodin[1] and I sleep on a featherbed.

September 9, 1920. Vladimir-Volynsk

The town is destitute, dirty, hungry, you can't buy anything with money, sweets cost twenty rubles and cigarettes. Dejection. Army headquarters. Gloomy. A council of trade unions, young Jews. I go to the economic councils and the trade unions, dejection, the military members make demands, act like louts. Sickly young Jews.

Magnificent meal—meat, kasha. Our only pleasure is food.

The new military commissar at headquarters—a monkey's face.

My landlord wants to barter for my shawl. I'm not going to let him hoodwink me.

My driver, barefoot with bleary eyes. Oy Russia![2]

A synagogue. I pray, bare walls, some soldier or other is swiping the electric light bulbs.

The bathhouse. A curse on soldiering, war, the cramming together of young, tormented, still-healthy people gone crazy.

The home life of my landlord and his wife, they are taking care of a few things, tomorrow is Friday, they are already preparing themselves, the old woman is good, the old man a little underhanded, they are only pretending to be poor. They say: Better to starve under the Bolsheviks than to eat fancy bread under the Poles.

September 10, 1920. Kovel

Half the day in the shattered, doleful, terrible train station in Vladimir-Volynsk. Dejection. The black-bearded Jew is working. We arrive in Kovel

1. An orderly at the headquarters of the Sixth Cavalry Division.
2. Babel uses "Rasseya," a folksy distortion of the word for Russia. —Ed.

at night. Unexpected joy: The Polit-otdel train.[3] Supper with Zdanevich,[4] butter. I spend the night in the radio station. Blinding light. A miracle. Khelemskaya is having an affair. Lymph glands. Volodya. She took off all her clothes. My prophecy came true.

September 11, 1920. Kovel

The town has kept traces of European-Jewish culture. They won't accept Soviet money, a glass of coffee without sugar: fifty rubles. A disgusting meal at the train station: 600 rubles.

Sun, I go from doctor to doctor, have my ear treated, itching.

I visit Yakovlev,[5] quiet little houses, meadows, Jewish alleys, a quiet hearty life, Jewish girls, youths, old men at the synagogues, perhaps wigs. Soviet power does not seem to have ruffled the surface, these quarters are across the bridge.

Dirt and hunger in the train. Everyone's emaciated, louse-ridden, with sallow faces, they all hate one another, sit locked up in their cubicles, even the cook is emaciated. A striking change. They are living in a cage. Khelemskaya, dirty, puttering about in the kitchen, her connection to the kitchen, she feeds Volodya, a Jewish wife "from a good home."

All day I look for food.

The district in which the Twelfth Army is located. Luxurious establishments: clubs, gramophones, conscientious Red Army fighters, cheerful, life is bubbling up, the newspapers of the Twelfth Army, Central Military News Service, Army Commander Kuzmin[6] who writes articles. As far as work goes, the Polit-otdel seems to be doing well.

The life of the Jews, crowds in the streets, the main street is Lutskaya Street, I walk around on my shattered feet, I drink an incredible amount of tea and coffee. Ice cream: 500 rubles. They have no shame. Sabbath, all the stores are closed. Medicine: five rubles.

I spend the night at the radio station. Blinding light, sassy radiotelegraphers, one of them is struggling to play a mandolin. Both read avidly.

September 12, 1920. Kivertsy

In the morning, panic at the train station. Artillery fire. The Poles are in town. Unimaginably pitiful flight, carts in five rows, the pitiful, dirty, gasping infantry, cavemen, they run over meadows, throw away their rifles, Borodin the orderly already sees the butchering Poles. The train moves out quickly, soldiers and carts come dashing, the wounded, their faces contorted, jump up into our train cars, a gasping political worker, his pants have fallen down, a Jew with a thin, translucent face, possibly a cunning Jew, deserters with broken arms jump on, sick men from the field hospital.[7]

The institution that calls itself the Twelfth Army. For every fighter there are four rear-line men, two ladies, two trunks filled with things—and even the actual fighter doesn't fight. The Twelfth Army is ruining the front and the Red Cavalry, it exposes our flanks and then sends us to stop up those

3. See note 3, p. 175.
4. V. Zdanevich, the editor-in-chief of the Red Cavalry newspaper *Krasny Kavalerist*, for which Babel wrote articles. (See "Reporting for *The Red Cavalryman*" in this volume.)
5. The political commissar of the Sixth Cavalry Division.
6. Nikolai Nikolayevich Kuzmin was the provisional commander of the Twelfth Army from August to November 1920.
7. See "Rabbi's Son." —Ed.

holes with ourselves. One of their units, the Urals Regiment or the Bashkir Brigade, surrendered, leaving the front open. Disgraceful panic, the army is unfit for combat. The soldier types: The Russian Red Army infantryman is barefoot, not only not modernized, but the embodiment of "wretched Russia," hungry and squat muzhiks, tramps, bloated, louse-ridden.

At Goloby all the sick, the wounded, and the deserters are thrown off the train. Rumors, and then facts: the Provision Unit of the First Cavalry sent into the cul-de-sac of Vladimir-Volynsk has been captured by the enemy, our headquarters has moved to Lutsk, a mass of fighters and equipment of the Twelfth Army has been captured, the army is fleeing.

In the evening we arrive in Kivertsy.

Life in the railway car is hard. The radio-telegraphers keep plotting to get rid of me, one of them still has an upset stomach, he plays the mandolin, the other keeps taunting him because he is an idiot.

Life in the railway car, dirty, malicious, hungry, animosity toward one another, unhealthy. Moscow women smoking, eating like pigs, faceless, many pitiful people, coughing Muscovites, everyone wants to eat, everyone is angry, everyone has an upset stomach.

September 13, 1920. Kivertsy

A bright morning, the forest. The Jewish New Year. Hungry. I go into the shtetl. Boys wearing white collars. Ishas Khakl[8] offers me bread and butter. She earns her money "herself," a hardy woman, a silk dress, she has tidied up the house. I am moved to tears, here the only thing that helped was talking things through, we spoke for a long time, her husband is in America, a shrewd, unhurried Jewess.

A long stop at the station. Dejection, like before. We get books from the club, we read avidly.

September 14, 1920. Klevan

We stop in Klevan for a day and a night, the whole time at the station. Hunger, dejection. The town of Rovno won't allow us passage. A railroad worker. We bake shortbread and potatoes at his place. A railroad watchman. They eat, say kind things, don't give us anything. I am with Borodin, his light gait. All day long we look for food, from one watchman to the next. I spend the night in the radio station in the blinding light.

September 15, 1920. Klevan

The third day of our agonizing stop in Klevan begins, the same hunt for food, in the morning we had a lot of tea with shortbread. In the evening I rode to Rovno on a cart of the First Cavalry's Air Force Department. A conversation about our air force, it doesn't exist, all the machines are broken, the pilots don't know how to fly, the planes are old, patched up, completely worthless. The Red Army fighter with a swollen throat—quite a type. He can barely speak, his throat must be completely blocked, inflamed, sticks in his fingers to scrape away the film in his gullet, they told him salt might help, he pours salt down his throat, he hasn't eaten for four

8. A distortion of the Biblical *eshet chayil* (Hebrew), "a woman of valor" (Prov. 31:10). —*Ed.*

days, he drinks cold water because nobody will give him hot. His talk is garbled, about the attack, about the commander, about the fact that they were barefoot, some advanced, others didn't, he beckons with his finger. Supper at Gasnikova's.

REPORTING FOR *THE RED CAVALRYMAN*

The pieces below published in *The Red Cavalryman* were signed by "the Military Correspondent of the Sixth Cavalry Division K. Lyutov" and, as far as we know, are Babel's only signed contributions to this newspaper. —*Ed.*

We Need More Men like Trunov[1]

We must add one more name now to our heroic, bloody, and sorrowful list, a name that will never be forgotten by the Sixth Division: the name of Konstantin Trunov, commander of the Thirty-fourth Cavalry Regiment, who died in the line of duty on August 3, near K. Another grave is now hidden by the shadows of the dense forests of Volhynia, another distinguished life marked by self-sacrifice and devotion to duty has been relinquished to the cause of the oppressed, another proletarian heart has been crushed so that its fiery blood will tint the red flags of Revolution. The story of Comr. Trunov's final years of life is inextricably linked with the titanic battle of the Red Army. He emptied his cup to the last drop, participating in every campaign from Tsaritsyn to Voronezh, and from Voronezh to the shores of the Black Sea. In the past he suffered hunger, deprivation, wounds, overwhelming battles fought alongside the best men in the front lines, and finally the bullet of the Polish nobleman which cut down the Stavropol peasant from the faraway steppes who was bringing the word of freedom to people who were strangers to him.

From the first days of the Revolution, Comrade Trunov took his true position without a moment's hesitation. We found him among the organizers of the first detachments of the Stavropol troops. In the Red Army, he subsequently took over the command of the Fourth Stavropol Regiment, the First Brigade of the Thirty-second Division, and the Thirty-fourth Cavalry Regiment of the Sixth Division.

In our military ranks his memory will not pale. Under the harshest conditions he triumphed over the enemy through his exceptional, selfless courage, his unbending persistence, and his immutable self-possession, and through his great influence over the men of the Red Army that was so close to him. If there were more Trunovs among us, the masters of this world would be finished.

The Knights of Civilization[2]

The Polish army has gone berserk. The Polish *Pans*, fatally bitten, expiring like dogs, are writhing in mortal agony, piling up crimes in stupidity,

---

1. *The Red Cavalryman*, August 13, 1920.
2. *The Red Cavalryman*, August 14, 1920.

dying and going to their graves in shame, cursed by their own people and by others. With the same feeling as before, they forge ahead not thinking of the future, forgetting that, according to their European governesses, they are the knights of European civilization, and therefore must act as the guardians of "law and order," a barrier against Bolshevik barbarity.

This is how this Polish barrier protects civilization:

Once upon a time there lived a modest, hardworking pharmacist in Berestechko, who always did his best. He worked without respite, taking care of his patients, his test tubes, and his prescriptions. He had no connection to politics at all, and quite possibly thought that Bolsheviks were monsters with ears above their eyes.

This pharmacist was a Jew. For the Poles that was enough: he was nothing but a cowering animal! Why even waste a bullet? Beat him, cut him down, torture him! They were quick to set him up. The peaceful pharmacist, who had happily saddled himself with hemorrhoids working with his little bottles, was accused of having somewhere, at some time, for some reason, killed a Polish officer, and was therefore an accomplice of the Bolsheviks.

What followed takes us back to the most oppressive years of the Spanish Inquisition. If I had not seen that lacerated face and that shattered body with my own eyes, I would never have believed that such shocking evil could exist in our era, cruel and bloody though it is. The pharmacist's body had been scorched with white-hot iron pokers, stripes like those on an officer's uniform had been burned into his legs ("We see you're in cahoots with those Cossack-Bolsheviks!"), burning needles had been driven under his nails, a Red Army star had been cut into his chest, his hair had been torn out, one hair at a time.

All this had been done at a leisurely pace, accompanied by little jibes at Communism and Jewish commissars.

But this wasn't all! The animalized Polish *Pans* razed the pharmacy to the ground and trampled on all the medicines. Not a single bottle was left untouched. Now the little town will doubtless perish without medical help. You will not find any powder against toothache in Berestechko. The population of twenty thousand has been left defenseless in the face of epidemics and disease.

And so now the Polish masters are perishing. Thus the evil, rabid dogs expire. Beat them, Red Fighters, clobber them to death, if it is the last thing you do! Right away! This minute! Now!

Murderers Who Have Yet to Be Clubbed to Death[3]

They wrought revenge on the workers in 1905. They set off on punitive expeditions in order to shoot and smother our dark slave-villages through which a fleeting breeze of freedom had blown.

3. *The Red Cavalryman*, September 17, 1920. The words of the Russian title, *Nedobitye ubiisty*—along with the related exhortations in the previous article and at the end of this one—mean literally "murderers who have not been finished off." Babel elaborates here on a particular Marxist motif. In Soviet propaganda, aimed at the largely illiterate and exhausted soldier peasants, the enemy was often presented as a feudal lord bent on restoring serfdom, or reversing the course of history. As a Marxist would see it, this enemy was already dead and buried, but if he managed to reemerge from the graveyard of history, as he apparently did in 1920, then the ascendant revolutionary class had to "finish him off" and to "stomp on his coffin lids." —*Ed.*

In October 1917, they threw off their masks and went after the Russian proletariat with fire and sword.[4] For almost three years they hacked at the land that had already been hacked to pieces. It looked like they were on their last legs. We left them to die a natural death, but they would not die.

Now we are paying for our mistake. His Excellency Wrangel[5] is strutting about the Crimea, while the pitiful remnants of the Black Hundred of the Russian Denikin[6] gangs are turning up in the ranks of the highly refined and most noble of Polish warriors. The ragtag and bobtail of Russia hurried to the aide of Counts Potocki and Taraszczynski to save culture and law from the Barbarians.

This is how culture was saved in the town of Komarov, occupied on August 28, by the Sixth Cavalry Division.

The valiant boys of Cossack Captain Yakovlev had spent the night in the little town—the same Captain Yakovlev who kept trying to talk us into returning to the sweet and peaceful life of our villages, which have been littered with the bodies of commissars, Yids, and Red Army soldiers. As our squadrons approached, these knights disappeared into thin air. But before they did, they managed to ply their trade.

We found the town's Jewish population robbed of everything it had, wounded and hacked to pieces. Our soldiers, who have seen a thing or two in their time and have been known to chop off quite a few heads, staggered in horror at what they saw. In the pitiful huts that had been razed to the ground, seventy-year-old men with crushed skulls lay naked in pools of blood; infants, often still alive, with fingers hacked off; and old women, raped, their stomachs slashed open, crouched in corners, with faces on which wild, unbearable desperation had congealed. The living were crawling among the dead, bumping into mangled corpses, their hands and faces covered with sticky, foul-smelling blood, terrified of leaving their houses, fearing that all was not yet over.

Hunched, frightened shadows roamed the streets of the dead town, cowering away from human voices, wailing for mercy at every sound. We came across houses over which a terrible silence hung—a whole family was lying next to an aged grandfather. Father, grandchildren—everyone in twisted, inhuman positions.

All in all, over thirty were killed and about sixty wounded. Two hundred women were raped, many of them tortured to death. To escape the rapists, women had jumped from second- and third-floor windows, breaking limbs and necks. Our medical officers worked all day without respite, and still could not meet the demands for help. The horror of the Middle Ages pales in comparison to the bestiality of the Yakovlev bandits.

The pogrom, needless to say, was carried out according to the rules. First, the officers demanded fifty thousand rubles in protection money from the Jewish population. Money and vodka were immediately brought, but still the

4. Babel refers to the activities of the Cossack riot police under the old regime and during the early days of the Revolution, when they were used to suppress popular protests. The units of the Cossack Captain Vadim Yakovlev were among the most notorious in 1917. —Ed.
5. General Pyotr Nikolayevich (Baron) Wrangel replaced General Anton Denikin as the commander of the anti-Bolshevik White Forces in April 1920. At the time of this article, the White Forces were occupying the Crimea. —Ed.
6. General Anton Ivanovich Denikin was the commander of the anti-Bolshevik White Forces in 1918–20. After a series of defeats in early 1920, his army disintegrated, and some of its elements—among them the units of Captain Vadim Yakovlev and his Don Cossack units—joined the Polish army. —Ed.

officers marched in the front lines of the pogromists and searched the cowering Jewish elders at gunpoint for bombs and machine guns.

Our answer to the Polish Red Cross's laments concerning Russian bestiality is: the event I have just described is only one among a thousand far worse.

The dogs that haven't yet been completely slashed to pieces have begun howling hoarsely. The murderers who haven't yet been completely clubbed to death are crawling out of their graves.

Slaughter them, Red Army fighters! Stamp harder on the rising lids of their rancid coffins!

Her Day[7]

I had a sore throat. I went to see the nurse of the First Squadron headquarters of the N. Division. A smoky hut, filled with fumes and rankness. The soldiers are lying on benches, smoking, scratching themselves, and using foul language. The nurse has set up shop in a corner. She bandages the wounded, one after the other, without much fuss or unnecessary ado. Some troublemakers hamper her work any way they can, each trying to outdo the other with the most blasphemous, unnatural curses. Suddenly—the alarm is sounded. The order to mount the horses. The squadron forms. We set off.

The nurse has harnessed her horse, tied a sack with oats to its muzzle, packed her bag, and ridden off. Her pitiful, thin dress flutters in the wind, and her frozen red toes show through the holes of her tattered shoes. It is raining. The exhausted horses can barely lift their hooves from the terrible, sucking, viscous Volhynian mud. The damp penetrates to the bone. The nurse has neither cloak nor coat. The men are singing a bawdy song. The nurse quietly hums her own song—about dying for the Revolution, about better days to come. A few men begin singing along with her, and our song, our unceasing call to freedom, spills out into the rainy autumnal dusk.

In the evening—the attack. Shells burst with soft, sinister booms, machine guns rattle faster and faster with feverish dread.

Beneath the most horrifying crossfire, the nurse bandages the wounded with disdainful calm, dragging them away from the battle on her shoulders.

The attack ends. The agonizing advance continues. Night, rain. The soldiers are darkly silent, only the heated whisper of the nurse, comforting the wounded, can be heard. An hour later, the same picture as before—a dark, dirty hut in which the platoon has settled down, and in the corner, by the light of a pitiable dwindling candle, the nurse keeps bandaging, bandaging, bandaging. . . .

Foul curses hang heavily in the air. The nurse, at times unable to restrain herself, snaps back, and the men laugh at her. Nobody helps her, nobody puts straw down for her to sleep on, nobody fluffs up her pillow.

These are our heroic nurses! Lift your hats and bow to them! Soldiers and commanders, honor your nurses! It is high time we distinguished between the camp girls who shame our army and the martyred nurses who ennoble it.

---

7. *The Red Cavalryman*, September 18, 1920.

The Caucasus

Towards the end of Babel's service with Budyonny's First Cavalry, his friends and family began to hear rumors that he had either died or been killed. But he managed to return to Odessa, albeit exhausted and ill. He took a long time to recover. Finally, to help mend his health while earning some money, Babel took an assignment in the Caucasus resort area in Abkhazia as a reporter for *Zarya Vostoka* (Dawn of the Orient), a Russian-language Georgian newspaper published in Tiflis (now Tbilisi). If Babel's foray into Poland was his first encounter with the West, his stint as a reporter in Abkhazia brought him face to face with the Muslim Orient. Unlike the Georgians, who are mostly Christian, Abkhazians are predominantly Muslim. For the writer, this was an opportunity to explore "Orientalism" as both a style and a subject matter. His business school training, too, proved useful, giving his articles on local industries a commercial crispness and depth. —Ed.

At the Workers' Retreat[1]

Beyond the veranda is the night, full of slow sounds and majestic darkness. An inexhaustible rain patrols the violet clefts of the mountains, and the gray rustling silk of its watery walls hangs over the cool and menacing dusk of the ravines. The blue flame of our candle flickers through the tireless murmur of the drumming water like a distant star, and twinkles on the wrinkled faces carved by the heavy, eloquent chisel of labor.

Three old tailors, gentle as nursemaids; the charming M., who not too long ago lost an eye at his loom; and I, who am worn out by the bitter, agonizing dust of our towns, are sitting on the veranda that extends into the night, the boundless, aromatic night. An ineffable calm rubs our sore, exhausted muscles with its maternal palms, and we sip our tea, unhurriedly and dreamily—three gentle tailors, the charming M., and I, a downtrodden but enthusiastic workhorse.

You petite bourgeoisie, as talentless and hopeless as a storekeeper's paunch, who built these "little dachas" for yourselves, if only you could see us rest in them! If only you could see our faces, ravaged by the steel-jawed machines, brighten up!

This silent, masculine kingdom of peace, these vulgar dachas that the miraculous power of events transformed into Workers' Retreats, embody the elusive and noble essence of careful, silent indolence, so revitalizing and peaceful. Oh, the peerless gesture of a worker's resting hands chastely frugal and wisely deliberate! I watch with fixed rapture these unswerving, convulsive black hands, used to the complex and unflagging soul of the machine. It is the machine that has given the exhausted body

1. *Zarya Vostoka,* June 22, 1922.

its resigned, silent, and deliberate immobility. How much I learned of the philosophy of respite[2] and the principles of resuscitating depleted energy on that noisy, clear evening, as the tailors and metal workers drank tea on the terrace in the Workers' Retreat in Mtskhet.[3]

Tipsy with tea, the boisterous champagne of the poor, we slowly and fervently sweat as we lovingly exchange subdued words and reminisce about how the Workers' Retreats came to be.

A year has passed since their birth. It was only last February that the Georgian Trade Union Commission came to Mtskhet for an initial survey. They found the dachas in a terrible state, uninhabitable, filthy, dilapidated. The Trade Union went to work with unflagging zeal to launch this blessed undertaking, the bourgeoisie pitching in to the extent its modest means allowed. As is well known, the penalties the Trade Union has imposed on storekeepers of every kind for violating labor laws have reached the comforting sum of six hundred million rubles. So a hundred and fifty million of this sum was spent turning the tumbledown dachas into Workers' Retreats—from which it clearly follows that the bourgeoisie's money, for which it had spat blood (emphasis on the blood), is supporting Georgia's first workers' spas, for which we bow our heads in thanks. There is an unshakable confidence in the air that, due to the intrinsic nature of the bourgeoisie, the influx of enforced donations will not flag, and will allow the Trade Union to unfurl a model Workers' Town over the blossoming slopes of Mtskhet in lieu of the present dachas. Unfortunately, the grandiloquent compliments paid the bourgeoisie above are tainted by the memory of the astonishing and heroic battles the owners of the dachas fought in their war against the Trade Union. The owners threatened to go "all the way to the Czar." And they did. Their path was long, and paved with the delicate poison of juridical pettifoggery. But "the Czar" (spelled VTs IK[4] in the new orthography) was prompt and just. The petitioners departed with a speed inversely proportional to the slowness of their arrival. The lesson that the dacha owners learned in their tireless quest for truth was that they had been born a good twenty years too late. An insightful lesson.

The dachas are set up to hold sixty people. The Department of Labor Protection intends to increase their capacity to a thousand, a thousand five hundred people per season, calculating a two-week stay per worker. In certain cases this stay can be extended up to a month. But one does have certain reservations, since in the overwhelming majority of cases a two-weeks' stay is not enough for our workers' worn-out constitutions.

The period of construction and reconstruction of the Mtskhet dachas is still continuing. Thus advice proffered with goodwill and love can be quite beneficial. For instance, the food which is, all told, healthy and abundant, should be increased at breakfast and dinnertime. Not to mention that it

2. "Respite" was how the Bolsheviks referred to the New Economic Policy (NEP), which replaced the rigors and privations of War Communism, with its confiscatory taxation in the countryside and universal rationing. The NEP established a mixed economy, encouraging private ownership and initiative of peasants and small entrepreneurs. Agriculture and consumer industries quickly recovered. This "respite" came to an end in 1928, when Stalin moved to abandon the NEP in favor of crash industrialization and the collectivization of agriculture, causing famine and massive dislocations. —Ed.

3. The ancient capital of Georgia, a resort known for its mineral water cure. —Ed.

4. The acronym for the All-Union Executive Committee, the name of the executive branch of the Soviet party-state. —Ed.

would be nice if they could eradicate the god-awful dormitory structure of these Workers' Retreats. We get sick and tired of it, we who have to live in furnished rooms, offices, and barracks. What we need in the blissful two weeks in which we get to stretch our wracked and wheezing chests is a little corner of cleanliness, coziness, and with a modicum of seclusion.

A library is already up and running. That's good. Little evening concerts will begin next week to entertain the resting workers. For the time being, we subsist on durachok.[5] But, by God, with what fire, with what unspent ebullience and passion we play this endless, tender game that warms us like a grandfatherly sheepskin coat. I will never forget these simple, shining faces bent over the tattered cards, and for a long time to come I will carry within me the memory of the happy, restrained laughter ringing beneath the sound of the dying rain and the mountain winds.

Bagrat-Ogly and the Eyes of His Bull[1]

I saw a bull of unparalleled beauty lying by the side of the road.

A boy was bending over it, crying.

"This boy is Bagrat-Ogly," said a snake charmer who was eating his scanty meal nearby. "Bagrat-Ogly, son of Kazim."

"He is as exquisite as twelve moons," I said.

"The green cloak of the Prophet will never cover the rebellious whiskers of Kazim," the snake charmer said. "He was a quarrelsome man, and left his son nothing but a pauper's hut, his plump wives, and a bull that was unrivaled. But Allah is great!"

"*Allah il'Allah!*" I said.

"Allah is great," he repeated, pushing away his basket of snakes. "The bull grew up to become the mightiest bull in Anatolia. Memed-khan, a neighbor, sick with envy, castrated it last night. Now no one will bring their cows to Bagrat-Ogly in the hope of conception. Now no one will pay Bagrat-Ogly a hundred piasters for the love of his bull. He is a pauper, Bagrat-Ogly. He weeps by the side of the road.

The silence of the mountains unfurled its violet banners above us. The snows glittered on the peaks. Blood trickled down the legs of the mutilated bull and bubbled onto the grass. And, hearing the bull moan, I looked into its eyes and saw the bull's death and my own death, and I fell to the ground in measureless torment.

"Traveler!" the boy then called, his face as rosy as the dawn. "You writhe, and foam bubbles from the corners of your lips. A black illness is fettering you with the ropes of its convulsions."

"Bagrat-Ogly!" I answered, sunk in exhaustion. "In the eyes of your bull I saw the reflection of the ever-watchful malice of our neighbors, the Memed-khans of this world. In the moist depths of its eyes I saw mirrors in which rage the green fires of the treachery of our neighbors, the

---

5. "The Little Fool," a simple Russian card game. —*Ed.*
1. First published in *Siluety* (Odessa) 12 (1923) with the title "Bagrat-Ogly i glaza ego byka" and the subtitle "From the Book Oforty."

Memed-khans of this world. In the eyes of the mutilated bull I saw my youth, barren and cut down, the prime of my life thrashing its way through the thorny undergrowth of indifference. The deserts of Syria, Arabia, and Kurdistan, which I have fathomed thrice, I saw within the eyes of your bull, O Bagrat-Ogly, and their flat sands leave me no hope. The hatred of the whole world has penetrated the eye sockets of your bull. Flee from the malice of our Memed-khan neighbors, O Bagrat-Ogly, and may the old snake charmer hoist his basket of pythons onto his back and flee at your side!"

And filling the ravines with my moans, I rose to my feet. I drank in the fragrance of the eucalyptus and walked away. A many-headed dawn soared above the mountains like a thousand swans. The steel waters of the Bay of Trebizond sparkled in the distance, and I saw the sea and the yellow decks of the feluccas. The freshness of the grass poured over the ruins of a Byzantine wall. The bazaars of Trebizond and the carpets of Trebizond rose before me. I came across a young highlander at a fork in the road outside the city. On his outstretched hand sat a pigeon hawk chained by its talon. The highlander walked with a light gait. The sun surfaced above our heads. And a sudden calm descended on my wanderer's soul.

Information[1]

In answer to your inquiry, I would like to inform you that I set out on my literary career early in life, when I was about twenty. I was drawn to writing by a natural affinity, and also by my love for a woman named Vera. She was a prostitute from Tiflis, and among her friends she had the reputation of being a woman with a good head for business. People came to pawn things with her, she helped young women launch their careers, and on occasion traded alongside Persians at the Eastern Bazaar. She went out on the Golovinsky Boulevard every evening, hovering before the crowds—tall, her face a radiant white—as the Mother of God hovers before the prow of a fishing boat. I saved up some money, crept after her silently, and finally mustered the courage to approach her. Vera asked me for ten rubles, leaned against me with her soft, large shoulders, and forgot all about me.

In the tavern where we ate kebabs she became flushed with excitement, trying to talk the tavern keeper into expanding his trade by moving to Mikhailovsky Boulevard. From the tavern we went to a shoemaker to get some shoes, and then Vera went off to a girlfriend's for a christening. Toward midnight we arrived at the hotel, but there too Vera had things to do.

---

1. In 1933, Babel submitted this story, under the title "Spravka," along with its longer version, "My First Fee," and the story "Froim Grach," to the almanac *God shestnadtsatyi* (Moscow, 1934), a miscellany marking the sixteenth year after the October Revolution. The submissions were rejected by the editors (perhaps even by Stalin himself). Still, "Information" was published in Babel's lifetime, in an English translation in the Soviet English-language journal *International Literature* 9 (1937). The shorter version of the story, published here, likely represents a later reduction by the author. Both versions can be found in *The Complete Works of Isaac Babel*. Antonina Pirozhkova recalled Babel telling her that the stories were based on an anecdote recounted by Babel's old Petrograd journalist friend P. I. Storitsyn (Kogan). —*Ed.*

An old woman was getting ready to go to her son in Armavir. Vera knelt on her suitcase to force it shut, and wrapped pies in oilpaper. Clutching her rust-brown handbag, the little old woman hurried from room to room in her gauze hat to say good-bye. She shuffled down the hallway in her rubber boots, sobbing and smiling through all her wrinkles.

I waited for Vera in a room with three-legged armchairs and a clay oven. The corners of the room were covered with damp splotches. Flies were dying in a jar filled with milky liquid, each fly dying in its own way. Other people's life bustled in the hallway, with peals of sudden laughter. It was an eternity before Vera came back into the room.

"We'll do it now," she said, closing the door behind her. Her preparations resembled those of a surgeon preparing for an operation. She lit the kerosene burner, put a pot of water on it, and poured the water into an enema bag that had a white tube hanging from it. She threw a red crystal into the enema bag, and began undressing.

"We've just sent Fedosya Mavrikevna off," Vera said. "I swear she was just like a mother to all of us. The poor old thing has to travel all alone, with no one to help her!"

A large woman with sloping shoulders lay in the bed, her flaccid nipples blindly pointing at me.

"Why are you sitting there so glum?" Vera asked, pulling me toward her. "Or are you sorry you gave me the money?"

"I don't care about the money."

"What do you mean, you don't care? You a thief or something?"

"I'm not a thief, I'm a boy."

"Well, I can see you're not a cow," Vera said with a yawn. Her eyes were falling shut.

"I'm a boy," I repeated, and went cold at the suddenness of my invention. There was no going back, so I told my chance companion the following story:

"We lived in Alyoshki in the district of Kherson"—is what I came up with as a beginning. "My father worked as a draftsman, and tried to give us children an education. But we took after our mother, who was only interested in cards and good food. When I was ten I began stealing money from my father, and a few years later ran away to Baku to live with some relatives on my mother's side. They introduced me to an old man. His name was Stepan Ivanovich. I became friends with him, and we lived together for four years."

"How old were you then?"

"Fifteen."

Vera was expecting to hear about the evil deeds of the man who had corrupted me.

"We lived together for four years," I continued, "and Stepan Ivanovich turned out to be an extremely trusting man—he trusted everyone. I should have learned a trade during those years, but I only had one thing on my mind—billiards. Stepan Ivanovich's friends ruined him. He gave them bronze promissory notes, and they cashed them in right away."

I have no idea how I came up with bronze promissory notes, but it was a very good idea. The woman believed everything once I mentioned these promissory notes. She wrapped herself in her red shawl, and it trembled on her shoulders.

"They ruined Stepan Ivanovich. He was thrown out of his apartment and his furniture was auctioned off. He became a traveling salesman. When he lost all his money, I left him and went to live with a rich old man, a church warden."

Church warden! I stole the idea from some novel, but it was the invention of a lazy mind. To regain ground, I squeezed asthma into the old man's yellow chest—asthma attacks and hoarse whistling as he gasped for breath. The old man would jump up in the middle of the night and, moaning, breathe in the kerosene-colored night of Baku. He died soon after. My relatives would have nothing to do with me, so here I was, in Tiflis, with twenty rubles to my name. The waiter at the hotel where I was staying promised to send me rich clients, but up to now had only sent me tavern keepers.

And I started jabbering about low-down tavern keepers and their coarse, mercenary ways, bits of information I had picked up somewhere. Self-pity tore my heart to pieces; I had been completely ruined. I fell silent. My story had come to an end. The kerosene burner had died out. The water had boiled and cooled down again. The woman walked silently through the room, her back fleshy and sad.

"The things men do," Vera whispered, opening the shutters. "My God, the things men do!"

A stony hillside framed by the window rose with a crooked Turkish road winding up it. The cooling flagstones on the street hissed. The smell of water and dust came rolling up the carriageway.

"So, have you ever been with a woman?" Vera asked, turning to me.

"How could I have? Who would have wanted me?"

"The things men do," Vera said. "My God, the things men do!"

I shall interrupt my story at this point to ask you, my dear friends, if you have ever watched a village carpenter helping a fellow carpenter build a hut for himself and seen how vigorous, strong, and cheerful the shavings fly as they plane the wooden planks.

That night a thirty-year-old woman taught me her trade. That night I experienced a love full of patience and heard women's words that only other women hear.

It was morning when we fell asleep. We were awakened by the heat of our bodies. We drank tea in the bazaar of the old quarter. A placid Turk carrying a samovar wrapped in a towel poured tea, crimson as a brick, steaming like blood freshly spilled on the earth. A caravan of dust flew toward Tiflis, the town of roses and mutton fat. The dust carried off the crimson fire of the sun. The drawn-out braying of donkeys mingled with the hammering of blacksmiths. The Turk poured tea and kept count of the rolls we ate.

Covered in beads of sweat, I turned my glass upside down and pushed two golden five-ruble coins over to Vera. Her chunky leg was lying over mine. She pushed the money away and pulled in her leg.

"Do you want us to quarrel, my little sister?"

No, I didn't want to quarrel. We agreed to meet again in the evening, and I slipped back into my wallet the two golden fivers—my first fee.

The Odessa Stories

This section includes Babel's stories and a play set in his native city of Odessa. Babel's work on *The Odessa Stories* began soon after he returned from the Polish campaign and proceeded parallel to his work on the *Red Cavalry* cycle. Sometimes stories from both appeared in the same journal issue, and both came to be associated with the phenomenon of Babel's spectacular ascent.

His work on *The Odessa Stories* was part of a long-range plan. As he announced to his Petrograd readers in 1916 ("Odessa"), he anticipated a "literary messiah from Odessa" to change the character and course of Russian letters hitherto dominated by the landed gentry and Petersburg traditions. This messiah had now arrived. While Babel's character Benya Krik was raiding the coffers of Odessa's Jewish bourgeoisie, the author Babel was stealing thunder from Russian writers and his Yiddish forerunner, Sholem Aleichem. The very name Benya *Krik* was a pun emphasizing the character's Jewish roots (Bentsion or Ben Zion) and echoing both the Russian word for yelling (*krik*) and its French cognate, as in *le dernier cri*. Babel believed he had concluded these two cycles in 1925–26, but he returned to them in the 1930s, adding new stories, albeit in a key more reminiscent of the unforgiving St. Petersburg than the colorful Cossacks or the jolly Odessa mobsters.

The writings comprising the Odessa cycle, including the play *Sunset*, appear here in a chronological order, tracing the trajectory of Babel's imagination over the first two decades of Soviet rule. —Ed.

The King[1]

The wedding ceremony ended, the rabbi sank into a chair, then he left the room and saw tables lined up the whole length of the courtyard. There were so many of them that the end stuck out of the gates onto Gospitalnaya Street. The tables, draped in velvet, coiled through the yard like a snake on whose belly patches of every color had been daubed, and these orange and red velvet patches sang in deep voices.

The rooms had been turned into kitchens. A rich flame, a drunk, plump flame, forced its way through the smoke-blackened doors. Little old women's faces, wobbly women's chins, beslobbered breasts, baked in the flame's smoky rays. Sweat, red as blood, pink as the foam of a rabid dog, dripped from these blobs of rampant, sweet-odored human flesh. Three cooks, not counting the scullery maids, prepared the wedding feast, and over them eighty-year-old Reizl reigned, traditional as a Torah scroll, tiny and hunchbacked.

---

1. The earliest known version of "The King" was published in the Odessa newspaper *Moryak,* June 23, 1921. This translation is based on a later, revised version. —Ed.

Before the feast began, a young man unknown to the guests wormed his way into the courtyard. He asked for Benya Krik. He took Benya Krik aside.

"Listen, King!" the young man said. "I have a couple of words I need to tell you. Aunt Hannah from Kostetskaya Street, she sent me."

"So?" Benya Krik, nicknamed "the King," answered. "So what's these couple of words?"

"Aunt Hannah, she sent me to tell you that a new chief of police took over at the police station yesterday."

"I've known that since the day before yesterday," Benya Krik answered. "Well?"

"The chief of police called the whole station together and gave a speech . . ."

"A new broom is always eager to sweep," Benya Krik answered. "He wants a raid. So?"

"But when does he want to raid, King, do you know that?"

"Tomorrow."

"King, it's going to be today!"

"Who told you that, boy?"

"Aunt Hannah, she said so. You know Aunt Hannah?"

"I know Aunt Hannah. So?"

"The chief called the whole station together and gave them a speech: 'We must finish off Benya Krik,' he said, 'because when you have His Majesty the Czar, you can't have a King too. Today, when Krik gives away his sister in marriage, and they will all be there, is when we raid!'"

"So?"

"Then the stool pigeons began to get worried. They said, 'If we raid them today, during his feast, Benya will get angry and a lot of blood will flow.' But the chief said, 'Our self-respect is more important to me!'"

"Good, you can go," the King said.

"So what do I tell Aunt Hannah about the raid?"

"Tell her Benya he knows from the raid."

And the young man left. Three or four of Benya's friends followed him. They said they would be back in about half an hour. And they were back in half an hour. That was that.

At the table, the guests did not sit in order of seniority. Foolish old age is just as pitiful as cowardly youth. Nor in order of wealth. The lining of a heavy money bag is sewn with tears.

The bride and groom sat at the table's place of honor. It was their day. Beside them sat Sender Eichbaum, the King's father-in-law. That was his due. You should know the story of Sender Eichbaum, because it's a story definitely worth knowing.

How did Benya Krik, gangster and King of gangsters, make himself Eichbaum's son-in-law? How did he make himself the son-in-law of a man who owned one milch cow short of sixty?[2] It all had to do with a robbery. A year or so earlier Benya had written a letter to Eichbaum.

---

2. An allusion to Sholom Aleichem's *Tevye the Milkman*, a famous character in Yiddish literature. The name of Babel's *milcher*, Eichbaum, is another allusion, this one to Boris Eikhenbaum, a Formalist critic. —*Ed.*

"Monsieur Eichbaum," he wrote. "I would be grateful if you could place twenty thousand rubles by the gate of number 17, Sofiyefskaya Street, tomorrow morning. If you do not, then something awaits you, the like of which has never before been heard, and you will be the talk of all Odessa. Sincerely yours, Benya the King."

Three letters, each clearer than the one before, remained unanswered. Then Benya took action. They came by night, ten men carrying long sticks. The sticks were wound with tarred oakum. Nine burning stars flared up in Eichbaum's cattle yard. Benya smashed the barn's locks and started leading the cows out, one by one. They were met by a man with a knife. He felled the cows with one slash and plunged his knife into their hearts. On the ground drenched with blood the torches blossomed like fiery roses, and shots rang out. The dairy maids came running to the cowshed, and Benya chased them away with shots. And right after him other gangsters began shooting into the air because if you don't shoot into the air you might kill someone. And then, as the sixth cow fell with a death bellow at the King's feet, it was then that Eichbaum came running out into the courtyard in his underpants.

"Benya! Where will this end?" he cried.

"If I don't have the money, you don't have the cows, Monsieur Eichbaum. Two and two make four."

"Benya, come into my house!"

And inside the house they came to an agreement. They divided the slaughtered cows between them, Eichbaum was promised immunity and given a certificate with a stamp to that effect. But the miracle came later.

At the time of the attack, that terrible night when the slashed cows bellowed and calves skidded in their mothers' blood, when torches danced like black maidens, and the milkmaids scattered and screeched before the barrels of the amicable Brownings—that terrible night, old Eichbaum's daughter, Zilya, had run out into the yard, her blouse torn. And the King's victory turned into his downfall.

Two days later, without warning, Benya gave back all the money he had taken from Eichbaum, and then came in the evening on a social call. He wore an orange suit, and underneath his cuff a diamond bracelet sparkled. He entered the room, greeted Eichbaum, and asked him for the hand of his daughter, Zilya. The old man had a small stroke, but recovered—there were at least another twenty years of life in him.

"Listen, Eichbaum," the King told him. "When you die, I'll have you buried in the First Jewish Cemetery, right by the gates. And, Eichbaum, I will have a monument of pink marble put up for you. I will make you the Elder of the Brodsky Synagogue. I will give up my career, Eichbaum, and I will go into business with you as a partner. We will have two hundred cows, Eichbaum. I will kill all the dairymen except you. No thief shall walk the street you live in. I shall build you a dacha at the Sixteenth Stop[3] . . . and don't forget, Eichbaum, you yourself were no rabbi in your youth. Who was it who forged that will? I think I'd better lower my voice, don't you? And your son-in-law will be the King, not some snotface! The King, Eichbaum!"

---

3. Bolshoy Fontan, an elegant resort spa outside Odessa.

And he got his way, that Benya Krik, because he was passionate, and passion holds sway over the universe. The newlyweds stayed for three months in fertile Bessarabia, among grapes, abundant food, and the sweat of love. Then Benya returned to Odessa to marry off Dvoira, his forty-year-old sister, who was suffering from goiter. And now, having told the story of Sender Eichbaum, we can return to the marriage of Dvoira Krik, the King's sister.

For the dinner at this wedding, they served turkeys, roasted chicken, geese, gefilte fish, and fish soup in which lakes of lemon shimmered like mother-of-pearl. Above the dead goose heads, flowers swayed like luxuriant plumes. But do the foamy waves of the Odessan Sea throw roasted chickens onto the shore?

On this blue night, this starry night, the best of our contraband, everything for which our region is celebrated far and wide, plied its seductive, destructive craft. Wine from afar heated stomachs, sweetly numbed legs, dulled brains, and summoned belches as resonant as the call of battle horns. The black cook from the *Plutarch*, which had pulled in three days before from Port Said, had smuggled in big-bellied bottles of Jamaican rum, oily Madeira, cigars from the plantations of Pierpont Morgan, and oranges from the groves of Jerusalem. This is what the foamy waves of the Odessan Sea throw onto the shore, and this is what Odessan beggars sometimes get at Jewish weddings. They got Jamaican rum at Dvoira Krik's wedding, and that's why the Jewish beggars got as drunk as unkosher pigs and began loudly banging their crutches. Eichbaum unbuttoned his vest, mustered the raging crowd with a squinting eye, and hiccuped affectionately. The orchestra played a flourish. It was like a regimental parade. A flourish, nothing more than a flourish. The gangsters, sitting in closed ranks, were at first uneasy in the presence of outsiders, but soon they let themselves go. Lyova Katsap smashed a bottle of vodka over his sweetheart's head, Monya Artillerist fired shots into the air. But the peak of their ecstasy came when, in accordance with ancient custom, the guests began bestowing gifts on the newlyweds. The synagogue *shamases* jumped onto the tables and sang out, above the din of the seething flourishes, the quantity of rubles and silver spoons that were being presented. And here the friends of the King proved what blue blood was worth, and that Moldavanka[4] chivalry was still in full bloom. With casual flicks of the hand they threw gold coins, rings, and coral necklaces onto the golden trays.

The Moldavanka aristocrats were jammed into crimson vests, their shoulders encased in chestnut-colored jackets, and their fleshy legs bulged in sky-blue leather boots. Drawing themselves up to their full height and sticking out their bellies, the bandits clapped to the rhythm of the music and, shouting "Oy, a sweet kiss for the bride!," threw flowers at her, and she, forty-year-old Dvoira, Benya Krik's sister, the sister of the King, deformed by illness, with her swollen goiter and eyes bulging out of their sockets, sat on a mountain of pillows next to a frail young

---

4. A lower-class quarter in Odessa, known for its criminal underworld and pockets of extreme poverty. Babel's parents resided in Moldovanka briefly, long enough for their son to be born there, a fact he referred to with irony and pride. —Ed.

man who was mute with melancholy who had been bought with Eich-baum's money.

The gift-giving ceremony was coming to an end, the *shamases* were growing hoarse, and the bass fiddle was clashing with the violin. A sudden faint odor of burning spread over the courtyard.

"Benya," Papa Krik, the old carter, known as a ruffian even in carting circles, shouted. "Benya! You know what? I think the embers have blazed up again!"

"Papa!" the King said to his drunken father. "Please eat and drink and don't let these foolish things be worrying you!"

And Papa Krik followed his son's advice. He ate and drank. But the cloud of smoke became ever more poisonous. Here and there patches of sky were turning pink, and suddenly a tongue of fire, narrow as a sword, shot high into the air. The guests got up and started sniffing, and their women yelped. The gangsters looked at one another. And only Benya, who seemed not to notice anything, was inconsolable.

"My feast! They're ruining it!" he shouted in despair. "My friends, please, eat, drink!"

But at that moment the same young man who had come at the beginning of the feast appeared again in the courtyard.

"King!" he said. "I have a couple of words I need to tell you!"

"Well, speak!" the King answered. "You always got a couple words up your sleeve!"

"King!" the young man said with a snigger. "It's so funny—the police station's burning like a candle!"

The storekeepers were struck dumb. The gangsters grinned. Sixty-year-old Manka, matriarch of the Slobodka[5] bandits, put two fingers in her mouth and whistled so shrilly that those sitting next to her jumped up.

"Manka! You're not at work now!" Benya told her. "Cool down!"

The young man who had brought this startling news was still shaking with laughter.

"About forty of them left the station to go on the raid," he said, his jaws quivering. "They hadn't gone fifteen yards when everything went up in flames! Run and see for yourselves!"

But Benya forbade his guests to go look at the fire. He himself went with two friends. The police station was in flames. With their wobbling backsides, the policemen were running up and down the smoke-filled staircases, throwing boxes out of the windows. The prisoners made a run for it. The firemen were bristling with zeal, but it turned out that there wasn't any water in the nearby hydrant. The chief of police, the new broom so eager to sweep, stood on the opposite sidewalk, chewing on his mustache which hung into his mouth. The new broom stood completely still. Benya walked past and gave him a military salute.

"A very good day to you, Your Excellency!" he said sympathetically. "What bad luck! A nightmare!" He stared at the burning building, shook his head, and smacked his lips: "Ai-ai-ai!"

5. A rough shantytown neighborhood on the outskirts of Odessa. —*Ed.*

When Benya came back home, the lantern lights in the courtyard were already going out and dawn was breaking across the sky. The guests had dispersed, and the musicians were asleep, their heads leaning against the necks of their bass fiddles. Only Dvoira hadn't gone to sleep yet. With both hands she was edging her timid husband toward the door of their nuptial chamber, looking at him lustfully like a cat which, holding a mouse in its jaws, gently probes it with its teeth.

How Things Were Done in Odessa[1]

I was the one who began.

"Reb Arye-Leib," I said to the old man. "Let's talk about Benya Krik. Let's talk about his lightning-quick beginning and his terrible end. Three shadows block the path of my thoughts. There is Froim Grach. The steel of his actions—doesn't it bear comparison to the power of the King? There is Kolka Pakovsky. The rage of that man had everything it takes to rule. And could not Chaim Drong tell when a star was on the rise? So why was Benya Krik the only one to climb to the top of the ladder while everyone else was clinging to the shaky rungs below?"

Reb Arye-Leib remained silent as he sat on the cemetery wall. Before us stretched the green calm of the graves. A man thirsting for an answer must stock up with patience. A man in possession of facts can afford to carry himself with aplomb. That is why Arye-Leib remained silent as he sat on the cemetery wall. Finally he began his tale:

"Why him? Why not the others, you want to know? Well then, forget for a while that you have glasses on your nose and autumn in your heart. Forget that you pick fights from behind your desk and stutter when you are out in the world! Imagine for a moment that you pick fights in town squares and stutter only among papers. You are a tiger, you are a lion, you are a cat. You can spend the night with a Russian woman, and the Russian woman will be satisfied by you. You are twenty-five years old. If the sky and the earth had rings attached to them, you would grab these rings and pull the sky down to the earth. And your papa is the carter Mendel Krik. What does a papa like him think about? All he thinks about is downing a nice shot of vodka, slugging someone in their ugly mug, and about his horses—nothing else. You want to live, but he makes you die twenty times a day. What would you have done if you were in Benya Krik's shoes? You wouldn't have done a thing! But he did. Because he is the King, while you only thumb your nose at people when their back is turned!

"He, Benchik, went to Froim Grach, who even back then peered at the world with only one eye and was just what he is now. And Benya told Froim, 'Take me on. I want to come on board your ship. The ship I end up on will do well by me.'

"Grach asked him, 'Who're you, where d'you come from, what's your bread and butter?'

---

1. First published in the supplement to *Izvestia* (Odessa), May 5, 1923. The title alludes to Boris Eikhenbaum's essay "How Gogol's Overcoat Was Made" (1919). Babel ironically matches Eikhenbaum's view of how Russian literature "was made" in St. Petersburg with his own—the way things were done in Odessa. —*Ed.*

"'Try me, Froim,' Benya answered, 'and let's stop wasting time spreading kasha on the table.'
"'Fine, we won't waste time spreading kasha on the table,' Grach said. 'I'll try you.'
"And the gangsters called a council together to decide about Benya Krik. I wasn't at that council, but word has it that they did call together a council. The elder back then was the late Lyovka Bik.
"'Anyone know what's going on under Benchik's hat?' the late Bik asked.
"And one-eyed Grach gave his opinion.
"'Benya talks little, but he talks with zest. He talks little, but you want that he'll say more.'
"'If that's so, we'll try him out on Tartakovsky,' the late Bik pronounced.
"'We'll try him out on Tartakovsky,' the council decided, and those who still housed a trace of conscience turned red when they heard this decision. Why did they turn red? If you listen, you'll find out.
"Tartakovsky was known as 'Yid-and-a-Half' or 'Nine-Raids.' They called him 'Yid-and-a-Half' because there wasn't a single Jew who had as much chutzpah or money as Tartakovsky had. He was taller than the tallest Odessa policeman, and heavier than the fattest Jewess. And they called Tartakovsky 'Nine-Raids' because the firm of Lyovka Bik and Company had launched not eight raids and not ten, but exactly nine raids against his business. To Benya, who was not yet King, fell the honor of carrying out the tenth raid on Yid-and-a-Half. When Froim informed Benya of this, Benya said yes, and left, slamming the door behind him. Why did he slam the door? If you listen, you'll find out.
"Tartakovsky has the soul of a murderer, but he's one of us. He sprang forth from us. He is our blood. He is our flesh, as if one mama had given birth to us. Half of Odessa works in his stores. Not to mention, his own Moldavankans have given him quite a bit of grief. They abducted him twice and held him for ransom, and once, during a pogrom, they buried him with chanters. The Slobodka thugs were beating up Jews on Bolshaya Arnautskaya. Tartakovsky ran away from them and came across the funeral march with chanters on Sofiyskaya Street.
"'Who are they burying with chanters?' he asked.
"The passersby told him that Tartakovsky was being buried. The procession marched to the Slobodka Cemetery. Then our boys yanked a machine gun out of the coffin and started shooting at the Slobodka thugs. But Yid-and-a-Half had not foreseen this. Yid-and-a-Half got the fright of his life. What boss in his place would not have been frightened?
"A tenth raid on a man who had already been buried once was a crass deed. Benya, who back then wasn't yet the King, knew this better than anyone else. But he said yes to Grach and on that very same day wrote Tartakovsky a letter, typical of those letters:

Most esteemed Rubin Osipovich,
   I would be grateful if by the Sabbath you could place by the rainwater barrel a . . . , and so on. Should you choose to refuse, which you have opted to do lately, a great disappointment in your family life awaits you.
                                                      Respectfully yours,
                                                      Ben Zion Krik

"Tartakovsky, not one to dither, was quick to answer:

Benya,
   If you were an idiot, I would write you as to an idiot. But from
what I know of you, you aren't one, and may the Lord prevent me
from changing my mind. You, as is plain to see, are acting like a
boy. Is it possible that you are not aware that this year the crop in
Argentina has been so good that we can stand on our heads but we
still can't unload our wheat? And I swear to you on a stack of Bibles
that I'm sick and tired of having to eat such a bitter crust of bread
and witness such trouble after having worked all my life like the
lowliest carter. And what do I have to show for my life sentence of
hard labor? Ulcers, sores, worries, and no sleep! Drop your foolish
thoughts, Benya.
                            Your friend, a far better one than you realize,
                            Rubin Tartakovsky

"Yid-and-a-Half had done his part. He had written a letter. But the mail
didn't deliver it to the right address. Getting no answer, Benya became
angry. The following day he turned up at Tartakovsky's office with four
friends. Four masked youths with revolvers burst into the room.
   "'Hands up!' they shouted, waving their pistols.
   "'Not so loud, Solomon!' Benya told one of the youths, who was
yelling louder than the rest. 'Don't get so jumpy on the job!' and he
turned to the shop assistant, who was white as death and yellow as clay,
and asked him:
   "'Is Yid-and-a-Half in the factory?'
   "'He's not in the factory,' said the shop assistant, whose family name
was Muginshtein, his first name Josif, and who was the unmarried son of
Aunt Pesya, the chicken seller on Seredinskaya Square.
   "'So who's in charge when the boss is out?' they asked poor Muginshtein.
   "'I'm in charge when the boss is out,' the shop assistant said, green as
green grass.
   "'In that case, with God's help, please open the safe!' Benya ordered,
and a three-act opera began.
   "Nervous Solomon stuffed money, papers, watches, and jewelry into a
suitcase—the late Josif Muginshtein stood in front of him with his
hands in the air, while Benya told stories from the life of the Jewish
people.
   "'Well, ha! If he likes playing Rothschild,' Benya said about Tartakovsky,
'then let him roast in hell! I ask you, Muginshtein, as one asks a friend: he
gets my business letter—so how come he can't take a five-kopeck tram to
come visit me at home, drink a shot of vodka with my family, and eat what
God has seen fit to send us? What stopped him from baring his soul to
me? Couldn't he have said—Benya, you know, such and such, but here's
my balance sheet, just give me a couple of days to catch my breath, to get
things rolling—don't you think I'd have understood? Pigs at a trough
might not see eye to eye, but there is no reason why two grown men can't!
Do you see what I'm saying, Muginshtein?'
   "'I see what you're saying,' Muginshtein answered, lying, because he
was at a loss as to why Yid-and-a-Half, a respected, wealthy man, one of

the foremost men in town, should want to take a tram so he could have a bite to eat with the family of Mendel Krik, a carter.

"But all the time misfortune was loitering beneath the windows, like a beggar at dawn. Misfortune burst loudly into the office. And though this time it came in the guise of the Jew Savka Butsis, it was as drunk as a water carrier.

"'Ooh, ooh, ah!' Savka the Jew shouted. 'I'm sorry I'm so late, Benchik!' And he stamped his feet and waved his hands. Then he fired, and the bullet hit Muginshtein in the stomach.

"Are words necessary here? There was a man, and now there's none. An innocent bachelor, living his life like a little bird on a branch, and now he's dead from sheer idiocy. In comes a Jew looking like a sailor and doesn't shoot at a bottle in a fairground booth to win a prize—he shoots at a living man! Are words necessary here?

"'Everyone out!' Benya shouted, and as he ran out last, managed to tell Butsis, 'On my mother's grave, Savka, you'll be lying next to him!'

"So tell me, a young gentleman like you who cuts coupons on other people's bonds, how would you have acted in Benya Krik's position? You wouldn't know what to do? Well, he did! That's why he was King, while you and I are sitting here on the wall of the Second Jewish Cemetery, holding up our hands to keep the sun out of our eyes.

"Aunt Pesya's unfortunate son didn't die right away. An hour after they got him to the hospital, Benya turned up. He had the senior doctor called in and the nurse, and, without taking his hands out of the pockets of his cream-colored pants, told them, 'I have a whole lot of interest that your patient, Josif Muginshtein, recovers. Just in case, let me introduce myself—Ben Zion Krik. Give him camphor, air cushions, a private room, from the depths of your heart! If you don't, then every doctor here, even if they're doctors of philosophy, will be doled out six feet of earth!'

"And yet, Muginshtein died that same night. It was only then that Yid-and-a-Half raised hell in all Odessa. 'Where do the police begin and Benya end?' he wailed.

"'The police end where Benya begins,' levelheaded people answered, but Tartakovsky wouldn't calm down, and to his amazement saw a red automobile with a music box for a horn playing the first march from the opera *I Pagliacci* on Seredinskaya Square. In broad daylight the car raced over to the little house in which Aunt Pesya lived. Its wheels thundered, it spat smoke, gleamed brassily, reeked of gasoline, and honked arias on its horn. A man jumped out of the automobile and went into the kitchen where little Aunt Pesya was writhing on the earthen floor. Yid-and-a-Half was sitting on a chair waving his arms. 'You ugly hooligan!' he shouted, when he saw the man. 'You damn bandit, may the earth spit you out! A nice style you've picked for yourself, going around murdering live people!'

"'Monsieur Tartakovsky,' Benya Krik said to him quietly. 'For two days and nights I have been crying for the dear deceased as if he were my own brother. I know that you spit on my young tears. Shame on you, Monsieur Tartakovsky! What fireproof safe have you hidden your shame in? You had the heart to send a paltry hundred rubles to the mother of our dear deceased Josif. My hair, not to mention my brain, stood on end when I got word of this!'

"Here Benya paused. He was wearing a chocolate jacket, cream pants, and raspberry-red half boots.

"'Ten thousand down!' he bellowed. 'Ten thousand down, and a pension till she dies—may she live to be a hundred and twenty! If it's 'no,' then we leave this house together, Monsieur Tartakovsky, and go straight to my car!'

"Then they started arguing. Yid-and-a-Half swore at Benya. Not that I was present at this quarrel, but those who were, remember it well. They finally agreed on five thousand cash in hand, and fifty rubles a month.

"'Aunt Pesya!' Benya then said to the disheveled old woman rolling on the floor. 'If you want my life, you can have it, but everyone makes mistakes, even God! This was a giant mistake, Aunt Pesya! But didn't God himself make a mistake when he settled the Jews in Russia so they could be tormented as if they were in hell? Wouldn't it have been better to have the Jews living in Switzerland, where they would've been surrounded by first-class lakes, mountain air, and Frenchmen galore? Everyone makes mistakes, even God. Listen to me with your ears, Aunt Pesya! You're getting five thousand in hand and fifty rubles a month till you die—may you live to be a hundred and twenty! Josif's funeral will be first-class. Six horses like lions, two hearses with garlands, chanters from the Brodsky Synagogue, and Minkovsky himself will come to chant the burial service for your departed son!'

"And the funeral took place the next morning. Ask the cemetery beggars about this funeral! Ask the synagogue *shamases*, the kosher poultry sellers, or the old women from the Second Poorhouse! Such a funeral Odessa had never seen, nor will the world ever see the like of it. On that day the policemen wore cotton gloves. In the synagogues, draped with greenery, their doors wide open, the electricity was on. Black plumes swayed on the white horses pulling the hearse. Sixty chanters walked in front of the procession. The chanters were boys, but they sang with women's voices. The elders of the Kosher Poultry Sellers Synagogue led Aunt Pesya by the hand. Behind the elders marched the members of the Society of Jewish Shop Assistants, and behind the Jewish shop assistants marched the barristers, the doctors, and the certified midwives. On one side of Aunt Pesya were the chicken sellers from the Stary Bazaar, and on the other the esteemed dairymaids from the Bugayevka, wrapped in orange shawls. They stamped their feet like gendarmes on parade. From their broad hips came the scent of sea and milk. And behind them plodded Rubin Tartakovsky's workers. There were a hundred of them, or two hundred, or two thousand. They wore black frock coats with silk lapels, and new boots that squeaked like piglets in a sack.

"And now I will speak as God spoke on Mount Sinai from the burning bush! Take my words into your ears. Everything I saw, I saw with my own eyes, sitting right here on the wall of the Second Cemetery, next to lisping Moiseika and Shimshon from the funeral home. I, Arye-Leib, a proud Jew living among the dead, saw it with my own eyes.

"The hearse rolled up to the synagogue in the cemetery. The coffin was placed on the steps. Aunt Pesya was shaking like a little bird. The cantor climbed out of the carriage and began the funeral service. Sixty chanters supported him. And at that very moment the red automobile came flying around the corner. It was honking *I Pagliacci* and came to a stop. The people stood, silent as corpses. The trees, the chanters, the beggars stood silent. Four men got out from under the red roof, and with quiet steps carried to the hearse a wreath of roses of a beauty never before seen. And when the funeral ended, the four men lifted the coffin onto their steel shoulders, and with burning eyes and protruding chests, marched with the members of the Society of Jewish Shop Assistants.

"In front walked Benya Krik, who back then nobody was yet calling the King. He was the first to approach the grave. He climbed onto the mound, and stretched out his arm.

"'What are you doing, young man?' Kofman from the Burial Brotherhood shouted, running up to him.

"'I want to give a speech,' Benya Krik answered.

"And he gave a speech. All who wanted to hear it heard it. I, Arye-Leib, heard it, as did lisping Moiseika, who was sitting next to me on the wall.

"'Ladies and gentlemen,' Benya Krik said. 'Ladies and gentlemen,' he said, and the sun stood above his head, like a guard with a rifle. 'You have come to pay your last respects to an honest toiler, who died for a copper half-kopeck. In my own name, and in the name of all those who are not present, I thank you. Ladies and gentlemen! What did our dear Josif see in his life? One big nothing! What did he do for a living? He counted someone else's money. What did he die for? He died for the whole working class. There are men who are already doomed to die, and there are men who still have not begun to live. And suddenly a bullet, flying toward the doomed heart, tears into Josif, when all he has seen of life is one big nothing. There are men who can drink vodka, and there are men who can't drink vodka but still drink it. The former get pleasure from the agony and joy, and the latter suffer for all those who drink vodka without being able to drink it. Therefore, ladies and gentlemen, after we have prayed for our poor Josif, I ask you to accompany Saveli Butsis, a man unknown to you but already deceased, to *his* grave.'

"Having finished his speech, Benya Krik came down from the mound. The people, the trees, and the cemetery beggars stood silent. Two gravediggers carried an unpainted coffin to an adjacent grave. The cantor, stuttering, ended the prayer. Benya threw the first spadeful of earth and walked over to Savka. All the barristers and ladies with brooches followed him like sheep. He had the cantor chant the full funeral rites for Savka, and sixty chanters sang with him. Savka had never dreamt of such a funeral—you can trust the word of Arye-Leib, an aged old man.

"Word has it that it was on that day that Yid-and-a-Half decided to close shop. Not that I myself was there. But I saw with my own eyes, the eyes of Arye-Leib—which is my name—that neither the cantor, nor the choir, nor the Burial Brotherhood asked to get paid for the funeral. More I couldn't see, because the people quietly slipped away from Savka's grave and started running, as if from a fire. They flew off in carriages, in carts, and on foot. And the four men who had arrived in the red automobile left in it. The musical horn played its march, the car lurched and hurtled off.

"'The King!' lisping Moiseika, who always grabs the best seat on the wall, said, following the car with his eyes.

"Now you know everything. You know who was the first to pronounce the word 'King.' It was Moiseika. Now you know why he didn't call one-eyed Grach that, nor raging Kolka. You know everything. But what use is it if you still have glasses on your nose and autumn in your heart? . . ."

Lyubka the Cossack[1]

In the Moldavanka, on the corner of Dalnitskaya and Balkovskaya Streets, stands Lyubka[2] Shneiweis's house. In this house there is a wine cellar, an inn, an oat store, and a dovecote for a hundred Kryukov and Nikolayev doves. All these as well as lot number forty-six in the Odessa quarry belong to Lyubka Shneiweis, nicknamed Lyubka the Cossack—only the dovecote is the property of Yevzel, a retired soldier with a medal. On Sundays, Yevzel goes to Okhotnitskaya Square and sells doves to officials from town and to the boys of the neighborhood. Also living in Lyubka's courtyard, besides the watchman, are Pesya-Mindl, cook and procuress, and Zudechkis, the manager, a small Jew with a build and beard like those of our Moldavanka Rabbi, Ben Zkharia. There are many stories I can tell about Zudechkis. The first is the story of how Zudechkis became the manager of the inn that belonged to Lyubka, nicknamed the Cossack.

About ten years ago Zudechkis was the middleman in the sale of a horse-drawn threshing machine to a landowner, and in the evening he brought the landowner over to Lyubka's to celebrate the sale. This landowner had not only a mustache, but also a goatee, and wore lacquered shoes. Pesya-Mindl served him gefilte fish, followed by a very nice young lady by the name of Nastya. The landowner stayed the night, and in the morning Yevzel woke Zudechkis, who was lying curled up by Lyubka's door.

"Well!" Yevzel said to him. "Last night you were boasting about how the landowner bought a threshing machine through you! Well, let me inform you that he stayed the night and then at dawn, like the lowest of the low, made a run for it. That'll be two rubles for the food and four rubles for the young lady. I can see you're a slippery old con!"

But Zudechkis wouldn't pay. So Yevzel shoved him into Lyubka's room and locked the door.

"Well!" the watchman said. "You're going to stay right here till Lyubka gets back from the quarry, and with the help of God she will beat the soul out of you! Amen!"

"Jailbird!" Zudechkis shouted after the soldier, and looked around the room. "All you know about is your doves, you jailbird! But I still have some faith in God who will lead me out of here, the way He led all the Jews first out of Egypt and then out of the desert!"

There was much more that the little middleman wanted to tell Yevzel,

---

1. First published in *Krasnaya nov* 5 (1924), subtitled "From The Odessa Stories." —*Ed.*
2. Among Russians, the name Lyubka is an informal diminutive of Lyubov (love), but among Yiddish speakers it was often a derivative of Leyba, itself a derivative of the Yiddish *leb* or lion. —*Ed.*

but the soldier had taken the key and left, his shoes thumping. Then Zudechkis turned around and saw the procuress, Pesya-Mindl, sitting by the window reading *The Miracles and Heart of Baal-Shem*.[3] She was reading the Hasidic book with gilt edges, and rocking an oak cradle with her foot. In the cradle lay Lyubka's son, Davidka, crying.

"I see you have a nice setup here in this Sakhalin prison camp!" Zudechkis said to Pesya-Mindl. "The child lies there, bawling its lungs out so that a man feels pity at the sight of it, while you, you fat woman, sit here like a stone in the woods and don't even give him a bottle."

"*You* give him a bottle!" Pesya-Mindl answered, without looking up from her book. "That's if he'll take a bottle from you, you old crook! He's as big as a pork butcher, and all he wants is his mama's milk, while his mama gallops around her quarries, drinks tea with Jews in the Medved Tavern, buys contraband down by the harbor, and thinks of her son as she might think of last year's snow!"

"Oy, poor Zudechkis!" the small middleman then said to himself. "You have fallen into the hands of the Pharaoh himself!" And he went over to the eastern wall of the room, muttered the whole Morning Prayer with addenda, and then took the crying infant in his arms. Davidka looked at him in bewilderment and waved his little crimson legs covered in infant's sweat, and the old man started walking up and down the room and, rocking like a *tsaddik* in prayer, began singing an endless song.

"Ah-ah-ah," he began singing. "Now all the children will get nothing-and-a-half, but our little Davidka will get some buns, so he will sleep both night and day . . . ah-ah-ah, now all the children will get a good punch in the . . ."

Zudechkis showed Lyubka's son his fist with its gray hairs, and repeated the song about getting nothing-and-a-half and buns until the boy fell asleep and the sun had reached the middle of the shining sky. It reached the middle and began quivering like a fly weakened by the heat. Wild muzhiks from Nerubaiska and Tatarka who were staying at Lyubka's inn crawled under their carts and fell into a wild and sonorous sleep; a drunken workman went out to the gates and, dropping his plane and his saw, collapsed on the ground and began snoring then and there, surrounded by the golden flies and the blue lightning of July. Wrinkled German settlers who had brought Lyubka wine from the borders of Bessarabia sat nearby in the shade. They lit their pipes, and the smoke from their curved chibouks blended with the silver stubble of their old, unshaven cheeks. The sun hung from the sky like the pink tongue of a thirsty dog, the immense sea rolled far away to Peresip, and the masts of distant ships swayed on the emerald water of Odessa Bay. The day sat in an ornate boat, the day sailed toward evening, and halfway toward evening, at five o'clock, Lyubka came back from town. She rode in on a little roan horse with a large belly and an overgrown mane. A fat-legged young man in a calico shirt opened the gate for her, Yevzel grabbed hold of the bridle of her horse, at which point Zudechkis called down to Lyubka from his prison cell, "My respects, Madam Shneiweis, and good day to you! You simply go off on a three-year trip, and throw your hungry child at me!"

---

3. In medieval Jewish folklore, a Baal Shem was a rabbi whose spirituality enabled him to perform miracles. The term also refers to Israel ben Eliezer (1698–1760), the founder of Hasidic Judaism, Baal Shem Tov. —*Ed.*

"Shut your ugly trap!" Lyubka shouted back at the old man, and jumped off the horse. "Who's that yelling out my window?"

"It's Zudechkis, a slippery old con," the soldier with the medal explained to his mistress, and began telling her the whole story about the landowner, but didn't get to the end because Zudechkis interrupted him, yelling with all his might.

"This is an outrage!" he yelled, hurling down his skullcap. "This is an outrage to throw a child at a stranger and simply go off on a three-year trip! Come here this instant and give him your breast!"

"You wait till I come up there, you crook!" Lyubka muttered, and ran to the stairs. She came into the room and pulled her breast out of her dusty blouse.

The child stretched toward her and gnawed at her monstrous nipple, but didn't strike milk. A vein protruded on the mother's brow, and, shaking his skullcap, Zudechkis said to her, "You're such a greedy woman, Lyubka! You want everything for yourself! You snatch at the whole world, the way a child snatches at a tablecloth to get at breadcrumbs! You always have to have the best wheat and the best grapes! You want to bake white bread in the blaze of the sun, while your little baby, your sweet little pumpkin, is drying up without milk!"

"How am I supposed to have milk!" the woman yelled, kneading her breast. "The *Plutarch* pulled into port today and I had to cover fifteen versts in the heat! But don't think you can hoodwink me with your stories, you old Jew! Give me my six rubles!"

But again Zudechkis wouldn't pay. He rolled up his sleeve, and jabbed his thin, dirty elbow into Lyubka's mouth.

"Choke, you jailbird!" he shouted, and spat into the corner.

Lyubka stood there for a while with the foreign elbow in her mouth, then took it out, locked the door, and went out into the courtyard. Waiting for her there was Mr. Trottyburn, who resembled a pillar of red meat. Mr. Trottyburn was the chief engineer on the *Plutarch*. He had brought Lyubka two sailors. One of the sailors was an Englishman, the other a Malay. The three of them were lugging into the courtyard contraband they had brought from Port Said. The box was heavy. They dropped it on the ground, and out of the box tumbled cigars tangled with Japanese silk. A horde of women came running to the box, and two wandering gypsy women came slyly edging nearer.

"Get out of here! Scum!" Lyubka yelled at them, and led the sailors to the shade of an acacia tree.

They sat down at a table. Yevzel brought them wine, and Mr. Trottyburn began unwrapping his merchandise. Out of his bale he took cigars and delicate silks, cocaine and metal jiggers, uncut tobacco from the state of Virginia, and black wine bought on the Island of Chios. Each item had a special price, and each figure was washed down with Bessarabian wine with its bouquet of sunshine and bedbugs. Twilight was already flooding the courtyard, twilight was flooding in like an evening wave over a wide river, and the drunken Malay, completely taken aback, poked Lyubka's breast with his finger. He poked it with one finger, then with each of his fingers, one after the other.

His yellow and tender eyes hung above the table like paper lanterns on a Chinese street. He started singing, barely audibly, and toppled onto the ground as Lyubka punched him with her fist.

"A nice literate fellow, that one!" Lyubka said to Mr. Trottyburn. "That Malaysian's making me lose my last drop of milk, while that Jew up there won't stop badgering me for it!"

And she pointed at Zudechkis, who was standing by the window, washing his socks. A small lamp was smoking in Zudechkis's room, his tub frothed and hissed, he leaned out the window sensing that they were talking about him, and in despair started yelling down to them.

"Save me, you people!" he yelled, waving his hands.

"Shut your ugly trap!" Lyubka yelled back, and burst out laughing. "Shut up!"

She threw a stone at the old man, but didn't manage to hit him. She then grabbed an empty wine bottle. But Mr. Trottyburn, the chief engineer, took the bottle away from her, aimed, and flung it through the open window.

"Miss Lyubka," the chief engineer said, rising, pulling his drunken legs toward himself. "Many worthy individuals have come to me, Miss Lyubka, to trade, but I trade with no one, not with Mr. Kuninson nor with Mr. Bats, nor with Mr. Kupchik, no one but you, because I find your conversation so agreeable, Miss Lyubka."

And, gaining a foothold on his wobbly legs, he grabbed his sailors by their shoulders—the one an Englishman, the other a Malay—and began dancing with them through the cooling courtyard. The men from the *Plutarch* danced in deeply pensive silence. An orange star had slid right down to the edge of the horizon and was staring them in the face. Then they took their money, grabbed each other by the hand, and went out into the street, swaying the way hanging lamps sway on a ship. From the street they could see the sea, the black waters of Odessa Bay, little toy flags on sunken masts, and piercing lights that had ignited in the spacious depths. Lyubka walked her dancing guests to the intersection. She stayed back alone in the empty street, laughed to herself, and went home. The sleepy young man in the calico shirt locked the gates behind her, Yevzel brought his mistress the proceeds of the day, and she went upstairs to sleep. There Pesya-Mindl, the procuress, was already slumbering, and Zudechkis was rocking the oak cradle with his bare feet.

"How you've tortured us, you shameless woman!" he said, and took the child out of the cradle. "But here, watch me and you might learn a thing or two, you foul mother, you!"

He laid a thin comb on Lyubka's breast and put her son into her bed. The child stretched toward his mother, pricked himself on the comb, and started to cry. Then the old man pushed the bottle toward him, but Davidka turned away from the bottle.

"Is this some spell you're putting on me, you old swindler?" Lyubka muttered, dozing off.

"Shut up, you foul mother, you!" Zudechkis said to her. "Shut up and learn, may the devil take you!"

The baby pricked himself on the comb again, hesitantly took the bottle, and began sucking.

"There!" Zudechkis said, and burst out laughing. "I have weaned your child! I can teach you a thing or two, may the devil take you!"

Davidka lay in his cradle, sucking on his bottle and dribbling blissfully. Lyubka woke up, opened her eyes, and closed them again. She saw her son, and the moon forcing its way through her window. The moon jumping into black clouds, like a straying calf.

"Well, fair enough," Lyubka said. "Unlock the door for Zudechkis, Pesya-Mindl, and let him come tomorrow for a pound of American tobacco."

And the following day Zudechkis came for a pound of uncut tobacco from the state of Virginia. He was given it, and a quarter pound of tea was thrown in. And within a week, when I came to buy a dove from Yevzel, I ran into the new manager of Lyubka's courtyard. He was tiny, like our Rabbi Ben Zkharia. Zudechkis was the new manager. He stayed at his post for fifteen years, and during that period I heard a great number of stories about him. And if I can manage, I will tell them one after another, because they are very interesting stories.

Sunset

A play in eight scenes[1]

CHARACTERS

Mendel Krik—owner of a horse carting establishment. 62 years old.

Nekhama—his wife, 60.

Their children:

   Benya—a dandyish young man, 26.

   Lyovka—a hussar on leave, 22.

   Dvoira—an unmarried girl past her prime, 30.

Arye-Leib—*shamas* of the Carting Union Synagogue, 65.

Nikifor—the Kriks' chief driver, 50.

Ivan Pyatirubel—a blacksmith and friend of Mendel Krik, 50.

Ben Zkharia—a rabbi of the Moldavanka, Odessa's Jewish section, 70.

Fomin—a contractor, 40.

Evdokiya Potapovna Kholodenko—sells live and slaughtered chickens at the market. She is a corpulent old woman with a twisted hip, and an alcoholic. 50.

Marusia—her daughter, 20.

Ryabtsov—a tavern keeper.

Mitya—a waiter at the tavern.

---

1. Babel wrote this play in 1926 soon after completing and publishing his script for the film *Benya Krik*, which ends with the bandit's execution by the Reds. *Sunset* was cleared by the theater censorship committee in October 1927 and premiered soon after in Baku and Odessa (where it was performed in both the Russian and Ukrainian theaters simultaneously), and on February 28, 1928 it opened in Moscow's MKhAT II Theater. It was first published in *Novy mir* 2 (1928). —*Ed.*

Miron Popyatnik—a flute player at Ryabtsov's tavern.

Madame Popyatnik—his wife. A gossip with frantic eyes.

Urusov—clandestine solicitor. He rolls his r's.[2]

Semyon—a bald peasant.

Bobrinets—a loud Jew. He is loud because he is rich.

Weiner—a rich man with a speech impediment.

Madame Weiner—a rich woman.

Klasha Zubaryeva—a pregnant girl.

Monsieur Lazar Boyarsky—the owner of the Chef d'Oeuvre ready-to-wear clothes factory.

Senka Topun.

Cantor Zwieback.

The action takes place in Odessa in 1913.

Scene One

The dining room in the KRIK *house. A low-ceilinged, homey, bourgeois room. Paper flowers, chests of drawers, a gramophone, portraits of rabbis, and next to them photographs of the* KRIK *family: stony dark faces, bulging eyes, shoulders like cupboards.*

The dining room has been prepared to receive guests. The table is covered with a red tablecloth and bottles of wine, preserves, and pies.

Old NEKHAMA KRIK *is making tea. To the side, on a small table, stands a boiling samovar.*

In the room, besides NEKHAMA, *are* ARYE-LEIB *and her son* LYOVKA, *in a hussar's parade uniform. His peakless yellow cap is cocked to the side above his brick-red face, and his military greatcoat is flung over his shoulders. Behind him he trails a curved sword.* BENYA KRIK, *decked out like a Spaniard at a village fair, is knotting his tie.*

ARYE-LEIB   Ha, fine, Lyovka, very fine indeed! I, Arye-Leib the Molda-vanka matchmaker and *shamas* at the carters' synagogue, am fully aware of what hacking things to pieces is all about! First they hack down reeds, then they start hacking down men! No one asks you whether you've got a mother or not! But explain this to me, Lyovka! Why can't a Hussar like you take an extra week off until your sister's happiness has been taken care of?

LYOVKA [*Laughs. His rough voice is thunderous.*]   An extra week? You're an idiot, Arye-Leib! An extra week off? The cavalry isn't the infantry, you know! The cavalry spits on the infantry! If I'm even an hour late, the sergeant major will drag me off to his office, squeeze the juice out of my soul and nose, and then have me court-martialed. Cavalrymen are judged by three generals, three generals covered with medals from the Turkish war.

ARYE-LEIB   Do they do this to everyone, or just to Jews?

---

2. A trait characteristic of a Yiddish or German accent. —*Ed.*

LYOVKA   A Jew who climbs onto a horse stops being a Jew and becomes a Russian. You're such a blockhead, Arye-Leib! What's this got to do with Jews?

[DVOIRA's *face pokes through the half-opened door.*]

DVOIRA   Mama, a girl can beat her brains out in this house before she finds anything! Where did you put my green dress?

NEKHAMA [*Mumbles without looking up.*]   Look in those drawers.

DVOIRA   I've already looked, it's not there.

NEKHAMA   How about the wardrobe?

DVOIRA   It's not there either.

LYOVKA   Which dress is it?

DVOIRA   The green one with the frills.

LYOVKA   I guess Papa swiped it.

[DVOIRA *enters the room. She is half dressed, her face heavily rouged, her hair curled. She is tall and plump.*]

DVOIRA [*In a dull voice.*]   Oy, I'm dying!

LYOVKA [*To his mother.*]   I bet you told him, you old cow, that Boyarsky is coming over today to take a look at Dvoira. Of course you did! Well, that's that, then! I saw Papa this morning. He harnessed Solomon the Wise and Muska, gulped some food, guzzled down his vodka like a hog, threw a green bundle into the cart, and drove off.

DVOIRA   Oy, I'm dying! [*She starts crying loudly, rips down the curtain from the window, jumps up and down on it, and throws it at her mother.*] There, take that!

NEKHAMA   May you die! May you die today!

[DVOIRA *runs out howling. The old woman shoves the curtain into a drawer.*]

BENYA [*Knotting his tie.*]   Our darling papa, you see, won't cough up the dowry.

LYOVKA   The old bastard should have his throat cut, like a pig!

ARYE-LEIB   Is this the way you talk about your father, Lyovka?

LYOVKA   Well, he shouldn't be such a bastard!

ARYE-LEIB   Your father's at least a Sabbath older than you are!

LYOVKA   Then he shouldn't be such a boor!

BENYA [*Sticks a pearl pin into his tie.*]   Last year Syomka Munsh wanted Dvoira, but our dear papa simply wouldn't cough up the dowry, if you know what I mean. He made kasha with sauce out of him and threw him down the stairs!

LYOVKA   The old bastard should have his throat cut, like a pig!

ARYE-LEIB   As the sage Ibn Ezra once said of an unlucky matchmaker like myself, "Should you take it into your head to become a maker of candles, the sun will surely stick like a clod in the sky and never set again!"

LYOVKA [*To his mother.*]   A hundred times a day the old man kills us, and you stand there, dumb as a post! Dvoira's future bridegroom could turn up any minute now. . . .

ARYE-LEIB   It was about an unlucky man like myself that Ibn Ezra said, "Take it into your head to sew shrouds for the dead, and not one man will die from now to the end of time, amen!"

BENYA [*Has knotted his tie, taken off the crimson band that keeps his hair in place, donned a tight-fitting jacket, and poured himself a vodka.*] Health to all present!

LYOVKA [*In a rough voice.*]   To our health!

ARYE-LEIB   May all go well!

LYOVKA   And may all go well!

[MONSIEUR BOYARSKY *rushes into the room. He is a cheerful, rotund man. He is an incessant talker.*]

BOYARSKY   Greetings! Greetings! [*He introduces himself.*] Boyarsky, pleased to meet you, excessively pleased! Greetings!

ARYE-LEIB   Lazar, you said you would be here at four, and it's six o'clock already!

BOYARSKY [*Sits down and takes a glass of tea from old* NEKHAMA KRIK.] God in heaven, we live in Odessa, and here in Odessa you have clients who squeeze the life out of you the way you squeeze pits out of a date—your best friends are ready to swallow you whole, suit and all, forget the salt! Cartloads of worries—a thousand scandals! When does a man have time to think about his health? You'll ask, what does a merchant need health for? I barely had time to get myself a hot seawater bath—and I came straight over!

ARYE-LEIB   You take seawater baths, Lazar?

BOYARSKY   Every day, like clockwork.

ARYE-LEIB [*To old* NEKHAMA.]   You can't get away for less than fifty kopecks a bath!

BOYARSKY   God in heaven, how fresh is the wine that flows in our Odessa! In the Greek Bazaar, Fankoni's—[3]

ARYE-LEIB   You eat at Fankoni's, Lazar?

BOYARSKY   I eat at Fankoni's.

ARYE-LEIB [*Triumphantly.*]   He eats at Fankoni's! [*To the old woman.*] You can't even get up from the table there for less than thirty kopecks—I won't tell you forty!

BOYARSKY   Forgive me, Arye-Leib, for daring—as a younger man—to interrupt you. Fankoni's costs me a ruble a day, even a ruble-and-a-half!

ARYE-LEIB [*Ecstatically.*]   What a spendthrift you are, Lazar! The world has never seen a rascal like you! A whole family can live on thirty rubles, send the children for violin lessons, and still save a kopeck—

[DVOIRA *rushes into the room. She is wearing an orange dress, and her powerful calves are squeezed into short, high-heeled boots.*]

ARYE-LEIB   This is our little Vera.

BOYARSKY [*Jumps up.*]   Greetings! Boyarsky!

DVOIRA [*Hoarsely.*]   Pleased to meet you.

[*Everyone sits down.*]

LYOVKA   Our Vera is a little dizzy today—too much ironing.

BOYARSKY   To get dizzy from ironing, that anyone can do, but not everyone can be a good person.

ARYE-LEIB   Thirty rubles a month up in smoke! . . . O Lazar, that you should ever have seen the light of day!

BOYARSKY   A thousand pardons, Arye-Leib, but this you must know about Boyarsky: he is not interested in capital. Capital is nothing. What Boyarsky is interested in is happiness! I ask you, dear friends,

3. A well-known elegant and expensive café in the center of Odessa. —Ed.

what good is it to me if my firm puts out a thousand—a thousand five hundred—suits, and then on top of that trousers to go with them, and then coats?

ARYE-LEIB [*To the old woman.*] That's five rubles clean, a suit—I won't tell you ten!

BOYARSKY So what good is my firm to me when my exclusive interest is happiness?

ARYE-LEIB And my answer to you, Lazar, is that if we do business like human beings, and not like charlatans, then you will be guaranteed happiness till the day you die—may you live to be a hundred and twenty! And I tell you this as a *shamas,* and not as a matchmaker!

BENYA [*Pours wine.*] May all our wishes come true!

LYOVKA [*In a rough voice.*] To our health!

ARYE-LEIB May all go well!

LYOVKA And may all go well!

BOYARSKY I was telling you about Fankoni's. Let me tell you a story, Monsieur Krik, about an impudent Jew. There I am, dropping in at Fankoni's, it's packed like a synagogue on Yom Kippur. Everyone is eating, spitting on the floor, worrying like crazy. One fellow worries because his business is bad, the next worries because business is good for his neighbor. And as for finding a place to sit down, forget it! . . . So then I bump into Monsieur Chapellon, a stately-looking Frenchman—and let me tell you, it's extremely rare for a Frenchman to be stately-looking—so he gets up to greet me, and invites me over to his table. Monsieur Boyarsky, he says to me in French, I hold your firm in the highest esteem, and I have some of the most marvelous coverings for coats—

LYOVKA Coverings?

BOYARSKY Coverings—heavy cloth for the outside of a coat—the most marvelous coverings for coats, he says to me, in French, and it would be an honor to invite you, as a firm, to drink two mugs of beer and eat ten crayfish with me—

LYOVKA I love crayfish.

ARYE-LEIB You'll be saying you love toads next.

BOYARSKY —and eat ten crayfish with me—

LYOVKA [*In a rough voice.*] I love crayfish!

ARYE-LEIB Crayfish, toads—same difference.

BOYARSKY [*To* LYOVKA.] Forgive me, Monsieur Krik, for saying this, but a Jew should not hold crayfish in high regard. This I am telling you from experience. A Jew who holds crayfish in high regard will go further with the female of the species than is right, he will utter obscenities at the table, and if he has children, then you can bet your last ruble that they'll turn into degenerates and billiard players. This I am telling you from experience. So let me tell you this story about an impudent Jew—

BENYA Boyarsky.

BOYARSKY Yes?

BENYA Give me an estimate, off the cuff, how much a winter suit will cost me.

BOYARSKY Double-breasted or single-breasted?

BENYA Single-breasted.

BOYARSKY   What kind of coattails—round or pointed?

BENYA   Round coattails.

BOYARSKY   Whose cloth—yours or mine?

BENYA   Your cloth.

BOYARSKY   What cloth—English, Polish, or Muscovite?

BENYA   Which is best?

BOYARSKY   English cloth, Monsieur Krik, that's good cloth; Polish cloth is just sackcloth with a pattern on it; and Muscovite cloth is sackcloth without a pattern on it.

BENYA   I'll go for the English.

BOYARSKY   Your trimmings or mine?

BENYA   Your trimmings.

BOYARSKY   So how much will that cost you?

BENYA   How much will that cost me?

BOYARSKY   [Struck by a sudden idea.]   Monsieur Krik, I'm sure we'll be able to give you a good deal!

ARYE-LEIB   I'm sure you'll be able to give him a good deal!

BOYARSKY   I'm sure we'll be able to give you a good deal—I was telling you about Fankoni's.

   [There is a clatter of metal-reinforced boot heels. MENDEL KRIK enters, carrying a whip, along with NIKIFOR, his head driver.]

ARYE-LEIB   [Suddenly timid.]   Let me introduce you. Mendel, this is Monsieur Boyarsky.

BOYARSKY   [Jumps up.]   Greetings! Boyarsky!

   [Stomping with his boots, old MENDEL crosses the room, ignoring everyone. He throws down the whip, sits down on the couch, and stretches out his long, fat legs. NEKHAMA kneels down and begins pulling off her husband's boots.]

ARYE-LEIB   [Stuttering.]   Monsieur Boyarsky was telling us about his company. It puts out a hundred fifty suits a month—

MENDEL   So you were saying, Nikifor?

NIKIFOR   [Leaning against the doorpost, staring up at the ceiling.]   I was saying, master, that people are laughing us out of town.

MENDEL   Why are they laughing us out of town?

NIKIFOR   People are saying that there are a thousand masters in your stable and seven Fridays in your week! Yesterday we carted wheat down to the harbor—so I went over to the office to get our money, and there they tell me—"Back off! The young master, Benchik, came over and gave us instructions to pay the money directly into the bank with a receipt."

MENDEL   Gave instructions?

NIKIFOR   Gave instructions!

NEKHAMA   [Has pulled off one of MENDEL's boots and unwrapped his dirty leggings. He stretches out his other leg to her. She looks up at her husband with intense hatred and mutters through clenched teeth.]   May you not live to see the light of day, you torturer!

MENDEL   So you were saying, Nikifor?

NIKIFOR   I was saying I was insulted by Lyovka today.

BENYA   [Drinks down his wine, his little finger extended.]   May all our wishes come true!

LYOVKA   To our health.

NIKIFOR   We took the mare Freilin over to the blacksmith to be shod today. So Lyovka suddenly bursts in and starts shooting off his mouth, ordering Pyatirubel the blacksmith to line the horseshoes with rubber. So I say to him, excuse me, who does he think we are to be using rubber on our horseshoes? Police chiefs? Czars? Nicholas the Seconds? The master, I tell him, said nothing to me about this. So Lyovka turns red as a beet and shouts: Who do you think is your master?
   [NEKHAMA *has pulled off the second boot.* MENDEL *gets up. He yanks the tablecloth. Plates, pies, and preserves fall on the floor.*]
MENDEL   So who do you think is your master, Nikifor?
NIKIFOR [*Sullenly.*]   You are my master.
MENDEL   And if I am your master [*he goes over to* NIKIFOR *and grabs him by his shirt collar.*] . . . if I am your master, then tear to pieces anyone who dares set foot in my stables—tear out his heart, his tendons, his eyes!
   [*He shakes* NIKIFOR *and then flings him to the side. Stooping forward, dragging his bare feet,* MENDEL *walks across the room to the door.* NIKIFOR *shuffles behind him. The old woman crawls on her knees to the door.*]
NEKHAMA   May you not live to see the light of day, you torturer!
   [*Silence.*]
ARYE-LEIB   What if I told you, Lazar, that the old man didn't attend one of the better finishing schools?
BOYARSKY   I'd believe you, and you wouldn't even have to give me your word.
BENYA [*Gives* BOYARSKY *his hand.*]   I hope you'll come visit us some other time.
BOYARSKY   Well, families being what they are, there's always something going on—sometimes cold, sometimes hot. Good-bye! Good-bye! I'll come again some other time.
   [BOYARSKY *hurries out.* BENYA *gets up, lights a cigarette, and throws his flashy coat over his arm.*]
ARYE-LEIB   Ibn Ezra once said about an unlucky matchmaker like myself, "Should you take it into your head to sew shrouds for the dead—
LYOVKA   The old bastard should have his throat cut, like a pig!
   [DVOIRA *leans back in her chair and starts screaming.*]
LYOVKA   Ha, there you go! Dvoira is having a fit!
   [*He pries open his sister's clenched teeth with a knife. She squeals louder and louder.* NIKIFOR *enters the room.* BENYA *flings his coat over his left arm, and with his right punches* NIKIFOR *in the face.*]
BENYA   Harness the bay horse to the buggy!
NIKIFOR [*A few drops of blood slowly trickle from his nose.*]   Give me my wages, I'm leaving.
BENYA [*Comes over to* NIKIFOR, *face-to-face, and speaks in a sweet and tender voice.*]   Nikifor, my dear friend, you will die today without eating supper!

Scene Two

Night. The KRIKS' *bedroom. Black wooden beams across the low ceiling. Blue moonlight weaves its way through the window.* MENDEL *and* NEKHAMA *are in a double bed. They are covered by a single blanket.* NEKHAMA, *her dirty gray hair disheveled, is sitting up in bed. She is grumbling in a low voice, grumbling endlessly.*

NEKHAMA   Other people live like people . . . other people buy ten pounds of meat for lunch, they make soup, they make meatballs, they make compote! The father comes home from work, everyone sits at the table, everyone eats, laughs. And us? God, oh, God, how dark my house is!

MENDEL   Let me be, Nekhama! Sleep!

NEKHAMA   And Benya, our little Benchik, as bright as the sun in the sky, and now look what he's come to! Today one policeman comes around, tomorrow another . . . one day people have a piece of bread in their hand, the next they find their legs in irons.

MENDEL   Let me breathe, Nekhama! Sleep!

NEKHAMA   And Lyovka! The child will come back from the army and also start marauding. What else is there for him to do? His father is a degenerate, he won't take his sons into his own business—

MENDEL   Let it be night, Nekhama! Sleep!

[*Silence.*]

NEKHAMA   The rabbi said, Rabbi Ben Zkharia . . . Come the new month, Ben Zkharia said, I won't let Mendel into the synagogue. The Jews won't allow me to—

MENDEL   [*Throws off the blanket and sits up beside the old woman.*] What won't the Jews allow?

NEKHAMA   Come the new moon, Ben Zkharia said—

MENDEL   What won't the Jews allow? And what have these Jews of yours ever given me?

NEKHAMA   They won't allow you in, into the synagogue.

MENDEL   A ruble with a chewed-off edge they gave me, these Jews of yours! And *you* they gave me, you old cow, and this bug-ridden grave!

NEKHAMA   And what did the Russian pork butchers give you? What did they give you?

MENDEL   [*Lies back down.*]   Oh, this old cow is sitting on my head!

NEKHAMA   Vodka, that's what the pork butchers gave you, and a mouth full of foul language, a rabid dog's mouth. . . . He's sixty-two years old, God, sweet God, and he's as hot as an oven, strong as an oven!

MENDEL   Pull my teeth out, Nekhama! Pour Jewish soup into my veins! Break my back!

NEKHAMA   Hot as an oven. . . . God, how ashamed I am! [*She takes her pillow and lies down on the floor in the moonlight. Silence. Then her grumbling starts up again.*] Friday evening people go outside their gates, people play with their grandchildren—

MENDEL   Let it be night, Nekhama!

NEKHAMA   [*Crying.*]   People play with their grandchildren . . .

[BENYA *enters the room. He is in his underwear.*]
BENYA Haven't you had enough for today, my little lovebirds?
[MENDEL *sits up in bed. He looks at his son in shock.*]
BENYA Or do I have to go to an inn to get some sleep?
MENDEL [*Gets out of bed. Like his son, he is in his underwear.*] You . . . you dare come in here?
BENYA Do I have to pay two rubles for a room in order to get some sleep?
MENDEL At night, at night you dare come in here?
BENYA She's my mother. Do you hear me, you cheap bastard?
[*Father and son stand face-to-face in their underwear. Slowly* MENDEL *moves closer and closer to his son. In the moonlight* NEKHAMA's *disheveled head of dirty gray hair is trembling.*]
MENDEL At night, at night you dare come in here. . . .

Scene Three

A *tavern on Privoznaya Square. Night.* RYABTSOV, *the tavern keeper—a stern, sickly man—is at the counter reading the Bible. His drab, dusty hair is plastered down on both sides of his head.* MIRON POPYATNIK, *a meek flutist, is sitting on a raised platform. They call him the major. A weak, tremulous melody comes from his flute. Gray-haired, black-mustached* GREEKS *sit at one of the tables playing dice with* SENKA TOPUN, BENYA KRIK's *friend. In front of* SENKA *are a sliced watermelon, a Finnish knife, and a bottle of Malaga wine. Two sailors are sleeping, their sculpted shoulders slumped on the table. In a far corner* FOMIN, *the contractor, is meekly sipping soda water. A drunken woman—* POTAPOVNA—*is heatedly trying to convince him of something.* MENDEL KRIK *is standing by a table in front. He is drunk, inflamed, colossal. With him is* URUSOV, *the solicitor.*

MENDEL [*Bangs his fist down onto the table.*] It's dark! I feel like I'm in a grave, Ryabtsov, in a black grave!
[MITYA *the waiter, a little old man with close-cropped silvery hair, brings a lamp and puts it down in front of* MENDEL.]
MENDEL I ordered all the lamps! I asked for singers! I ordered you to bring me all the lamps in the tavern!
MITYA They don't give us kerosene for free, you know. That's just how it is—
MENDEL It's dark in here!
MITYA [*To* RYABTSOV.] He wants extra light.
RYABTSOV That'll be a ruble.
MITYA Here's a ruble.
RYABTSOV Got it.
MENDEL Urusov!
URUSOV Present!
MENDEL How much blood did you say runs through my heart?
URUSOV According to science, two hundred *pood* of blood run through a man's heart every twenty-four hours. And in America they invented a—

MENDEL   Hold it! Hold it! . . . And if I want to go to America—is that free?

URUSOV   Totally free. You just up and go!

[POTAPOVNA *waddles over to the table, wiggling her crooked hip.*]

POTAPOVNA   Mendel, sweetie, it's not America we're going to, we're going to Bessarabia, to buy orchards.

MENDEL   You mean I just up and go?

URUSOV   According to science, you have to cross four seas—the Black Sea, the Ionian Sea, the Aegean Sea, the Mediterranean—and two world oceans, the Atlantic and the Pacific.

MENDEL   And you said a man can actually fly across the seas?

URUSOV   He can.

MENDEL   And can a man fly over mountains, high mountains?

URUSOV [*Sternly.*]   He can.

MENDEL [*Grabs his disheveled head.*]   There's no end, no limit. . . . [*To* RYABTSOV.] That's it, I'm going! I'm going to Bessarabia.

RYABTSOV   And what are you going to do in Bessarabia?

MENDEL   I'll do whatever I want!

RYABTSOV   What can you want?

MENDEL   Listen here, Ryabtsov, I'm still alive—

RYABTSOV   You're not alive if God killed you!

MENDEL   When is it he killed me?

RYABTSOV   How old did you say you were?

A VOICE FROM THE TAVERN   All in all, he's sixty-two!

RYABTSOV   It's sixty-two years that God's been killing you.

MENDEL   Listen Ryabtsov, I'm a lot cleverer than God.

RYABTSOV   Maybe you're cleverer than the Russian God, but not cleverer than the Jewish God.

[MITYA *brings in another lamp. Following him in single file are four fat, sleepy girls in grease-stained smocks. Each is carrying a lit lamp. A blinding light fills the tavern.*]

MITYA   Well, a bright and happy Easter to you! Girls! Surround this poor fool with lamps!

[*The girls put down the lamps in front of* MENDEL. *The radiance lights up his crimson face.*]

A VOICE FROM THE TAVERN   So we're turning night into day, Mendel?

MENDEL   There is no end!

POTAPOVNA [*Pulls* URUSOV *by the sleeve.*]   Sir, I beg you, please, have a drink with me. . . . You see, I sell chickens at the market, and those damn peasants always foist the oldest and scrawniest hens on me. Do I have to be chained to those damn hens? My daddy was a gardener, the best gardener that ever was! If an apple tree grows wild, you should see me prune it!

A VOICE FROM THE TAVERN   Are we turning Monday into Sunday, Mendel?

POTAPOVNA [*Her jacket has fallen open over her fat breasts. Vodka, heat, and rapture are stifling her.*]   Mendel will sell off his business and, with the Lord's help, we'll get some money and set off with my pretty daughter for those orchards. Lime blossoms, sir, will rain down on us, you know. . . . Mendel, darling, I'm a gardener, you know, I'm my daddy's daughter!

MENDEL [*Walks over to the counter.*] Ryabtsov, I used to have eyes . . . listen to me, Ryabtsov, my eyes were stronger than telescopes, and what did I do with my eyes? My legs ran faster than locomotives, my legs could walk on water, and what did I do with my legs? I ran from eating slops to the outhouse, from the outhouse to eating slops. I've mopped floors with my face, but now I'm going to garden!

RYABTSOV So go ahead and garden! Who's stopping you?

A VOICE FROM THE TAVERN I'm sure there are one or two people at home who might very well stop him! They'll step on his tail, and that'll be that!

MENDEL I ordered songs! Hey, you, musician! Let's have a military tune. . . . You're boring me to death! Come on, let's have some life here! Come on!

[*Quavering, faltering,* MIRON POPYATNIK'*s flute lets out a piercing melody.* MENDEL *dances, stamping his iron-shod boots.*]

MITYA [*Whispering to* URUSOV.] Are you ready for Fomin, or is it early yet?

URUSOV It's early yet. [*To the musician.*] Go for it, Major!

A VOICE FROM THE TAVERN There's no point him going for it, the singers are here. Pyatirubel has dragged in the singers.

[*The singers enter—blind men in red shirts. They bump into chairs, waving their canes in front of them.* PYATIRUBEL, *the blacksmith, is leading them. He is a boisterous man, a friend of* MENDEL'*s.*]

PYATIRUBEL I dragged these devils out of their beds. We're not going to play, they tell me. It's night, they tell me, night all over the world, we can't play anymore. . . . Do you know who I am, I tell them!

MENDEL [*Throws himself at the lead singer, a tall, pockmarked blind man.*] Fedya, I'm going to Bessarabia!

THE BLIND MAN [*In a thick, deep bass.*] Good luck, master!

MENDEL A song, one last song for me!

THE BLIND MAN Shall we sing "The Glorious Sea"?

MENDEL One last song!

THE BLIND MEN [*Start tuning their guitars. They begin singing in deep bass voices.*]

> "O holy Baikal—glorious sea,
> My barrel of salmon, my ship so free!
> Hey, oarsman, whip the waves to-and-fro,
> For this brave man has far to go."

MENDEL [*Hurls an empty bottle at the window. The window shatters.*] Hit it!

PYATIRUBEL Damn! He's a hero, the son-of-a-bitch!

MITYA [*To* RYABTSOV.] How much shall we charge for the window?

RYABTSOV That'll be a ruble.

MITYA Here's a ruble.

RYABTSOV Got it.

THE BLIND MEN [*Sing.*]

> "Long was I shackled in heavy chains,
> Over mountains I wandered in the rains.
> An old comrade helped me run,
> And I survived to see the sun."

MENDEL [*With a blow of his fist he knocks out the window frame.*] Hit it!

PYATIRUBEL He's Satan incarnate, the old bastard!

VOICES FROM THE TAVERN
Go for it! Now he's really celebrating!
What do you mean, really celebrating? For him this is normal!
It can't be, someone must have died!
No one's died! This is his normal celebrating!
So, what's the reason? What's he celebrating?

RYABTSOV Go find the reason! With one man it's money—he celebrates his wealth, with the next it's lack of money—he celebrates his poverty. People are always celebrating.

[*The song rings out louder and louder. The sound of the guitars reverberates against the walls, and inflames hearts. A star flickers through the broken window. The sleepy girls stand by the door and sing, propping up their breasts with their rough hands. A sailor, his big legs spread apart, sways and sings in a clear tenor.*]

"Shilka and Nerchinsk no longer scare me,
Guards in the mountains did not snare me,
By beasts of the forest I wasn't torn apart.
Henchmen's bullets didn't pierce my heart."

POTAPOVNA [*Drunk and happy.*] Mendel, darling, drink with me! Let's drink to my sweet pretty daughter!

PYATIRUBEL He punched the post office clerk in the face! That's the way the old dog is! Then he ripped out the telegraph poles and carried them home on his back. . . .

"I walked all night and all day long,
With watchful eye through towns I flew.
Village women gave bread to make me strong,
And village men the tobacco they grew."

MENDEL Break my back, Nekhama! Pour Jewish soup into my veins!
[*He throws himself onto the floor, rolls about, moans, laughs.*]

VOICES FROM THE TAVERN
He's like an elephant . . .
I've seen elephants cry real tears . . .
You're lying! Elephants don't cry . . .
I tell you, I've seen them cry real tears . . .
At the zoo once I taunted an elephant . . .

MITYA [*To* URUSOV.] Are you ready for Fomin, or is it early yet?

URUSOV It's early yet.
[*The singers sing with all their might. The song thunders. The quivering, quaking guitars play full force.*]

"O holy Baikal—O glorious sea,
A glorious sail, my caftan fluttering free!
Hey oarsman, whip the waves to and fro,
I hear the thunder louder grow."

[*The blind men sing the last lines with vehement, joyful, weeping voices. Finishing the song, they rise and leave as one.*]

MITYA Is that all?

THE LEAD SINGER That's all.

MENDEL [*Jumps up.*] I want a war song! Musicians, some life!

MITYA [*To* URUSOV.]   Is it time for Fomin, or is it early yet?

URUSOV   It's time.

[MITYA *winks at* FOMIN, *who is sitting in a far corner.* FOMIN *quickly walks over to* MENDEL'*s table.*]

FOMIN   I wish you a pleasant evening.

URUSOV [*To* MENDEL.]   Now, my dear friend, this is what we'll do—there's a time for work, and a time for play. [*He takes out a piece of paper covered with writing.*] Shall I read it out loud?

FOMIN   If you're not in the mood to dance, then I guess you should.

URUSOV   Should I just read the final amount?

FOMIN   I am in agreement with your suggestion.

MENDEL [*Stares at* FOMIN *and moves away.*]   I ordered some songs!

FOMIN   Don't worry, we'll sing, we'll celebrate, and when it's time to die, we'll die!

URUSOV [*Reads, rolling his r's.*]   "In accordance with the aforementioned points, I cede my carting establishment, with all its assets, as itemized below, to Vasili Eliseyevich Fomin—"

PYATIRUBEL   Fomin, you clown, do you realize what horses you're buying? These horses have carted millions of bushels of corn and half the world's coal! With these horses you're dragging away everything we've got here in Odessa!

URUSOV   "—in total, for the sum of twelve thousand rubles, of which a third is to be paid on signing, with the additional sum—"

MENDEL [*Points at the* TURK, *serenely smoking his hookah in the corner.*]   That man sitting there, he's judging me.

PYATIRUBEL   That's true, he's judging you. . . . Come on, let's drink to it! [*To* FOMIN.] Just watch, he's going to kill somebody!

FOMIN   I doubt it.

RYABTSOV   You're crazy, you fool! That man over there, that Turk, is a holy man!

POTAPOVNA   I'm daddy's little girl.

FOMIN   Right here, Mendel, that's where you have to sign.

POTAPOVNA [*Thumps* FOMIN *on the chest.*]   This is where he keeps his money, that's where it is!

MENDEL   I should sign, you said? [*Dragging his feet, he walks across the tavern to the* TURK *and sits down next to him.*] Ha, the girls I've had in my time, my dear fellow! The happiness I have seen! I built a house, I had sons—and the price they're offering me for all that, my dear fellow, is twelve thousand! And then that's that—you lie down and die!

[*The* TURK *bows, and with his hand touches first his heart and then his forehead.* MENDEL *kisses him tenderly on the lips.*]

FOMIN [*To* POTAPOVNA.]   Are you trying to make a Yenkel of me?

POTAPOVNA   He'll sell, Vasili Eliseyevich! On my life, he'll sell!

MENDEL [*Returns to his table, shaking his head.*]   How boring!

MITYA   What's boring is that you have to pay up!

MENDEL   Go away!

MITYA   No, you have to pay!

MENDEL   I'll kill you!

MITYA   Then you'll pay for that too!

MENDEL [*Lays his head on the table and spits. Saliva hangs from his mouth like a rubber band.*]   Go away, I want to sleep. . . .

MITYA You won't pay? *Oy,* I'll kill him!

PYATIRUBEL Hold on a minute before you start killing him! First, how much have you been swindling out of him per pint?

MITYA [*Flares up.*] I'm no pushover! I'll rip you to pieces!

[*Without lifting his head,* MENDEL *pulls from his pocket some coins and throws them. They roll on the floor.* MITYA *runs after them, picking them up. A sleepy girl blows out the lamps. It is dark.* MENDEL *sleeps, his head resting on the table.*]

FOMIN [*To* POTAPOVNA.] You couldn't hold back, could you? Your tongue scampers like a running dog! You ruined everything!

POTAPOVNA [*Wiping her tears from her deep, grimy wrinkles.*] Vasili Eliseyevich. It's my daughter I'm sorry for!

FOMIN You don't know what sorrow is yet!

POTAPOVNA The Yids have surrounded us like lice!

FOMIN A Yid is no obstacle for a clever man.

POTAPOVNA He will sell, Vasili Eliseyevich! He'll swagger about a bit, but then he'll sell!

FOMIN [*Slowly, menacingly.*] But if he doesn't sell, then I swear to you, old woman, by Jesus Christ our Lord, I will come for you and tear the skin off your back!

Scene Four

POTAPOVNA's *attic.* POTAPOVNA *is wearing a colorful new dress, and is leaning out the window chatting with a neighbor. There is a view of the harbor and the sparkling sea from the window. On the table is a big pile of purchases: rolls of cloth, shoes, a silk umbrella.*

NEIGHBOR'S VOICE Come over and show off some of your new things!

POTAPOVNA Don't worry, I'll be over to see you!

NEIGHBOR'S VOICE Here we've been selling chickens in the same market row for nineteen years now, and suddenly—no more Potapovna!

POTAPOVNA Maybe I won't have to stay chained to those damn chickens for the rest of my life after all. It looks now like I won't have to suffer all my life.

NEIGHBOR'S VOICE It looks like you won't.

POTAPOVNA I bet people can't believe my luck!

NEIGHBOR'S VOICE No, they can't! Everyone would want to have your luck! You could bake it and sell it by the pound!

POTAPOVNA [*Laughs, her large body shaking.*] Not everyone, you see, has a pretty daughter.

NEIGHBOR'S VOICE They say, though, your daughter's a bit too skinny.

POTAPOVNA Don't worry, dear! The nearer to the bone, the sweeter the meat!

NEIGHBOR'S VOICE They say his sons are scheming against you.

POTAPOVNA The girl will outweigh the sons.

NEIGHBOR'S VOICE That's what I say, too!

POTAPOVNA It's not like an old man will just drop a young girl like that.

NEIGHBOR'S VOICE I hear he'll buy you some orchards.

POTAPOVNA So, what else are people saying?

NEIGHBOR'S VOICE   Nothing, really, they're just prattling. I can't make heads or tails of it!

POTAPOVNA   I can! I definitely can! What are they saying about the linen?

NEIGHBOR'S VOICE   They say the old man set you up with fifteen yards.

POTAPOVNA   Thirty-five yards!

NEIGHBOR'S VOICE   A pair of shoes . . .

POTAPOVNA   Three pair!

NEIGHBOR'S VOICE   When old men fall in love—it's deadly!

POTAPOVNA   Yes, it looks like we won't have to stay chained to those damn chickens. . . .

NEIGHBOR'S VOICE   I guess you won't! Come on, dress up and hop over here to show off some of your new things.

POTAPOVNA   I'll be over in a bit! See you later, dear!

NEIGHBOR'S VOICE   See you later, dear!

> [POTAPOVNA *leaves the window. She waddles about the room humming, and opens the closet. She climbs onto a chair and reaches up to the top shelf, where there is a big bottle of liquor. She drinks, and then eats a cream puff.* MENDEL, *festively dressed, enters the room with* MARUSIA.]

MARUSIA [*Boisterously.*]   Look where our little birdie has hopped up to! Mama, run over to Moseyka, will you?

POTAPOVNA [*Climbing down from the chair.*]   What do you want me to get?

MARUSIA   Some watermelons, and a bottle of wine, and half a dozen smoked mackerel. . . . [*To* MENDEL.] Give her a ruble!

POTAPOVNA   A ruble won't be enough.

MARUSIA   Don't try that on me! It'll be enough, there'll even be change!

POTAPOVNA   A ruble really won't be enough.

MARUSIA   It will! Come back in an hour. [*She shoves her mother out the door, slams it shut, and turns the key.*]

POTAPOVNA'S VOICE   I'll be sitting by the gate! If you need me, call!

MARUSIA   Fine! [*She throws her hat onto the table, shakes out her golden hair, and starts plaiting it into a braid. In a ringing voice full of strength and joy, she resumes her interrupted story.*] So we arrive at the cemetery, we look—it's one o'clock and the funeral is over. No one's there, only people kissing in the bushes. My godfather's grave was so pretty, you wouldn't believe it! So I took out the booze, the Madeira you gave me, two bottles of it, and ran to get Father Yoann. You know Father Yoann—he's the little old man with little blue eyes.

> [MENDEL *is watching* MARUSIA *adoringly. He is trembling and mumbles something in answer—what, is unclear*]

MARUSIA   Father Yoann sang the psalms for the dead, then I poured him a glass of Madeira, wiped the glass with a towel, and he drank. I poured him a second. [MARUSIA *has finished braiding her hair, and fluffs the end of her braid. She sits down on the bed, and unties the laces of her fashionable yellow boots.*] Xenia, in the meantime, is acting like she's forgotten she's at her father's grave. She's putting on airs, acting like a mouse in a bag of wheat, all made up and everything, ogling her fiancé, Sergey Ivanovich, who all the while is making me one sandwich after another! So to spite her I say: Excuse me, Sergey Ivanovich, shouldn't you be paying at least a little attention to your fiancée, Xenia Matveyevna? Though I said it straight out, it went in one ear and out the other! So we all drank the Madeira you gave me. [MARUSIA *takes off her boots and her stockings. She walks barefoot to the window and pulls the curtain shut.*] My godmother couldn't stop crying, but then got pink in the face like a little girl, so pretty, you wouldn't believe it! I was drinking too—so I say to Sergey Ivanovich [MARUSIA *uncovers the bed.*]: C'mon, let's all go to Langeron beach for a swim! And he says: Okay, let's go! [MARUSIA *laughs and struggles to take off her dress, which is too tight.*] And I bet you Xenia's back is covered with pimples, and she hasn't washed her feet in three years—you should have heard some of the things she called me! [MARUSIA *is hidden from her head to her waist by the dress she is trying to struggle out of.*] Ha, she tells me, you're just acting up, all snooty, hankering after the old man's money—ha, they won't let you get your hands on it! [MARUSIA *pulls off the dress and jumps into the bed.*] So I say to her— you know what, Xenia, darling—I say to her—let sleeping dogs lie! Sergey Ivanovich hears us and dies laughing! [*She stretches out her exquisite, bare, girlish arm to* MENDEL, *and pulls him toward her. She takes off his jacket, and throws it on the floor.*] So . . . come here and say, "Marusia, darling!"

MENDEL   Marusia, darling!

MARUSIA   Say: "Marusia, my sweet little darling!"

[*The old man wheezes, shivers, half laughing, half crying.*]

MARUSIA [*Sweetly.*]   You ugly little pugface, you!

Scene Five

The Carting Union Synagogue in the Moldavanka, Odessa's Jewish quarter. Friday evening worship. Lit candles. CANTOR ZWIEBACK, *wearing a tallith and boots, is standing in the pulpit. The congregation—red-faced carters—is in deafening communion with God, rocking back and forth, spitting, wandering about the synagogue. Stung by the sudden bee of grace, they emit loud exclamations, sing along with the cantor in rough voices, falter and start muttering to themselves, and then loudly start lowing again, like oxen awakened from slumber. In the depths of the synagogue two ancient Jews—bony, hunchbacked giants, their long yellow beards swept to the side—are bent over a volume of the Talmud.* ARYE-LEIB, *the shamas, marches grandly back and forth between the rows of worshipers. A fat man with flushed, puffy cheeks is sitting on the front bench with his ten-year-old son between his knees. He is forcing the boy to look at the prayer book.* BENYA KRIK *is sitting on a side bench. Behind him sits* SENKA TOPUN. *They give no sign that they know each other.*

CANTOR [*Proclaims.*]   Lkhu nranno ladonai noriio itsur isheinu!

[*The carters start singing along. The drone of prayer.*]

CANTOR   Arboim shono okut nbdoir vooimar . . . [*In a throttled voice.*] Arye-Leib, rats!

ARYE-LEIB   Shiru ladonai shir khodosh . . . Oy, let's sing a new song to God! [*He goes over to a praying* JEW.] How are hay prices doing?

THE JEW [*Rocking back and forth.*]   They're up.

ARYE-LEIB   A lot?

THE JEW   Fifty-two kopecks.

ARYE-LEIB   We'll hold out—watch it hit sixty!

CANTOR   *Lifnei adonai ki vo, ki vo mishpoit goorets* . . . Arye-Leib, rats!

ARYE-LEIB   Enough already, you ruffian!

CANTOR [*In a throttled voice.*]   If I see one more rat, there'll be trouble!

ARYE-LEIB [*Serenely.*]   *Lifnei adonai ki vo, ki vo* . . . Oy, I am standing, oy, I am standing before God . . . where do oats stand?

SECOND JEW [*Without interrupting his prayer.*]   A ruble and four, a ruble and four!

ARYE-LEIB   I'm going crazy!

SECOND JEW [*Rocks back and forth bitterly.*]   It'll hit a ruble ten, it'll hit a ruble ten!

ARYE-LEIB   I'm going crazy! *Lifnei adonai ki vo, ki vo* . . .

> [*Everyone is praying. In the silence, snippets of muffled conversation between* BENYA KRIK *and* SENKA TOPUN *are heard.*]

BENYA [*Bends over his prayer book.*]   Well?

SENKA [*From behind* BENYA.]   I have a job in the works.

BENYA   What job?

SENKA   Wholesale.

BENYA   What is it?

SENKA   Cloth.

BENYA   A lot?

SENKA   A lot.

BENYA   Police?

SENKA   Don't worry.

BENYA   Night watchman?

SENKA   He's in on it.

BENYA   Neighbors?

SENKA   They've agreed to be asleep.

BENYA   What cut d'you want?

SENKA   Half.

BENYA   Forget it.

SENKA   Why, as it is, you're about to lose your inheritance.

BENYA   I'm going to lose my inheritance, am I?

SENKA   So where do you stand?

BENYA   Forget it!

> [*There is a gunshot—*CANTOR ZWIEBACK *has shot a rat that was running past the altar. The bored ten-year-old, trapped between his father's knees, flails about, trying to break loose.* ARYE-LEIB *stands frozen to the spot, his mouth hanging open. The* TALMUDISTS *raise their large, indifferent faces.*]

THE FAT MAN WITH THE FLUSHED CHEEKS   Zwieback! That's a pretty low-down trick!

CANTOR   My understanding was that I would pray in a synagogue, not a rat-infested pantry! [*He clicks open his revolver and throws the empty cartridge on the floor.*]

ARYE-LEIB   Oy, you bastard! Oy, you lout!

CANTOR [*Pointing at the dead rat with his revolver.*]   Look at this rat, O Jews, call in the people! Let the people judge if this is not a rat the size of a cow!

ARYE-LEIB   Bastard! Bastard! Bastard!

CANTOR [*Cold-bloodedly.*]   May there be an end to these rats!

[*He wraps himself up in the tallith and holds a tuning fork to his ear. The boy finally wriggles free from his father's knees, dashes over to the cartridge, snatches it up, and runs off.*]

FIRST JEW   All day long you break your neck working, you come to the synagogue to relax a little—and then this!

ARYE-LEIB [*Shrieks.*]   Jews, this is a sham! Jews, you know not what is taking place here! The Milkmen's Union is paying this bastard an extra ten rubles! So why don't you go to the milkmen, you bastard, and kiss their you-know-whats!

SENKA [*Bangs his fist down on his prayer book.*]   Can we have some quiet? This isn't a marketplace!

CANTOR [*Solemnly.*]   Mizmoir ldovid!

[*Everyone prays.*]

BENYA   So?

SENKA   There are people we can use.

BENYA   What people?

SENKA   Georgians.

BENYA   They have weapons?

SENKA   They have weapons.

BENYA   Where do you know them from?

SENKA   They live next to your buyer.

BENYA   What buyer?

SENKA   The one who's buying your business.

BENYA   What business?

SENKA   Your business—your lands, your house, your carting establishment.

BENYA [*Turns around.*]   Are you crazy?

SENKA   He said so himself.

BENYA   Who said?

SENKA   Mendel, your father, said so himself! He's going with Marusia to Bessarabia to buy orchards.

[*The hum of prayer. The JEWS are moaning intricately.*]

BENYA   Are you crazy?

SENKA   Everyone knows it.

BENYA   Swear it's true!

SENKA   May I not see happiness in this life!

BENYA   Swear on your mother!

SENKA   May I find my mother lying in a pool of blood!

BENYA   Swear again, you piece of shit!

SENKA [*Scornfully.*]   You're such a fool!

CANTOR   Borukh ato adonai . . .

Scene Six

The KRIKS' *courtyard. Sunset. It is seven o'clock in the evening.* BENYA *is sitting by the stable on a cart with its shafts raised, cleaning a revolver.* LYOVKA *is leaning against the stable door.* ARYE-LEIB *is explaining the profundities of The Song of Songs to* IVAN, *the boy who had run out of the synagogue on Friday evening.* NIKIFOR *is nervously pacing up and down the courtyard. He is obviously worried about something.*

BENYA   The time is coming! Make way for time!

LYOVKA   He should have his throat cut, like a pig!

BENYA   The time is coming. Step aside, Lyovka! Make way for time!

ARYE-LEIB   *The Song of Songs* teaches us: "By night on my bed I sought him whom my soul loveth"—What does the great commentator Rashi tell us about these words?

NIKIFOR   [*Points at* BENYA *and* LYOVKA, *and says to* ARYE-LEIB]   Look at them! They've planted themselves by the stable like oak trees!

ARYE-LEIB   This is what the great Rashi tells us: "By night" means "by day and by night." "On my bed I sought"—who was seeking? Rashi asks. Israel was seeking! The People of Israel were seeking! "Him whom my soul loveth"—whom does Israel love? Rashi asks! Israel loves the Torah, and the Torah loves Israel!

NIKIFOR   What I want to know is, what are they loafing by the stable for?

BENYA   That's right, go on shouting!

NIKIFOR   [*Pacing up and down the courtyard.*]   I know what I know. . . . My horse collars keep disappearing. I can suspect whoever I want!

ARYE-LEIB   Here an old man is trying to teach the law to a child, and you, Nikifor, keep interfering!

NIKIFOR   Why have they planted themselves by the stable like damn oak trees?

BENYA   [*Takes his revolver apart and cleans it.*]   Nikifor, I see you're all nerves.

NIKIFOR   [*Shouts, but his voice is weak.*]   I'm not your slave! If you want to know, I have a brother who lives out in the country, still in his prime! If you want to know, my brother would gladly take me in!

BENYA   Shout, shout as much as you want before you die!

NIKIFOR   [*To* ARYE-LEIB.]   Old man, tell me why they're doing this to me!

ARYE-LEIB   [*Raises his bleary eyes and looks at* NIKIFOR.]   I'm trying to teach the law, and you're bellowing like a cow! Is this how things should be in this world?

NIKIFOR   Your eyes are open, old man, but you do not see!
      [NIKIFOR *leaves.*]

BENYA   Our Nikifor seems a little worried!

ARYE-LEIB   "By night on my bed I sought . . ." Whom was she seeking? What does Rashi teach us?

THE BOY   Rashi teaches us: "She was seeking the Torah."
      [*Loud voices are heard.*]

BENYA   The time is coming. Step aside, Lyovka! Make way for time!
      [MENDEL, BOBRINETS, NIKIFOR, *and* PYATIRUBEL *enter.* PYATIRUBEL *is slightly tipsy.*]

BOBRINETS   [*Deafeningly loud.*]   If you're not going to cart my wheat down to the harbor, Mendel, then who the hell will? If I'm not going to come to you Mendel, then who should I go to?

MENDEL   I'm not the only carter in the world. There's other carters besides me.

BOBRINETS   You're the only carter in Odessa—or are you trying to send me over to Butsis with his three-legged mules, or to Zhuravlenko with his broken-down tubs?

MENDEL [*Not looking at his sons.*]   Someone's hanging around my stables again!

NIKIFOR   They've struck root there, like damn oak trees.

BOBRINETS   You'll harness ten pairs of horses for me tomorrow, Mendel, you'll cart the wheat for me, you'll get the money, down a bottle of vodka, sing a few songs. . . . Ai, Mendel!

PYATIRUBEL   Ai, Mendel!

MENDEL   Why are people hanging around my stables?

NIKIFOR   Master, for God's sake!

MENDEL   Well?

NIKIFOR   Run for it, master . . . your sons . . .

MENDEL   My sons what?

NIKIFOR   Your sons are out to get you!

BENYA [*Jumps down from the cart. His head down, he speaks distinctly.*]

Papa, I happened to hear, from strangers, no less—both my brother, Lyovka, and I, we both heard—that you intend to sell the family business into which we have sunk a gold ruble or two and our own sweat!

[*Neighbors working in their yards come to see what is happening.*]

MENDEL [*Looking down.*]   People, neighbors . . .

BENYA   Did we hear right, me and my brother Lyovka?

MENDEL   People, neighbors, take a look at my own flesh and blood [*He raises his head, and his voice gets stronger.*], my very own flesh and blood, lifting a hand to strike me. . . .

BENYA   Did we hear right, me and my brother Lyovka?

MENDEL   You won't get me! [*He throws himself at* LYOVKA, *punches him in the face, and knocks him down.*]

LYOVKA   We will get you!

[*The sky is flooded by a blood-red sunset.* MENDEL *and* LYOVKA *roll on the ground, punching each other in the face. They roll behind a shed.*]

NIKIFOR [*Leaning against the wall.*]   Oh, what sin!

BOBRINETS   Lyovka! Hitting your own father!

BENYA [*In a desperate voice.*]   I swear to you on my life! He has thrown everything—our horses, our house, our life—he has thrown everything at the feet of that whore!

NIKIFOR   Oh, what sin!

PYATIRUBEL   I'll kill anyone who tries to separate them! Don't anyone dare touch them!

[*Wheezing and groaning is heard from behind the shed.*]

PYATIRUBEL   The man is yet to be born who can stand up to Mendel!

ARYE-LEIB [*To the boy.*]   Ivan, get out of the yard!

PYATIRUBEL   I'm ready to put a hundred rubles down—

ARYE-LEIB   Ivan, get out of the yard!

[MENDEL *and* LYOVKA *roll out from behind the shed. They jump to their feet, but* MENDEL *knocks* LYOVKA *down again.*]

BOBRINETS   Lyovka! Hitting your own father!

MENDEL   You won't get me! [*He starts kicking his son.*]

PYATIRUBEL   I'm ready to put a hundred rubles down for anyone who's interested!

[MENDEL *has won. Some of* LYOVKA's *teeth are broken, tufts of his hair have been pulled out.*]

MENDEL   You won't get me!

BENYA   Just watch us!
[*With great force* BENYA *hits his father on the head with the butt of his revolver.* MENDEL *falls down. Silence. The sunset's blazing forests of cloud sink lower and lower.*]

NIKIFOR   They've killed him!

PYATIRUBEL [*Bends over* MENDEL, *who is lying motionless on the ground.*] Mendel?

LYOVKA [*Gets up, steadying himself with his fists. He is crying, stamping his feet.*]   He kicked me below the belt, the bastard!

PYATIRUBEL   Mendel?

BENYA [*Turns to the crowd of bystanders.*]   What are you all doing here?

PYATIRUBEL   And I say it's not night yet! Night is still a thousand versts away!

ARYE-LEIB [*On his knees next to* MENDEL, *to* PYATIRUBEL.]   Oy, Russian man, why say that it's not night yet when it is plain to see that this man is as good as gone!

LYOVKA [*Crooked streams of tears and blood run down his face.*]   He kicked me below the belt, the bastard!

PYATIRUBEL   Two against one! [*He staggers toward the exit.*]

ARYE-LEIB [*To the boy.*]   Get out of the yard, Ivan.

PYATIRUBEL   Two against one . . . it's a disgrace, a disgrace for all Moldavanka! [*He stumbles off.*]
[ARYE-LEIB *wipes* MENDEL's *injured head with a wet handkerchief. On the other side of the courtyard,* NEKHAMA—*wild, dirty-gray—is hovering about in disbelief. She comes and kneels down next to* ARYE-LEIB.]

NEKHAMA   Don't be silent, Mendel!

BOBRINETS [*To* MENDEL, *in a deep voice.*]   Stop fooling around, you old clown!

NEKHAMA   Yell something, Mendel!

BOBRINETS   Get up, you old carter! Wet your whistle, down a bottle of vodka!
[LYOVKA *is sitting on the ground with his legs apart. Slowly he spits out long ribbons of blood.*]

BENYA [*Chases the crowd of bystanders into a corner of the courtyard. He grabs a young man of about twenty by his shirt.*]   Get the hell out!
[*Silence. Evening. A blue darkness has fallen, but above the darkness the sky is still hot, crimson, and pitted with fiery holes.*]

Scene Seven

The KRIKS' *cart shed—a pile of horse collars, unharnessed buggies, harnesses. A part of the courtyard is visible.* BENYA *is sitting at a small table near the doors, writing something.* SEMYON, *an awkward, bald-headed peasant, is arguing with him, while* MADAME POPYATNIK *paces up and down.* MAJOR, *his legs dangling, sits out in the yard, on a cart with its shafts raised. A new sign is leaning against the wall. On it, in gold letters:*

"Horse-Carting Establishment, Mendel Krik & Sons." Garlands of horseshoes and crossed whips surround the letters.

SEMYON I don't care! What I want is my money!

BENYA [*Continues writing.*] Why so rude, Semyon?

SEMYON Give me my money, or I'll cut your throat!

BENYA My dear man, I spit on you!

SEMYON Where did you hide the old man?

BENYA The old man is sick.

SEMYON Right here on the wall, this is where he wrote how much he owed for the oats, how much for the hay—all nice and clear. And he always paid up! Twenty years I drove for him, and he was always fair and square!

BENYA [*Gets up.*] You drove for him, but you're not going to drive for me—he wrote on the wall, but I'm not going to write on the wall—he paid you, but as for me, I very well might not pay you, because—

MADAME POPYATNIK [*Looks at the peasant with extreme disapproval.*] When a man is such an idiot—it's disgusting!

BENYA —because, with me, my dear fellow, you might well die before you eat your supper tonight!

SEMYON [*Frightened, but still defiant.*] I want my money!

MADAME POPYATNIK I am no philosopher, Monsieur Krik, but I can plainly see that there are people in this world who have no right to be alive!

BENYA Nikifor!

[NIKIFOR *enters, looking about sheepishly. He speaks reluctantly.*]

NIKIFOR Present.

BENYA Settle up with Semyon and go over to Groshev's.

NIKIFOR The day laborers are here and want to know who will be doing the hiring.

BENYA I'll be doing the hiring.

NIKIFOR And the cook is kicking up a fuss too because she pawned off her samovar to the master. Now she wants to know who she has to pay to get it back.

BENYA She has to pay me. Settle up the business with Semyon, and bring back five hundred *poods* of hay from Groshev.

SEMYON [*Stunned.*] Five hundred? Twenty years I've been carting—

MADAME POPYATNIK When a man has money, he can buy hay, and oats, and even nicer things.

BENYA And oats, two hundred *poods*.

SEMYON I wouldn't say no to carting for you!

BENYA Semyon, lose my address!

[SEMYON *kneads his hat, looks away, walks off, returns for a moment, and then walks off again.*]

MADAME POPYATNIK A damn peasant giving you all this trouble! My God, if everyone suddenly remembered who owes them money! This very morning I was telling my husband, Major: "Husband, darling, I would never ask for those miserable two rubles that Mendel Krik owes us."

MAJOR [*In a hoarse, melodious voice.*] One ruble, ninety-five kopecks.

BENYA What two rubles?

MADAME POPYATNIK   Please, it's not even worth mentioning, really, good heavens, it's not even worth mentioning! Last Thursday, you see, Monsieur Krik was in a fabulous mood, and ordered marching tunes. . . . [*To her husband.*] How many were there?

MAJOR   Marching tunes? Nine.

MADAME POPYATNIK   And then he wanted dance tunes.

MAJOR   Twenty-one dance tunes.

MADAME POPYATNIK   That comes to one ruble, ninety-five. Paying musicians has always been a top priority with Monsieur Krik.

[NIKIFOR *enters, dragging his feet. He is looking to the side.*]

NIKIFOR   Potapovna is here.

BENYA   What do I care who's here and who isn't!

NIKIFOR   She's making threats.

BENYA   What do I care who's—

[POTAPOVNA *bursts in, hobbling, waving her enormous hip. She is drunk. She throws herself to the floor and stares up at* BENYA *with dull, fixed eyes.*]

POTAPOVNA   Czars in heaven!

BENYA   Yes, Madame Potapovna?

POTAPOVNA   Czars in heaven!

NIKIFOR   She's come to make trouble.

POTAPOVNA   [*Winks.*]   Y-Y-Y-Yid bubbles are humming . . . the bubbles are bouncing about in my head—y-y-y.

BENYA   Get to the point, Madame Potapovna!

POTAPOVNA   [*Bangs her fist on the floor.*]   You're right! You're right! Let the clever man measure, and the pig dance the measureka.

MADAME POPYATNIK   What a sophisticated lady!

POTAPOVNA   [*Throws some coins on the floor.*]   Here are the forty kopecks I earned today. . . . I got up before dawn, it was still dark, and waited for the peasants on Baltskaya Street. . . . [*She lifts her head to the sky.*] I wonder what time it is now. Maybe three o'clock?

BENYA   Get to the point, Madame Potapovna!

POTAPOVNA   Y-Y-Y, blew bubbles . . .

BENYA   Nikifor!

NIKIFOR   Yes?

POTAPOVNA   [*Wags her fat, weak, drunken finger at* NIKIFOR.]   And now, Nikisha, my own daughter is knocked up!

MADAME POPYATNIK   [*Totters, burning with excitement.*]   Oh, what a scandal! What a scandal!

BENYA   What are you doing here, Madame Popyatnik? What do you want?

MADAME POPYATNIK   [*Staggers, her eyes sparkling and fluttering with excitement.*]   I'm going, I'm going! God willing we will meet again . . . in happiness, in joy, in a blessed hour, in a happy minute!

[*She grabs her husband by the hand and starts backing out of the room. She turns around, her eyes crossed and flickering like black flames.* MAJOR *follows his wife, wiggling his fingers. They leave.*]

POTAPOVNA   [*Smearing her tears over her flabby, wrinkled face.*]   At night I went to her, felt her breasts—I feel her breasts every night—they're already filled with milk, they don't even fit my hands anymore!

BENYA [*His sparkle has left him. He speaks quickly, glancing furtively behind him.*] What month?

POTAPOVNA [*She stares fixedly up at* BENYA *from where she's lying on the floor.*] Fourth.

BENYA You're lying!

POTAPOVNA Okay, third.

BENYA What do you want from us?

POTAPOVNA Y-Y-Y, blew bubbles . . .

BENYA What do you want?

POTAPOVNA [*Tying her kerchief.*] A cleanup costs one hundred rubles.

BENYA Twenty-five!

POTAPOVNA I'll bring in the dockworkers!

BENYA You'll bring in the dockworkers? Nikifor!

NIKIFOR Present.

BENYA Go upstairs and ask my papa if I should hand over twenty-five—

POTAPOVNA A hundred!

BENYA —twenty-five rubles for a cleanup, or doesn't he want one?

NIKIFOR I won't go.

BENYA You won't?

[BENYA *rushes over to the calico curtains that divide the carting shed in two.*]

NIKIFOR [*Grabs* BENYA *by the arm.*] Young man, I'm not afraid of God— I saw God and wasn't frightened—I will kill without being frightened!

[*The curtain stirs and parts.* MENDEL *enters. He is carrying his boots slung over his shoulder. His face is blue and swollen, like the face of a dead man.*]

MENDEL Unlock the gates.

POTAPOVNA Oh, my God!

NIKIFOR Master!

[ARYE-LEIB *and* LYOVKA *approach the cart shed.*]

MENDEL Unlock the gates.

POTAPOVNA [*Crawls on the floor.*] Oh, my God!

BENYA Go back upstairs to your wife, Papa.

MENDEL Unlock the gates for me, Nikifor, old friend—

NIKIFOR [*Falls on his knees.*] I beg you, master, don't grovel before me, a simple man!

MENDEL Why won't you unlock the gates, Nikifor? Why won't you let me leave this courtyard where I have served my life sentence? [MENDEL's *voice becomes more powerful, his eyes glitter.*] This courtyard, it has seen me be the father of my children, the husband of my wife, the master of my horses. It has seen my strength, and that of my twenty stallions and my twelve carts, reinforced with iron. It has seen my legs, huge as pillars, and my arms, my evil arms . . . but now unlock the gates for me, my dear sons, today let me for once do as I wish! Let me leave this courtyard that has seen too much. . . .

BENYA Go back in the house, Papa, to your wife.

[*He approaches his father.*]

MENDEL Don't hit me, Benchik.

LYOVKA Don't hit him.

BENYA What low-down people! [*Pause.*] How could you . . . [*Pause.*] How could you say what you just said?

ARYE-LEIB [*To the onlookers.*]   Don't you all see that you shouldn't be here?

BENYA   Animals! Animals!

[BENYA *rushes out.* LYOVKA *follows him.*]

ARYE-LEIB [*Leads* MENDEL *to the couch.*]   We'll rest a bit, Mendel, we'll take a little nap. . . .

POTAPOVNA [*Gets up from the floor and begins to cry.*]   They've killed the poor darling!

ARYE-LEIB [*Helps* MENDEL *onto the couch behind the curtain.*]   You'll take a little nap, Mendel. . . .

POTAPOVNA [*Throws herself onto the floor by the couch, and starts kissing* MENDEL'*s hand, which is hanging down limply.*]   My little son, my sweet little darling!

ARYE-LEIB [*Covers* MENDEL'*s face with a kerchief, sits down, and begins speaking in a quiet, distant voice.*]   Once upon a time, in the distant past, there lived a man named David. He was a shepherd and then he was a king, the King of Israel, of Israel's army and Israel's wise men.

POTAPOVNA [*Sobbing.*]   My sweet darling!

ARYE-LEIB   David experienced wealth and experienced glory, but he was not satiated. Strength brings thirst, only grief quenches the heart. Having grown old, King David saw Bathsheba, General Uriah's wife, on the roofs of Jerusalem, under the skies of Jerusalem. Bathsheba's breasts were beautiful, her legs were beautiful, her gaiety was great. And General Uriah was sent into battle, and the king coupled with Bathsheba, the wife of a man not yet dead. Her breasts were beautiful, her gaiety was great . . .

Scene Eight

The KRIKS' *dining room. Evening. The room is brightly lit by a homemade hanging lamp, candles in candelabras, and old-fashioned blue lamps fixed to the wall.* MADAME POPYATNIK, *wearing a silk dress, is busy bustling about a table decorated with flowers and filled with food and wine.* MAJOR *is sitting silently in the back of the room. His paper shirtfront is jutting out, his flute is lying on his knees. He is twiddling his fingers and bobbing his head from side to side. There are many guests. Some are strolling in groups about the open rooms, others sitting along the walls. The pregnant* KLASHA ZUBARYEVA *enters the room. She is wearing a shawl with a gigantic flower pattern.* LYOVKA, *wearing a hussar's parade uniform, stumbles in after her, drunk.*

LYOVKA   [*Barks out cavalry orders.*]
　　　　　　　　　Horsemen, friends!
　　　　　　　　　Forward trot!
　　　　　　　　　If your horses are hungry,
　　　　　　　　　Then feed them a lot!

KLASHA [*Laughs out loud.*]   Oy, my belly! Oy, I'm going to miscarry!

LYOVKA　　　　　　*Mount your horses, left leg high,*
　　　　　　　　　Hold on tight, or you will fly!

KLASHA   Oy, I'm dying!

[*They stroll on, passing* BOYARSKY, *who is wearing a frock coat, and* DVOIRA KRIK.]

BOYARSKY Mademoiselle Krik, I don't call black white, nor am I the kind of man who would permit himself to call white black. With three thousand, we can set up a prêt-à-porter boutique on Deribasovskaya Street, and get happily married.

DVOIRA It's got to be the whole three thousand, all at once?

BOYARSKY Right now we're in the middle of July, and July isn't September. Light overcoats move in July, ladies' coats in September. And after September, you ask? Nothing! September, October, November, December. I don't call night day, nor am I the kind of man who would allow himself to call day night. . . .

[*They stroll on.* BENYA *and* BOBRINETS *enter.*]

BENYA Is everything ready, Madame Popyatnik?

MADAME POPYATNIK Even Czar Nicholas II wouldn't turn up his nose at such a table.

BOBRINETS Explain your idea to me, Benya.

BENYA This is my idea: A Jew no longer in the prime of life, a Jew who used to go about naked, barefoot, and filthy like a convict on Sakhalin island! And now that, thank God, he is getting up there in years, it is time to put an end to this life sentence of hard labor—it is time to turn the Sabbath into Sabbath.

[BOYARSKY *and* DVOIRA *stroll by.*]

BOYARSKY September, October, November, December . . .

DVOIRA But then, Boyarsky, I also want you to love me, at least a little.

BOYARSKY What am I supposed to be doing with you if I won't be loving you? Turn you into meatballs? You make me laugh!

[*They stroll by. Near the wall, under a blue lamp, sit a poised cattle dealer and a thick-legged young man in a three-piece suit. The young man is carefully cracking sunflower seeds with his teeth and putting the shells in his pocket.*]

THICK-LEGGED YOUNG MAN Pow! A right hook in the face! Pow! A left hook—and wham, the old man went down!

CATTLE DEALER Ha! Even the Tartars respect their elders! "Walking through life, oh the toil, oh the strife."

THICK-LEGGED YOUNG MAN If he had lived by the book, but he . . . [*He spits out a shell.*] he did whatever he wanted. So what's there to respect?

CATTLE DEALER You're an idiot!

THICK-LEGGED YOUNG MAN Benya bought more than a thousand *poods* of hay.

CATTLE DEALER For the old man a hundred was enough!

THICK-LEGGED YOUNG MAN Either way, they're going to cut the old man's throat.

CATTLE DEALER Yids? Their own father?

THICK-LEGGED YOUNG MAN They'll slit the old man's throat, all right.

CATTLE DEALER You're an idiot!

[BENYA *and* BOBRINETS *stroll by.*]

BOBRINETS But what do you want, Benya?

BENYA I want the Sabbath to be Sabbath. I want us to be people as good as anyone else. I want to walk with my legs on the ground and my head held high. . . . Do you understand what I'm saying, Bobrinets?

BOBRINETS   I understand what you're saying, Benya.

[*By the wall, next to* PYATIRUBEL, *sit* MR. *and* MADAME WEINER, *smothered by the greatness of their wealth.*]

PYATIRUBEL [*Seeking their sympathy in vain.*]   He used to rip the belts off policemen and beat the clerk at the main post office. He'd down a gallon of vodka on an empty stomach. He had all of Odessa by the throat. That's what the old man was like!

[WEINER *keeps rolling his heavy, slobbering tongue, but it's impossible to make out what he is saying.*]

PYATIRUBEL [*Timidly.*]   The gentleman has a speaking problem?

MADAME WEINER [*Viciously.*]   What do you think!

[DVOIRA *and* BOYARSKY *stroll by.*]

BOYARSKY   September, October, November, December . . .

DVOIRA   And I *do* want a child, Boyarsky.

BOYARSKY   Absolutely! A child in a prêt-à-porter boutique is very pretty—it looks good. As for a child without a business, how will that look?

[MADAME POPYATNIK *bursts in with great excitement.*]

MADAME POPYATNIK   Ben Zkharia is here! Rabbi . . . Ben Zkharia!

[*The room fills with guests. Among them are* DVOIRA, LYOVKA, BENYA, KLASHA ZUBARYEVA, SENKA TOPUN, *pomaded* CART DRIVERS, *waddling* SHOPKEEPERS, *and giggling* PEASANT WOMEN.]

THICK-LEGGED YOUNG MAN   When money beckons, even the rabbi comes running. And here he is!

[ARYE-LEIB *and* BOBRINETS *wheel in a large armchair. Almost hidden in its plush depths is* BEN ZKHARIA's *shriveled little body.*]

BEN ZKHARIA [*Shrilly.*]   Dawn has only sneezed, and in heaven the Lord is washing Himself with red water—

BOBRINETS [*Laughs out loud, expecting an intricate answer.*]   Why red, Rabbi?

BEN ZKHARIA   —and I am still lying on my back, like a cockroach—

BOBRINETS   Why on your back, Rabbi?

BEN ZKHARIA   Every morning God turns me on my back so I cannot pray. My prayers are getting on God's nerves. . . .

[BOBRINETS *roars with laughter.*]

BEN ZKHARIA   The chickens haven't gotten up yet, and Arye-Leib wakes me: Quick! Get over to the Kriks, Rabbi! They're having a feast! You'll get food, you'll get drink. . . .

BENYA   You'll get food, you'll get drink, whatever your heart desires, Rabbi!

BEN ZKHARIA   Whatever my heart desires? You mean you'll give away your horses too?

BENYA   I will give away my horses too!

BEN ZKHARIA   In that case, Jews, run to the Funeral Brotherhood and harness his horses to their hearse and take me to . . . where do you think?

BOBRINETS   Where to, Rabbi?

BEN ZKHARIA   To the Second Jewish Cemetery, you idiot!

BOBRINETS [*Roars with laughter, snatches the yarmulke off the* RABBI's *head, and kisses his bald, pink pate.*]   Oy, he's a wild man! . . . Oy, he's a clever man!

ARYE-LEIB [*Introduces* BENYA.]   That's him, Rabbi, Mendel's son, Ben Zion.

BEN ZKHARIA [*Chews his lip.*]   Ben Zion . . . son of Zion . . . [*He is silent.*] Nightingales are not fed with fables, son of Zion, nor women with wisdom. . . .

LYOVKA [*In a deafening voice.*]   Get to your chairs, you riffraff, get your backsides to some stools!

KLASHA [*Shakes her head, smiles.*]   Oy, he's a lively one!

BENYA [*Throws his brother an indignant look.*]   My dear friends, please be seated! Monsieur Bobrinets will sit next to the rabbi.

BEN ZKHARIA [*Squirms in his armchair.*]   Why should I sit next to this Jew who's as long as our exile from the Holy Land has been? [*He points at* KLASHA.] Let the National Bank sit next to me. . . .

BOBRINETS [*Anticipating a new witticism.*]   Why National Bank?

BEN ZKHARIA   She's better than the National Bank. Make a nice deposit in her, and she'll yield such a percentage that wheat will wilt with envy. Make a bad deposit in her, and all her guts will creak in order to change your broken-down kopeck into a golden one! She's better than a bank, better than a bank!

BOBRINETS [*Raises his finger.*]   You must listen to his words!

BEN ZKHARIA   But where is our Star of Israel? Where is the master of this house? Where is Rabbi Mendel Krik?

LYOVKA   He is sick today.

BENYA   No, he is feeling well. . . . Nikifor!

[NIKIFOR *appears in the doorway in his shabby peasant coat.*]

BENYA   Have Papa and his wife come down.

[*Silence.*]

NIKIFOR [*In a desperate voice.*]   Ladies and gentlemen! . . .

BENYA [*Very slowly.*]   Have Papa come down.

ARYE-LEIB   Benya, we Jews don't cover our fathers with shame in front of everyone.

LYOVKA   Rabbi, no man has ever tortured a wild boar the way Benya is torturing Papa.

[WEINER *babbles indignantly, splattering spit.*]

BENYA [*Bends down to* MADAME WEINER.]   What is he saying?

MADAME WEINER   He is saying—"Shame and disgrace!"

ARYE-LEIB   Jews don't do such things, Benya!

KLASHA   You raise sons and—

BENYA   Arye-Leib, old man, old matchmaker, *shamas* of the Carters' Synagogue and funeral cantor, why don't you tell me how things should be done properly? [*He bangs his fist down on the table, and speaks with a pause after each word, accompanied by a thump of his fist.*] Have Papa come down!

[NIKIFOR *disappears.* BENYA *is standing in the middle of the room, his head hanging, his legs far apart. The blood is slowly rising to his head. Utter stillness. Only* BEN ZKHARIA's *senseless muttering breaks the agonizing silence.*]

BEN ZKHARIA   God bathes in red water in heaven. [*He falls silent, squirms in his armchair.*] Why red, why not white? Because red is merrier than white. . . .

[*The two halves of the side door creak, groan, and then open. All faces turn in that direction.* MENDEL *appears, his face bruised and powdered. He is wearing a new suit. With him is* NEKHAMA, *wearing a bonnet and a heavy velvet dress.*]

BENYA   My friends, sitting here in my house! Permit me to raise this glass to my father, the hardworking Mendel Krik, and his wife, Nekhama Borisovna, who have walked thirty-five years along the road of life together. Dear friends! We know, we know full well, that no one has paved this road with cement, no one has placed benches along this long road! And then there's all the hordes of people who come running down that road, who haven't made it any easier, they've made it harder! My friends, sitting here in my house! What I ask is that you don't water the wine in your glasses, or the wine in your hearts!

[WEINER *babbles rapturously.*]

BENYA   What is he saying?

MADAME WEINER   He is saying—"Hurrah!"

BENYA   [*Without looking at anyone.*]   Teach me, Arye-Leib. . . . [*He pours wine for his mother and father.*]   Our guests are honoring you, Papa. Say a word or two!

MENDEL   [*Looks around, and very quietly says.*]   To your health. . . .

BENYA   What Papa is trying to say is that he's donating a hundred rubles.

CATTLE DEALER   And then they talk about Jews. . . .

BENYA   Papa is donating five hundred! To whom should he donate, Rabbi?

BEN ZKHARIA   To whom? Jews! A girl's milk should not be left to curdle! He must donate the money to brides with no dowries!

BOBRINETS   [*Bursts out laughing.*]   Oy, he's a wild man! . . . Oy, he's a clever man!

MADAME POPYATNIK   Do we want a flourish from the band now?

BENYA   Yes, we do!

[*A doleful flourish resounds through the room. A row of guests with glasses in their hands files toward* MENDEL *and* NEKHAMA.]

KLASHA ZUBARYEVA   To your health, Grandpa!

SENKA TOPUN   A wagonload of fun, Papa! A hundred thousand in pocket money!

BENYA   [*Without looking at anyone.*]   Teach me, Arye-Leib!

BOBRINETS   Mendel, may God give me a son like your son!

LYOVKA   [*Calls out across the table.*]   Papa! Don't be angry! Papa, you've had your fun and games. . . .

CATTLE DEALER   And then they talk about Jews! I know twice as much about Jews as you do!

PYATIRUBEL   [*Makes his way across to* BENYA *and tries to kiss him.*]   You'll buy us and you'll sell us, you devil, you, and then tie us in a knot!

[*Loud sobbing is heard behind* BENYA. *Tears are flowing down* ARYE-LEIB's *cheeks and into his beard. He shudders, and kisses* BENYA's *shoulder.*]

ARYE-LEIB   Fifty years, Benchik! Fifty years together with your father! [*He shouts hysterically.*]   He was a good father to you, Benya!

WEINER   [*Suddenly attains the gift of speech.*]   Take him away!

MADAME WEINER   Well, I'll be damned!

BOYARSKY   Arye-Leib! You're mistaken, this is a time for laughter!

WEINER   Take him away!

ARYE-LEIB [*Sobs.*]   You had a good father, Benya. . . .
[MENDEL *turns ashen under his powder. He holds out a new
handkerchief to* ARYE-LEIB, *who uses it to wipe away his tears.*
ARYE-LEIB *is laughing and crying.*]
BOBRINETS   You blockhead, you're not in your cemetery now!
PYATIRUBEL   You can search the whole world over, you'll never find a
second Benchik! I'll wager anything. . . .
BENYA   Dear friends, be seated!
LYOVKA   Get your backsides to some stools, you riffraff!
[*The thunder of chairs being moved. They seat* MENDEL *between
the* RABBI *and* KLASHA ZUBARYEVA.]
BEN ZKHARIA   Jews!
PYATIRUBEL   Quiet, now!
BEN ZKHARIA   The old fool Ben Zkharia wants to say a word. . . .
[LYOVKA *slumps forward onto the table, snorting with contempt,
but* BENYA *shakes him, and he becomes quiet.*]
BEN ZKHARIA   Jews! Day is day, and night is night. Day drenches us with
the sweat of our toil, but night offers its fans of divine coolness.
Joshua, son of Nun, who stopped the sun, was nothing but a crazed
fool! Jesus of Nazareth, who stole the sun, was an evil madman. And
here is Mendel Krik, a member of our synagogue, who has turned out
to be no cleverer than Joshua, son of Nun. He wanted to warm himself
in the sun all his life, all his life he wanted to stand where he stood at
midday. But God has policemen on every street, and Mendel Krik had
sons in his house. The policemen come and see to it that things are as
they should be. Day is day, and night is night. Jews! Everything is as it
should be! Let's down a glass of vodka!
LYOVKA   Let's down a glass of vodka!
[*The shrill sound of flutes, the clinking of glasses, incoherent
shouts, thunderous laughter.*]

Karl-Yankel[1]

In the days of my childhood there was a smithy in Peresyp[2] that belonged
to Jonas Brutman. Horse dealers, carters—known as *bindyuzhniks* in
Odessa—and butchers from the town slaughterhouses gathered in this
smithy. It was on the Balta Road, and it was quite handy as a lookout
post for intercepting muzhiks carting oats and Bessarabian wine into
town. Jonas was a small, timid man, but he knew his way around wine. In
him dwelled the soul of an Odessa Jew.

1. First published in *Zvezda* 7 (1931), this story subtly echoes Babel's own personal drama of the
adoption of his son Mikhail by Tamara Kashirina's new husband, Babel's old friend and fellow
writer Vsevolod Ivanov. Ivanov was an intensely jealous husband and could not tolerate any contact with Babel. During the adoption he legally changed his son's date and year of birth. The appearance of the Kirghiz nursemaid volunteer at the end of the story alludes to Ivanov's famous
1922 novella "Dityo" (Baby). —*Ed.*
2. Odessa's eastern suburb by the harbor.

In my day he had three growing sons. He only came up to their waists.
It was on the beach of Peresyp that I first reflected on the power of
the forces in nature. The boys, three fattened bulls with crimson shoulders and feet big as shovels, carried shriveled-up little Jonas to the water
the way one carries an infant. And yet it had been he, and no one else,
who had sired them. There was no doubt about that. The blacksmith's
wife went to the synagogue twice a week, on Friday evenings and on
the morning of the Sabbath. It was a Hasidic synagogue, where on
Passover they whirled themselves into an ecstasy like dervishes. Jonas's
wife paid tribute to the emissaries sent by the Galician *tsaddiks* to
our southern provinces. The blacksmith did not interfere in his wife's
relationship with God. After work, he went to a wine shop next to
the slaughterhouses, and there, sipping his cheap pink wine, listened
meekly to what people were talking about—politics and the price of
cattle.

His sons resembled their mother in strength and build. As soon as
they came of age, two of the boys went and joined the partisans. The
elder was killed at Voznesensk, the other, Semyon, went over to Primakov[3] and joined a Red Cossack division. He was chosen to be commander of a Cossack regiment. He and a few other shtetl youths were
the first in this unexpected breed of Jewish fighters, horsemen, and partisans.

The third son became a blacksmith like his father. He works at the
Ghen plow factory.[4] He has not married and has not sired anyone.

The children of Semyon, the Cossack commander, tagged along from
place to place with his division. But the old woman needed a grandchild
to whom she could tell stories about the Baal-Shem. She was expecting a
grandchild from her youngest daughter Paulina. Paulina was the only
one in the whole family who resembled little old Jonas. She was timid,
nearsighted, and had delicate skin. Many came around asking for her
hand in marriage. Paulina chose Ofsey Byelotserkovsky. We could not
understand why she chose him. Even more surprising was the news that
the young couple was happy. A woman runs her household as she wills,
an outsider cannot see pots breaking. But in this case it was Ofsey
Byelotserkovsky who was to break the pots. A year into their marriage, he
dragged Brana Brutman, his mother-in-law, to court. The old woman
had taken advantage of Ofsey's being away on a business trip and
Paulina's being in the hospital for a breast inflammation to abduct her
newborn grandson and take him to the neighborhood charlatan, Naftula
Gerchik. And there, in the presence of ten doddering wrecks—ten
ancient and impoverished men, denizens of the Hasidic synagogue—the
rites of circumcision were performed.

Ofsey Byelotserkovsky did not find out what had happened until after
his return. Ofsey had put himself forward as a candidate to join the
Party. He decided to seek the advice of Bychach, the secretary of the
local cell of the State Trade Committee.

---

3. Vitaly Markovich Primakov (1897–1937), a Red Commander who had taken part in the storming
   of the Winter Palace. In 1918, he had formed the first Red Cossack Regiment, and was later both
   commander and military commissar of the Eighth Cavalry Division.
4. One of the largest agricultural machinery factories of the time.

"You've been morally bespattered!" Bychach told him. "You must pursue this matter further."

Odessa's public prosecutor's office decided to set up a model public trial at the Petrovsky factory.[5] Naftula Gerchik, the neighborhood charlatan, and Brana Brutman, sixty-two years of age, found themselves on the defendants' bench.

Naftula was as much an Odessan fixture as the statue of the Duke of Richelieu.[6] Naftula used to walk past our windows on Dalnitskaya Street carrying his tattered, grease-stained midwife's bag. In that bag he kept his simple instruments. Sometimes he took a little knife out of it, sometimes a bottle of vodka and a piece of honey cake. He'd sniff the honey cake before he drank his vodka, and having drunk it would rattle off some prayers. Naftula was as redheaded as the first redheaded man on earth. When he sliced off what was his due, he did not strain off the blood through a glass funnel, but sucked it with puckered lips. The blood smudged his tousled beard. He appeared tipsy before the guests. His bearlike eyes twinkled cheerfully. Redheaded as the first redheaded man on earth, he whimpered a blessing over the wine. With one hand Naftula pitched his vodka into his mouth's overgrown, crooked, fire-spitting pit, while in the other he held a plate. On this plate lay the little knife, reddened with the infant's blood, and some gauze. As he collected his money, Naftula went from guest to guest with his plate, elbowing his way through the women, falling on them, grabbing their breasts. "Fat mamas!" he howled for the whole street to hear, his little coral eyes glittering. "Go churn out some boys for Naftula, thresh some corn on your bellies! Do your best for Naftula! Go churn out some boys, fat mamas!"

The husbands threw money onto his plate. The women wiped away the blood from his beard. The courtyards of Glukhaya and Gospitalnaya Streets did not lack offspring. They seethed with children, as the mouths of rivers seethe with roe. Naftula went trudging around with his bag, like a tax collector. Orlov, the investigating magistrate, brought Naftula's rounds to an end.

The investigating magistrate thundered from the bench, endeavoring to prove that the neighborhood charlatan was a priest in a cult.

"Do you believe in God?" he asked Naftula.

"Let him who won two thousand believe in God," the old man answered.

"Were you not surprised when Comrade Brana Brutman came to you at such a late hour in the rain, carrying a newborn in her hands?"

"I am surprised when a person does something reasonable," Naftula said. "When a person does idiotic things, then I'm not surprised!"

These answers did not satisfy the investigating magistrate. The matter of the glass funnel came next. He charged that by sucking blood with his lips, the defendant was exposing children to the danger of infection.

5. One of the largest steelworks of the time. Its more than eight thousand workers had played a key role in the Revolution. Holding this trial at the Petrovsky factory indicated that the new Soviet government wanted to make a landmark case out of it.
6. A French émigré nobleman, governor general of Odessa from 1803–1814, on whom Lord Byron modeled his Don Juan. The famous bronze statue of him, sculpted by Ivan Martos, stands at the head of the Odessa Steps.

Naftula's head, that shaggy nut of his, hung almost to the ground. He sighed, closed his eyes, and wiped his drooping mouth with his fist.

"What are you muttering about, Comrade Gerchik?" the judge asked him.

Naftula fixed his extinguished eyes on Orlov, the investigating magistrate.

"The late Monsieur Zusman, your late Papa," Naftula said to him with a sigh, "he had a head the likes of which you can't find nowhere in the world. And praised be God, that your papa did not have an apoplectic fit when he had me come over to perform your *bris*. And we can all see plain enough that you grew into a big man in the Soviet government, and that Naftula did not snip off along with that little piece of *shmokhtes* anything you might have needed later on."

He blinked with his bearlike eyes, shook his red-haired nut, and fell silent. There were volleys of laughter, thunderous guffawing salvos. Orlov, né Zusman, waved his arms in the air and shouted out something that could not be heard in the cannonade. He demanded that the record reflect that . . . Sasha Svetlov, one of the satirists of the *Odessa News*, sent him a note from the press box. "You're a nincompoop, Syoma," the note went. "Finish him off with irony, only what is funny will kill! Your Sasha."

The room quieted down when they brought Byelotserkovsky to the witness box.

Byelotserkovsky reiterated what was in his deposition. He was lanky and wore riding breeches and cavalry jackboots. According to Ofsey, the Tiraspol and Balta Party Committees had been fully cooperative in the business of acquiring livestock feed. In the heat of the negotiations he had received a telegram announcing the birth of his son. After discussing the matter with the Balta Party Committee's head of operations, he decided not to interrupt the transaction and to restrict himself to dispatching a congratulatory telegram. He did not return home for another two weeks. Sixty-four thousand *poods* of livestock feed had been gathered throughout the region. No one was at home, except for the witness Kharchenko—a neighbor and laundress by profession—and his infant son. His wife was away at the hospital, and the witness Kharchenko was rocking the cradle and was engaged in the now-obsolete practice of singing a lullaby. Knowing the witness to be an alcoholic, he did not find it necessary to try making out the words of this song, but he was taken aback to hear her call the boy Yankel, when he had expressly given instructions that his son be named Karl, in honor of our esteemed teacher Karl Marx. Unwrapping the child's swaddling clothes, he came face-to-face with his misfortune.

The investigating magistrate asked a few questions, the defense did not. The bailiff led in the witness Paulina Byelotserkovskaya. She staggered toward the bar. The bluish tremor of recent motherhood twisted her face, and there were drops of sweat on her forehead. She looked over to her father, the little blacksmith, dressed to the nines in a bow tie and new boots as if for a feast, and to her mother's coppery, gray-mustached face. The witness Paulina Byelotserkovskaya did not answer the question as to what she knew about the matter at hand. She said that her father was a poor man, who had worked in the smithy on the road to Balta for forty years. Her mother had given birth to six children, of whom three had died. One brother was a Red commander, the other worked in the Ghen factory. "My mother is very devout, everyone knows that, and she always suffered because her children were not religious. She could not bear the idea that her grandchildren would not be Jews. You must take into consideration in what kind of a family my mother was raised. Everyone knows the shtetl of Medzhibozh,[7] the women there are still wearing wigs."

"Will the witness please tell us," a sharp voice interrupted her. Paulina fell silent, the drops of sweat darkening on her forehead as if blood were seeping through her delicate skin. "Will the witness please tell us," repeated the voice of Samuel Lining, a former barrister. Were the Sanhedrin[8] to exist nowadays, Lining would have been its head. But the Sanhedrin no longer exists, and Lining, who had learned to read and write Russian at twenty-five, had begun in his fourth decade to write appeals to the government indistinguishable from the treatises of the Talmud. The old man had slept throughout the trial. His jacket was covered in cigarette ash. But he had woken up when Paulina Byelotserkovskaya had appeared. "Will the witness please tell us"—his fishlike rows of bobbing blue teeth were clacking—"if you had been aware of your husband's decision to name his son Karl?"

"Yes."

"What name did your mother give him?"

"Yankel."

"And what about you, Comrade Witness? What do you call your son?"

"I call him 'sweetie.'"

"And why 'sweetie,' of all things?"

"I call all children 'sweetie.'"

"Let us proceed," Lining said. His teeth slipped out, but he caught them with his nether lip and slid them back into his mouth. "Let us proceed. In the evening, when the child was taken over to the defendant Gerchik, you were not at home. You were at the hospital. Is my statement in accordance with the facts?"

"I was at the hospital."

"At what hospital were you being treated?"

"The one in Nezhinskaya Street, at Dr. Drizo's."

"Dr. Drizo was treating you?"

"Yes."

"Are you sure of this?"

"Why wouldn't I be?"

"I would like to introduce this here document into evidence." Lining's lifeless face rose over the table. "From this document the court will ascertain that during the period of time in question, Dr. Drizo was away at a congress of pediatricians in Kharkov."

The investigating magistrate did not object to the introduction of the document.

"Let us proceed," Lining said, his teeth clacking.

7. A shtetl in western Ukraine in the district of Khmelnitsky, home of the founder of Hasidism, Israel ben Eliezer, Baal Shem Tov.
8. The highest court of the ancient Jewish nation.

The witness leaned her whole body against the bar. Her whisper was barely audible.

"Maybe it wasn't Dr. Drizo," she said, resting her whole weight against the bar. "I can't remember everything. I am exhausted."

Lining raked his pencil through his yellow beard. He rubbed his stooping back against the bench and joggled his false teeth.

Paulina was asked to produce her official medical report, but she told the court she had misplaced it.

"Let us proceed," the old man said.

Paulina ran her palm over her forehead. Her husband sat at the end of the bench, away from the other witnesses. He sat there stiffly, his long legs in their cavalry boots pulled in under him. The rays of the sun fell on his face, packed with a framework of minute, spiteful bones.

"I will find my medical record," Paulina whispered, and her hands slid off the bar.

At that moment a bawling baby was heard. A child was crying and mewling outside the doors.

"You see, Paulina?" the old woman suddenly yelled out in a hoarse voice. "The child hasn't been fed since this morning! He's shriveling up with hollering!" Startled Red Army fighters snatched up their rifles. Paulina began to slide lower and lower, her head falling back to the floor. Her arms flew up, flailed, and then tumbled down.

"The court is adjourned!" the public prosecutor shouted.

An uproar erupted in the room. Byelotserkovsky stalked over to his wife with cranelike steps, a green sheen on his hollow cheeks.

"Feed the child!" people were shouting from the back rows, cupping their hands like megaphones around their mouths.

"They're already feeding him!" a woman's voice shouted back. "You think they were waiting for you?"

"The daughter's tangled up in all of this," said a worker sitting next to me. "The daughter's got her hand in it."

"It's a family thing," the man sitting next to him said. "One of those dark, nighttime jobs. At night they go tangling up things that in daylight you just can't untangle."

The sun cut through the room with its slanting rays. The crowd stirred heavily, breathing fire and sweat. Elbowing my way through, I reached the corridor. The door to the Red Corner[9] stood ajar. I could hear Karl-Yankel's mewling and slurping inside. Lenin's portrait hung in the Red Corner, the portrait in which he is giving a speech from the armored car on the square in front of the Finland Station. It was surrounded by multicolored production graphs showing the Petrovsky factory's output. The walls were lined with banners and rifles on wooden mounts. A woman worker with a Kirghiz face, her head bent forward, was feeding Karl-Yankel, a plump little fellow about five months old with knitted socks and a white tuft of hair on his head. Fastened to the Kirghiz woman by his mouth, he gurgled, banging her breast with his little clenched fist.

9. Part Communist Party shrine, part reading room, and part meeting place, the Red Corner—traditionally the name for the corner where the icon was hung—existed in most public buildings and contained the portraits of the leaders, propaganda literature, banners, and other paraphernalia. —Ed.

"What are they shouting for?" the Kirghiz woman said. "There's always someone who'll feed a baby."

There was also a girl of about seventeen puttering about the room in a red kerchief, her cheeks puffed out like pine cones. She was wiping dry Karl-Yankel's changing-mat.

"He's going to be a fighter, he is," the girl said. "Look at those punches he's throwing!"

The Kirghiz woman gently pulled her nipple out of Karl-Yankel's mouth. He began growling, and in desperation threw back his head with its white tuft of hair. The woman took out her other breast and gave it to him. He looked at her nipple with dull eyes that suddenly lit up. The Kirghiz woman looked at Karl-Yankel, squinting her black eyes at him.

"Not a fighter, no," she crooned, fixing the boy's cap. "He'll be an aviator. He will fly through the sky, he will."

In the other room the hearing had resumed.

A battle was now raging between the investigating magistrate and the experts who were giving vague and inconclusive testimony. The public prosecutor got up from his seat and began banging the desk with his fist. I could see the public in the first few rows—Galician *tsaddiks*, their beaver hats resting on their knees. They had come to the Petrovsky factory, where, according to the Warsaw papers, the Jewish religion was being put on trial. The faces of the rabbis sitting in the first row hovered in the stormy, dusty brightness of the sun.

"Down with them!" shouted a member of the Young Communist League who had managed to fight his way right up to the podium.

The battle raged with growing force.

Karl-Yankel, staring blankly at me, sucked at the Kirghiz woman's breast.

The straight streets that my childhood and youth walked unfurled outside the window—Pushkin Street went to the train station, Malo-Arnautskaya Street jutted out into the park by the sea.

I grew up on these streets. Now it was Karl-Yankel's turn. But nobody had fought over me the way they were fighting over him, nobody had cared much about me.

"I can't believe that you won't be happy, Karl-Yankel," I whispered to myself. "I can't believe you won't be happier than me."

The End of the Almshouse[1]

In the days of the famine, no one lived better in all Odessa than the almsfolk of the Second Jewish Cemetery. Kofman, the cloth merchant, had built an almshouse for old people by the wall of the cemetery in memory of his wife Isabella, a fact that became the butt of many a joke at Café Fankoni.[2] But Kofman turned out to be right in the end. After the Revolution, the old men and women who found refuge by the cemetery immediately grabbed positions as gravediggers, cantors, and body

1. First published in the journal *30 dney* 1 (1932), subtitled "From The Odessa Stories." —*Ed.*
2. A famous elegant and expensive café in the center of Odessa. —*Ed.*

washers. They got their hands on an oak coffin with a silver-tasseled pall, and rented it out to the poor.

There were no planks to be found anywhere in Odessa in those days. The rental coffin did not stand idle. The dead would lie in the oak coffin at home and at the funeral service—but then they were pitched into their graves wrapped in a shroud. This was a forgotten Jewish custom.

Wise men had taught that one is not to hinder the union of worm and carrion—carrion is unclean. "For dust thou art and unto dust shalt thou return."

Because of the revival of the forgotten custom, the rations of the old folk grew in ways which in those days no one could even dream of. In the evenings they got drunk in Zalman Krivoruchka's cellar, and threw their leftover scraps to poorer companions.

Their prosperity remained undisturbed until the rebellion in the German settlements. The Germans killed Garrison Commander Gersh Lugovoy.

He was buried with honors. The troops marched to the cemetery with bands, field kitchens, and machine guns on *tachankas*. Speeches were given and vows made over his open grave.

"Comrade Gersh joined the Revolutionary Social Democratic Workers' Party of the Bolsheviks in 1911, where he held the position of propagandist and liaison agent!" Lenka Broytman, the division commander, yelled at the top of his lungs. "Comrade Gersh was arrested along with Sonya Yanovskaya, Ivan Sokolov, and Monozon in the town of Nikolayev in 1913. . . ."

Arye-Leib, the elder of the almshouse, lay in waiting with his comrades. Lenka hadn't yet finished his farewell speech over the grave when the old men heaved up the coffin in order to tip it onto its side so that the deceased, covered with a flag, would come tumbling out. Lenka discreetly jabbed Arye-Leib with his boot spur.

"Beat it!" he hissed. "Go on, beat it! . . . Gersh served the Republic . . ."

Before the eyes of the horrified old folk, Lugovoy was buried along with the oak coffin, the tassels, and the black pall onto which the Star of David and verses from an ancient Hebrew prayer for the dead had been woven in silver.

"We've all just attended our own funeral!" Arye-Leib told his comrades after the burial. "We have fallen into Pharaoh's hands!" And he rushed off to see Broydin, the overseer of the cemetery, with a request that planks for a new coffin and cloth for a pall be issued immediately. Broydin made promises, but did nothing. His plans did not include the enrichment of the old folk.

"My heart aches more for the unemployed municipal employees than for these entrepreneurs," he told the others at the office.

Broydin made promises, but did nothing. In Zalman Krivoruchka's wine cellar, Talmudic curses rained down on his head and the heads of the Union of Municipal Workers. The old folk cursed Broydin's bone marrow and that of the members of the union, along with the fresh seed in the wombs of their wives. They called down every kind of paralysis and boil upon each and every one of them.

The old folk's income shrank. Their rations now consisted of bluish soup with boiled fish bones, with a second course of barley kasha without a single dab of butter in it.

An aged Odessan is ready enough to eat any kind of soup, regardless what it's made of, as long as there's garlic, pepper, and a bay leaf in it. There were none of these in the old folk's soup.

The Isabella Kofman Almshouse shared in the common lot. The rage of its famished inmates grew. Their rage rained down upon the head of the person who least expected it. This person was Dr. Judith Shmayser, who had come to the almshouse to administer smallpox vaccinations.

The Provincial Executive Committee had issued an order for mandatory vaccination. Judith Shmayser laid out her instruments on the table and lit a little alcohol burner. Outside the windows stood the emerald walls of the cemetery hedges. The blue tongue of the flame mingled with the June lightning.

Meyer Beskonechny, a haggard old man, stood closest to Judith. He watched her preparations sullenly.

"I'll give you a jab now," Judith said to him, beckoning him over with her tweezers. She pulled his thin, bluish strap of an arm out of his rags.

"There's nowhere for you to jab me," the old man said, jerking back his arm.

"It's not going to hurt," Judith exclaimed. "It doesn't hurt when you're given a jab in the flesh."

"I don't have no flesh!" Meyer Beskonechny said. "There's nowhere for you to jab."

Muffled sobs came from one of the corners. Doba-Leya, a former cook at circumcision feasts, was sobbing. Meyer twisted his decayed cheeks.

"Life is shit," he muttered. "The world's a brothel, everyone's a swindler!"

The pince-nez on Judith's nose bounced, her breasts swelled out of her starched coat. She opened her mouth to explain the benefits of vaccination, but Arye-Leib, the elder of the almshouse, stopped her.

"Young lady," he said. "Our mamas gave birth to us just like your mama gave birth to you! And this woman, our mama, gave birth to us so we would live, not so we would suffer! She wanted for us to live well, and she was as right as a mother can be. A person who is pleased with what Broydin provides him, that person is not worth the material that went into him. Your aim, young lady, is to inoculate smallpox, and with God's help, you are inoculating it. Our aim is to live out our life, not torture it! But we are not achieving our aim!"

Doba-Leya, a whiskered old woman with a leonine face, started sobbing even louder on hearing these words. She sobbed in a deep bass.

"Life is shit," Meyer Beskonechny repeated. "Everyone's a swindler!"

Paralyzed Simon-Volf, screeching and twisting his hands, clutched at the steering wheel of his invalid cart and went rolling toward the door. His yarmulke slid over his swollen, crimson head. Thirty growling and grimacing old men and women tumbled out onto the cemetery walk behind Simon-Volf. They shook their crutches and brayed like starving donkeys.

When he saw them, the watchman slammed the cemetery gates shut. The amazed gravediggers stopped digging and raised their shovels, clumps of earth and grass roots still clinging to them.

The noise brought out bearded Broydin in his tight little jacket, leggings, and cycling cap.

"You swindler!" Simon-Volf shouted. "There's nowhere for us to be jabbed! We've got no meat on our arms!"

Doba-Leya began snarling and growling. She grabbed Simon-Volf's invalid cart and tried to ram Broydin with it. Arye-Leib, as always, began spouting allegories and parables that crept up on byways toward an end that was not always clearly apparent.

He began with the parable about Rabbi Osiya, who had given his property to his children, his heart to his wife, his fear to God, and his levy to Caesar, keeping for himself only a place beneath an olive tree where the setting sun shone the longest. From Rabbi Osiya, Arye-Leib moved on to planks for a new coffin, and to rations.

Broydin spread his long-legginged legs, and listened without raising his eyes. The brown fringe of his beard lay motionless on his new jacket. He seemed immersed in sad, tranquil thought.

"Forgive me, Arye-Leib," Broydin sighed, turning to the cemetery sage. "Forgive me, but I must say that I cannot but see ulterior motives and political goals here. Standing behind you, I cannot but see people who know exactly what they are doing, just as you know exactly what you are doing."

Broydin raised his eyes. In a flash they filled with the white water of fury. He trained the trembling hills of his pupils on the old folk.

"Arye-Leib!" Broydin said in his powerful voice. "I want you to read this telegram from the Tatar Republic, where an immense number of Tatars are starving like madmen! Read the petition of the Petersburg proletariat who are working and waiting, hungering by their benches!"

"I don't have time to wait!" Arye-Leib interrupted Broydin. "I have no time!"

"There are people," Broydin continued without listening, "who have it worse than you do, and there are thousands of people who have it worse than the people who have it worse than you do! You are sowing trouble, Arye-Leib, and a whirlwind is what you shall reap. You are as good as dead if I turn my back on you. You will die if I go my way and you go yours. You will die, Arye-Leib. You will die, Simon-Volf. You will die, Meyer Beskonechny. But tell me one thing, just one thing, before you die—do we have a Soviet government, or could it be that we do not? If we do not have a Soviet government, if it's all in my imagination, then I would be grateful if you would be so kind as to take me back to Mr. Berzon's on the corner of Deribasovskaya and Ekaterininskaya Streets, where I worked as a tailor sewing vests all my life! Tell me, Arye-Leib, is the Soviet government all in my imagination?"

And Broydin came right up to the old cripples. His quivering pupils broke loose and went hurtling over the groaning, petrified herd like searchlights, like tongues of flame. Broydin's leggings crackled, and sweat stewed on his furrowed face. He came closer and closer to Arye-Leib, demanding an answer to whether it was all in his imagination that the Soviet government was now in power.

Arye-Leib remained silent. This silence might have been the end of him, had not Fedka Stepun appeared at the end of the walk, barefoot and in a sailor's shirt.

Fedka had been shell-shocked near Rostov and lived in a hut next to the cemetery, recovering. He wore a whistle on an orange police cord and carried a revolver without a holster.

Fedka was drunk. The locks of his rock-hard curls rested on his fore-head. Beneath his locks his face, with its high cheekbones, was twisted by convulsions. He walked up to Lugovoy's grave, which was surrounded by wilted wreaths.

"Where were you, Lugovoy, when I took Rostov?" Fedka asked the dead man.

Fedka gnashed his teeth, blew his police whistle, and pulled the revolver from his belt. The revolver's burnished muzzle glittered.

"They've trampled on the czars," Fedka shouted. "There are no czars! Let them all lie without coffins!"

Fedka was clutching his revolver. His chest was bare. On it were tattooed the name "Riva" and a dragon, its head inclined toward a nipple.

The gravediggers crowded around Fedka with their raised shovels. The women who were washing corpses came out of their sheds ready to join Doba-Leya in her howling. Roaring waves beat against the locked ceme-tery gates.

People with dead relatives on wheelbarrows demanded to be let in. Beggars banged their crutches against the fence.

"They've trampled on the czars!" Fedka shouted, firing into the sky.

The people came hopping and jumping up the cemetery walk. Broy-din's face slowly turned white. He raised his hand, agreed to all the demands of the almsfolk, and, with a soldierly about-turn, went back to his office. At that very instant the gates burst open. Pushing their wheel-barrows in front of them, the relatives of the dead briskly hurried down the paths. Self-proclaimed cantors sang "El moley rakhim"[3] in piercing falsettos over open graves. In the evening the old folk celebrated their victory at Krivoruchka's. They gave Fedka three quarts of Bessarabian wine.

"Hevel havolim," Arye-Leib said, clinking glasses with Fedka. "You're one of us, one of us! Kuloy hevel."[4]

The mistress of the wine cellar, Krivoruchka's wife, was washing glasses behind the partition.

"When a Russian man is blessed with a good character," Madame Krivoruchka commented, "it's a rare luxury!"

Fedka was led out of the wine cellar after one in the morning.

"Hevel havolim." He muttered the dire, incomprehensible words as he tottered along Stepovaya Street. "Kuloy hevel."

On the following day the old folk of the almshouse were each given four sugar cubes, and there was meat in their borscht. In the evening they were taken to the Odessa City Theater to a performance organized by the Department of Social Assistance. A performance of Carmen. It was the first time in their lives that these invalids and cripples saw an Odessa theater's gilt tiers, the velvet of its loges, and the oily sparkle of its chandeliers. During intermission they were given liver-sausage sand-wiches.

---

3. Hebrew: El maley rakhamim, God is filled with mercy. A prayer traditionally chanted at burials.
4. Hebrew quotations from the Bible (Ecclesiastes 12:8), Hevel havolim, "vanity of vanities," and Kuloy hevel, "All is vanity."

An army truck took them back to the cemetery. It rolled through the deserted streets, banging and sputtering. The old folk slept with full stomachs. They belched in their sleep and shuddered with satiation, like dogs who have run so much they can run no more.

The next morning, Arye-Leib got up earlier than the rest. He faced east to say his prayers and saw a notice pinned to the door, in which Broydin announced that the almshouse was going to be closed for renovations and that all its wards were to report immediately to the local Department of Social Assistance for their employability to be reassessed.

The sun emerged over the green treetops of the cemetery grove. Arye-Leib raised his hand to his eyes. A tear dropped from the spent hollows.

The shining chestnut walk stretched toward the mortuary. The chestnuts were in bloom, the trees bore tall white blossoms on their spreading boughs. An unknown woman with a shawl tied tautly under her breasts was working in the mortuary. Everything had been redone—the walls decorated with fir branches, the tables scraped clean. The woman was washing an infant. She nimbly turned it from side to side, the water pouring in a diamond stream over its crushed, blotchy little back.

Broydin was sitting on the mortuary steps in his leggings. He sat there like a man of leisure. He took off his cap and wiped his forehead with a yellow handkerchief.

"That's exactly what I said to Comrade Andreychik at the union," said the melodious voice of the unknown woman. "We're not afraid of work! Let them go ask about us in Ekaterinoslav—Ekaterinoslav knows how we work.[5]

"Make yourself at home, Comrade Blyuma, make yourself at home," Broydin said placidly, sticking his yellow handkerchief into his pocket. "I'm easy enough to get along with, yes, I'm easy enough to get along with!" he repeated, and turned his sparkling eyes to Arye-Leib, who had dragged himself all the way up to the stoop. "As long as you don't spit in my kasha."

Broydin did not finish what he was saying. A buggy harnessed to a large black horse pulled up at the gate. Out of the buggy stepped the director of the Communal Economics Department, wearing a fine shirt. Broydin rushed over to help him out of the buggy and, bowing and scraping, took him to the cemetery.

The former tailor's apprentice showed his director a century of Odessan history resting beneath the granite tombstones. He showed him the vaults and memorials of the wheat exporters, shipping brokers, and merchants who had built Russia's Marseille on the site of Khadzhibei.[6] They all lay here, their faces toward the gate, the Ashkenazis, Gessens, and Efrussis—the lustrous misers and philosophical bon vivants, the creators of wealth and Odessa anecdotes. They lay beneath their labradorite and rose-marble memorials, shielded by chains of acacias and chestnut trees from the plebes clumped against the wall.

5. Broydin has hired cemetery workers from outside Odessa to take over the funerary duties of the old folk from the almshouse. Ekaterinoslav in eastern Ukraine has been renamed Dnipropetrovsk.
6. Khadzhibei was the small Turkish settlement where in 1794 Czarina Catherine II decided to build a large Black Sea port, which she then renamed Odessa.

"They wouldn't let us live while they were alive," Broydin said, kicking a memorial with his boot. "And after their death they wouldn't let us die."

Inspired, he told the director of the Communal Economics Department about his reorganization program for the cemetery and his campaign plan against the Jewish Burial Brotherhood.

"And get rid of them over there too," the director said, pointing to the beggars who had gathered by the gate.

"I am already seeing to that," Broydin answered. "Step by step, everything's being taken care of."

"Well, keep up the good work," Mayorov,[7] the director, said. "I see you have things under control here. Keep up the good work!"

He placed his boot on the buggy's footboard, but suddenly remembered Fedka.

"By the way, who was that clown back there?"

"Just some shell-shocked fellow," Broydin said, lowering his eyes. "There are times when he loses control of himself—but he's been straightened out, and he apologizes."

"That Broydin knows his onions," Mayorov told his companion, as they drove off. "He's handling things well."

The large horse took Mayorov and the director of the Department of Public Services into town. On the way, they passed the old men and women who had been thrown out of the almshouse. They were hobbling along the road in silence, bent under their bundles. Spirited Red Army fighters were herding them into lines. The invalid carts of the paralyzed were screeching. Asthmatic whistling and humble wheezing tore from the chests of the retired cantors, wedding jesters, circumcision-feast cooks, and washed-up sales clerks.

The sun stood high in the sky. The heat tore into the hearts of the heaps of rags dragging themselves along the earth. Their journey lay along a joyless, scorched, stony high road, past shacks of straw and clay, fields smothered by rocks, gutted houses mangled by shells, and past the plague mound.[8] This inexpressibly sad Odessan high road led from the town to the cemetery.

Froim Grach[1]

In 1919, Benya Krik's men ambushed the rear guard of the Volunteer Army,[2] slaughtered the officers, and captured part of their supply unit. As a reward, they demanded that the Odessa soviet allow them three days of "peaceful insurrection," but as they were not given permission, they looted all the stores lining the Alexandrovsky Boulevard. Then they

7. Mikhail Moiseyevich Mayorov (born Meyer Biberman, 1890–1938), like Broydin also originally a tailor by profession, became the director of the Communal Economics Department in July 1920.
8. A huge sepulchral mound in which victims of the 1812 plague were buried.
1. Babel wrote this story in 1933 or earlier and gave it, along with three other stories, to Gorky, who headed the editorial committee of the almanac *God XVI*, celebrating the sixteenth year of Soviet power. The committee rejected Babel's submission, and the story was not published until 1963, in the New York miscellany *Vozdushnye puti 3*. —Ed.
2. The anti-Bolshevik White forces (1918–21), which began as an officer volunteer army. —Ed.

set their sights on the Mutual Credit Society. They let all the customers enter first, and then requested that the porters carry all the bags of money and valuables outside to a car parked nearby. Within a month Benya Krik's men were being lined up and shot. There were people who said that Aron Peskin, a workshop owner, had had a hand in their capture and arrest. What kind of workshop it was, nobody knew. There was a machine in it—a long device with a warped lead roller—and on the floor, surrounded by sawdust, lay pasteboards for binding books.

One spring morning Misha Yablochko, one of Peskin's friends, knocked on the door of his workshop.

"The weather's great outside," Misha said to him. "You see before you a man who is about to grab a bottle of vodka along with some food and go for a ride to Arkadia.[3] Don't laugh—sometimes I love to just walk away from it all!"

Peskin put on his jacket and set out with Misha Yablochko in his buggy to Arkadia. They rode about until evening. At dusk, Misha Yablochko entered the room in which Madame Peskin was bathing her fourteen-year-old daughter in a tub.

"Greetings," Misha said, lifting his hat. "We had such a nice time. The air there—simply out of this world! Though talking to your husband is like pulling teeth. What a tiresome man he is!"

"You can say that again!" Madame Peskin said, grabbing her daughter by the hair and yanking her head every which way. "Where is he, that vagabond?"

"He's unwinding outside in the garden."

Misha lifted his hat again, excused himself, and left in his buggy. Madame Peskin went straight outside. Her husband was sitting there in a Panama hat, leaning against the garden table with a grin on his face.

"You vagabond!" Madame Peskin said to him. "How dare you just sit there laughing, while that daughter of yours is driving me to an early grave! She won't wash her hair! I want you to go inside right now and have a word with her!"

Peskin sat there silently, still grinning.

"You fool!" Madame Peskin said. She peered under her husband's Panama hat and started screaming.

The neighbors came running.

"He's not alive," she told them. "He's dead!"

That wasn't true. Peskin had been shot twice in the chest and his skull was broken, but he was still alive. They took him to the Jewish hospital. Doctor Silberberg in person operated on the wounded man, but Peskin was out of luck. He died under the knife. That same night the Cheka[4] arrested a man nicknamed The Georgian, and his friend Kolya Lapidus. One of them was Misha Yablochko's coachman, the other had lain in wait for the buggy in Arkadia by the bend in the road that leads from the seashore out into the steppes. The two arrested men were shot after a brief interrogation. But Misha Yablochko managed to slip the net. He disappeared from sight, and a few days later an old woman selling sunflower seeds came hobbling into Froim Grach's yard. She was carrying a basket of seeds on

3. A resort area outside Odessa by the sea.
4. See note 1, p. 52.

her arm. One of her eyebrows was arched in a furry, coal-black line above her eye, the other, barely visible, lay sagging on her eyelid. Froim Grach was sitting near the stable with his legs apart, playing with Arkadi, his grandson. The boy had come tumbling out of his daughter Basya's powerful womb three years ago. Froim held out his finger to Arkadi, who grabbed it and began to swing from it as if it were a crossbeam.

"You little scoundrel, you!" Froim said to his grandson, peering at him with his single eye.

The old woman came up to him with her furry eyebrow and her men's boots tied with string.

"Froim," she said. "I tell you these people have not a drop of soul in them. They don't say a word, they just kill us in their cellars like dogs. And they don't give us a chance to open our mouths before we die. We should tear these men to pieces with our teeth, and rip out their hearts! Why are you silent?" the old woman—Misha Yablochko—asked Froim. "Our men are waiting for you to break your silence!"

Misha got up, moved the basket to his other arm, and left, lifting his black eyebrow. He ran into three girls with braided hair walking with their arms around each other's waists outside the church on Alekseyevskaya Square.

"Hello girls," Misha Yablochko said to them. "Sorry I can't invite you for tea and cake."

He scooped up some sunflower seeds with a little glass mug, poured them into the pockets of their dresses, and walked off, disappearing around the church.

Froim Grach remained alone in his yard. He sat motionless, his single eye staring into the distance. Mules captured from imperialist troops were munching hay in the stables, and fattened mares were grazing with their foals on the meadow. Carters were playing cards in the shade of the chestnut trees and drinking wine from broken cups. Hot gusts of air swept over the whitewashed walls, and the sun in its blue rigidity poured over the yard. Froim got up and went out into the street. He crossed Prokhorovskaya Street, which was blackening the sky with the destitute, melting smoke of its kitchens, and Tolkuchy market, where people laden with curtains and drapes were trying to sell them to each other. He walked up Ekaterininskaya Street, made a turn by the statue of the Empress, and went inside the building of the Cheka.

"I am Froim," he told the commandant. "I want to see the boss."

The chairman of the Cheka back then was Vladislav Simen, who had come from Moscow. When he heard that Froim was there to see him, he called in Borovoi, one of his investigators, and asked for information on him.

"A first-rate fellow!" Borovoi told him. "Odessa begins and ends with him!"

And old Froim, in his canvas overalls, red-haired and big as a house, a patch over one eye and his cheek disfigured, was led into the office by the commandant.

"You know who you're killing off, boss?" he said as he walked into the room. "You're killing off all the lions! And you know what you'll be left with if you keep it up? You'll be left with shit!"

Simen leaned forward and opened his desk drawer.

"Don't worry, I'm clean," Froim told him. "Nothing in my hands, nothing in my boots—and I didn't leave nobody waiting outside neither. Let my boys go, boss! Just name your price!"

Simen had the old man sit down in an armchair, and offered him some cognac. Borovoi left the room and called together all the investigators who had come from Moscow.

Borovoi told them how it was one-eyed Froim and not Benya Krik who was the real boss of the forty thousand Odessa thugs. Froim might never show his hand, but he was the brains behind everything—the looting of the factories and the Odessa Treasury, and the ambushing of both the anti-Bolshevik army and its allies. Borovoi waited for Froim to come out of Simen's office so he could have a word with him. But Froim did not appear. Tired of waiting, Borovoi went to look for him. He searched through the whole building until he finally looked out into the backyard. Froim Grach was lying there stretched out under a tarpaulin by a wall covered in ivy. Two Red Army men stood by his body, smoking.

"Strong as an ox," the older of the two said when he saw Borovoi. "Strength like you wouldn't believe! If you don't butcher an old man like that, he'll live forever. He had ten bullets in him and he was still going strong!"

The Red Army man's face reddened, his eyes sparkled, and his cap slipped to the side.

"You're shooting your mouth off!" the second soldier cut in. "He died just like they all do!"

"No, not like they all do!" the older soldier shouted. "Some holler and beg, some don't say a word! So what do you mean, 'like they all do'?"

"To me they're all the same," the younger Red Army man repeated obstinately. "They all look the same, I can't even tell them apart!"

Borovoi bent down and pulled back the tarpaulin. The old man's face was frozen in a grimace.

Borovoi went back to his office. It was a round chamber with walls covered in satin. A meeting was under way about new rules for prosecuting cases. Simen was reprimanding the staff on the irregularities he had come upon, about the haphazard way verdicts were written up, and the absurd method with which protocols of the investigations were drawn up. The investigators were to split into groups and work with legal experts, so that from now on matters would be conducted according to the codes and statutes instituted by the Cheka headquarters in Moscow.

Borovoi sat in his corner, listening. He sat alone, far away from the rest. Simen came up to him after the meeting and took him by the hand.

"I know you're angry at me, Sasha," Simen said to him, "but you mustn't forget that now we are the power, the state power! You must remember that!"

"I'm not angry at you," Borovoi said, turning away. "It's just that you're not an Odessan, you can't understand what the old man represented."

They sat side by side, the chairman of the Cheka, who had just turned twenty-three, and his subordinate. Simen was holding Borovoi's hand in his and pressing it.

"Tell me one thing as a Chekist, as a revolutionary," Simen said to him after a moment of silence. "What use would that man have been to the society we are building?"

"I don't know," Borovoi said, staring motionlessly in front of him. "I suppose no use at all."

He pulled himself together and chased away his memories. Then, livening up, he continued telling the Chekists who had come from Moscow about the life of Froim Grach, about his ingenuity, his elusiveness, his contempt for his fellow men, all the amazing tales that were now a thing of the past.

Collectivization and the
Five-Year Plan

The adoption of the First Five-Year Plan in 1928–29—the collectivization of agriculture and crash industrialization—was known in Soviet history books as the Great Break and in the West as the Stalin Revolution. Both terms convey the scale of suffering, dislocation, and regeneration that would soon make the country unrecognizable. Writers were mobilized, along with everyone else, to participate in "socialist construction." Babel traveled to industrial sites and visited rural areas where peasants were forced to relinquish their property and join the collective farms. Millions perished from starvation and deportations. As Babel once confided to a friend, what he saw in Ukrainian villages was more horrifying than anything he had encountered during the civil war. He retained from his trips to rural Ukraine "the sharpest memory of all my life." Experienced in describing brutality and violence, the author of *Red Cavalry* set out to write *The Great Krinitsa*, a book of stories about a village in the throes of collectivization. Only two stories from this cycle have survived. We know that there was at least one other, "Ivan Marinets," but Babel must have felt discouraged from finishing the cycle. Stalin did not like "Gapa Guzhva" (see his letter to Kaganovich on p. 434), and there was little chance that the rest would ever be published. As to industrialization, "Petroleum" is the sole story Babel seems to have devoted to the subject. —*Ed.*

Gapa Guzhva[1]

Six weddings were held in Velikaya Krinitsa on Shrovetide in 1930. They were celebrated with a wild abandon, the likes of which had not been seen for a long time. Old customs were reborn. The father of one of the bridegrooms got drunk and demanded that he be allowed to try out the bride, a custom that had been discontinued some twenty years back. The father-in-law had already taken off his sash and thrown it to the ground. The bride, shaking with laughter, was tugging at the old man's beard. He puffed out his chest closer and closer to her, guffawed, and stamped his boots. And yet there was not much for the old man to be worried about. Of the six sheets that were hung up over the huts after the wedding night, only two were stained with virginal blood. As for the other brides, they had gone on late-night walks and come back soiled.

---

1. First published in *Novy mir* 10 (1931), subtitled "The First Chapter from the Book *Velikaya Krinitsa*." The prototype for the village was Velikaya Staritsa of the Borispol district outside Kiev. — Ed.

One of the sheets was grabbed by a Red Army soldier who was home on leave, and Gapa Guzhva climbed up for the other one. She jumped onto the roof, kicking away the men behind her, and clambered up the pole, which bent and swayed under her weight. She tore down the reddened rag and came sliding down the pole. A table and a stool stood on the gable of the roof, and on the table was a half liter bottle of vodka and slices of cold meat. Gapa tipped the bottle into her mouth, and with her free hand waved the sheet. The crowd down below roared and danced. The stool slid out from under her, shook, and fell apart. Berezan herdsmen, driving their oxen to Kiev, stared at the woman drinking vodka on the roof under the sky.

"She's no woman, that one!" the villagers told them. "Our widow's the devil, she is!"

Gapa threw bread, twigs, and plates from the roof. She finished the vodka and smashed the bottle against the chimney ledge. The muzhiks who had gathered below roared. The widow jumped off the roof, untied her shaggy-bellied mare who stood dozing by the wooden fence, and rode off to get some wine. She came back weighed down with flasks, as a Circassian tribesman is weighed down with ammunition. Her horse was panting heavily and tossing its muzzle. Its belly, heavy with foal, surged and bulged, and equine madness quivered in its eyes.

At the weddings, the villagers danced holding handkerchiefs, with lowered eyes, their boots shuffling in one spot. Only Gapa whirled around, as they do in the towns. She danced with Grishka Savchenko, her lover. They held each other as if they were wrestling. They tugged at each other's shoulders with headstrong anger. They drummed the ground with their boots, and tumbled down as if they had been knocked off their feet.

The third day of the wedding feasts began. The couples' best men wore their sheepskin coats inside out and ran smeared with soot through the village, banging on oven doors. Bonfires were lit in the streets. People jumped through them, horns painted on their foreheads. Horses were harnessed to troughs that were dragged hurtling through the flames over clods of grass. Men fell to the ground, overpowered by sleep. Housewives threw broken pots and pans into their yards. The newlyweds washed their feet and climbed into tall beds, and only Gapa was still dancing alone in an empty shed. She whirled in circles, holding a tarred boat pole in her hand, her hair untied. She pounded the pole against the walls, leaving sticky black wounds, the thuds jolting the shed.

"We bring fire and death," Gapa whispered, waving the pole over her head.

Planks and straw rained down on her as the walls caved in.

She danced with loose hair among the ruins, in the din and dust of the crumbling wattle and the flying splinters of the breaking planks. Her delicate red-rimmed boots whirled through the rubble, drumming the ground.

Night fell. The bonfires were dying out in the thawing snow pits. The shed lay in a tangled heap on the hill. A light began to flicker in the village council hut across the street. Gapa threw away her pole and ran over to the hut.

"Ivashko!" she yelled, as she rushed into the room. "Come have some fun with us, let's drink our life away!"

Ivashko was the representative of the Regional Commission for Collectivization. For two months now he had been trying to talk the villagers into collectivizing. He was sitting in front of a pile of crumpled, tattered papers, his hands resting on the table. The skin on either side of his forehead was wrinkled, and in his eyes hung the pupils of an ailing cat. Above them bulged the arches of his bare pink eye sockets.

"Are you sneering at our peasants?" Gapa yelled, stamping her foot.

"I'm not sneering," Ivashko said gloomily. "But it would be inappropriate for me to join you all."

Gapa danced past him, tapping her feet and waving her arms.

"Come break bread with us," she said to him. "And then tomorrow we'll do exactly as you say, Comrade Representist! We will tomorrow, not today!"

Ivashko shook his head.

"It would be inappropriate for me to break bread with you," he said. "You people aren't human—you bark like dogs! I've lost fifteen pounds since I came here!"

He chewed his lip and closed his eyes. He stretched out his hand, groped for his canvas bag, got up, staggered forward, and made his way toward the door with dragging feet, as if he were walking in his sleep.

"Comrade Ivashko is pure gold," Kharchenko, the council secretary, said after he had left. "He's a kind fellow, but our village has been too rough on him."

An ash-blond forelock[2] hung over Kharchenko's button nose and pimples. He was reading a newspaper, his feet resting on the bench.

"Just wait till the judge from Voronkov[3] comes over," Kharchenko said, turning a page of his newspaper. "Then you'll all sit up straight."

Gapa slipped a bag of sunflower seeds out of her cleavage.

"How come all you think about's your duties, Comrade Secretary?" she asked. "Why are you afraid of death? Who ever heard of a muzhik turning away from death?"

Outside, a swollen black sky was seething around the village belfry, and wet huts crouched and slithered away. The stars struggled to ignite above them, and the wind crept along the ground.

Gapa heard the dull murmur of an unfamiliar, husky voice in the front room of her hut. A woman pilgrim had come to spend the night and was sitting on the bench above the stove with her legs pulled in under her. The icon lamp's crimson threads of flame threw a net on the wall. A stillness hung over the clean hut. An odor of apple liquor seeped from the walls and partitions. Gapa's fat-lipped daughters, craning their necks, were staring at the beggar woman. Short horsy hair covered their heads, and their lips were large and puffed out. A dead, greasy sheen lay on their narrow foreheads.

"Keep up your lies, Grandma Rakhivna," Gapa said, leaning against the wall. "I love it when you tell your lies."

---

2. It was a custom among Ukrainian villagers to shave their heads except for a forelock.
3. A town southeast of Kiev.

Rakhivna sat on the bench above the stove with her head against the low ceiling, plaiting her hair into braids, which she then coiled in rows over her little head. Her washed, misshapen feet rested on the edge of the stove.

"There's three patriarchs in this world," the old woman said, lowering her wrinkled face. "Our government has imprisoned the Patriarch of Moscow, the Jerusalem Patriarch is living among Turks. It is the Antioch Patriarch who now rules all of Christianity. He sent forty Greek priests onto Ukrainian soil to curse the churches from which our government took down the bells. The Greek priests passed Kholodny Yar, they've already been seen at Ostrogradsk, and come next Sunday they'll be here in Velikaya Krinitsa!"

Rakhivna closed her eyes and fell silent. The light of the icon lamps flickered over the hollows of her feet.

"The judge from Voronkov," the old woman suddenly said. "He collectivized the whole of Voronkov in a single day! He stuck nine squires in a cold cell, and on the following day they were to march in the chain gangs to Sakhalin. I tell you, daughter, there's people everywhere, Christ is gloried everywhere! The squires were kept in a cold cell all night—then in come the guards to take them, the guards open the dungeon door, and what do their eyes behold in the full light of the morning? Nine squires dangling from the rafters on their belts!"

Before she lay down, Rakhivna fussed about for a long time, sorting through her rags, whispering to her God as she would have whispered to her old man lying next to her. Then her breathing suddenly became light. Grishka Savchenko, the husband of one of the village women, was lying on a bench by the wall. He lay curled up, right on the edge as if he had been crushed, his back twisted, his vest bunched up over it, and his head sunk in pillows.

"A man's love," Gapa said, prodding and shaking him. "I know all there is to know about a man's love. They turn their snouts away from their wives and shuffle off, like this one here! *He* didn't go home to his wife Odarka, no, he didn't!"

Half the night they rolled on the bench in the darkness, their lips tightly clenched, their arms stretching out in the darkness. Gapa's braid went flying over the pillow. At dawn Grishka started up, moaned, and fell asleep with a snarl on his lips. Gapa gazed at her daughters' brown shoulders, low foreheads, thick lips, and dark breasts.

"What camels!" she said to herself. "How could they have come from me?"

Darkness receded from the oak-framed window. Dawn opened a violet streak in the clouds. Gapa went out into the yard. The wind enveloped her like cold river water. She harnessed her sledge and loaded it with sacks of wheat—during the wedding celebrations everyone had run out of flour. The road slithered through the fog and mist of dawn.

It snowed all day. At the mill they couldn't start grinding till the following evening. At the edge of the village, short-legged Yushko Trofim, wearing a soaked cap, came out from inside a sheet of snow to meet Gapa. His shoulders, covered in a sea of flakes, were surging and falling.

"Well, they finally got up," he muttered. He came up to her sledge and raised his bony black face up to her.

"What's that supposed to mean?" Gapa asked him. She pulled at her reins.

"All the big men came to our village last night," Trofim said. "They've already dragged off that old biddy staying with you and arrested her. The head of the Collectivization Commission and the secretary of the District Party Committee. They've nabbed Ivashko and now the Voronkov judge is stepping in."

Trofim walked off, his walrus whiskers bobbing, snowflakes slithering down them. Gapa shook the reins but then tugged at them again.

"Trofim! What did they drag the old biddy off for?"

Trofim stopped and yelled back from far away through the whirling, flying snow.

"They said it was because of her propaganda campaign about the world coming to an end!"

He walked on, limping on one foot, and in an instant his wide back was swallowed up by the sky that melted into the earth.

Gapa rode up to her hut and tapped on the window with her whip. Her daughters were lounging around the table dressed in shawls and shoes as if they were at a feast.

"Mama," the oldest said. "Odarka came over while you were out and took her husband back home."

The daughters set the table and lit the samovar. Gapa ate, and then went to the village council, where she found the elders of Velikaya Krinitsa sitting in silence along the walls. The window, smashed some time back during a debate, was boarded up, the glass of the lamps had worn thin, and a sign saying "No Smoking" had been nailed to the pockmarked walls. The judge from Voronkov, his shoulders hunched, sat at the table reading. He was reading through the record ledger of the village council of Velikaya Krinitsa. He had raised the collar of his shabby little coat. Kharchenko, the council secretary, was sitting next to him, drawing up a formal charge against his own village. On columned sheets of paper he was entering all the crimes, arrears, and fines—all the wounds, visible and invisible. When Judge Osmolovsky from Voronkov had arrived in the village, he had refused to call a general meeting of the citizens, as the representatives before him had done. He did not give speeches, but simply asked for a list of quota dodgers and former merchants, an inventory of their property, crops, and farmsteads.

The elders of Velikaya Krinitsa sat quietly on the benches, while Kharchenko's bustling, whistling pen crackled through the silence. There was a flurry of movement when Gapa came into the room. Evdokim Nazarenko's face lit up when he saw her.

"Here's our number one activist, Comrade Judge!" Evdokim said, guffawing and rubbing his palms together. "Our widow here has been actively ruining all our village youths."

Gapa stopped by the door and narrowed her eyes. A sneer flitted over Judge Osmolovsky's lips, and he crinkled his thin nose.

"Good morning," he said, nodding to her.

"She was the first one to sign up for the collective farm," Evdokim said, trying to chase away the brewing storm with a gush of words. "But then the good people of the village had a chat with her, and she de-signed up."

Gapa didn't move. Her face flushed brick red.

"The good people of the village say that in the collective farm everyone is to sleep under the same blanket!" she said in her sonorous voice. Her eyes twinkled in her fixed face.

"Well, I for one am against sleeping wholesale! We like sleeping in twos, and we like our home-brewed vodka, goddamn it!"

The muzhiks burst out laughing, but immediately fell silent. Gapa peered at the judge. He raised his inflamed eyes and nodded to her. Then he slumped even lower, took his head in his thin, red-haired hands, and once again immersed himself in the record ledger of Velikaya Krinitsa. Gapa turned around, and her stately back flashed out of the room.

In the yard, Grandpa Abram, overgrown with raw flesh, was sitting on some wet planks with his knees pulled up. A yellow mane of hair hung to his shoulders.

"What's wrong?" Gapa asked him.

"I'm sad," the old man said.

Back at home, her daughters were already in bed. Late at night, a little slanting flame, its mercurial tongue flickering, hovered across the road in the hut of Nestor Tyagay, a member of the Young Communist League. Judge Osmolovsky was lodging there. A sheepskin coat had been laid out on a bench, and his supper was waiting for him. A bowl of yogurt, an onion, and a thick slice of bread. The judge took off his spectacles and covered his aching eyes with his palms. He was known throughout the district as Comrade Two-Hundred-and-Sixteen-Percent—that had been the percentage of grain which he had managed to exact from the renegade town of Voronkov. Osmolovsky's percentage had given rise to tales, songs, and folk legends.

He chewed the bread and the onion, and spread out in front of him *Pravda*, the instructions of the District Committee, and the collectivization reports of the People's Commissariat for Agriculture. It was late, after one in the morning, when the door opened and Gapa, her shawl tied across her chest, came in.

"Judge," she said to him, "what's going to happen to the whores?"

Osmolovsky raised his eyes, his face covered in rippled light.

"They will no longer exist."

"Won't the whores be allowed to earn their living?"

"They will," the judge said. "But in a different, better way."

Gapa stared into a corner of the room with unseeing eyes. She fingered the necklace that hung across her chest.

"I'm glad to hear that!"

Her necklace clinked. Gapa left, closing the door behind her.

The piercing, frenzied night hurled itself down on her with thickets of low-hanging clouds—twisted ice floes lit up by black sparks. Silence spread over Velikaya Krinitsa, over the flat, sepulchral, frozen desert of the village night.

Kolyvushka[1]

Four men entered Ivan Kolyvushka's courtyard: Ivashko, the representative of the Regional Commission for Collectivization, Evdokim Nazarenko, the head of the village council, Zhitnyak, the chairman of the newly formed kolkhoz,[2] and Adrian Morinets. Adrian walked like a tower that had uprooted itself and was on the march. Ivashko had hurried past the barns, pressing his canvas briefcase to his side, and came bursting into Kolyvushka's house. Kolyvushka's wife and two daughters were sitting by the window spinning yarn on blackened spindles. They looked like nuns, with their kerchiefs, their long bodices, and their small, clean, bare feet. Photographs of Czarist ensigns, schoolmistresses, and townsfolk at their dachas hung on the walls between embroidered towels and cheap mirrors. Ivan Kolyvushka came into the house after his guests, and took off his hat.

"How much tax does Kolyvushka pay?" Ivashko asked, turning to face the others.

Evdokim, the village council head, watched the whirling wheels of the spindles with his hands in his pockets.

Ivashko snorted when he was told that Kolyvushka paid two hundred and sixteen rubles.

"Surely he can swing more than that!"

"It looks like he can't."

Zhitnyak stretched his dry lips in a thin line. Evdokim continued watching the spindles. Ivan Kolyvushka stood in the doorway and winked at his wife, who went and pulled a receipt out from behind an icon and handed it to Ivashko, the representative of the Collectivization Commission.

"And what about the seed fund?" Ivashko asked abruptly, impatiently digging his foot into the floorboards.

Evdokim raised his eyes and looked around the room.

"This household has already been cleaned out, Comrade Representative," Evdokim said. "This isn't the kind of household that doesn't pay its share."

The whitewashed walls curved up into a low, warm cupola over the guests' heads. The flowers in glass jars, the plain cupboards, the polished benches, all sparkled with an oppressive cleanliness. Ivashko jumped up and hurried out the door, his briefcase swinging.

"Comrade Representative!" Kolyvushka called out, hurrying after him. "So will instructions be sent to me, or what?"

"You'll be notified!" Ivashko shouted, his arms dangling, and rushed off.

Adrian Morinets, inhumanly large, rushed after him. Timish, the cheerful bailiff, bobbed past the gate close at Ivashko's heel, wading with his long legs through the mud of the village street.

---

1. Part of the planned book about the collectivization of agriculture in Ukraine, *Velikaya Krinitsa* (The Great Krinitsa), this story was not published in Babel's lifetime. It first appeared in the New York almanac *Vozdushnye puti* 3 (1963). —Ed.
2. Collective farm.

"What's this all about?" Kolyvushka called out, waving him over and grabbing him by the sleeve. The bailiff, a long cheerful stick, bent forward and opened his mouth, which was packed with a purple tongue and set with rows of pearls.

"They are about to confiscate your house."

"What about me?"

"You'll be sent off for resettlement."

And Timish rushed after Ivashko and the others with cranelike steps.

A horse harnessed to a sledge was standing in Kolyvushka's courtyard, and the red reins had been thrown over some sacks of wheat piled up in the sledge. There was a tree stump with an axe stuck in it in the middle of the yard by a stooping lime tree. Kolyvushka ran his fingers over his hat, pushed it back, and sat down. The mare came over to him, dragging the sledge behind her. She hung out her tongue and then curled it up. She was with foal, and her belly was heavily swollen. She playfully nudged and nuzzled her master's shoulder. Kolyvushka looked down at his feet. The trampled snow lay in ripples around the tree stump. Hunching over, Kolyvushka grabbed the axe, held it up high in the air for an instant, and brought it down on the horse's forehead. One of her ears lunged back, the other fluttered and then slumped down. She moaned and bolted to the side, the sledge toppling over, the wheat flying in curved ribbons over the snow. She reared her forelegs into the air, tossing back her muzzle, and got caught in the spikes of a harrow by the shed. Her eyes peered out from under a streaming curtain of blood. She sang out in lament. The foal turned within her. A vein puffed up on her belly.

"Forgive me!" Ivan said, stretching out his hand to her. "Forgive me, my one and only!"

He held out his palm to her. The mare's ear hung limply, her eyes rolled, rings of blood sparked around them, her muzzle lay in a straight line with her neck. She curled back her upper lip in despair. She stretched out her neck and scuttled forward, pulling the jumping harrow behind her. Ivan raised the axe over his head. The blow hit her between the eyes, her foal again turned inside her tumbling belly. Ivan walked across the yard to the shed and dragged out the winnowing fan. He swung the axe down with wide, slow blows, smashing the machine, dragging the axe into the drum and the delicate grid of the wheels. His wife came out onto the stoop in her long bodice.

"Mother!" Kolyvushka heard her faraway voice. "Mother! He's smashing everything up!"

The door opened. Out of the house came an old woman in canvas trousers, steadying herself on a stick. Yellow hair hung over the hollows of her cheeks, and her shirt clung to her thin body like a shroud. The old woman stepped into the snow with her shaggy stockings.

"Murderer!" she said to her son, grabbing the axe out of his hand. "Do you remember your father? Do you remember your brothers in the labor camps?"

The neighbors began to gather in the yard. The muzhiks stood in a semicircle and looked away. A woman lunged forward and began to shriek.

"Shut up, you foolish cow!" her husband told her.

Kolyvushka stood leaning against the wall. His rasping breath echoed through the courtyard. It was as if he were working strenuously, panting heavily.

Kolyvushka's Uncle Terenti was shuffling about the gate, trying to lock it.

"I am a man!" Kolyvushka suddenly said to the people around him. "I am a man, a villager like you! Have you never seen a man before?"

Terenti hustled the villagers out of the yard. The gates creaked and fell shut. They swung open again in the evening, and a sledge piled high with possessions came sweeping out of the yard, the women perched on bales like frozen birds. A cow, tethered by her horn, came trotting behind. The sledge passed the outskirts of the village and disappeared into the flat, snowy desert. The wind spiraled in this desert, pummeling and moaning, scattering its blue waves behind which stretched the metallic sky, through which a mesh of diamonds wound sparkling.

Kolyvushka walked down the street to the village council, his eyes fixed straight ahead. A meeting of the new kolkhoz named "Renaissance" was under way. Hunchbacked Zhitnyak sat slouching behind the desk.

"The great change in our lives—what's this great change all about?" he said.

The hunchback's hands pressed against his torso, and then went flying up.

"Fellow villagers! We are redirecting ourselves into dairy production and market gardening! This is of momentous importance! Our fathers and grandfathers trudged over great treasures with their boots, and the time has now come for us to dig these treasures up! Is it not a disgrace, is it not an outrage that though we are only some sixty versts from our regional capital, we haven't developed our farming according to scientific methods? Our eyes were closed, my fellow villagers, we've been running away from ourselves! What does sixty versts mean? Does anyone here know? In our country that is equal to an hour—but even that one hour belongs to us! It is worth its weight in gold!"

The door of the village council opened. Kolyvushka came in and walked over to the wall in his voluminous fur jacket and tall sheepskin hat. Ivashko's fingers jumped and went scuttling into the pile of papers in front of him.

"I must ask all individuals without a voting right to immediately leave this meeting," he said, looking down at the papers.

Outside the window, beyond the dirty glass, the sunset was spilling out in green emerald streams. In the twilight of the village hut, sparks glittered faintly in the raw clouds of rough tobacco. Ivan Kolyvushka took off his hat, and his mop of black hair came pouring forth.

He walked up to the table around which the committee was sitting: Ivga Movchan, a woman who worked as a farmhand, Evdokim, the head of the village council, and silent Adrian Morinets.

"My people!" Ivan Kolyvushka said, stretching out his hand and laying a bunch of keys on the table. "My people, I am cutting all ties with you!"

The iron keys clanked and lay on the blackened boards. Adrian's haggard face appeared from within the darkness.

"Where will you go, Ivan?"

"My people won't have me, maybe the earth will!"

Kolyvushka walked out quietly, his head lowered.

"It's a trick!" Ivashko yelled the moment the door fell shut. "It's a provocation! He's gone to get his rifle, that's what! He's gone to get his rifle!"

Ivashko banged his fist on the table. Words about panic and the need to keep calm tried to struggle through his lips.

Adrian's face again retreated into its dark corner. "No, Comrade Chairman," he said from within the darkness. "I don't think he went to get his rifle."

"I have a proposal to make!" Ivashko shouted.

The proposal was that a guard be set up outside Kolyvushka's place. Timish the bailiff was voted to be the guard. Grimacing, he took a bentwood chair out onto the stoop, slumped down on it, and laid his shotgun and his truncheon by his feet. From the heights of the stoop, from the heights of his village throne, Timish bantered with the girls, whistled, shouted, and thumped his shotgun on the ground. The night was lilac and heavy, like a bright mountain crystal. Veins of frozen rivulets lay across it. A star sank into a well of black clouds.

The following morning Timish reported that there had been no incidents. Kolyvushka had spent the night at Grandpa Abram's, an old man overgrown with raw flesh.

In the evening Abram had hobbled off to the well.

"Why go there, Grandpa Abram?" Kolyvushka asked.

"I'm going to put on a samovar," Grandpa said.

They slept late. Smoke rose above the hut. Their door remained shut.

"He's run for it!" Ivashko said at the kolkhoz meeting. "Are we going to cry tears over him? What d'you think, villagers?"

Zhitnyak sat at the table, his sharp, quivering elbows spread wide, entering the particulars of the confiscated horses. The hump on his back cast a moving shadow.

"How much more are we going to stuff down our throats?" Zhitnyak pronounced philosophically as he wrote. "Now we suddenly need everything in the world! We need crop sprinklers, we need plows, tractors, pumps! Gluttony, that's what this is! Our whole country has been seized by gluttony!"

The horses that Zhitnyak entered in the book were all bay or skewbald, with names like "Boy" and "Little Miss." Zhitnyak had the owners sign against their surnames.

He was interrupted by a noise, a faraway, muffled clatter of hooves. A tidal wave was rolling toward Velikaya Staritsa[3] and came crashing over it. A crowd poured over the ravished street, legless cripples hobbling in front. An invisible banner was fluttering above their heads. They slowed as they arrived at the village council and drew into formation. A circle opened in their midst, a circle of ruffled-up snow, a gap as for a priest during a church procession. Kolyvushka was standing in the circle, his shirt hanging loose beneath his vest, his head completely white. The night had silvered his gypsy locks, not a black hair was left. Flakes of snow, weak birds carried by the wind, drifted across the warming sky. An old man with broken legs jostled his way forward and peered avidly at Kolyvushka's white hair.

3. Apparently the surviving copy of "Kolyvushka" predated Babel's decision to present the actual Velikaya Staritsa as a fictional Velikaya Krinitsa. —Ed.

"Tell us, Ivan," the old man said, raising his arms. "Tell us what is in your soul!"

"Where will you chase me to, my fellow villagers?" Kolyvushka whispered, looking around. "Where shall I go? I was born here among you."

The crowd began to rumble. Morinets elbowed his way to the front.

"Let him be," he said in a low, trembling voice, the cry trapped in his powerful chest. "Let him be! Whose share will he grab?"

"Mine!" Zhitnyak said, and burst out laughing. He walked up to Kolyvushka, shuffling his feet, and winked at him.

"I slept with a woman last night!" the hunchback said. "When we got up she made pancakes, and me and her, we gobbled them down like we was hogs—ha, we blew more farts than you could shake a stick at—"

The hunchback stopped in midsentence, his guffaws broke off, and the blood drained from his face.

"So you've come to line us up against the wall?" he asked in a lower voice. "You've come to bully us with that white head of yours, to turn the thumbscrews on us? But we won't let you, the time for thumbscrews has passed!"

The hunchback came nearer on his thin, bowed legs. Something whistled inside him like a bird.

"You should be killed," he whispered, an idea flitting through his mind. "I'll go get my gun and finish you off."

His face brightened. He gave Kolyvushka's hand a spirited tap and hurried off into the house to get Timish's gun. Kolyvushka wavered for a moment, and then walked off. His silver head disappeared in the tangled mesh of houses. He stumbled as he walked, but then his strides grew firmer. He took the road to Ksenevka.

No one ever saw him again in Velikaya Staritsa.

Petroleum[1]

I have a lot of news to tell you, as always. Sabsovich was given a prize at the oil refinery, walks about decked out in flashy "foreign" clothes, and has been given a promotion. When people heard about this promotion, they finally saw the light: the boy is moving up the ladder. This is the reason I stopped going out with him. "Now that he has moved up the ladder," the boy feels that he knows the truth hidden from us lesser mortals and has turned into "Comrade Perfect," so orthodox ("orthobox," as Kharchenko calls it) that you can't even talk to him anymore. When we ran into each other two days ago, he asked me why I hadn't congratulated him. I asked him whom I should congratulate, him or the Soviet government. He understood my point right away, hemmed and hawed, and said, "Well, call me sometime." But his wife was quick to pick up the scent. Yesterday I got a call. "Claudia, darling, if you need any underwear, we now have great connections at the Restricted Access Store." I told her that I was hoping to get by with my own underwear ration coupons till the outbreak of the World Revolution.

---

1. First published in the Moscow newspaper *Vechernyaya Moskva*, February 14, 1934. —*Ed.*

Now a few words about myself. You'll have heard by now that I am the section head at the Petroleum Syndicate. They dangled the position before me for the longest time, but I kept turning them down. My argument: no aptitude for office work, and then I also wanted to enroll at the Industrial Academy. Four times at Bureau Meetings they asked me to accept the position, so finally I had to accept. And I must say I don't regret it. From where I am I have a clear picture of the whole enterprise, and I've managed to get a thing or two done. I organized an expedition to our part of Sakhalin, stepped up the prospecting, and I deal a lot with the Petroleum Institute. Zinaida is with me. She's well. She'll be giving birth soon, and has been through quite a lot. She didn't tell her Max Alexandrovich (I call him Max-and-Moritz)[2] about the pregnancy until she was already in her third month. He put on a show of enthusiasm, planted an icy kiss on her forehead, and then gave her to understand that he was on the brink of a great scientific discovery, that his thoughts were far from everyday life, and that one could not imagine anyone less suited to family life than he, Max Alexandrovich Solomovich, but, needless to say, he wouldn't hesitate to sacrifice everything, etc., etc. Zinaida, being a woman of the twentieth century, burst into tears but kept her aplomb. She didn't sleep all night, gasping, her head thrashing about. The moment it was light, she put on a tattered old dress and rushed off to the Research Institute, looking dreadful, her hair in tangles. There she made a scene, begging him to forget what had happened the previous night, saying that she would destroy the child, but that she would never forgive the world—all this in the halls of the Research Institute, teeming with people! Max-and-Moritz goes bright red, then pale. "Let's discuss it on the phone, we'll get together for a chat," he mutters.

Zinaida didn't even let him finish, but rushed out and came running to me. "I'm not coming to work tomorrow!" she told me.

I blew up, and, seeing no reason to control myself, bawled her out. Just think—she's over thirty, has no looks worth mentioning, no man worth his salt would even wipe his nose with her, and then this Max-and-Moritz fellow turns up (not that he's hot for her, he's hot for the fact that she's not Jewish and has aristocratic ancestors), she gets herself knocked up, so she might as well keep the baby and raise it. As we all know, Jewish half-castes come out quite well—just look at the specimen Ala produced. And when if not now does she intend to have a child, now when her gut muscles are still working and her breasts can still make milk? But she has only one answer to whatever I say: "I cannot bear the idea of my child growing up without a father." She tells me it's still like in the nineteenth century, "and my papa, the general, will come stalking out of his study carrying an icon and lay a curse on me (or maybe without an icon—I don't know how they used to curse back then), after which the women will take the baby to a foundling home or send it to a wet nurse in the countryside."

"Nonsense, Zinaida!" I tell her. "Times have changed, we'll make do without Max-and-Moritz!"

---

2. Two boys who terrorize the neighborhood with their funny practical jokes in the story in verse, *Max and Moritz*, by the German humorist Wilhelm Busch.

I was still in midsentence when I was called to a meeting. At that time the matter of Viktor Andreyevich had to be dealt with immediately. The Central Committee had decided to revoke the former Five-Year Plan and raise petroleum extraction in 1932 to forty million tons. The figures for analysis were handed to the planners, in other words to Viktor Andreyevich. He locks himself in his office, then calls me over and shows me his letter. Addressed to the Presidium of the Supreme National Economic Council. Contents: I hereby renounce all responsibility for the planning department. I consider the figure of forty million tons to be wholly unjustified. We're supposed to get more than a third of it from unprospected regions, which is like selling a bearskin not only before you've actually killed the bear, but even before you've tracked it down! Furthermore, from three oil refineries functioning today the new plan expects us to have a hundred and twenty up and running by the end of the Five-Year Plan. And all this with a shortage of metal and the fact that we have not yet mastered the extremely complex refinery system. And this is how he ended the letter: Like all mortals, I prefer to support accelerated production quotas, but my sense of duty, and so on and so forth. I read his letter to the end.

So then he asks me: "Should I send it, or not?"

And I tell him: "Viktor Andreyevich! I find your arguments and attitude completely unacceptable, but I do not see myself as having the right to advise you to hide your views."

So he sent the letter. The Supreme National Economic Council's hair stood on end. They called a meeting. Bagrinovsky himself came from the council. They hung a map of the Soviet Union on the wall, pinpointing new deposits and pipelines for crude and refined oil. "A country with fresh blood in its veins," Bagrinovsky called it.

At the meeting the young engineers of the "omnivore" type wanted to make a meal of Viktor Andreyevich. I stepped forward and gave a forty-five-minute speech: "Though I do not doubt the knowledge and good will of Professor Klossovsky, and even have the utmost respect for him, I spurn the fetishism of numbers that is holding him captive!" That was the gist of my argument.

"We must reject our multiplication tables as guidelines for governmental wisdom. Would it have been possible to foretell on the basis of mere figures that we were going to manage to fulfill our five-year crude-oil quarrying quota within just two and a half years? Would it have been possible to foretell on the basis of mere figures that by 1931 we would have increased the bulk of our oil export by nine times, putting us in second place after the United States?"

Muradyan got up and spoke after me, attacking the route of the oil pipeline from the Caspian Sea to Moscow. Viktor Andreyevich sat in silence, taking notes. His cheeks were covered with an old man's flush, a flush of venous blood. I felt sorry for him. I didn't stay to the end and went back to my office. Zinaida was still sitting there with clasped hands.

"Are you going to give birth or not?" I asked her.

She looked at me with unseeing eyes, her head shaking, and said something, but the words were soundless.

"I'm all alone with my sorrow, Claudia, as if they've just nailed my coffin shut," she tells me. "How quickly one forgets—I can't even remember how people live without sorrow."

That's what she said to me, her nose turning red and growing even longer, her peasant cheekbones (yes, some aristocrats do have them!) jutting out. I doubt Max-and-Moritz would get all fired up seeing you like that, I think to myself. I started yelling at her, and chased her off to the kitchen to peel potatoes. Don't laugh—when *you* come here, I'll have you peeling potatoes too! We were given such a stringent time frame for designing the Orsky factory that the construction crew and the draftsmen are working night and day, and Vasyona cooks them potatoes and herring and makes them omelets, and off they go to work again.

So off she went to the kitchen, and a minute later I heard a scream. I run—Zinaida is lying on the floor without a pulse, her eyes rolled up. I cannot even begin to tell you what she put us through—Viktor Andreyevich, Vasyona, and me! We called in the doctor. She regained consciousness at night and touched my hand. You know Zinaida, how incredibly tender she can be. I could see that everything inside her had burned out and something new was about to well up. There was no time to lose.

"Zinusha," I tell her, "we'll call Rosa Mikhailovna (she's still our main specialist in these matters) and tell her that you've had second thoughts, that you won't go and see her. Can I call her?"

She made a sign—yes go ahead, you can. Viktor Andreyevich was sitting next to her on the sofa, taking her pulse incessantly. I walked away, but listened to what he said to her. "I'm sixty-five, Zinusha," he told her, "my shadow falls more and more weakly on the ground before me. I am an elderly, learned man, and God (God does have His hand in everything), God willed that the final five years of my life are to coincide with this—well, you know what I mean—this Five-Year Plan. So now I won't get a chance to have a breather or a quiet moment till the day I die. If my daughter didn't come to me in the evenings to pat me on the back, if my sons didn't write me letters, I would be unhappier than words could say. Have the baby, Zinusha, and Claudia Pavlovna and I will help raise it."

While the old man goes on mumbling, I call Rosa Mikhailovna—well, my dear Rosa Mikhailovna, I tell her, I know Zinaida promised to come see you tomorrow, but she's reconsidered. And I hear Rosa's sprightly voice on the phone: "Oh, I'm so happy she's reconsidered! That's absolutely marvelous!" Our specialist is always like this. Pink silk blouse, English skirt, hair neatly curled, showers, exercise, admirers.

We took Zinaida home. I tucked her in bed, made tea. We slept in each other's arms, we even cried, remembered things best forgotten, talked everything through, our tears mingling, until we fell asleep. All the while my "old devil" was sitting nice and quiet at his desk translating a German technical book. Dasha, you wouldn't recognize my "old devil"—he's all shriveled up, has run out of steam and become quiet. It really upsets me. He spends the whole day working himself to death on the Five-Year Plan, and then at night he does translations.

"Zinaida will have the baby," I tell him. "What shall we call the boy?" (It's definitely not going to be a girl.) We decided on Ivan. There are far too many Yuris and Leonids about the place. He'll most probably be a beast of a little boy, with sharp teeth, with teeth enough for sixty men.

We've produced enough fuel for him, he'll be able to go on drives with young ladies to Yalta, to Batumi, while we've had to make do with the Vorobyovi Hills.[3] Good-bye, Dasha. My "old devil" will write you separately. How are things with you?

CLAUDIA.

P.S. I'm scribbling this at work, there's a great racket overhead, the plaster is falling from the ceiling. Our building still seems strong enough, and we're adding another four stories to the four that we have. Moscow is all dug up and full of trenches, pipes and bricks everywhere, a tangle of tram lines, machines imported from abroad are banging, rumbling, swinging their cranes, there's the stench of pitch, and there's smoke everywhere, like at a wildfire. Yesterday on Varvarskaya Square[4] I saw a young man with sandals on his bare feet, his red, shaven head shining and his peasant shirt without a belt. He and I went hopping from one little mound to another, from one earth pile to another, climbing out of holes, falling back into them again.

"This is what it's like once a battle has begun," he tells me. "Moscow has now become the front, lady, Moscow is at the heart of the battle!"

He had a kind face, smiling like a child. I can still picture him before me.

---

3. The hilly district on the western edge of Moscow overlooking the city. —Ed.
4. One of the oldest neighborhoods in Moscow, not far from the Kremlin and the Moscow River and close to Babel's house. —Ed.

Paris

Babel and his wife, Evgeniya, loved Paris and planned to live there as early as 1924, but circumstances changed when, as a newly famous writer, he became involved with Tamara Kashirina. In November 1925, Evgeniya settled in Paris for good. Babel joined her in the fall of 1927, but returned to Russia in October 1928, in debt and anxious to resume his career as a Soviet writer. Eight months later, their daughter Nathalie was born. Now Babel had a family in Paris. It took him months to obtain permission to leave Russia, which he did thanks to intervention by Maxim Gorky. This time, he spent almost a year abroad, most of it with his family in Paris. His attempts to make a living there were unsuccessful, and he went back to Russia where he could earn money as a writer. He tried to convince his wife to move back to Russia but she refused. Babel was told by the authorities that his travel abroad was conditional on his publication output. Failing to meet these expectations, he was trapped. Unexpectedly, pressed by André Malraux and André Gide, the Politburo appointed Babel, along with Boris Pasternak, delegates to the anti-fascist congress in Paris in June 1935. Babel stayed in Paris for two months, collecting material for a series on the city of light. This was his last trip abroad. Babel's two novellas that follow are all we have left of his planned cycle of *The Paris Stories.* —Ed.

Dante Street[1]

The Hotel Danton, where I was staying, was rattled to its foundations by moans of love from five until seven in the evening. Experts were at work in the rooms. Having arrived in France with the conviction that its people had lost their spark, I was somewhat taken aback by their vigor. In our country, we do not bring women to such a boiling pitch. Nowhere near it.

"*Mon vieux*," Monsieur Bienalle, my neighbor, once told me, "in our thousand years of history we have created woman, food, and literature. No one can deny this."

Jean Bienalle, a secondhand car dealer, did more for my knowledge of France than all the books I had read and all the French towns I had seen. The first time we met he asked me which restaurant I ate at, what café I went to, and which brothel I frequented. My answer appalled him.

"*On va refaire votre vie!*"[2]

And the changes were undertaken. We ate lunch at a tavern across the street from the Halles aux vins, frequented by cattle dealers and wine merchants.

---

1. First published in *30 dney* 3 (1934), the original manuscript has the subtitle "From *The Paris Stories*" (*Iz parizhskikh rasskazov*). A small street off Boulevard St. Germaine and close to the Sorbonne. —Ed.
2. French: We shall change your ways!

Village girls in slippers served us lobster in red sauce, roast rabbit stuffed with garlic and truffles, and wine you could find nowhere else. Bienalle ordered, I paid, but I only paid as much as the French paid. It wasn't cheap, but it wasn't the foreigner's price. And I also paid the Frenchman's price at the brothel funded by a group of senators next to the Gare St. Lazare. Bienalle had to put more effort into introducing me to the inmates of that house than if he had attempted to introduce me to a session of Parliament while a cabinet is being overthrown. We capped off the evening at the Porte Maillot at a café where boxing promoters and race car drivers gathered. My tutor belonged to the half of the nation that sells cars. The other half buys them. He was an agent for Renault and did most of his trade with the Balkans, those most ambiguous of countries, and with Rumanian speculators, the dirtiest of speculators. In his free time Bienalle taught me the art of buying a used car. According to him, one had to go down to the Riviera toward the end of the season, when the English were leaving for home, abandoning in local garages cars they had only used for two or three months. Bienalle himself drove a dilapidated Renault, which he drove the way a Siberian tribesman drives his sled dogs. On Sundays we drove 120 kilometers to Rouen in his bouncing vehicle to eat duck, which the locals there roast in its own blood. We were accompanied by Germaine, who sold gloves on Rue Royale. She spent every Wednesday and Sunday with Bienalle. She always came at five o'clock. Within seconds their room echoed with growls, the thud of tumbling bodies, frightened gasps, after which the woman's tender death throes began: "Oh, Jean . . ."

I added it all up: Germaine went into his room, closed the door behind her, they gave each other a kiss, she took off her hat and gloves, laid them on the table, and, according to my calculations, that was all there was time for. He wouldn't even have had time to undress. Not uttering a word, they bounced about like rabbits between the sheets. They moaned for a while, and then burst out laughing and chatted about everyday things. I knew as much as any neighbor living on the other side of a thin board partition. Germaine was having trouble with Monsieur Heinrich, the store manager. Her parents lived in Tours, where she visited them. On one Saturday she bought herself a fur wrap, on another she went to see *La Bohème* at the opera. Monsieur Heinrich had his saleswomen wear tailored dress suits. Monsieur Heinrich anglicized Germaine, turning her into one of those brisk, flat-chested, curly-haired businesswomen painted with flaming, brownish rouge. But her fine chunky ankles, her low, nimble laugh, the sharp gaze of her sparkling eyes, and that death-throe moan—"Oh, Jean!"—were all left untouched for Bienalle.

Germaine's powerful, lithe body moved before us in the smoke and gold of the Paris evening. She laughed, throwing back her head and pressing her delicate pink fingers to her breasts. My heart glowed during these hours. There is no solitude more desperate than solitude in Paris. This town is a form of exile for all who come to it from far away, and I realized that Germaine was more important to me than she was to Bienalle. I left for Marseilles with this thought in mind.[3]

3. In the original typed manuscript, the paragraph ended with this passage: "There I saw my native city—Odessa—what it would have become in twenty years, had its development not been blocked; I saw the unrealized future of our avenues, embankments, and ships." —*Ed.*

After a month in Marseilles, I returned to Paris. I waited for Wednesday to hear Germaine's voice.

Wednesday came and went, but nobody disturbed the silence of the room next door. Bienalle had changed his day. A woman's voice rang out on Thursday, at five o'clock as always. Bienalle gave his visitor time to take off her hat and gloves. Germaine had not only changed her day, she had also changed her voice. It was no longer the gasping, imploring "Oh, Jean!" followed by silence, the harsh silence of another person's happiness; it had turned into a hoarse domestic clamor with guttural exclamations. The new Germaine gnashed her teeth, flung herself heavily onto the sofa, and during the interludes pontificated in her thick, dragging voice. She said nothing about Monsieur Heinrich, growled until seven o'clock, and then got ready to go. I opened the door a crack to say hello to her, but saw a mulatto woman in the corridor with a cockscomb of horse-like hair and large, dangling, hoisted-up breasts. She was coming down the corridor, her feet shuffling in worn-out shoes with no heels. I knocked on Bienalle's door. He was lolling about in bed in his shirt and washed-out socks, ashen and crumpled.

"So, *mon vieux*, you've pensioned off Germaine?"

"*Cette femme est folle*,"[4] he said with a shudder. "Mademoiselle Germaine does not care that on this earth there is winter and summer, a beginning and an end, and that after winter comes summer and then the opposite. She heaves a heavy burden on you and demands that you carry it—but where to, nobody but Mademoiselle Germaine knows!"

Bienalle sat up in bed. His trousers stretched over his thin legs. His pale scalp shimmered through his matted hair, and his triangular mustache twitched. A bottle of Macon, four francs a liter, lifted my friend's spirits again. As we waited for our dessert, he shrugged his shoulders and said as if in answer to my thoughts, "There's more than everlasting love in this world—there are Rumanians, promissory notes, men who go bankrupt, cars with broken chassis. *Oh, j'en ai plein le dos!*"[5]

He grew more cheerful over a cognac at the Café de Paris. We sat on the terrace under a white awning with wide stripes running down it. The crowd streamed past over the sidewalk, blending with the electric stars. A car, long as a torpedo, stopped across the street from us. From it emerged an Englishman with a woman in a sable wrap. She sailed past in a cloud of perfume and fur, inhumanly long with a small, shining head of porcelain. Bienalle sat up when he saw her, stretched out his leg in his tattered trousers, and winked at her the way one winks at the girls on the rue de la Gaîté. The woman smiled with the corner of her carmine mouth, gave a barely visible nod with her tightly wrapped pink head, and, swinging and swaying her serpentine body, disappeared, with the stiff, crackling Englishman in tow.

"*Ah, canaille!*"[6] Bienalle said after them. "Two years ago anyone could have had her for an aperitif."

The two of us parted late. I had decided that I would go see Germaine that Saturday, take her to the theater, go to Chartres with her if she was in

4. French: That woman is mad.
5. French: Oh, I've had it up to here!
6. French: Ah, the bitch!

the mood. But as things turned out, I was to see Bienalle and his former girlfriend before then. The following evening, all the doors of the Hotel Danton were cordoned off by the police, their blue capes swirling through our vestibule. They let me go up after they verified that I was one of Madame Truffaut's lodgers. I found policemen standing outside my room. The door to Bienalle's room stood open. He was lying on the floor in a pool of blood, his lusterless eyes half closed. The stamp of street death was upon him. My friend Bienalle had been stabbed, stabbed to death. Germaine was sitting at the table in her tailored dress suit and her delicate, close-fitting hat. She greeted me and hung her head, and with it the feather on her hat hung too.

All this took place at six in the evening, the hour of love. There was a woman in every room. They hastily applied rouge and drew black lines along the edges of their lips before leaving half dressed, with stockings up to their thighs like pageboys. Doors opened and men with untied shoes lined up in the corridor. In the room of a wrinkled Italian racing cyclist a barefoot little girl was crying into the pillow. I went downstairs to tell Madame Truffaut. The girl's mother sold newspapers on the Rue St. Michel. All the old women of our street, the Rue Dante, misshapen piles of goiterous meat, whiskered, wheezing, with cataracts and purple blotches, had already gathered in the little office: market women, concierges, sellers of roasted chestnuts and potatoes.

"Voilà qui n'est pas gai," I said as I went in. "Quel malheur!"[7]

"C'est l'amour, monsieur. . . . Elle l'aimait."[8]

Madame Truffaut's lilac breasts tumbled in her lace blouse, her elephantine legs strode through the room, her eyes flashed.

"L'amore!" Signora Rocca, who ran a restaurant on Rue Dante, called out from behind her like an echo. "Dio castiga quelli, chi non conoscono l'amore!"[9]

The old women huddled together, all muttering at the same time. A variolar flame lit their cheeks, their eyes bulging out of their sockets.

"L'amour," Madame Truffaut repeated, hobbling toward me. "C'est une grosse affaire, l'amour!"[1]

A siren sounded in the street. Skillful hands dragged the murdered man downstairs and out to the ambulance. My friend Bienalle had turned into a mere number, losing his name in the rolling waves of Paris. Signora Rocca went over to the window and looked out at the corpse. She was pregnant, her belly jutting out threateningly. Silk lay on her protruding hips, and the sun washed over her yellow, puffy face and soft yellow hair.

"Dio," Signora Rocca said. "Tu non perdoni quelli, chi non amano!"[2]

Dusk descended on the tattered net of the Latin quarter, the squat crowd scuttling into its crevices, a hot breath of garlic pouring from its yards. Darkness covered the house of Madame Truffaut, its gothic facade with its two windows, and the remnants of turrets and volutes, ivy turned to stone.

7. French: Well, this isn't very cheerful. How dreadful!
8. French: It is love, monsieur. . . . She loved him.
9. Italian: Love! God punishes those who do not know love!
1. French: Love is a nasty business!
2. Italian: God, you do not forgive those who do not love!

Danton[3] had lived here a century and a half ago. From his window he had seen the Conciergerie,[4] the bridges strewn across the Seine, and the same cluster of little blind hovels huddling by the river. The same breath had wafted up to him. Rusty beams and signs of wayside inns had creaked, rattled by the wind.

The Trial[1]

Madame Blanchard, a sixty-one-year-old woman, met Ivan Nedachin, a former lieutenant colonel, in a café on the Boulevard des Italiens. They fell in love. Their love was more a matter of sensuality than common sense. Within three months the lieutenant colonel had disappeared with Madame Blanchard's stocks and the jewelry she had given him to be appraised by a jeweler on the Rue de la Paix.

"Accès de folie passagère,"[2] the doctor diagnosed Madame Blanchard's ensuing fit.

Regaining consciousness, the old woman confessed everything to her daughter-in-law. Her daughter-in-law went to the police. Nedachin was arrested in a wine cellar in Montparnasse where Moscow gypsies sang. In prison Nedachin turned yellow and flabby. He was tried in chamber number fourteen of the criminal court. First there was a case involving an automobile matter, followed by the case of sixteen-year-old Raymond Lepique, who had shot his girlfriend out of jealousy. The lieutenant colonel came after the boy. The gendarme pushed him out into the light, as a bear is pushed into a circus arena. Frenchmen in badly sewn jackets were shouting loudly at each other, and submissively rouged women fanned their teary faces. In front of them, on the podium beneath the republic's marble coat of arms, sat a red-cheeked man with a Gallic mustache, wearing a toga and a little hat.

"Eh bien, Nedachin," he said, on seeing the accused man, "eh bien, mon ami." And his fast burred speech washed over the shuddering lieutenant colonel.

"As a descendant of the noble line of the Nedachins," the presiding judge loudly proclaimed, "you, my friend, are listed in the heraldic books of the province of Tambov. An officer of the Czar's army, you immigrated with Wrangel[3] and became a policeman in Zagreb. Discrepancies in the question of what was government property and what was private property," the presiding judge continued sonorously, the tips of his patent leather shoes darting in and out under the hem of his gown. "These discrepancies,

3. A leading figure in the French Revolution, Georges Danton (1759–1794) was a member of the Committee for Public Safety. He initially supported the Terror but then turned against it, only to become one of its more famous victims. —Ed.
4. The oldest prison in Paris, especially notorious during the French Revolution when many of its inmates, including Danton and later Robespierre, were transported through the city to Place de la Révolution (later Concorde) to be publicly guillotined. —Ed.
1. First published in the weekly Ogonyok 23 (1938), subtitled "From the Notebook" (Iz zapisnoy knizhki). —Ed.
2. French: A fit of temporary insanity.
3. Baron Peter Nikolayevich Wrangel (1878–1928), commander of the White anti-Bolshevik army, was forced to evacuate 150,000 soldiers and civilians by sea from the Crimea to Constantinople in November 1920. This evacuation marked the end of the Russian Civil War.

my friend, forced you to bid the hospitable kingdom of Yugoslavia farewell
and set your sights on Paris."

"In Paris,"—here the judge ran his eyes over some papers lying before
him—"in Paris, my friend, the taxi driver test proved a fortress you could
not conquer, at which point you concentrated all the powers left to you
on Madame Blanchard, who is absent from this hearing."

The foreign words poured over Nedachin like a summer shower. He
towered over the crowd—helpless, large, with dangling arms—like an
animal from another world.

"*Voyons*,"[4] the presiding judge said unexpectedly. "From where I am
sitting, I can see the daughter-in-law of the esteemed Madame Blanchard."

A fat, neckless woman, looking like a fish jammed into a frock coat,
hurried with lowered head over to the witness box. Panting, lifting her
short little arms to heaven, she began listing the stocks stolen from
Madame Blanchard.

"Thank you very much, madame," the presiding judge interrupted her,
nodding to a gaunt man with a well-bred, sunken face, who was sitting
next to him.

The public prosecutor, rising slightly, muttered a few words and sat
down again, clasping his hands. He was followed by the defense attorney, a naturalized Kiev Jew, who ranted about the Golgotha of the Russian military officers in an offended tone, as if he were in the middle of
an argument. Incomprehensibly pronounced French words came sputtering out of his mouth, sounding increasingly Yiddish toward the end of his
speech. The presiding judge peered blankly at the attorney for a few
moments without saying a word, and then suddenly lunged to the side—
toward the gaunt old man in the toga and the little hat—then lunged to
the other side, to another old man just like the first.

"Ten years, my friend," the presiding judge said meekly, nodding his
head at Nedachin, and hurriedly grabbed the papers for the next case,
which his secretary slid over to him.

Nedachin stood rigidly to attention. His colorless eyes blinked, his
small forehead was covered with sweat.

"*T'a encaissé dix ans*," the gendarme behind him said. "*C'est fini, mon
vieux*."[5] And, quietly pushing the crowd out of the way, the gendarme led
the convicted man toward the exit.

---

4. French: Let's see.
5. French: He's locked you up for ten years. It's over, old boy.

Autobiographical Fiction: Childhood

The surviving unfinished story "At Grandmother's" is datelined "Saratov 11.12.15," indicating that Babel began exploring the theme early while under the influence of his idols, Leo Tolstoy and Maxim Gorky, each the author of his own *Childhood*. However, Babel's childhood cycle did not emerge until a decade later, after much of the *Red Cavalry* and *The Odessa Stories* had been written and published. Apparently Babel needed first to establish his public persona—as a Russian Jewish author inspired by the revolution—before he could begin his "cherished work," as he once referred to the cycle in a letter to his mother. The first to be published was "The Story of My Dovecote" (1925), subtitled "the opening of my autobiographical long fiction", followed by its companion piece, "First Love" (1925). But it took years for Babel to add three more stories, which together make up what we know as his book about childhood. Significantly, this "autobiographical long fiction" did not include the 1915 story, "At Grandmother's." Its young protagonist did not fit the character of the boy who would later evolve into the mythic author-narrator of *Red Cavalry*. —Ed.

At Grandmother's[1]

On Sabbaths after six classes I came home late. Walking through the streets didn't seem to me pointless. I could daydream remarkably well as I walked, and I felt that everything, everything around me was part of my being. I knew the signs, the stones of the houses, the windows of the stores. I knew them in a very special way, a very personal way, and I was firmly convinced that I saw the fundamental secret within them—what we grown-ups call the "essence" of things. Everything about them was deeply imprinted on my soul. When grown-ups mentioned a store in my presence, I envisioned its sign, the worn, golden letters, the little scratch in the left corner, the young lady with the tall coiffure at the cash register, and I remembered the air around this store that was not around any other. I pieced together from these stores, from the people, the air, the theater posters, my own hometown. To this day I remember, feel, and love this town—feel it, as one feels one's mother's scent, the scent of her caresses, words, and smiles, and I love this town because I grew up in it, was happy, melancholy, and dreamy in it. Passionately and singularly dreamy.

---

1. First published in *Literaturnoe nasledstvo. Iz tvorcheskogo naslediya sovetskikh pisateley*, vol. 74 (Moscow, 1965). The manuscript is titled "Childhood. At Grandmother's" and date lined Saratov, 11.12.1915. "Babel was at that time in Saratov, where the Kiev Commercial Institute had been evacuated after the start of World War I. —Ed.

I always walked down the main street—that is where most of the people were.

The Sabbath I want to tell you about was a Sabbath in early spring. At that time of year, our air does not have the quiet tenderness, so sweet in central Russia, resting upon its peaceful streams and modest valleys. Our air has a sparkling, light coolness that blows with a shallow, chilly passion. I was no more than a young boy then and didn't understand a thing, but I felt the spring, and I blossomed and reddened in the chill.

The walk lasted a long time. I stared at the diamonds in the jeweler's window, read the theater posters from A to Z, and once I even studied the pale pink corsets with their long, wavy suspenders in Madam Rosalie's store. As I was about to walk on, I collided with a tall student who had a big black mustache. He smiled at me and asked, "So you're examining these closely, are you?" I was mortified. Then he patronizingly patted me on the back and said in a superior tone, "Keep up the good work, dear colleague! My compliments! All the best!" He roared with laughter, turned, and walked away. I felt very flustered, avoided looking at Madam Rosalie's display window, and quickly headed for home.

I was supposed to spend the Sabbath at my grandmother's. She had her own room at the very end of the apartment, behind the kitchen. A stove stood in the corner of this room, grandmother always felt cold. The room was hot and stuffy, which made me feel melancholy and want to escape, to get out into the open.

I dragged my belongings over to grandmother's, my books, my music stand, and my violin. The table had already been set for me. Grandmother sat in the corner. I ate. We didn't say a word. The door was locked. We were alone. There was cold gefilte fish for dinner with horseradish (a dish worth embracing Judaism for), a rich and delicious soup, roasted meat with onions, salad, compote, coffee, pie, and apples. I ate everything. I was a dreamer, it is true, but a dreamer with a hearty appetite. Grandmother cleared away the dishes. The room became tidy. There were wilting flowers on the windowsill. What grandmother loved best among all living things were her son, her grandson, Mimi her dog, and flowers. Mimi came over, rolled herself up on the sofa, and immediately fell asleep. She was kind of a lazy pooch, but a splendid dog, good, clever, small, and pretty. Mimi was a pug dog. Her coat was light-colored. Even in old age she didn't get flabby or heavy, but managed to remain svelte and slim. She lived with us for a long time, from birth to death, the whole fifteen years of her dog life, and, needless to say, she loved us, and most of all our severe and unbending grandmother. I shall tell about what tight-mouthed, secretive friends they were another time. It is a very interesting and tender story.

So there we were, the three of us—grandmother, Mimi, and me. Mimi slept. Grandmother, kind, wearing her holiday silk dress, sat in the corner, and I was supposed to study. That day was difficult for me. There were six classes in the high school, and Mr. Sorokin, the music teacher, was supposed to come, and Mr. L., the Hebrew teacher, to make up the lesson I had missed, and then maybe Peysson, my French teacher. I had to prepare for all these lessons. I could deal with L. easily enough, we were old friends, but the music and the scales—what anguish! First of all, I started on my homework. I spread out my notebooks and painstakingly began to do my mathematics problems. Grandmother didn't interrupt me, God forbid. The tension inside her, and her reverence for my work, gave her face a dazed look. Her eyes, round, yellow, transparent, never left me. I would turn a page—and her eyes would slowly follow my hand. Another person might have suffered greatly under her persistent, watchful, unwavering stare, but I was used to it.

Then grandmother listened to me recite my lessons. It has to be said that her Russian was bad—she had her own peculiar way of mangling words, mixing Russian with Polish and Hebrew. Needless to say, she couldn't read or write Russian, and would hold books upside down. But that didn't deter me from reciting my lesson from beginning to end. Grandmother listened without understanding a word, but to her the music of the words was sweet, she bowed before science, believed me, believed in me, and wanted me to become a "bogatyr"[2]—that is what she called a rich man. I finished my lessons and began reading a book. At the time, I was reading "First Love" by Turgenev. I liked everything in it, the clear words, the descriptions, the conversations, but the scene that made me shiver all over was the one in which Vladimir's father strikes Zinaida's cheek with a whip. I could hear the whip's whistling sound—its lithe leather body sharply, painfully, instantly biting into me. I was seized by an indescribable emotion. At that point in the book I had to stop reading, and pace up and down the room. And grandmother sat there stock-still, and even the hot, stupefying air did not stir, as if it sensed I was studying and shouldn't be disturbed. The heat in the room kept rising. Mimi began snoring. Until then there had been silence, a ghostly silence, not a sound. Everything seemed uncanny at that moment and I wanted to run away from it all, and yet I wanted to stay there forever. The darkening room, grandmother's yellow eyes, her tiny body wrapped in a shawl silent and hunched over in the corner, the hot air, the closed door, and the clout of the whip, and that piercing whistle—only now do I realize how strange it all was, how much it meant to me. I was snatched out of this troubled state by the doorbell. Sorokin had come. I hated him at that moment, I hated the scales, the incomprehensible, pointless, shrill music. I must admit that Sorokin was quite a nice fellow. He wore his black hair cropped very short, had large red hands, and beautiful thick lips. On that day, under grandmother's watchful stare, he had to work for a whole hour, even longer, he had to push himself to the limit. For all of this he got absolutely no recognition. The old woman's eyes coldly and persistently followed his every move, remaining distant and indifferent. Grandmother had no interest in outside people. She demanded that they fulfill their obligations to us, and nothing more. We began our lesson. I wasn't frightened of grandmother, but for a full hour I had to brave poor Sorokin's boundless zeal. He felt extremely ill-at-ease in this remote room, in the presence of a dog peacefully asleep and a coldly watchful, hostile old woman. Finally he took his leave. Grandmother gave him her hard, wrinkled, large hand with indifference, without shaking it. On his way out, he stumbled into a chair.

---

2. The grandmother is confusing Bogatyr, a Herculean hero in Russian folklore, with *bogaty*, "rich man."

I also survived the following hour, Mr. L.'s lesson, longing for the moment that the door would close behind him too.

Evening came. Faraway golden dots ignited in the sky. Our courtyard, a deep cage, was dazzled by the moon. A woman's voice next door sang the ballad "Why I am madly in love." My parents went to the theater. I became melancholy. I was tired. I had read so much, studied so much, seen so much. Grandmother lit a lamp. Her room immediately became quiet. The dark, heavy furniture was softly illuminated. Mimi woke up, walked through the room, came back to us again, and waited for her supper. The maid brought in the samovar. Grandmother was a tea lover. She had saved a slice of honey cake for me. We drank large quantities. Sweat sparkled in grandmother's deep, sharp wrinkles. "Are you sleepy?" she asked. "No," I said. We began to talk. And once more I heard grandmother's stories. Long ago, many, many years ago, there was a Jew who ran a tavern. He was poor, married, burdened with children, and traded in bootleg vodka. The commissar came and tormented him. Life became difficult. He went to the *tsaddik* and said, "Rabbi! The commissar is vexing me to death! Speak to God on my behalf!" "Go in peace," the *tsaddik* said to him. "The commissar will calm down." The Jew left. At the threshold of his tavern he found the commissar. He was lying there dead, with a purple, swollen face.

Grandmother fell silent. The samovar hummed. The woman next door was still singing. The moon still dazzled. Mimi wagged her tail. She was hungry.

"In olden times, people had beliefs!" grandmother said. "Life on earth was simpler. When I was a girl, the Poles rebelled. Near where we lived was a count's estate. Even the Czar came to visit the count. Seven days and seven nights they made merry. At night I ran over to the count's castle and looked through the bright windows. The count had a daughter and the finest pearls in the world. Then came the uprising. Soldiers dragged him out onto the square. We all stood there crying. The soldiers dug a pit. They wanted to blindfold the old man. He said, "That will not be necessary!" The count stood before the soldiers and ordered, "Fire!" He was a tall, gray-haired man. The muzhiks loved him. Just as they began burying him, a messenger came galloping up. He brought a pardon from the Czar.

The samovar had gone out. Grandmother drank her last, cold glass of tea, and sucked on a piece of sugar with her toothless mouth.

"Your grandfather," she began, "knew many stories, but he had no beliefs whatsoever, he only believed in people. He gave away all his money to his friends, and when his turn came to ask them for something they kicked him down the stairs, and he lost his mind."

And then grandmother told me about my grandfather, a tall, haughty, passionate, and despotic man. He played the violin, wrote literary works at night, and knew all the languages. He was governed by an unquenchable thirst for knowledge and life. A general's daughter fell in love with their eldest son, who traveled a lot, played cards, and died in Canada at the age of thirty-seven. All grandmother had left was one son and me. It was all over. Day slips into evening, and death slowly approaches. Grandmother falls silent, lowers her head, and begins crying.

"Study!" she suddenly said forcefully. "Study and you can have everything—wealth and glory. You must know everything. Everyone will fall on their knees before you and bow to you. Let them envy you. Don't believe in people. Don't have friends. Don't give them your money. Don't give them your heart!"

Grandmother stops talking. Silence. Grandmother is thinking of bygone years and sorrows, is thinking about my fate, and her severe testament rests heavily, eternally, on my weak, young shoulders. In the dark corner, the incandescent cast-iron stove is blazing intensely. I'm suffocating, I can't breathe, I want to run out into the air, into the open, but I don't have the strength to lift my drooping head.

Dishes clatter in the kitchen. Grandmother goes there. We're going to have supper. I hear her angry, metallic voice. She is shouting at the maid. I feel strange and troubled. Just a short while ago she had been breathing peace and sorrow. The maid snaps back at her. Grandmother's unbearably shrill voice rings out in an uncontrollable rage, "Get out of here, you dreck! I'm the mistress here. You are destroying my property. Get out of here!" I cannot bear her deafening voice of steel. I can see grandmother through the half-open door. Her face is distorted, her lips are trembling thinly and relentlessly, her throat has thickened, as if it were bulging out. The maid answers back. "Get out of here," grandmother says. Then there is silence. The maid bows, and quietly, as if she were afraid of offending the silence, slips out of the room.

We eat our dinner without talking. We eat our fill, abundantly and long. Grandmother's transparent eyes are staring immovably—what they are staring at, I do not know. After supper, she [. . .][3]

More than that I do not see because I fall into a deep sleep, a child's sleep behind seven locks[4] in grandmother's hot room.

The Story of My Dovecote[1]

For Maxim Gorky

As a child I wanted a dovecote very badly. In all my life I have never desired anything more intensely. I was nine years old when my father promised to give me the money to buy some planks and three pairs of doves. The year was 1904. I was getting ready for the examinations for the preparatory class of the Nikolayev Gymnasium.[2] My family lived in Nikolayev, in the province of Kherson. This province no longer exists; our town was absorbed into the district of Odessa.

I was only nine years old, and was frightened of the examinations. In both Russian and mathematics I could not afford to get less than five, the highest

3. Gap in manuscript.
4. An expression from Russian fairy tales. —*Ed.*
1. Published in *Krasnaya gazeta* (Leningrad), May 18, 19, and 20, 1925. It came out almost simultaneously in Moscow in *Krasnaya nov* 4 (1924), with an author's note calling it the "opening of an autobiographical long fiction" (*avtobiograficheskaya povest*). —*Ed.*
2. Imperial Russia had two types of primary/secondary schools to qualify students for higher education. One was the gymnasium, distinguished by its classical curriculum requiring both Latin and Greek, whose graduates were eligible to apply to universities; the other type included the "commercial school" and *realnoe uchilishche*, which emphasized sciences and practical knowledge, including modern languages, and whose graduates were eligible to apply to polytechnic schools or other specialized colleges. —*Ed.*

grade. The Jewish entry quota for our gymnasium[3] was harsh, only five percent. Out of forty boys, only two Jews could be admitted into the preparatory
class. The teachers would come up with the most cunning questions for these
two boys; nobody was given the kind of complicated questions we were. So
my father promised to buy me doves on condition that I manage to get two
five-pluses. He tormented me more than I can say, I tumbled into a never-
ending daydream—the long, desperate dream of a child—and though I went
to the examination immersed in that dream, I still fared better than the rest.

I was good at learning. The teachers, though they tried every trick, did not
manage to waylay my mind and my sharp memory. I was good at learning,
and so got two fives. But then the situation changed. Khariton Ephrussi,[4]
the grain merchant who exported wheat to Marseilles, proffered a five-
hundred-ruble bribe for his son, I was given a five-minus instead of a five,
and the gymnasium admitted Ephrussi junior in my place. My father was
deeply pained by this. From the time I was six, he had taught me all the subjects you could imagine. That minus drove him to desperation. He wanted
to beat Ephrussi up, or to hire two dockworkers to beat him up, but mother
talked him out of it, and I began preparing myself for the examination next
year for the following grade. Behind my back, my family talked my tutor into
going over the lessons for both the preparatory class and the first class
within one year, and, as we were completely desperate, I ended up learning
three books by heart. These books were Smirnovsky's grammar, Yevtu-
shevsky's book of mathematical problems, and Putsikovich's introduction to
Russian history. Children no longer study these books, but I learned them
by heart, line by line, and the following year Karavayev, the schoolmaster,
gave me those unattainable five-pluses in my Russian language examination.

Karavayev was a ruddy-faced, indignant man who had been a student in
Moscow. He was barely thirty. His manly cheeks blossomed with the flush
seen on the cheeks of peasant children. He had a wart on his face from
which a tuft of ashen, feline hair sprouted. Also present at the examination
besides Karavayev was the deputy warden, who was considered an important
figure not only in the gymnasium but in the whole province. The deputy warden asked me about Peter I, and a blankness came over me, a feeling that the
end, the abyss, was near, a dry abyss surrounded by delight and despair.

I knew by heart the passage about Peter the Great in Putsikovich's
book and Pushkin's poems. I recited the poems in sobs. Faces swarmed
into my eyes, mixing and shuffling deep inside like a fresh deck of cards,
while I, shivering, straight-backed, shouted out Pushkin's verses with all
my might, as fast as I could. I went on shouting the verses for a long
time, nobody interrupting my crazed rambling. Across my crimson blindness, across the freedom that had taken hold of me, I only saw Pyatnitsky's old face leaning forward with its silvery beard. He did not interrupt
me, but turned to Karavayev, who was rejoicing in Pushkin and me, and
whispered, "What a nation! The devil is in these Yids!"

When I finished he said, "Very good, off you go now, my little friend."

I left the classroom and went out into the corridor, and there, leaning
against the unpainted wall, I woke from the convulsions of my dreams.

---

3. The gymnasium "Jewish quota" was much more restrictive than that of a commercial school, which
   often had no quotas while offering a superb education. Babel himself attended a commercial
   school, not a gymnasium; incidentally, so did the aristocratic Vladimir Nabokov (1899–1977), —Ed.
4. The Ephrussi family was one of the oldest and wealthiest Jewish merchant families in Odessa.

Russian boys were playing all around me, the school bell hung nearby over the official-looking flight of stairs, a watchman was dozing on a broken chair. I gazed at him and began to come back to my senses. Children came creeping toward me from all sides. They wanted to poke me and get me to play with them, but suddenly Pyatnitsky appeared in the corridor. Passing by me, he stopped for an instant, his frock coat undulating in a heavy slow wave over his back. I saw emotion in his large, fleshy, gentlemanly back, and I went up to him.

"Children," he told the schoolboys. "Leave this boy alone!" And he laid his fat, tender hand on my shoulder. "My little friend," Pyatnitsky said, turning to me. "You can go and tell your father that you have been accepted into the first class."

A magnificent star shone on his chest, medals tinkled by his lapel, and hemmed in by the murky walls, moving between them like a barge moves through a deep canal, his large, black, uniformed body marched off on rigid legs and disappeared through the doors of the headmaster's office. A little attendant brought him tea with solemn ceremony, and I ran home to our store.

In our store a muzhik customer sat scratching his head in the grip of indecision. When my father saw me, he abandoned the muzhik and drank in my story without a moment's doubt. He shouted to his sales clerk to close the store, and rushed over to Sobornaya Street to buy me a cap with the school emblem on it. My poor mother barely managed to wrest me away from my delirious father. She stood there, pale, trying to foresee my fate. She kept caressing me and then pushing me away in disgust. She said that a list of all the children admitted into the gymnasium was always published in the newspapers, and that God would punish us and that people would laugh at us, if we bought a school uniform ahead of time. My mother was pale, she was trying to foresee my fate in my eyes, and looked at me with bitter pity, as if I were a little cripple, for she was the only one who fully realized how luckless our family was.

All the men of our clan had been too trusting of others and too quick to take unconsidered action. We had never had any luck in anything. My grandfather had once been a rabbi in Belaya Tserkov, had been chased out of town for blasphemy, and then lived in scandal and poverty for another forty years, learned foreign languages, and started going insane in his eightieth year. My Uncle Lev, my father's brother, studied at the Yeshiva in Volozhin, evaded conscription in 1892, and abducted the daughter of a quartermaster serving in the Kiev military district. Uncle Lev took this woman to California, to Los Angeles, where he abandoned her, and he died in a house of ill repute among Negroes and Malays. After his death, the American police sent us his belongings—a large trunk reinforced with brown iron hoops—from Los Angeles. In this trunk were dumbbells, locks of a woman's hair, uncle's *tallith*, whips with gilded tips, and herbal tea in little boxes trimmed with cheap pearls. The only men left in the family were mad Uncle Simon, who lived in Odessa, my father, and me. But my father was too trusting of others, he offended people with his exhilarating welcome of first love. They did not forgive him for this, and so cheated him. This was why my father believed that his life was governed by a malevolent fate, an inscrutable being that pursued him and that was unlike him in every way. So in our family I was my mother's only hope. Like all Jews, I was short in stature, weak, and plagued by headaches from too much study. My mother could see this clearly. She had never been blinded by her husband's destitute pride and his incomprehensible belief that our family would one day be stronger and richer than other people in this world. She did not foresee any success for us, was frightened of buying a school uniform ahead of time, and only acceded to my having my picture taken by a portrait photographer.

On September 20, 1905, a list of all those who had managed to enter the first class was posted outside the gymnasium. My name was on that list. My whole family went to look at this piece of paper—even Grandpa Shoyl, my great-uncle, went to the gymnasium. I loved this braggart of an old man because he sold fish in the market. His fat hands were moist, covered with fish scales, and reeked of wonderful, cold worlds. Shoyl was also different from other people because of his fabricated stories about the Polish uprising of 1861. In the distant past, he had been an innkeeper in Skvira. He had witnessed the soldiers of Nicholas I shoot Count Godlewski and other Polish insurgents. But then again, maybe he hadn't witnessed this. Now I know that Shoyl was no more than an old fool and a naive teller of tall tales, but I have not forgotten those little tales of his, they were good tales. So even foolish Shoyl went over to the gymnasium to read the list that had my name on it, and in the evening he danced and stamped his feet at our beggarly feast.

My father organized a feast of celebration and invited his comrades—grain merchants, estate brokers, and itinerant salesmen who sold agricultural machines in our region. These itinerant salesmen sold machines to everyone. Both muzhiks and landowners were afraid of them, as they could not get rid of them without buying something. Of all the Jews, the itinerant salesmen are the most worldly and cheerful. At our feast they sang drawn-out Hasidic songs made up of only three words, but with many funny intonations. Only those who have celebrated Passover with the Hasidim, or who have visited their boisterous synagogues in Volhynia, know the charm of these intonations. Old Liberman, who taught me Hebrew and the Torah, also came to our house that evening. My family always addressed him as Monsieur Liberman. He drank more Bessarabian wine than he should have, the traditional silk strings slipped out from under his red vest, and he called out a toast in my honor in Hebrew. In this toast the old man congratulated my parents, and said that by passing this examination I had won a victory over all my foes, I had won a victory over the fat-cheeked Russian boys and the sons of our roughneck rich. Thus in ancient times had David, the King of the Jews, won a victory over Goliath, and just as I had triumphed over Goliath, so too would our people, through its sheer power of mind, triumph over the foes that surround us, eager for our blood. Monsieur Liberman wept, pronounced these words weeping, drank some more wine, and yelled, "Vivat!" The dancing guests took him into the circle and danced with him the ancient quadrille, as at a shtetl wedding. Everyone was joyful at our feast, even my mother took a little sip of wine, though she did not like vodka and did not understand how anyone could. Which is why she thought all Russians were mad, and why she could not understand how women could live with Russian husbands.

But our happy days were to begin later. For my mother they began when she started making me sandwiches in the morning before I left for school, when we went from store to store buying festive supplies—a pencil box, a piggybank, a schoolbag, new books with hard covers, and notebooks with glossy covers. No one in the world has a stronger response to new things than children. They shudder at the smell that new things give off, like dogs at the scent of a rabbit, and experience a madness, which later, when one is an adult, is called inspiration. And this clean, childish feeling of ownership of new things infected my mother too. It took us a whole month to get used to the pencil box and the morning twilight, when I would drink tea at the edge of the large, brightly lit table and gather my books into my schoolbag. It took us a whole month to get used to our happy life, and it was only after the first school term that I remembered the doves.

I had gotten everything ready for them—the one and a half rubles and the dovecote made out of a box by Grandpa Shoyl. The dovecote was given a coat of brown paint. It had nests for twelve pairs of doves, a series of little slats on its roof, and special grating I had invented so that it would be easier for other doves to come in too. Everything was ready. On Sunday, October 22, I set off to the wild game market, but I ran into unexpected obstacles along the way.

The story I am relating here, in other words my entry into the first class of the gymnasium, took place in the autumn of 1905. Czar Nicholas was in the process of giving the Russian people a constitution, and orators in threadbare coats were clambering onto podiums outside the buildings of the town councils and giving speeches to the people.[5] On the streets at night shots were fired, and my mother did not want to let me go to the wild game market. Early in the morning on October 20, the boys from next door were flying a kite right outside the police station, and our water carrier, abandoning all his duties, strolled pomaded and red-faced along the street. Then we saw the sons of Kalistov, the baker, drag a leather vaulting horse out onto the street and start to do their exercises right in the middle of the road. Nobody tried to stop them. Semernikov, the constable, was even egging them on to jump higher. Semernikov was wearing a homemade silk waistband, and his boots that day had been polished to a shine they had never before achieved. An out-of-uniform constable frightened my mother more than anything else, and it was because of him that she would not let me go out. But I crept out onto the street through backyards, and ran all the way to the wild game market, which lay behind the train station.

Ivan Nikodimich, the dove seller, was sitting at his usual place in the market. Besides doves, he was also selling rabbits and a peacock. The peacock, its tail fanned out, sat on a perch, darting its dispassionate head from one side to the other. Its foot was tied with a twisted string, the other end of the string lay wedged under Ivan Nikodimich's wicker chair. The moment I got there, I bought from the old man a pair of cherry-red doves with wonderful ruffled tails, and a pair of crested ones, and hid

---

5. Defeated by Japan in the Russo-Japanese war, Russia was in turmoil throughout 1905. In October, the country was paralyzed by a general strike. Heeding his liberal advisors, Nicholas II agreed to replace absolute autocratic rule with a limited constitutional monarchy and an elected parliament, the Duma. The edict, known as the October Manifesto, was issued on October 17. In the Pale of Settlement, the ultramonarchists saw the reform as a political and economic concession to the Jews (identified with the left and capitalism) and provoked a wave of pogroms. The anti-Jewish riots in Nikolayev started, as in Odessa, on October 19 and lasted two days, until the police and the military intervened to restore order. —Ed.

them in a sack under my shirt. I still had forty kopecks after my purchase, but the old man wouldn't give me a male and female Kryukov dove for that price. What I liked about Kryukov doves was their beaks, which were short, mottled, and amiable. Forty kopecks was the right price for them, but the old man overpriced them and turned away his yellow face, harrowed by the unsociable passions of the bird-catcher. As the market started closing, Ivan Nikodimich called me over, seeing that there weren't going to be any other buyers. Things turned out my way, things turned out badly.

Shortly before noon, or a little after, a man in felt boots walked across the square. He walked lightly on swollen feet, his lively eyes twinkling in his haggard face.

"Ivan Nikodimich," he said, as he walked past the bird-catcher. "Gather up your bits and bobs, in town the nobles of Jerusalem are being given a constitution. On Rybnaya Street they've just served Grandpa Babel a helping of death."

He made his way lightly among the cages, like a barefoot plowman walking along a field path.

"This is wrong!" Ivan Nikodimich muttered after him. "This is wrong!" he shouted more adamantly, gathering up the rabbits and the peacock, and pushing the Kryukov doves into my hands for forty kopecks.

I hid them under my shirt and watched the people run from the market. The peacock on Ivan Nikodimich's shoulder was the last to disappear. It sat like the sun in a damp autumn sky, like July on a rosy riverbank, a scorching July in long cold grass. There was no one left at the market, and shots were thundering not too far away. Then I ran to the train station, cut across the little park, which suddenly seemed to turn upside down, and I dashed into a deserted alley tamped with yellow earth. At the end of the alley sat legless Makarenko in a wheelchair, in which he rode around town selling cigarettes from a tray. The boys from our street bought cigarettes from him, the children liked him, I went running toward him in the alley.

"Makarenko," I said, breathless from running, and patted the legless man on the shoulder. "Have you seen Shoyl?"

The cripple didn't answer, his rough face of red fat and fists and iron was shining translucently. He was fidgeting in his chair, his wife, Katyusha, turning her puffed-up backside toward us, was riffling through things that lay scattered on the ground.

"How many have you counted?" the legless man asked her, pitching away from the woman with his whole body, as if he knew in advance that he wouldn't be able to bear her answer.

"Seven pairs of spats," Katyusha said, without straightening up, "six duvet covers, now I'm counting the bonnets."

"Bonnets!" Makarenko shouted, choked, and made a sound as if he were sobbing. "Obviously, God has chosen me to bear the Cross, Katyusha! People are carting off whole bales of cloth—these people get nice and proper things, and what do we get? Bonnets!"

And sure enough, a woman with a beautiful, fiery face went running down the alley. She was holding a bunch of fezzes in one hand and a bolt of cloth in the other. In a happy, desperate voice she was calling out to her children, who had disappeared. A silk dress and a blue jacket trailed after her scuttling body, and she didn't hear Makarenko, who went rushing after her in his wheelchair. The legless man couldn't catch up with her. His wheels rattled, he moved the levers with all his might.

"Madame!" he yelled deafeningly. "Madamochka! Where did you get the calico?"

But the woman with the scuttling dress was no longer to be seen. A rickety cart came flying around the corner where she had just disappeared. A young peasant was standing upright in the cart.

"Where's everyone run off to?" the young man asked, raising the red reins above his nags, who were straining in their collars.

"Everyone's on Sobornaya Street," Makarenko whined in an imploring voice. "Everyone's there, my dearest, my very dearest friend! Whatever you can grab, bring it here to me—I'll buy everything!"

The young man leaned forward over the front of his cart and whipped his skewbald nags. They bounced in their dirty cruppers like colts and went galloping off. The yellow alley was once again left yellow and empty. The legless man glared at me with his dead eyes.

"Well, am I not the man that God singled out?" he said lifelessly. "Am I not the Son of Man, huh?"

And he stretched out a hand flecked with leprosy.

"What've you got there in that bag?" he said, snatching away the sack that had warmed my heart.

The cripple's fat hand turned the sack upside down and he pulled out a cherry-red dove. The bird lay in his palm, its feet sticking up.

"Doves!" Makarenko said, and rolled up to me with squeaking wheels. "Doves!" he repeated, and slapped me across the face.

He hit me hard with the palm of his hand, crushing the bird. Katyusha's puffed-up backside loomed before my eyes, and I fell down in my new overcoat.

"Their seed has to be stamped out!" Katyusha said, getting up from the bonnets. "I cannot abide their seed and their stinking men!"

She also said other things about our seed, but I no longer heard anything. I lay on the ground, the innards of the crushed bird trickling down the side of my face. They trickled, winding and dribbling, down my cheek, blinding me. The dove's tender entrails slithered over my forehead, and I closed my uncaked eye so that I would not see the world unravel before me. This world was small and ugly. A pebble lay in front of my eyes, a pebble dented like the face of an old woman with a large jaw. A piece of string lay near it and a clump of feathers, still breathing. My world was small and ugly. I closed my eyes so I wouldn't see it, and pressed myself against the earth that lay soothing and mute beneath me. This tamped earth did not resemble anything in our lives. Somewhere far away disaster rode across it on a large horse, but the sound of its hooves grew weaker and vanished, and silence, the bitter silence that can descend on children in times of misfortune, dissolved the boundary between my body and the unmoving earth. The earth smelled of damp depths, of tombs, of flowers. I breathed in its scent and cried without the slightest fear. I walked down a foreign street filled with white boxes, walked in my raiment of blood-drenched feathers, alone on sidewalks swept clean as on a Sunday, and I cried more bitterly, more fully and happily than I would ever cry again. Whitened wires hummed above my head, a little mongrel mutt was running in front of me, in a side street a young muzhik in a vest was smashing a window frame in the house of Khariton Ephrussi. He was smashing it with a wooden hammer, his whole body steeped in the movement. He breathed in deeply, smiled in all directions the gentle smile of drunkenness, of sweat and hearty strength. The whole street was filled with the crackling, crashing song of shattering wood. All this muzhik wanted was to flex his back, to sweat, and to yell out bizarre words in an unknown, not Russian language. He shouted them and sang, opening his blue eyes wide, until a religious procession appeared on the street, marching from the town council.

Old men with painted beards were carrying the portrait of a neatly combed Czar, banners with sepulchral saints fluttered above the religious procession, inflamed old women were running in front of it. When the muzhik in the vest saw the procession, he pressed the hammer to his chest and went running after the banners, while I, waiting for the procession to pass, carefully made my way to our house. It was empty. Its white doors stood open, the grass by the dovecote was trampled down. Kuzma, our janitor, was the only one who had not left our courtyard. Kuzma was sitting in the shed, laying out Shoyl's dead body.

"The wind brings you in like a bad splinter," the old man said when he saw me. "You were gone for ages! See how the townsfolk have hacked our Grandpa down?"

Kuzma began sniffling, turned away, and pulled a perch out of the fly of Grandpa's trousers. Two perches had been shoved into Grandpa—one into his fly, the other into his mouth—and although Grandpa was dead, one of the perches was still alive and quivering.

"Just our Grandpa's been hacked down, no one else!" Kuzma said, throwing the perches to the cat. "You should have heard him curse their goddamn mothers up and down! What a sweet man he was. You should lay two fivers on his eyes."

But back then, just ten years old, I had no idea what dead people needed fivers for.

"Kuzma," I whispered, "save us!"

And I went over to the janitor, embraced his old, bent back with its crooked shoulders, and peered at Grandpa Shoyl from behind the janitor's back. Grandpa Shoyl was lying there in the sawdust, his chest crushed, his beard pointing up, rugged shoes on his bare feet. His legs, spread apart, were dirty, purple, dead. Kuzma was bustling around them. He bound Grandpa's jaws, and kept looking to see if there was anything else he had to do for the deceased. He was bustling about as if some new object had just been delivered to his house. He only calmed down after he finished combing the dead man's beard.

"He cursed their goddamn mothers," he said, smiling, and looked at the corpse lovingly. "If they had been Tatars attacking him, he'd have fought them off—but it was Russians who came, women too, damn Russians; those damn Russians think it's an insult to forgive someone, I know those Russians well!"

The janitor poured sawdust under the dead man. He took off his carpenter's apron and grabbed hold of my hand.

"Let's go to your father," he mumbled, squeezing my hand harder and harder. "Your father's been looking for you since this morning, he must be half dead with worry!"

And I went with Kuzma to the house of the tax inspector, where my parents had hidden from the pogrom.

First Love[1]

When I was ten years old I fell in love with a woman by the name of Galina Apollonovna. Her surname was Rubtsov. Her husband, an officer in the army, had gone to the Japanese War and returned in October 1905. He brought many trunks back with him. These trunks were full of Chinese things: folding screens, precious weapons—all in all, thirty *poods*. Kuzma told us that Rubtsov had bought them with money he had made serving in the engineering corps of the Manchurian Army. Others said the same thing. People found it hard to gossip about the Rubtsovs, because the Rubtsovs were happy. Their house lay right next to our property. Their glass veranda cut into a piece of our land, but my father had not quarreled with them about it. Old Rubtsov, the tax inspector, was known in our town as a fair man, he counted Jews among his acquaintances. And when his son, the officer, returned from the Japanese War, we all saw how lovingly and happily he and his wife settled down together. For days on end Galina Apollonovna would hold her husband's hand. She didn't take her eyes off him, as she hadn't seen him for a year and a half. But I was horrified at her gaze, and looked away, shivering. In the two of them I was watching the strange and shameful life of all the people in the world, and I wanted to fall into a magic sleep to forget this life that surpassed all my dreams. Sometimes Galina Apollonovna would walk about her room in red shoes and a Chinese dressing gown, her braid hanging loose. Beneath the lace of her low-cut chemise I could see the deepening onset of her pressed-down breasts, white and swollen, and on her dressing gown dragons, birds, and hollow trees embroidered in silk.

All day she trailed about the house, a vague smile on her wet lips, bumping into the trunks that had not yet been unpacked and the exercise ladders that lay around on the floor. Whenever Galina bruised her leg, she would lift her dressing gown above her knees and croon to her husband, "Kiss my little booboo!"

And the officer, bending his long legs in dragoon's breeches, spurs, and tight kidskin boots, got down on the dirty floor, and, smiling, shuffled crawling on his knees to her and kissed the bruised spot, the spot where her garter had left a puffy crease. I saw those kisses from my window. They caused me great suffering, but it is not worth describing because the love and jealousy of a ten-year-old boy resembles in every way the love and jealousy of a grown man. For two weeks I did not go to my window and avoided Galina, until a coincidence threw us together. The coincidence was the pogrom that broke out in 1905 in Nikolayev and other towns inside the Jewish Pale. A crowd of hired killers ransacked my father's store and killed my Grandpa Shoyl. All this happened without me. That morning I had been out buying doves from Ivan Nikodimich,

---

1. First published in *Krasnaya gazeta* (Leningrad), May 24 and 25, 1925, and soon after in the almanac *Krasnaya nov*, June 1925. —*Ed.*

the hunter. For five of my ten years I had dreamed with all the fervor of my soul about having doves, and then, when I finally managed to buy them, Makarenko the cripple smashed the doves against the side of my face. After that Kuzma had taken me to the Rubtsovs. A cross had been drawn in chalk on the Rubtsovs' gate, no one would harm them, and they had hidden my parents. Kuzma took me to their glass veranda. There, in the green rotunda, sat my mother and Galina.

"We're going to have to wash our face," Galina said to me. "We're going to have to wash it, my little rabbi. Our whole little face is covered in feathers, and the feathers are all bloody."

She hugged me and led me along the corridor with its sharp aroma. My head was leaning against Galina's hip, and her hip moved and breathed. We went into the kitchen, and she put my head under the tap. A goose was frying on the tiled oven, flickering kitchenware hung along the walls, and next to the kitchenware, in the cook's corner, hung Czar Nicholas I, decorated with paper flowers. Galina washed off the remains of the dove that were caking my cheeks.

"As handsome as a bridegroom, my pretty little boy," she said, then kissed me on the lips with her puffy mouth and turned away.

"Your Papa," she suddenly whispered, "your Papa is very troubled right now. All day long he has been wandering aimlessly through the streets. Go to the window and call him!"

Outside the window I saw the empty street with the enormous sky above it, and my red-haired father walking along. He wasn't wearing a hat, and his red hair was tousled and wispy. His paper shirtfront was twisted to the side and fastened haphazardly with a button, but not the right one. Vlasov, a haggard workman in patched-up soldier's rags, was doggedly following my father.

"No, we don't need it!" he was saying in a fervent, wheezing voice, patting my father tenderly with both hands. "We don't need freedom just so the Yids can trade freely![2] Just give a working man a life of bright . . . brightfulness . . . for all his big horrible toil! Give it to him, my friend! You hear me? Give it to him!"

The workman was patting my father, beseeching him. In his face, flashes of pure drunken inspiration alternated with drowsy despondence.

"Like the Molokans,[3] that's what our lives should be like," he muttered, swaying on unsteady legs. "Our lives should be just like the Molokans, only without that God of the Old Believers—it's from Him the Jews make a profit, no one else does!"[4]

And Vlasov began shouting desperately about the God of the "Old Betrievers," who took pity on no one but the Jews. Vlasov howled, stum-

---

2. In the first publication, this passage read: " 'Babel,' he was saying in a fervent, wheezing voice, patting my father tenderly with both hands, 'We don't need freedom just so the Yids can trade freely!' " —Ed.

3. The Molokans, a Russian Protestant Christian sect that emerged in central Russia in the seventeenth century, focus their worship exclusively on the Scripture (God's "spiritual milk"; hence their name, literally, "the drinkers of milk"); they are opposed to violence and in many ways resemble the Quakers and the Mennonites. —Ed.

4. Old Believers, also known as schismatics, are the Orthodox Christians of the "Ancient Rite," who split from the Orthodox Church after it adopted the reforms of Patriarch Nikon in the seventeenth century. Some of the wealthiest Russian merchants were Old Believers, which is probably why Vlasov associates them with the Jewish capitalists, confusing believers in the God of the Old Testament (the Hebrew Bible) with the Old Believers of the Orthodox Christian faith. —Ed.

bled, and tried to catch up with his mysterious God, but at that moment a mounted Cossack patrol blocked his path. An officer in striped trousers, wearing a silver parade belt, was riding at the head of the detachment. A tall peaked cap was perched on his head. The officer rode slowly, without looking left or right. He rode as if he were riding through a ravine where one can only look forward.

"Captain," my father whispered, when the Cossack reached his side. "Captain," my father repeated, falling to his knees in the mud and clasping his head.

"What can I do for you?" the officer answered, still looking forward, lifting his hand in its lemon suede glove to his peaked cap.

Up ahead, at the corner of Rybnaya Street, thugs were smashing our store and throwing out into the street boxes of nails, tools, and also the new portrait photograph of me in my gymnasium uniform.

"Over there," my father said, without getting up from his knees. "They're smashing everything I've worked for all my life, Captain! Why are they doing this?"

The officer muttered something, tapped his cap with his lemon suede glove, and tugged the reins, but his horse didn't move. My father had crawled on his knees in front of it, brushing against its kindly, short, slightly shaggy legs.

"I will see to it!" the captain said, tugged at the reins, and rode off. The Cossacks followed him.

They sat dispassionately on their high saddles, riding through their imaginary ravine, and disappeared around the corner of Sobornaya Street.

Galina again pushed me toward the window.

"Get your Papa to come home," she said. "He hasn't eaten anything since this morning."

And I leaned out the window.

My father turned around when he heard my voice.

"My darling son," he called out with indescribable tenderness.

He and I went up to the veranda of the Rubtsovs, where mother was lying in the green rotunda. Next to her bed lay dumbbells and an exercise machine.

"Those damn kopecks!" my mother said to us as we came in. "People's lives, and children, and our luckless luck. You gave them everything! Those damn kopecks!" she shouted in a hoarse voice unlike her own. She shuddered convulsively, and lay quiet on the bed.

Then, in the silence, I began to hiccup. I stood by the wall with my cap pulled down and couldn't stop hiccuping.

"Shame on you, my pretty little boy," Galina said, smiling her haughty smile at me, and tapping me with the stiff flap of her dressing gown. She went over to the window in her red shoes and began to hang Chinese curtains on the extraordinary rod. Her bare arms drowned in the silk, the live braid moved over her hip. I looked at her with delight.

Learned boy that I was, I looked at her as at a distant stage lit by many lights. And I imagined I was Miron, the son of the coal merchant who sold coal on our street corner. I imagined myself in the Jewish Self-defense Brigade. I could see myself walking around, just like Miron, in tattered shoes tied together with string. A dingy rifle hangs on a green strap from my shoulder, and I'm kneeling by the old wooden fence, firing shots at the murderers. Beyond the fence lies a vacant lot with heaps of dusty coal. My old rifle shoots badly, the murderers with their beards and white teeth are edging ever closer to me. I feel the proud sensation of impending death, and high, high up, high in the blue heavens, I see Galina. I see an opening cut into the wall of a gigantic fortress built with myriads of bricks. This crimson building looms over the side street with its badly tamped gray earth. On the parapet stands Galina. With her haughty smile she smiles from that inaccessible opening, her husband, the half-dressed officer, standing behind her back, kissing her neck.

In my attempt to stop hiccuping, I imagined all this in order to make my loving her more bitter, hot, and hopeless, and perhaps because so much grief is overwhelming for a ten-year-old boy. These foolish fantasies helped me forget the death of the doves and the death of Shoyl. I would have perhaps forgotten these deaths if Kuzma had not come onto the veranda with that terrible Jew, Aba.

It was twilight when they came. A weak little lamp, hiding in a corner, shone on the veranda—a twinkling lamp, a disciple of misfortune.

"I have prepared Grandfather," Kuzma said as he came in. "Now he's lying nice and pretty—I brought the *shamas* too so he can say some words over the old man."

And Kuzma pointed to *shamas* Aba.

"Let him whine a little," Kuzma said amiably. "Stuff a *shamas'* guts, and the *shamas* will pester God all night."

Kuzma stood on the threshold, his good-natured, broken nose jutting in all directions, and warmly began telling us how he had bound the dead man's jaw. But my father interrupted him.

"I would be thankful, Reb Aba, if you would pray over the deceased, I will pay you," my father said.

"Pay me? But I'm worried you won't pay," Aba answered in a weary voice, laying his squeamish bearded face on the tablecloth. "I am worried that you will take my ruble and run off to Argentina, to Buenos Aires, and open a wholesale business there with that ruble of mine! A wholesale business!" Aba said. He chewed his disdainful lips and picked up the newspaper *Son of the Fatherland*, which was lying on the table. In this newspaper there was an article about the Czar's manifesto of October 17, and about freedom.[5]

"Citizens of free Russia," Aba read haltingly, and chewed his beard, which he had stuffed into his mouth. "Citizens of free Russia, Easter greetings on this Holy Sunday. The old *shamas* held the shaking newspaper sideways in front of him. He read it drowsily, in a singsong voice, pronouncing the Russian words he did not know in the strangest way. Aba's pronunciation of these words resembled the muffled babble of a Negro who has just arrived at a Russian port from his native land. It even made my mother laugh.

"I am being sinful," she shouted, leaning out of the rotunda. "You are making me laugh, Aba! You should tell us how you and your family are doing?"

"Ask me about something else," Aba mumbled without releasing his beard from between his teeth, and continued reading the newspaper.

5. Aba's is making fun of the October Manifesto. The first part is a verbatim quote from the Manifesto of October 17, but the "greeting" part is Aba's mockery of the Manifesto's content. Aba's joke is that the Manifesto's promise is as good as Easter in October, which is another reason for the boy's mother to burst out laughing. —*Ed.*

"Ask him something else," my father repeated, walking over to the middle of the room. His eyes, smiling at us through their tears, suddenly began rolling and fixed themselves on a spot invisible to all.

"Oy, Shoyl!" my father uttered in a flat, false, theatrical voice. "Oy, beloved Shoyl!"

We saw that he was getting ready to start hollering, and my mother forewarned us.

"Manus!"[6] she shouted, tearing at my father's breast, her hair becoming instantly disheveled. "Look what a state our child is in, can't you hear him hiccuping? Can't you?"

Father fell silent.

"Rakhel," he said timorously, "I cannot tell you how unhappy I am about Shoyl."

Aba went to the kitchen and came back with a glass of water.

"Drink, you little *shlemazl*," he said, coming over to me. "Drink this water, which will help you as much as incense helps a dead man!"

And sure enough, the water did not help me in the least. My hiccups became stronger and stronger. A growl tore out of my chest. A swelling, pleasant to the touch, expanded in my throat. The swelling breathed, widened, covered my gullet, and came bulging out over my collar. Within the swelling gurgled my torn breath. It gurgled like boiling water. By nightfall I was no longer the silly little boy I had been all my life, but had turned into a writhing heap. My mother, now taller and shapelier, wrapped herself in her shawl and went to Galina, who stood watching stiffly.

"My dear Galina," my mother said in a strong, melodious voice. "We are imposing on you and dear Nadyezhda Ivanovna, and all your family so much. My dear Galina, I am so embarrassed!"

With fiery cheeks my mother jostled Galina toward the door, and then came hurrying over to me, stuffing her shawl into my mouth to smother my groans.

"Hold on, my little darling," mother whispered. "Hold on for Mama."[7]

But even if I could have held on, I wouldn't have, because I no longer felt any shame at all.[8]

That was how my illness began. I was ten years old at the time. The following morning I was taken to the doctor. The pogrom continued, but no one touched us. The doctor, a fat man, diagnosed an illness of the nerves.[9]

He told us to go to Odessa as quickly as we could, to the specialists, and to wait there for the warm weather and bathing in the sea.

And that is what we did. A few days later I left for Odessa with my mother to stay with Grandfather Levy-Itskhok and Uncle Simon. We left in the morning on a ship, and by midday the churning waters of the Bug

6. The elder Babel's actual first name (Manus, Man', Emmanuel Babel). —*Ed.*
7. In the early printed version, the passage read: " 'Hold on, sonny,' she whispered, 'Hold on, my poor Babel, hold on for your mother's sake.' " —*Ed.*
8. In the earlier printed version, Babel elaborated further: "I thrashed about the bed and sliding off it was not taking my eyes off Galina. Fear tormented her and made her swoon; I groaned in her face in order to prolong my power over her, and as I was sobbing, triumphant and exhausted, with the last efforts of love, I gushed forth at her with a green liquid right from my heart." —*Ed.*
9. In the early version, the text continued as follows: " 'This illness,' said he, 'occurs only among Jews, and among Jews only among women.' For this reason, the doctor was surprised to have found such a strange illness in me." —*Ed*

changed to the heavy green waves of the sea. This was the beginning of my life in the house of my crazed Grandfather Levy-Itskhok. And I bade farewell forever to Nikolayev, where I had lived the first ten years of my childhood.[1]

The Awakening[1]

All the people of our circle—middlemen, storekeepers, clerks in banks and steamship offices—sent their children to music lessons. Our fathers, seeing they had no prospects of their own, set up a lottery for themselves. They built this lottery on the bones of their little children. Odessa was in the grip of this craze more than any other town. And sure enough, over the last few decades our town had sent a number of child prodigies onto the stages of the world. Mischa Elman, Zimbalist, Gawrilowitsch all came from Odessa—Jascha Heifetz started out with us.[2]

When a boy turned four or five, his mother took the tiny, frail creature to Mr. Zagursky.[3] Zargursky ran a factory that churned out child prodigies, a factory of Jewish dwarfs in lace collars and patent leather shoes. He went hunting for them in the Moldavanka slums and the reeking courtyards of the old bazaar. Zagursky gave them the first push, then the children were sent off to Professor Auer[4] in Petersburg. There was powerful harmony in the souls of these little creatures with their swollen blue heads. They became acclaimed virtuosi. And so—my father decided to keep up with them. I had passed the age of child prodigies—I was almost fourteen—but because of my height and frailness I could be mistaken for an eight-year-old. Therein lay all our hopes.

I was brought to Zagursky. Out of respect for my grandfather, he agreed to take me at a ruble a lesson—a low fee. My grandfather was the laughing-stock of the town, but also its ornament. He walked the streets in a top hat and tattered shoes, and provided answers to the murkiest questions. People asked him what a Gobelin was, why the Jacobins had betrayed Robespierre, how synthetic silk was made, what a cesarean section was. My grandfather knew the answers to all these questions. It was out of respect for his knowledge and madness that Zagursky charged us only a ruble a lesson. And he put a lot of effort into me, fearing Grandfather, though putting any effort into me was pointless. Sounds scraped out of my violin like iron filings. These sounds cut even into my own heart, but my father would not give up. All anyone talked about at home was Mischa Elman; the Czar himself had absolved him from military service. Zimbalist, from what my father had heard, had been presented to the King of England and had played at Buckingham Palace. Gawrilowitsch's parents had bought two houses in Peters-

1. In the earlier version, the ending continued: "And now, recalling those sad years, I discover in them the origin of the maladies tormenting me today and the reason for my premature decay." —Ed.
1. First published in *Molodaya gvardiya* 17–18, 1931. —Ed.
2. Mischa Elman (1891–1967), Efrem Zimbalist (1890–1985), and Jascha Heifetz (1901–1987) were among the foremost violinists of the twentieth century. Ossip Gabrilowitsch (1878–1936), was a prominent pianist and conductor.
3. Zagursky's prototype was Pyotr Solomonovich Stolyarsky (1871–1944), a friend of Babel's family, a famous violin instructor, and founder of the Odessa City Music School named after him. He was also famous for his absurd maxims and aphoristic malapropisms. —Ed.
4. Leopold Auer (1845–1930), world-famous professor of violin at the St. Petersburg Conservatory.

burg. The child prodigies brought wealth to their parents. My father was prepared to resign himself to a life of poverty, but he needed fame.

"It's unthinkable," people who went out dining with my father at his expense assured him, "absolutely unthinkable, that the grandson of a grandfather like his wouldn't become . . ."

But I had other things in my head. Whenever I practiced my violin I placed books by Turgenev or Dumas on my music stand, and, as I scraped away, devoured one page after another. During the day I told stories to the neighborhood boys, at night I put them down on paper. Writing was a hereditary occupation in our family. Grandpa Levy-Itskhok, who had gone mad in his old age, had spent his life writing a novel with the title *The Headless Man*. I followed in his footsteps.

Laden with violin case and music scores, I dragged myself over to Zagursky's on Witte Street, formerly Dvoryanskaya Street.[5] There, along the walls, Jewesses sat, waiting flushed and hysterical for their turn. They pressed to their weak knees violins more magnificent than those destined to play at Buckingham Palace.

The door of the inner sanctum opened. Large-headed, freckled children came bustling out of Zagursky's chamber, their necks thin as flower stalks, a convulsive flush on their cheeks. Then the door closed, swallowing up the next dwarf. In the adjacent room Zagursky, with his red curls, bow tie, and thin legs, sang and conducted in ecstasy. The founder of this freakish lottery filled the Moldavanka and the back alleys of the old bazaar with specters of pizzicato and cantilena. This incantation of his was then fine-tuned to a diabolical brilliancy by old Professor Auer.

I had no business being a member of his sect. I too was a dwarf just as they were, but I heard a different calling in the voice of my ancestors.

This was an arduous apprenticeship for me. One day I set out from home, laden with my music, my violin, its case, and the sum of twelve rubles, the fee for a month of lessons. I walked down Nezhinskaya Street, and should have turned into Dvoryanskaya Street to get to Zagursky's place. Yet I walked down Tiraspolskaya and ended up in the port. My allotted three hours flew past in the Prakticheskaya harbor. That was the beginning of my liberation. Zagursky's waiting room was never to see me again. More important things were occupying my mind. My classmate Nemanov and I got in the habit of going on board the *Kensington* to visit an old sailor called Mr. Trottyburn. Nemanov was a year younger than I, but from the time he was eight years old he had engaged in the most complex trading you could imagine. He was a genius at anything having to do with trade, and always delivered what he promised. Now he is a millionaire in New York, the general manager of General Motors, a company as powerful as Ford. Nemanov took me along because I obeyed his every command. He bought smuggled tobacco pipes from Mr. Trottyburn. These pipes had been carved by the old sailor's brother in Lincoln.

"Mark my words, gentlemen," Mr. Trottyburn said to us. "You have to make your children with your own hands. Smoking a factory-made pipe is like sticking an enema tube in your mouth. Do you know who Benvenuto

---

5. The street had been renamed in honor of Sergey Witte, an Odessan who had been Russia's Minister of Finance and who was appointed Prime Minister after the Manifesto of October 17, 1905, a document that he had helped draft. —*Ed.*

Cellini was? He was a master! My brother in Lincoln could tell you about him. My brother lives and lets live. The one thing he believes in is that you have to make your children with your own hands, you can't leave that sort of thing to others. And he is right, gentlemen!"

Nemanov sold Trottyburn's pipes to bank managers, foreign consuls, and rich Greeks. He made a hundred percent profit.

The pipes of the Lincoln master exuded poetry. Each and every one of them contained a thought, a drop of eternity. A little yellow eye twinkled from their mouthpieces. Their cases were lined with satin. I tried to imagine how Matthew Trottyburn, the last of the pipe-carving masters, lived in an England of old, defying the winds of change.

"He is right, gentlemen, you have to make your children with your own hands!"

The heavy waves by the harbor wall separated me more and more from a home reeking of onions and Jewish fate. From the Prakticheskaya harbor I moved on to the breakwater. There, on a stretch of sandbar, the boys of Primorskaya Street hung out. They went without pants from morning till night, they dove under fishing boats, stole coconuts for food, and waited for the time when carts carrying watermelons rolled in from Kherson and Kamenki, and they could split these watermelons open on the moorings of the dock.

My dream now was to learn how to swim. I was ashamed of admitting to those bronzed boys that I, though born in Odessa, had not even seen the sea until I was ten, and that I still could not swim at fourteen.

How late I learned the essential things in life! In my childhood, nailed to the Gemara,[6] I led the life of a sage, and it was only later, when I was older, that I began to climb trees.

It turned out that the ability to swim was beyond my reach. The hydrophobia of my ancestors, the Spanish rabbis and Frankfurt money changers, dragged me to the bottom. Water would not carry me. Battered, doused in salt water, I went back to the shore, to my violin and my music scores. I was attached to my instruments of crime, and dragged them along with me. The battle of the rabbis with the sea lasted until the local water god—Efim Nikitich Smolich, a proofreader for the *Odessa News*—took pity on me. In that athletic chest of his there was a warmth for Jewish boys. Nikitich led crowds of frail little creatures, gathering them up from the bedbug-ridden hovels of the Moldavanka. He took them to the beach, built sand castles with them, exercised and dived with them, taught them songs, and, baking in the hard rays of the sun, told them tales of fishermen and animals. To grown-ups, Nikitich explained that he was simply a devotee of natural philosophy. Nikitich's stories made the Jewish children collapse with laughter. They squealed and frolicked like puppies. The sun spattered them with creeping freckles, freckles the color of lizards.

Nikitich silently watched me combat the waves single-handed. Seeing that there was no hope I would ever learn to swim on my own, he let me join the other little lodgers of his heart. His cheerful heart was completely devoted to us. It was never disdainful, never miserly, and never agitated. He lay among us by the breakwater, the king of these melon and

6. Part of the Talmud, the Gemara is a rabbinical commentary on the Mishna, the first codification of ancient Jewish oral laws.

kerosene waters, with his copper shoulders, his head that of an aging gladiator, and his lightly crooked, bronze legs. I loved him as only a boy afflicted with hysteria and headaches can love an athlete. I didn't leave his side, and tried to please him every way I could.

"Calm down," he told me. "Steady your nerves, and swimming will come of its own accord. . . . What do you mean, the water won't hold you up? Why shouldn't it?"

Seeing how I was reaching out to him, Nikitich made an exception for me among all his pupils, and invited me to come up to his place, a clean, spacious garret covered in mats, and showed me his dogs, his hedgehog, his tortoise, and his doves. In gratitude for his generosity I brought him a tragedy I had written the night before.

"I knew you were a scribbler!" Nikitich said. "You have that look in your eyes. You're no longer looking at things."

He read my play, shrugged his shoulders, ran his fingers through his stiff, gray locks, and paced up and down the garret.

"I believe," he said in a slow drawl, pausing between words, "that there is a divine spark in you."

We went out into the street. The old man stopped, banged his stick hard on the sidewalk, and peered at me.

"There's something lacking in your work, but what is it? That you are young is no problem—that will pass in time. What you lack is a feel for nature."

He pointed his stick at a tree with a reddish trunk and a low crown. "What kind of tree is that?"

I didn't know.

"What's growing on this bush?"

I didn't know that either. We walked through the little park on Aleksandrovsky Boulevard. The old man poked at all the trees with his stick, grabbed my shoulder whenever a bird flew by, and had me listen to their different calls.

"What bird is that singing?"

I couldn't answer. The names of birds and trees, what families they belonged to, where the birds flew, on which side the sun rose, when the dew was at its heaviest—all this was unknown to me.

"And you have the audacity to write? A man who does not exist in nature the way a stone or an animal exists in it will not write a single worthwhile line in all his life. Your landscapes resemble descriptions of stage sets. Goddamn it! What could your parents have been thinking of these past fourteen years?"

What had they been thinking of? Of contested bills and the mansions of Mischa Elman. I didn't tell Nikitich that, I remained silent.

At home, at the dinner table, I didn't touch my food—it wouldn't go down.

"A feel for nature!" I thought. My God, why hadn't this occurred to me? Where could I find someone to tell me what the different birdcalls and the names of trees were? How much did I know about these things? I could perhaps identify lilacs—that is, if they were in bloom. Lilacs and acacias. Deribasovskaya and Grecheskaya Streets were lined with acacias.

At dinner, father told us a new story about Jascha Heifetz. On his way to Robyn's, father had run into Mendelson, Jascha's uncle. It turned out that the boy was getting eight hundred rubles a performance: "So go ahead and add up how much that comes to at fifteen concerts a month!"

I added it up. The result was twelve thousand a month. As I multiplied the number, carrying the four in my head, I looked out the window. My music teacher, Mr. Zagursky, wearing a lightly billowing cape, red ringlets jutting out from under his soft hat, and propping himself up with his cane, came marching through our cement yard. It cannot be said that he had been quick to notice my absence: more than three months had already passed since the day my violin had sunk to the sandy bottom off the breakwater.

Zagursky came up to our front door. I rushed off to the back door. It had been boarded up the night before to keep out thieves. So I locked myself in the toilet. Within half an hour my whole family had gathered outside the toilet door. The women were crying. Auntie Bobka, quivering with sobs, was grinding her fat shoulder against the door. My father was silent. He began speaking more quietly and distinctly than ever before in his life.

"I am an officer," my father said. "I have an estate. I ride out on hunts. The muzhiks pay me rent. I sent my son to the Cadet Corps. There is no reason for me to lose any sleep over my son."

He fell silent. The women sniffled. Then a terrible blow came crashing against the toilet door. My father began throwing himself on it with his whole body; he took runs and hurled himself against it.

"I am an officer!" he howled. "I ride out on hunts! I will kill him! That's it!"

The hook went hurtling off the door, but the bolt was still there, held by a single nail. The women threw themselves on the floor, grappling for my father's legs. Raving, he tried to tear himself loose. Hearing the rumpus, my old grandmother, my father's mother, came hurrying in.

"My child," she said to him in Yiddish. "Our sorrow is great, it knows no bounds. The last thing we need in our house is blood. I do not want to see blood in our house!"

My father moaned. I heard his footsteps receding. The latch was hanging on its last nail.

I sat in my fortress till nightfall. When everybody had gone to bed, Auntie Bobka took me to my grandmother's. It was a long walk. The moonlight froze on unknown shrubs, on nameless trees. An invisible bird whistled once and then was quiet, perhaps it had fallen asleep. What kind of bird was it? What was it called? Was there dew in the evenings? Where was the constellation of the Great Bear in the sky? On what side did the sun rise?

We walked along Pochtovaya Street. Auntie Bobka held my hand tightly so that I wouldn't run away. She was right. I was thinking of running away.

In the Basement[1]

I was a boy who told lies. This came from reading. My imagination was always aroused. I read during class, between classes, on my way home, and

---

1. First published in *Novy mir* 10, 1931. —Ed.

under the table at night, hidden by the tablecloth that hung down to the floor. Reading books, I missed out on everything the world around me had to offer: skipping classes to go to the port, the coming of billiards to the coffee shops along Grecheskaya Street, swimming at Langeron.[2] I had no friends. Who would have wanted to spend time with someone like me?

One day I saw the brightest student in our class, Mark Borgman, with a book about Spinoza. He had just read it and was dying to tell the boys around him about the Spanish Inquisition. What he told them was nothing but scientific prattle. There was no poetry in Borgman's words. I could not stop myself from cutting in. To whoever would listen, I talked about old Amsterdam, about the gloom of the ghetto, about the philosopher diamond cutters. I added quite a lot of spice to what I had read in books. I couldn't resist. My imagination sharpened dramatic scenes, altered endings, steeped the beginnings in more mystery. Spinoza's death, his lonely death in freedom, appeared to me in my imagination as a battle. The Sanhedrin had tried to compel the dying man to repent, but he held fast. It was at this point that I blended in Rubens. I imagined Rubens standing at the head of Spinoza's bed, casting a death mask of the corpse's face.

My schoolmates listened to my outlandish tale with open mouths. I told my tale with gusto. When the bell rang we reluctantly dispersed. Borgman came up to me during the following break, took me by the arm, and we went for a walk together. Soon we were seeing eye to eye. Borgman wasn't a bad specimen of top student. To his powerful brain, high school learning was only a scribble in the margin of the book of life. And he sought that book with ardor. Even as foolish little twelve-year-olds, we were all very aware that a wondrous and erudite life lay before him. He didn't even prepare for classes, he just sat there and listened. This reserved, sober boy was drawn to me because of my knack for twisting things, even the simplest things you could imagine.

That year we moved up to the third class. My report card was full of C-minuses. I was so strange, with all the outlandish gibberish bouncing through my mind, that my teachers, after much deliberation, decided against giving me twos.

At the beginning of summer, Borgman invited me to come to his dacha. His father was the director of the Russian Bank for International Trade. He was one of those men who was turning Odessa into a Marseilles or Naples. The core of the old Odessa merchant was within him. He was one of those pleasant but skeptical bon vivants who avoided speaking Russian, preferring instead the rough, choppy language of the Liverpool ship captains. When an Italian opera came to Odessa in April, Borgman invited the whole cast to dinner. The puffy banker, the last of the Odessa merchants, had a little two-month liaison with the buxom prima donna. She took with her memories that did not burden her conscience along with a necklace chosen with taste but not costing too much.

The old man also held the position of Argentinean consul, and was chairman of the stock exchange committee. And I had been invited to his house. My Auntie Bobka ran out into the courtyard trumpeting the

2. A beach in Odessa, named after the French count, Alexander Langeron, who was governor general of Odessa from 1816–22.

news. She dressed me up as best she could. I took the train to the sixteenth stop at Bolshoy Fontan.[3] The dacha stood on a low, red cliff right by the shore. A flower garden of fuchsias and clipped thuya shrubs covered the cliff.

I came from a loud, impoverished family. The Borgman dacha filled me with awe. White wicker chairs glittered in walks covered with foliage. The dinner table was filled with flowers, the windows fitted with green casings. A low wooden colonnade opened up before the house.

The bank director came to the dacha in the evenings. After dinner he placed his wicker chair at the very edge of the cliff in front of the shifting plain of the sea, stretched out his legs in his white trousers, lit a cigar, and began to read the *Manchester Guardian*. The guests, Odessa ladies, played poker on the veranda. A narrow samovar with ivory handles was sputtering on the edge of the table.

The women—card-playing gourmands, sluttish coquettes, and furtive debauchees with large hips and perfumed undergarments—fluttered black fans and staked their gold. The sun pierced its way to them through the copse of wild vines. Its fiery globe was immense. Copper sparks weighed down the women's black hair. Flashes of sunset pierced their diamonds— diamonds that hung everywhere: in the deep hollows of breasts pressed apart, from powdered ears, and on plump and bluish female fingers.

Evening fell. A bat rustled by. The sea rolled blacker against the red cliff. My twelve-year-old heart surged with the cheer and ease of others' wealth. My friend and I ambled hand in hand down the long walks. Borgman told me that he would become an aviation engineer. There was a rumor that his father would be appointed the London representative of the Russian Bank for International Trade. Borgman would be educated in England.

At our house, Auntie Bobka's house, no one talked of such things. I had nothing with which I could match this uninterrupted splendor. So I told Borgman that although things back at my place were very different, my grandfather Levy-Itskhok and my uncle had traveled the whole world over and had thousands of adventures under their belts. I described these adventures one after the other. Within seconds, I lost all sense of reality, and took Uncle Volf from the Russian-Turkish War to Alexandria and Egypt.

Night rose in the poplars, stars pressed down on stooping branches. I spoke with wild gesticulations. The fingers of the future aviation engineer trembled in my hand. He emerged with difficulty from the hallucination, and promised to come visit me at my place the following Sunday. Braced by his promise, I took the ferry back home to Auntie Bobka's.

The whole following week I imagined I was a bank director. I brought about millions of transactions with Singapore and Port Said. I acquired a yacht, and sailed it single-handedly. By Sabbath reality struck. Little Borgman was to come visiting the following day. Nothing of what I had told him actually existed. What did exist was far more extraordinary than anything I had invented, but at the age of twelve I had no idea how to grapple with the truth of my world. Grandpa Levy-Itskhok, a rabbi chased out of his shtetl for forging Count Branitsky's signature on prom-

---

3. "Large Fountain" was an elegant beach spa outside Odessa.

issory notes, was considered a madman by neighbors and street boys alike. Uncle Simon-Volf I could not stand because of his loud eccentricity, full of mad fire, yelling, and harassment. Auntie Bobka was the only one I could count on. She was very proud that the son of a bank director was my friend. She saw this friendship as the beginning of a bright career and baked a fruit strudel and a poppy-seed pie for our guest. Into that pie she put the heart of our tribe, the heart that had withstood so many tribulations. We hid my grandfather, with his tattered top hat and his swollen feet bound in rags, with our neighbors the Apelkhots, and I begged him not to show himself until our guest left. I also dealt with Simon-Volf. He went off with his profiteer pals to drink tea at the Medved Tavern. Tea there was braced with vodka, and it was safe to assume that Simon-Volf would be delayed. It has to be said that my family was not your typical Jewish family. There were drunks in our clan, we had run away with the daughters of generals and then abandoned them before crossing the border, and our grandfather had forged signatures and written blackmailing letters for abandoned wives.

All my efforts went into keeping Simon-Volf away for the whole day. I gave him the three rubles I had managed to save up. Spending three rubles took some doing, Simon-Volf would come back late, and the bank director's son would never know that the tales of my uncle's kindness and strength were all lies. It must, however, be said that were one to appraise things purely with one's heart, then my tale could be seen as true and not a lie at all. But when you first came face-to-face with the loud and dirty Simon-Volf, this intangible truth was not to be discerned.

On Sunday morning, Bobka put on her brown, raw-cloth dress. Her fat, kindly breasts bounced in all directions. She tied on her kerchief with the black floral print, the kind of kerchief worn in the synagogue on Yom Kippur and Rosh Hashanah. Bobka arranged the pies, jam, and pretzels on the table and waited. We lived in the basement. Borgman raised his eyebrows as he walked over the corridor's crooked floor. A barrel of water stood by the entrance. The instant Borgman was inside, I began entertaining him with every conceivable marvel. I showed him the alarm clock which my grandfather had constructed down to the last screw—a lamp was hooked up to the clock, and every time the clock reached a full or half hour, the lamp would light up. I also showed him our little keg of shoe wax. Grandpa Levy-Itskhok had invented that shoe wax recipe, and he would not reveal it to anyone. Then Borgman and I read a few pages from my grandfather's manuscript. He wrote in Yiddish, on square sheets of yellow paper large as maps. The manuscript was called *The Headless Man*. In it was a description of all Levy-Itskhok's neighbors over a period of sixty years—first in Skvira and Belaya Tserkov, then in Odessa. Undertakers, cantors, Jewish drunks, cooks at *bris* feasts, and the charlatans who performed the ritual operation—these were Levy-Itskhok's characters. They were all loud and offensive people, with crude speech and fleshy noses, pimply faces, and twisted backsides.

As we were reading, Bobka appeared in her brown dress. She came floating in, engulfed by her fat, kindly breasts, carrying a tray on which stood a samovar. I introduced them. "Pleased to meet you," Bobka said, reaching out her sweaty, stiff fingers and doing a little scraping bow. I couldn't have wished for things to go better. Our neighbors the Apelkhots wouldn't let grandfather leave their place. I dragged out all his treasures one by one: grammars of every language you could imagine, and sixty-six volumes of the Talmud. Borgman was dazzled by the keg of shoe wax, the wondrous alarm clock, and the mountain of Talmuds—all things one would never see in any other home.

We each drank two glasses of tea with our strudel. Bobka left, bowing her head and shuffling backward out of the room. I fell into a joyful state of mind, struck a pose, and began declaiming the verses that I loved more than anything in the world. Antony, bending over Caesar's dead body, speaks to the people of Rome.

> Friends, Romans, countrymen, lend me your ears;
> I come to bury Caesar, not to praise him.[4]

That is how Antony begins his performance. I gasped and pressed my hand to my heart.

> He was my friend, faithful and just to me:
> But Brutus says he was ambitious;
> And Brutus is an honorable man.
> He hath brought many captives home to Rome
> Whose ransoms did the general coffers fill:
> Did this in Caesar seem ambitious?
> When that the poor have cried, Caesar hath wept:
> Ambition should be made of sterner stuff:
> Yet Brutus says he was ambitious;
> And Brutus is an honorable man.

Brutus's face hovered before my eyes, in the mists of the universe. His face turned whiter than chalk. The people of Rome began closing in on me menacingly. I raised my arm—Borgman's eyes obediently followed it—my clenched fist was quaking, I raised my arm, and through the window saw Uncle Simon-Volf walk through the yard with Leykakh the junk dealer. They were carrying a rack made of antlers, and a red trunk with handles in the form of lions' jaws. Bobka also saw them from the window. Forgetting my guest, she came running into the room and grabbed hold of me with trembling hands.

"Oh my poor heart! He's been buying furniture again!"

Borgman rose in his school uniform, and bowed to Auntie Bobka in bewilderment. They were pounding on the door. The thud of boots and the clatter of the trunk being dragged across the floor came rumbling from the corridor. The thundering voices of Simon-Volf and redheaded Leykakh were deafening. Both were tipsy.

"Bobka!" Simon-Volf yelled. "Guess how much I paid for these antlers!"

He blared like a trumpet, but there was a hint of uncertainty in his voice. Drunk though he was, he knew how much we hated redheaded Leykakh, who spurred him on to keep buying things, flooding our place with useless and ridiculous furniture.

Bobka stood there in silence. Leykakh said something to Simon-Volf in his wheezing voice. To drown out his snakelike hissing and my anxiety, I started shouting Anthony's words.

---

4. Shakespeare's *Julius Caesar* III. ii. —*Ed.*

But yesterday the word of Caesar might
Have stood against the world; now lies he there.
And none so poor to do him reverence.
O masters, if I were disposed to stir
Your hearts and minds to mutiny and rage,
I should do Brutus wrong, and Cassius wrong,
Who, you all know, are honorable men . . .

Suddenly there was a thud. Bobka had fallen down, knocked off her feet by her husband's blow. She must have made a sharp remark about the antlers. The daily ritual began. Simon-Volf's brassy voice thundered to high heaven.

"You are squeezing the glue out of me!" my uncle roared. "You are squeezing the glue out of me so you can stuff those damn dog faces of yours! My soul's been crushed by work, I've nothing left to work with, no hands, no legs, nothing! You've hung a millstone around my neck, a millstone hangs from my neck!"

He heaped Yiddish curses on Bobka and me, he wished that our eyes would leak out, that our children would rot and wither in their mothers' wombs, that we would not live to bury each other, and that we would be dragged by our hair to a pauper's grave.

Little Borgman stood up. He looked around the room, his face pale. He did not understand the ins and outs of Jewish blasphemy, but he was familiar enough with Russian swearing. And Simon-Volf did not refrain from slipping into Russian. The bank director's son stood there kneading his cap. My eyes saw him double as I struggled to shout away all the evil in the world. My mortal agony and Caesar's death became one. I was dead and I was shouting. A wheeze rose from the depths of my being.

If you have tears, prepare to shed them now.
You all do know this mantle: I remember
The first time ever Caesar put it on;
'Twas on a summer's evening, in his tent,
That day he overcame the Nervii:
Look, in this place ran Cassius' dagger through:
See what a rent the envious Casca made:
Through this the well-beloved Brutus stabb'd;
And as he pluck'd his cursed steel away,
Mark how the blood of Caesar follow'd it . . .

No one would have had the power to drown out Simon-Volf. Bobka sat on the floor, sobbing and blowing her nose. Leykakh, unruffled, was dragging the trunk along behind the partition. And it was at this very moment that my crazed grandfather got it into his head to come to my rescue. He tore himself loose from the Apelkhots next door, crawled over to the window, and began sawing away at his violin, most probably so that people wouldn't hear Simon-Volf's cursing. Borgman looked out the window, which was at ground level, and stumbled back in horror. My poor grandfather was twisting his rigid blue mouth into wild grimaces. He had on his crooked top hat and his black quilted cloak with its bone buttons; the remnants of what had been shoes clung to his elephantine feet. His sooty beard hung in tatters and blew into the window. Borgman ran for the door.

"Please don't worry," he muttered, as he ran for freedom. "Please don't worry."

His uniform and his cap with the raised brim flashed through the yard. With Borgman's departure my agitation began to subside. I waited for evening to come. After grandfather lay down in his cot and went to sleep, having filled a sheet of paper with Yiddish scribbles (describing the Apelkhots, at whose house, through my ministrations, he had spent the whole day), I went out into the corridor. It had a dirt floor. I moved through the darkness, barefoot, in my long, patched-up nightshirt. The cobblestones shimmered like blades of light through the cracks in the boards. The barrel of water stood as always in the corner. I lowered myself into it. The water cut me in two. I plunged my head under, choked, and came up for air. Our cat gazed at me sleepily from high up on a shelf. The second time I held out longer. The water swished around me, swallowing my moan. I opened my eyes and saw my billowing shirt and my legs pressed against each other. Again I didn't have enough strength. I came up. My grandfather was standing next to the barrel in his nightshirt. His single tooth jiggled in his mouth.

"My grandson." He spoke these words distinctly and with contempt. "I shall go and drink some castor oil so that I will have something to dump on your grave."

I started shouting and thrashing, plunging into the water with all my might. I was pulled up by my grandfather's weak hand. I cried for the first time that day, and the world of tears was so immense and beautiful that everything except my tears disappeared from before my eyes.

When I regained consciousness, I was lying wrapped in blankets in my bed. Grandfather was pacing up and down the room, whistling. Fat Bobka was warming my hands on her breasts.

"Look how he is shivering, our silly little boy!" Bobka said. "And how does he have the strength to shiver like that?"

Grandfather tugged at his beard, whistled, and began walking up and down the room again. In the next room Simon-Volf was snoring with tormented breath. He always yelled himself out during the day, and so never woke in the night.

Di Grasso[1]

I was fourteen years old. I belonged to the fearless battalion of theater ticket scalpers. My boss was a shark with an eye that always squinted and a large, silky mustache. His name was Kolya Shvarts. I fell in with him that dark year when the Italian Opera went bust. The impresario,

1. First published in the weekly *Ogonyok* 23, 1937. Di Grasso (1873–1930) was a famous Sicilian actor, originally a puppeteer, who successfully toured with his troupe in Europe and the United States beginning in 1908 and well into the 1920s. He performed in a dialect incomprehensible outside Sicily, but made up for it by intensely passionate acting. He had famous admirers, among them Gabriel D'Annunzio, Edward VII, and the Bolshevik culture commissar Anatoly Lunacharsky. Di Grasso toured Russia in late 1908 and early 1909, when Babel, like his narrator, was fourteen years old. The play that made Di Grasso famous in this story was *Feodalesimo* by Àngel Guimerà. Babel did not exaggerate the antics; according to a Russian reviewer, they were part of the production. —*Ed.*

swayed by the theater critics, had not signed up Anselmi and Tito Ruffo as guest stars, concentrating instead on a strong ensemble. He was punished for this, went broke, and so did we. To set things right, we were promised Chaliapin, but Chaliapin wanted three thousand a performance. So Di Grasso, the Sicilian tragic actor, came with his troupe instead. They were taken to their hotel in carts loaded with children, cats, and cages in which Italian birds fluttered.

"We can't push this merchandise!" Kolya Shvarts said when he saw the motley procession rolling in.

The moment the actor arrived, he went down to the bazaar with his bag. In the evening, carrying a different bag, he turned up at the theater. Barely fifty people came to the premiere. We hawked tickets at half price, but could find no buyers.

That evening Di Grasso's troupe performed a Sicilian folk drama, with a plot as humdrum as night and day. The daughter of a rich peasant became engaged to a shepherd. She was true to him, until one day the squire's son came visiting from town in a velvet vest. The girl chatted with the visitor, tongue-tied and giggling at all the wrong moments. Listening to them, the shepherd darted his head about like a startled bird. Throughout the whole first act he crept along walls, went off somewhere in his fluttering trousers, and then came back again, looking around shiftily.

"We have a turkey on our hands!" Kolya Shvarts said during the intermission. "This is merchandise for Kremenchug, not Odessa!"

The intermission gave the girl time to prime herself for the betrayal. In the second act she was unrecognizable. She became intolerant and dreamy, and eagerly gave back the engagement ring to the shepherd. The shepherd led her to a tawdry painted statue of the Holy Virgin.

"Signorina! It is the Holy Virgin's will that you hear me out!" he said in a bass voice in Sicilian dialect, turning away from her. "The Holy Virgin will give Giovanni, the visitor from town, as many women as he wills. But I, Signorina, need nobody but you! The Virgin Mary, our Immaculate Protectress, will tell you the same if you ask her."

The girl stood with her back to the painted wooden statue. As the shepherd talked, she tapped her foot impatiently. On this earth—oh, woe to us!—there isn't a woman who is not gripped by folly at the very moment when her fate is being decided. A woman is alone at such moments, with no Holy Virgin she can appeal to.

In the third act, Giovanni, the visitor from town, met his fate. The village barber was shaving Giovanni as he sat with his powerful masculine legs sprawled out over the proscenium. The pleats of his vest shone beneath the Sicilian sun. The stage set portrayed a village fair. The shepherd stood in the far corner. He stood there silently, among the carefree crowd. He hung his head, then raised it, and under the weight of his burning, fixed gaze, Giovanni began to fidget and squirm in his chair. He jumped up and pushed the barber away. In a cracking voice Giovanni demanded that the policeman remove all shady and suspicious-looking people from the village square. The shepherd—played by Di Grasso—hesitated for a moment, then smiled, soared into the air, flew over the stage of the Odessa City Theater, alighted on Giovanni's shoulders, and sunk his teeth into his neck. Muttering and squinting at the audience, he sucked the blood from the wound. Giovanni fell to the ground and the curtain came down in menacing silence, hiding the murderer and the murdered man. Not wasting a single moment, we rushed off to Theater Alley, Kolya Shvarts leading the pack. The box office was already selling tickets for the following day. Next morning the *Odessa News* informed the few people who had been at the performance that they had seen the most incredible actor of the century.

During his Odessa performances, Di Grasso was to play *King Lear*, *Othello*, *Civil Death*, and Turgenev's *Parasite*, convincing us with every word and movement that there was more justice and hope in the frenzy of noble passion than in the joyless rules of the world.

The tickets for these performances sold at five times their price. The public in its frantic quest for tickets ran to the taverns, where they found howling, red-faced scalpers spouting innocent blasphemies.

A stream of dusty pink heat poured into Theater Alley. Storekeepers in felt slippers brought green bottles of wine and casks of olives out onto the street. Macaroni was boiling in foaming water in cauldrons in front of stores, the steam melting into the distant skies. Old women in men's boots sold cockleshells and souvenirs, chasing wavering customers with their loud yells. Rich Jews, their beards combed and parted, rode in carriages to the Hotel Severnaya, and knocked discreetly at the doors of fat, black-haired women with mustaches—the actresses of Di Grasso's troupe. Everyone in Theater Alley was happy, except for one person, and that person was me. Disaster was hovering over me. It was only a matter of time before my father would realize that I had taken his watch and pawned it with Kolya Shvarts. Kolya had had enough time now to get used to the idea that the gold watch was his, and as he was a man who drank Bessarabian wine instead of tea at breakfast, he could not bring himself to return the watch, even though I had paid him back his money. That was the kind of person he was. His personality was exactly like my father's. Caught between these two men, I watched the hoops of other people's happiness roll past me. I had no choice but to escape to Constantinople. Everything had already been arranged with the second engineer of a steamer, *The Duke of Kent*, but before setting out to sea, I decided to bid Di Grasso farewell. He was to appear one last time in the role of the shepherd whisked into the air by an otherworldly force. Odessa's whole Italian colony had come to the theater, led by the trim, bald-headed consul, followed by fidgety Greeks and bearded externs staring fanatically at a point invisible to all. Long-armed Utochkin[2] was also there. Kolya Shvarts even brought his wife in her fringed, violet shawl, a woman as robust as a grenadier and as drawn-out as a steppe, with a crinkled, sleepy face peeking out at its borderland. Her face was drenched with tears as the curtain fell.

"You no-good wretch!" she shouted at Kolya as they left the theater. "Now you know what *real* love is!"

With mannish steps Madame Shvarts plodded heavily down Langeron Street, tears trickling from her fishlike eyes, her fringed shawl shuddering on her fat shoulders. Her head shaking, she yelled out for the whole

2. Sergey Isayevich Utochkin, 1874–1916, an aviation pioneer, was a prominent and dashing Odessan figure.

street to hear a list of women who lived happily with their husbands. "Sugar puff—that's what those husbands call their wives! Sweetie pie! Baby cakes!"

Kolya walked meekly next to his wife, quietly blowing into his silky mustache. Out of habit, I walked behind them. I was sobbing. Catching her breath for a second, Madame Shvarts heard me crying and turned around.

"You no-good wretch!" she shouted at her husband, her fishlike eyes widening. "May I not live to see another happy hour if you don't give that boy back his watch!"

Kolya froze, his mouth falling open, but then he came to his senses, and, pinching me hard, shoved the watch into my hands.

"What does he give me?" Madame Shvarts's rough, tearful voice lamented, as it receded into the distance. "It's animal stuff today, it's animal stuff tomorrow! I ask you, you no-good wretch, how long can a woman wait?"

They walked to the corner and turned onto Pushkin Street. I stayed back, clutching my watch, and suddenly, with a clarity I had never before experienced, I saw the soaring columns of the Town Council, the illuminated leaves on the boulevard, and Pushkin's bronze head with the moon's pale reflection on it. For the first time I saw everything around me as it really was—hushed and beautiful beyond description.

SELECTED LETTERS OF ISAAC BABEL TO HIS SISTER AND MOTHER, 1926–1939

Selected Letters of Isaac Babel
to His Sister and Mother
1926–1939

One of the most peripatetic writers, with a vast and varied body of kin, friends, and associates, Babel generated an enormous corpus of correspondence; unfortunately, much of it perished, along with his own archive after he was arrested in May 1939. For the most part, his own letters met a similar fate: some disappeared into the black hole of the NKVD, along with their addressees, or were destroyed by them as evidence of their association with "a known enemy of the people." As Nathalie Babel once explained to me, her mother destroyed Babel's letters for fear that in Nazi-occupied France they might identify her as the wife of a prominent Soviet antifascist, costing her and her daughter their lives. Still, many letters have survived. Babel's sister managed to hold on to most of Babel's letters to her and their mother (some nine hundred pieces in all!). Russian state archives have preserved parts of Babel's epistolary legacy, and hitherto unknown pieces of his correspondence keep coming to the surface to this day.

This selection is meant to aid the reader in tracing the life and career of Isaac Babel from a personal, often entirely quotidian, perspective. Like most of their compatriots, the Babels lost almost everything in the Revolution, and after the death of his father in May 1924, he assumed responsibility for the welfare of his family. Given the borders, restrictions on travel, and the increasingly stringent Soviet currency regulations, not to mention the vagaries of freelancing, this was a difficult, almost impossible task; hence, the subterfuges and codes Babel had to resort to in order to send money to his family in Brussels and Paris.

The letters published here are addressed to Babel's sister Mary Chapochnikoff (1899–1987), who emigrated to Belgium in February 1925 to join her fiancé Grigory Chapochnikoff (*Chap* or *Esculapius* in the letters), who was finishing his medical studies at the University of Louvain; they soon settled in Brussels. After July 1926, the letters are, for the most part, addressed to both Mary and Babel's mother, Faina Aaronovna (Feiga, Fenya, née Shvevel, or Shvekhvel, 1868–1942), who joined her daughter and son-in-law in Brussels. Some letters refer to *Zhenya*, Evgeniya Borisovna Babel (née Gronfain, 1897–1957), Babel's wife and mother of his daughter Nathalie (1929–2006). She and Babel were married in Odessa in August 1919 but had known each other since Babel's student years at the Kiev Commercial Institute (1911–15). In the letters, she is referred to as *Zhenya*, *Evgeniya Borisovna*, and/or *Yenta*—a nickname the thoroughly middle-class Babels had given her to poke fun at her upper-class manners and refinement. She and Babel had planned on an extended stay in France, but Babel's affair with Tamara Ivanova (née Kashirina; see her memoirs in this volume) prompted Evgeniya to leave for Paris alone in November 1925. Breaking off his relationship with Kashirina, Babel rejoined his wife in Paris in July 1927. For a biographical background to this correspondence, see "Isaac Babel: A Chronology" in this volume.

All sixty-four letters in this section are from *Isaac Babel: The Lonely Years, 1925–1939: Unpublished Stories and Correspondence*, edited and with an introduction by Nathalie Babel, translated from the Russian by Andrew R. MacAndrew and Max Hayward. Copyright © 1964, renewed 1992 by Farrar, Straus, and Giroux, LLC. Reprinted by permission of Farrar, Straus, and Girox, LLC, and The Estate of Nathalie Babel. —*Ed.*

Moscow, January 1, 1926

* * * I must admit very frankly that I have gone backward rather than forward. I haven't done a thing as far as serious literature goes for about ten months, but have simply been hanging around in Moscow in search of big pay-offs, that is, taken the line of least resistance, a road which is loathsome to me. It turned out that I had neither the strength nor the foresight to avoid this odious road, but now I must at least find the strength within myself to stop. There are many unfulfilled obligations weighing on me. If I manage to hand in the work for which I have orders now, during the course of January, then I must go to Paris or to some even more exotic place, where I could straighten out my burdened spirit and do some real work. These considerations, and above all the fact that my only hope of salvation in 1926 lies in my not having to earn money, force us to think of the future, and, above all, about Mama. She and I both consider a journey abroad unnecessary. That's out. And since it's out, it wouldn't be so bad if you made yourselves a home in Russia, where (I and many other sensible people consider) it is possible to arrange one's life better, more honorably and more fruitfully than anywhere else. It would only be possible, however, for you to set yourself up here with my assistance. What can I offer you? A job—for you and for Shap.—right away, that is, a good living wage. Your knowledge of foreign languages, of course, would be a great help. Then, we can offer you a comfortable apartment in Leningrad which certainly would be no worse than the one you have in Brussels. But it is easier to live and to earn enough in Moscow than in Leningrad. I don't think there would be any great difficulty in exchanging our excellent room for two rooms, with very little additional outlay. Thus, by early spring, we could fix you up with two rooms. That's the maximum it would be possible to obtain with the present apartment crisis in Moscow. That's what I can offer you in the material sense, and as to spiritual life in Russia—and *scientific opportunities*—there's no need for me to tell you that they are richer and have a greater future than what you can expect in the West.

* * *

Moscow, March 31, 1926

Dear Stone Quarry,

As it is now clear beyond doubt that you ought not to move, we have decided to make the move ourselves. So this very day we are starting to liquidate several unnecessary things (we'll keep the necessary ones), and we'll hand in our application for a passport, etc. So you must let us know *at once* about the renewal of Mama's visa. She will leave May 1 at the latest. During the next few days we will transfer a hundred dollars to Mme. Braude and one hundred dollars to you. Please put this money (which must not be touched) in the bank in dollars and also let me know the *addresses*. You must do all this at once. Enough dilly-dallying. I'm expecting an immediate reply and confirmation of the visa from you. I'm taking the opportunity to send you by registered book-mail my little book *The Story of My Dovecote*.* They sent me from Berlin my book [*The Odessa Stories*] published by Malik Verlag. It's a very nice edition. I imagine you can buy it in Brussels. *Red Cavalry* is coming out in Russian and in German in April.

*   *   *

Moscow, November 15, 1926

*   *   *

The chances are I'll soon have my play* in stageable condition. The Arts Theater is waiting for it impatiently. I'm working hard, like an ox, a forced laborer, a hired hand, but that gives me real satisfaction. As before, I am living in the House of Rest of the Soviet People's Commissariat—a very luxurious establishment, quiet, separate room, a garden. I am housed free here. Am keeping my address a secret from everyone. Never show my nose in Moscow. I have had enough of idiots. The hell with them. Why shouldn't I, too, live the way I need to for once? Lola promises to pay Zhenya a hundred rubles for Volodka [Vladimir Seliger, Zhenya's brother-in-law].

*   *   *

January 28, 1927

*   *   *

I have lots of things to do in Moscow and I'll probably spend another two or three weeks here. My literary affairs are in quite good shape. I can't understand why I haven't received notification that you got the money. Tomorrow, I'm sending you fifty dollars through the Torgovo-Promyshleny Bank [Commercial and Industrial Bank]. * * * Why does she [Mary] write to me that she is in a desperate mood? If she is worried about material matters, *I swear* that within the next few weeks your financial situation will be radically improved. Now if it is about me that she's worrying, try to explain to her that I am not one of those you can bend into a ram's horn. * * * What a moaning crew! There is actually no reason for you to moan. When I go through moments of despair, I think

---

* Babel was then writing the play *Sunset,* which shares characters and setting with *The Odessa Stories.*

of Papa. What he expected and wanted from us was success not moaning. Remembering him, I feel a surge of strength, and I urge myself forward. Everything I promised him, not in words but in thought, I shall carry out, because I have a sacred respect for his memory. And it hurts me to think you should drown the only sacred memory I have in your needless tears and weakness.

* * *

Paris, May 21, 1928

* * *

A collection of articles about me has just come out in Russia. It makes very amusing reading—quite incomprehensible. It was written by frightfully scholarly fools. Reading it, I get the impression that I'm reading about a dead man—what I am doing now is so different from what I did before.

* * *

Rostov, July 20, 1929

Dear Grandma, Aunt and Uncle,
    She turned out to be a girl [daughter Nathalie]. Wise people say that a devoted daughter will provide for the old parents better than a lazy son. So let us thank the Creator and try to live the best we know how.

* * *

Moscow, April 27, 1930

Leading beauties *du royaume des Belges,*
    I've really had enough of your worries. A young man whose mental and physical gifts are in full bloom has better things to do than keep up a correspondence with retired Odessans. Writers' funerals alone take up so much time. You should have thought of that yourselves!!!
    V.M.'s death [Vladimir Mayakovsky's suicide] completely bewildered me. His main reason, as they say, was an unhappy love, but of course, years of accumulated weariness played its part too. It's difficult to make out because the letter he left doesn't provide a single clue. Mama probably remembers him, huge and blooming, when he came to see us back in Odessa. . . . A monstrous death.

* * *

Moscow, December 15, 1930

Gosizdat just informed me that the latest edition of *Red Cavalry* has been sold in record time—something like seven days—and that they are going to put out yet another printing, which means a new payday for me.

I have written to Zhenya to say that it looks as if this horsey will keep pulling us along until spring.

*   *   *

Molodenovo, February 11, 1931

*   *   *

My program is the following: I spend a few days in Moscow and then go to the south, via Kiev. In Kiev I have to go to see the administration of VUFKU [Ukrainian Film Studios], for whom I do some nondescript work from time to time, and then I also want to go to unforgettable Velikaya Staritsa, of which I have retained one of the sharpest memories of all my life. Then I'll go farther south for a few days to the new Jewish "peasant" colonies. Then back to Molodenovo.

*   *   *

Molodenovo, July 7, 1931

*   *   *

Life has become much gayer for me than before. I don't remember whether I've already told you that Alexei Maximovich [Gorky] has settled down less than a mile from Molodenovo in the former Morozov house. (They picked the best of the places around Moscow for him.) And since, for old times' sake, the rules that regulate the stream of people around him do not apply to me, I sometimes go to visit him in the evening. There's no need to tell you how instructive it is and what an unexpected pleasure to have him for a neighbor. It brings back my youth, and the good thing about it is that our relationship, formed in my youth, hasn't changed to this day.

*   *   *

Molodenovo, July 22, 1931

Mamachen,

How are you getting along in your health resort? It's sunny here now, just like in our home town. After lunch I sun myself and swim. The river has really become so shallow that you lie in it like in a bath. It's true I need a little rest, but I mustn't even think of it at this time because every day of lazing around separates me for that much longer from my family. And that's why I'm driving myself. Physically, I feel wonderful, only my brains would like to take it easy, and then too, surrounded by such beauty, you want to enjoy it. Starting today, I've introduced an innovation—I work only until lunchtime, and not the whole day as I did before.

I'm hoping to entice Katya [Babel's aunt] to Molodenovo. They've invited her to Odessa but she quite rightly supposes that she won't get a chance to rest there. If she goes, it'll be a real loss to me. She is my guardian angel and, most important, my wet nurse.

I.

Molodenovo, October 14, 1931

Before leaving I asked Katya to send you and Zhenya each a copy of the magazine *Molodaya Gvardia*. In it, I make my debut, after several years of silence, with a small extract from a book which will have the general title of *The Story of My Dovecote*. The subjects of the stories are all taken from my childhood, but, of course, there is much that has been made up and changed. When the book is finished, it will become clear why I had to do all that.

* * *

Moscow, January 2, 1932

* * *

In general, what's being published is a quite insignificant part of my work—I am writing the main bulk of it only now. It is too early to shower me with praise—we'll see what there is to come. The only thing I know I have gained is the feeling of having become a professional writer and a will and eagerness for work such as I have never experienced before.

* * *

Moscow, April 5, 1932

I presented my papers [permission to travel to France] again yesterday, this time in a more hopeful atmosphere than before. The case will probably be given special attention and sped through. I have declared that I must leave no later than May. In case of further difficulties, I'll go to Alexei Maximovich [Gorky] who is now in Moscow.

* * *

Moscow, September 4, 1932

Yesterday they gave me my passport for travel abroad and I sent you a wire.

* * *

Paris, October 6, 1932

* * *

Send me her [mother's] passport and I will have it extended, and I'm sure I will be able to send her the visa at any time. I have made the acquaintance of [Anatole] de Monzie and I'll have no difficulty with it.

Starting tomorrow, Zhenya will have a Viennese maid who's been recommended to her by Madame Birkham. Then she won't be so tied down in the house.

I have ordered a full wardrobe at a good tailor's: two suits and a winter coat, and bought myself a few more things, so very soon I will look like a prospective cabinet minister.

* * *

Sorrento, May 5, 1933

Yesterday, I spent the whole day in Naples with Gorky. He took us to the museums, showed us ancient sculpture (I'm still breathless with admiration), paintings by Titian, Raphael and Velasquez. We had lunch and dinner together. The old man drank, and he drank plenty. In the evening, we went to a restaurant located on a hill above the town (a fairy-tale view from there). Everyone in the establishment has known him for thirty years and they all got up when he came in. The waiters rushed to kiss his hands [sic] and immediately sent for the old-timers who sing Neapolitan songs. They came running—seventy-year-olds who remembered Gorky well—and they sang in their cracked old voices in a way I will never forget. Gorky wept unrestrainedly, drank constantly and when they tried to take his glass away from him, kept saying: "It's the last time in my life." For me, it was an unforgettable day.

I am trying hard to speed Zhenya's and Natasha's coming. I hope that they will arrive in ten days or so.

I have been advised to send my play [*Maria*] by mail. Of course, I really ought to take it myself. I haven't decided yet what I will do. The Gorkys are leaving on the ninth—there's a Soviet ship going from London to Odessa and it is, of course, most convenient for them to take it. Besides me, there'll only be Marshak, [Samuil] our superb children's poet, in the house, and I hope he will take to Natasha. Marshak also has a sister in Brussels and possibly we will all go to Belgium together.

Gorky has taken three of my new stories for his almanac. I am really quite pleased with one of them—I only hope the censors will pass it. Gorky has promised to send me my fees in foreign currency.

* * *

Nalchik, November 2, 1933

* * *

I haven't started working yet, because I'm still roaming about this wonderland. Today I'm leaving to visit a German collective farm—one of the richest and most modern collective farms in the region—and I'll set my mind working there. Went hunting with Yevdokimov and Kalmykov.* They killed several wild boar (I didn't take part, of course) 6,000 feet up, among the alpine pastures and with a view of the whole Caucasian range, from Novorossysk to Baku.

* * *

Prishibskaya Cossack Settlement, December 13, 1933

I'm living in an old, pure-blooded Cossack settlement. The change-over to the collective farm system was not easy here and they have suffered hardships, but now it's all going ahead with a great deal of bustle. In another couple of years, they will be so well off that it will overshadow anything that these Cossack settlements have seen in the past—and they didn't have much to complain about. The collective-farm movement has made great progress this year and now limitless vistas are opening up—the land is being transformed. I don't know just how long I'll stay here. It is both interesting and essential for me to witness the new economic relations and forms. Use my Nalchik address as before. They'll forward the mail from there.

I can also tell you that I've finished the play [Maria]. In the next few days I'll copy it and send it off to Moscow. The most remarkable thing about all this is that I've already started on another one, and it looks as if I have stumbled on a gusher. I've learned from my previous efforts.

The winter here is extraordinarily mild and beautiful. There's a lot of snow. I feel well. We eat roast pheasant for dinner and drink young wine supplied by the German collective farms.

---

* Efim Georgievich Yevdokimov (1891–1940), a high-level Cheka official and party functionary, deputy security chief of the Southwestern and Southern Front during the Soviet-Polish War (when Babel may have befriended him), chief of state security in the North Caucasus Region in 1932 and its party boss in 1934. He was arrested in September 1938 and executed in February 1940. Betal Edykovich Kalmykov (1898–1940) was the legendary party boss of Kabardino-Balkaria, a republic in the North Caucasus, and the subject of a book planned by Babel. Arrested in November 1938, Kalmykov was executed on February 26, 1940. Both Evdokimov and Kalmykov were posthumously cleared of all charges. Their names, along with Babel's, were on the list of three hundred and forty-six individuals (nos. 6, 89, and 123) marked for execution and signed by Stalin on January 17, 1940. —Ed.

Moscow, February 13, 1934

It's such a long time since I wrote to you that yesterday, in a fit of remorse, I sent you a telegram to say I was well and everything was all right. The Paris events [the February '34 right-wing riots.—Tr.—MacA.] worry me very much and I have sent a wire asking whether my family are all right. I think of Natasha a thousand times a day and my heart contracts.

I'm still busy with theater matters. Rehearsals are starting simultaneously in the Vakhtangov Theater and in the Jewish Theater. I'm negotiating with some provincial towns too. The play that I have completed is really only a trial work. I am writing the next one at full steam and attach much greater importance to it.

My Molodenovo is finished for me. I'm going to look over a country house outside the city where I could work, because I just don't know how to refuse people and in Moscow I'm so encumbered with other people's affairs that I don't have a moment to think of myself. There's enormous animation in all fields of endeavor here—feverish activity.

*　*　*

Moscow, March 3, 1934

Katya has left to go to see Iosif [her husband, then in prison]. I had to supply her with money. In general, I have to bear the full moral and financial weight of the business.

As before, I'm doing things for numerous people and there's little time left for myself, and yet I have an endless quantity of work before me.

*　*　*

Moscow, April 5, 1934

[A postcard.]

*　*　*

I stroll around Moscow which is all torn up like a field of battle—they're building the subway. The first line should be opened in November of this year.

I've started work on the scenario based on Bagritsky's poem. When the libretto is ready, I'll take it to Kiev. I hope to be able to insist on their moving the production to the Odessa film studios. If they did, I would be able to live in Odessa for a while. At the same time, I'm working on my play. I would very much like to finish it by the fall.

There's been some improvement in Iosif's "case." I am trying to arrange for him to be allowed to come back to Moscow some time in the course of this month. I ate up my matzos. My maid has gone to the store to get the flour, cottage cheese and other things which go to make up *kulich* and *paskha* for Easter.

* * *

Moscow, May 13, 1934

* * *

We were having summer weather up till yesterday, but today it's overcast.* * * The city is a very interesting place right now. It is full of life and is being thoroughly rebuilt. And culturally, we are becoming part of Europe. Concerts by eminent musicians, and so on. Materially, our life is incomparably better and, if it weren't for Berta Davydovna [Babel's ailing mother-in-law cared for by Evgeniya], I would put the question of Zhenya's and Natasha's coming here in the sharpest way. I think about it all the time now. If they came, nine-tenths of all my difficulties would fall away.

* * *

Uspenskoye, June 18, 1934

I'm still living at Gorky's. As they say in Odessa—a real thousand and one nights. My memories of this will last me my whole life. * * *

Have been busy doing some editing for Gorky all this time and so neglected my work on the scenario. I'm taking it up again now: I want to finish it quickly and take it to Kiev, otherwise it'll be in the way of my further work.

* * *

The Ehrenburgs have arrived. Hope they've brought greeting from Zhenya and Natasha.

* * *

Moscow, June 20, 1934

* * *

I've come into Moscow to see the Ehrenburgs and Malereau [sic*] and shall spend two days here. Gorky has loaded me down with tons of edito-

---

* André Malraux (1901–1976), French author and statesman, then on a visit to the Soviet Union with his wife Clara (see her memoirs in this volume) to attend the First Congress of Soviet writers. Babel makes a pun out of his name. —Ed.

rial work which has caused me to neglect my scenario. It doesn't look as if I'll ever catch up.

*   *   *

Moscow, November 14, 1934

My worthy distant relatives,

If I write seldom it is not because something untoward has happened to me but simply because of the complications of life. These complications arise from three causes: one—literature, two—the fact that I must get hold of more money than what's coming to me and, three—the softness of my character because of which I get weighed down with all sorts of requests and am forced to run around for other people.

I am working more than ever before but, as you can see, I have nothing tangible to show for it. Life refuses to linger at my desk, be it for five minutes only. It is a rewarding assignment to express the philosophy of this stormy movement in my art, but it presents difficulties such as I've never had to face before.

I am incapable of compromise, be it internal or external, and so I have to suffer, retreat inside myself, and wait. Much of my time is taken up by all sorts of nondescript jobs done for money and I receive enough of it to have built myself a house in town and a villa in the country, to have bought a car and go driving all over the Crimea, the Caucasus or wherever. But instead, it all goes to pay the old Paris debts and to send money to Yenta, to whom it is just a drop in the ocean, while here it is a whole fortune. And so, I am even deprived of the moral satisfaction of really helping her. All this should be radically changed, and if I could have a breathing spell, lay aside the money jobs and turn to short stories (for translation), it would make more sense. But it seems quite impossible for me to get the breathing spell I need. All this means that I haven't spare minute for myself.

Nowadays, writing doesn't mean sitting at one's table. It means rushing all over the country, participating in active life, doing research, establishing close contact with some enterprise, and suffering a constant feeling of impotence at one's inability to be everywhere one ought to be.

I have already told you that material conditions are improving here with amazing speed. I am sure that Natasha could be incomparably better brought up here than in France and it is becoming senseless to remain there.

Now, with winter approaching, I cannot demand that they come over here right away, but I'll start a real campaign in January or February. The stumbling block in the business is, of course, B.D., [mother-in-law] but I shall explain to Lyova [brother-in-law] in no uncertain terms what I think about it all.

With all sorts of people staying in my place, there's been a lot of talk; but now, they're gradually dispersing and they will all be gone by December 1st.

As soon as they have left, I'll go to Kiev, a trip which is long overdue and has been postponed several times. Generally speaking, I am longing to make myself a foothold somewhere around Odessa, because the tempo of life in Moscow is so fast that, with my habits and my need for lengthy meditation, I am having a very difficult time. Today Moscow is one of the noisiest of European cities, and in the scope of its development and the revolutions that take place daily in its streets and squares, there is no doubt that even New York is no match for it. Yes, I must say that now, every day, we can see the outlines of a country of unprecedented might more and more clearly and, by now, there is no doubt in anyone's mind as to the realizability of the slogan "to catch up and surpass."

I'm going to take two days off and will then send you some books and the newspapers, which are becoming more and more interesting. Now, since you have more time on your hands than I, do not keep any accounts in our correspondence in the form of credits and debits—just write as often as you can. I miss you very badly. I won't write about Natasha but the fact that I am forced to live without her will soon cause an emotional explosion. I feel it coming.

So long, my dear ones, write and tell me when Mama is coming over here.

Your reinforced-concrete son and brother,

I.

Moscow, January 7, 1935

* * *

I have finished most of the writing I had to do on order, and feel I can live a life that is natural for me. I would like to convey to the world what I know of the old Odessa, after which I could move to the new Odessa. I dream of seeing you, all or separately, in the spring, and I shall do everything in my power to see that that dream comes true. I am not good at reaping financial benefits from my literary efforts at the time and the place of my choice, but I hope that this time things will work out by themselves.

In our apartment, the fires are burning in the stoves, the samovar is boiling and my German is keeping the place clean.* I am now the owner of an eight-cylinder Ford just received from America, which we share equally. We have a chauffeur. That makes life much easier and more pleasant. It would be hard for you to imagine how thick the Moscow traffic is, even thinking of Paris. In a month, the first line of the subway, between Sokolniki and Devichie Polye, will be opened. That will ease the congestion a bit, although we really need ten lines rather than one. The subway is being built at a feverish rate.

* * *

---

* An Austrian engineer, Bruno Steiner (d. 1942) with whom Babel shared an apartment and housekeeping from 1933 to 1936, when Steiner's Soviet visa was revoked. —Ed.

Moscow, February 4, 1935

[A postcard.]

* * * The Party Congress [Seventh Congress of Soviets] is taking place now. All my comrades are climbing uphill and so am I, little by little. They are starting to rehearse my play and it has already gathered some ardent fans. I hope to be able to arrange things for Katya and intend to send something to Zhenya.

*   *   *

Moscow, February 18, 1935

*   *   *

Lately, I've been leading an extremely social life—I've been attending the Congress sessions and sat through four days of a conference of collective farmers in the Kremlin. It has all left an indelible impression upon me.

Karpych, my former Molodenovo landlord, came to stay with me here. He has been doing the following things in Moscow: for the first time in the sixty-five years of his life, he spoke on the phone, for the first time went to the movies (we saw the marvelous Soviet film, *Chapayev* and he was one of the first Soviet citizens to take a ride on the subway, which will be open to the general public in two or three weeks. Now they are doing trial runs and it takes a lot of pull to get a pass. It is a fantastic affair that can't be compared either with the Paris or the Berlin subways, and I even think it's rather too luxurious.

I will soon be finished with the orders I have received. The film in which I had a hand will be shown soon [*Lyotchiki*]. It was extremely warmly received at the previews. We'll see what will come later. I am working on a new play. It looks as though they will soon publish *Maria* and, who knows, perhaps stage it too.

*   *   *

Yevdokimov and Kalmykov are urging me to go to the Caucasus, a region which we may say we own nowadays. I haven't decided as yet what I'll do.

*   *   *

Moscow, February 24, 1935

*   *   *

A piece of news for you: they've decided to publish *Maria* and the play will appear in the March or April issue. This gives it a good chance of being staged.

The comedy I am working on is progressing, although slowly. It would be great if I managed to finish it by May.

A strange change has come over me—I don't feel like writing in prose. I want to use only the dramatic form.

* * *

Our eight-cylinder Ford is serving us with distinction. Perhaps one day it will appear at your doorstep and bring you back home.

Spring has arrived here—everything is thawing and, with the arrival of the warm weather, I am turning into a different and cheerful man.

This will have to be a short letter because I'm dying to sleep.

Today, my Kabarda hero, Kalmykov, left. We talked from eight o'clock in the evening to seven in the morning. I saw him off to the station and then went to a private showing of the American film *Viva Villa* and so haven't slept one minute since the night before last.

A lady friend of mine is leaving for Paris on the twenty-eighth and she's taking some presents with her.

* * *

Moscow, March 23, 1935

* * *

Guess whom I met yesterday? Stolyarsky [Babel's childhood violin teacher]. You must have read that there has been a contest of musicians in Warsaw and in Leningrad. As usual, Stolyarsky's pupils reaped the honors. He is now a famous professor. * * * We met in the foyer and fell into each other's arms. He is fresh, red as a ripe apple and was wearing a bright necktie with a pin in it, and spats. He was accompanied by his fat, heavily made-up daughter who wore a beauty patch.

Just as before, Stolyarsky is mass-producing child prodigies and supplies violinists for the concert halls of the world. I am the only one he cannot boast about. He remembered everything—our dining room, our courtyard on Tiraspolskaya Street and my determined resistance. I'm going to give a solemn dinner to mark this occasion. He recognized me right away and in his first outburst of enthusiasm declared that I hadn't changed in the least.

* * *

Moscow, March 31, 1935

* * *

I am not sure what the Frenchman will tell me tomorrow, but I have good reason to believe that Zhenya's financial situation is a difficult one. It would seem that I could easily have put it right by sending articles to France. But, not to mention the fact that that sort of writing is not my forte, something seems to have put a spell on my hand: I can no longer write prose [fiction]. This has happened to me before and I know that the only thing I can do is to wait for things to change. The only form that attracts me now is drama. And so, for many months, I've been sitting over a play which I haven't been able to bring off, but now, only a couple of weeks ago, to my great joy I saw a flash of light and it looks as though I'll be able to finish it. Anyway, there's no going back now—too much effort has gone into it as it is and, besides, the theaters are waiting and are hanging over me like a heavy storm cloud.

As you already know, *Maria* is being published; as soon as it is out, I'll send you a copy of the magazine.

Mikhoels—from the Jewish Theater—has decided to put on *Sunset* after the big success of *King Lear*. They are looking for a translator now and will start rehearsals in the summer. In addition, *Sunset* will be staged by the Jewish Theater of Byelorussia and it looks as if the Russian theaters may give it another run.

And "to topple all this," as Stolyarsky, whom I saw a few days ago, would say, a very funny business is going on now, in which I secretly have a part. I believe I wrote to you that I was given an order—to rewrite an unusable screenplay. Well, I rewrote it very thoroughly but, since I didn't believe that the film would have any success, I demanded that the movie producers should not mention my name. But now that film, *Pilots* [*Lyotchiki*], is having a success approaching the reception meted out to *Chapayev*. Well, those involved know what's what, of course, but for me it's too late to back out of my decision. So the whole story is causing a lot of excitement and merriment among the movie people and the writers.

I have written a small piece on Bagritsky and am awaiting the hour when I will again be able to write prose. There's something beginning to seethe inside me and, who knows, perhaps it will come off.

Spring is coming. Friends are trying to drag me off to Kabarda, to the northern Caucasus, to Pyatigorsk. Schmidt [Academician Otto Schmidt, polar explorer, 1891–1956] wants me to go to the North Pole. But I think I'd better stay put and work, for that is the only way I can help Zhenya and you. If I could gather in my scattered tribe, my heart would recover its peace. Physically and mentally I feel I am better fitted for work than ever before.

Moscow, April 17, 1935

My uninteresting relatives,

It's the first *seder* tonight, a fact that I am bringing to your attention with a special telegram. I have managed to get matzos, and not from Katya who . . . [illegible] . . .

I'm going to a certain patriarchal house tonight. Three days ago, sent a hundred rubles to Sonya [cousin]. My trip abroad [1932–33] has brought me to the brink of bankruptcy and, to this day, I cannot get rid of the debts, humiliations and unpleasantnesses, and there's no telling how much of my energy, nerves and spirit have had to be spent on hack work. And so all I can do is send short stories, especially since we know that there is a demand for them. In recent years, however, my stories haven't been coming off too well—certain mental and literary changes have taken place within me that are beyond my control, changes that take no account of publishers' requirements and that aren't interested in whether Lyova's business is good or bad. I have started to write articles again that might help Yenta and Mama, but one can never be sure of anything in this business. And then my literary endowment is such that I can only handle ideas that I have thoroughly worked out, ideas that, on top of that, must be original, otherwise they don't interest me, and even if my own life depended on it or my child was dying before my eyes, I would be unable to get results by trying to force myself.

That's one thing, and the other is that if I do nothing here in Moscow I have an income that would enable my family to live not only passably but regally in comparison with their present life, as far as clothing, food, housing, summerhouses, medical care, seaside places, Natasha's [daughter Nathalie's] education, etc., etc., go. And besides, I would be free immediately from having to humiliate myself over money matters, I could do some serious work, go to the places I must go to (it is indispensable now for me to travel all over the Soviet Union and study life intensively, in order to be able to write about it) and I would at last accomplish what I can and must accomplish in my writing. So why is it a matter of vanity on my part? It is a matter of logic, it is a desire for moral and material stability in life. And, after all, why must Natasha be brought up in French lycées among an alien people, struggling through the depression and misery besetting the Western world, when she happens to be a citizen of a young and flourishing country full of sap and vigor, and with a future! Well, do I have the right to wish for it or not? In my opinion, Natasha belongs with all her being to Russia and her severance from us will cripple her. I am afraid that this will be realized only when it is too late.

Now for point number three. Let us assume that the cycle of short stories I am working on now comes off. Then Zhenya and Mama will receive a sum of money each. But what after that? The same situation again? I have already sent many messengers to Zhenya and they have told her that from the material viewpoint my life is something quite beyond her dreams. Well, shouldn't that convince her after all? I haven't written to her because I feel miserable and I don't want to make her already gloomy life even gloomier. And so I'll work in a very unpropitious mental state and, although I'll do my damned best, I really don't know what I fear more—to write successful short stories and thus prolong our dispersion or to fail in what I am trying to do. I am not really afraid of the latter because in these things my doggedness and energy are inexhaustible. I am longing for privacy, for meditation, for a life organized according to my own recipe, and that is all possible here. But I am being pulled out into the public market place, into the world of fuss and business and bargaining, into which I don't fit.

I am not writing all this to make you feel bad. On the contrary—I'll use whatever strength I have to make a better life for my family.

I am enclosing a copy of my published play.

Next time, I'll write a lighter and more cheerful letter.

I.

Moscow, June 13, 1935

* * *

When I think of the life I'll lead in the northern Caucasus, I feel ashamed before you, because it'll be a palatial one. The supreme chief of the northern Caucasus is an old friend of mine and the preparations made for my arrival will be such that I don't even feel like going—makes me feel rather awkward. After the cure, I'll visit Nalchik, Pyatigorsk, Dagestan and other enchanted places. . . .

* * *

My nice Mama, if I write seldom it is not because my life is hard—compared with millions of people, my life is easy, happy and privileged—but because it is uncertain and this uncertainty derives from nothing else but changes and doubts connected with my work. In a country as united as ours, it is quite inevitable that a certain amount of thinking in clichés should appear and I want to overcome this standardized way of thinking and introduce into our literature new ideas, new feelings and rhythms. This is what interests me and nothing else. And so I work and think with great intensity, but I haven't any results to show yet. And, inasmuch as I myself do not see clearly how and by what methods I will reach these results (I do see my inner paths clearly, though), I am not sure myself where and in what kind of environment I ought to live if I am to achieve my goal, and that is what causes my reluctance to drag anyone along behind me and makes me the insecure and wavering man who causes you so much trouble.

I am not worried about myself. I have faced trials of this sort before and finally triumphed over them. But the thought of you hurts me.

Paris, June 27, 1935

* * *

The Congress actually ended yesterday.* My speech, or rather my ad lib talk (delivered under awful conditions, at nearly one o'clock in the morning) went down very well with the French.

I'll spend the short time assigned to me in Paris in roaming around the place in search of material like a hungry wolf. I will try to make some systematic notes of what I know of *la Ville Lumière*, and perhaps have them published one day.

---

* International Congress for the Defense of Culture (Congrès international des écrivains pour la défense de la culture), Paris, June 21–25, 1935. Organized by Ilya Ehrenburg, Mikhail Koltsov, and André Malraux, it was a follow-up to the Moscow First Congress of Soviet Writers (August 1934), with which it shared a nonsectarian antifascist agenda. But things did not go smoothly. Gorky, who was to preside over the event, cancelled out at the last moment. To make matters worse, the official Soviet delegation lacked celebrities familiar to Western intellectuals. Malraux and André Gide threatened to walk out unless Babel and Boris Pasternak were included. Informed of this demand, the Politburo in Moscow acted quickly and invited Babel and Pasternak, who arrived in Paris on June 24 and spoke before the Congress closed. Babel stayed on until August. It was his last trip abroad (see Boris Souvarine's reminiscences in this volume). —*Ed.*

September 11, 1935

I am sailing along the Dnieper on a steamer. * * * I've had an amazing ten-day trip through the settlements and villages of Kiev Province. I have been to Korsuna, Belaya Tserkov, Cherkassy and many other places. It would be no exaggeration to describe what I found there as miraculous. Some villages already have two or three schools, a hospital, including a maternity ward, a movie theater and a hairdresser's, and many of them have electricity. And you must remember that they stand in places where four or five years ago there was emptiness.

*   *   *

Odessa, September 19, 1935

* * *

I came to Odessa on the sixteenth and stayed at the London Hotel where I lived like a lord, then, yesterday, I moved to Arkadia which is quite unrecognizable now with its palms, neat walks and umbrellas on the beach.

In other respects Odessa is lagging—she is poor and provincial, but as beautiful as ever.

*   *   *

While in Kiev I attended the war games and saw a few things that other mortals haven't seen.

Some vague business is demanding my presence in Moscow but I'll try and stay here as long as I can, for I feel I am being resurrected both mentally and physically.

*   *   *

Odessa, October 19, 1935

* * *

My stay in Odessa has done me a tremendous amount of good—my soul and my brains have been thoroughly refreshed. Perhaps I am also enjoying living here so much because I'm liked by the people. Completely unknown street cleaners, news vendors and what not, come up to me in the street, say hello and engage me in the most incredible conversations. The other evening I went to the Sibiryakovsky Theater. At one point, I was asked to say a few words. Then, when I left, there were thousands of young people thronging about in Kherson Street. They barred the road to my automobile, shouted, hollered and prevented me from leaving. As you can see, the nice Odessa people are still there.

I've met many of my old schoolmates. They are all bookkeepers or something of the sort and all look henpecked and subdued. I seem to be the only one unaffected either by place or time.

*   *   *

I don't think I know who the [Soviet] ambassador [in Brussels] is but it'd be easy enough for me to make his acquaintance.

Moscow, January 28, 1936

*   *   *

On top of all my work, I have a lot of people coming to see me: Kalmuks from Kabarda, miners from the Donets Basin, old pals from Kiev. . . . And all these people must be fed dinners and entertained until four in the morning. I just don't have the physical stamina for it.

*   *   *

Unlike in past years, I'm leading a disciplined, austere, hardworking life. However, despite all my efforts, human waves come breaking against my monastic cell and it shakes like a tree in a storm [Babel's mixed metaphor.—Tr.—MacA.]. Well, I hope I'll still manage somehow.

I recall with elation the weeks spent in Odessa. Ah, what a nice life that was.

*   *   *

Moscow, March 1, 1936

*   *   *

Financially, I am doing rather well now. I keep driving myself and am working *comme un nègre*. I hope that by the end of March I'll be clear of all my debts and will be able to work without thinking about tomorrow.

*   *   *

Akademia has entrusted me with the editing of Sholom Aleichem's works. I read him in my spare hours and roll around with laughter; it brings my young years back to me.

*   *   *

Moscow, March 5, 1936

Unexpected news: am leaving for the Crimea this evening, to go and see Gorky with Mikhail Koltsov and Malereau, who is here from Paris. I'll return on the 11th. I'm very sad at not having managed to get through to you on the phone—Malraux's [André Malraux] arrival has disrupted all my plans. I have been going out for a few days now and there is no trace of my grippe left.

I hope that this letter will find Zhenya in Brussels. I've received confirmation from old man Gaikis.

Kiss my rowdy daughter for me.

We're traveling in a special car. Will write to you tomorrow.

Moscow, June 2, 1936

* * *

No news from Vienna except a word from my publisher informing me that the money will be sent to Fenya in the course of June so that she'll be able to move to some spa on July first.

Am writing to Zhenya today. * * *

In the course of June, I will become a landowner and the owner of a house. A comfortable summer settlement has been established about twenty miles from Moscow [Peredelkino] and now they are building a two-story house with all modern convenience there for me. The house will be ready by June 20th and it will include half a hectare of forest land. It would really be ideal if it wasn't a special settlement for writers, but anyway, we've all agreed to keep to ourselves and to abstain from visiting one another.

* * *

Moscow, June 7, 1936

I am very depressed. It doesn't look as if Alexei Maximovich [Gorky] will get away with it this time. Although the doctors sound a bit more hopeful today, I don't believe them.

* * *

Moscow, June 17, 1936

* * *

The state of Gorky's health is still rather precarious but he is fighting for life like a lion and we keep swinging from despair to hope. In the past few days, the doctors have sounded a little bit more optimistic. André Gide is flying in today. I am going to meet him.

* * *

Moscow, June 19, 1936

It is a great loss for our entire country and it is also a personal blow to me. That man was my conscience and my judge, an example to me. I was linked to him by twenty years of unspoiled friendship and affection. The way for me to live up to his memory now is to live and work, and to do both those things well. Gorky's body is lying in state in the Hall of Columns, and endless crowds file past his coffin. It's a hot summer day. I think I'll go out for a bit. I'll write again soon.

Odessa, September 1, 1936

Yesterday in the streetcar I had my watch cut off me. It was one of my favorite possessions. Well, since once upon a time I used to make up epics about such thieves, I have no right to complain. This is the major piece of news I have to report.

I've had a guest: on his way to Yalta, [Sergei] Eisenstein stopped over at my place. In a few days they are beginning to shoot my screenplay [*Bezhin Meadow*] and we revised the last few scenes together. Most likely I'll take a little trip to Yalta toward the end of September, eat some grapes there and attend the shooting of the most important scenes. Eisenstein told me that I am hardly recognizable, both physically and mentally, since he saw me last in Moscow. I work ten times better than I did in Moscow.

I.B.

Odessa, November 24, 1936

* * *

This is the third day now that I haven't worked. I have finished my rough draft and now I must stop for a while, busy myself with something else, catch my breath and, then, get back to it. I reckon to whip it into shape for publication in two or three months.

I have been spending my rest period on reading the newspapers and catching up with the news. Ah, what threatening clouds on the horizon! Even little Belgium is in turmoil. Please write to me more often. How do you feel? How is Grisha's [Chapochnikoff] work? Things are not too quiet in France either. It's all very bad. The only hope is that the instinct of self-preservation will triumph in the end.

Moscow, December 7, 1936

I am once again in Moscow's iron grip but this time I am behaving more intelligently. I am not squandering my energy and am trying to stick to my Odessa work schedule. * * * My screenplay for Eisenstein is complete and now I have to do one for [Grigory] Alexandrov (the director of the films *Gay Children* and *Circus*). Every minute of my time is assigned to some task and I have to act like a Parisian businessman now and invite business acquaintances of mind to dinner every day, for I can't find any other time to see them.

I hope my book will be published next spring. Slowly but surely it is moving toward completion. In my opinion, it is quite interesting.

* * *

Moscow, December 12, 1936

I have no time to write, no time even to scribble a postcard. Formerly, I did one thing at a time and it was either for my soul or for profit, and I used to manage, but now I have to do both simultaneously. I must finish one more screenplay for Alexandrov, the director of *Gay Children* and *Circus*; it is difficult work and, I must admit, rather unwelcome. Now that I want to write (which, as we all know, doesn't happen very often) I am forced to busy myself with something else. I am trying to combine both things but then I really have to give up letter-writing, social life and reading, not only books but even newspapers. My most hectic month will be December. After that, things will ease up a bit.

Yesterday I had a free evening and spent it with Gorky's family. We sat in his rooms and recalled the past, feeling both easy and sad at the same time.

*   *   *

Each day I open my newspaper with apprehension. There are heavy stormclouds on the political horizon and, besides general, civic worries, I have people whose destiny worries me directly.

*   *   *

Moscow, March 11, 1937

Just returned from the countryside and am going back there again to-morrow.

*   *   *

I have nothing else to report except, perhaps, the fact that I have started making a neat copy of the fruits of my many years of meditation—as usual, I find that instead of weighty volumes I have less than a sparrow's beak to show and that's sure to cause a great outcry.

I am enjoying my life in the country house tremendously: I've grown accustomed to the uncanny atmosphere and to the absence of the master. . . . The mystical aspect of the matter is that twenty years ago I made my start in his house, and now, in another house of his, with the master gone, I must continue.

*   *   *

Moscow, May 17, 1937

Have spent a few days in town attending the stormy literary meetings, the gravity of which you know from the newspapers. Their beneficent effect upon the future is beyond doubt but in the meantime it keeps breaking one's writing rhythm. Today, I am going back home to the countryside. As I grow older, my thirst for work increases.

*   *   *

Moscow, July 10, 1937

* * *

I've had a letter from Zhenya. She says she intends to go and spend a month with you. I am delighted about it.

* * *

Zhenya worked for a month in our pavilion at the Exhibition [World's Fair in Paris] but, alas, she got overtired very quickly and went off on a trip. That rather saddens me because she had a good opportunity there to strengthen her position among the Soviet colony and she failed to take full advantage of it.

* * *

Moscow, July 30, 1937

* * *

I am comparatively poor now since I have discarded all extraneous work, reserving myself exclusively for pure literature. I reckon that this period of poverty will come to an end in a couple of months and then there won't be any need for me to take on assignments from outside. I have written a few new stories and I will send them to you one by one as they are published. As before, I'm hoping I'll be able to go to Odessa toward the end of August.

* * *

Moscow, August 26, 1937

* * *

Please, have your picture taken more often because those pieces of cardboard give me tremendous joy. I only wish I could have completed our family group personally.

* * *

Moscow, September 6, 1937

In the first place, allow me to inform you that today is Rosh Hashanah and also to congratulate you on this new, many-thousand-year-old Jewish year.

On Yom Kippur, I'll go to the synagogue.

In the second place—I still haven't recovered from the excitement that gripped me when I heard Natasha's and Zhenya's voices. I hope that Zhenya will have a phone installed in her house now. Natasha's accent is very amusing and moving. Write to me about her in more detail.

* * *

Kiev, January 3, 1938

The situation is unchanged, if I chose to disregard the fact that my Moscow publishers, the studios and other creditors, furious at my protracted absence, are threatening me with frightful vengeance. However, I have decided, and I believe correctly, not to move from here until I have completed the important assemblage work for which I am responsible. Its completion will enable me to rest for a while and have a bit of time to myself.

*   *   *

Quite by accident, I have met my best school-friend, Mirosha Berkov, here. He is still the same warm and comforting person he used to be. He has worked in a bank for twenty years, is married to a friend of Mera's— Kadya Fran. We spent a sentimental evening devoted to reminiscences of Odessa and the dispatching of prayers to the former God that he may send you well-being, health, money and all sorts of achievements.

*   *   *

Moscow, April 16, 1938

(1) From yesterday on, have been eating the finest matzos brought in from somewhere around Minsk. (They were presented to me by some kind-hearted old woman.) I wish you had some of the same. Are you celebrating this best of all Judaic festivals? Have you kosherized your crockery for Passover? Well, in brief, a happy Passover to you.

*   *   *

In a few days, I am moving to what is supposed to be my private villa. At first I didn't want to live in the so-called writers' settlement, but when I realized that the villas were quite far away from one another and that I wouldn't have to meet my brother authors, I decided to move there.

*   *   *

Moscow, July 26, 1938

*   *   *

Despite the Egyptian heat wave, I'll stay in Moscow for a couple of days for change and relaxation. My summer villa is my working place and the city is a place of relaxation.

*   *   *

Today I'll attend the Physical Culture Day show (a repetition of the parade of Physical Culturists on Red Square). It is an absolutely magical sight, involving thirty-five thousand participants. If we could borrow a bit of health from one of them, it would take care of all our troubles.

Moscow, September 20, 1938

*   *   *

I don't remember whether I wrote to you about the ecstatic impression left upon me by Yasnaya Polyana—I found myself standing in Tolstoi's ascetic rooms and felt that his thought still continued its furious activity there.

*   *   *

Peredelkino, September 26, 1938

We are having beautiful and sunny although quite cool days, The leaves are falling.

Everything would be so nice and quiet if it weren't for the newspapers that are brought to me from town and that fill me with anxiety. After reading them, I have to do violence to myself to regain my composure and go on with my work.

Am leaving for Moscow for a couple of days. I want to look for books to send to Natasha. I reckon to be back on the 28th, in the evening.

I have a stock of firewood for the winter. In the coming days, the house will undergo an overhauling—the foundation will be strengthened and the rather dried-up floors will be relaid, I hope it'll be nice and warm here in the winter. I have brought all my books from town and, at night, sit by the fire reading Sholom Aleichem in our highly original tongue.

Peredelkino, December 2, 1938

*   *   *

I have walked and worked a great deal—incomparably more effectively than in Moscow. Tomorrow I am going into town. Besides other more pressing matters, I want to see the new Eisenstein film *Alexander Nevsky* and my friend, the astounding Jewish actor Michoels, in the stage version of Sholom Aleichem's *Tevie, the Milkman*. (By the way, I'd like to translate a few chapters of that book.) I intend to come back here in a few days.

*   *   *

Moscow, January 2, 1939

*   *   *

And so, a happy New Year to you. If I were God, you'd live better than anyone ever dreamed of living. But since I am not endowed with divine powers, I must content myself with wishes, the scope and content of which you are well aware of. As to me, the year 1939 finds me in great working form. The only trouble is that I haven't enough time for creative writing.

*   *   *

Moscow, January 28, 1939

Except for a feeling of sadness left in me in the mornings after I have read the war communiqués I have nothing new to tell you. I am working hard and dreaming of more poetic and less time-consuming work. We are having a wonderful winter and only recently did we have a real snowfall. I go out for walks and sometimes stand for hours by the fence of the ice-skating rink at Chistyye Prudy, admiring the people and the radiance of the light on the ice and enjoying the pure, icy air. Of the news from everyday life, I ought to report the appearance of bananas in the stores—the first in twenty years—on which we all pounce with greed and joy.

*   *   *

Moscow, February 7, 1939

*   *   *

I get your letters regularly. Of course, I couldn't manage to finish everything by February first, but I did hand in a fair share of it. I am moving relentlessly ahead and I hope that in a few days my life will be devoted to pure sounds and prayers.

*   *   *

Moscow, February 24, 1939

*   *   *

In the morning I drove out to Peredelkino. The overhaul of the villa is coming to an end and it'll be a real reinforced concrete house. They have built a new brick foundation, relaid all the flooring on the ground floor and are now putting down parquet there. Everything will be ready by the first and then I'll really have a house that will last me for years. And although

I have no neighbors too close by, I want, nevertheless, to put up a high wall around my garden. My pigeons are all there. My house help had bought a new cow. Now, having returned from my villa, I am having my lunch (for hors d'oeuvre, I'm having radish with goose dripping). Afterward, I'll go to the hippodrome. I haven't been there for four months. Then I'll go with a friend to a restaurant which specializes in shashlyk. And that's my complete program for the day.

Moscow, March 6, 1939

Today is an important day for sports lovers—the Winter Derby. * * * Yesterday, I went to my estate: the laying of the new brick foundation and of the flooring has been completed and now they are laying the parquet. I reckon I'll be able to move in there by the tenth. I am very pleased about it. The rest is fine and unchanged. I can hear hooting downstairs—it is the car that is taking me to the race track. Write more often and don't be put off by a lack of topics to write about—to me you are the most interesting of writers.

Moscow, March, 18, 1939

According to my calculations, in a couple of weeks I'll be a well-off man, well rid of daily drudgery. * * *
I will go to my Peredelkino villa at the end of this month—the main part of the overhaul has been completed and now I have only to wait for the paint to dry and for the parquet to be planed and polished, and a supply of ice put into the cellar.
The day before yesterday my first pigeon chick came out of its egg and today we are expecting the second one.
I still hope to go to Odessa for the summer.

* * *

Astoria Hotel, Leningrad, April 22, 1939

* * *

Went to dinner at [Mikhail] Zoshchenko's yesterday, after which, until five o'clock in the morning, sat with my 1938 publisher, who goes back to my Gorky period. Then, at dawn, I walked down Kamenostrovsky Parade, across the Troitsky Bridge, past the Winter Palace, in this amazing city, so quiet at that hour. Am leaving tonight.

* * *

Peredelkino, May 10, 1939

For your information, it has been snowing for two days now. Talk of a May 10th! I suppose even your Brussels climate would envy this.

I am already installed in my country seat and am feeling wonderful, except that I am bored with having to go on lighting fires. Am going to Moscow for one day tomorrow. Perhaps there will be a letter from Mera there; I wonder how her trip has been. It is such a shame Mama couldn't go with her on that excursion.

I have sent off some books for Natasha and now that the grand-daughter has been taken care of, I must think of her grandmother and will try to get some recent literature for her too tomorrow.

Nothing new about me—I'm absorbed in work. I am finishing my last assignment—for the movies (a film about Gorky) and will soon devote myself to the final polishing of my true work. I reckon to hand it in to the publishers by the fall. Write more often because I have no time for reading long books and your messages are the best reading there is for me. How is Grisha? How is Boris? Do you see him often?

ISAAC BABEL
THROUGH THE EYES
OF HIS CONTEMPORARIES

NATHALIE BABEL

[The Family]†

I grew up wishing that someday, somewhere, a door would open and my father would come in. We would recognize each other immediately and without seeming surprised, without letting him catch his breath, I would say: "Well, here you are at last. We've been puzzled about you for so long; although you left behind much love and devotion, you bequeathed us very few facts. It's so good to have you here. Do sit down and tell us what happened." [Now we know some of what happened, and even today when I am 75 years old, I still feel deeply the pain of having been abandoned by my father.[1]]

* * *

As Babel tells us, he was born July 13, 1894 (June 30 by the old calendar) in the Moldavanka, a suburb of Odessa. Though the name "Moldavanka" today evokes a vision of gangsters inhabiting dirty hideouts, the district had, at least at that time, less colorful people living there as well—such as the newlyweds Emmanuel Isaakovich Babel and his wife. Babel could scarcely have remembered much about the suburb as it was then; the family moved, shortly after his birth, to Nikolayev, another Black Sea port, where his sister was born in 1899. The Babel house in Nikolayev had a garden, a dovecote, and a courtyard, which became a skating rink in winter.

Babel's mother taught him to read in Nikolayev, and there he went to primary school and began his study of English, French and German, languages which he spoke well later in life.

Though I have no intention here of discussing my father's work *per se*, some mention of it should be made, apropos of Nikolayev. Because Babel often wrote in the first person, his stories have been thought to be autobiographical;[2] actually they are a blend of fact and fiction.[3] Two good examples are "The Story of my Dovecote," and "First Love," both of which have Nikolayev as their setting and a pogrom as their central event.

It is true that as a child Babel witnessed a pogrom and, evidently, was deeply shaken by the experience. But the Babel family, though, of course, terrified, was not physically harmed. Nor would his father have had to kneel at a Cossack's feet and beg that his store be spared, for the simple reason that Babel's father did not own a store. He owned a warehouse, which was neither broken into nor plundered during the pogrom. I must add (and this may be a disillusionment to readers of "First Love") that no member of the Babel family was red-headed, that my grandmother's

† Nathalie Babel, Isaac Babel's daughter, was born in Paris in 1929. She grew up in France, emigrating to the United States in the late 1950s. She has edited and contributed introductions and commentary to several editions of her father's writings. Excerpts from "Introduction" from *The Lonely Years* by Isaac Babel. Copyright © 1964, renewed 1992 by Farrar, Straus, and Giroux, LLC. Reprinted by permission of Farrar, Straus, and Giroux, LLC, and the Estate of Nathalie Babel.
1. Nathalie Babel asked the editor to insert this sentence shortly before her death in December 2005.
2. For example, see L. Trilling's introduction (p. 469, this volume) and R. Rosenthal's "The Fate of Isaak Babel," *Commentary*, Feb., 1947.
3. See Babel's letter of Oct. 14, 1931: "The subjects of the stories are all taken from my childhood, but, of course, there is much that has been made up and changed."

name was Fanny, not Rachel, nor would she ever have thought of addressing her husband in the terms used by the woman in the story; she was a
modest, sensitive woman. It is, of course, not impossible that there was a
charming girl named Galina who wore a Chinese peignoir, and who excited the passions of my father at the age of ten. But if she did exist, my
father was the only member of the family who had the privilege of knowing her.

I could cite many more such examples. Of course, sifting the facts and in-
ventions out of the stories has no bearing on their quality, but it does help
to restore the biography of the author.

At the beginning of 1905, Babel entered the Commercial School of
Odessa, an institution open to the sons of Jewish merchants who were
members of the first or second guild. He lived at the time with his two aunts
and his maternal grandmother on Tiraspolskaya Street. One of his aunts
was a midwife, and the other, Katya, was a dentist. More than once these
poor women were in danger of being burned alive while they slept, for their
nephew, instead of being in bed, sat hidden by the tablecloth under the
dining-room table reading by a kerosene lamp. Later that year, Emmanuel
Babel decided to return to Odessa. At first the family lived with the aunts,
but several months later rented an apartment at 17 Reschelevskaya Street,
a street considered one of the prettiest in Odessa. The family lived there
until 1923, the year my grandfather died. After his death, his widow and
his daughter moved to Moscow.

*   *   *

On his return to Odessa, he established his own business, opening an
office on Politsiskaya Street where most of the various export-import
firms were located. It can be said of him that he was a self-made man,
and like many self-made men, had his financial ups and downs; but this
was certainly his most prosperous period. Dandyish, elegant, good-
looking, he was a man of imposing physique and impetuous nature. His
rages were legendary. One of his ambitions was to educate his children as
well as possible—especially his son for whom he had a scarcely concealed
preference. Nothing was too good for the boy. For Emmanuel Babel education meant that his son must speak a number of foreign languages,
study music and Hebrew. And my father had an unusual gift for languages but none whatsoever for music. Despite his obvious lack of interest in the violin, his musical training continued under the supervision of
his paternal grandmother, a rather formidable and wicked old lady with a
great passion for her grandson. When it was time to practice, my father
would saw away at his fiddle with a book, instead of a score, opened before him on the music stand. The more agonizing the sound that issued
from the instrument, the happier the old woman became. One day Mr.
Stolyarsky, my father's violin teacher, a most eminent man, stopped by at
the house to inquire about the health of his pupil who had not shown up
for his lesson, ostensibly because of illness. But the "patient" was down at
the harbor, a favorite hangout, which he found more fascinating than
Mozart. Thus ended my father's career as a virtuoso. Only my great-
grandmother wept.

Because of the *numerus clausus*, or Jewish quota, Babel was unable to go to the University of Odessa. His father therefore decided to send him to Kiev to continue his studies in the Institute of Financial and Business Studies. Babel entered the Institute in 1911. At the beginning of the First World War, the school was moved to Saratov, and it was there that Babel received his degree.

While he was still living in Kiev, Babel was introduced to Boris Venyaminovich Gronfein, a manufacturer and importer of agricultural machinery who had been dealing with Emmanuel Babel for years. Naturally Gronfein was happy to entertain his friend's son. Babel was then sixteen years old, a graceless, blushing, puffy-cheeked young provincial.

The atmosphere at the Gronfeins' was relaxed and elegant. Boris Gronfein was a cultured, indulgent, generous man. His opinions and style of living were thoroughly westernized. His wife was a handsome but somewhat melancholy woman who devoted much of her time to reading and playing chess. The couple had a son and two daughters. Leon (Lyova) had been brought up as a young princeling, and was busier at this time establishing his reputation as a dandy and a Don Juan than in working in his father's business. Actresses apparently found him irresistible. Raya, the elder of the girls, had just become engaged to Volodya Seiliger, a violinist; Volodya would bring his friends to the house where they held concerts in the parlor around the white Bechstein piano.

Evgenia (Zhenya), the younger, who was to marry Babel, was then fifteen, a handsome, shy, romantic girl already planning a career as an artist. The Italian Renaissance, Sir Walter Scott, Goethe, Strindberg, and Balzac were more familiar and less disturbing to her than the outside world. Even years later, after many sorrows she could still find serenity and renewed courage by absorbing herself completely in a book or a beautiful object. My mother and father, from adolescence on, shared a commitment to art and a belief that one ought to sacrifice everything for it.

This was an era of social unrest and intellectual exaltation; my parents were determined to live heroically. My mother refused to wear the furs and pretty dresses her parents gave her. My father, to harden himself, would walk bareheaded in the dead of winter without an overcoat, dressed only in a jacket. These Spartan efforts ended abruptly one day when my parents were walking, in their usual costume, and a woman stopped, and, apparently mesmerized by what she saw, pointed at my father, and shouted "A madman!" Thirty years later my mother was still mortified when she remembered this incident. Nor had she forgotten her astonishment when her fiancé took her out for tea for the first time and she watched him gobble down cake after cake with dizzying speed. At the Gronfeins, he refused everything but tea. The explanation was simple. "When I start eating cake, I can't stop," he said. "So it's better for me not to start at all."

Babel went to St. Petersburg in 1915, ostensibly as a student, but it is unlikely that he did much studying. My guess is that in his autobiography he somewhat dramatized that stay in the capital. His father still sent him money. Moreover, although Jewish students were allowed to remain in Petersburg only for a limited period of time, this period could be extended. Then, too, the residence permit for Jews was abolished in 1917.

Though he had been exempted from military service in 1914, he volunteered for the army in October, 1917. He was thus able to start in on that apprenticeship to life which Gorky had exhorted him to seek. Babel served on the Rumanian front until 1918 when, having contracted malaria, he was evacuated back to Odessa.

Babel was again in St. Petersburg in 1919. His schoolfriend Alexander Fraenkel, remembers that in the spring of that year Babel spent his days sleeping in his unpretentious but quite adequate room on the Nevsky Prospect and his nights losing himself in the city. However, in that period he also seems to have found time to work for the People's Commissariat of Enlightenment.

It was also in 1919 that my parents were married. Then in 1920, during the civil war, my father rejoined the army, where he was assigned to Budyonny's cavalry,[4] and acted as correspondent in the army for ROSTA, the predecessor of TASS. On his first day of duty, and very likely his first experience as a horseman, he had to ride for about fifty miles. He not only managed to survive the ordeal; he also fell in love with horses. At the end of that year he was reported dead, but ultimately returned, completely exhausted, covered with vermin, and suffering from acute asthma.

For a while he worked in a government publishing house, but he was still very ill. To facilitate his recovery, my parents took a house in the Caucasus in the neighborhood of Batum, where on the side of a mountain my mother was initiated into the mysteries of housekeeping. To go marketing, one had to walk several miles in country that was far from safe, and my father's asthma was still so bad that he was unable to make the trips himself. He taught my mother how to do the laundry without bruising her hands. Once she served him soup so thick that he took his knife and pretended to cut it. Finally he introduced her to an old Tartar who taught her the arts of steaming rice and roasting pieces of lamb over an open fire. They found themselves penniless, and for a very strange reason. Boris Gronfein had given them a thousand-ruble note, which they kept concealed in a clothes brush. Unfortunately, they could never find anyone in the district rich enough to change the bill.

It was in 1923 during his stay in the mountains that my father began to work on the stories which eventually appeared in *Red Cavalry*. Achieving the form that he wanted was an endless torture. He would read my mother version after version; thirty years later she still knew the stories by heart.

* * *

4. Budyonny's cavalry was one of the military units of the Red Army that during the summer of 1920 pushed back the Poles from the Ukraine (where the Polish Army had occupied Kiev), from White Russia, and Lithuania to the suburbs of Warsaw. At Warsaw the Poles made a stand and prevented the Russians from capturing the city. This was later called "The Miracle on the Vistula."

M. N. BERKOV

We Knew Each Other since Childhood[†]

I entered the third form of the Odessa Nicholas I Commercial Academy in 1906. I was seated at the desk next to Babel. In subsequent years we shared a desk, which helped us to become friends.

The commercial academy we attended was funded mainly by donations from the Odessa merchant community. The academy trained future qualified banking and commercial clerks, and the merchant community supported their education with great generosity.

The Academy was situated in a big three-story building with spacious classrooms, meeting halls, offices, and labs. Outside, there was the academy's large yard, a park, and even our own church.

The program was identical to that of a classical gymnasium minus Latin and Greek. Instead, we had a few specialized subjects: chemistry, commodity analysis, accounting, commercial calculus, law, political economy. Many hours were allotted to foreign languages: French, German, and English.

The *numerus clausus* for Jews in commercial academies and at the Commercial Institute was very high, which is why Babel, though he was not interested in commercial disciplines, studied at two commercial schools, first the academy and later the institute.

As a student at the academy, Babel showed no special aptitude for letters. He was good in literature classes and received excellent grades, but other students also got good grades for their class work and compositions.

And yet there were some traits that distinguished him from his classmates. He showed exceptional perseverance and concentration in pursuit of his goals. He loved history and as a child read many books on the subject. At the age of thirteen or fourteen, he read all eleven volumes of Karamzin's *History of the Russian State*. He used to tell me how he read Karamzin at night under the table covered with a large tablecloth hanging all the way to the floor. He read his books by the light of a small kerosene lamp, which he had bought much earlier when he still lived in Tiraspolskaya Street in 1907 and 1908.

The subject of history was taught by the Academy's director, A. V. Vyrlan. Babel's responses in class were deeper and broader than what Vyrlan was giving us. We listened to Babel with greater interest than we did to Vyrlan, who taught to the textbook. In the senior year, Vyrlan was replaced by Vandraczek, who knew and taught history magnificently. He and Babel became friends.

Our French teacher was Vadon, who succeeded in exciting in many of us an interest in French literature. Babel began studying French with enthusiasm. He was not satisfied by the thumbnail sketches of French classics and their works provided by Vadon. One could often see Babel with the volumes of Racine, Corneille, and Molière; whenever possible he tried to do his homework for his French tutor during classtime. German classes were most suitable for this activity, because the German teacher,

† M. N. Berkov, "My byli znakomy s detstva," N. Pirozhkova and N. N. Yugeneva, eds., *Vospominaniya o Babele* (Moscow, 1989), pp. 203–07.

Herr Osetzki, was nearsighted and conducted his lessons from his desk; this made it difficult for him to see what his students were doing. At his lessons, Babel became totally absorbed in his French. As he finished his assignment, he would make a loud noise—a sigh of satisfaction or something. Ozetski would turn to Babel (he called him *Babyl*) and utter one of his phrases: "Babyl, machen sie keine faulen Witzen!" or "Aber, Babyl, sind Sie verrückt?"[1]

During our senior year, Babel was unhappy with the German we were getting at school and decided to study it in greater depth. He suggested that we do it together. We bought a textbook by Tüssen and Langescheit and went to work. Soon it became clear to me that I had neither Babel's perseverance nor his concentration, and I fell behind.

Even when he was a student at the academy, he displayed unusual talent in reciting and telling stories.

In 1909, a group of students decided to mark the fifth anniversary of Chekhov's death. The parents of one of our classmates, Watman, offered us a big room in their house at Rishelievskaya, at the corner of Novorybnaya. I cannot reconstruct the details of this evening, but I remember clearly Babel's small figure kneeling before a chair with an inkpot and a piece of paper on it. He was doing an impression of Chekhov's Vanka slowly writing out words on a sheet of paper and reading aloud his letter "to Grandpa in the village." I think I remember Babel so well because his unusual recitation moved me so deeply: I had a lump in my throat and tears in my eyes.

That Babel himself was a writer we found out in 1911–1914, during one of Babel's trips back to Odessa from Kiev.

He gathered a few of us together and read to us his play. I remember neither the title nor the content of the play but judging by the mood it created, perhaps because of Babel's special reading skill, it resembled Chekhov. I remember that as he was describing the setting of the last act, Babel put special emphasis on one detail: a pool of light from the lamp illuminating a letter on the heroine's bedtable.[2] We were very impressed by the fact that Babel had written a play and touched by his reading.

When he finished, we all got up and clustered around him. We tried to convince him that he should take the play to Petersburg and show it to some editor there who might publish it. Babel was moved by our response and, perhaps, also by his own reading; he declared to us that he could not negotiate with anyone the sale of what had been written with his heart's blood. These were his student years when he was supported by his father and was free of material want. As is well known, he subsequently changed his attitude to publishing his work.

One more episode made me think about Babel as a writer. During one of his trips to Odessa in 1912 or 1913, Babel proposed that we visit a pub called Gambrinus, the one that Kuprin had described in his story by the same name. This pub had a bad reputation because its clientele—prostitutes, sailors, and pimps—often started fights, and one could easily get hit in the general melee for absolutely no reason. I had no desire to go

1. German: "Babel, don't make such off-color jokes!" "But, Babel, are you crazy?"
2. A similar image appears in Babel's play *Maria* in the description of the setting in Scene Five.

there, but I did not like the idea of Babel taking me for a coward. We spent one and a half or two hours at Gambrinus. I had ants in my pants and could not wait for Babel to decide to leave. Babel calmly observed the clientele and exchanged a few words with some of them. On our way back I asked him why we had to spend two hours in a dive where the air was befouled by alcohol and tobacco when we could have had a pint of beer in more respectable surroundings. Babel looked at me and said, "From an ethnographic point of view, this is a very interesting place."

During the early years after the Revolution, we met rarely. He would drop by my place during his trips to Odessa.

I remember well his story about an episode that had a rather sad ending for him. When the Red Cavalry was retreating towards Kiev under Polish pressure, Budyonny's Cossacks staged pogroms in Jewish towns. In one shtetl, Babel got into an argument with them. The Cossacks brutally beat him up, but afterwards they put him into their cart, sick and beaten, and took him into the rear, never abandoning him, not even in the most dangerous moments. According to what he told me then, some three hundred Cossacks who had been most active in instigating the pogroms were shot on Trotsky's orders.

During four months at the end of 1937 and the beginning of 1938, Babel lived in Kiev. He came there on the invitation of the Kiev Film Studios to write a script based on the novel *How the Steel Was Tempered*.[3] We met several times then. I still cannot forgive myself for not having written down the stories he told us about his meetings with prominent interesting people. He told stories with such skill and magnetism that on one occasion my wife, myself, and a couple of our friends spent the whole night listening to his tales about Gorky, Feuchtwanger, Stanislavsky, André Gide, and others.

When I asked why he stopped writing, he replied, "There is a children's game that goes like this: a lady has sent you a hundred rubles; you can go and buy whatever you want, but you must not say 'yes' or 'no,' nor must you mention 'white' or 'black,' nor must you shake your head. I can't write according to such rules. Besides, I have a bad temper. By contrast, Valentin Kataev[4] has a good temper. When he describes a poor and hungry boy and takes his work to the editor, and the editor says to him that a Soviet boy cannot be poor and hungry, then Kataev goes back to his place and quietly changes the boy into a healthy one with red cheeks and a big red apple in his hand. I have a bad temper—I can't do that."

I very much wanted to find out what Babel thought about the mass repressions and arrests taking place at that time. In that time of terror, mutual mistrust, and most importantly an inability to comprehend what was happening, one could not expect someone to offer an open and true interpretation of those events. Babel did not answer my question . . .

This was our last meeting. In 1939 I came to Moscow on business and learned that Babel had been arrested.

3. A famous Soviet novel written in 1932–34 by Nikolay Ostrovsky (1904–1936).
4. A popular novelist and playwright (1897–1986), and a native of Odessa.

PYOTR PILSKY

[The Young Babel]†

He is volatile, he is nervous, he is talented.

I remember:

One day, Efim Zozulya,[1] then only beginning his literary career, brought to my Petersburg apartment the little Babel. He was wearing his student uniform and impressed me very favorably with his simple manners, his reserve, and his youthful credulity. He was not only a very merry man—he was prone to mirth. When he visited us, he often stayed late, sometimes spending the night. Only later did I find out that Babel did not have his residence permit then[2] and that he wore his student uniform as a suit of armor to shield himself from the inquisitive concierges and the police. He was then renting a room from some noisy and ever-inebriated waiter.

The Babel of those days exuded a sense of inner anxiety and fatigue. He was very animated, not to say fussy—the sign of unsettled nerves and lack of self-confidence. He spoke little but was acutely observant, and one could sense the tension of desire in the intensity with which he registered everything he saw. In general, he lived his life guardedly.

That was in 1916.

Once, Zozulya showed me a story by Babel. Painfully modest, Babel did not dare to draw someone's attention towards himself by means of what was apparently one of his first experiments in short fiction. I read it: one could see a strong influence of Maupassant. In general, Babel was a captive of the French. At first, he was teased by Maupassant, then dumbfounded by Barbusse.[3]

Three years later—in 1919—I heard him read his new story in the Palace of Peasants in Odessa. It was the same thing: Maupassant.

* * *

Of course, he is talented. But however talented he may be, however observant, Babel is still a victim type. His quiet strength is not great; as an author he is not prolific; his career will be short. He is all impermanence. And as I recall my old acquaintance with the little black-uniformed Babel—his soft, thinning hair, his tensely raised eyebrows, his high forehead, and his animated, fussy gesturing—when I read his books now, I realize that Babel the author, too, is a miniature, his pieces are miniatures, and he himself is a tender, anxious, and delicate creature. In the field of literature, he stands like a heron, on one leg.

---

† Pyotr Moiseyevich Pilsky (1879–1940), famous Russian literary critic and journalist and one of the most important voices in the Russian émigré press in Estonia and Latvia in the interwar period. This excerpt is from his book of reminiscences and essays *Zatumanivshiysya mir* (Gramatu Daugs: Riga, 1929), pp. 157–64.
1. Efim Davydovich Zozulya (1891–1941), journalist, fiction writer, and editor, was a native of Odessa, where he began as a reporter, and a lifelong friend of Isaac Babel's.
2. Babel briefly visited Petrograd at the end of 1915 and may not have had a residence permit then. When he returned in the fall of 1916, having been admitted to the faculty of law of the Petrograd Psycho-Neurological Institute, he had the benefit of such a permit, routinely issued to Jewish students at the Institute.
3. Henri Barbusse (1873–1935), French novelist, veteran of World War I, and author of the antiwar novel *Le Feu* (Under Fire), which made him famous when it was published in 1916.

ELENA PILSKY

[Babel in Odessa, 1919–1920]†

* * * Remembering Babel, I cannot help thinking about our travails of 1919–1920 in Odessa. The Bolsheviks had conquered the city but they were still unsure of their victory and tried to eliminate their opponents brutally and with dispatch. Their automobiles, nicknamed "black crows," crisscrossed the city; people were seized and often disposed of on the spot without trial. Early in the morning one could see trucks stacked full of dead bodies, with bare feet sticking out from under the tarp. Many perished that way. Finally, it came the turn of the journalists. One night we had a visit from our little friend Babel. He told us that my husband was soon to be arrested, that the decision had already been made, and that he had to go into hiding at once or, at the very least, avoid spending the night at home. We followed his advice for several nights. My husband would return in the morning. On the third night, the "guests" came, searched all the rooms, closets, and wardrobes. Finding nothing, they went away but their leader stayed.

For some reason, in moments of great danger I feel a strange calm. Reaction comes later. That night, I staged a comedy, pretending to be interested only in my acting career; I showed my guest all of my new costumes, which I needed for the coming production of Bernard Shaw's *Man and Superman*. The effect was salutary. When two of the "guests" returned in the morning and announced that they were taking me to the Cheka, my new fan came to my defense. He told them to put me under house arrest and left me alone guarded by some masculine-looking female, who was armed to the teeth. At eleven actors from the theater called, surprised that I had missed the rehearsal. I glanced at my guard; they understood everything and went directly to the powers that be, warning them that the theater would have to close since I had control of the repertoire. The Bolsheviks patronized the theater, and the petition was granted, but I was still tailed by their agents. All this time Babel made sure my husband was safe. He tracked Pilsky down in the morning on his way home and warned him about the "guests." Babel also took care of him subsequently during the three months that my husband was in the "underground." He often visited me telling me that I must really be happy to be the wife of such a brilliant man. I agreed with him and told him that even our quarrels have an aspect of brilliance.

Babel helped my husband to escape from Odessa with the help of Mikhail Koltsov.[1] Without exaggeration, I can say that in those terrible times Babel saved my husband's life, because Pilsky's [earlier] hard-hitting articles against communism posed a grave threat.[2] * * *

---

† Elena Pilsky (E. S. Kuznetsova; d. 1972), theater actress and the second wife of Pyotr Pilsky. This little memoir, "Venok pamyati Babelya" (A Memorial Wreath for Babel), was published in *Novoe Russkoe Slovo* (NY), June 8, 1966, p. 3.
1. Babel was no doubt involved in saving Pilsky from the Odessa Cheka in winter–spring 1920, but by the time Pilsky made his escape from Odessa to Rumania in August 1920 Babel was marking his fourth month at the Polish front. Possibly it was Babel who put Pilsky in touch with his powerful friend from Petrograd, Mikhail Koltsov (1898–1940). The future famous Soviet journalist and cultural entrepreneur was then in Odessa as the head of the Southern Division of the Soviet Telegraph Agency (YugROSTA) and was in a position to perform "miracles."
2. On May 9, 1918, the Petrograd newspaper *Petrogradskoe ekho* published Pilsky's article "Put Them in a Straitjacket!" in which he described top Bolshevik leaders as clinically mad. In response, the

KONSTANTIN PAUSTOVSKY

Life's Novel. The Time of Great Expectations[†]

* * * Izya Livshits[1] was the one who brought Babel to the editorial offices of *Moryak*.[2] I have never met a man who looked so unlike a writer. At first glance, this man—stooped, with practically no neck and suffering from a congenital case of Odessa asthma, with a nose like a duck's beak, a wrinkled brow, and small eyes with an oily sheen—this man could elicit little interest. But as soon as he began to speak, this impression changed. Until then, he could have been mistaken for a door-to-door salesman or a broker.

As soon as he began to speak, everything changed. His thin voice rang with irony.

Many people could not stand Babel's direct gaze, which seemed to burn through them. By nature, Babel was a demystifier. He liked it when people were taken aback by him, and for this reason he had the reputation of someone difficult and dangerous.

Babel came into the editorial office of *Moryak* with a volume of Kipling in his hands. As he was talking to the editor, Zhenya Ivanov, he put the book on the table but all during the conversation he cast impatient and even predatory glances on it. He fidgeted in his chair, got up from it and sat down again. He was clearly impatient. All he wanted to do was to read, not carry on this forced, polite discussion.

Soon he changed the subject to Kipling. One must write, he said, in the same iron prose as Kipling and have the clearest notion of what was to flow from one's pen. A story must be precise as a report from the field of battle or a bank cheque. It must be written in the same firm and straight hand as military orders and cheques. And Kipling, as it happens, had such a handwriting.

After taking off his glasses, which made his face seem helpless and kind, he finished his discourse on Kipling with a surprising statement. "Here in Odessa," he said with a mocking twinkle in his eyes, "we will never have our own Kiplings. We are peaceful lovers of life. Instead, we will have our own Maupassants, because we have much sea, sunshine, beautiful women, and much food for thought. That we shall have our own Maupassants—I guarantee."

Thereupon he recounted his visit to Maupassant's last apartment in Paris. He told us about the rosy-colored lace lampshades, warmed by the sun and resembling the underdrawers of rich courtesans, about the scent of brilliantine and coffee, about the rooms with enormous space that tor-

---

authorities incarcerated him for six months and charged him with "insanity." He was released on parole and with his wife fled to the Ukraine, then under German occupation. They made their way to Odessa at the end of 1919. According to Mikhail Koltsov, Pilsky earned his living in Odessa writing orthodox Bolshevik copy for the local papers, without, however, signing his own name. Mikhail Koltsov, "Stradaniya Kalibana," *Sobranie sochineny*, 3 vols., vol. 2 (Moscow, 1934), pp. 259–61.

[†] Paustovsky (1892–1968), a master of Soviet literature, a stylist known for his humanity and love of nature, who avoided ideological didacticism and who after Stalin's death supported liberal causes. The recollections excerpted here refer to 1921 and were written in 1958: *Povest o zhizni. Vremya bolshikh ozhidany* (M. 1966).

1. Isaak (Izya) Livshits (1892–1978), journalist, editor, Babel's lifelong friend and correspondent.

2. *Moryak* (Sailor), an Odessa newspaper and an outlet for some of Babel's early Odessa stories.

mented the frightened and sick author, who had for years practiced the discipline of restraint and brevity in his writing.

In the process, Babel gave us a brief sketch of the topography of Paris.[3] Babel spoke good French.

The few remarks Babel made convinced me that he was unusually strong-willed, a man who grasped things quickly, who wanted to see everything, who was open to any kind of knowledge, who wished to be seen as someone skeptical—even cynical—but in fact believed deeply in the naïve and kind human soul. This explains why he liked to repeat a Biblical aphorism: "Power makes you thirst for more, and only grief sates the heart."[4] * * *

YURI ANNENKOV

Isaac Babel[†]

* * * Strange as it may sound, I met Babel in person only in Paris one evening, in 1925,[1] at Ilya Ehrenburg's: we were either drinking tea or drinking wine.

Unlike many Russian writers and poets of our time, largely a moody lot, Isaac Emmanuilovich Babel was invariably cheerful, quick to laugh, and had a youthful demeanor. He and I used to wander around Paris for days on end, amuse ourselves at street fairs, turn somersaults on swings, test our marksmanship by shooting at the little round targets made of plaster—almost hitting the bull's eye!—and, of course, hung around the Montparnasse.

Soon after our first encounter at Ehrenburg's, Babel became one of my most frequent visitors, a "habitué." He would arrive at my place on rue Boileau, ring the bell, and ask when the door was opened: "Will you allow me to pay a visit to the old-world landowners?"

The old-world landowners, that is, my wife and I, were always very glad to see Babel. His wife, Evgeniya Borisovna, a woman of extraordinary cultivation but always preoccupied with caring for her family, came less often than her husband. Babel's visits and our conversations almost always ended in our going for a walk.

"Shall we go and take a look at things?" Babel would ask.

In Paris, there are always plenty of things to look at. At the time, Babel was especially interested in painting, and in those days galleries had two or three *vernisages* a week. I often accompanied Babel on his visits to these exhibitions and toured museums with him. In painting, he was particularly curious about the Impressionists and the transition to abstract art. What

---

3. Babel visited Paris for the first time in 1927.
4. This "aphorism" is not actually found in the Bible.
† Yuri Pavlivich Annenkov (1889–1974), Russian modernist painter, graphic artist, theater and film set designer, studied art in Petersburg (alongside Marc Chagall) and in Paris; in 1916–24 he became famous for his book illustrations and portraits; he left Russia in 1924 and settled in Paris. He wrote his "Isaac Babel" recollections in 1963, including them in the two volumes of his memoirs, *Dnevnik moikh vstrech* (*Diary of My Encounters*), published in New York in 1965–66. Although Annenkov does not always get his dates right, his memoirs, based on a set of short notes (*poste pneumatique*) exchanged between him and Babel, have an authentic ring.
1. Babel was in Paris for the first time in 1927–28. Annenkov must be referring to this sojourn.

attracted Babel to the Impressionists was their air of intimacy, informality, and warmth.

"Impressionism," he once said when we talked about Renoir, "that's, well, a calmingly colorful kind of thing."

I was struck then by the precision and truth of this definition—even in the technical sense. And that was true not only about Renoir: just look at the canvases by Claude Monet, Degas, Pissarro, Sisley, Berthe Morisot, or their disciples—Seurat, Signac, Vuillard, Bonnard, up to and including our own Ivan Puni.[2] * * *

For a while, after Babel returned to Paris [at the end of 1932], we saw each other almost every week, sometimes more frequently, sometimes less. In a matter of months, Babel's mood had turned. True, he still joked a lot and spoke in a comical argot, but the subject of our conversations changed. His last few months in the Soviet Union and the growing government interference in literature and the arts had completely disillusioned Babel.[3] To be an author within the framework of the "official Soviet ideology" was becoming intolerable, but he did not know how he could live without being one. * * *

We met after a long hiatus. The conversation centered exclusively on the question of what to do:

"I have a family: my wife, my daughter," Babel kept saying. "I love them and must support them. But under no circumstances do I want them to go back to the Soviets. They must live here where they are free. What about me? Should I stay here and become a cab driver like Gayto Gazdanov?[4] But he has no children! Should I go back to our Proletarian Revolution? Revolution! Just try and find it! Proletarian? The proletariat raced by like an old carriage and wound up cracking up its wheels! It has lost its wheels. Now, believe me, it's all kinds of Central Committees that are doing the pushing, and they are quite a bit more formidable. They don't need any wheels—they have machine guns instead! The rest is clear and requires no comments, as they say in polite society . . . [5] No, it's unlikely I will become a taxi driver, although, as I've told you, I passed the driving test long ago. A taxi driver here is much freer than our university presidents . . . But, taxi driver or not, I shall be a free citizen . . ."

He wrote to me on 18 January 1933: "Dear Yu. P., I am very sorry you missed me. Let's agree—*sauf contre-ordre* [unless countermanded]: I'll come to your place on Monday between 4 and 5. If you'd like, we'll do a *balade* [excursion]. * * *

We did this *balade* in my car and, of course, ran into a street fair with tents, merry-go-round, etc.; we did our target practice, looked at half-naked female acrobats in the circus, listened to phonograph records of Jeanne Mistingett and Maurice Chevalier . . .

2. Ivan Albertovich Puni (Jean Pougny, 1892–1952), Russian avant-garde artist, close to the Futurists and active in Petrograd in 1916–18; associate of Kazimir Malevich and Marc Chagall; left Russia in 1920 and in 1923 emigrated to France.
3. Babel was told to "produce" if he wished to be allowed to travel abroad. It took months of lobbying by Babel and, ultimately, Gorky for Babel to obtain permission to travel to his family in France. See Freidin's essay in this volume.
4. Gayto (Georgy) Ivanovich Gazdanov (1903–1971), veteran of the White Army and French Resistance (in France since 1923), along with Vladimir Nabokov, a leading Russian émigré writer of the interwar and post-WWII period.
5. A similar thesis is conveyed in Babel's play *Maria*. See also Freidin's essay in this volume.

"*Balade* must go on!" Babel declared firmly. "It must—no matter what! France alone will no longer suffice—I have not traveled to other countries yet! It's time I go!"

* * * Babel came to see me [at the end of March 1933], but he was still busy with his work, still waiting for what he called the "good life" to begin. Nonetheless, this did not prevent us from having a splendid dinner in a small bistro, arguing about literature, and even paying a visit to a cinematograph. The "good life" began in a month and a half when Babel was already in Rome. * * *

[Babel was back in France, when] on 24 July 1933 came his letter [saying that he was] "inexplicably recalled to Moscow" and was "leaving under the most dramatic circumstances, without money and loaded with debts." He was, he concluded, "glad to be going to Moscow; the rest was bitterness and uncertainty."

*   *   *

DMITRY FURMANOV

Notes from the Diary 1925–1926[†]

[. . . Babel:] I've gone way past the deadline with the *Red Cavalry* manuscript; I've cheated you ten times already. I would like to ask you only one thing now: please grant me another extension.

Another extension? Well, why not, I say, "but let's nail down a firm date and *basta!*"[1]

"January 15!"

"That'll do."

We decided that he would submit the entire book on January 15 [1926]. It's going to be like this: he's got about twenty chapters written and already published; another twenty have been written but are still unpublished. Ten more are being written now. These are long, serious chapters; they'll have positive things to say about the cavalry; their purpose is to fill the gap . . . fifty chapters altogether.

Babel lives in Sergievo. He has the best conditions for writing there. It's completely quiet. He lives there alone with his mother.

"Unfortunately, all sorts of pleaders and go-betweens have figured out that I am a sellable commodity, and they have snowed me with offers. Were I to agree, I could be making literally hundreds a day. But I am resisting

---

† Dmitry Furmanov (1891–1926), Bolshevik commissar during the civil war, writer and editor, chiefly known for his semiautobiographical novel *Chapaev* (1923). The novel is based on Furmanov's service as a commissar alongside V. I. Chapaev, a gifted but barely literate commander of Red guerrilla forces on the eastern front. A rather conventional narrative, *Chapaev* has much in common with Babel's *Red Cavalry*: the civil war setting and, more important, the tension between an educated political officer (Furmanov, though of peasant origin, studied at Moscow University) before World War I (who tries to civilize (and discipline) the unruly force of a popular revolt. Furmanov was Babel's editor at the State Publishing House when Babel was preparing the first edition of *Red Cavalry*.

1. Italian: Enough!

even though I have no money. I torment myself a lot. I write with great difficulty. I keep thinking, thinking, then I'll put it down on paper, recopy it, and then when it's almost ready, I tear it all up. My friends are wondering: none of them writes that way. I write with difficulty. I trust I am a man of two or three books! I doubt I can write more, have the time for more. I started writing late: in 1916. At first, I just toyed with writing but then I decided to drop by *Letopis*. I remember clearly it was on a Tuesday. Gorky comes out, I give him the manuscript and ask: When should I come back?

" 'Friday'," he says. That's *Letopis* for you!

"I came back on Friday—he spoke with me for an hour and half. This hour and a half are unforgettable. They decided my fate as a writer.

" 'Write,' he said to me.

"Well, I did, but much of it was off the mark. He said to me: 'Go and apprentice among people,' that is, go and study life.

"I did, and since then I've learned a lot, especially during the Revolution. I held sixteen hundred positions and duties; I've done it all: a bookbinder, a typesetter, a menial worker, an editor, soldiered in a squadron under Budyonny . . . What I saw in Budyonny's army is what I've told [in *Red Cavalry*] . . . I realize I have not told anything about the political workers, and not much about the Red Army, but I will later, if I can. But this isn't coming out as spicy as what I've done before. I guess one has only the gift for the things that one has the gift for.

"But just think what my upbringing was like! I grew up surrounded by the most refined conditions, I learned French from a French teacher so well that even as a youth I knew well the French classics. My grandfather was a defrocked [sic] rabbi. He was the most intelligent, the most honest man, an atheist, a serious man with depth. His grandchildren have inherited some of it. I am a man of unrestrained temper, this was so especially when I was eighteen to twenty. Now I use thought and will to control this temper. The most important thing for me now is literature." * * *

Babel came to see me yesterday. We spent some four hours together [and talked] into the early hours. * * *

He does not like keeping books around; there are almost none at his house. He was surprised by their abundance at my place. He gorged himself on the books about the civil war.

Then all of a sudden, without any preliminaries, he started talking in great detail about the articles by Kamenev-Zinoviev-Stalin on the subject of Trotskyism; he even began comparing them: he liked Stalin's the least and thought Kamenev's to be the most valuable. I was very pleased by his taking an interest in these articles, and, I must admit, greatly surprised. Just look at this fellow! He remembers even Rykov's articles, and as to Dzerzhinsky,[2] he is full of admiration for him. "What precision, what brevity, and how practical!" He then told me that he wanted to write a big book about the Cheka.

"I don't know, though, if I can manage it—my view of Cheka is just too one-sided. The reason is that the Chekists that I know, they are, well, they are simply saintly people, even those who did the shooting with their own

2. By 1925–26, Leon Trotsky had already lost decisive battles, but he still had a numerous and powerful following in the party and the military, and the deadly strife at the party's highest level spilled out into the open, onto the pages of the daily press. Felix Dzerzhinsky (1877–1926), the head and founder of the Cheka, the political police, tried to keep above the fray.

hands . . . And I fear it may come out too saccharine. On the other hand, I don't know enough. I just have no idea of the mood of those who inhabited the cells. Somehow, I am not even interested. Still, I think I am going to do it." * * *

SEMYON GEKHT

By the Walls of the Passion Monastery on a Summer Day in 1924[†]

* * * Did Babel's philosophical restraint have an influence on Esenin?[1] Perhaps. But what happened during the night of Esenin's wedding[2] suggests a reverse influence. Under the sway of Esenin's will, Babel turned all of a sudden into a debauched drunkard. Though no one could believe it then and it is hard to believe now, he returned home early with no wallet or passport, so hungover from devil-may-care merriment that he could not remember anything at all. Babel used to smirk: "That was the first and last time."

Esenin was the only person who could bend Babel to his will. Babel could not recall what they ate, drank, or talked about, where they went, or whom they quarreled with, but still he retained the memory of the way Esenin read or, rather, sang his verse that night.

Why then do I remember so little from their conversation under the linden tree by the monastery wall, even though they sat there for a long time, for several hours? Surely the conversation between two such people would have imprinted itself on my memory forever. Or perhaps I did not understand what great talents these two were? Oh, I knew that! The reason is simple: both kept silent for long periods of time. A little gypsy girl came up to us, shaking her shoulders in a dance gesture. Babel dipped into his pocket for change, and Esenin, too, gave her a coin. Both did this hurriedly, anxious to get rid of this cheerless sight. The clicks of the horses' hooves around us were so loud that they muffled the ringing of the A-Tram passing by. * * *

* * * These two thirty-year-old sages were sitting on a bench at sunset, as I wrote above, by the walls of the Passion Monastery.[3] Despite their youth, these men had the gift of knowing and they knew a lot. Whence the wisdom which allowed Esenin to complain: "I myself know not where my pain comes from"—and which prompted Babel to write a sad confessional story, "At Trinity's."[4] As I understand the story now, it was a drama about the approach of old age, about regrets over a wasted life, "the stings of the

[†] Semyon Gekht, "U steny Strastnogo monastryrya v letniy den 1924 goda," in A. N. Pirozhkova and N. N. Yurgeneva, eds., *Vospominaniya o Babele* (Moscow, 1989), pp. 54–63. Gekht (1903–1973), poet, journalist, writer, and native of Odessa, was one of Babel's younger friends and a protégé.
1. Sergey Esenin (1895–1925), premier Russian poet of the post-Symbolist generation whose poetry explored the tension between the poet's peasant origins and modern urban civilization.
2. The wedding in July 1925 of Sergey Esenin and Sofia Andreevna Tolstaya (1900–1957), Leo Tolstoy's granddaughter.
3. The Passion Monastery was situated in what is today Pushkin Square in Moscow, at the site of the park with the statue of Pushkin. The statue was relocated from its original spot at the opposite side of the square after the monastery was demolished in 1937.
4. This story has been lost.

heart's serpent—conscience."[5] The setting was the beer hall at Samotech-naya Square, close to Trinity Lanes, whence the title of the story. It was that same beer hall that Gorky decided to visit in 1930. In hopes of con-cealing himself, the renowned writer put on a big cab driver's beard, but people still recognized him, and his attempt to remain anonymous came to naught. Gorky read Babel's "At Trinity's."

During collectivization, Babel asked the regional authorities to appoint him secretary of the village council in Molodenovo, not far from Moscow. He lived in a hut at the edge of a ravine, in a dark room, like a poor man. But on the table in the room of this strange village council secretary there were stacks of racing programs, and among the visitors who dropped by his humble hut at the edge of the ravine were military men with the rank of army corps commanders.[6] Two kilometers from Molodenovo stood the old estate of the merchant magnate Savva Morosov. This mansion with white columns became the residence of Maxim Gorky. Babel used to visit him and show him what he had written. "At Trinity's" is not a cheerful story, and to grasp its message, I suggest that you take a look at Pushkin's poem "When for a mortal the noisy day dies down" ["Recollection," 1828]. * * *

KORNEI CHUKOVSKY

Diary (1901–1969)[†]

[Early Fame]

Monday, April 13, 1925 (Leningrad)

* * * On Sunday, I had a visit from I. Babel. When I saw him last, he was a student with rosy cheeks skillfully affecting excitement and naïveté. Now this same affection is less convincing but I trust and love him as be-fore. I asked him:

"Do you still have the same name and patronymic now?"

"Yes, but I no longer use them."[1]

He told very funny stories about his vacations in Kislovodsk, where he was placed in a residence along with Rykov, Kamenev, Zinoviev, and Trotsky.[2]

5. A line from Pushkin's elegy "Vospominanie" (Recollection, 1828).
6. The second or third highest rank in the Red Army until the reintroduction of traditional Russian army ranks, which had been abolished in 1917.
† Kornei Ivanovich Chukovsky (Nikolai Vasilyevich Korneichukov, 1882–1969), Russian literary and cultural critic, theorist of translation, diarist, and writer for children. Dates refer to the en-tries in his diary that contain the excerpts. The titles in square brackets are those of the editor. K. I. Chukovsky, *Dnevnik 1901–1969*, 2 vols. (OLMA Press: Moscow, 2003).
1. Isaac Babel's official records (birth certificate, school documents) list him as Isaac Manyevich Bo-bel, a name redolent of the shtetl. For career and cultural reasons, his father, Man (Manus) Bo-bel, assumed a more cosmopolitan-sounding business alias of Emmanuil Babel early in the 1900s, but his son's official papers remained unchanged. Babel followed his father, assuming a pen name Isaac (Emmanuilovich) Babel. It is not known when exactly Isaac Manyevich Bobel changed his passport to Isaac Emmanuilovich Babel, but it appears from this entry no earlier than 1925.
2. Apart from Stalin, these were the most powerful men in Soviet Russia at the time: Aleksei Ivanovich Rykov (1881–1938), Chairman of the Soviet of People's Commissars (prime minister) of the USSR (1924–30); Lev Borisovich Kamenev (1883–1936), Chairman of the Council for La-bor and Defense; Grigori Evseyevich Zinovyev (1883–1936), Chairman of the Petrograd (Leningrad) Soviet and Chairman of the Communist International; Lev Davydovich Trotsky

He wears his fame lightly and cheerfully: "It's some kind of a joke—what happened to me." He complains about censorship. "They cut out the phrase: 'He looked at her the same way that a girl yearning for the discomforts of conception looks at a popular professor.'" He told me stories about Pyotr Storitsyn,[3] who is spreading false rumors and horrible gossip about Babel. When Babel learned that Storitsyn fell on hard times, he decided to give Storitsyn a chervonets[4] and to say to him:

"One does not get money for nothing. You are welcome to lie about me, but, please, do so up to a certain level. Now, let's set the level."

[Money Orders]

March 3, 1926 (Leningrad)
* * * The day before yesterday, I met Babel at the editorial office of *Krasnaya gazeta*; he had just received a 300 ruble advance from Iona.[5] He treats me, as before, with real delicacy. I, too, asked Iona for an advance, of 100 rubles, and Iona willingly obliged. Babel and I went together to the accounting office of *Krasnaya gazeta* to get our money. After a lot of torturous red tape, we finally got our money. Babel is just as he used to be: a darling face of a Jewish student, a mixture of cynicism and lyricism. "Oh, I see you have your lunch in your briefcase! Damn bag lunches! Let's go to the Evropeyskaya Hotel—it'll be my treat." "Let's go." But I never got my treat because Babel dropped in at the State Bank to cable 100 rubles to his wife in Paris. "It'll just be a second, Kornei Ivanovich!" But half an hour later, he ran out of the bank: "I am not done yet. So much red tape!" And he dragged me into the bank.

I would not have waited for him if it had not been for another appointment at the Evropeyskaya. * * * I took out my lunch and ate it while Babel was standing in the queue and kept running up to me. After we left the bank, he said: "Oh, I have lied to you, K.I.! I had, not one but two money orders to send—to my sister in Brussels and the other, to my wife in Paris." And those same dimples on his cheeks.

[Babel's "First Story"]

March 26, 1928 (Leningrad)
* * * I met Vengrov[6] at the State Publishing office a week ago. He did a good job retelling the first story by Isaac Babel, "Le beau pays France."

(1879–1940), People's Commissar of Naval and Military Affairs, Chairman of the Revolutionary-Military Council. All four were members of the party's Politburo. Kamenev and Zinovyev were at the time siding with Stalin against Trotsky. Eventually, all four fell victim to Stalin.
3. Pyotr Ilyich Storitsyn (P. E. B. Kogan, 1873–1941), native of Elizavetrag, son of a Kiev sugar magnate, chemist, Tolstoyan, journalist, poet, patron of the arts and literary entrepreneur; financed and participated in poetry almanacs of Odessa poets during WWI; freelance journalist associated with the Leningrad *Krasnaya gazeta* in the 1920s. See also Note to the story "Information" and Viktor Shklovsky's "A Critical Romance."
4. Originally, a colloquial term for a ten-ruble note, it became a new gold-backed currency unit introduced by the Soviet government in 1922, its value pegged officially at 11,400 rubles. In 1924, the value of one chervonets was approximately the same as that of one US dollar. In 1925, the official rate for one chervonets was set at 10 paper rubles.
5. Chukovsky means "chervonets," at the time, approximately $300. Ilya Ionovich Ionov (Bernshtein, 1887–1942), one of the early Bolshevik activists, political prisoner under the old regime, poet, head of the Leningrad branch of State Publishing, and brother-in-law of the chief of the Leningrad Party organization, Grigory Zinovyev. He was arrested in 1937 and died in jail.
6. Natan Vengrov (1894–1962), poet, head of the Moscow State Publishing department for children and youth, and an ideological nemesis of Chukovsky as a writer for children.

Vengrov was there when Babel brought this story to Gorky (I am now on my second dose of sleeping potion, so I am not sure I have the details right). It's a story about a Parisian woman who joins her husband, a teacher of French, in a provincial Russian town and decides to find herself a lover. She does not know anyone in this town. She writes letters to herself, mails them, and every day comes to the post office to collect them, and in this way makes her acquaintance with the postmaster. The postmaster would not mind 'having a fling' with a Parisienne. So, a week later, she takes him to some place outside the town to make love. A plaid blanket in one hand and a picnic basket in the other, she marches on, stepping with determination on the wooden planks of the pavement—and he is trudging after her like a lamb to the slaughter. Once they reach a grove, she spreads the blanket, takes sandwiches out of the basket—and in general prepares everything for love Parisian style. Vengrov was enthusiastic about the story. * * *

[How Budenny Lost His Argument with Gorky]

May 2, 1953. Moscow
* * * I met General Vasily Stepanovich Popov.[7] He told me how Semyon Budenny's [70th birthday] was celebrated. "We pooled the money and bought him a vase with a [martial] painting by Boris Grekov. During the supper, a conversation started, people saying that the Cavalry Army had not yet been hailed in literature. 'Not only has it not been hailed yet,' someone picked it up, 'on the contrary, it has been defamed by Babel.'
" 'I went to see Gorky to complain about it,' replied Budenny, 'but Gorky was no help. He took Babel's side. I went to see Lenin [sic].[8] Lenin said: Gorky is the one who is in charge of literature. Let's leave it to him to decide. It's a bad idea to quarrel with him.' "

[Paustovsky on Babel and Babel's Father]

February 17, 1963. Moscow
Paustovsky came to see me yesterday. * * * On Babel. [Paustovsky said that Babel] lied to everyone, even about trivial things. He liked surrounding himself with a mysterious aura. Preparing to leave for St. Petersburg, he told everyone, even a ten-year-old girl from next door: "I am off to Kaluga."
Once Babel's father, who kept a warehouse of McCormick's agricultural equipment in Odessa, was paid a visit by the commissars searching for valuable things to confiscate. As they started the search in the apartment, his wife, Babel's mother, locked her husband in his room for fear he would blurt something out. The police search was going well—they found nothing. But she let go of her old man too early. He leapt out of his room and gave the departing commissars the finger: "That's what you get! Couldn't find anything, could you!" The commissars went back in, lifted up the floor boards and found a heap of dollars and gold coins.

7. V. S. Popov (1894–1967), Hero of the Soviet Union, at the time of the entry, served on the General Staff.
8. Chukovsky, of course, used "Lenin" here as a code word for Stalin, afraid to put down the name of the dreaded dictator in this sensitive context even three weeks after Stalin's demise on 5 April 1953. Budenny simply could not have complained to Lenin, who had been incapacitated for months before his death on January 21, 1924, the time when the first Red Cavalry stories were published in the Moscow journals, LEF and Krasnaya nov.

[*The Young Babel and The Wrath of Dionysus*]

14 April–10 May 1969
  Once [in 1916?] I ran into Mikhail Kuzmin[9] in the restaurant "Vienna."
He was surrounded by a large company of people I did not know, and he
invited me to join them. He pointed to the corpulent lady sitting opposite
him and said:
  "You are obsessed with writing about Nekrasov[1] but you are not aware
that this Bacchant is the actual daughter of Avdotya Yakovlevna Panaeva.[2]
* * *
  The Bacchant turned out to be Nagrodskaya,[3] the author of the much-
talked-about novel *The Wrath of Dionysus*. * * * She casually let it out that
she had in her possession a notebook completely covered in Nekrasov's
handwriting.
  I had to get hold of this notebook.
  Nagrodskaya lived in Pavlovsk. Unsure of my own abilities, I decided to
take with me my two friends: Emile Krotky[4] and Isaac Babel. On the way
to Pavlovsk, I told them how significant this notebook could be for the
Nekrasov scholarship. Emile Krotky never stopped telling jokes; Babel was
silent and kept looking out of the window. In those days, he affected great
deference toward me and would begin every phrase addressed to me with
the words "Allow me, Kornei Ivanovich." He often accompanied me in my
peregrinations across St. Petersburg. Of course, I was aware that this deference was an affectation, that underneath it there was plenty of irony,
but I was happy to be playing along.
  I took Emile Krotky with me to talk to Nagrodskaya. Babel stayed outside in the courtyard. Krotky at once spoiled everything. He began by
telling this lady that she was in possession of a most precious document
and how much posterity shall cherish every line written in Nekrasov's
hand, etc., etc.
  I managed to get rid of this clumsy comrade-in-arms and called on Babel
for help. Babel, gloomy-faced, heard us out in a way that a great actor hears
out some awkward dilettantes, then made a sign for us to keep silent.
  "Allow me, Elena (or Elizaveta?) Apollonovna, to speak with you *intime*,"
he said, "just the two of us."
  They retreated into another room. It was clear that she favored him more
than us. No doubt, his likable face with its dimples made an impression.
  We waited for a long time. At last, Babel reemerged, red-faced and with
beads of sweat on his high brow. In his hand he held a black (now famous)

9. Mikhail Alekseevich Kuzmin (1872–1936), poet, composer, novelist, a major figure of Russian
   modernism.
1. Nikolai Alekseevich Nekrasov (1821–1878), poet, tireless editor, and publisher. His poetry, often
   based on folk rhythms, combined lyricism with social criticism more typical of the novel or journalism. Chukovsky's passion for Nekrasov enhanced Nekrasov's reputation among Russian mod-
   ernists.
2. Panaeva (1820–1893), writer, a long-time companion of Nekrasov, and his editorial collaborator.
3. Evdokiya Apollonovna Nagrodskaya (1866–1930), writer and advocate of a radical reevaluation
   of sexual mores whose novel *The Wrath of Dionysus* (Gnev Dionisa) was one of the most-talked-
   about and radical critiques of the conventions of sex and gender. A first-person story about the
   carnal love of a masculine woman artist, the narrator, for an effeminate male engineer, *The Wrath*
   went through five printings in 1910–15.
4. Emil Krotky (Emmanuil German, 1892–1963), well-known comic and satirical poet, a native of
   Odessa.

notebook which he handed to me with his customary semi-ironic bow. I handed to Nagrodskaya a signed promissory note; my hands trembled.

As soon as we left, I asked Babel what kind of magic spells he used to persuade her to part with this real treasure.

"I spoke with her, not about Nekrasov, no, but about her novel, *The Wrath of Dionysus*. I praised it to the sky. I told her that for me she was greater than Flaubert and Huysmans, and that I myself was under the sway of her influence. She invited me to come to her next Friday; she will read to me the first part of her new novel . . . 'What do you need them for—these yellow sheets of bygone times,' I said to her, 'you who commands the present and the future!' 'You have no idea what a great talent you have.'"

"But *The Wrath of Dionysus* is a talentless novel!" I said.

"I don't know—haven't read it," replied Babel.

TAMARA IVANOVA (KASHIRINA)

A Chapter from My Life
(Memoirs. Letters of I. Babel)[†]

* * * I am twenty-five years old [in 1925], and I am terribly bored. I am more bored than I have been before or since.

By all appearances I have a full life. I have a husband, a child. I am an actress at Vsevolod Meyerhold Theater. I am studying to be a stage director. I am acting in Sergey Tretyakov's *Earth Rearing Up* and Ilya Ehrenburg's *Trust DE*. I go to classes. I study biomechanics, boxing, fencing, etc. I teach classes at clubs for workers and Red Army soldiers. I write theater reviews, and they are sometimes published in the journal *Theater*; I attend public debates.

And yet, I feel terribly bored.

You can be this bored only when you are in full bloom and not in love, though your whole being is unconsciously striving for it.

Many found me appealing then, many in my circle sought my love but I could not respond in kind because my feelings for them were not reciprocated. Instead, I settled for my habitual, if pale, relationship with my husband.

At the time I was teaching an amateur theatrical class at the soldiers' club for the Kremlin security regiment. In collaboration with my students, I staged and directed Vsevolod Ivanov's *Armored Train* (though I did not know Ivanov at the time[1]).

The man in charge of all of the amateur theatrical classes for the Kremlin security regiment was Vasily Alexandrovich Reginin.[2] Every time he ran into me, he would invite me over for a visit. Once, after my class, I agreed.

---

† Tamara Ivanova (Kashirina), "Glava in zhizni: Vospominaniya i pisma Isaaka Babelya (A Chapter from My Life: Recollections and Letters of Isaac Babel), *Oktyabr* 5 (May 1992), pp. 183–87.
1. Tamara Kashirina married the playwright Vsevolod Ivanov in 1928.
2. A friend of Isaac Babel's, Reginin was a journalist and editor of the journal *30 dney*, where Babel published his stories in the 1930s.

"You won't regret it," he was saying to me as we rode to his place. "I have interesting guests every night; I am sure there is somebody there already waiting and talking to my wife."

And indeed, somebody was: his name was Isaac Emmanuilovich Babel. I had already read his stories in *LEF*[3] and greatly admired their artistry but I had never before seen the author.

Babel, who was the wittiest interlocutor, an inimitable raconteur, was at his best that night. We stayed late. Babel accompanied me home on foot from Krasnye vorota all the way to Razgulyay, where I lived. The whole way there, Babel for some reason talked about his getting old and some inner alarm bells that warned him to live his life with greater intensity.

The power of suggestion is a remarkable thing. Even though he was only seven years my senior, he was able to convince me by his power of suggestion that he was indeed an "old man." My husband is eight years my senior, and still I consider him to belong to my own generation. But when I returned home, I told my husband that some "old man" had seen me home.

Be that as it may, I took an interest in this "old man," even though at first he elicited no romantic feelings in me. Quite the contrary. He seemed to me repulsively ugly (and I pitied him for that). I thought of him as a very old man exhausted by life's struggles.

The next day we met again. At the Reginins, I invited everyone to come to the theater for Sergey Treyakov's *Earth Reared Up.* * * *

After supper, Babel again saw me home, but this time he hired a cab. It was a long journey. As we rattled along in the cab, Babel kept on talking—this time not about his old age but about horses. The "horse problem," he said to me, held for him the meaning of life. I would have ignored this talk altogether (horses did not interest me), if it had not been for his repeated insistence that I was missing the point.

After these two encounters, Babel often dropped by to see me either at the theater or at one of the amateur theater clubs where I was teaching.

We took walks; if I was free in the evening, we would go to the cinema or theater. And he always saw me home but never came in.

Gradually and without noticing it, I not only stopped thinking about Babel as an old man but I began to see a certain charm in his unprepossessing looks (his balding head, his odd build: an excessively short neck and excessively long arms).

As for him, he did not so much as mention his erstwhile old age; nor did he bother with his horses. Now he talked more about feelings—both theoretically as they related to literature and art and concretely as they related to me.

What's more, he had an ability to combine passion with irony and mockery even concerning himself.

At that time I was a straightforward and trusting sort, and for that reason I accepted all of Babel's hyperbolic assurances at face value. I believed him when he said he had actually fallen in love for the first time in his life, and that he had never felt anything even resembling what he was now feeling towards me.

---

3. Vladimir Mayakovsky edited this journal of Russian Futurists, in which Babel made his Moscow debut in 1924.

During our daily encounters, however, he pleaded with me to keep our meetings secret—ostensibly because he was sending his wife abroad and if she found out about us, she would refuse to leave.

My naïveté, multiplied by my excessive self-assurance, led me to believe in the exclusive quality of his love for me. I could not even imagine that he himself was planning to go abroad or, at the very least, had promised his wife to return to her eventually, even though his pleas for secrecy led logically to such a conclusion.

I did not tolerate "secrets" in my emotional life, and I was about to tell my husband some of what I was feeling, even though I myself had not yet responded to Babel's declarations of love. At that time, there was nothing between the two of us except for abstract conversations and Babel's amorous entreaties.

I decided to "switch off" our relationship. I told Babel that I was busy and spent my free time with some of my old admirers whom I had rejected but who were still pursuing me.

But nothing came of these schemes. I became even more upset because I now realized that no one could distract me, that what I needed was Babel and nobody else, and that I simply could not live without hearing his daily declarations of love.

Still I persevered and showed no signs of yielding.

This rejection made Babel so furious and prompted such an explosion of emotions—expressed with such artistry—that I fell, as I had been ready to fall, under the sway of their intensity and was overtaken by them once and for all.

Getting ahead of the story, I must say that had I been skilled in the game of love, and not a plain young woman who believed only in truth and sincerity in love relationships, I probably would have learned to control Babel's very complicated character, with its penchant for playing games.

A few months went by, and our relationship became reciprocal. But our meetings took place only in the street or in other public places.

I was then rehearsing for the role of Tamarochka in Erdman's[4] play *The Mandate*. * * * But this role was utterly unsuitable for me. * * * Taking advantage of my dissatisfaction with the role and my inner confusion, Babel convinced me to "run away."

"This role makes you act falsely," he would say. "It is impossible not to be false when you play it. What do you need it for? Let's run away to Leningrad."

In Leningrad, we stayed at the Evropeiskaya in a two-bedroom suite.

Babel again told me we must keep everything secret, this time "for the sake of my own interests." I had told the theater that I was sick and I would only embarrass myself if I was seen walking around Leningrad. I agreed. I had no idea with whom I was dealing. We went out for a walk. On the way back, he asked to be excused for a few minutes. (As it turned out, he went to a flower shop to have flowers sent to me at the hotel.) I let him go and went shopping for a gift for my daughter Tanya. On returning I discovered first a basket of orchids with a "passionate" note from Babel, which needless to say touched me, and second a barrage of phone

---

4. Nikolay Robertovich Erdman (1900–1970), playwright and scriptwriter, a comic genius of the 1920s and early 1930s who spent some time in the Gulag for his jokes.

calls (in the space of an hour, he had already "secretly" announced to people that he was in town, and they had begun showering him with invitations).

We did go to one such get-together—a dinner at the home of the writer Nikolay Nikitin. There we met Lydia Nikolaevna Seifullina, who became my lifelong friend from then on, and her husband, Valerian Pravdukhin. The dinner dragged on, and so did the "literary" discussions, which held no interest for me then. The talk was about some writers whom I had neither met nor read. As I listened I suddenly began to miss my theater and the role I had abandoned. I could no longer follow the conversations. I was angry with Babel. I stood up from the table, said good-bye to the host, and walked towards the door. They all rushed after me, but I said to them rather rudely: "You, writers, have your own interests; I am an actress, and I have mine; in any case, you didn't even talk about literature—you were just gossiping, and it's boring to listen to you."

My rudeness made quite an impression, and Lydia Yakovlevna told me later she admired me for it. Not yielding to their entreaties, I left. Babel, of course, left with me and begged me not to be angry with him. On the way to the hotel I gradually calmed down and even laughed as Babel regaled me with jokes making fun of the guests and of himself.

When we returned to the hotel, another surprise awaited me. One of the rooms in the suite was packed with Babel's friends who, as he assured me, had appeared entirely uninvited. I had to restrain myself not to turn on him—I was not in the least mollified by another basket of flowers, this time hyacinths, delivered with a note from him while we were away. He realized that things were going from bad to worse and began getting rid of his friends; as he did so, he whispered in my ear that he would be back in a minute, and left with them.

He soon returned but I was very upset and did not even wish to speak with him. Oh, what tricks he resorted to then in the hopes of softening my anger! In the end, of course, he had his way. I knew only how to be sincere, whether in anger or happiness. I felt upset and offended, not on account of Meyerhold (who would have forgiven me, even if he knew I was not really ill); and I concealed nothing from my husband. What hurt, indeed offended me, was that Babel did not value our first opportunity to be alone with each other. But I forgave him because I loved him and could not stand to be without him.

I was totally gripped, overwhelmed by love. Given my temperament and my upbringing, as well as the principles I had absorbed from *belles lettres*, I was convinced that people in love must want to be together. I simply could not stand living apart from him, but he left for Kiev with the express purpose of "settling for good" (his words) the affairs of his wife; she was about to go abroad and was staying for the time being with her parents in Kiev.

Babel wrote to me from Kiev practically every day. It is remarkable how a person—myself, in this case—could misread letters. I read into them what I myself was feeling, that is to say, love and desire for a complete fusion of our two lives. * * * As to the hints that my beloved still preferred to keep our relationship secret and that he was in no haste to affirm our union—I paid no attention because I had no desire to see it. * * *

VYACHESLAV POLONSKY

Diary, 1931–1932[†]

* * * Oh, what a disgusting bunch these writers are. Greed and petty bourgeois attitudes reign supreme among them. Not only do they want to live with a full stomach but they want to live *comfortably*, too. In the country that is building socialism, where the working class lives in the most appalling conditions, pushing themselves to the limit, knowing no respite in order to work—I mean shock workers, the socialist competition—these types literally try to snatch the last shirt off the workers' backs just for sake of furnishing their own apartments, bathing in affluence and saving for a rainy day. All the while they try to create an impression that they are devoted to the interests of the working class. And what is the fruit of their labor? Rehashing some old stuff, or else imitations. * * *

Among them, Babel is an original. He has not published anything new in seven years.[1] All this time he has been living off the "interest" from his published works. His skill at extracting advances is astonishing. There is hardly anybody from whom he has not received an advance or to whom he does not owe something; his collateral is always his "new stories and novellas ready for publication." Three years ago *Zvezda* published an excerpt from his work in its prospectus with a note saying that the entire work was in their portfolio.[2] As soon as he received the advance, Babel stopped by the editorial office, asked to see the manuscript for a minute in order to "insert a word," leafed through the the pages, told the secretary he would bring the manuscript back the next day, and took it home with him. It has been four years since the *Zvezda* editors have laid eyes on that manuscript. I advanced him twenty-five hundred rubles on the basis of a contract. I have revised the contract several times, given new extensions—he has repeatedly assured me that the manuscripts are ready, sitting on his desk, that he will send them to me tomorrow—if only I can give him some money.

Babel called. Once again he has a thousand and one excuses. He tells me he has consulted with Gorky, and Gorky is counseling him against publishing the stories he has given me. But he has written a "rough draft" of two stories about collectivization (I heard about these rough drafts three years ago) and he is now working on them. He will give them to me within a month.[3]

[†] Vyacheslav Polonsky (Gusin, 1886–1932) was a leading Bolshevik figure in the cultural sphere. A journalist, literary critic, art critic, and theorist, he founded and edited several journals, including *Novy mir* (1926–31) while chairing the Supreme Military Editorial Council. A true believer, he was not doctrinaire in literary matters, had a weakness for talent, and did everything to promote writers such as Babel and Boris Pasternak.
  Reprinted here are the excerpts from Polonsky's diary that deal with Babel. Some of these were first published in *Vospominaniya o Babele* (pp. 195–99), others came from the publication "Iz dnevnika Vyach. Polonskogo. Mart-aprel 1931 goda," *Vstrechi s proshlym*, vyp. 9 (Moscow, 2000), pp. 308–10.
1. This exaggeration, typical of contemporary discussions of Babel, sounds particularly strange here: Polonsky's own *Novy mir* published Babel's play *Sunset* in its second issue of 1928.
2. Babel's only publication in *Zvezda* was in the July (no. 7) issue of 1931 ("Karl-Yankel").
3. Probably "Gapa Guzhva," published in *Novy mir* 10 (1931), and "Kolyvushka," not published in Babel's lifetime. Three other stories announced for publication in *Novy mir* for 1931–32 were "Adrian Marinets," "Honey," and "Spring." Together with the other two, they were supposed to comprise the book cycle *Velikaya Krinitsa*, dealing with the collectivization of agriculture. At least one of them and possibly all three were actually completed by Babel, but none has survived. It was a minor miracle, attributable to the considerable authority of Polonsky as well as his courage, that one of them, "Gapa Guzhva," saw the light of day in 1931.

Four years ago he even gave me the title of a story that he promised to send me on August 15. I announced the impending publication of his piece—and to this day I have not seen it.[4] * * * He is in debt everywhere and many have writs against him; but his address is unknown, he does not live in Moscow, he travels nobody knows where in the provinces outside Moscow, and he has no property. He is elusive, invincible like a ghost. Occasionally, he would write me a letter, promising to send the manuscripts in a day or two, and then he would disappear without a trace.
* * *

What a strange fate for a writer! On the one hand, there is no question that he is "honest" and is incapable of adapting. On the other hand, it is becoming increasingly clear that he is extremely alien to the Revolution—alien and in his heart of hearts, probably hostile to it. This means that when he issues his proclamations of love for socialist construction and the village, etc., he is just pretending.
* * *

Babel dropped by. He came in the evening—a small, rotund figure in a cotton shirt of some indefinite grey-blue color, a veritable high-school student with a pointed little nose, clever shining little eyes behind round glasses. A smiling, happy man, simple at first glance. Only rarely, when he stops pretending to be a jolly fellow, his gaze deepens and darkens, the face changes: there emerges a different man, with an air of deeply guarded secrets. He read me his new pieces: "In the Basement," and another story that was not part of *Red Cavalry*, "Argamak,"[5] about a horse. A few days ago he submitted three manuscripts—all erotic through and through.[6] They can't be published. They would destroy his reputation as a fellow-traveler. To be silent for eight years[7] and all of a sudden to explode with a bouquet of densely erotic pieces—can this be what we expect from a fellow-traveler! But these are wonderful pieces. His laconic style is more powerful than before. His language is now simpler, without mannerism, spiciness, and complex phrasing. He gave them to me, as he put it, to shut up the accounting office. He owes *Novy mir* two thousand rubles. The accounting office is threatening legal action. He submitted the manuscript to pacify the accounting office. He promises to give us more pieces in August, the kind we can publish in the journal. He is a strange man. These are marvelous pieces but he does not want to publish them now. He really does dote over his manuscripts. He is anxious about them. He looks up quizzically: "Is it good?" "I write with difficulty," he says, "for it's a torture. I write a few sentences in one day, then I pace back and forth, torment myself, change one word after another."
* * *

He is indifferent to fame. He would like to be forgotten. He complains about a large number of dependents; if it were not for them, his life would have been easier.

4. The title of the story announced in *Novy mir* was "Marie Antuanette." Apparently while in Paris, Babel continued to work on the subject at the Bibliothèque Nationale.
5. Both stories were published in *Novy mir,* in the issues 10 (1931) and 3 (1932), respectively.
6. Polonsky is probably referring to "Guy de Maupassant," published in *30 dney* 6 (1932), and a version of "Information" ("My First Fee"), which was published in Babel's lifetime but only in English. Some of Babel's "village stories," too, may have been too pungent for people living under the strictures of socialist construction.
7. Babel's most recent major work, his play *Sunset,* was published in *Novy mir* 2 (1928), a little over three years earlier. *Red Cavalry* was first published as a book in 1926, five years earlier.

Babel says: "I do not understand Pasternak. I simply cannot understand sometimes what he is saying."

In 1918, I printed his pieces in *Vechernyaya zvezda*[8] after his first stories appeared in *Letopis*. I was doing him a big favor. When he ran into me in Moscow in 1922—he had brought his *Red Cavalry* with him—he literally choked me in his embraces and assured me that he had come to Moscow to see me, that he had been looking for me everywhere, and so on. He was lying, of course.

Why is he not publishing? The reason is clear. He has truly been writing. He is a wonderful writer. And the fact that he is not rushing, that he has not been infected by vanity, shows that he believes his pieces will not go out of date so it will do no harm to publish them later. But he knows that he will do himself harm if he publishes them earlier. I have not read these pieces. Voronsky tells me that they are all counter-revolutionary. That is, they are not publishable: for their material is such that they can hardly be published today. Babel worked not only in the First Cavalry Army. He also worked in the Cheka. His appetite for blood, death, murders, for everything terrifying, his almost sadistic passion for suffering—all this has limited the material he can work with.

He was present at executions, he watched people die before a firing squad, he has collected enormous amounts of material about the cruelties of the Revolution. Tears and blood—that is his material. He needs the exceptional, the spicy, the deadly. All of *Red Cavalry* is like this. And what he is holding onto now is probably about the Cheka. He joined the First Cavalry Army just so he could collect material of this sort. He is afraid to publish it now, because he has gained the reputation of a fellow-traveler.

Recently some reporter for a Polish newspaper published an interview Babel had given him somewhere on the Riviera. This interview showed that even for a fellow-traveler Babel was too critical. Babel denounced this publication [as a fabrication].[9] Somewhere along the way, he mentioned in the *Literary Gazette* that he was living in a village, observing the birth of collectivized agriculture, and that these days one must not write the way people, including himself, used to write. One must write in a special way, and behold, he himself will soon write in that special way, making proud both the collectivization of agriculture and socialism. His letter to the newspaper did the trick. He rewrote his contracts, got an advance from the State Publishing House, and then he "split." Now he lives somewhere outside Moscow, in some Zhavoronki or other, at a stud farm where he studies horse breeding. He has been writing to me assuring me of his loyalty and pleading with me to trust him: he is just about to send me his new pieces. Not very likely. What repulses me is his coldness. What makes him tick? But he has a rich inner life. No question about it. It's the old, deep Jewish culture.

8. A Bolshevik newspaper Polonsky edited in Petrograd in 1917–18; one of its issues that has now been lost contained the first of a two-installment piece by Babel, "Notes on Odessa" ("Listki ob Odesse"). The second installment appeared on March 9 and is published in *TCB* as "The Aroma of Odessa."
9. Apprently this was indeed a fabrication, and the author of the "interview" in the Polish *Wiadomosci literackie*, Alexander Dan, admitted as much. See J. Solajczyk, "Polski epizod w biografii Izaaka E. Babla," *Zeszyty naukowe wyzszej szkoly pedagogicznej im. Powstancow slaskich w Opolu. Filologia rosyjska* IX. Seria A. (Opole, 1972), p. 103–11.

Babel came yesterday and brought a new story to read. He was all pink in the face, wore a shirt of a dark color, a new jacket and a black leather coat, there was a whiff of wine on his breath; he has been having a good time. * * * He read a story about a village. Simple, short, condensed—powerful.[1] His village is like his *Red Cavalry*—blood, tears, sperm. That's his métier: peasants, village councilmen and kulaks, cretins, cripples, degenerates. He read another story about an execution by a firing squad—a story of terrifying power.[2] The story is overwhelmingly realistic and at the same time laconic in the extreme and sharply metaphoric. He renders images palpable to the point of total illusion. And he achieves this effect by what seems the simplest of means. "I work like a specialist," he says. "I want to make my pieces the way a master craftsman makes his. For me the method of treating my material means everything. I am proud of this piece of work. I've produced something. And I feel good about it."

He was very emotional as he was reading. He is happy in his solitude. He lives alone in a village. He has his slippers, his tea with lemon, his room heated to a temperature not below 26 degrees Celsius. He does not want to see anybody.
* * *

Babel came today and brought the rough draft of the stories he has started working on.

"I don't have finished pieces—what can I do?" True, there is nothing to be done. I reproached him: he had promised a story, did not deliver, and let me down. He promised one in December. I announced it, but the story never came. He read me an excerpt from a story about an Odessan by the name Babichev; the story begins with the praise of Bagritsky, Kataev, and Olesha, and shows a certain disdain for Russian literature, which the men of Odessa had raided.[3]

His wife lives in Paris. They have been living apart for a few years now. He tells me his wife sent him a cable: if you don't come in a month, I am going to marry someone else. He stated very matter-of-factly that two years ago his wife gave birth to their daughter. He is indifferent, laughing.

Babel told me how he used to be friends with a maid at Rudzutak's dacha.[4] The groundskeeper knew him, too. Now this dacha is occupied by Gorky. He went to visit Gorky and entered the house not through the servants' entrance but through the front door. The groundskeeper had no idea who Babel actually was; he did not even know his real name. Nor did the scullery maid. He told Babel not to loiter in the entryway but to go to the backyard. Babel did not react and kept going. The groundskeeper yelled at him: "We don't let anybody in, not even a People's Commissar, so what are you doing coming in here!" But Gorky's son Maxim noticed Babel through the window and called out to him to come in. The maid was trembling when she served food. There at the table was her man, her friend, her partner in gossip slouched in his seat—conversing with Gorky like an equal.

---

1. Probably "Gapa Guzhva," published in *Novyi mir* 10 (1931).
2. No such story by Babel has survived.
3. No such story by Babel has survived.
4. Ian Ernestovich Rudzutak (1887–1938), a leading Bolshevik, People's Commissar of Communications in 1924–30 and a secretary of the Party's Central Committee.

Stalin–Kaganovich Correspondence[†]

Stalin to Kaganovich. June 7, 1932[1]

Greetings, Comrade Kaganovich!

1. I have finally read Demyan Bedny's play "How the Fourteenth Division Went to Paradise" (see *Novy mir*). In my opinion, the piece did not come out very well. A mediocre, crude piece, it exudes the atmosphere of a tavern, full of tavern jokes. Whatever educational significance it has is negative. * * *

2. *Novyi mir* is serializing the new novel by Sholokhov, *Virgin Soil Upturned*. What an interesting work! One can see that Sholokhov has made a thorough study of collective farming on the Don. In my opinion, Sholokhov possesses great artistic talent. Besides, he is a deeply conscientious writer: he writes about things that he knows well—unlike "our" fidgety and slippery Babel, who does little else but write about things that he knows nothing about (*Horse Army* [sic], for example).[1] * * *

Greetings!
I. Stalin.

Kaganovich to Stalin. June 23, 1932

Greetings, Comrade Stalin!

At today's meeting of the Politburo, we have decided to call a plenary meeting of the Central Committee at the end of September.
* * *

P.S. A. M. Gorky appealed to the Central Committee to permit Babel to go abroad for a short period of time. Although I have told them that we doubt such a trip is advisable, I receive phone calls from Gorky every day. Apparently, Gorky is rather upset. Knowing that in such circumstances you treat him with exceptional sensitivity, I am reporting to you about this and ask for your guidance.

L. Kaganovich

---

† O. V. Khlevnyuk et al., eds., *Stalin i Kaganovich. Perepiska. 1931–1936 gg.* (M, 2001), pp. 149, 188–89, 197. Joseph Stalin (1878–1953), leader of the Soviet Union, was spending the summer of 1932 in the Caucasus. In the absence of reliable long-distance telephones, the business of state was conducted by government courier on a daily basis. Lazar Moiseyevich Kaganovich (1893–1991) was one of Stalin's closest and most loyal associates since the mid-1920s. He was appointed the head of the Ukrainian CP in 1925 and became the head of the Moscow city and the Moscow Region Party Committee in 1930, presiding over the reconstruction of Moscow in 1930–35, and filling key party posts throughout Stalin's rule.

1. The letter is Stalin's review of *Novy mir* for the previous year or so, which included the writings on collectivization by both Babel and Sholokhov. Alexander Sholokhov's *Virgin Soil Upturned* was serialized in *Novy mir* beginning with the first issue (January) of 1932. The serialization had Stalin's own imprimatur and was in part a result of the first meeting between Sholokhov and Stalin, arranged and hosted by Gorky in July 1931. Sholokhov made his name earlier with a story-cycle book about the Civil War, *The Don Tales*, published, like Babel's *Red Cavalry*, in 1926. The serialization of his Civil War epic, *The Quiet Don*, in 1928 met critical acclaim. Babel's "collectivization" story, "Gapa Guzhva," was published in *Novy mir* 10 (1931).

Stalin to Kaganovich (and Molotov). June 26, 1932

Comrade Sheboldaev raises in his memorandum an altogether pressing question.

* * *

My response:

1. We should limit ourselves to establishing one more Donbass district in Ukraine.
2. Regarding the grain exports, my recommendation is to reduce sharply the Rozengolts plan (for the third quarter).
3. In my opinion Babel is not worth our spending hard currency on for his trip abroad.

I. Stalin

Gorky's Letter to Babel about *Maria*[†]

My dear Babel—

When you—in Sorrento—read to me your play, you must have noticed, perhaps, that I was unable to say anything definite or comprehensible about it or a related subject.

Probably then, as now that I have read it in manuscript, the play surprised me but caused in me no excitement. I need not say that it is put together artfully and that the subtle and telling details in it are presented masterfully, but on the whole, the play is cold, its function is undefined, the author's purpose elusive.

All who sincerely love literature, myself included, see you in an exceptional light: you, who are so talented and wise, are expected to produce works that are clear and far-reaching.

This play does not justify the expectations that you have created. Personally, I am repelled by its Baudelaire-like passion for spoiled meat. In it, beginning with the invalids, all the people have gone rotten, reek badly, and practically all have been infected or enslaved by an aggressive sensuality.

Perhaps, this is the sensuality of despair felt by people who, as they are perishing, wish to leave after them a memory and to avenge themselves by leaving stains of rot on the floor and on the walls.

The task of "grand" art is: to show people in all their complexity, as a psychological writer would, or definitely repulsive, as a critical realist would, or to elicit respect and sympathy for the people, to romanticize them.

You, in essence, appear to be a romantic but for some reason, you have resolved not to be one.

Maria, whose presence in the play is only epistolary, along with the last act, confirm your inclination towards romanticism, but it is expressed through the characters who do not appear successful and indeed suggest

† *Gorkii i sovetskie pisateli. Literaturnoe nasledstvo*, vol. 70 (M., 1963), pp. 43–44. Gorky's letter is undated and survives in a carbon copy. Most likely, it was written or dictated in May 1933, shortly after Babel read the play to him in Sorrento and left for Paris. On May 29, 1933, Babel wrote from Paris to Anna Slonim about his disappointment. "The play's done—but it's no good. I cannot decide, though, whether the failure is final or reparable."

to one that they have been introduced into the play as a "concession" to some external demand, and not as a counterpoint that is emotionally justified by the author. The last scene in its entirety is attached to the play mechanically—that is the impression. In it, reason alone acts, whereas in the rest of the play one feels a clear presence of intuition.

It is hard and I would not like to assume that a clash or fracture between *intuitio* and *ratio* was organically yours; my personal conviction is that this antagonism is of a purely technical nature.

I do not consider myself a dramatist, but, perhaps, I can write more or less interesting scenes for the stage, which explains my "success" in the theater. I think you are not a dramatist either, since this form demands a light and clever touch, but your hand is heavy. Between us, good, true drama is a rare phenomenon: all that's left of Gutzkow[1] is *Uriel Acosta*, Ostrovsky,[2] *The Storm*, etc.—only those dramas survive that are kin to the "lofty art" of tragedy; and comedy, too, is vital, and it is comedy that should be the basis for contemporary theater.

And so I think that you, a man with a sense of humor that often shades into sarcasm—you should try your hand at comedy. You tend to construct your drama on the basis of some large but undermined, fractured force.

In particular, what I don't like most in your play is Dymshits, who reminds one of Grzhebin.[3] You put him in a position that is too comfortable for the Judeophobes. All that I am saying, I am afraid, is not very clear but the conclusion to be drawn from it is as follows: do not stage the play in this version. The critics will tell you that the play is not in tune with reality, that all that you show are the bygones and not typical enough to be worth showing. And five or so sentences will be taken out of the dialogue to give the opportunity to the volunteers of this sort to draw political conclusions hostile to your own person.

BORIS SOUVARINE

My Last Conversations with Babel[†]

* * * During our endless conversations—at his place, at mine, in cafés, in the street, even in the metro, even on our walks—it never occurred to me to

---

1. Karl Gutzkow (1811–1878), German playwright and author, most famously, of *Uriel Acosta* (1847)
2. Aleksandr Nikolayevich Ostrovsky (1823–1886), Russian playwright, the author of *Storm* (1860).
3. Zinoviy Isayevich Grzhebin (1869–1929), publisher who collaborated with Leonid Andreyev and Gorky, a legendary figure who founded his famous Russian publishing house in Berlin in 1920. Gorky perhaps refers to Grzhebin's well-known materialism and his Odessa accent, two elements marking the character of Dimshits. The cue must have been given by Dimshit's readiness to publish Mukovnin's history. Babel may have met Grzhebin during his stay in France in 1927–28.
† Boris Souvarine (Livshits Cohn, 1895–1984) was born in Russia and educated in France; a founder of the French Communist Party, he lived in Moscow in 1918–25, when he was expelled from the party for his loyalty to Leon Trotsky. After his return to France, Souvarine gradually distanced himself from Trotsky and later on from communism, becoming a critic of the Soviet Union and, in particular, of Stalin; he was one of the earliest Kremlinologists. His recollections of Isaac Babel, excerpted here, were first published in *Kontinent* 23 (1980):343–78, and later as part of the volume Boris Souvarine, *Souvenirs sur Isaac Babel, Panàt Istrati, Pierre Pascal; suivi de Lettre Alexandre Soljenitsyne* (Paris, 1985).

take notes (in those days I had an elephant's memory). For the most part we talked about Russia, literature, Soviet politics. But I loved his meditations on France and Paris because as an acute and humorous observer, he would point out things that the jaded eye of an old Parisian like myself would pass over, taking no notice of them. These observations prompted in him funny and perceptive aphorisms. It was only during our three conversations in 1932 that I felt the need to take down his observations on paper. At that time, I was working on a biography of Stalin,[1] and I felt compelled to include several key moments in the history of Communism in the historical record. I also jotted down some notes in 1935 during Babel's last visit to France.

I do not mean to suggest that I have retained a literal record of our conversations, but thanks to the notes I took, it is possible to reconstruct the conversations. My own commentary will not contain any generalizations, analysis or explanations. All I offer are some details of past times, colored, more often than not, by Babel's humor. As he used to say, "a life without humor is not livable." All of his statements were accompanied by subtle changes in his facial expressions, meaningful pauses, and variations in intonations which after so many years are hard to convey.

Habent sua fata libelli . . .[2] As do manuscripts. The Gestapo and the GPU,[3] which worked in such touching harmony in occupied France in 1940 and 1941, cleaned out my apartment, my library, and my archives. But the notes I took on Babel have survived in the country house of friends who gave me refuge. This makes it possible to piece together our conversations, which we carried on in Russian or in French, depending on which language allowed Babel to express his thoughts with greater precision and compactness. All students of Babel's prose remark on its economy, intensity, and precision. His speech displayed the same qualities. * * *

Tuesday, October 18, 1932

In light of Babel's close relations with Gorky and his acquaintance with Voroshilov and other well-informed bigwigs, I decided to ask him about Stalin. Babel felt obligated to Gorky, who had supported his first efforts as a writer. Moreover, when Budyonny attacked Babel in the press in 1924 and 1928, castigating him for *Red Cavalry*, Gorky came to Babel's defense in the press, and Voroshilov did the same among the military. This helps to explain their personal relations.

Here is a brief record of Babel's response to my first question. He replied in short phrases uttered in a phlegmatic tone.

Babel: Stalin is distancing himself from everybody. He paces back and forth in his study, puffing on his pipe. He thinks. From time to time, he telephones one of his subordinates. He gives orders. Now he has gone to the Caucasus for three months.[4] In his absence, the "boss" is Kaganovich; he is the number-two man in the political leadership of the country. More generally, the number-two man is Gorky. Do you know what people

---

1. Souvarine, *Staline: aperçu historique du bolchévisme* (Paris, 1935).
2. Latin: Books have their fates.
3. A replacement for the Bolsheviks' first political police organization, Cheka, the State Political Directorate (*Glavnoe politicheskoe upravlenie*), or GPU, was decreed in 1922, to be replaced by the NKVD in 1934, MGB in 1953, and KGB in 1954.
4. In 1932, Stalin, who was seriously ailing at the time, took the longest vacation of his career, from May 29 through August 27.

whispered after Stalin departed, leaving the country's affairs in such a sorry state, especially the economy? He shat and quit . . .

* * *

Stalin loves the Moscow Art Theater and ballet. He goes there often. He holds court in his box. Members of the Politburo are invited to join him. When in his own milieu, he gets bored. He was really delighted to find in Gorky an interlocutor at his own level. Now his favorites are Ordzhonikidze and Mikoyan . . . He speaks slowly, mulling over each word for five minutes . . .

Souvarine: Tell me about Gorky.

Babel: He is a remarkable personality in many respects. His memory is astounding. He has a broad and complex understanding of the modern world and its problems.

Souvarine: You have just mentioned Kaganovich.

Babel: A hard worker. He grasps things quickly. In addition to his other functions, he is now the censor of the Moscow Art Theater and two other theater companies.

Souvarine: What happened to Pyatakov?[5]

Babel: On the ascendant. Drinking . . .

Souvarine: And Preobrazhensky?[6]

Babel: Drinking . . .

Souvarine: Serbriakov?[7]

Babel: Drinking . . .

* * *

Souvarine: I trust the dissolution of RAPP[8] was Gorky's initiative?

Babel: You are mistaken. Stalin decides everything himself, on his own initiative. For two weeks he received and listened to Averbakh[9] and his types, Bezymensky[1] and his types, and so on. Then he made his decision: nothing good will come out of working with these people. At the Politburo meeting, he made a surprising proposal [to dissolve RAPP]. Nobody batted an eyelash.

* * *

Babel: That's how Stalin does it. He invites several comrades to his place, offers them a drink, pours a big glass of vodka or Caucasian brandy and gives it to Averbakh, for instance, and says: "Drink!" Averbakh is baffled. He mumbles: "But . . . Comrade Stalin . . . the problem is . . . I don't

5. Georgy Leonïdovich Pyatakov (1890–1938), a leading Bolshevik figure and government official, purged in the Great Terror.
6. Eugeny Alexeyeviah Preobrazhensky (1886–1937), leading Bolshevik economist and an ally of Trotsky. He recanted his Trotskyism in 1929, recovered his party membership, and returned to government service. Purged again in 1933, he perished in the Great Terror.
7. Leonid Petrovich Serebriakov (1890–1937) joined the Bolsheviks in 1905 and after 1917 held key posts in military, industrial, and party organizations. An ally of Trotsky's, he lost his membership in the party in 1927 but after recanting recovered it in 1930 and returned to government service. He was arrested in 1936 and tried and shot in 1937.
8. The Russian Association of Proletarian Writers, known by its Russian acronym RAPP, was the ideological scourge of the late 1920s and early 1930s, with its leading journal *On Guard*. It brought together some of the most orthodox Bolshevik cultural figures who tried to, and for a while at least succeeded in, fashioning themselves into the party's ideological control instrument in the cultural sphere. They were especially opposed to Trotsky's cultural policy, with its rejection of "proletarian culture" and reliance on "fellow-travelers," i.e., non-party but loyal writers, as the foundation of Soviet cultural construction. RAPP's ideological "subcontract" came to an abrupt end in April 1932, when it was dissolved by a special party decree to be replaced by a more inclusive Union of Soviet Writers.
9. Leopold Averbakh (1903–1939), a Marxist literary critic, the head of RAPP, and fortuitously the son-in-law of the GPU chief Genrikh Yagoda.
1. Alexander Ilyich Bezymensky (1898–1973) was known as a Young Communist poet, an epigone of Mayakovsky, and a leading figure in RAPP.

drink alcohol . . ." Stalin orders: "Drink! What is it—you don't want to drink?" Averbakh is frightened: "But Comrade Stalin . . . you know . . . I can't . . ." Stalin is enraged: "Drink! What's the matter—you are refusing to drink!?" (Imitating Stalin, Babel tries to assume a malicious and frightening expression; he stresses every word and raises his voice to a yell.) Stalin: "Drink! Oh, you are still refusing to drink! Eh! You are afraid! You are af-raid of di-vulg-ing some-thing!!!"

* * *

Friday, October 25, 1932

* * *

Souvarine: And what are people saying about Trotsky, after all these years?

Babel: He is very popular, even among the peasantry—because he is a leader, a hero. He made a bad impression by collaborating with the *Daily Telegraph*[2] and publishing his memoirs.[3] But on the whole, he is respected *because he is not surrendering.* (Babel put a very strong emphasis on these last words.) In case of war or a critical situation, the former Trotskyists will demand his return.

Souvarine: Do people have any idea about the scope of political repressions?

Babel: Approximately ten thousand Trotskyists have been put under arrest or sent into exile. Now there are about fifteen hundred to two thousand left. The total number of prisoners is about three million.

Souvarine: Why did Trilisser fall into disfavor?

Babel: He had a series of failures. The Besedovsky affair in Paris[4] was the last drop; the cup overflowed.

Souvarine: And how is Agranov?[5]

Babel: A brilliant career. He has total power over the Moscow Region. This means government security is in his hands. That's no joke.

(Having run through the GPU bosses whom I used to know earlier—all of whom were subsequently shot because of Stalin's murderous paranoia—I asked about another man, Kamenev.)

Babel: He edited the marvelous collected works of Herzen with a marvelous introduction. He now works for the publishing house Academia.[6]

2. After being exiled from Russia in 1929, Trotsky wrote a column for the London *Daily Express*, a popular daily then known for its good international coverage.

3. Babel refers to Trotsky's autobiography, which came out in German, Russian, and English in 1930. In English it was published as *My Life: The Rise and Fall of a Dictator* (London, 1930).

4. Babel refers to the defection of the number-two Soviet diplomat in Paris, Grigory Besedovsky, in September 1929. The international embarrassment caused by the defection—Besedovsky condemned the brutalities of the regime—led to the promulgation of a new law making defection by a Soviet official equivalent to high treason and punishable by death. The scandal cost Mikhail Trilisser (1883–1938) his job as the head of the foreign intelligence service.

5. Yakov Saulovich Agranov (Sorenson, 1893–1938) was a senior official of the GPU/NKVD whose brief career included oversight of the intelligentsia elite, including academics, writers, and artists. He was on friendly terms with many in the literary milieu of the 1920s and early 1930s, including Vladimir Mayakovsky, who committed suicide with a gun that Agranov had given him as a present. Apparently Babel was only partially informed about Agranov's assignments. He was indeed the GPU man in charge of the Moscow Region from September 1, 1931, to February 21, 1933. More important (and unmentioned by Babel), Agranov was the head of perhaps the most important unit in the GPU, the Secret-Political Department, in charge of both political surveillance and information gathering. A close associate of Genrikh Yagoda's, Agranov was, like his boss, a victim of the purges, arrested in 1937 and executed in 1938.

6. Lev Borisovich Kamenev (Rozenfeld, 1883–1936) was a leading Bolshevik, a close ally of Lenin's, and a major political figure in the 1920s until his demise in 1926–27, when he was expelled from the Politburo, Central Committee, and the party (his membership was subsequently restored

(At this point, for some reason, I made a note: The "Writers' House" in Moscow.)

Babel: It's a sewer.

* * *

During Babel's last trip to Paris [in 1935], Pierre Drieu La Rochelle[7] asked me to organize a meeting with Babel. They met at my place and talked while I listened in silence. Drieu was worried and obsessed by the possibility of a new war, apprehensive about the fate of France and Europe, and torn between Communism and fascism. He was seeking ultimate arguments that would enable him to resolve his doubt. He kept pestering Babel with questions, to which Babel responded with exceptional delicacy and subtle, ineffable restraint. For he was not the kind of man who could say in the presence of a foreign bourgeois even one word that might suggest a critical attitude towards his native country, or the regime that "history" had established. I sensed Drieu's puzzlement. He wanted a straight answer but this unusual Soviet citizen had decided to stick to a loyal line when it came to the authorities who were in charge of his foreign passport. I cannot reproduce a single phrase from this dialogue: after almost half a century, the evasive subtlety displayed by Babel has dissipated without a trace. Perhaps there are notes [pertaining to this encounter] in Drieu's archive?

* * *

I was not among those who tried to persuade Babel [in 1935] to remain in France. For I knew his immutable reaction to friendly advice of this sort: "I am a *Russian* writer; if I could no longer live among the Russian people, I would cease being a writer; I would be like a fish out of water." My heart ached and I could barely conceal my emotions when we parted. * * *

ILYA EHRENBURG

A Book for Adults[†]

* * * I must now speak about Babel if for no other reason than that Babel is not a poet, not a Cubist painter, not a shaman, not a man whose life ended in tragedy. He has a funny nose, an impossibly curious one, he has written stories about Benka Krik, he cannot resist life. It would seem he has no

---

twice and twice taken away). Accused along with Grigory Zinoviev of fomenting opposition, he was sent into exile in 1932–33 but, in part because of Gorky's intercession on his behalf, was allowed to return and assume editorship of the publishing house Academia in 1933. He was arrested in the wake of Sergey Kirov's assassination in December 1934. In August 1936, he was convicted in the first major show trial of the Great Terror, condemned to death, and shot. Like most other victims of the Stalinist purges he was posthumously cleared of all charges.

7. Pierre Drieu La Rochelle (1893–1945), noted French novelist and political activist, known for his vacillation between communism and fascism. Despite his shift to the Right in the mid-1930s, he remained on friendly terms with André Gide and André Malraux, both, like Boris Souvarine, determined antifascists. His break with the Left took place not long after his interview with Babel. During the German occupation of France, he advocated active collaboration with the Nazi regime. As editor of *La Nouvelle Review Française* (1940–43), he turned the famous publication into a pro–Nazi mouthpiece while enticing known antifascist authors like Gide and Louis Aragon to publish in the journal. Apparently, he remained conflicted in his loyalties and, according to his diary, nursed a secret admiration for Stalin. Facing prosecution after the liberation of Paris, he went into hiding with the help of his friend André Malraux and committed suicide in 1945.

† From *Kniga dlya vzroslykh* (Moscow, 1936), pp. 153–54.

place in these memoirs.[1] When we first met, he said to me: "Man lives for pleasure, to sleep with a woman, laugh, and on a hot day eat ice cream." I once came to see him; he was sitting naked—the day was very hot—he was not eating ice cream, he was writing. Few work with as much torment as Babel. I am now thinking about Flaubert, about the fate of Bouvard and Pécuchet. Babel becomes excited about everything in life; in fact, he continues to work even when he is eating gefilte fish somewhere in the Moldavanka. He has written several slim volumes; every day he discovers in life several thick novels. His own fate resembles one of these unwritten books: he himself is incapable of untangling it. Once, he was about to visit me. His little daughter[2] asked him, "Where are you going?" He had to tell her. Then he thought it over and decided not to come my to place. Like a badger, he digs circuitous, complicated passages through life. He should not be spooked. He loves racehorses. He cannot walk fast—he has asthma. He has described love and death many times; he reeks of them like a dog. This vital, curious man works like a monk, hiding now at a stud farm, now in a village hut. In Paris he rented a room from a mad old woman only because it was absolutely quiet. The old woman was afraid of Babel because his face resembles Benka Krik's more than it does Flaubert's. At night she would lock him in his room, fearing she might be slaughtered by her strange boarder. He did not mind; he sat there and wrote. In order to escape with its life, an octopus ejects ink, yet it gets caught and eaten. The favorite Spanish dish is "octopus in its own ink."

* * *

People, Years, Life[†]

At the end of 1937, I came to Moscow straight from the outskirts of Teruel.[1] When I give an account of those days further on, it will be come clear why it was so important for me to see Babel right away.[2] I found the "wise rabbi" sad but as courageous, as witty, and as gifted a raconteur as ever.

Once he told me a story about his visit to a factory where confiscated books were recycled into pulp to produce paper; it was a very funny and very terrifying story. On another occasion he told me a story about orphanages for children whose parents are still living.[3] Our parting in May 1938 was ineffably sad.[4]

* * *

1. This piece on Babel, written four years before his death, follows vignettes on Boris Pasternak and André Malraux.
2. Nathalie Babel.
† Ehrenburg's memoirs were first serialized in *Novy mir* in 1960 and published separately in two volumes in 1961. The excerpt translated here is from the latest edition: Ehrenburg, *Memoirs: 1921–1941*, trans. Tatiana Shebunina in collaboration with Yvonne Kapp (New York: The Universal Library, Grosset and Dunlap, 1966), pp. 117–118.
1. The battle of Teruel, which began on December 15, 1937, was one of the most heroic, legendary, and decisive battles of the Spanish Civil War. The Republican forces seized the town on December 17, but the Nationalists recaptured it on January 7, 1938. The tide was turning in favor of Franco's forces.
2. A close friend of Ehrenburg's, Babel was one of the best-informed people in Moscow and one of very few with whom Ehrenburg could speak frankly. However, the first person to brief Ehrenburg on what was going on was their mutual friend, Mikhail Koltsov. At that time, Babel was in Kiev from the end of December 1937 to early March 1938. He and Ehrenburg met on March 12, 1938.
3. A reference to the mass terror of the late 1930s, when children of the "enemies of the people" were placed in special orphanages.
4. After considerable difficulties, Ehrenburg received Stalin's permission to continue with his journalistic assignment in Paris; he left from Odessa in May 1938.

Babel was arrested in spring 1939. I learned about it late—I was then in France. The streets of Paris were filled with recently mobilized soldiers, Parisian women went out for a stroll holding gasmasks, windowpanes were crisscrossed by tape. And I was thinking that I had lost a man who helped me walk not along the meadow in May, but along the very difficult road of life.

. . . Our kinship was based on an understanding of the writer's duty, on our sense of our age: we wanted the new world to have a place for some very old things—for love, beauty, art . . .
* * *

CLARA MALRAUX

The Sound of Our Steps: Suddenly Summer Comes†

"I want to go back to Paris, I want to see my baby!" He said this one afternoon—we had been in Moscow for four months—and for me this was a sign [of his affection]. Let's go back, let's go as soon as possible. Today it may not work, so tomorrow . . .

Tomorrow came. André joined me less than a week later.

I had fastened my suitcases, I had my tickets in my purse. Those who knew about my impending departure came to say good-bye. Among them was Babel.

"Would you like to take one last walk to remember Moscow by before the sun goes down?"

The multitudes of onion domes are barefly distinguishable from the pinkish grey sky. What a difference to be walking alongside a man not much bigger than myself.

"I will tell you things that I did not tell you until now, not because I did not trust you, but because as long as one stays here, it is better not to know too much about this place. But you are about to leave . . . Clara, I am a man who has an easy life."

I knew it: he was rich, his good friends attributed to him seven mistresses living in seven different apartments. I had been introduced to one of them; she combined a certain charm with a capacity to dress almost as well as Gorky's daughter-in-law.

"I am a friend of Gorky's, which means I can be present almost every week at his evenings with Stalin."

I knew that too: from time to time, with just an hour's advance notice, the Kremlin telephoned Gorky to announce the impending arrival of the august visitor. Then the three of them would arrange themselves before the fireplace to chat and relax, or to pretend to.

† From *Le Bruit de Nos Pas: Voici Que Vient L'Été*, vol. 4 (Bernard Grasset: Paris, 1973), pp. 285–287. © 1973, Grasset & Fasquelle, Paris. Clara Malraux (1897–1982), author and first wife of André Malraux until their separation in the late 1930s. She accompanied André Malraux on his visit to the Soviet Union in the summer 1934 to attend the First Congress of Soviet Writers; he had just been awarded the prestigious Goncourt Prize for *La Condition Humaine* and was perhaps the most distinguished foreign visitor at the Congress. The conversation she recorded in her memoirs took place sometime in late September 1934.

"What advantage do you believe I take of these flattering friendships?"
I believed nothing.

His diction became precise:

"The right to be a writer who does not write. Yes, I may not publish books for years and still remain a member of the Writers' Union. A situation exceptional enough for me to be grateful, don't you think? I won't die of starvation, my little Clara, I shall not know financial difficulties either . . . I am, all in all, a man in a good position."

I am laughing: is it because we are in Moscow that this sounds like something I have heard from Dostoevsky's characters? The man walking alongside me is the author of *Red Cavalry*, one of the best books of the 1920s; he welcomed the Revolution; at present, though, he feels passion only for women, horses, and horseracing.

Is it necessary, then, in order to create the new man, to destroy those who witnessed his birth? Is it necessary that those who bore testimony to the hopes and suffering of others disappear in silence? Passersby gazed at the river; Babel continued in his rhythmic French:

"I have the right not to write. But I am a writer. A writer writes. I have two novels in my desk drawer: if they are found, I am a dead man."

Three hours later I had boarded the train. Around 1950, I learned, like everyone else, that Babel had been shot; it was, I believe, at the beginning of the war.

VALENTINA KHODASEVICH

Babel as I Saw Him[†]

* * * The year was 1926. All of a sudden my husband was under arrest. At the time we were living in Leningrad, I took food parcels to his prison at Shpalernaya, had to stand in line from morning till night. There were crowds of people like me. It was the time of inexplicable mass arrests. Prison visits were not allowed, and we were given no information.
* * *

While standing in these lines, I contracted chicken pox and spent the next few months in bed. There were rumors then that because of the abuses at the Leningrad GPU, Moscow was sending a special commission "to investigate and purge the Leningrad GPU."

One day the theater director S. E. Radlov, a good friend of mine and frequent collaborator, dropped by to see me. He told me that Babel had just arrived in Leningrad and they had a date to discuss, if I remember correctly, the upcoming production of his play *Sunset* at the Moscow Art Theater II. Babel had friends among the Moscow Commission members, and

† V. Khodasevich (1894–1970) was a well-known artist and theater set designer; she studied art in Munich and Paris and was closely associated with the World of Art and the Russian avant-garde. She was a close friend of Gorky's and had an illustrious career as a set designer for Pirandello's theater in Rome, the Mariinsky in Leningrad, and Bolshoi in Moscow. The reminiscences excerpted here come from "Babel kakim ya ego videla," A. N. Pirozhkova and N. N. Yurgeneva, eds., *Vospominaniya o Babele* (Moscow, 1989), pp. 63–73. These reminiscences come from Valentina Khodasevich's book of memoirs, *Portrety slovami* (Moscow: Galart, 1995).

Radlov invited me to come by to introduce myself to Babel, to tell him about my husband, and to ask him to intercede.

When I arrived at Radlov's, Babel was already there.

At first, I trembled, stuttered, and felt very nervous. But the goodwill I read in Babel's eyes, which were looking straight into mine; his melancholy, almost bitter, and barely perceptible smile; and the unhurried way in which he queried me about all of the details of the case—all this put me at ease.

* * * A day later, Babel informed me that the Commission was going to ask to see my husband's case and I should be patient for a little while longer. "We shall see, we shall see," he said to me and smiled with great tenderness.

Needless to say, it was not the following day. But soon after my husband was released—without any charges because there was no "case."
* * *

Meetings at A. M. Gorky's Country House
Before and After His Death

* * * Alexey Maksimovich led a rather solitary life in Gorki[1] and immersed himself deeply in his work. * * * A lot of people wished to see him, and his secretary kept a waiting list and enforced it strictly. But one category of people could "sidestep" the secretary and sneak in "illegally," something Gorky enjoyed very much.

Among the "illegals" were Isaac Emmanuilovich Babel, Solomon Mikhailovich Mikhoels, Samuil Yakovlevich Marshak, and Mikhail Koltsov.
* * *

Next to Gorky's country estate was the village of Molodenovo where, as we found out, Babel had settled back in 1930. He lived either there or in Moscow. He told us that he was interested in horses and in all the details of their lives; he studied them at the nearby breeding farm where he had friends both among the employees and the horses. He was going to write a "horse novel."

Babel either visited Gorki often or disappeared for long stretches of time. I remember how we would sit down to lunch and Alexey Maksimovich would say: "Shouldn't we still wait a bit longer for Babel—perhaps, he is just a little late . . ." * * * All of us at the table would look out of the window hoping to see Babel walking towards the house . . .

It felt particularly cozy during the winter when, against a backdrop of white snow, the little gate would open and Babel would slowly waddle in wearing his winter hat with earflaps, a warm jacket, and holding a walkingstick in his hand. "Now he is going to tell us," Alexey Maksimovich would say, "a lot of interesting things about horses and other matters." It was impossible to be bored in Babel's presence. He has a special sense of his audience and could move from one subject to another without letting your attention flag. It was most gemütlich in the winter, when Babel would enter the quiet and emptiness of the enormous house, full of literary and other kinds of news from Moscow.

1. More precisely, Gorki 10, the government compound outside Moscow where Gorky resided, former estate of Savva Morozov in the village Uspenskoe.

He and Alexey Maksimovich often held informal professional discussions. Gorky had a great need of them but there were few such opportunities for him.

He had great confidence in Babel and Marshak and somehow (this may seem strange applied to Gorky) he could let his hair down before them. Babel often recalled Odessa and told Gorky stories about it. Some of these were lyrical stories about the lives of Odessans, others were comical. One could always feel, though, how much he loved Odessa and, "just in case," each individual Odessan.

But he could also become mischievous and come up with all kinds of funny eccentric schemes. Unfortunately, I cannot remember any details. However, when he and Mikhoels met at Gorky's, they would always start recalling their times of "fun and games."

They told stories about endless practical jokes they would play on each other or that they would both play on someone else—a soft drink vendor or some other utterly innocent target. * * * I had the pleasure of being present at these dinner-table "shows" at Gorky's. Someone would start a conversation, then Babel and Mikhoels would wink at each other, begin to pipe in, and from then on, the audience not only would be afraid to interrupt their tales and dialogue but even to miss a single gesture or word. Alexey Maksimovich would move his plate aside and arming himself with a lit cigarette and a handkerchief (to wipe off the tears from laughing too hard), he would become attention personified.

After they left, Alexey Maksimovich and all of us would spend a long time discussing the "show" and its two talented performers. Alexey Maksimovich would say: "When two such different yet somehow similar Jews as Babel and Marshak gather at the table, the effect is certainly marvelous; but Babel and Mikhoels form a real 'duet'; when it is Babel and Marshak, then each tries to perform 'solo' and each gets a little jealous if the other begins to outstrip him." Alexey Maksimovich loved and valued all three men—Babel, Mikhoels, and Marshak.

It is summer, a warm moonlit evening. A huge bonfire is lit in the park in Gorki. I remember Babel standing with Alexey Maksimovich by the fire. They exchange occasional phrases but never take their eyes off the huge flame. * * * Or another memory. Babel is standing to the side, alone, leaning on his staff or against a tree—his eyes scan the people around him and then come to rest, with a long, serious, and loving gaze, on the figure of Alexey Maksimovich.

Once, already after Alexey Maksimovich had died, * * * Babel told us with a somewhat embarrassed smirk that he had married a remarkable woman with an astonishing biography: the daughter of an illiterate mother, she worked as an engineer at the Moscow Metro Construction, and her name—Pirozhkova—often appeared on the honor roll board. At the end of the day he would rush to the gates of the Metro Construction to greet her and would look anxiously at the honor roll board to see if she was there today.

One day, he arrived at Gorki from Molodenovo with a delightful, very beautiful young woman, exceptionally feminine-looking but still visibly domineering, strong-willed, and full of energy.

He said to us: "Here is Pirozhkova, Antonina Nikolaevna. Let me introduce her." And he went on, with a giggle, to rehearse her biography. Antonina

Nikolaevna lifted her light eyes at him—huge eyes practically covering her entire face—and gave him a hard look. No, this did not embarrass him, but he somehow froze in his tracks. Still, he had a very happy face. * * *

NKVD Reports on Babel†

Special Report of the Secret-Political Department of the Chief Directorate of State Security of the NKVD of the USSR Regarding the "Progress in the Work of the First Congress of Soviet Writers" (August 31, 1934)

* * * During a discussion with the Ukrainian writers, Semenko, Bazhan, and Savchenko, with the Moscow writers, Babel, Pilnyak, and Aseyev, the most critical position was expressed by Babel and Semenko.

Babel We are supposed to demonstrate to the world the unanimity among literary forces of the Union. But because everything has been organized superficially and by threats, the Congress proceedings are as deadly as a Tsar's parade; needless to say, nobody abroad believes this parade. No matter how much our press inflates its stupid ideas about the delegates' colossal unity, there are also foreign correspondents here who truthfully report on this funeral wake. Look at Gorky and Demyan Bedny. They hate each other, but here at the Congress they sit next to each other like two little doves. I can imagine with what high spirits they would have led their followers to do battle.

Semenko Everything is going so smoothly that I am gripped by the desire to take a hunk of shit or a dead fish and throw it at the presidium of the Congress. Maybe this would liven things up a bit. * * *

Report of the First Section of the Secret-Political Department of the Chief Directorate of State Security of the NKVD of the USSR Regarding the Attitudes of I. E. Babel in Connection with the Arrests of Former Oppositionists (July 5, 1936)

Emmanuel called Pirozhkova at her work. She said to him over the phone: "I am terribly glad to hear your voice. I was very worried about you. I wanted to call you but I simply did not want to risk being told that you were not there." Emmanuel agreed to meet her after work the same day. He did and he saw her home. Emmanuel asked her why she had been worried. Pirozhkova replied: "What? You don't know anything? I am surprised they haven't laid their hands on you. A huge number of people have been arrested. I have the impression that everyone without exception who had anything to do with the Trotskyists has been arrested." When asked who exactly had been arrested, Pirozhova replied: "Among my friends, they've taken away Marusya Soln-tseva, Efim and Sonya Dreytser,[1] Okhotnikov's last wife, Shura Solomko,

† Andrei Artizov and Oleg Naumov, compilers, *Vlast i khudozhestvennaya intelligentsiya: Dokumenty TsK RKP(b)–VKP(b), VCheka-OGPU-NKVD o kulturnoy politike. 1917–1953 gg.* (Moscow, 1999), pp. 233, 316–18, 325–26.

1. Efim Alexovich Dreytser (1894–1936), civil war hero, commissar, military and industrial leader, and Trotsky loyalist (for a while the commander of Trotsky's personal security detail), for which he was expelled from the party. He recanted in 1930 and served as deputy director of a large industrial enterprise. He was accused, convicted, and shot in August 1936.

Lyola Gayevskaya. What's more, Yasha Okhotnikov[2] has been arrested."
Pirozhkova has the impression that people are being arrested wholesale
and she has even begun to worry about herself and Babel.

Pirozhkova said she had asked Babel: "Can you be arrested?" Babel
responded: "While the Old Man (Gorky) was alive, this was impossible.
And now, well, it's still rather difficult." It was Sonya Dreitser who told
them about the arrest of Yefim Dreitser; regarding Sonya's arrest,
Pirozhkova learned herself when she found the police seal on the door of
their apartment. Solntseva's present husband, Dzhango Goglidze (Gogob-
eridze), informed her about Solntseva's arrest. The former, a Party member, is incensed by the arrest and has asked Babel several times to intervene
in this matter. He said to Babel: "Solntseva is always treated as some sort
of an appendage either to Okhotnikov or Lominadze.[3] But she is her own
person!"

Pirozhkova said that Babel had discussed it with her and decided to
intervene. Babel decided to intervene specifically on behalf of Maria Solntseva, in whose innocence he believes more than that of the others. Babel
decided to go to Gorki when Yagoda is there and to speak to him in the
presence of Nadezhda Alekseevna Peshkova[4], whom Yagoda likes.

Pirozhkova told Emmanuel that on June 26, they hosted a dinner at their
place for André Gide. Eisenstein was there too, along with some other
French writer. The brother of André Malraux, Roland Malraux, lives in
Babel's apartment. He is staying in the Soviet Union to work as a film director.

Emmanuel asked: "And what about Gide and other French friends of
Babel, do they know about these arrests?" Pirozhkova replied that she
thought they did not know. Over the course of the entire dinner, according
to Pirozhkova, André Gide did nothing but express his admiration for what
he had seen in the USSR, and he spoke about everything with fervor. After
the guests left, Babel asked Pirozhkova if she could understand what Gide
was saying (she was studying French). Pirozhkova replied that she understood how much he admired everything that was going on here. Babel said
to her then: "Don't trust this admiration. He is devilishly clever. We do not
yet know what he will write when he returns home. He is not so easy to
deceive. Compared to him, Gorky is just a village sexton. He (Gide) may
play a devilish trick on us when he returns to France."[5]

Pirozhkova and Emmanuel were talking in Nogin Square when they ran
into Babel, who was waiting for a tram. Pirozhkova said to Babel: "Here is
Roman, who, it turns out, has not been arrested." Babel asked Emmanuel

---

2. Yakov Osipovich Okhotnikov (1896–1937), one of Babel's most colorful civil war friends. As a student at a military academy, this Trotsky loyalist was known to have physically attacked Stalin during the military parade in Red Square on November 7, 1927. Curiously, this attack had no
immediate consequences for him. He was arrested and tried in 1933 and spent three years in
Magadan before being rearrested in 1936. Accused of belonging to a terrorist organization, he was
shot in 1937.
3. Visarion Visarionovich Lominadze (1897–1935), a leading Party and government figure; expecting
to be arrested, he committed suicide after learning of the arrest of several of his close friends.
4. N. A. Peshkova (née Vedenskaya, 1901–1971), the widow of Gorky's son Maxim Peshkov. She was
rumored to be the lover of Genrikh Yagoda (1891–1938), who headed the NKVD in 1934–37 and
had a dacha next to Gorky's country residence in Gorki.
5. The dinner conversation must have provided Babel with clues about Gide's increasingly grim view
of Stalin's Russia. Babel was prescient. André Gide's *Retour à l'URSS* was an indictment, albeit
qualified and polite, of the repression and incompetence of the regime governing the Soviet
Union and its alarming similarity to that of Nazi Germany. A major international embarrassment,
the book was denounced in Moscow's *Literary Gazette* on December 12, 1936. When the scandal
broke, Babel was editing a translation of Gide's work into Russian.

in jest: "Aren't you ashamed that you haven't been arrested?" He asked if
Emmanuel was employed. Emmanuel replied he was not. "Are you not
allowed to work, or don't you want to?" Emmanuel replied that he has
been having difficulties finding a job. Babel said: "That may be the very
thing that has saved you—you are not registered anywhere." The three of
them reached Babel's apartment, and Babel asked Emmanuel to come and
have lunch with them. Babel began asking Emmanuel about the arrests.
Emmanuel replied that he had not seen anyone and had learned about the
arrests today from Pirozhkova. Babel asked him if he knew of any of the
former Trotskyists who had not yet been arrested. Emmanuel replied that
he had a neighbor, N. V. Poluyan,[6] an old friend whom he dropped in on
from time to time. He knows she has not been arrested.

Babel asked Emmanuel about Smilga,[7] where he was, and how long his
sentence was. Babel said that try as he might, he had not been able to find
out or understand the reason for the recent mass arrests, and that even if
there were sufficient reasons, he could not see what this had to do with
people like Yashka Okhotnikov and Noah Bliskovetsky—for these two had
spent the last three years isolated and in prison. For Okhotnikov and Noah
Bliskovetsky, a new arrest and new verdict would mean the end. "In
effect," Babel said, "this is a firing squad in slow motion."

"If there is a need to colonize Kolyma," Babel said, "it would be simpler
to make them an offer to go and work there in a way that they would not
be able to refuse."

When Babel went into his room, Pirozhkova told Emmanuel several
pieces of gossip about the leadership of the Communist Party in connection with Gorky's death.

After lunch, Babel went into his room to take a nap, and when parting
asked Emmanuel to drop by for lunch.

Asked if he knew anything about the fate of A. K. Voronsky, Babel
replied, "Of course I do. Voronsky has been expelled from the Party, but he
has not been arrested either, and they have even allowed him to keep his
apartment."

> Assistant to the Chief of the First Section
> of the Secret-Political Department
> of the State Security Directorate,
> Bogen

Report of the Secret-Political Department of the State Security Directorate of the USSR NKVD Re. the Attitudes of I. E. Babel . . . (September 22, 1936)

After the publication of the verdict of the Supreme Court Military Col-
legium regarding the members of the Trotskyte-Zinovievite Bloc, the infor-
mant, who was then in Odessa, met the writer I. E. Babel in the presence

---

6. Sister of Yan Vasilievich Poluyan (1891–1937), a prominent Bolshevik party and government
   leader, purged and executed in 1937.
7. Ivar Tenisovich Smilga (1892–1938), a major party and military leader, member of the Revolutionary Military Council of the southern and western fronts during the Polish campaign. He
   shared the fate of other high-level Trotsky loyalists who recanted and were allowed to resume
   their careers. Arrested early in 1935 following the assassination of S. M. Kirov, Smilga spent the
   next four years in prison until he was tried, convicted, and shot in 1938.

of the film director Eisenstein. The conversation took place in a room in a hotel where Babel and Eisenstein were staying.

Touching, for the most part, on the concluding part of the trial, Babel said:

"You cannot even imagine, cannot even absorb what enormous personalities have perished and what effect this will have on history.

"It's a terrible business. Of course, you and I know nothing; for reasons having to do with personal relations, a struggle against the 'boss' has been going on—and still is.

"Who were the people who made the Revolution? Who were the members of the first Politburo?"

Babel took a sheet of paper and began making a list of the members of the Central Committee and the Politburo of the first post-revolutionary years. Then, one by one, he began to cross out the names of those who had died, were expelled, and finally those accused at the most recent trial. After that, Babel tore up the sheet and said:

"Do you comprehend who has been shot or is about to be executed? Take Sokolnikov. Lenin liked him a lot because of his extraordinarily intelligence. True, Sokolnikov has been a 'big skeptic'; he is an armchair leader who literally hates having to organize masses of people. For Sokolnikov, Lenin alone could command authority, and his entire struggle has been a struggle against the influence of Stalin. This is why the relations between Stalin and Sokolnikov have deteriorated to this extent.

"Or take Trotsky. You cannot even imagine the power of his charm and his influence on the people who come into contact with him. No doubt about it: Trotsky will continue his struggle, and many will support him.

"Among the executed, Mrachkovsky is the most remarkable figure.[8] He was a worker, and he organized a guerrilla movement in Siberia; he was a man of extraordinary willpower. I have been told that shortly before he was arrested he had an eleven-hour conversation with Stalin.

"I am very sorry for those executed, because they were true human beings. Take Kamenev, for example. He is the most brilliant connoisseur of Russian literature and language since Belinsky.

"I do not think this is a struggle with counter-revolutionaries; I think it is a struggle against Stalin, based on personal relations.

"You can imagine how this is seen in Europe and how they will treat us from now on. I know that after Kamenev, Zinoviev and others were executed, Hitler said: 'Now I will have Thaelmann shot.'

"Oh, what troubled times! I have a terrible premonition!"

Eisenstein did not object to any of the statements made by Babel.

Deputy Chief of the Secret-Political Department
of the State Security Directorate,
Senior Major of State Security,
V. Berman

---

8. Sergey Vitalyevich Mrachkovsky (1888–1936), an old Bolshevik and leading figure in the Party, the military, and industry after the Revolution. He was expelled from the party in 1927 for his opposition to Stalin, arrested in 1935, and tried and executed along with Kamenev and Zinoviev in August 1936.

ERWIN SINKO

A Novel about a Novel. Moscow Diary[†]

February 9, 1936

The Soviet humor magazine *Krokodil* and the *Literary Gazette* endlessly ask, "Where is Babel staying?"—"What is going on with Babel?"—"Why has Babel not produced anything for such a long time?" Sometimes in light banter, sometimes scolding, I ask him: What is the joke? Because we share a phone, I witness all day long—whether I want to or not—how different editorial offices (which I would be only too happy to know) seek out Babel, desire to speak to him and pursue him regularly. For his part, Babel plays hide and seek with them: sometimes he refuses, other times he promises them manuscripts just so he can ask the editor in question for an extension. He invents excuses and obstacles, makes jokes, and in the end comes up again with new promises. He tries in vain to shake off his pursuers. These editors, publishers, offices, whose business it is to solicit manuscripts, are just as tenacious in demonstrating that there is a demand for him, that—whether he wants it or not—his work, his existence, and he himself are considered socially valuable. He has a place here and without him, we would be orphaned and empty. By contrast, I am a Hungarian writer in Soviet Russia and they need me here as little as they need me in France or Vienna.

* * * Babel, unlike me, did not seem very troubled by it all; instead, he grew more agitated and morose. Still, he reciprocated my confidence. He probably understands me, he replied, but I don't understand him. I would be very mistaken if I took his situation literally. Yes, he receives continuous phone calls. Yes, he is being pestered in public. But it is impossible to say openly why he is not working—and it is not true that he is not.

What, then, does one do from morning till night and from night till morning if not work? I love horses, I often go to see horses, I look at the horses and spend a lot of time with them, but that's not all. Besides the horses, I love only work—and Paris where it was so good to live. Now I am left only with horses and work. Imagine a musician being told: we trust you, we will wait for your work, for your work alone. One might envy the musician to whom such words are addressed— but only as long as one forgets that this ideal musician, who is being cajoled, actually produces music that pleases the people who are telling him such things—as is the case, say, with Dunayevsky. When I

[†] From *Roman jednog romana; biljeske iz moskovskog dnevnika od 1935 do 1937 godine* (Zagreb: Zora, 1955), pp. 351–54. Sinko (1898–1967) was, as Babel used to joke, the most improbable man: a Jew, a Hungarian, a citizen of Yugoslavia, and a Communist. As a young man Sinko participated in the Hungarian revolution, later describing his experiences in the novel *The Optimists*. A political émigré and a protégé of Romain Rolland, he finally made his way to Moscow with his wife, a doctor, joining a community of Hungarian communist expatriates. An old friend of Babel's housemate, Austrian engineer Bruno Steiner, Sinko and his wife were "house-sitting" for Steiner in 1935–37, while he was on extended leave, and became friends with Babel. His attempts, ultimately unsuccessful, to have his novel about the Hungarian revolution published in Soviet Russia is the leitmotif of his Moscow Diary. Fortunately for the Sinkos, their Soviet visa was revoked in 1937 and they were able to leave the Soviet Union for France, untouched by the Great Terror. After World War II, Sinko taught philosophy at the University of Zagreb.

do not publish, I am merely reproached for my laziness. If I publish, however, I might bring down on my balding head serious and dangerous accusations. I feel like a pretty girl at a ball—everyone wants to dance with her. To go soft and yield would turn everyone at the ball against me. As soon as I began to dance, it would become clear that I was pretty only when I stood on the sidelines. To dance at this ball as I would dance—that would be a gross impropriety, yes, an impropriety setting a wild and dangerous example!

He puts his slightly crooked index finger to his thick lips and, bending toward me, whispers in my ear with an air of mystery and agitation: "Among those who invite me to the dance in speeches and in print, many do it only because they know that should I begin my first dance, then. . . ." He laughed loudly and bitterly, then waved his hand in a farewell gesture and concluded: "*Adio, mare!*"

All of a sudden it became clear to me: this man is frightened. And perhaps, not just sometimes. Most of the time he probably maintains a pretense. He puts on displays of *joie de vivre* not only to deceive others but also himself.

Again Babel speaks about Gorky. When Babel's book about Budyonny's Red Cavalry appeared, Budyonny, whose name crops up throughout the book, felt insulted. He thought the book harmed him personally, insulted the Revolution, the ideal of the Revolution, one of its *miles gloriosus.* There were others, too, who found the conjuncture of revolutionary romanticism and theatricality disturbing, but Budyonny denounced it in the most violent terms. The only person to come to the defense of *Red Cavalry* was Gorky who, in view of the danger, turned directly to Stalin. Stalin uttered one word that called off the chase. Once during a supper he mumbled under his mustache something to the effect that *Red Cavalry* "is not so bad, yes, it's quite a good book indeed"—but he mumbled it in such a way that hardly anyone else could hear it.

"So why doesn't he mumble something similar to protect Shostakovich?"[1]

Since the *Pravda* editorial that denounced him, it was tactless even to mention Shostakovich's name. It was the first time that I raised this subject with Babel. He did not take offense at my question. He looked at me, however, with a disdainful but not unfriendly expression, waving his hand like a teacher who tries to restrain noisy pupils, indicating either that it was getting too late or was still too early, and that we should be mindful of the fact that M. had to go to work. But M. responded. It was her impression that the attack on Shostakovich was much more general and that it concerned more than just the person of Shostakovich and his opera—that it went deeper than the controversy surrounding *Red Cavalry* and was, it seemed, a prelude to a comprehensive campaign. She asked Babel if that was how he understood it.

"The one thing that I don't understand is how one can stand living with a woman as smart as your Irma Yakovlevna?" replied Babel and turned to me. This jocular comment, which Babel found so amusing, was his answer, but it was also no answer at all. Having adopted this tone, Babel

1. The conversation recounted by Sinko here took place soon after the famous attack on Dmitry Shostakovich's opera *Lady Macbeth of Mtzensk* in a *Pravda* editorial on January 28, 1936, which inaugurated a new wave of cultural repression, known as the Campaign Against Formalism.

leaned against the kitchen door and relayed to us the latest gossip that Antonina Nikolaevna had heard at the tailor's. And Antonina Nikolaevna always had to report at great length because Babel madly enjoyed the gossip one heard at the tailor's. Babel was practically crying with laughter as he showed us with his whole body how a buxom old lady tried on an evening gown and had difficulties fitting her bosom into it.

NADEZHDA MANDELSTAM

Hope Against Hope[†]

"Who needs this cursed regime?" Lev Bruni[1] had said as he gave M.[2] the money to pay his fare to Maly Yaroslavets. In the autumn it began to seem advisable to move from Savelovo, and we again started studying the map of the Moscow region. Lev recommended Maly Yaroslavets. * * *

In autumn it gets dark very early, and apart from the railroad station, there was no lighting at all in Maly Yaroslavets. We walked up the streets, which were slippery from mud, and we saw not a single streetlamp or lighted window—nor were there any passersby. Once or twice we had to knock on windows to ask the way, and each time a fear-contorted face peered out. But when we simply asked the way, the faces were at once transformed and wreathed in smiles, and we were given very detailed instructions with extraordinary friendliness. When we at last arrived at Nadia Bruni's and we told her what had happened when we knocked on windows, she explained that there had been more and more arrests in recent weeks, not only of exiles, but of local people too. As a result, everybody was just sitting at home, waiting with bated breath. During the Civil War, people did not have lights in their windows for fear of attracting the attention of all the freebooters then roaming the country. In the towns occupied by the Germans, people also sat without lights. In 1937, however, it made no difference, since people were picked up not at random but on individual warrants. All the same, everybody went to bed early to avoid putting the lights on. Perhaps it was the most primitive animal instinct—better sit in the darkness of your burrow than in the light. I know the feeling very well myself— whenever a car stops outside the house, you want to switch off the light.

We were so horrified by the darkened town that after spending the night at Nadia Bruni's we fled back to Moscow the next morning. We didn't follow Lev's advice because we would have needed the strength of mind of the meek and gentle Nadia Bruni to stand the terror that lay like a pall

† From chapter 68, "Eclipse," in Mandelstam, *Hope Against Hope: A Memoir,* trans. Max Hayward. Copyright © 1970 by Atheneum Publishers. Reprinted by permission of the Random House Group Ltd. and Simon & Schuster, Inc. The events described take place in the summer or fall of 1937. Osip Mandelstam was arrested in May 1934 for his epigram against Stalin and sentenced to internal exile in Voronezh. His sentence expired in May 1937, but he was not permitted to settle in major cities. By then contrite—he had composed an elaborate plea for forgiveness, the "Ode to Stalin"—Mandelstam spent the next few months trying to rehabilitate himself and obtain the right to return to his apartment in Moscow. He was arrested again on May 3, 1938, sentenced to five years at a labor camp, and died in a transit camp in the Far East on December 31, 1938.
1. Lev Alexandrovich. Bruni (1894–1948), a well-known Russian artist.
2. Nadezhda Mandelstam refers to her husband Osip Emilievich Mandelstam, as "M." in her memoirs.

over the town. It was the same throughout the whole country, of course, but in the villages and small towns it was generally less overpowering.

The next person we consulted was Babel. I do not think he ever lived in any of the apartment buildings reserved for writers, but always managed to find peculiar places of his own. With great difficulty we tracked him down in a strange house that must formerly have been a private villa. I have a vague recollection that there were foreigners living in this house, and that Babel rented rooms from them on the second floor. But perhaps he just said so to astonish us—he was very fond of startling people like this. At that time foreigners were avoided like the plague—you could lose your head for the slightest contact with them. Who in his right mind would have lived in the same house as foreigners? I still remember my astonishment, and still cannot understand it. Whenever we saw Babel, he gave us something to be surprised about.

We told him our troubles, and during the whole of our long conversation he listened with remarkable intentness. Everything about Babel gave an impression of all-consuming curiosity—the way he held his head, his mouth and chin, and particularly his eyes. It is not often that one sees such undisguised curiosity in the eyes of a grownup. I had the feeling that Babel's main driving force was the unbridled curiosity with which he scrutinized life and people.

With his usual ability to size things up, he was quick to decide on the best course for us. "Go out to Kalinin," he said. "Erdman[3] is there—his old women just love him." This was Babel's cryptic way of saying that all Erdman's female admirers would never have allowed him to settle in a bad place. He also thought we might be able to get some help from them—in finding a room there, for instance. But Babel, as it turned out, had exaggerated Erdman's hold over his "old women"—when we went to Kalinin, we found that none of them lived out there with him, and that he had to come into Moscow to see them.

Babel volunteered to get the money for our fare the next day, and we then started talking about other things. He told us he now spent all his time meeting militiamen and drinking with them. The previous evening he had been drinking with one of the chief militiamen of Moscow, who in his drunken state had declared that "he who lives by the sword shall perish by the sword." The chiefs of the militia, he said, were disappearing one after another and "today you're all right, but you don't know where you'll be tomorrow."

The word "militia" was of course a euphemism. We knew that Babel was really talking about Chekists. M. asked him why he was so drawn to "militiamen": was it a desire to see what it was like in the exclusive store where the merchandise was death? Did he just want to touch it with his fingers? "No," Babel replied, "I don't want to touch it with my fingers—I just like to have a sniff and see what it smells like."

It was known that among the "militiamen" Babel visited was Yezhov himself.[4] After the arrest of Babel, Katayev and Shklovsky said he had

---

3. Nikolay Erdman (1902–1970), dramatist and screenwriter known not only for his successful plays but also for risqué political jokes, which led to his arrest in 1933 (indirectly witnessed by his friend Babel) and internal exile to the town of Kalinin.

4. Nikolay Ivanovich Yezhov (1897–1940), head of the NKVD in 1936–38 and Stalin's chief executioner. Babel was an old friend and a one-time lover of his wife, Evgeniya Solomonovna Khayutina (1905–1938), the de facto editor of USSR in Construction, a journal to which Babel frequently

visited Yezhov because he was so frightened, but that it hadn't saved him—
Beria had had him arrested precisely on this account. I am convinced that
Babel went to see Yezhov not out of cowardice but out of sheer curiosity—
just to have a sniff and see what it smelled like.

The question "What will happen to us tomorrow?" was the chief topic
of all our conversations. Babel, with his storyteller's gift, put it into the
mouth of his "militiamen." M. was generally silent about it—he knew too
well what awaited him. Only once did he blurt out something when we
happened to run into Shervinski on the street. He was no friend of ours,
but M. suddenly told him it couldn't go on like this—"I am right in front
of their noses all the time and they must have no idea what to do with
me—in other words, they will soon have to pick me up." Shervinski listened to this brief outburst and said nothing at all. After M.'s death I
sometimes met him, but he never mentioned it to me. I should not be surprised if he had forgotten—there was so much unpleasantness in our lives
that this was the only thing to do.

TATYANA STAKH

[The Search]†

* * * I saw Babel for the last time not long before that terrible sunrise,
which I shall remember forever.

One quiet spring evening, we were drinking tea in his dining room. The
phone rang in his study. Babel picked up the phone. It was Alexander
Fadeev[1] calling. The conversation was brief. Babel responded in monosyl-
lables; one could hear some of them:

"Thank you, not yet . . . No, no plans . . . I think soon . . . I don't know
yet . . ."

When he returned to the dining room, he looked a little perturbed. He
was wiping his glasses and said almost offhandedly: "He was asking me if
I had any plans to go somewhere . . . Hmm . . . The boss,[2] he said, has
been asking why I haven't published any books of late. Hmm . . ."

That was the end of the conversation.

Soon afterwards Babel left for Peredelkino.

. . . One evening, I felt an urge to go and see Antonina Nikolaevna
[Pirozhkova]; we talked and talked, time flew by quickly and before long I

contributed. A visitor to Evgeniya's informal literary salon, Babel had the opportunity to observe
Yezhov on several occasions. Yezhov's wife committed suicide in November 1938. Yezhov was
arrested in April 1939 and gave testimony against Babel.

† Tatyana Stakh, editor and translator, was the wife of Babel's old friend Boris Stakh (1894–1953),
the head of the Odessa Party Committee Agitprop and later the director of the Odessa State
Ukrainian Theater. Tatyana and her husband preserved the sole copy of Babel's civil war diary.
This is an excerpt from her reminiscences of Babel, "Kakim ya pomnyu Babelia" (Babel as I
Remember Him), published in the Kiev Russian-language journal *Raduga* 7 (1995).

1. Alexander Alexandrovich Fadeev (1901–1956), renowned Soviet writer, head of RAPP, and one of
the most powerful members of the Writers' Union (in 1946–54 he was its General Secretary). As
a top literary bureaucrat, he was implicated in the arrests—and sometimes in the protection—of
many writers. Fadeev committed suicide in 1956 during the de-Stalinization campaign.

2. Boss (*khozyain*) was a well-known euphemism for Joseph Stalin.

realized—this used to happen often—that I had missed the last train to Lianozovo, where we lived then. For the first time in my life, I spent the night in Babel's town flat. I slept in his study. It was a small square room with a low ceiling, painted floorboards and two windows, one of them looking out into a garden. Opposite the door, there stood a big wardrobe containing his clothes, with the letters and manuscripts kept in the lower drawer; to the left of the window, there was a big shelf full of books; to the right, a big wide sofa. Over it hung a few photographs of horses and the jockeys who were his friends. To the right of the door stood a big writing desk with a phone, a desk lamp, and few file folders. The walls were bare, and only the curtains on both windows and a small rug on the floor gave it some warmth.

The window was half open. I fell asleep.

I woke up at sunset with a strange feeling that there was someone standing nearby. Outside birds were singing and their outrageous chirping seemed particularly loud against the quiet of the early hours. I saw two men standing by the desk and doing something with the telephone. I was surprised that the repairmen came so early to work on the phone and tried to go back to sleep. But I did not sleep long. The unconscious alarm again awakened me. The room was empty. But I heard some shuffling and muted voices behind the door. I got up, folded the bedding, and walked out into the hallway. The doors of both rooms were wide open. Several men—one wore a military uniform—were conducting a search in the bedroom. One of them was pulling things out of the wardrobe using as an implement an old rusty sword stuck in its scabbard that Babel had been awarded for his service in the army. Another was rifling through the contents of the drawers. I still could not understand what was going on. Finally I decided that they had come for Esther Grigorievna, whose husband was doing time.[3] It took a while for me to realize that the object of the search was Babel.

Antonina Nikolaevna [Pirozhkova] was standing there totally petrified. The little Lydia[4] woke up and was rubbing her eyes. Esther Grigorievna was standing over her trying in vain to get her to go back to sleep.

"And who are you?" asked one of the NKVD men.

"A friend of the family."

"And why are you spending the night here?"

I gave my explanation.

"Don't leave."

When I protested, he interrupted me:

"We'll contact whoever necessary, if need be."

Bewildered, I returned to Babel's study with a plan to take something important from his desk. I knew he was working on a new novel about the Rostov Cheka. I always carried with me a small valise instead of a pocketbook, and I thought that I would be able to secrete something inside it. My naïveté in those days bordered on idiocy! The desk drawers were already empty. I took his blue blazer out of the wardrobe and wrapped it around

3. Esther Makotinsky, the wife of an old friend of Babel's from Kiev, M. Ya. Makotinsky, a physician with impressive revolutionary credentials. He was arrested in 1932, survived the camps, and was released sometime before 1956. After the arrest in 1938 of Makotinsky's daughter, Valentina Makotinskaya, Babel gave refuge to Esther in his Moscow apartment.
4. Babel's daughter, born in 1937.

my shoulders, pretending it was my coat. It was the only thing I could save . . . The lower drawer of the wardrobe had been locked.

　* * *

The search was drawing to a close. The abovementioned saber was recorded as a weapon.

It was eight in the morning.

Now came the most terrifying moment.

Some of the NKVD men were going to Peredelkino. Antonina Niko-laevna pleaded with them to take her along. She wanted to be the one to give the news to Babel, because she feared for his health. He suffered from asthma and frequently complained about his heart . . .

I cannot say exactly what happened in Peredelkino but from the spare report by Antonina Nikolaevna I know that Babel was calm; in the car he passed her the money he had on him, the key to the apartment, and remarked: "Poor Tanya—what bad luck! She comes so rarely—and now this!"

In the meantime, things were winding down in Babel's town flat in Nikolo-Vorobinsky Lane. Babel's study was sealed. I was asked to put my name to the search document as a witness and to sign a nondisclosure form. My hands were trembling, my eyes could not make out what I was signing, but I signed as asked. At last, I was allowed to leave but not before I received a warning to keep my mouth shut.

I left the house as if in a dream.

I hardly had the time to get to Vorontsov Lane when I ran into Semyon Gekht. He looked perplexed and was rushing somewhere . . .

"Tatyana," he stammered, "You know Babel has been arrested . . ."

. . . More than once a thought crossed my mind later: could it be that Fadeev was perhaps trying to give Babel a warning—to suggest that he go away somewhere? . . . But this is only a guess . . . * * *

ANTONINA PIROZHKOVA

At His Side: The Last Years of Isaac Babel[†]

Babel told me that most of the time he did not live in Moscow, where it was hard to find the solitude he needed to work. Instead he stayed in the village of Molodenovo, near Gorky's house in Gorki. He invited me to go out there the next time I had a day off from work.

He called for me early in the morning and we went down to Belorussian Station to catch a train. We got off at Zhavoronki, where a horse and car-riage awaited us, something Babel had obviously arranged in advance. The road first took us through a cluster of summer cottages, then through fields, and then through a grove of oak trees. Babel was in very good spir-its and for some reason he told me a story about a husband bringing his

† From At His Side: The Last Years of Isaac Babel, by A. N. Pirozhkova; published by Steerforth Press of Hanover, New Hampshire. Copyright © 1996 by A. N. Pirozhkova. Translation copyright © 1996 by Anne Frydman and Robert L. Busch.

wife home from their wedding. Along the way, the husband's horse refused to obey him on the count of "one," and again on the count of "two." After the count of "three," he hacked the animal to death. This made such an impression on his wife that from then on, her husband had only to say "one" for her to carry out his command at once, for she always remembered what followed "three."

The house that Babel lived in was on the very outskirts of town and stood at the edge of a ravine. A little stream flowed along the bottom, emptying eventually into the Moscow River. Inside the vestibule of the house two doors led off to separate wings.

The first wing, occupied by the landlord Ivan Karpovich and his family, consisted of a kitchen, a living room, and a bedroom facing the street. The second, in which Babel lived, consisted of just one big room whose windows faced the kitchen garden. It was furnished very modestly, with a simple table, two or three stools, and two narrow beds in the corners.

Babel was determined to show me all the sights of Molodenovo so we started off right away on foot to see the stud farm. There we were shown the newly foaled colts, including one that had been born just the night before and was named "Vera, Come Back!" for the wife of one of the trainers who had left him for another man.

We looked around the whole stud farm, where everyone knew Babel and wanted to tell him everything in complete detail, which I found surprising and for some reason amusing. Then we headed over to see the mares in foal, which were grazing separately on the banks of the Moscow River.

The conversation Babel had with a trainer there was highly specialized and full of expressions that I was to understand only much later—"high runner," "having a fine exterior," "leading by a nose." It seemed to me that Babel had forgotten all about me. Finally, he came over and started talking about the mares. The first filly was, in his words, a complete hysteric; the second was a prostitute; the third one managed to produce first-rate offspring no matter how poor the sire, i.e., she improved the breed; while the fourth, as a general rule, made it worse.

Both on the way to the stud farm and on the way back we walked past the gate of a white house with columns where Maxim Gorky lived. Past the house, we turned off the road and went down to the river, and after a swim we headed back to Molodenovo through a magnificent birch grove. Then Babel took me to meet an old beekeeper, a very tall man with a large beard who was a confirmed Tolstoyan and a vegetarian. He gave us tea to drink and honey in honeycombs.

We returned again to the railway station by horse and carriage. On the way, Babel said to me: "Here you are, an educated young lady who has just spent the day with a rather well-known writer, and you haven't asked him even one literary question." Without letting me answer, he said: "You were perfectly right to do so."

Later I came to understand fully how much Babel disliked talking about literature; indeed, he would do almost anything to avoid it.

Babel was very familiar with the operations of the Molodenovo kolkhoz, or collective farm, and he had even helped run it for a while before we met. He had done this not for money, of course, but just to learn about life on a kolkhoz. Everyone there called him Manuilych.

Not long before he went off to France, Babel persuaded me to move to Nikolo-Vorobinsky during his stay abroad. He was afraid that during the interim someone might be moved into the empty apartment. Steiner[1] was still abroad at the time. Babel was hopeful that, if it proved necessary, I would be able to find people who could keep the apartment from being filled with strangers. I moved into one of Babel's rooms upstairs and lived there for five or six months with a fine young woman named Ellie, Steiner's maid.

[OCTOBER 1936]

After breakfast Babel and Eisenstein would work on the scenario. Babel was supposed to supply the dialogue, but he also helped in creating scenes. So as not to get in the way, I would go for a walk or sit on the balcony and read. They often argued and even quarreled with each other. After one such fairly tempestuous scene I asked Babel what they had been fighting about.

"Sergey Mikhailovich is always going beyond the bounds of reality. I keep having to bring him down to earth," Babel said. He explained that they had come up with a scene in which an old woman, the mother of a kulak, sits in her hut with a sunflower in her hands; under instructions from the kulaks, she removes the sunflower seeds and replaces them with matches whose sulphur tips protrude. This flower is thrown beside a fuel tank at a Tractor Station so that one of the kulaks can set it on fire with a match or a cigarette butt. The match-filled sunflower bursts into flame, sets fire to the fuel tank, and eventually burns down the whole Tractor Station.

"So this old woman is sitting in her hut and replacing the seeds with matches," Babel said, "and she keeps looking over at the icons. She fully understands that what she is doing is utterly un-Christian, and she fears that the Lord will punish her. Here fantasy gets the better of Eisenstein, and he says: 'Suddenly the ceiling of the hut cracks, the Heavens open, and Almighty God appears in the clouds . . . The old woman faints.' That's how Eisenstein wanted to shoot the scene. Meanwhile, he's got little Stepok, wounded, wandering through the wheat field wearing a halo around his head. Sergey Mikhailovich himself has told me many times he prefers what isn't there in actuality—the *isn'tness*. He is so strongly drawn to the fantastic, the unreal. But unrealism around here is unrealistic," concluded Babel.

[MAY 1939]

We made plans for all of us to move out to the dacha at the end of May when the weather got warm. Work on the film scenario for *My Universities* was almost over, and shooting had already begun. "I feel I owe it to Gorky," Babel said. He had been involved to some degree or other with all the filming of Gorky's works—*Childhood, My Apprenticeship*, and finally *My Universities*. He told me, "My mind is on other things right now, but Ekaterina

---

1. Babel shared the apartment with an Austrian engineer, Bruno Steiner (d. 1942), who represented a German electrical firm in Moscow. Steiner went home for an extended visit in 1936, and while he was still abroad Soviet authorities cancelled his visa.

Pavlovna[2] asked me to keep an eye on these filmmakers to be sure they don't distort his work or do something in bad taste."

As he left for Peredelkino, Babel said good-bye cheerfully and remarked: "I won't be returning to this house soon."

He asked me to bring Mark Donskoy and his assistants out to see him on May 15, as it was Donskoy who was directing *My Universities*. We arranged for them to pick me up at Metroproject after work.

At the time, the only people at home besides me were our housekeeper, Shura, and Ester Grigorevna Makotinskaya, who took care of little Lida.[3]

On May 15, 1939, at five o'clock in the morning, I was awakened by a knock on the door of my room. When I opened it, two men in army uniforms entered and said they were searching for someone and needed access to the attic.

It turned out that four men had entered. Two climbed up to the attic and two stayed downstairs. One of them announced that they needed to see Babel, who could tell them where this person was, and that I should drive out to the dacha in Peredelkino with them. I got dressed and we set off. I was accompanied by two men in addition to the driver, who knew the way perfectly and did not once ask me for directions.

When we arrived at the dacha, I woke up the watchman and entered through the kitchen with the two men behind me. Hesitant, I stopped in front of the door to Babel's room. With a gesture one of the men ordered me to knock. I did so and heard Babel say, "Who's there?"

"Me."

Then he got dressed and opened the door. Pushing me away from the door, the two men walked right up to Babel and commanded, "Hands up!" Then they felt his pockets, frisking him for weapons. Babel kept silent.

We were ordered into another room—mine. There we sat down, huddling close together and holding each other's hands. Talking was beyond us.

After the search of Babel's room was completed, they put all his manuscripts into folders and ordered us to put on our coats and go to the car. Babel said to me: "They didn't let me finish." I understood that he was speaking of his book "New Stories." Then, in a very low tone, he said: "Inform André." He meant André Malraux.

In the car, one of the men sat in the back with Babel and me while the other one sat in front with the driver. "The worst part of this is that my mother won't be getting my letters," Babel said, and then he was silent for a long time.

I could not say a single word. Babel asked the secret policeman sitting next to him, "So, I guess you don't get much sleep, do you?" And he even laughed.

As we approached Moscow, I said to Babel, "I'll be waiting for you. It will be as if you've gone to Odessa . . . Only there won't be any letters . . ."

He answered, "I ask you to see that the child not be made miserable."

"But I don't know what my fate will be . . ."

At this point, the man sitting beside Babel said to me: "We have no claims whatsoever against you."

---

2. E. P. Peshkova, Gorky's first wife.
3. The daughter of Pirozhkova and Babel.

We drove up to the Lubyanka prison and through the gates. The car stopped before the massive, closed door, where two sentries stood guard.

Babel kissed me hard and said: "Someday we'll see each other . . ." And without looking back, he got out of the car and went through that door.

I turned to stone and could not even cry. For some reason I kept thinking, "Will they at least give him a glass of hot tea? He can't start the day without it."

* * *

CRITICISM

VIKTOR SHKLOVSKY

Isaac Babel: A Critical Romance[†]

I find myself somehow reluctant to take a close look at Babel. An author's success must be respected, and the reader should be given the opportunity to learn to like a writer before trying to figure out the reasons for his success. I'm ashamed to take a close look at Babel. His story "The Rabbi's Son" contains this passage: "The girls, planting their unpretentious bandy doe legs on the floor, stared coldly at his sexual organs, that stunted, tender, curly-haired masculinity of a wasted Semite."[1]

So for my article on Babel I have chosen the method of a lyrical warm-up. Once there was old Russia, enormous, like a mountain spread wide with furrowed slopes.

Some people wrote upon her with pencils, "This mountain shall be saved." That was before the Revolution.

Some of those who had written on the mountain in pencil worked on Gorky's *Chronicle* (*Letopis*). Gorky had just arrived. He was stooped, discontented, sick, and he wrote the article "Two Souls."[2] A highly erroneous article. * * *

A story by Babel appeared in one issue. It concerned two young girls who did not know how to perform an abortion.[3] Their father held the post of prosecutor in Kamchatka. Everyone noticed that story and remembered it. Then I met Babel himself. Average height, high forehead, huge head, a face unlike a writer's, quiet dress, entertaining conversation.

Came the Revolution, and the mountain was cleared away. There were some who still ran after it with pencils in their hands. There was nothing left for them to write on.

Just then Sukhanov[4] started to write. Seven volumes of reminiscences. They say he wrote them before the events happened, since he foresaw everything.

I arrived from the front. It was autumn. Gorky's *Novaya Zhizn* was still being published.

In it Babel wrote some comments under the heading "New Everyday Life." He was the only one who maintained his stylistic sangfroid throughout the Revolution.

Babel's sketches dealt with such things as how plowing is done today. It was then that I became better acquainted with him. He turned out to be an imperturbable man with a concerned voice, and a lover of fine feeling.

For him fine feeling was as necessary as a dacha.

I met Babel for the third time in Petersburg in 1919. Petersburg was

---

† First published in *LEF* 6 (1924), pp. 152–62. Trans. Edward Pearson in Edward J. Brown, ed., *Major Soviet Writers: Essays in Criticism* (1973). Copyright Oxford University Press, Inc. Used by permission of Oxford University Press, Inc.
1. See p. 174 in this Norton Critical Edition.
2. Printed in the inaugural issue of *Letopis* (1, 1915), Gorky's essay "Two Souls" (Dve dushi) appealed to the Russian intelligentsia to take a critical look at the "Russian national character" and "learn to understand what it inherited from Asia—its weak will, passive anarchy, pessimism, desire for intoxication, dreaming—and what it has absorbed from Europe, dynamic through and through, inexhaustibly active, believing only in the power of reason, study, and science." —Ed.
3. See "Mama, Rimma, and Alla."
4. Nikolay Sukhanov (1882–1939), socialist politician and author of the famous *The Russian Revolution of 1917: A Personal Record* (1922).

covered with snow in winter, as if the city itself stood snowbound in the middle of a road, only it was something like a latticed snow fence along a railroad track. In summer Petersburg was covered by a deep blue sky. There was no smoke from the chimneys, and the sun hung over the horizon; no one interfered with it. Petersburg was empty—its inhabitants were at the front. Among the cobblestones on the streets the grass in little shoots of green flame struggled up towards the sun.

Side streets were already grassed over.

In front of the Hermitage, on the wooden pavement that was resonant right at that place, children played at skittles with torn up blocks. The city was beginning to be grown over, like an abandoned military camp.

Babel lived on 25th of October Street, No. 86.

He lived alone in his hotel room; his visitors came and went. Maidservants saw to his needs, cleaned the rooms, emptied the buckets with bits of unfinished food floating in them.

Babel lived, contemplating at leisure the city's hungry lechery. His room was clean. He would tell me that "nowadays" women could be had only before six, since the streetcars stopped running after that.

He had no feeling of alienation from life. But I had the impression that when he went to bed, Babel would sign his name to each completed day as though it were a story. The tools of the man's trade had left their mark on him.

A samovar inevitably graced Babel's table, and even sometimes bread. And that was a rarity in those days.

He was always a warm and willing host. A certain retired chemist used to visit him, a Tolstoyan and also a teller of incredible anecdotes.

He was the man who, having publicly insulted the duke of Baden, appeared at his own trial in Petersburg to testify against himself. (However, he was pronounced insane and punished only by having his laboratory confiscated.) He was a bad poet and an indifferent critic, that most unlikely man, Peter Storytsin. And Babel valued Storytsin.[5]

Kondrat Yakovlev visited him, a few others, I myself, and some veterans from Odessa who were always ready to tell a tale, along with other assorted Odessites, who told all the stories that were written in them.

Babel wrote little, but steadily. It was always the same story—about two Chinamen in a brothel.

He loved that story as he loved Storytsin. The Chinamen and the women kept changing. They grew young, aged, broke windows, beat up a woman, organized this or that.

A good many stories resulted from all this, and not just one. Though he had not really finished with his Chinamen, Babel went away one sunny autumn day, leaving me his grey sweater and leather satchel. . . . There was no word at all from Babel; it was as though he'd gone to Kamchatka to talk to the prosecutor about his daughters.

Once a visiting Odessite, after having spent all night losing at cards in a well-known house, and having borrowed enough the next morning to cover his loss, offered me as a sign of gratitude the information that Babel was either translating from the French or putting together a book of stories from a book of anecdotes. Later, when I was wounded and was passing through Kharkov, I heard that Babel had been killed while with the Red Cavalry.

5. Petr Ilych Storitsyn (Kogan, 1877–1941), a native of Odessa, a Tolstoyan, a dentist turned Petrograd reporter, and a theater critic.

Fate, in its own time, worked a hundred changes in each of us.
In 1924 I again met Babel. I learned from him that he had not been killed, though he'd been beaten at great length.
He hadn't changed. He could tell even more interesting stories. From Odessa and the front he had brought with him two books. The Chinamen had been forgotten, stowed away in one particular story.
The new pieces were beautifully written. I don't think there's anyone else nowadays who writes as well as he does. He has been compared to Maupassant, because readers sense a French influence, and they are quick to name a sufficiently worthy object of comparison. But I prefer another name—Flaubert. The Flaubert of *Salambô*.[6] The Flaubert of that marvelous operatic libretto.
The shiniest jackboots, handsome as young girls; the whitest riding breeches, bright as a standard against the sky; even a fire blazing as bright as Sunday cannot be compared with Babel's style.
A stranger from Paris—from Paris alone, with no touch of London—Babel saw Russia as a French writer a century earlier, conscripted into Napoleon's Grande Armée, might have seen it.
The Chinamen were no longer needed; their place had been taken by Cossacks from French illustrations.
Connoisseurs of lovemaking say that its very effective to "sweet talk" in abusive language. "The peculiar meaning and force that results from the use of words whose lexical color is the opposite of their intonation effect is due precisely to this contrast." (Yury Tynyanov, *The Problem of Poetic Language*). Babel's principal device is to speak in the same voice of the stars above and of gonorrhea.
Babel's lyrical passages are not successful.
His description of Brody ("Road to Brody") and its Jewish cemetery are not too good.
When he sets out to describe something, Babel adopts an elevated tone and enumerates many beautiful things. He writes:

> You and I are walking through this enchanted garden, this marvelous Finnish forest. To our dying day we will not encounter anything better, and you, you cannot even see the rosy, ice-crusted edges of the waterfall, over there, on the river. The weeping willow, leaning over the waterfall—you cannot see its Japanese delicacy. The red trunks of the pine trees heaped with snow! The granular sparkle that scintillates over the snows! It begins as a frozen line above the tree's wavy surface, like Leonardo's line, crowned by the reflection of the blazing clouds. And what about Fröken Kirsti's silk stockings, and the line of her maturing legs?

True, this passage ends with: "Get yourself some eyeglasses, Aleksandr Fyodorovich, I beseech you" ("Line and Color").
Babel is gifted, and he is able, by the device of an irony communicated just in time, to render acceptable the highly colored objects he describes.
Without the irony it would be painful to read such things.
He even anticipates our objections and provides an explanatory sign over his tableaux—"this is opera":

6. A historical novel (1862) by Gustave Flaubert (1821–1880), *Salambô* is renowned for its orientalist exoticism.

The burned-out town—broken columns and the hooks of evil old women's fingers dug into the earth—seemed to me raised into the air, comfortable and unreal like a dream. The naked shine of the moon poured over the town with unquenchable strength. The damp mold of the ruins blossomed like a marble bench on the opera stage. And I waited with anxious soul for Romeo to descend from the clouds, a satin Romeo singing of love, while backstage a dejected electrician waits with his finger on the button to turn off the moon. [Italian Sun"]

I used to compare Red Cavalry with Gogol's Taras Bulba. There are decided similarities in certain techniques. That "letter" telling of the murder of a father by his son is a Gogolian plot turned inside out. Babel also uses the Gogolian trick of enumerating family names, a device that may have its roots in the classical tradition.

But with Babel the enumeration is suddenly broken off. The Cossack Melnikov writes:

For thirteen days I've been fighting with the rear guard, protecting the invincible First Cavalry, and am finding myself under hot rifle, artillery, and air fire from the enemy. Tardy has been killed, Lukhmannikov has been killed, Lykoshenko has been killed, Gulevoy has been killed, Trunov has been killed, and the white stallion is no longer under me, so, in line with the changing fortunes of war, don't count on seeing your beloved divisional commander Timoshenko, Comrade Melnikov, but we'll meet again, in—to be blunt about it—the kingdom of heaven, though rumor has it the old man in heaven hasn't a kingdom, but a regular whorehouse, and there's plenty of clap on earth already, so maybe we won't see each other after all. So long then, Comrade Melnikov. ["The Continuation of the Story of a Horse"]

Babel's Cossacks are all insufferably and ineffably handsome. "Ineffable" is a favorite word of Babel's.

Babel makes use of two contradictions, which in his work take the place of plot: 1) his style is in contrast to the life he describes, and 2) that life *is* in contrast to the author himself.

He is a stranger in the army, a foreigner who has a right to be surprised. When he describes the military way of life, he accentuates the "weakness and despair" of the observer.

In addition to Red Cavalry, Babel has written Odessa Tales. These are full of descriptions of various bandits. The atmosphere of banditry and the bandits' motley chattels Babel requires as a justification of his own style.

We recall that the divisional commander had "jackboots that looked like girls"; but consider the aristocrats of the Moldavanka district, who "were girded in crimson vests. Russet jackets covered their steely shoulders, and azure leather burst its seams around their fleshy feet" ("The King").

Babel is a stranger in both worlds. He is a stranger even in Odessa. There he's told: "Forget for a time that you've spectacles on your nose, but autumn in your heart. Stop raising hell at your writing desk and stammering in public. Imagine for a moment that you raise hell on the streets and stammer on paper." Of course those remarks don't describe Babel. He isn't like that at all; he doesn't stammer. He's a brave man. I even think that "he could spend the night with a Russian woman and the Russian woman would be satisfied."

Because the Russian woman loves eloquence. Babel plays the part of a foreigner because that device, like irony, facilitates his writing. And even Babel would not dare attempt high emotion without irony.

When Babel writes, he keeps the music to himself while describing the motions of the dance, yet at the same time he renders the whole piece in a high register. No doubt it was from the epic that he borrowed the device of giving answers which repeat the questions.

Benya Krik in the *The Odessa* Stories talks that way:

> Grach asked him:
> "Who are you, where do you come from, and what do you fill your lungs with?"
> "Try me out, Froim," answered Benya, "and let's stop playing around."
> "Let's stop playing around," said Grach. "I'll try you out."

And the Cossacks in "The Letter" speak in the same way:

> And Senka asked Timofey Rodionych:
> "Are you doing all right, Dad, in my hands?"
> "No," Dad said . . . "doing badly."
> Then Senka asked:
> "And Fedya, when you cut him up, was he doing all right?"
> "No," said Dad, "Fedya did badly."

Babel's books are excellent books. Russian literature is as gray as a siskin:[7] it needs crimson riding breeches and boots of sky-blue leather.

It also needs the thing that Babel understood when he left his Chinamen to fend for themselves and set off with the "Red Cavalry."

Literary heroes, girls, old people and young people in all their possible situations are long since played out. Literature needs concreteness, and it must interbreed with our new everyday life in order to create a new form.

SEMYON BUDYONNY

The Babism of Babel from *Red Virgin Soil*[†]

Under the resonant, clearly speculative title "From the book *Red Cavalry*,"[1] the not-so-clever author attempts to paint the everyday life, customs, and traditions of the First Cavalry Army during the heyday of its heroic struggles on the Polish and other fronts.

In order to describe the heroic, historically unprecedented class struggle, one must understand first of all the essence of this struggle and the nature of classes; that is, one must be a dialectician, a Marxist artist.

---

7. Shklovsky probably meant a common sparrow, not a siskin (Russian *chizhyk, Spinus spinus Linnaeus*), which is a colorful black-and-yellow bird.
† Trans. G. Freidin. From *Oktyabr* 3 (1924). Reprinted by permission of *Oktayabr*. Budyonny makes a pun on Babel's last name and the similar sounding Russian designation, often pejorative, for a peasant woman, *baba* (an ignorant woman, a wench, an "old wife"); the addition of an "-ism" endowed this new coinage with the air of an alien ideology. The issue containing the article came out in September 1924; by then, more than a dozen of Babel's *Red Cavalry* stories had appeared in *Red Virgin Soil (Krasnaya nov* and *LEF).*
1. Many of the *Red Cavalry* stories first appeared in print with the subtitle "From the Book *Red Cavalry.*"

The author is neither of these.

This is why he does not care why and for what purpose the First Cavalry Red Army fought while serving as one of the greatest instruments of class struggle. Even though the author belonged to the ranks of the glorious Cavalry Army (assigned to the rear), he failed to notice with his eyes, ears, and brain its heroic struggle, its terrible, inhuman suffering and privations. Small-minded and ideologically alien by nature, he failed to notice the giant sweep of its struggle.

Citizen Babel recounts to us old wives' gossip about the Cavalry Army. He is rifling through old wives' junk and underwear, relating to us with frightened indignation that some Red Army soldier took from someone a loaf of bread and a chicken; he invents fairy tales, pours dirt over the best communist commanders, indulges in fantasy, and just lies.

The author needed the resonant title most likely in order to impress the reader, to force him to believe the old tales about our revolution, saying that it was made not by a class mature enough to understand its class interests and to seize power directly but by a bunch of brigands, thieves, bandits, and prostitutes who have brazenly grabbed power by force.

This is the old song of misters Suvorin, Milyukov, Denikin,[2] and their ilk, who used to scream until they were hoarse, write, and hiss on the subject of the thick-skulled, crude, stinking, and hateful peasantry; but even they have now come to their senses and stopped.

I am not puzzled by this, but what puzzles me is how it was possible that our Soviet literary and general interest journal, headed by a communist editor, permitted in our country, the USSR, in the year 1924, the singing of such songs without first checking their ideological significance and historically-correct content.

Citizen Babel was unable to see the greatest tremors of class struggle; it was alien to him, repulsive; but instead he sees with the passion of a sick sadist the trembling breasts of a Cossack woman, her bare haunches, and so forth. He looks at the world as a "meadow traversed by naked wenches, studs, and mares."

Yes, with imagination like this, what else could he have written—except lies—about Red Cavalry.

For us, there is nothing new in the fact that the old intelligentsia is rotten, degenerate, dirty, and vice-ridden. Its brilliant representatives— Kuprin, Artsybashev (his novel *Sanin*),[3] and others—have naturally found themselves on the other side of the barricades, but Babel, who has stayed here either because he is stupid or by accident, keeps feeding to us this old drivel refracted through the prism of his sadism and degeneracy, and then has the gall to call it "From the book *Red Cavalry*."

Could it be that Comrade Voronsky[4] loves these stinking Baba-Babelian piquancies so much that he allows these irresponsible fairy tales to be

2. Alexey Suvorin (1834–1912), conservative literary and social critic and publisher; Pavel Milyukov (1859–1943), historian, leader of the Constitutional Democrats, and minister of the Provisional Government; and General Anton Denikin (1872–1947), commander of the White Army.
3. Alexander Ivanovich Kuprin (1870–1938): native of Odessa, journalist and fiction writer, famous for his novel *The Pit* (Yama, 1910) about a house of ill repute in a provincial Russian town. Mikhail Petrovich Artsybashev (1878–1927): author of the erotic novel *Sanin* (1907), which scandalized the reading public in Russia and abroad and led to the author being charged with writing pornography in Russia as well as Austria-Hungary and Germany.
4. Alexander Konstantínovich Voronsky, the founder and editor-in-chief of *Red Virgin Soil*, a well-known Marxist critic allied with Leon Trotsky as well as a friend and admirer of Babel's.

published in such a responsible journal? Not to speak of the fact that Comrade Voronsky knows well the names of those individuals at whom the literary degenerate Babel spits with his artistic spittle of class hatred.

LIONEL TRILLING

The Forbidden Dialectic†

A good many years ago in 1929, I chanced to read a book which disturbed me in a way I can still remember. The book was called *Red Cavalry*; it was a collection of stories about Soviet regiments of horses operating in Poland. I had never heard of the author, Isaac Babel—or I. Babel as he signed himself—and nobody had anything to tell me about him, and part of my disturbance was the natural shock we feel when, suddenly and without warning, we confront a new talent of great energy and boldness. But the book was disturbing for other reasons as well.

In those days one still spoke of the "Russian experiment" and one might still believe that the light of dawn glowed on the test tubes and crucibles of human destiny. And it was still possible to have very strange expectations of the new culture that would arise from the Revolution. I do not remember what my own particular expectations were, except that they involved a desire for an art that would have as little ambiguity as a proposition in logic. Why I wanted this I don't wholly understand. It was as if I had hoped that the literature of the Revolution would realize some simple, inadequate notion of the "classical" which I had picked up at college; and perhaps I was drawn to this notion of the classical because I was afraid of the literature of modern Europe, because I was scared of its terrible intensities, ironies, and ambiguities. If this is what I really felt, I can't say that I am now wholly ashamed of my cowardice. If we stop to think of the museum knowingness about art which we are likely to acquire with maturity, of our consumer's pride in buying only the very best spiritual commodities, the ones which are sure to give satisfaction, there may possibly be a grace in those moments when we lack the courage to confront, or the strength to endure, some particular work of art or kind of art. At any rate, here was Babel's book and I found it disturbing. It was obviously the most remarkable work of fiction that had yet come out of revolutionary Russia, the only work, indeed, that I knew of as having upon it the mark of exceptional talent, even of genius. Yet for me it was all too heavily charged with the intensity, irony, and ambiguousness from which I wished to escape.

There was anomaly at the very heart of the book, for the Red Cavalry of the title were Cossack regiments, and why were Cossacks fighting for the Revolution, they who were the instrument and symbol of Tsarist repression? The author, who represented himself in the stories, was a Jew; and a Jew in a Cossack regiment was more than an anomaly, it was a joke, for between Cossack and Jew there existed not merely hatred but a polar

† The Introduction to *Isaac Babel: The Collected Stories*, ed. and trans. Walter Morison (New York: The New American Library, 1955). Reprinted by permission of S. G. Phillips, Inc.

opposition. Yet here was a Jew riding as a Cossack and trying to come to terms with the Cossack ethos. At that first reading it seemed to me— although it does not now—that the stories were touched with cruelty. They were about violence of the most extreme kind, yet they were composed with a striking elegance and precision of objectivity, and also with a kind of lyric joy, so that one could not at once know just how the author was responding to the brutality he recorded, whether he thought it good or bad, justified or not justified. Nor was this the only thing to be in doubt about. It was not really clear how the author felt about, say, Jews; or about religion; or about the goodness of man. He had—or perhaps, for the sake of some artistic effect, he pretended to have—a secret. This alienated and disturbed me. It was impossible not to be overcome by admiration for *Red Cavalry*, but it was not at all the sort of book that I had wanted the culture of the Revolution to give me.

And, as it soon turned out, it was not at all the sort of book that the Revolution wanted to give anyone. No event in the history of Soviet culture is more significant than the career, or, rather, the end of the career, of Isaac Babel. He had been a protégé of Gorky, and he had begun his career under the aegis of Trotsky's superb contempt for the pieties of the conventional "proletarian" aesthetics. In the last years of the decade of the twenties and in the early thirties he was regarded as one of the most notable talents of Soviet literature. This judgment was, however, by no means an official one. From the beginning of his career, Babel had been under the attack of the literary bureaucracy. But in 1932 the Party abolished RAPP—the Russian Association of Proletarian Writers—and it seemed that a new period of freedom had been inaugurated. In point of fact, the reactionary elements of Soviet culture were established in full ascendancy, and the purge trials of 1937 were to demonstrate how absolute their power was. But in the five intervening years the Party chose to exercise its authority in a lenient manner. It was in this atmosphere of seeming liberality that the first Writers' Congress was held in 1934. Babel was one of the speakers at the Congress. He spoke with considerable jauntiness, yet he spoke as a penitent—the stories he had written since *Red Cavalry* had been published in a volume at the end of 1932 and since that time he had written nothing, he had disappointed expectation.

His speech was a strange performance. It undertook to be humorous; the published report is punctuated by the indication of laughter. It made the avowals of loyalty that were by then routine, yet we cannot take it for granted that Babel was insincere when he spoke of his devotion to the Revolution, to the Government, and to the State, or when he said that in a bourgeois country it would inevitably have been his fate to go without recognition and livelihood. He may have been sincere even when he praised Stalin's literary style, speaking of the sentences "forged" as if of steel, of the necessity of learning to work in language as Stalin did. Yet beneath the orthodoxy of this speech there lies some hidden intention. One feels this in the sad vestiges of the humanistic mode that wryly manifest themselves. It is as if the humor, which is often of a whimsical kind, as if the irony and the studied self-depreciation, were forlorn affirmations of freedom and selfhood; it is as if Babel were addressing his fellow-writers in a dead language, or in some slang of their student days, which a few of them might perhaps remember.

Everything, he said at one point in his speech, is given to us by the Party and the Government; we are deprived of only one right, the right to write badly. "Comrades," he said, "let us not fool ourselves: this is a very important right, and to take it away from us is no small thing." And he said, "Let us give up this right, and may God help us. And if there is no God, let us help ourselves."

The right to write badly—how precious it seems when once there has been the need to conceive of it! Upon the right to write badly depends the right to write at all. There must have been many in the audience who understood how serious and how terrible Babel's joke was. And there must have been some who had felt a chill at their hearts at another joke that Babel had made earlier in his address, when he spoke of himself as practicing a new literary genre. This was the genre of silence—he was, he said, "the master of the genre of silence."

Thus he incriminated himself for his inability to work. He made reference to the doctrine that the writer must have respect for the reader, and he said that it was a correct doctrine. He himself, he said, had a very highly developed respect for the reader; so much so, indeed, that it might be said of him that he suffered from a hypertrophy of the faculty of respect—"I have so much respect for the reader that I am dumb." But now he takes a step beyond irony; he ventures to interpret, and by his interpretation to challenge, the official doctrines of "respect for the reader." The reader, he says, asks for bread, and he must indeed be given what he asks for—but not in the way he expects it; he ought to be surprised by what he gets; he ought not be given what he can easily recognize as "a certified true copy" of life—the essence of art is unexpectedness.

The silence for which Babel apologized was not broken. In 1937 he was arrested. He died in a concentration camp in 1939 or 1940. It is not known for certain whether he was shot or died of typhus. Both accounts of the manner of his death have been given by people who were inmates of the camp at the time. Nor is it known for what specific reason he was arrested. Raymond Rosenthal, in an admirable essay on Babel published in *Commentary* in 1947, says, on good authority, that Babel did not undergo a purge but was arrested for having made a politically indiscreet remark. It has been said that he was arrested when Yagoda was purged, because he was having a love affair with Yagoda's sister. It has also been said that he was accused of Trotskyism, which does indeed seem possible, especially if we think of Trotsky as not only a political but a cultural figure.

But no reason for the last stage of the extinction of Isaac Babel is needed beyond that which is provided by his stories, by their method and style. If ever we want to remind ourselves of the nature and power of art, we have only to think of how accurate reactionary governments are in their awareness of that nature and that power. It is not merely the content of art that they fear, not merely explicit doctrine, but whatever of energy and autonomy is implied by the aesthetic qualities a work may have. Intensity, irony, and ambiguousness, for example, constitute a clear threat to the impassivity of the State. They constitute a secret.

Babel was not a political man except as every man of intelligence was political at the time of the Revolution. Except, too, as every man of talent or genius is political who makes his heart a battleground for conflicting tendencies of culture. In Babel's heart there was a kind of fighting—he was captivated by the vision of two ways of being, the way of violence and the way of peace, and he was torn between them. The conflict between the two ways of being was an essential element of his mode of thought. And when Soviet culture was brought under full discipline, the fighting in Babel's heart could not be permitted to endure. It was a subversion of discipline. It implied that there was more than one way of being. It hinted that one might live in doubt, that one might live by means of a question.

It is with some surprise that we become aware of the centrality of the cultural, the moral, the personal issue in Babel's work, for what strikes us first is the intensity of his specifically aesthetic preoccupation. In his school days Babel was passionate in his study of French literature; for several years he wrote his youthful stories in French, his chief masters being Flaubert and Maupassant. When, in an autobiographical sketch, he means to tell us that he began his mature work in 1923, he puts it that in that year he began to express his thoughts "clearly, and not at great length." This delight in brevity became his peculiar mark. When Eisenstein spoke of what it was that literature might teach the cinema, he said that "Isaac Babel will speak of the extreme laconicism of literature's expressive means—Babel, who, perhaps, knows in practice better than anyone else that great secret, 'that there is no iron that can enter the human heart with such stupefying effect, as a period placed at just the right moment.'" Babel's love of the laconic implies certain other elements of his aesthetic, his commitment (it is sometimes excessive) to le mot juste, to the search for the word or phrase that will do its work with a ruthless speed, and his remarkable powers of significant distortion, the rapid foreshortening, the striking displacement of interest and shift of emphasis—in general his pulling all awry the arrangement of things as they appear in the "certified true copy."

Babel's preoccupation with form, with the aesthetic surface, is, we soon see, entirely at the service of his moral concern. James Joyce has taught us the word epiphany, a showing forth—Joyce had the "theory" that suddenly, almost miraculously, by a phrase or a gesture, a life would thrust itself through the veil of things and for an instant show itself forth, startling us by its existence. In itself the conception of the epiphany makes a large statement about the nature of human life; it suggests that the human fact does not dominate the scene of our existence—for something to "show forth" it must first be hidden, and the human fact is submerged in and subordinated to a world of circumstance, the world of things; it is known only in glimpses, emerging from the danger or the sordidness in which it is implicated. Those writers who by their practice subscribe to the theory of the epiphany are drawn to a particular aesthetic. In the stories of Maupassant, as in those of Stephen Crane, and Hemingway, and the Joyce of Dubliners, as in those of Babel himself, we perceive the writer's intention to create a form which shall in itself be shapely and autonomous and at the same time unusually responsible to the truth of external reality, the truth of things and events. To this end he concerns himself with the given moment, and, seeming almost hostile to the continuity of time, he presents the past only as it can be figured in the present. In his commitment to event he affects to be indifferent to "meanings" and "values"; he seems to be saying that although he can tell us with unusual accuracy what is going on, he does not presume to interpret it, scarcely to understand it, certainly not to judge it. He arranges that the story shall tell itself, as it were; or he tells it by means of a narrator who somehow makes it clear that he has no personal concern with the outcome of events—what I have called Babel's lyric joy in the midst of violence is in effect one of his devices for achieving the tone of detachment. We are not, of course, for very long deceived by the elaborate apparatus contrived to suggest the almost affectless detachment of the writer. We soon enough see what he is up to. His intense concern with the hard aesthetic surface of the story, his preoccupation with things and events, are, we begin to perceive, cognate with the universe, representative of its nature, of the unyielding circumstance in which the human fact exists; they make the condition for the epiphany, the showing forth; and the apparent denial of immediate pathos is a condition of the ultimate pathos the writer conceives.

All this, as I say, is soon enough apparent in Babel's stories. And yet, even when we have become aware of his pathos, we are, I think, surprised by the kind of moral issue that lies beneath the brilliant surface of the stories, beneath the lyric and ironic elegance—we are surprised by its elemental simplicity. We are surprised, too, by its passionate subjectivity, the intensity of the author's personal involvement, his defenseless commitment of himself to the issue.

The stories of *Red Cavalry* have as their principle of coherence what I have called the anomaly, or the joke, of a Jew who is a member of a Cossack regiment—Babel was a supply officer under General Budyonny in the campaign of 1920. Traditionally the Cossack was the feared and hated enemy of the Jew. But he was more than that: The principle of his existence stood in total antithesis to the principle of the Jew's existence. The Jew conceived his own ideal character to consist in his being intellectual, pacific, humane. The Cossack was physical, violent, without mind or manners. When a Jew of Eastern Europe wanted to say what we mean by "a bull in a china shop," he said "a Cossack in a succah"—in, that is, one of the fragile decorated booths or tabernacles in which the meals of the harvest festival of Succoth are eaten: he intended an image of animal violence, of aimless destructiveness. And if the Jew was political, if he thought beyond his own ethnic and religious group, he knew that the Cossack was the enemy not only of the Jew—although that in special—but the enemy also of all men who thought of liberty; he was the natural and appropriate instrument of ruthless oppression.

There was, of course, another possible view of the Cossack, one that had its appeal for many Russian intellectuals, although it was not likely to win the assent of the Jew. Tolstoy had represented the Cossack as having a primitive energy, passion, and virtue. He was the man as yet untrammeled by civilization—direct, immediate, fierce. He was the man of enviable simplicity, the man of the body and of the horse, the man who moved with speed and grace. We have devised an image of our lost freedom which we mock in the very phrase by which we name it: the noble savage. No doubt the mockery is justified, yet our fantasy of the noble savage represents a reality of our existence, it stands for our sense of something unhappily surrendered, the truth of the body, the truth of full sexuality, the truth of open aggressiveness. Something, we know, must inevitably be surrendered for the sake of civilization; but the "discontent" of civilization which Freud describes is our self-recrimination at having surrendered too much. Babel's view of the Cossack was more consonant with that of Tolstoy than with the traditional view of his own people. For him the Cossack was indeed the noble savage—all too savage, not often noble, yet having in his savagery some quality that might raise strange questions in a Jewish mind.

I have seen three pictures of Babel, and it is a puzzle to know how he was supposed to look. The most convincing of the pictures is a photograph, to which the two official portrait sketches bear but little resemblance. The sketch that serves as the frontispiece to Babel's volume of stories of 1932 makes the author look like a Chinese merchant—his face is round, impassive, and priggish; his nose is low and flat; he stares through rimless glasses with immovable gaze. The sketch in the Literary Encyclopedia lengthens his face and gives him horn-rimmed spectacles and an air of amused and knowing assurance: a well-educated and successful Hollywood writer who has made the intelligent decision not to apologize for his profession except by his smile. But in the photograph the face is very long and thin, charged with emotion and internality; bitter, intense, very sensitive, touched with humor, full of consciousness and contradiction. It is "typically" an intellectual's face, a scholar's face, and it has great charm. I should not want to speak of it as a Jewish face, but it is a kind of face which many Jews used to aspire to have, or hoped their sons would have. It was, surely, this face, or one much like it, that Babel took with him when he went among the Cossacks.

We can only marvel over the vagary of the military mind by which Isaac Babel came to be assigned as a supply officer to a Cossack regiment. He was a Jew of the ghetto. As a boy—so he tells us in his autobiographical stories—he had been of stunted growth, physically inept, subject to nervous disorders. He was an intellectual, a writer—a man, as he puts it in striking phrase, with spectacles on his nose and autumn in his heart. The orders that sent him to General Budyonny's command were drawn either by a conscious and ironical Destiny with a literary bent—or at his own personal request. For the reasons that made it bizarre that he should have been attached to a Cossack regiment are the reasons why he was there. He was there to be submitted to a test; he was there to be initiated. He was there because of the dreams of his boyhood. Babel's talent, like that of many modern writers, is rooted in the memory of boyhood, and Babel's boyhood was more than usually dominated by the idea of the test and the initiation. We might put it that Babel rode with a Cossack regiment because, when he was nine years old, he had seen his father kneeling before a Cossack captain who wore lemon-colored chamois gloves and looked ahead with the gaze of one who rides through a mountain pass.

Isaac Babel was born in Odessa in 1894. The years following the accession of Nicholas II were dark years indeed for the Jews of Russia. It was the time of the bitterest official anti-Semitism, of the Pale, of the Beilis trial, of the Black Hundreds and the planned pogroms. And yet in Odessa the Jewish community may be said to have flourished. Odessa was the great port of the Black Sea, an eastern Marseille or Naples, and in such cities the transient, heterogeneous population dilutes the force of law and tradition, for good as well as for bad. The Jews of Odessa were in some degree free to take part in the general life of the city. They were, to be sure,

debarred from the schools, with but few exceptions. And they were sufficiently isolate when the passions of a pogrom swept the city. Yet all classes
of the Jewish community seem to have been marked by a singular robust-
ness and vitality, by a sense of the world and of themselves in the world.
The upper classes lived in affluence, sometimes in luxury, and it was possible for them to make their way into a Gentile society in which prejudice
had been attenuated by cosmopolitanism. The intellectual life was of
a particular energy, producing writers, scholars, and journalists of very
notable gifts; it is in Odessa that modern Hebrew poetry takes its rise with
Bialyk and Tchernikovsky. As for the lower classes, Babel himself represents them as living freely and heartily. In their ghetto, the Moldavanka,
they were far more conditioned by their economic circumstances than by
their religious ties; they were not at all like the poor Jews of the shtetln,
the little towns of Poland, whom Babel was later to see. He represents
them as characters of Breughel-like bulk and brawn; they have large,
coarse, elaborate nicknames; they are draymen and dairy farmers; they are
gangsters—the Jewish gangs of the Moldavanka were famous; they made
upon the young Babel an ineradicable impression, and to them he devoted
a remarkable group of comic stories.

It was not Odessa, then, it was not even Odessa's ghetto, that forced
upon Babel the image of the Jew as a man not in the actual world, a man
of no body, a man of intellect, or wits, passive before his secular fate. Not
even his image of the Jewish intellectual was substantiated by the Odessa
actuality—Bialyk and Tchnernikovsky were anything but men with spectacles on their noses and autumn in their hearts, and no one who ever encountered in America the striking figure of Dr. Chaim Tchernowitz, the
great scholar of the Talmud and formerly the Chief Rabbi of Odessa, a
man of Jovian port and large, free mind, would be inclined to conclude
that there was but a single season of the heart available to a Jew of Odessa.

But Babel had seen his father on his knees before a Cossack captain on
a horse; the captain said, "At your service," and touched his fur cap with
his yellow-gloved hand and politely paid no heed to the mob looting the
Babel store. Such an experience, or even a far milder analogue of it, is
determinative in the life of a boy. Freud speaks of the effect upon him
when, at twelve, his father told of having accepted in a pacific way the
insult of having his new fur cap knocked into the mud by a Gentile who
shouted at him, "Jew, get off the pavement." It is clear that Babel's relation
with his father defined his relation to his Jewishness. Benya Krik, the
greatest of the gangsters, he who was called King, was a Jew of Odessa,
but he did not wear glasses and he did not have autumn in his heart—it is
in writing about Benya that Babel uses the phrase that sets so far apart the
intellectual and the man of action. The exploration of Benya's preemi-
nence among gangsters does indeed take account of his personal
endowment—Benya was a "lion," a "tiger," a "cat"; he "could spend the
night with a Russian woman and satisfy her." But what really made his
fate was his having had Mendel Krik, the drayman, for his father. "What
does such a father think about? He thinks about drinking a good glass of
vodka, of smashing somebody in the face, of his horses—and nothing
more. You want to live and he makes you die twenty times a day. What
would you have done in Benya Krik's place? You would have done nothing.
But he did something." But Babel's father did not think about vodka, and

smashing somebody in the face, and horses; he thought about large and serious things, among them respectability and fame. He was a shopkeeper,
not well to do, a serious man, a failure. The sons of such men have much
to prove, much to test themselves for, and, if they are Jewish, their Jewishness is ineluctably involved in the test.

Babel, in the brief autobiographical sketch to which I have referred,
speaks with bitterness of the terrible discipline of his Jewish education.
He thought of the Talmud Torah as a prison shutting him off from all
desirable life, from reality itself. One of the stories he tells—conceivably
the incident was invented to stand for his feelings about his Jewish
schooling—is about his father's having fallen prey to the Messianic delu-
sion which beset the Jewish families of Odessa, the belief that any one of
them might produce a prodigy of the violin, a little genius who could be
sent to be processed by Professor Auer in Petersburg, who would play before
crowned heads in a velvet suit, and support his family in honor and comfort. Such miracles had occurred in Odessa, whence had come Elman,
Zimbalist, Gabrilowitsch, and Heifetz. Babel's father hoped for wealth,
but he would have foregone wealth if he could have been sure, at a minimum, of fame. Being small, the young Babel at fourteen might pass for
eight and a prodigy. In point of fact, Babel had not even talent, and certainly no vocation. He was repelled by the idea of becoming a musical
"dwarf," one of the "big-headed freckled children with necks as thin as
flower stalks and an epileptic flush on their cheeks." This was a Jewish
fate and he fled from it, escaping to the port and the beaches of Odessa.
Here he tried to learn to swim and could not: "the hydrophobia of my
ancestors—Spanish rabbis and Frankfurt money-changers—dragged me
to the bottom." But a kindly proofreader, an elderly man who loved nature
and children, took pity on him. "How d'you mean, the water won't hold
you? Why shouldn't it hold you?"—his specific gravity was no different
from anybody else's—and the good Yefim Nikitich Smolich taught him to
swim. "I came to love that man," Babel says in one of the very few of his
sentences over which no slightest irony plays, "with the love that only a
boy suffering from hysteria and headaches can feel for a real man."

The story is called "Awakening," and it commemorates the boy's first
effort of creation. It is to Nikitich that he shows the tragedy he has composed and it is the old man who observes that the boy has talent but no
knowledge of nature and undertakes to teach him how to tell one tree or
one plant from another. This ignorance of the natural world—Babel refers
to it again in his autobiographical sketch—was a Jewish handicap to be
overcome. It was not an extravagance of Jewish self-consciousness that led
him to make the generalization—Maurice Samuel remarks in *The World of
Sholom Aleichem*[1] that in the Yiddish vocabulary of the Jews of eastern Europe
there are but two flower names (rose, violet) and no names for wild birds.

When it was possible to do so, Babel left his family and Odessa to live
the precarious life, especially precarious for a Jew, of a Russian artist and
intellectual. He went to Kiev and then, in 1915, he ventured to St. Petersburg without a residence certificate. He was twenty-one. He lived in a cellar
on Pushkin Street, and wrote stories which were everywhere refused until

1. Maurice Samuel, *The World of Sholom Aleichem* (New York: Knopf, 1943).

Gorky took him up and in 1916 published in his magazine two of Babel's stories. To Gorky, Babel said, he was indebted for everything. But Gorky became of the opinion that Babel's first stories were successful only by accident; he advised the young man to abandon the career of literature and to go "among the people." Babel served in the Tsar's army on the Rumanian front; after the Revolution he was for a time a member of the Cheka; he went on grain-collecting expeditions in 1918; he fought with the northern army against Yudenich. In 1920 he was with Budyonny in Poland, twenty-six years old, having seen much, having endured much, yet demanding initiation, submitting himself to the test.

The test, it is important to note, is not that of courage. Babel's affinity with Stephen Crane and Hemingway is close in many respects, of which not the least important is his feeling for his boyhood and for the drama of the boy's initiation into manhood. But the question that Babel puts to himself is not that which means so much to the two American writers; he does not ask whether he will be able to meet danger with honor. This he seems to know he can do. Rather, the test is of his power of direct and immediate, and violent, action—not whether he can endure being killed but whether he can endure killing. In the story "After the Battle" a Cossack comrade is enraged against him not because, in the recent engagement, he had hung back, but because he had ridden with an unloaded revolver. The story ends with the narrator imploring fate to "grant me the simplest of proficiencies—the ability to kill my fellowmen."

The necessity for submitting to the test is very deeply rooted in Babel's psychic life. This becomes readily apparent when we read the whole of Babel's canon and perceive the manifest connection between certain of the incidents of *Red Cavalry* and those of the stories of the Odessa boyhood. In the story "My First Goose" the newcomer to the brigade is snubbed by the brilliant Cossack commander because he is a man with spectacles on his nose, an intellectual. "Not a life for the brainy type here," says the quartermaster, who carries his trunk to his billet. "But you go and mess up a lady, and a good lady too, and you'll have the boys patting you on the back." The five new comrades in the billet make it quite clear that he is an outsider and unwanted; they begin at once to bully and haze him. Yet by one action he overcomes their hostility to him and his spectacles. He asks the old landlady for food and she puts him off; whereupon he kills the woman's goose in a particularly brutal manner, and, picking it up on the point of a sword, thrusts it at the woman and orders her to cook it. Now the crisis is passed; the price of community has been paid. The group of five reforms itself to become a group of six. All is decent and composed in the conduct of the men. There is a general political discussion, then sleep. "We slept, all six of us, beneath a wooden roof that let in the stars, warming one another, our legs intermingled. I dreamed: and in my dreams I saw women. But my heart, stained with bloodshed, grated and brimmed over." We inevitably read this story in the light of Babel's two connected stories of the 1905 pogrom, "The Story of My Dovecote" and "First Love," recalling the scene in which the crippled cigarette vendor, whom all the children loved, crushes the boy's newly bought and long-desired pigeon and flings it in his face. Later the pigeon's blood and entrails are washed from the boy's cheek by the young Russian woman who is sheltering the Babel family and whom the boy adores. It is after her caress that the boy sees his father on his knees before the Cossack captain; the story ends with his capitulation to nervous illness. And now again a bird has been brutally killed, now again the killing is linked with sexuality, but now it is not his bird but another's, now he is not passive but active.

Yet no amount of understanding of the psychological genesis of the act of killing the goose makes it easy for us to judge it as anything more than a very ugly brutality. It is not easy for us—and it is not easy for Babel. Not easy, but we must make the effort to comprehend that for Babel it is not violence in itself that is at issue in his relation to the Cossacks, but something else, some quality with which violence does indeed go along, but which is not in itself merely violent. This quality, whatever it is to be called, is of the greatest importance in Babel's conception of himself as an intellectual and an artist, in his conception of himself as a Jew.

It is, after all, not violence and brutality that make the Cossacks what they are. This is not the first violence and brutality that Babel has known— when it comes to violence and brutality a Western reader can scarcely have, unless he sets himself to acquire it, an adequate idea of their place in the life of Eastern Europe. The impulse to violence, as we have learned, seems indigenous in all mankind, but among certain groups the impulse is far more freely licensed than among others. Americans are aware and ashamed of the actuality or potentiality of violence in their own culture, but it is nothing to that of the East of Europe; the people for whom the mass impalings and the knout are part of their memory of the exercise of authority over them have their own appropriate ways of expressing their rage. As compared with what the knife, or the homemade pike, or the boot, can do, the revolver is an instrument of delicate amenity and tender mercy—this, indeed, is the point of one of Babel's stories. Godfrey Blunden's description of the method of execution used by the Ukrainian peasant bands is scarcely to be read. Nor is it only in combat that the tradition of ferocious violence appears, as is suggested by the long Russian concern with wifebeating as a national problem.

The point I would make is that the Cossacks were not exceptional for their violence. It was not their violence in itself that evoked Tolstoy's admiration. Nor is it what fascinated Babel. Rather he is drawn by what the violence goes along with, the boldness, the passionateness, the simplicity, and directness—and the grace. Thus the story "My First Goose" opens with a description of the masculine charm of the brigade commander Savitsky. His male grace is celebrated in a shower of epithet—we hear of the "beauty of his giant's body," of the decorated chest "cleaving the hut as a standard cleaves the sky," of "the iron and flower of that youthfulness," of his long legs, which were "like girls sheathed to the neck in shining riding boots." Only the openness of the admiration and envy— which constitutes, also, a qualifying irony—keeps the description from seeming sexually perverse. It is remarkably not perverse; it is as "healthy" as a boy's love of his hero of the moment. And Savitsky's grace is a real thing. Babel is not ready to destroy it by any of the means that are so ready to the hand of the intellectual confronted by this kind of power and charm; he does not diminish the glory he perceives by confronting it with the pathos of human creatures less physically glorious, having more, or a higher, moral appeal because they are weaker and because they suffer. The possibility of this grace is part of what Babel saw in the Cossacks.

It is much the same thing that D. H. Lawrence was drawn by in his imagination or archaic cultures and personalities and of the ruthlessness, even the cruelty, that attended their grace. It is what Yeats had in mind in his love of "the old disturbed exalted life, the old splendor." It is what even the gentle Forster represents in the brilliant scene in *Where Angels Fear to Tread* in which Gino, the embodiment of male grace, tortures Stephen by twisting his broken arm. This fantasy of personal, animal grace, this glory of conscienceless self-assertion, of sensual freedom, haunts our culture. It speaks to something in us that we fear, and rightly fear, yet it speaks to us.

Babel never for a moment forgets what the actualities of this savage glory are. In the story "The Brigade Commander" he speaks of the triumph of a young man in his first command. Kolesnikov in his moment of victory had the "masterful indifference of a Tartar Khan," and Babel, observing him with genuine pleasure, goes on to say that he was conscious of the training of other famous leaders of horse, and mentions "the captivating Savitsky" and "the headstrong Pavlichenko." The captivating Savitsky we have met. The headstrong Pavlichenko appears in a story of his own; this story is his own account of his peasant origin, of the insults received from his aristocratic landlord, of how when the Revolution came, he had wiped out the insult. "Then I stomped on my master Nikitinsky; trampled on him for an hour or maybe more. And in that time I got to know life through and through. With shooting . . . you only get rid of a chap. Shooting's letting him off, and too damn easy for yourself. With shooting you'll never get at the soul, to where it is in a fellow and how it shows itself. But I don't spare myself, and I've more than once trampled an enemy for over an hour. You see, I want to get to know what life really is." This is all too *raffiné*—we are inclined, I think, to forget Pavlichenko and to be a little revolted by Babel. Let us suppose, however, that he is setting down the truth as he heard it; let us suppose too that he has it in mind not to spare himself—-this is part, and a terrible part, of the actuality of the Cossack directness and immediacy, this is what goes along with the grace and charm.[2]

In our effort to understand Babel's complex involvement with the Cossack ethos we must be aware of the powerful and obsessive significance that violence has for the intellectual. Violence is, of course, the contradiction of the intellectual's characteristic enterprise of rationality. Yet at the same time it is the very image of that enterprise. This may seem a strange thing to say. Since Plato we have set violence and reason against each other in reciprocal negation. Yet it is Plato who can tell us why there is affinity between violence and the intellectual life. In the most famous of the Platonic myths, the men of the Cave are seated facing the interior wall of the Cave, and they are chained by their necks so that it is impossible for them to turn their heads. They can face in but one direction, they can see nothing but the shadows that are cast on the wall by the fire behind them. A man comes to them who has somehow freed himself and gone into the world outside the Cave. He brings them news of the light of the sun; he

---

2. The celebration of the Cossack ethos gave no satisfaction to General Budyonny, who, when some of Babel's *Red Cavalry* stories appeared in a magazine before their publication in a volume, attacked Babel furiously, and with a large display of literary pretentiousness, for the cultural corruption and political ignorance which, he claimed, the stories displayed. Budyonny conceived the stories to constitute a slander on the Cossacks.

tells them that there are things to be seen which are real, that what they
see on the wall is but shadows. Plato says that the men chained in the
Cave will not believe this news. They will insist that it is not possible, that
the shadows are the only reality. But suppose they do believe the news!
Then how violent they will become against their chains as they struggle to
free themselves so that they may perceive what they believe is there to be
perceived. They will think of violence as part of their bitter effort to know
what is real. To grasp, to seize—to apprehend, as we say—reality from out
of the deep, dark cave of the mind—this is indeed a very violent action.

The artist in our time is perhaps more overtly concerned with the apprehension of reality than the philosopher is, and the image of violence
seems often an appropriate way of representing the nature of his creation.
"The language of poetry naturally falls in with the language of power,"
says Hazlitt in his lecture on *Coriolanus* and goes on to speak in several
brilliant passages of "the logic of the imagination and the passions" which
makes them partisan with representations of proud strength. Hazlitt carries his generalization beyond the warrant of literary fact, yet all that he
says is pertinent to Babel, who almost always speaks of art in the language
of force. The unexpectedness which he takes to be the essence of art is
that of a surprise attack. He speaks of the maneuvers of prose, of "the
army of words . . . the army in which all kinds of weapons may be brought
into play." In one of his most remarkable stories, "Di Grasso," he describes
the performance of a banal play given by an Italian troupe in Odessa; all is
dreariness until in the third act the hero sees his betrothed in conversation with the villainous seducer, and, leaping miraculously, with the power
of levitation of a Nijinsky or a panther, he soars across the stage, falls
upon the villain and tears out his enemy's throat with his teeth. This leap
makes the fortune of the Italian company with the exigent Odessa audience; this leap, we are given to understand, is art. And as the story continues, Babel is explicit—if also ironic—in what he demonstrates of the
moral effect that may be produced by this virtuosity and power, of what it
implies of human pride and freedom.

The spectacles on his nose were for Babel of the first importance in his
conception of himself. He was a man to whom the perception of the world
outside the cave came late and had to be apprehended, by strength and
speed, against the parental or cultural interdiction, the Jewish interdiction;
it was as if every beautiful violent phrase that was to spring upon reality
was a protest against his childhood. The violence of the Revolution, its sudden leap, was cognate with this feral passion for perception—to an artist
the Revolution might well have seemed the rending not only of the social
but of the perceptual chains, those that held men's gaze upon the shadows
on the wall; it may have seemed the rush of men from the darkness of the
cave into the light of reality. Something of this is suggested in a finely-
wrought story "Line and Color"—like other stories of the time of Babel's
sojourn in France in the early thirties, written in French—in which Kerensky is represented as defending his myopia, refusing to wear glasses, because, as he argues very charmingly, there is so much that myopia protects
him from seeing, and imagination and benign illusion are thus given a
larger license. But at a great meeting in the first days of the Revolution he
cannot perceive the disposition of the crowd and the story ends with Trotsky coming to the rostrum and saying in his implacable voice, "Comrades!"

But when we have followed Babel into the depths of his experience of violence, when we have imagined something of what it meant in his psychic life and in the developing conception of his art, we must be no less aware of his experience of the principle that stands opposed to the Cossack principle.

We can scarcely fail to see that when in the stories of *Red Cavalry* Babel submits the ethos of the intellectual to the criticism of the Cossack ethos, he intends a criticism of his own ethos not merely as an intellectual but as a Jew. It is always as an intellectual, never as a Jew, that he is denounced by his Cossack comrades, but we know that he has either suppressed, for political reasons, the denunciations of him as a Jew that were actually made, or, if none were actually made, that he has in his heart supposed that they were made. These criticisms of the Jewish ethos, as he embodies it, Babel believes to have no small weight. When he implores fate to grant him the simplest of proficiencies, the ability to kill his fellowman, we are likely to take this as nothing but an irony, and as an ironic assertion of the superiority of his moral instincts. But it is only in part an irony. There comes a moment when he should kill a fellowman. In "The Death of Dolgushov," a comrade lies propped against a tree; he cannot be moved, inevitably he must die, for his entrails are hanging out; he must be left behind and he asks for a bullet in his head so that the Poles will not "play their dirty tricks" on him. It is the narrator whom he asks for the coup de grâce, but the narrator flees and sends a friend, who, when he has done what had to be done, turns on the "sensitive" man in a fury of rage and disgust: "You bastards in spectacles have about as much pity for us as a cat has for a mouse." Or again, the narrator has incurred the enmity of a comrade through no actual fault—no moral fault—of his own, merely through having been assigned a mount that the other man passionately loved, and riding it badly so that it developed saddle galls. Now the horse has been returned, but the man does not forgive him, and the narrator asks a superior officer to compound the quarrel. He is rebuffed. "You're trying to live without enemies," he is told. "That's all you think about—not having enemies." It comes at us with momentous force. This time we are not misled into supposing that Babel intends irony and a covert praise of his pacific soul; we know that in this epiphany of his refusal to accept enmity he means to speak adversely of himself in his Jewish character.

But his Jewish character is not the same as the Jewish character of the Jews of Poland. To these Jews he comes with all the presuppositions of an acculturated Jew of Russia, which were not much different from the suppositions of an acculturated Jew of Germany. He is repelled by the conditions of their life; he sees them as physically uncouth and warped; many of them seem to him to move "monkey-fashion." Sometimes he affects a wondering alienation from them, as when he speaks of "the occult crockery that the Jews use only once a year at Eastertime." His complexity and irony being what they are, the Jews of Poland are made to justify the rejection of the Jews among whom he was reared and the wealthy assimilated Jews of Petersburg. "The image of the stout and jovial Jews of the South, bubbling like cheap wine, takes shape in my memory, in sharp contrast to the bitter scorn inherent in these long bony backs, these tragic yellow beards." Yet the Jews of Poland are more than a stick with which Babel beats his own Jewish past. They come to exist for him as a spiritual fact of consummate value.

Almost in the degree that Babel is concerned with violence in the stories of *Red Cavalry*, he is concerned with spirituality. It is not only Jewish spirituality that draws him. A considerable number of the stories have to do with churches, and although they do indeed often express the anticlerical feeling expectable in the revolutionary circumstances, the play of Babel's irony permits him to respond in a positive way to the aura of religion. "The breath of an invisible order of things," he says in one story, "glimmers beneath the crumbling ruin of the priest's house, and its soothing seduction unmanned me." He is captivated by the ecclesiastical painter Pan Apolek, he who created ecclesiastical scandals by using the publicans and sinners of the little towns as the models for his saints and virgins. Yet it is chiefly the Jews who speak to him of the life beyond violence, and even Pan Apolek's "heretical and intoxicating brush" had achieved its masterpiece in his Christ of the Berestechko church, "the most extraordinary image of God I had ever seen in my life," a curly-headed Jew, a bearded figure in a Polish greatcoat of orange, barefooted with torn and bleeding mouth, running from an angry mob with a hand raised to ward off a blow.

Hazlitt, in the passage to which I have referred, speaking of "the logic of the imagination and the passions," says that we are naturally drawn to the representation of what is strong and proud and feral. Actually that is not so: we are, rather, drawn to the representation of what is real. It was reality that Babel found in the Jews of the Polish provinces. "In these passionate, anguish-chiseled features there is no fat, no warm pulsing of blood. The Jews of Volhynia and Galicia move jerkily, in an uncontrolled and uncouth way; but their capacity for suffering is full of a somber greatness, and their unvoiced contempt for the Polish gentry unbounded."

Here was the counterimage to the captivating Savitsky, the image of the denial of the pride of the glory of the flesh to which, early or late, every artist comes, to which he cannot come in full sincerity unless he can also make full affirmation of the glory. Here too is the image of art that is counter to Di Grasso's leap, to the language in arms—the image of the artist's suffering, patience, uncouthness and scorn.

If Babel's experience with the Cossacks may be understood as having reference to the boy's relation to his father, his experience of the Jews of Poland has, we cannot but feel, a maternal reference. To the one Babel responds as a boy, to the other as a child. In the story "Gedali," he speaks with open sentimentality of his melancholy on the eve of Sabbaths—"On those evenings my child's heart was rocked like a little ship upon enchanted waves. O the rotted Talmuds of my childhood! O the dense melancholy of memories." And when he has found a Jew, it is one who speaks to him in this fashion: "All is mortal. Only the mother is destined to immortality. And when the mother is no longer living, she leaves a memory which none yet has dared to sully. The memory of the mother nourishes in us a compassion that is like the ocean, and the measureless ocean feeds the rivers that dissect the universe."

He has sought Gedali in his gutted curiosity-shop ("Where was your kindly shade that evening, Dickens?") to ask for "a Jewish glass of tea, and a little of that pensioned-off God in a glass of tea." He does not, that evening, get what he asks for; what he does get is a discourse on revolution, on the impossibility of a revolution made in blood, on the International that is never to be realized, the International of the good.

It was no doubt the easier for Babel to respond to the spiritual life of the Jews of Poland because it was a life coming to its end and having about it the terrible strong pathos of its death. He makes no pretense that it could ever claim him for its own. But it established itself in his heart as an image, beside the image of the other life that also could not claim him, the Cossack life. The opposition of these two images made his art—but it was not a dialectic that his Russia could permit.

EFRAIM SICHER

Midrash and History: A Key to the Babelesque Imagination[†]

The use of myth in Babel's fiction gives an illusion of the epic while mocking it and reads both unorthodox interpretations and essential truths into history. For Babel, the myths of history and religion were a subtle and ironical medium for allegorical parallels, as well as allusions to a moral message. This is an essentially midrashic approach to history, following the ancient Jewish storytelling tradition that imaginatively elaborates on biblical and historical narrative, usually for exegetic or homiletic purposes, and playfully draws on intertextual, verbal, and semantic associations. Often new, contemporary meaning is introduced into the reading of familiar stories, or biblical verses are given unexpected levels of figural meaning that dramatizes biblical figures as human.

Babel draws on biblical references and, indeed, on the gamut of Jewish and Christian culture not only in symbolic imagery, but also in the plot construction of *Red Cavalry*. We may find a key to Babel's view of history in the art of the Polish painter in *Red Cavalry*. Apolek is himself an instance of the introduction of myth. Like the French avant-garde poet Apollinaire, Apolek is christened Apollinarius, which identifies him with the muse Apollo, god of poetry and music, representative, in direct opposition to Dionysus, of the intellect and of civilization. Apollo has a confused history in Greek mythology, but out of his many functions it is as Apollo Smintheus that Apolek is recognized: Apolek wanders the earth with two white mice tucked behind his shirt, although here they are a Babelian epithet for the archetypal victim. Apolek lacks his classical forebear's lyre, but he does have the blind musician Gottfried to play to him. The prototype of the blind musician who plays Heidelberg songs can be traced back to Windermeier, the blind musician from Tubingen in The Concert in Katerinenstadt" (1918),[1] and it is in Western Europe, to whose influence Babel, as an Odessa Jew, was naturally predisposed, that we must seek clues to Babel's hagiography of *Pan* Apolek.

In the diary Babel wrote while on the Polish-Soviet front in 1920, which served as raw material for the later *Red Cavalry* stories, there is no

† From *The Slavonic and East European Review* 60, no. 4 (October 1982), © 1982 by the University of London. Reprinted by permission of the author. This version has been slightly revised and abridged for this Norton Critical Edition.
1. *TCB*, p. 543.

mention of a Polish painter, but in the ruins of Catholic churches and in the home of the priest Tuzinkiewicz, with its ancient tomes and Latin manuscripts, Babel stumbles upon the Catholic mystery, which provides him, a Jew from Orthodox Russia, with a startling revelation. The narrator first comes across the art of *Pan* Apolek in the story "*Pan* Apolek." In his exposition to the story, the narrator takes vows to the aesthetic ideal of Apolek's art, a "gospel that had remained hidden from the world," and writes with hindsight that the saintly life of *Pan* Apolek "went to his head like old wine": it later transpires that Apolek is a drunken heretic. The invented aesthetic model of the Polish painter expresses in characteristically visual imagery Babel's concept of art and history. It is an ideal, moreover, that awakens a sense of destiny and a sense of his own failings in the mind of the alienated Jewish intellectual torn between his roots in his doomed ancestral past and the Revolution. It is an ideal that juxtaposes the real and the ideal. The narrator chats to Apolek about the romantic past of the Polish gentry and about Luca della Robbia, the fifteenth-century sculptor who created a spiritual beauty in his church art, but the treatise on Apolek's artistic ideal ends with the narrator returning to the gruesome reality of his plundered Jews; the story concludes with his loneliness, homelessness, and impossible idealism:

> По городу слонялась бездомная луна. И я шел с нею вместе, отогревая в себе неисполнимые мечты и нестройные песни.

> [The vagrant moon trailed through the town and I tagged along, nurturing within me unfulfillable dreams and dissonant songs.[2]]

The first of Apolek's chefs-d'oeuvre to be exhibited is his portrait of St John. This is evidently a portrait of Saint John the Baptist, for his head lies on a clay dish after his execution, but at the same time it is of Saint John the Apostle-Evangelist, for out of the mouth issues a snake, a reference to the legend in which a snake saved John the Apostle's life by extracting the venom from a poisoned chalice. The dead Saint John's face seems familiar to the narrator, and he has a presentiment of the truth: the severed head is drawn from *Pan* Romuald. *Pan* Romuald, we recall, was the treacherous viper of "The Church in Novograd", the runaway priest's assistant who was later shot as a spy. His venomous character is introduced in that story by the image of his cassock snaking its way through the dusk and his soul is merciless, like a cat's. Incidentally, the association of Romuald with the serpent and the cat makes him both the natural and mythological enemy of Apollo the mouse-god and slayer of the python. The monkish eunuch Romuald, as in the ascetic yet decadent theology of the established church (in which he would have become a bishop had he not been shot as a spy), stands in direct contrast to the aesthetic and doctrinal heresy of Apolek. *Pan* Robacki, who pours anathema on the heretical painter in "*Pan* Apolek," is also likened to a cat, and his "gray ears" help to equate him with the "gray old men with bony ears" in "The Church in Novograd," all senile attributes of a dead world opposed to the life-giving, joyful art of Apolek.

2. For the Russian passage, see Isaac Beicl, *Detstvo i drugie nasskazy*, comp., ed., annot., E. Sicher (Jerusalem: Biblioteka Aliya 1979), p. 120; for the English translation, see this NCE, p. 102.

The narrator finds himself halfway toward solving the riddle of Apolek's iconography when he spots the Madonna hanging over the bed of *Pani Eliza*, the priest's housekeeper, for it is she who is portrayed as a rosy-cheeked Mary. Apolek first came to Novograd-Volynsk thirty years before, as the narrator relates in his apocryphal rendering of the coming of this questionably holy fool, who sparked a long and bitter war with the established church. Like Michelangelo in the Sistine Chapel, Apolek climbs along the walls of the Novograd church and paints into his frescoes a psychological, though ahistorical, truth. The lame convert Janek is depicted as Paul, who was disabled with blindness in the story of his conversion (Acts 9:1–19). The scene of the stoning of the adulteress (compare John 8:3–11) is referred to as the stoning of Mary Magdelene, appropriately depicted as the Jewish prostitute Elka, for all three are fallen women. Apolek's heresy is to elevate ordinary folk into mythical heroes with the haloes of saints, while bringing divine, supernatural myths down to the level of comprehension of mortals. In the same way that Renaissance painters flattered their patrons, Apolek wins a smile and a glass of cognac from the old priest who recognizes himself among the Magi, and he peoples the homes of the local population with peasant Josephs and Marys. For an extra ten złoty, their enemy can be depicted as Judas Iscariot. Apolek even offers to paint the narrator as Saint Francis of Assisi, with a dove or a goldfinch on his sleeve, an ironical reference to the horse's head insignia on the sleeve of the narrator's Red Cavalry uniform.

Apolek realizes in ordinary folk with all their human vices their potential for spirituality and epic deeds. Above all, Apolek brings out the aesthetic beauty of human flesh, which he colors like a "tropical garden." Lush and sensuous, Apolek's paintings beatify mundane existence as if mythical, while the mythical is revitalized to reveal hidden truths. Apolek's scenes of the nativity resemble Babel's impressions of the religious paintings of Rembrandt, Murillo, and the Italian masters, which he saw in a Polish church in Beresteczko. The hint at the pre-Christian and pagan origins of the Church in the "Chinese carved rosary," which the Novograd priest holds as he blesses the infant Jesus in Apolek's painting, is also clear in the description in Babel's diary entry for August 7, 1920:

великолепная итальянская живопись, розовые патеры, качающие младенца Христа, великолепный темный Христос, Рембрандт, Мадонна под Мурильо, а может быть Мурильо, и главное—эти святые упитанные иезуиты, фигурка китайская жуткая за покрывалом, в малиновом кунтуше, бородатый еврейчик, лавочка, сломанная рака, фигура святого Валента. Служитель трепещет, как птица, корчится; мешает русскую речь с польской, мне нельзя прикоснуться, рыдает. Зверье, они пришли, чтобы грабить, это так ясно, разрушаются старые боги.

[Magnificent Italian art, pink *Paters* rocking the infant Jesus, a magnificent mysterious Christ, Rembrandt, a Madonna after Murillo or perhaps a real Murillo, and the main thing is these pious, well-fed Jesuits, a weird Chinese figurine behind the veil, (Jesus is) a bearded little Jew in a crimson-colored cloak, a bench, the shattered shrine, the figure of Saint Valentine. The beadle, shivering like a bird, cowers, mixes up his Russian with Polish, I mustn't touch, he sobs. The beasts, they came to ransack. It's very clear, the old gods are being destroyed. (translation revised)]

The scene of the ransacking of a church, from which this extract is taken, is transformed into the desecration by the Cossacks in "At Saint Valentine's." This transformation tells us much about Babel's recognition of the power of myth to make supernatural or historical events relevant to the present day, an aesthetic concept that the author places at the center of the art of that mythical myth-maker, *Pan* Apolek, and that is modeled on the masters of the Renaissance. The result is an unexpected historical perspective in which the historical is seen as real and the real as legendary.

This brings us into the realm of *midrash*, the homiletic rereading and supranarration of Jewish history and lore. In *Red Cavalry*, Jewish legends of the desecration of the Temple are made appropriate to the persecution of East European Jewish communities in 1919–1920. For example, the Babylonian Talmud (Gittin 56b) relates how Titus entered the Temple and committed an obscenity on the Scroll of the Law. Then he drew a sword and pierced the curtain in front of the Holy of Holies in the middle of the Temple. By a miracle blood oozed out and he started to shout that he had killed the God of the Jews. (There is another version of this tale in the midrashic compilation *Vayikra raba* 20, 5.) In Babel's "At Saint Valentine's," the curtain falls away to reveal Jesus, a bleeding, suffering, persecuted Polish *shtetl* Jew, who frightens a Cossack soldier in the Polish-Soviet war whose comrades and ancestors have persecuted so many Jewish communities. In an excised passage, the Cossacks commit an obscenity with the brigade nurse Sashka in this holy place against the background of a further destruction of the Jewish community.

Apolek's reweaving of the Gospel stories, like Babel's imagery, transposes the sacred and the profane, rendering the supernatural grotesquely earthy and the everyday almost superhuman. As the fence and cemetery watchman Witold declares in Apolek's defense to the church dignitary investigating the local outbreak of blasphemy, Apolek's art conveys to the sinful, ignorant masses the sort of truth Jesus told, which was as unpalatable to the authorities then as now. And is there not more truth, he asks, in Apolek's paintings, which ennoble the spectator, who is also depicted as participating in them, than in the angry and condescending words of the clergy? Italian prelates and Polish priests, it would seem, are not at all out of place in nativity scenes set in the Renaissance, painted in the 1890s and viewed by the narrator in 1920 when the Roman Catholic Church was being sacked by Slav hordes.

The messianic theme is related to the Revolution and the Civil War not only through the device of Apolek's paintings. One Sabbath eve at the Zhitomir rebbe's ("The Rabbi"), the narrator sees in the rebbe's son an unrecognized herald of the Messiah in a violent apocalypse. This Elijah (Ilya) profanes the Sabbath by smoking, he has the "emaciated face of a nun" and the "forehead of Spinoza"—that other Jewish heretic—and the Hasidim around him are likened to "fishermen and apostles." Like the boy-narrator in Babel's Childhood stories and like the Jewish intellectual narrator of the *Red Cavalry* stories, Ilya has tried to escape from the traditional Jewish home and ancestral past—he is described as a recaptured "runaway prisoner." Later, in "The Rabbi's Son," he renounces his mother (reminding us of Matthew 12:46–50) in the name of a new messianic ideology, the Revolution. Ilya dies, sexually impotent, and while the narrator, his ancient Jewish memory stirred, identifies with his spiritual brother, it is clear that the synthesis of Jewish values (Song of Songs, Maimonides, and phylacteries) with revolutionary ideals (communist leaflets, Lenin, and revolver cartridges) remains an impossible dream.

There is evidence in Babel's 1920 diary and in the drafts of the *Red Cavalry* that he wished to build the messianic theme into the framework of *Red Cavalry* and that he intended historical and religious myths to convey a topical message. In the draft "Smert' Trunova" ("The Death of Trunov") there is explicit mention of the coming days of the Messiah:"И я поверил бы в воскресенье Ильи, если бы не аэроплан, коротый заплывал и т.д." ["And I would have believed in the resurrection of Elijah, if it had not been for the airplane which was winging its way, etc."] But in the story "Squadron Commander Trunov," the Elijah whose name is shouted by the quarreling Jews is Elijah the Vilna Gaon (1720–1797), the antagonist of the Hasidim: the Jews argue over old sectarian differences as if there were no war or Revolution. Further evidence for the messianic theme is found in a projected story, "Demidovka," which refers several times to Jeremiah and was based on an incident in a *shtetl* on the Fast of the Ninth of Av, when Jews mourn the anniversary of the destruction of the Temple and read Jeremiah's lament over the fall of Jerusalem. As Babel recorded in his diary, the Cossacks forced the local Jews to cook food for them on the eve of the fast, which happened to be a Sabbath, when all work is prohibited. Everything was as in the days of the destruction of the Temple, Babel wrote, and elsewhere he speaks of the "same old story," when time and again he witnesses the pillaging and torture of the long-suffering Jewish population at the hands of Poles and Cossacks. For example, the diary entry for July 18, 1920 specifies the point-for-point repetition of history in a description of a Jewish cemetery that has seen Khmelnitsky and now Budyonny, a parallel important for understanding the subtext of "The Cemetery in Kozin."

As if to sharpen the historical analogy still further, the Cossacks marching into Beresteczko in *Red Cavalry* pass the watchtower of the hetman Bogdan Khmelnitsky, responsible for massacring many Jewish communities, where he was routed by the Poles in 1651. An old man crawls out of the Cossack burial mounds to sing of past glories. In the tradition of Khmelnitsky, the first act of the Cossacks on entering the town is to murder a Jew. The irony is that the Cossacks marching past the memorials of their epic past are greeted by silence and shuttered windows. The Jewish quarter of Beresteczko "reeks in anticipation of a new era." The town's ex-masters are a lunatic countess and her impotent son. A fragment of a letter in French, a fragment of the past dated 1820, one hundred years before the incursion of the Bolsheviks and the arrival of the narrator, recalls the Napoleonic Wars and Napoleon's death. As the narrator reads the letter, apparently from a mother to a husband long departed for war— a letter that epitomizes the Raciborskis and the dying Polish nobility—a revolutionary council is being elected below the old Polish château. The historical parallel between the Napoleonic and Revolutionary wars, between the dying Polish nobility's romantic past and its degenerate heirs, also involves a stylistic contrast and leads to an ironic story ending: power is supposedly being handed over to a bewildered petty bourgeoisie and to plundered Jews.

Allusion to historical and religious myths and specifically to the apocalyptic motif can be seen too in the viewpoint of the alienated Jewish intellectual. The sun has set over the traditional Jewish past from which he is trying to break out, but he is instinctively drawn to his roots and childhood memories, to Gedali's Dickensian Curiosity Shop with its Winchester dated 1810. Gedali (Gedaliah in Hebrew) is the name of the governor of Judaea after the destruction of the First Temple (586 B.C.E.), whose assassination signaled the end of Jewish sovereignty (see Jeremiah 41). Nor can we miss the messianic allusion in the anomaly that the Zhitomir rebbe, Motale, is named Bratslavsky and called "last rebbe of the Czernobyl dynasty." This presages the apostasy and death of his son. Yet the Czernobyl dynasty belonged to the Twersky, not the Bratslav, sect of Hasidism, and the Bratslav rebbe, Nakhman, had left no male heir at his death in 1810 (the date engraved on Gedali's Winchester, as if time had not moved forward for East European Jews). Bratslav may be considered the most messianic of Hasidic sects, and it is surely significant that the fictional son of a long-dead rebbe should be known as Elijah. Anti-Semitism has throughout Jewish history reawakened messianic expectations based on the writings of the Hebrew prophets, as may be witnessed by the following for the false messiah, Shabtai Tsvi, in the wake of the 1648 Khmelnitsky massacres, and, true to the paradigm of Jewish lamentation literature, the scenes of despair and devastation in *Red Cavalry* are accompanied by a hope, albeit disappointed, for future justice and salvation.

In "Crossing the River Zbrucz," the opening *Red Cavalry* story, the crossing of the river suggests a road on the way to a red Calvary under apocalyptic portents in the blood-red sky. A drowning soldier defames the Virgin Mary. The fording of the river takes place amid nocturnal chaos and death. The Zbrucz may be interpreted as a symbolic boundary that relates the crossing to the Exodus from Egypt, with all the overtones of redemption in the Passover story, evoked by the smashed Passover crockery, representing fragments of the narrator's Jewish past that he encounters on entering the home of the pregnant Jewess. If the first half of the story is permeated by violation of nature (emphasized by the monastic and virginal image of the buckwheat) and death in nature, then the second part introduces the idea of unborn life and future deliverance out of death and destruction, an idea embodied in the Jewish mother-to-be. Moreover, her plea for compassion at the end of the story is echoed by the prayer for justice and respite from death for the Jewish victims of persecution that closes "The Cemetery in Kozin."

Karl-Yankel, in the Odessa story of that name, is another ambivalent symbol of salvation, the firstborn who heralds an era of justice. But the hope that the unfortunate baby, named after the Marxist and Biblical patriarchs Karl Marx and Jacob (Yankel in Yiddish), will benefit from the struggle over its fate is fraught with ironies. Such ironies fill Babel's stories. Benya Krik, the gangster in "How Things Were Done in Odessa," is proclaimed "King" by Arye-Leyb, an eloquent Aaron speaking on behalf of a lisping Moses. Arye-Leyb speaks out of a burning bush on Mount Sinai (the mountain of divine revelation and the giving of the law) after Benya has spoken from "on high" at the funeral of Joseph Muginshteyn, a strange kind of Sermon on a Mount in which he declares Joseph to be a scapegoat (in a further mix of biblical allusions) for the whole working-class. This is, of course, a perverse irony, as is Benya's earlier complaint that God made a mistake in settling the Jews in Russia, where they were tormented worse than in hell, for he is mostly concerned with buying off his guilt for Joseph's death during the gangsters' raid on the premises of Reuben Tartakovsky.

Nevertheless, as we are reminded in the play *Sunset* (1928), Benya is Bentsion, the "son of Zion." Benya's *coup* in the Krik household puts an end to the injustices of Mendel's reign of terror and reinstates the natural order of cyclical changeover from father to son. The allegory of King David's love for Batsheva in Scene Seven is instructive, for Mendel wishes to cheat his sons of their inheritance by running off to Bessarabia with Marusya, but they seize the throne in their father's old age (compare 2 Samuel 11:1–26 and 1 Kings 1:1–40). The repeated references to sunset and the coming of the Sabbath reinforce the idea that historical change is cyclical and that no force can halt the setting of the sun. In the stage directions, sunset coincides with the beating of Mendel, and later Benya speaks of making the Sabbath a Sabbath. In the play's concluding speech, the local rabbi, Ben-Zkharya, warns that Joshua the prophet (compare Joshua 10:12–15 and Midrash Kohelet 111, 114) and Jesus of Nazareth (a reference to Luke 23:44–55, omitted in all but the first edition of the play) were mistaken in thinking that they could alter the natural, divinely ordained course of events by symbolically stopping the sun:

День есть день, евреи, и вечер есть вечер. День затопляет нас потом трудов наших, но вечер держит наготове веера своей божественной прохлады. Иисус Навин, остановивший солнце, всего только сумасброд. Иисус из Назарета, укравший солнце, был злой безумец. И вот Мендель Крик, прихожанин нашей синагоги, оказался не умнее Иисуса Навина. Всю жизнь хотел он жариться на солнцепеке, всю жизнь хотел он стоять на том месте, где его застал полдень. Но Бог имеет городовых на каждой улице, и Мендель Крик имел сынов в своем доме. Городовые приходят и делают порядок. День есть день, и вечер есть вечер. Все в порядке, евреи. Выпьем рюмку водки! (Babel, *Zakat* 95-6)

[Day is day, Jews, and evening is evening. Day crushes us with the sweat of our labors, but evening holds in readiness the fan of its divine coolness. Joshua the Prophet, who stopped the sun, was a bit crazy. Jesus of Nazareth, who stole the sun, was an evil madman. And here is Mendel Krik, a member of our synagogue, who has turned out to be no cleverer than Joshua the Prophet. All his life he wanted to bask in the heat of the sun, all his life he wanted to stand where the midday sun stood. But God has policemen on every street and Mendel Krik had sons in his house. Policemen come and make order. Day is day, and evening is evening. Everything is in order, Jews. Let's drink a glass of vodka! (translation revised)][3]

Among several possible interpretations of *Sunset*, the allegorical sunset of traditional Jewish society in Russia is one that fits the historical situation of 1913, but seen from a non-Marxist and anachronistic view of 1928. Benya does not fulfill any mission as a savior and, while the sun literally salutes the zenith of his power in "How Things were done in Odessa," his role as king of the gangsters is something of a comic parody. In the 1927 movie script *Benya Krik*, Babel shows him being shot by the Reds during the civil war, as was Misha Yaponchik in real life after he defended Odessa's Jews from the Whites and offered his services to the Bolsheviks. Only in the later play *Maria* (1933, published 1935 but repressed while in rehearsal), which contains clear marianic motifs as well as quotations from the Gospels, is there a portrayal of the new, nascent social order. The final curtain falls in *Maria* on a scene somewhat reminiscent of Kuzma Petrov-Vodkin's painting *1918 in Petrograd*, in which a proletarian Madonna figure is portrayed against the background of the socialist city. Here, the worker Safonov's pregnant wife admires the apartment of General Mukovnin's family, which is now their home, while the enormous Nyushka, bathed in sunlight, cleans the windows; Elena is about to give birth in the new maternity hospital in a former palace, but she is not confident she will deliver a healthy child. The play ends on a mixed note of hope and uncertainty about the future.

In *Red Cavalry*, the red dawn of the promised Bolshevik utopia fails to brighten the horizon and Ilya Bratslavsky lacks sufficient artillery to bring a messiah to the apocalyptic confrontation between Bolshevik Russia and Catholic Poland. By contrast with the semen-oozing seductive crucifixes of the established Church, described in "The Church in Novograd," the portrayal of Jesus presents a rather un-messianic, earthly figure. Apolek's, or rather Babel's, Jesus is as aesthetically sensual and human as the virginal theology of the "winking madonnas" is ascetic and inhuman.

Apolek's parable of Jesus and Deborah, in the *Red Cavalry* story "Pan Apolek," may have some basis in popular folklore or the rich Jewish tradition of stories denigrating Jesus, such as the fourteenth-century *Toldot Yeshu* (in which Joseph sires Jesus when he disguises himself as Mary's bridegroom Yokhanan), but it certainly demonstrates Babel's love of the apocryphal. Apolek not only demythicizes Jesus but rewrites the Gospels, relating that the wedding night of the Israelite virgin Deborah ended in tears of shame when she took fright at her approaching bridegroom and vomited. Jesus takes pity on her by dressing in the clothes of her bridegroom, just as it is Jesus who sends the angel Alfred to Arina in "The Sin of Jesus" (1922). "The Sin of Jesus" is a hilarious tale of the drunken lust of a Russian peasant woman who crushes the angel Alfred in her inebriated sleep and then refuses to forgive Jesus for her life of incessant sex and pregnancy; it seems to derive from a tale by Boccacio about a monk who disguises himself as the angel Gabriel and visits a Venetian merchant's wife, though in the end he is discovered. The all-embracing love of Jesus in Apolek's parable is explicitly a union of the flesh. Lying in holy adultery

3. For the Russian, see Isaac Babel, *Zakat* (Moscow: "Krug," 1928); for the English, see p. 305 in this volume.

Kuzma Sergeevich Petrov-Vodkin, *1918 in Petrograd* (Tretyakov Gallery, Moscow), Russia / Giraudon / The Bridgeman Art Library.

with Deborah, Jesus proves his compassion more just than the law. Deborah is Hebrew for a bee, and Babel clearly means this to refer to the "bee of sorrow" that stings Jesus:

> Смертельная испарина выступила на его теле, и пчела скорби укусила его в сердце.

> [His body was drenched with mortal sweat, for the bee of sorrow had stung his heart.

Stricken by postcoital remorse, Jesus leaves unnoticed to join John in the desert.

The bee may represent here the deadliness of human passion, and we may compare the bestial desire of Dvoyra (the Yiddish form of Deborah), who drags off her bridegroom at the end of "The King", looking at him like a cat holding a mouse. The bee also figures prominently in Afonka Bida's parable of the crucifixion in "The Road to Brody." There the bee, by extension of the Christian virtue of industriousness essentially a proletarian creature, refuses to sting Jesus on the cross out of class solidarity, for Jesus came from a carpenter's family.

The propensity for suffering and compassion are the attributes of Jesus that are brought out in the syphilitic shepherd Sashka Konyayev, whose meekness earns him the nickname "The Christ." It is by explicitly sexual compassion and an earthy acceptance of sin that Sashka, like Jesus in Apolek's parable, becomes himself something of a Jesus figure. His stepfather Tarakanych is a carpenter, like Mary's husband Joseph. Sashka begs his stepfather to be allowed to become a shepherd, because "all the saints" were shepherds, but Tarakanych mocks the idea of a saint with syphilis. That night Sashka has a vision from heaven in which he sees himself in a rosewood cradle hanging from the sky on two silver cords. A syphilitic Russian peasant, he too has aspirations to be supernaturally born. There is, however, an unstated irony in Sashka's exchange of his mother's sexual purity for permission to join the shepherds.

Babel's use of biblical and mythical sources is, to say the least, unorthodox, and his mixture of Jewish and Christian sources is as irrelevant as Chagall's nativity scenes, but then, as a non-believing Jew, he was not interested in allegorical interpretations of the role of the Christian savior, such as in Blok's *The Twelve,* although the background of Marxist and religious messianism in pre-Revolutionary and Revolutionary Russia is surely relevant. Babel's retelling of myth aimed to convey the contemporary mores of the Cossack and Russian masses. Matvey Pavlichenko in his saintly *zhizneopisaniye* (biography—that is, his hagiography) in *Red Cavalry* differs from his patron saint (compare Matthew 5:38–39) in not being able to turn the other cheek. His cheek burns with personal as well as revolutionary vengeance, and in retribution he tramples his former master to death.

Myth and mystification throw serious scholars into confusion because Babel disregards the niceties of geographical and historical accuracy, not to mention ideologically acceptable historicity. Instead, the inventive fantasy of imagination vividly visualizes inner truths and historical parallels in much the same way that the boy-narrator of the childhood story "In the Basement" transforms the dull, unpoetic details of a book about the life of Spinoza into a dramatic account of old Amsterdam, ending with a fantastic scene of the heretic's relentless, lonely death-struggle while Rubens (anachronistically!) stands by his bed taking a deathmask. Just as the lies of the "untruthful little boy" expose hidden truths about his grandfather, so too Babel's playful use of historical and religious myths poeticizes the narrator's view of actuality and thereby affords a novel interpretation of the contemporary meaning of legendary or supernatural events. In the transformation of myth several key devices of Babel's poetics are deployed, such as parallelism or juxtaposition of the real and the ideal, the sacred and the profane, the divine and the earthly. The lurid rich colors that stream from *Pan* Apolek's palette are Babel's own, and in the author's taste for the heretical and the apocryphal may be sensed his belief in the potential of ordinary mortals for the epic and the spiritual. The Roman Catholic churches in *Red Cavalry* are as unredeemably doomed as the Jewish *shtetl,* yet despite the aesthetic revelations they offer, the disoriented Jewish intellectual does not feel for them the nostalgia and sympathy evoked by the Jewish areas he visits. It is, however, *Pan* Apolek who offers a version of Babel's own aesthetics, suggesting, as Babel declared in his speech at the First Congress of Soviet Writers in 1934, that art must emphasize the unexpected, surprising the reader with a renewed perception of life.

Often, it must be said, Babel needs myth for no more than a playful irony. In the scene of the Adoration of the Magi in the Odessa story "Lyubka the Cossack," for example, three guests arrive from strange lands and present exotic gifts to the Jewish mother—traditionally one of the wise gentiles is dark-skinned, although in this case he is a Malay, not an Ethiopian—and, as the three sailors dance, an orange star speeds across the sky, looking down on them (compare Matthew 2:9–12). These are not, however, gifts for a holy infant, but contraband Lyubka is purchasing. If the baby apparently lacks an earthly father, then this only emphasizes Lyubka's masculinity. She is, after all, a failed mother. The sleight of hand performed by Tsudechkis is, in a way, a "miracle," as perhaps implied by the Jewish dealer's name (after the Polish *cud*, miracle). But if there is any allusion to the christological myth it is as an ambiguous hope for the new breed of Jews represented by the firstborn Davidka and Karl-Yankel, born into the aftermath of the pogroms and on the eve of a new era.

The historical parallels in Babel's stories are not without ironic paradoxes, but these in no way detract from the author's more serious intent. An illustration of the structural function of historical myth is the narrator's apostrophe in "The Church in Novograd":

> Нищие орды катятся на твои древние города, о Польша, песнь об единении всех холопов гремит над ними, и горе тебе. Речь Посполитая, горе тебе, князь Радзивилп, и тебе, князь Сапега, вставшие на час! . . . (Babel, *Detstvo* 104)
>
> [Hordes of beggars are converging on your ancient towns, O Poland! The song of all the enslaved is thundering above them, and woe unto you, Rzeczpospolita polska, woe unto you, Prince Radziwiłł, and you, Prince Sapieha, who have risen to rule but for an hour! translation revised)]

Prince Janusz Radziwiłł (1880–1939/40), head of the Polish Conservatives, and Prince Eustachy Sapieha (1881–1963), Polish Foreign Minister, are continuing, as it were, their ancestors' ancient conflict with Muscovy as part of Pilsudski's plan to resurrect the Poland of the eighteenth century. (Lew Sapieha, 1557–1633, planned to include Muscovy in the Polish-Lithuanian Commonwealth, and Janusz Radziwiłł, 1612–1655, sent punitive expeditions against Khmelnitsky, the legendary forebear of Budyonny.)

Such perceptive and sophisticated use (or creation) of historical myth calls up the historical background without need for an ideologically risky elaboration, as in "Crossing the River Zbrucz," where the Red soldiers march along the "ever-memorable highway from Brest to Warsaw built on the bones of peasants by Nicholas I." Novograd, taken by Soviet troops in this story, is situated on the Słucz, not the Zbruch, a hundred miles to the southwest, and fell on June 27, 1920, at which time the rear guard could not have been strung out along the Brest-Warsaw road. What Babel wishes to convey, however, in the succinctness of his fiction is the symbolic nature, historically and artistically, of the crossing of the Zbrucz, which signaled the reversal of the Polish invasion of the Ukraine, as well as stressing the personal significance of the narrator's entry into Poland, with its East European Jewish population and Western heritage, and into the world of the First Red Cavalry. The army of Cossacks and peasants, treading the path of destiny of tsarist serfs along the road built by them, form part of the Bolshevik advance through Brest in the direction of Warsaw—the goal on the way to international revolution, which was, of course, never reached. To speak of building a road on peasants' bones is to visualize a historical memory of tsarist serfdom, but also to prepare for the symbolic crossing of a Styx by blaspheming peasants and Cossacks who are supposedly liberating the world in a travesty of the Exodus story, fording the passage from the promised land of socialism into the land of bondage. At the same time, the story sets up an intertextual connection with a very different parallel in Russian history, the triumphant Russian victory over Napoleon, in K. N. Batyushkov's uncompleted "Perekhod russkikh voisk cherez Neman 1 yanvarya 1813 goda" ("The Crossing of the Nieman by Russian Forces on January 1, 1813," published 1830). In this neoclassic description of the young tsar Alexander I and his elderly general, Kutuzov, surveying the troops at the beginning of the campaign to repulse Napoleon from the Russian empire, the sky is indeed dark and the light over the corpses somber, but the outcome is very different from the Russian repulsion of the Poles from the Ukraine and the invasion of Poland in *Red Cavalry*. The irony in Babel's reversal of this poetic *topos* can be seen if we compare Batyushkov's "Perekhod cherez Rein" ("The Crossing of the Rhine," published 1817), which celebrates the crossing into Western Europe of Russian troops, following the Roman legions, covered with glory and honor:

> Меж тем как воины вдоль идут по полям,
> завидя вдалеке твои, о, Рейн, волны,
>   Мой конь, веселья полный,
> От строя отделясь, стремится к берегам . . .
> (Batiushkov, *Sochineniya*, 158–59)

> [Meanwhile as the warriors go through the fields,
> Catching a distant glimpse of your waves, Oh Rhine,
>   My horse, filled with merriment . . .
> Leaves the formation and rushes to your shores. . . .
> (my translation)]

The closing scene, with the shouts and curses falling silent, contrasts sharply with the shouted obscenity and chaos of the army crossing the Zbrucz, described as a violation of the virginal pastoral landscape. The highway that Nicholas I used to check the abortive insurrection by Poles in 1830 is an ironic reminder of absolutist tyranny, for it is now being used to bring questionable liberation from tsarist repression. It suggests a reversal of the propaganda slogans about an international revolution and subtly points to the failure of the Polish campaign.

The play on historical and religious myth was to become muted in Babel's prose of the late twenties and thirties, and it is absent from the fragment that has survived of the novella *Yevreyka* ("The Jewess," begun around 1927), which draws a poignant picture of the final demise of the Jewish *shtetl* and the move of a Jewish Red Army officer's family to Moscow. Similarly, Babel drew on his colorful metaphors and sensuous imagery more sparsely and thus more devastatingly in his search for a new style and form after the mid-twenties. He nevertheless remained aware of the aesthetic power of myth as demonstrated in his midrashic interpretation of history.

WORKS CITED

Бабель, Исаак. *Закат*. Москва: Артель писателей «Круг», 1928.

Бабель, Исаак. *Детство и другие рассказы*. Подгот. текста и комментарии Э. Зихера. Иерусалим: Библиотека Алия, 1979.

Батюшков, К.Н. *Сочинения*. Редакция и комментарии Д.Д. Благого. Москва, 1934.

GREGORY FREIDIN

The Other Babel

"A vicious night" is how Babel opened his story "Chink," datelined "Petrograd 1918." Barely three pages long in the original, it drew on Babel's minimalist central casting: a prostitute, combining business and affection; her aristocratic hanger-on, an emblem of the old civilization compromised by trade; and a Chinese worker, a stranger, and the prostitute's customer, with just enough pigeon Russian to conclude the exchange. With the vividness of an expressionist painting, Babel shows just how merciless that night was:

> Slashing wind. A dead man's fingers pluck at the frozen entrails of Petersburg. The crimson pharmacies on street corners freeze over. A pharmacist's prim head lolls to the side. The frost grips the pharmacy by its purple heart. And the pharmacy's heart dies.
> The Nevsky Prospekt is empty. Ink vials shatter in the sky. It is two in the morning. The end. . . .[1]

Fifteen years later, as he surveyed his life in art, Babel adopted this setting for his play *Maria*. What meaning did this gesture hold for the celebrated author of the colorful *Odessa Stories* and *Red Cavalry*, who had once claimed the title of Russian "literature's messiah from the sun-drenched steppes by the sea?"[2]

*   *   *

The second and third years of the civil war in the former imperial capital were the harshest, coldest, and most brutal. The metropolis, as Evgeny Zamyatin saw it in his Petrograd stories, was lapsing into the ice age, each apartment morphing into a cave and each resident into a savage cave dweller. As hostilities unfolded in 1918 the Bolsheviks abolished all forms of private commerce and much of the money economy, installing in its place a centralized system that they could totally control. Before long life in the communist utopia was reduced to its bare minimum, and even that could hardly be supported by the starvation rations of the civil war. The black market ballooned, crime proliferated, the streets emptied of traffic. Petrograd—an abandoned capital since 1918, when the new government moved to Moscow—was sinking into a state of nature.

In the winter, giant snowdrifts covered the city and people either froze or starved to death. And then, in the words of one contemporary, came something worse than hunger: the city's plumbing froze. Soon, as Victor Shklovsky intrepidly recorded in his *Sentimental Journey*, all the surfaces of the former capital, even roofs, were covered in human excrement. In the spring, side streets of the dying city became overgrown with weeds, and on the scarcely traveled Nevsky Prospekt young grass broke through the cobblestones.

---

1. "Khodya" (Chink, 1923), p. 38.
2. "Odessa," p. 21, was published in December 1916, soon after Babel's debut in *Letopis* (see also his "Autobiografiya" and "Nachalo" in *Sochineniya*).

The poet Osip Mandelstam considered this a sign of true modernity, the dawning of a "world without man." Nature was reclaiming this western-most outpost of the Eurasian colossus. "Humanism collapsed," averred Russia's premier poet Alexander Blok with approval, and its passing was now making way for the return of the "younger barbarian masses"—the new guardians of "true culture." Whether it was because of the "younger barbarian masses," or members of Russia's disproportionately small edu-cated elite, or, closer to the truth, various combinations of both, life was losing, in the parlance of the day, all the pretenses of civilization. What mattered were the instincts, the will, and the wits of the men and women inhabiting the subarctic Hobbesean world. As a writer, who "must know everything,"[3] Babel was in his element—a witness to the primordial jungle breaking through the cracks in the carapace of modernity. For him, still in Odessa in December 1917 and aspiring, as he put it, "to conquer Peters-burg," *being there* was a matter of life and death, both literally and figura-tively. His story "The Road" (1932) conveys this sense exquisitely. Before long, he came, he saw, he conquered—even if it took him seven more years to realize his dream.

As late as 1922, Babel planned a collection of his pieces under the title *Petersburg 1918*, but he abandoned this project in favor of *Red Cavalry* and *The Odessa Stories*. These two cycles, which defined Babel for the rest of his life, were written between 1921 and 1926—an ironic celebration of Rabelaisian humanity and its life of abandon. They were read as a victory of the sunny south over the gloomy St. Petersburg, as much its northern cast as its style and outlook. *Petersburg* retreated, making way for the dawn of a new age. But the victory did not last.

Already in 1926, the Petersburg tradition—Pushkin's *Bronze Horseman*, the late stories of Nikolay Gogol, and practically the entire corpus of Dostoevsky—had crept back and taken hold of Babel's imagination. Ilya Ehrenburg remembered Babel confessing to him a few years later that he now preferred Gogol's "Overcoat," an archetypal Petersburg tale, to the vis-ceral exuberance of Gogol's earlier Ukrainian cycles. Despite Babel's vows to exorcise it with sunshine ("Odessa"), despite the exuberance of his Jew-ish gangsters or the equestrian brio of his Red Cossacks, *Petersburg* now haunted Babel with its familiar settings and memories of his experience in the early days of the civil war. The city of Dostoevsky, Zamyatin, and Blok returned as a vehicle for Babel's self-expression, and to account for it, we must look at the interplay of life, history, and art at the heart of Babel's writing.

* * *

As with many of Babel's works, *Maria* has powerful autobiographical over-tones, including echoes of his most famous adventure during the Polish offensive of April–October 1920. But the background to the play's setting proper must be traced to Babel's sojourn in St. Petersburg (Petrograd) from early February or March 1918 to the winter of 1918–19 when he resided at Nevsky 86.[4] A good half of *Maria*'s action takes place at that

3. See "At Grandmother's" in this Norton Critical Edition, p. 343.
4. Nevsky Prospekt was then renamed Prospekt dvadtsat pyatogo Oktyabrya (October 25 Avenue) in honor of the date of the October Revolution, according to the old-style Julian calendar.

particular venue, one of the grand Yusupov palaces transformed into a seedy residential hotel. This insignificant detail was recorded by Victor Shklovsky in one of the earliest and sharpest critical appreciations of Babel's writings—the 1924 essay "Isaac Babel: A Critical Romance."[5] Apparently, the address mattered to Babel a lot, and it is referred to repeatedly throughout the play. Babel made sure that whatever his *Maria* was meant to convey, it sent a distinct autobiographical message, one that his close friends would understand and that readers in posterity would be able to decode. Grasped in this way, the play emerges as an autobiographical statement.

*   *   *

During his residency at Nevsky 86, Babel combined, as he claimed rather dubiously, a career as a translator for the Petrograd Cheka with that of a staff writer for the journal *Novaya zhizn* (New Life), contributing pieces about the everyday life of the dying city. The All-Russia Extraordinary Commission for the Struggle against Counter-Revolution and Sabotage (Cheka) was decreed on December 20, 1917. By the time Babel allegedly commenced his career there (no earlier than February 1918),[6] it was already much feared, although it had not yet become as infamous as it would in response to the assassination of its Petrograd chief, Moisey Uritsky, and the unsuccessful attempt at Lenin's life in August 1918.

By contrast, *Novaya zhizn,* edited by Babel's loyal patron and literary godfather, Maxim Gorky, maintained—despite its self-identification as "Social-Democratic"—a clear anti-Bolshevik stance. Babel's first story in it appeared on March 9, 1918, and his last in the July 2 issue, right before the journal was shut down by authorities unwilling to tolerate even this relatively loyal opposition to its policies. Soon afterwards, Babel traveled to the Volga region with a food-provisioning detachment. After returning to Petrograd in October, he continued to publish his pieces in another Petrograd journal, *Zhizn iskusstva* (Life of Art). He stayed in Petrograd through the winter 1919 before leaving for Odessa sometime after April of that year.[7]

*   *   *

As much as *Maria* draws on Babel's experience in and his writings about civil war Petrograd and the Polish front, it is propelled by Babel's sense of his works and days in the late 1920s and early 1930s. Many have written about Babel's difficulties with the Soviet cultural and political establishment and its pressures to conform to the party line in the arts and the civil war mythology being constructed by Budyonny, Voroshilov, and Stalin. Yet however much Babel chafed from Soviet censorship and political correctness, made worse by Budyonny's attacks on him, he was also subject to stresses of a different sort. His personal life was becoming increasingly complicated and now demanded great logistical ingenuity as well as substantial amounts of cash. From 1925 to 1932, Babel had to maintain his

5. See p. 463 of this Norton Critical Edition.
6. On the questions surrounding Babel's alleged service in the Cheka, see note 23, p. 55.
7. The Petrograd period of Babel's life, 1918–19, is recalled in Viktor Shklovsky, *A Sentimental Journey* (1923) and his essay in this volume (p. 463).

commitments to his mother and sister, who settled in Brussels; closer to home, in Moscow and Leningrad, he had to support, appease, mollify, and somehow manage his tempestuous relationship with Tamara Kashirina, who was simultaneously his friend, lover, and the mother of his first child, Mikhail (born in 1926); he had to remain loyal, despite his infidelity, to his wife, Evgeniya, who left for Paris in 1925, whom he rejoined there in 1927–28, and who bore him his daughter Nathalie in 1929; and as of summer 1932, he had to juggle, in addition, a budding romance with Antonina Pirozhkova, who bore him his last child, daughter Lydia, early in 1937.

Additional pressures came from unrealistic and unrealized commitments to publishers and film studios, as well as the complicated financial schemes he resorted to in order to discharge his financial obligations—real or imagined—to his mother in Brussels, Kashirina and their son in Moscow, and his wife and daughter in Paris. Perhaps no other Soviet author equaled Babel in the art of generating advances on unwritten stories, novels, plays, and film scripts. But sooner or later the time came to pay up, and for Babel, with his literary perfectionism and the compulsion to take months to polish a single story, the weight of these obligations was intolerable, sometimes crushing. Seen in this light, his passion for horses and the racing world offered, if not escape, then relief from the pressures of "economic rationality," his life as a literary moneymaking machine.

Indeed, there was not one but two Isaac Babels. One was a writer, a bohemian who romanced Russian women (Babel's two significant "other women" were not Jewish), who was bound to nothing but his Muse, and who needed to live the life of a vagabond à la Gorky, all in order to gather material and gain inspiration for his writings. The other was a responsible if grossly overtaxed *pater familias*, husband, father, son, and lover, with ideas about constancy and loyalty that were rather old-fashioned for his times and that he, to his chagrin, often failed to live by. This other Babel had to calculate and plan ahead, to meet deadlines and to sign binding contracts. In short, he had to be a proper bourgeois Jew. (For Babel, as for many of his coreligionists, there was a natural affinity between these two terms, as there was for Karl Marx and Babel's contemporaries Georg Simmel and Werner Sombart.)[8] For this "rationalized" Babel, his literary gift, the only possible form of divine grace in the secular age, was nothing but a métier, a trade, a way of maintaining his family, his status, and—in this order—of paying his bills. This shuttling between the world of responsibility and the world of spontaneity makes more comprehensible the inner conflict tearing at Babel's personal and professional life and, by extension, the polarities of the play *Maria*.

Allegories of the inner conflict between these two Babels were already visible in his first known play, *Sunset* (1927),[9] about the struggle between

---

8. See, for example, Karl Marx, "On the Jewish Question" (1844). In Babel's own time, Marx's position became the foundation for a popular sociological study by Werner Sombart, *Jews and Economic Life* (*Die Juden und das Wirtschaftsleben*, 1911), which Babel no doubt studied at the Kiev Commercial Institute. A similar position is expressed in Georg Simmel's famous essay "Stranger" ("Exkurs über den Fremden," 1908). Both Sombart and Simmel were well-known in Russian in the 1910s.

9. See p. 276 of this Norton Critical Edition.

Babel's two alter egos: one was the old teamster Mendel Krik, scheming to run away with his young Russian consort, Marusya, and to take with him the family cashbox; the other was his gangster son, Benya Krik, bent on bourgeois propriety and anxious to turn the old-fashioned horse-and-cart outfit into a modern, rationally run concern. This Benya Krik had all of his transendant *joie de vivre* leeched out of him by a passion for respectability and cash. Babel was *sunsetting* his larger-than-life Odessa—the site, as he now saw it, of his lost illusions. *Sunset* celebrated the victory of "economic rationality" over the life of exuberant violence and indefatigable romance—qualities that aesthetically redeemed a petty-bourgeois Jewish identity.

In *Sunset* this message may have been blurred by the gaudiness of its setting, its association with *The Odessa Stories,* and the pungency of its Odessa humor. Now, in *Maria,* Babel made sure that the picture would come out monochromatic and perfectly sharp. For the author of *The Odessa Stories* and *Red Cavalry,* this play, set in the merciless world of civil-war Petrograd, was a scream, albeit muted, of disenchantment and loss.

* * *

Babel began to cultivate this somber mood in the early 1930s by going back to his Petrograd days in several autobiographical stories. The first among them to be published, "The Road" (based on the 1922 "An Evening with the Empress"), is a miniature fictional memoir about Babel's arrival in Petrograd in 1918. Set first in the harsh landscape of provincial Russia and then in the winter desolation of revolutionary Petrograd, "The Road" compares the arrival of the aspiring author, exhausted and freezing to death in the former imperial capital, with the legend of a medieval Jewish poet crushed by the hooves of an Arab cavalry before he could reach his desired Zion. The analogy with Budyonny's attacks on Babel, accompanied evidently by threats of physical violence against the author of *Red Cavalry,* is here hidden in plain view. Budyonny's renewed attack on Babel and Gorky, published in *Pravda* in October 1928, when Gorky was becoming a state cult figure in the Soviet Union, had to have the highest sanction, namely that of Stalin himself. (It would have been like Stalin first to unleash Budyonny and then come to the defense of his friend Gorky, creating a good impression and indebting Gorky to himself.)[1] Babel understood this machinery and had every reason to be concerned, if not yet for his life then for his future as a writer in Soviet Russia.[2]

In "The Road," to drive home the point about his sense of danger, Babel draws another oblique analogy—between himself and the life story of the Danish princess Dagmar. Like the story's narrator, she too had come from afar and, in Simmel's striking phrase, was a "stranger who came yesterday and stayed tomorrow." She sailed from her cozy Copenhagen to the unforgiving city of Peter to become the wife of Alexander III,

---

1. See Babel's story about Stalin and *Red Cavalry* in Erwin Sinko's memoirs in this Norton Critical Edition, p. 450.
2. See Kornei Chukovsky's diary entry for May 2, 1953, on p. 424 in this volume.

Empress of Russia Maria Fedorovna, the mother of Russia's next and, as it turned out, last tsar. She lived long enough to learn that her issue, her "birthing blood," as Babel referred to the royal family, "fell on the merciless granite of St. Petersburg." The story was meant for publication in Stalin's Russia, and for obvious reasons Babel chose not to spell out the horrors of the murder of the royal family, but any reader his age or older would have picked up the clue at once. Hounded by Budyonny, pressed by his editors, and threatened with evisceration by the censors, the clever Babel was still able to wonder in his published story whether his "children"—his literary legacy—were destined to share the fate of Maria Fedorovna's murdered offspring. Yes, the story ends nicely. Babel's alter ego finds employment—no, not as a reporter for Gorky's *New Life*—but as a translator for the Cheka, where he receives an advance: a uniform, boots, food rations, and life-long friends (in that order). This obviously tacked-on ending, along with the loud silence about his work for Gorky's *Novaya Zhizn*, serves to amplify the story's two tragic analogies that Babel drew to his own increasingly dangerous career as a Soviet author—a stranger who had come from afar, and stayed.

In the second story of this *Petersburg* cycle, "The *Ivan and Maria*" (based on "The Concert at Katerinenstadt," 1918), Babel recalls his encounter with a larger-than-life Russian character who seems to have stepped out of Gorky's catalogue of provincial eccentrics (the steamboat cook Smury from *My Apprenticeship*[3] comes to mind). In the story, Babel travels with a food-procurement expedition consisting of a team of cripples (compare with the smugglers in *Maria*) to a German colony in the Volga region. There he meets a remarkable steamboat captain who ferried ammunition for Red Army detachments. This captain, with his exuberant and expansive Russian personality, is on a superhuman drinking binge, and uses up the boat's fuel for a dangerous nighttime run to procure more liquor. He succeeds but ends up with his brains splattering the wheels of a peasant cart, shot by a Red commander for wasting precious army fuel. Having set the sun on his own high-spirited Jewish bandit Benya Krik, Babel was now drawing the curtain on Gorky's odd and colorful Russian characters.

The final story of the cycle, "Guy de Maupassant" (1932), is set in the Petrograd winter of 1916. A budding author is hired to help an amateur translator of Maupassant—a rich young Jewess married to a financial magnate—to edit her translations for publication.[4] The regular editorial sessions of the two over Maupassant's volumes culminate one night in what readings of this sort have often culminated in, at least since Paolo and Francesca. In the dead of winter, the two admirers of Maupassant become intoxicated by the lusty sunshine of his story "L'aveu." United in their passion for literature and aided by a good, very good, wine from the husband's cellars, the translator and the editor collapse into each other's arms.

"L'aveu" is a story about a simple peasant girl's regular trips to market, for which she dutifully pays her garrulous coachman until one day he

---

3. The second book (1918) of Gorky's autobiographical trilogy.
4. This job was very similar to Babel's main moonlighting trade, doctoring scripts and rewriting dialogue for talkies throughout the 1930s.

allows her to keep her fare in exchange for a little sex. More trips lead to more savings until she gets pregnant, disgraced, and ruined for life. Quite the opposite, it seems, happens to Babel's autobiographical narrator: he receives good money for his editorial magic and on top of that gets to make love, magically without consequences, to an attractive married woman. But as Babel's story draws to an end, we learn that the merciless sun of "L'aveu"—associated, for Babel, with the Odessa sunshine of his own career as a writer—exacted its toll on the commercially and in every other way successful French author. Having made many lucrative trips to the literary marketplace, and many yachts and houses later, Maupassant dies at the end of Babel's story a raving syphilitic. "I felt touched by a premonition of being initiated into a mystery," Babel concludes the story, hiding in the cryptic phrase the simple truth of Maupassant's tale, one that he now understood only too well: for a writer, as for anyone else, there is no free ride. Sooner or later, one is called to account.

Other stories written and published around the same time, even though unconnected to St. Petersburg, sound a similar note. "Karl-Yankel" (1931) is a thinly veiled story of Babel's bereavement over the loss of his son, who had been adopted by Kashirina's new husband, the writer Vsevolod Ivanov. As Kashirina confirmed in her memoirs, the son Mikhail was forbidden by Ivanov to have any contact with his father. The story came out in July 1931, the month of Babel's and Mikhail's birthdays (they were born on the same day, thirty-two years apart), and should be read as an ironic farewell to Babel's sole male progeny.

Suffice it to say that the Kirghiz woman in the story who volunteers enthusiastically to nurse the baby Karl-Yankel at her own breast referred the knowing reader to Ivanov's "Dityo" ("Babe," 1921), a story emblematic of the debut of this other protégé and friend of Gorky. As in the case of "The Road," the optimistic ending Babel tacks onto "Karl-Yankel" sounds hollow—too hollow to drown out the absurdities and cruelties of Soviet life that are the subject of the story.

In the 1932 "The End of the Almshouse," the old men feeding off Odessa's Jewish cemetery, who once provided Babel with material for his gangster tales, are forcibly removed to a Soviet retirement home. As the title ironically suggests, neither the old shamus Arye-Leyb, nor by analogy the writer who made a career out of *retelling* his stories, can any longer make a living off the city's past glories and its myths. A similar theme of grudging accommodation and genuine grief over loss sounds in "Froim Grach" (1933), a story, like "The End of the Almshouse," clearly linked to the Odessa cycle but unpublished in Babel's lifetime. In "Froim Grach," Babel returns to the second most exotic figure of his Jewish gangster tales, a giant of a man and the elder of the Odessa bandits, only to have him, unarmed and unsuspecting, *liquidated* in the backyard of the Odessa Cheka. The orders came from an unsentimental officer from Moscow. He had no interest in the mythic figures of Odessa's history or its local color, nor did he think that it was wise for others to be curious about such things.

Red Cavalry too underwent a revision: a 1932 novella, "Argamak," became the final story of the civil war cycle and radically altered the book's trajectory. In "Argamak," the familiar bespectacled narrator, Babel's alter ego Lyutov, comes by chance into possession of a prize steed but, an unskilled rider, causes horrible sores on the animal's back and practically destroys it; worse, he begins to draw to himself the angry stares of Cossacks. Feeling ashamed and tormented by guilt, Lyutov gives up Argamak and gets in return a docile mare which he soon learns to ride well and, at long last, blends in with the Cossacks. The author was trading the Pegasus of his *Red Cavalry* inspiration for a tame mount—all for the sake of passing in Stalin's Russia.

Babel, it seems, was closing his books. It was time for the final tally, and *Maria* may be read as such a summing-up.

* * *

From the very opening of *Maria,* Babel cranks up the tension between his two autobiographical extremes by giving each a street address o its own. Economic rationality, with its Jewish "accent"—Isaac Dimshits—resides at the hotel at Nevsky 86 and traffics in all manner of commodities through his team of grotesque invalids. The all-too-Russian unrealistic, romantic dreaming—General Mukovnin's family—inhabits an old-fashioned apartment on Millionnaya, across the street from the great Hermitage and the Winter Palace. For a biographer of *Isaac* Babel, it is not hard to recognize in *Isaac* Dimshits a distillation of Babel's own authorial persona— a writer who became a commercial success through his stories about all manner of twisted and debased humanity. Babel's 1918 sketch, "The Concert in Katerinenstadt," and his more elaborate 1932 version of it, "The Ivan and Maria," lend support to this reading. He wrote in November 1918,

> Two weeks ago I arrived in Katerinenstadt with unusual people, I arrived with some cripples. We organized them in Petersburg into a food procurement detachment for the cripples and departed in search of bread from the Volga German colonies.[5]

The scheme, though not predatory, was akin to that devised by the character of Isaac Dimshits, who shared with Babel both a first name and a place of residence at Nevsky 86, not to mention the Odessa origins. The similarities do not end there. Dimshits's family situation—his wife and children live elsewhere out of harm's way—and his appetite for Gentile women have striking parallels with Babel's own.

Babel places a Russian noble family, the Mukovnins, and their entourage. Millionnaya street—opposite the Hermitage (the world of high art) and the Winter Palace (the old regime). These are General Mukovnin, his daughters Maria and Luudmila, their cousin Katya Veltsen, the old nanny, and Maria's old lover manqué Prince Golitsyn. Crushed by the Revolution and now in rapid decline, the Mukovnins and their circle nevertheless manage to retain aspects of Dostoevskian spirituality (Golitsyn and Katya), Russian Populist penitence before the people and willingness to collaborate with the Bolsheviks for the sake of the country (the General), cultural refinement (a taste for ballet at the Mariinsky), and book culture

5. I Babel, "The Concert in Katerinenstadt," subtitled "Diary" and published in *Zhizn iskusstva,* November 13, 1918, *The Complete Works of Babel,* p. 543.

and learning (Mukovnin, like his prototype, General Aleksey Ignatyev,[6] is writing a history of the abuses against the lower ranks in the imperial army). Underneath it all is the Mukovnins' fervent desire to survive and fit into the new world.

The two Mukovnin daughters, Luudmila (literally beloved of the people or popular) and Maria, choose different strategies. Babel employs a familiar Greek dichotomy: one, a twentieth-century version of Aphrodite Pandemos (Ludmila), takes the low road and is willing to sell herself to a rich Jew; the other, her heavenly counterpart, Aphrodite Urania (in the Christian vocabulary the Mary of Martha and Mary), prefers the high road and, like Babel, joins Budyonny's Red Cavalry. Allegories proliferate.

Even the Mukovnin family name defines their sociohistorical type— *muki* is Russian for "torment"—and readily recalls the intelligentsia's cult of martyrdom. Appropriately, as it deals with a similar intelligentsia family caught in the Revolution, the Mukovnin name also recalls Aleksey Tolstoy's famous civil war trilogy *Khozhdenie po mukam* (known as *Road to Calvary*). It too revolves around the fate of two sisters, and its first installment, *Sisters* (1921), like Babel's *Maria*, was written abroad. Eventually it proved Tolstoy's loyalty to the new regime when he returned to Soviet Russia from emigration in 1923. The title of Tolstoy's trilogy is borrowed from the tenth-century apocryphal story "Descent of the Mother of God to Hell" and literally means "walking through torments." In the "Descent," Maria Mother of God comforts sinners and pleads successfully before her son to grant them some respite.

In an allegorical allusion to this tale, the entire Mukovnin household is condemned to the living hell of 1920 Petrograd. Their only hope is to be saved by the family's favorite child, Maria, a decent, strong, beautiful woman who incarnates the pure romance of the Revolution. But they wait for her in vain: like Godot or the Messiah, the divine Maria never appears and only sends an emissary with a spare pair of boots—a signal to the family to get packing, whether to go into internal exile or emigration.

Readers in Babel's milieu had no trouble recognizing in the character of Maria a version of Babel's own authorial persona—an old-world intellectual redeemed by the Revolution—an image that Babel assiduously cultivated with the appearance of *Red Cavalry*. Dimshits and Maria, then, define the play's opposite poles, embodying two conflicting and/or complementary aspects of what it meant for Babel to be a writer—a person called upon to combine transcendence with commerce, not dissimilar to Babel's other favorite professional type, the prostitute, who mixed romance and profit. The play was the melancholy meditation of a desperate man. In 1933, approaching forty and still unable to make a choice in his personal life, Babel was haunted by the thought of never repeating his coup of the mid-1920s, when *Red Cavalry* and *The Odessa Stories* brought him to the apex of fortune and fame.

* * *

6. Aleksey Alekseyevich Ignatyev (1877–1954), Russian diplomat and general, took the side of the Soviets after the Revolution and served at the Soviet legation in Paris in 1927–37; the author of *Fifty Years in the Ranks* (Pyatdesyat let v stroyu, 1940, translated as *A Subaltern in Old Russia*, 1944). Babel befriended him in Paris in 1932–33.

Rooted as *Maria* is in Babel's anecdotes of civil war Petrograd,[7] there are indications that Babel may have conceived the play late in 1929, prompted by Vladimir Mayakovsky, in anticipation of the tenth anniversary of Budyonny's First Cavalry Army. If so, he was soon preempted by Vsevolod Vishnevsky, who fulfilled his "social command" by producing the play *The First Cavalry Army* in time for the anniversary and in accordance with the script of Budyonny and his coterie. Babel, however, did not give up on the idea. According to Babel's letter to Solomon Mikhoels, his good friend and the head of the State Jewish Theater, Babel had received an advance on the play, produced some unsatisfactory drafts, and was postponing further work until he could finish a cycle of stories.[8] Another letter (hitherto unpublished), addressed to actor and director Vasily Kuza, the deputy chair of the Vakhtangov Theater Artistic Council, speaks directly of Babel's continued attempts finish the play in January 1932:

> Dear V.V., if I do not arrive at your theater at the end of February with a finished play, then it means nothing has worked out. I simply won't have enough strength to continue working on it any further. Let's give it one last try. Yours, I.B.

Nothing came of it, it seems, until Babel arrived at Gorky's villa in Sorrento in April 1933. There, away from his family and enjoying Gorky's famous hospitality, he wrote the first full draft of *Maria* in the space of two weeks (something similar happened to him with his other play, *Sunset*, in 1926). There Babel's writer's block mysteriously lifted and the play was born.

What ten years earlier Alexey Tolstoy's novel *Sisters* did for that author, *Maria* was to do for Babel, serving as his "return ticket" to Soviet Russia. In September 1932 he had been grudgingly given permission to travel to France for two months, ostensibly in order to collect his wife and daughter and bring them back to the USSR.[9] He had now overstayed his allotted two months by another five, lending credence to the rumors then rife in Moscow that he was planning to settle abroad for good, perhaps in the manner of a "loyal émigré" like Evgeny Zamyatin, who had been granted this dispensation by Stalin himself. Whether or not he entertained such plans seriously, by the time Babel arrived in Sorrento he had decided to go back to the Soviet Union and felt it in his interest to have something new and substantive to show for his overextended stay abroad. His generous host Gorky must have thought so too; he had interceded on Babel's behalf before Kaganovich and Stalin[1] when Babel's request for permission to go to France was being blocked—apparently by Stalin—in the spring and

7. Sergey Povartsov, the eminent Babel scholar, draws a connection between some elements of the plot of *Maria* and one of Babel's 1918 Petrograd sketches, entitled "About a Georgian, Kerensky Rubles, and a General's Daughter (A Modern Tale)," published in Gorky's *Novaya zhizn* 83 (April 21, 1918). S. Povartsov, "Pyesa Babelya *Mariya*: opyt kommentariya," *Uchenye zapiski Moskovskogo oblastnogo pedinstituta* (*Sovetskaya literatura 10*) 265 (1970): 77–87.
8. Babel's letter to Solomon Mikhoels, November 28, 1931, in Isaak Babel, *Sochineniya*, 2 vols. (Moscow, 1990), ed. A. N. Pirozhkova, vol. 1, p. 320.
9. Babel's letter to Kaganovich, June 27, 1932, in Andrey Artizov and Oleg Naumov, comp., *Vlast i khudozhestvennaya intelligentsiya: dokumenty TSK RKP(b)-VKP(b), VChK-OGPU-NKVD o kul'-turnoï politike, 1917–1953 gg.* (Moscow: Mezhdinarody Fond "Demokratiya," 1999), p. 180.
1. See Kaganovich's letter to Stalin on p. 434.

summer 1932. It was only after Stalin's arrival in Moscow at the end of August 1932 that Babel was miraculously waved through. The permission to travel came on September 3, 1933. No doubt Babel and Gorky were aware that the author of the miracle was none other than Stalin himself. Eight months later it was payback time. *Maria* was supposed to, if not cancel his debts, then at least extend his credit.

The biggest outstanding item was Babel's diminished productivity, and a play, especially a successful play, could help chase the wolf away from the door. Another weighty debt was owed to the Red Cavalry Commander Semyon Budyonny. *Maria* was supposed to convey a long overdue conciliatory gesture to his powerful critic as well as his superior, Kliment Voroshilov, Stalin's trusted civil war comrade-in-arms and since 1925, People's Commissar of Defense. Since the end of the civil war, and especially since the ouster of their former nemesis Leon Trotsky in 1927, both were busy concocting their own heroic legend and linking it to Stalin's progressively inflated civil war record. A runaway success at home and abroad, Babel's *Red Cavalry* was a threat to this mythology, as it told the story of one of the biggest fiascos of the war, the Soviet defeat in the Polish campaign, in which Stalin may have played an invidious role when he disobeyed orders to have Budyonny's army link forces with Mikhail Tukhachevsky's outside Warsaw.[1] It is this rout of the Soviet forces that provides the setting for "The Rabbi's Son," the last story of the original *Red Cavalry.* Stalin, Budyonny, and Voroshilov would have crushed Babel despite his international acclaim and would have forced him into emigration had it not been for Gorky's powerful protection. For his part, Babel, who had no interest in joining the fray and even less so in adjudicating military appointments at the highest level, had tried to mend fences before—but never in such an elaborate fashion as he did in *Maria.*

Well-placed veterans of the Polish campaign of 1920 (and there were many) would have easily understood that Maria Mukovnin, the eponymous protagonist of the play, was modeled on Maria Denisova, a famous Odessa beauty and the original inspiration (the "Giaconda") of Mayakovsky's great love epic *Cloud in Pants.*[2] A modern, independent woman with strong leftist convictions and, apparently, a young illegitimate daughter, Denisova studied sculpture and art in Switzerland during World War I until the Swiss expelled her as a political undesirable in 1919. Back in Russia, she joined what was to become Budyonny's First Cavalry Army. Like Babel, she worked for the Army's Political Department, designing posters and conducting political education classes among the ranks during the Polish campaign.

Most important for Babel's rehabilitation scheme, during this time Denisova met and soon afterwards married Efrem Afanasyevich Shchadenko ("Akim Ivanych" in the play). Shchadenko was the Red Cav-

---

1. Robert C. Tucker, *Stalin as Revolutionary, 1879–1929: A Study in History and Personality* (New York: W. W. Norton, 1974), pp. 204–05, and Dmitry Volkogonov, *Stalin: Triumph and Tragedy,* trans. Harold Shukman (Rocklin, Ca.: Prima Publishing, 1996), p. 361.
2. Alexey Tolstoy knew Maria Denisova and apparently interviewed her and used her stories as he was preparing the last edition of his trilogy. Thus Denisova became, along with the Krandievsky sisters, a prototype for the two female heroines in the Tolstoy trilogy. Babel may have further hinted at his affinity with Tolstoy by giving one of his characters the name of Alexey Tolstoy's second wife (1907–14), the avant-garde artist Sofia Isaakovna Dimshits (1889–1963).

alry's number-three man after Voroshilov and Budyonny, and like them he would climb to the highest ranks of the Soviet armed forces, accelerating his career during Stalin's infamous Red Army purge.[4] Although Denisova's marriage was unhappy,[5] she shared her husband's (and Budyonny's) passion for the official myth of the Polish campaign, not as a defeat but as a feat of superhuman heroism, and would have had no trouble recognizing herself in the character of Babel's Maria. The naïve pathos of Maria's description of the Red Cossacks in her letter home contrasts with the stifling atmosphere of the play and served as an olive branch, which Babel was offering—without fawning—to the powerful Red Cavalry trio, along with their patron on high. We can only guess if Babel's conciliatory message reached its intended addressees; perhaps it helped to thin some of the clouds that had been gathering around him in the mid-1930s. Be that as it may, it would be a mistake to see in this "auxiliary function" of the play an artistic compromise.

The romantic pathos of the Polish campaign, muted by its distance from the play's setting, is counterpoint to the play's other dominant motif of helplessness, cynicism, and darkness. These two poles—the detached, naïve pathos and the all-too-palpable despair—account for the play's overall message. Even in the sunny, springtime final scene, there is enough ambivalence to amplify the dark side of this polarity. Thus we shall never know if Elena, the worker's pregnant wife who moves into Mukovnin's luxurious digs, will give birth to a healthy child. Babel has her worried by her "narrow hips," leaving the question mark hanging over the cliché allegory of the Revolution—the new world born of the Russian proletariat. The Cossack ballad being sung by a peasant wench as the curtain falls sounds a dissonant chord, as it tells of misfortune and betrayal.

While the play leaves little doubt about the death of the old world, the last scene asks to be seen as an allegory of a disoriented working class unsure of its future and overshadowed by the "uncivilized" Russian peasantry. Apparently Babel shared Gorky's earlier apprehensions about the fate of the Revolution: the drowning of Russia's minuscule intelligentsia and a small urban working class in the sea of ignorant peasants (e.g., Gorky's 1924 essay "V. I. Lenin"). Pointedly it is not the "narrow-hipped" working-class Elena but the peasant Nyushka, singing in her male "bass voice," who resounds as the concluding chord of *Maria*. Standing in the window, with her skirts tucked up, this giantess dwarfs the Atlantes of the New Hermitage across the street and dominates the final scene of *Maria* with the power and confidence of the famous 1927 sculpture, "Peasant Woman," by Vera Mukhina. In his art, Babel could be subtle, even cryptic, but where he chose to be a true artist, he eschewed compromise.

* * *

4. In 1937, Stalin appointed Shchadenko (1885–1951) Deputy People's Commissar of Defense to head the all-important Personnel Department of the Red Army.
5. As she complained to her friend Vladimir Mayakovsky in the 1920s, Denisova chafed under the traditional housewife role imposed on her by her husband and as a result felt frustrated as an artist. There are indications that in his 1930 play *The Bath House*, Mayakovsky modeled the selfish Soviet bureaucrat Pobedonosikov and his unhappy, suicidal wife, Paula, on Shchadenko and Denisova.

Vera Mukhina. *Peasant Woman.*
1927. Bronze, 2 meters. Tretyakov
Gallery.

Gorky had a mixed reaction to the play's first complete draft. He was not discouraging when Babel recited it to him in Sorrento, but reversed himself after reading the manuscript. He found the play's message "elusive," its action excessively grotesque, some of the dialogue easy fodder for anti-Semitism, and the happy ending artificially tacked on. Clearly, Gorky could not get used to "the other Babel," could not—or did not wish to—understand Babel's "Baudelaire-like passion for spoiled meat," ignored the pointedly autobiographical subtext, and prodded his protégé to revive his erstwhile sunny disposition.[6] He remained indifferent to Babel's formal innovations, in which Chekhovian depth combined with expressionist satire in the manner of Mayakovsky and Brecht, all of it shaped into a new cinematic structure.[7] Gorky wished to see a sunny Babel.

The paradoxes posed by the play destined it to run afoul of the Soviet censor. As Babel admitted in a letter to his mother, *Maria* did not tow the "general line."[8] Yet none of this seemed insurmountable. In 1933–34, with the worst horrors of collectivization receding into the past, the Soviet Union was going through a political and cultural thaw that brought with it an increased tolerance in the cultural sphere. Babel had great hopes for *Maria* as a stage success and, more important, as a work inaugurating a new period in his career: he now felt drawn to the dramatic form as never before. This new creative spurt after a dry spell of some seven years would put an end to the rumors—no doubt noticed by Stalin—that his "silence" was an expression of opposition to the party-state.

Thematically, *Maria* could be seen as a play after the fashions of the late 1920s and early 1930s. Several civil war dramas had been produced enjoying both critical acclaim and box office success. Babel hoped that *Maria*

6. See Gorky's letter to Babel about the play *Maria* on p. 435.
7. Suggested by Carl Weber, who directed the Stanford University production of *Maria* in 2004, the play's premiere in the United States.
8. Letter of May 2, 1933. Nathalie Babel, ed., *Isaac Babel: The Lonely Years, 1925–1939*, p. 232.

508   GREGORY FREIDIN

might do as well.[9] His earlier play *Sunset* premiered in Moscow in his absence and had a mixed reception. This time, he took great care in orchestrating his comeback in order to maximize both visibility, along with income from advances. Parts of the play were published early in 1934 in Moscow and Leningrad. Babel gave public readings at various venues, feeding the excitement and paving the way for what he imagined would be the play's triumph onstage. For a while, everything proceeded according to plan; *Maria* was considered simultaneously by two Moscow companies (the Vakhtangov Theater and the State Jewish Theater, where it was to play in Yiddish) and one in Leningrad.

But on December 1, 1934, the world changed. The assassination of Kirov, the Leningrad Party Secretary and a rising member of the Politburo—the crime of the century, as Robert Conquest put it—abolished the softer rules of the game and signaled the beginning of a new round of repression and purges.[1] Staging a new play, one that was ideologically ambiguous by an author as controversial as Babel, became too risky an enterprise for anyone to undertake.

Having at first resisted the publication of the play (he wanted the public to be surprised by the play onstage), now Babel thought that once vetted by the censor and published *Maria* would seem less dangerous to the theater establishment. And appear it did in the journal *Teatr i dramaturgiya* in April 1935. But it came into the world carrying its own ball and chain. Running parallel with the text of the play was a patronizing and discouraging review by the influential arts editor of *Pravda*, Isay Lezhnev, who clearly understood Babel's take on the fate of the Revolution. Now *Maria* seemed doomed but for a glimmer of hope. Citing the author's private communication and some of the play's details, suggesting that *Maria* was intended as the second play in a trilogy, the authoritative reviewer advised Babel, if he wished to see his *Maria* staged, to tone down the sex and to clarify his ideological stand in the other parts of the trilogy.

Babel, it appears, tried to oblige, though without much success or enthusiasm. References to some version of *Maria II* crop up from time to time in Babel's correspondence in 1934 and 1935 but they soon trail off, suggesting that the project was abandoned. It had the same fate as Babel's earlier planned peacetime sequel to *Red Cavalry* (his unfinished novel *The Jewess*). Busy with his lucrative assignments for the Soviet film industry, he now focused his efforts in the literary arena on preserving his legacy—negotiating new editions of his writings, with a few new or unpublished stories to justify republication.[2]

Still an important cultural figure, he saw signs that he was again falling out of favor, but friends abroad, associated with the antifascist Popular Front, continued to provide support. After André Gide and André Malraux threatened to walk out of the Congress of Writers in Defense of Culture

9. These acclaimed productions included Vsevolod Ivanov's *Armored Train 14–69* (1927), Konstantin Trenev's *Lyubov Yarovaya* (1926), Vsevolod Vishnevsky's *First Cavalry Army*, (1930) and, of course, Mikhail Bulgakov's *The Days of the Turbins* (1927), which after Stalin's personal intervention became the mainstay of the Maly Theater repertoire.
1. Robert Conquest, *The Great Terror: A Reassessment* (New York and Oxford: Oxford University Press, 1990).
2. The fullest edition of Babel's work during his lifetime came out in a printing of 50,000 copies in September 1936.

and Peace in Paris, Babel and Pasternak were retroactively included in the Soviet delegation and rushed to France in June 1935.[3] This new role in the Soviet antifascist charm offensive in the West, along with the continued protection afforded by Gorky, must have influenced Babel's decision to return to Russia in 1935. But the sense of security, however relative, did not last past the beginning of 1936, when a new campaign of cultural repression was inaugurated by an abusive editorial in *Pravda* against the composer Dmitry Shostakovich. In this atmosphere of increasing ideological *diktat* accompanied by mounting terror, Babel had few illusions left. As he explained his reluctance to publish to his friend Erwin Sinko, the appearance in print of any new work by him meant that he was exposing himself to greater danger.[4] What happened to *Maria* was certainly a case in point. Gorky's illness and death in June 1936 made Babel especially vulnerable, According to a secret police report filed on July 5, 1936, Babel told Antonina Pirozhkova that he had felt invincible as long as Gorky was alive, but he now could no longer be sure.[5] As the Great Terror gathered force, Babel grew desperate. In 1938, perhaps encouraged by Ilya Ehrenburg's surprising departure for France, he pleaded with Malraux to write to Stalin asking him to allow Babel to travel to Paris. For whatever reason (possibly suspecting that Babel might defect), Malraux never complied. He was now busy supporting the Republican cause in Spain and did not wish to find himself on the wrong side of Stalin, whom he considered the Republicans' last hope.[6] In a gesture reminiscent of *Maria*, Malraux sent Babel a warm coat and a copy of his novel, *L'Espoir*.

As Babel's friends were disappearing one after another, his own chances for survival grew bleaker by the day. At times, he tried to remain cheerful when communicating with his mother, but as we know from his letter to Anna Slonim, he often felt paralyzed and depressed. His association with the leaders of antifascist causes in the West was losing its value to the regime now secretly negotiating an alliance with Nazi Germany. Maxim Litvinov, People's Commissar for Foreign Affairs, known for his pro-Western orientation, was sacked on May 3, 1939. As if following the script from *Maria* (page 80), "two citizens came calling" on Babel twelve days later. The charges were standard issue for the Great Terror: spying for France and Austria and conspiring to assassinate the leaders of the Soviet party and state. Beaten and tortured for days by his interrogators, Babel complied with their demands and "confessed," only to renounce his testimony later. Perhaps he believed that the fantastic nature of the charges would open the court's eyes to the sheer absurdity of the indictment against him. But this strategy, if indeed it *was* a strategy, had no effect.

Seven months after his arrest, Babel stood before the rubber-stamp

3. From Mikhail Koltsov's testimony at the Lubyanka on April 9, 1939: "On the third day of the Congress, A. Gide conveyed via Ehrenburg an ultimatum for A.S. Shcherbakov and me: either Babel and Pasternak are sent to Paris immediately or A. Gide and his friends leave the Congress. * * * A. Gide said that only they could be trusted about the information regarding the USSR: 'they alone tell the truth, the rest are bought and paid for.'" Viktor Fradkin, *Delo Koltsova* (Moscow: Vagrius, Mezhdunarodny fond "Demokratiya." 2002), pp. 90–91.
4. See Erwin Sinko's entry in his diary for February 9, 1936, on p. 450.
5. See the secret police report on p. 446.
6. Curtis Cate, *André Malraux: A Biography* (New York: Fromm International Publishing Corp., 1995), p. 264.

court, which took twenty minutes to examine his case and to pronounce him guilty of most charges. He was shot in the Lubyanka basement a few hours later and buried in the same unmarked grave at the Donskoy Monastery in Moscow as were his friends, executed around the same time. Among them were the writer and editor Mikhail Koltsov; the old Chekist friend Efim Evdokimov; the former party boss of Kabardino-Balkaria, Betal Kalmykov; the theater director Vsevolod Meyerhold; and paradoxically the former head of the NKVD, Nikolay Ezhov, whose wife, Evgeniya Solomonovna, had been a close, sometimes intimate, friend of Babel's.[7] Different as they were, all identified with the promise of the Revolution, and all were betrayed—like the Cossack and his bride in the folk ballad that the peasant girl Nyushka belts out as the curtain falls on the final scene of *Maria*.

For the "Messiah from Odessa," once so eager to bring sunshine to Russian letters, it was a vicious night indeed.

---

7. She committed suicide in November 1938.

Isaac Babel: A Chronology

1894   Isaac Bobel (Babel) born to Feyga (later, Faina, 1868–1942),
           née Shvekhvel, and Manus Bobel (later, Emmanuel Babel,
           1865–1924) in the Moldavanka district of Odessa. The family
           soon moves to Nikolayev where Emmanuel Babel begins his
           career as a dealer in agricultural machinery.
           Nicholas I ascends the Russian throne. Odessa celebrates its
           centennial.
1899   Babel's sister Maria (Mera, Mary) born in Nikolayev.
1902   Moscow premiere of Maxim Gorky's play *Lower Depths*; be-
           ginning of Gorky's worldwide fame, second only to that of Leo
           Tolstoy.
1903   Anti-Jewish pogrom in Kishinev.
           Babel denied admission to preparatory class of the Count
           Witte Commercial School in Nikolayev "for lack of vacancies."
1904   Russo-Japanese War begins.
           Death of Anton Chekhov.
           Babel enrolls in the first grade at the Count Witte Commercial
           School.
1905   Revolution of 1905. General strike compels Nicholas I to issue
           the October Manifesto establishing a constitutional monarchy.
           Pogroms sweep the Pale of Settlement, including Nikolayev and
           Odessa.
           Babel leaves Nikolayev to live with his aunts in Odessa at the
           end of 1905.
1906–11   Babel transfers to the second grade of the Odessa Nicholas I
           Commercial School. Babel's parents and sister move back to
           Odessa, and the family eventually settles down in the city cen-
           ter at Richilieu Street 17; Babel takes violin lessons, learns
           French, English, German; studies Hebrew as part of religious
           instruction; frequents theater and opera.
1910   Death of Leo Tolstoy.
1911   Babel enrolls in the Kiev Commercial Institute to study eco-
           nomics and business; meets his future wife Evgeniya Gronfain
           (1897–1957), daughter of a wealthy Kiev industrialist and
           business associate of his father.
1913   Publication of Babel's first known story, "Old Shloyme," in the
           left-wing Kiev weekly *Ogni*.
           Beilis trial in Kiev ends in acquittal.
1914   Babel (reservist III class) granted temporary exemption from
           military service for health reasons; plans to go abroad for
           treatment are thwarted by the outbreak of World War I.

1915   Babel drafted into civil defense corps, military service deferred;
            follows the Kiev Commercial Institute as it is evacuated to
            Saratov where he writes "At Grandmother's."
1916   Completes studies and examinations at the Kiev Commercial
            Institute in Saratov, moves to Petrograd, enrolling in law school
            at the Petrograd Psycho-Neurological Institute; meets Gorky
            who encourages his writing and publishes two of his stories. Ba-
            bel begins to contribute regularly to the Petrograd press.
1917   Babel charged with pornography for one of his stories.
            Nicholas I abdicates; Provisional Government takes power (the
            February Revolution).
            Babel continues to contribute to the Petrograd press through
            April; on Gorky's prompting, leaves Petrograd to "apprentice
            among people," travels as a reporter and, *he claims*, volunteers
            at the Rumanian front.
            Bolshevik coup d'état (the October Revolution).
            The Kiev Commercial Institute issues Babel the diploma of
            Candidate of Economic Science Second Degree, dated Novem-
            ber 10, 1917.
1918   Russian Civil War (1918–21). End of World War I. Josef Pil-
            sudski becomes head of independent Poland, proposes a Feder-
            ation of Poland, Lithuania, Belarus, and Ukraine (Międzymorze
            or Border Federation). Russia adopts Gregorian calendar (Janu-
            ary 31 becomes February 14).
            Babel resumes publication in the Petrograd *Evening Star* and
            Gorky's anti-Bolshevik *New Life* in March; contributes regu-
            larly to *New Life* while working, *he claims*, as translator for the
            Petrograd Cheka.
            After *New Life* is banned in July, Babel is drafted into food-
            procurement expeditions and travels to the Volga region; works
            for the People's Commissariat of Enlightenment; resides at
            Nevsky 86, continues to publish in the Petrograd press.
1919   Red Army retakes Odessa from the Whites in April as French
            occupation forces evacuate.
            Babel, *as he claims*, participates in defense of Petrograd from
            the attacking forces of General Yudenich.
            Returns to Odessa and works in a printing house; marries
            Evgeniya Gronfain on August 9.
            General Denikin's White forces retake Odessa on August 18.
            Beginning of the Russo-Polish War (1919–1920).
1920   The Reds take over Odessa (January).
            Polish forces briefly occupy Kiev; Red Army's successful coun-
            teroffensive threatens Warsaw; Second Congress of the Com-
            intern meets in Petrograd and Moscow. Defeated outside
            Warsaw (August), Red Army retreats; the Curzon Line accepted
            as permanent border between Poland and Russia.
            Babel works for the State Publishing House in Odessa; in April,
            with identity papers in the name of Kiril Vasilyevich Lyutov, joins
            Semyon Budyonny's First Cavalry Army as reporter for *The Red
            Cavalryman* and serves for the duration of the Polish Campaign;

	reports of Babel's death; Babel returns to Odessa in failing health.

1921 End of civil war and War Communism; beginning of the New Economic Policy (NEP, 1921–28), a regime of mixed economy accompanied by relative ideological and cultural tolerance. Famine devastates the Volga region. After his appeals for international relief succeed, the ailing Maxim Gorky leaves Soviet Russia.

Babel's "The King" published in Odessa's newspaper *The Mariner,* the first of *The Odessa Stories.*

1922 Babel travels in Georgia and the Caucasus to improve his health while on assignment for *The Dawn of the Orient,* a Russian-language Georgian newspaper.

Gorky denounces the show trial of Socialist Revolutionaries underway in Moscow.

1923 Publication of *Red Cavalry* stories in Odessa's *Izvestia.*

"Line and Color" and "Pan Apolek" are published in the Moscow fellow-travelers' journal *Red Virgin Soil,* edited by Alexander Voronsky.

Friendship with Vladimir Mayakovsky, poet and editor of the Moscow avant-garde journal *LEF.*

1924 Lenin dies; Stalin in ascendancy.

Stories from *Red Cavalry* and the *Odessa* cycles appear in January in *LEF* and *Red Virgin Soil.* Beginning of Babel's fame. Mayakovsky recites Babel's story "Salt" at public performances. Emmanuel Babel dies in Odessa; Babel and family move permanently to Moscow.

Budyonny attacks Babel for "defaming" the First Cavalry Army.

1925 Publication of *Stories,* Babel's first book, in edition of 50,000 copies.

Babel begins his long and productive career as a screen writer; collaborates with Sergey Eisenstein on the script for *Benya Krik,* based on *The Odessa Stories*; writes intertitles for *Jewish Luck* starring Solomon Mikhoels; writes the script for the film *Salt,* based on his story.

Romance with Tamara Kashirina.

Babel's sister emigrates to Belgium; his wife, Evgeniya, leaves for France. Publication of "The Story of My Dovecote" and "First Love." Babel's third book of stories, *Lyubka Kazak,* printed in edition of 25,000 copies. Friendship with poet Sergey Esenin; Esenin's suicide.

1926 Babel reads from his work at a private meeting with Leon Trotsky.

Publication of the book *The Story of My Dovecote,* followed by the first edition of *Red Cavalry* (soon translated into German and French).

Kashirina gives birth to Babel's first child, Mikhail. Babel writes *Sunset,* his first known play; Babel's mother emigrates to join her daughter in Belgium.

1927   Trotsky and his supporters, including Voronsky, are expelled
         from the party.
         Release of films *Benya Krik* (soon banned) and *Wandering
         Stars* based on Babel's scripts and with his intertitles. In Kiev,
         Babel helps secure the Gronfain property after the death of his
         father-in-law; breaks with Kashirina, leaving her his Moscow
         lodgings, and departs for France; during a stopover in Berlin
         has a brief affair with Evgeniya Khayutina, the future wife of
         Nikolay Yezhov; rejoins his wife in Paris in July, finishes script
         of *Chinese Mill* (released in 1928).

1928   Adoption of First Five-Year Plan inaugurating crash industrial-
         ization and collectivization of agriculture. Writers are mobi-
         lized to depict socialist construction; increasing ideological
         diktat in the cultural sphere; Maxim Gorky visits the USSR to
         take part in official, countrywide celebrations of his sixtieth
         birthday.
         Babel's play *Sunset* produced in Baku, Odessa, and Moscow.
         Publication of *Sunset* and three stories in an almanac.
         Babel returns to Russia in October, travels in the south of
         Russia and North Caucasus, avoids Moscow.

1929   First American edition of *Red Cavalry*.
         Trotsky is exiled from the USSR.
         Gorky praises Babel comparing him to Nikolay Gogol; defends
         Babel against Budyonny's attacks.
         Babel's daughter, Nathalie, is born to Evgeniya Babel in Paris.

1930   Visits Ukrainian countryside outside Kiev to study collectiviza-
         tion and is deeply moved by its horrors; settles in Molodenovo,
         a village outside Moscow near a stud farm; serves as secretary
         for the collective farm council.
         Suicide of Vladimir Mayakovsky.
         Critics begin to speak of Babel's "silence" as a writer.
         Babel falsely accused of making anti-Soviet statements while
         abroad; successfully clears his name but the taint lingers.
         Fourth edition of *Red Cavalry*.

1931   Babel publishes two new childhood stories, one new Odessa
         story, and another about a Ukrainian village, ostensibly part of a
         book on the collectivization of agriculture; hopes to go abroad.
         Resumes direct contact with Gorky, who has just returned to
         the USSR and lives on a country estate near Molodenovo.
         Evgeny Zamyatin receives Stalin's permission to leave the USSR.

1932   Babel finds new lodgings in Moscow, sharing an apartment
         with its owner, Austrian engineer Bruno Steiner.
         Under pressure to produce, Babel publishes four new stories
         and continues to seek permission to visit his family abroad,
         but his travel plans are blocked at the highest level.
         Romance with a young mining engineer, Antonina Pirozhkova.
         Gorky repeatedly intercedes on Babel's behalf, Stalin relents,
         and Babel promptly leaves for Paris to rejoin his wife and
         daughter.

1933   Hitler and the Nazi party come to power in Germany. Publica-
         tion of *Stories* and *Red Cavalry* (eighth edition).

Works on a film project about Evno Azef, a Socialist Revolutionary terrorist and double agent; writes a treatment and a script based on *Red Cavalry* for the French film studio, Pathé. Rumors spread in Moscow about Babel's decision to remain abroad.

Babel visits Gorky in Sorrento and there drafts his play *Maria*. On the way back to Paris, stops in Rome and Florence, on Gorky's bidding, to observe fascism in action.

Gorky returns to the USSR. A delegation of Soviet writers organized by Gorky departs on a boat tour of the White Sea Canal constructed by convict labor and managed by the OGPU.

Babel travels back to Russia via Berlin where he witnesses the burning of proscribed books, *Red Cavalry* among them; in Moscow, penniless and in debt; speaks publicly about the literary scene in France (praises Céline and Nabokov) and Italian fascism.

Travels to the Caucasus to conduct research on a book about Kabardino-Balkaria and its party boss Betal Kalmykov.

Boar hunting in the Caucasus with his important friends.

1934   Seventeenth Party Congress (the "Congress of Victors") celebrates the conclusion of the first Five-Year Plan and reaffirms Stalin's supremacy. Babel travels to the Donbass region to conduct research for a book on industrialization.

Babel's play *Maria* rehearsed in Moscow in the Vakhtangov Theater and the Jewish State Theater, but production is delayed and ultimately cancelled.

Babel works on new drama projects; publishes two new stories.

Stays at Gorky's estate, assisting in preparations for the First Congress of Soviet Writers.

Meets André Malraux, in Moscow, where he attends the Writers' Congress.

At the Congress, Babel exhorts Soviet writers to be less effusive in their panegyrics and learn from Stalin's laconic oratorical style; refers to himself as a "great master of the genre of silence." *Pravda* and *Izvestia* print the speech.

Babel's name crops up in secret police reports on the disloyal attitudes of writers.

Soviet Union begins to support the Popular Front, a coalition of Western left forces, including the communists, against fascism.

Assassination of Leningrad's party boss Sergey Kirov (December 1); introduction of "expedited judicial procedures" in the organs of state security; purges intensify.

1935   Babel attends the Congress of Soviets where a draft of the new constitution is discussed; at night, entertains his important friends who are among the delegates.

The play *Maria* is published.

In Paris, disappointed at the composition of the Soviet delegation, André Malraux and André Gide demand the presence of Babel and Boris Pasternak at the International Congress of Writers in Defense of Culture and Peace. Babel and Pasternak journey to Paris together and speak at the Congress. Afterward, Babel travels in France and Belgium.

Wife Evgeniya refuses to return to Russia with their daughter Nathalie.

In Moscow, Babel sets up household with Antonina Pirozhkova.

1936   Dmitry Shostakovich's opera *Lady Macbeth of Mtsensk* is denounced in *Pravda*, triggering the Campaign against Formalism.

Rumors of Gorky's plan to unite the intelligentsia into a party.

André Malraux, accompanied by Babel and Mikhail Koltsov, visits Gorky in the Crimea to discuss joint projects of the International Association of Writers and to complain about the campaign.

Babel is one of the first writers to be awarded a dacha in the "writers village" in Peredelkino.

Gorky's illness and death.

André Gide begins his tour of the USSR. Babel hosts him in Moscow.

Spanish Civil War begins.

The first trial of the "Trotskyite-Zinovyevite Block" ends in death sentences for former Bolshevik leaders, inaugurating the Great Terror.

Babel collaborates with Eisenstein and travels to Yalta and Odessa for the reshooting of *Bezhin Meadow,* now based on Babel's script.

Publication of *Stories,* the most complete collection of Babel's works to appear in his lifetime, in edition of 50,000 copies.

Gide's *Retour de l'URSS,* critical of the Soviet regime, published in France and denounced in the USSR.

Adoption of the new Soviet Constitution.

1937   The second major show trial opens in Moscow; along with other writers, Babel denounces the accused in *The Literary Gazette.*

Pirozhkova gives birth to Lydia, Babel's second daughter.

Bezhin Meadow attacked in *Pravda*; authorities order the film stock destroyed.

Babel designs the special issue of *USSR In Construction* (journal edited by Evgeniya Yezhov) devoted to Maxim Gorky.

Sweeping purges of the political, military, and cultural elites, including many of Babel's friends and associates.

Publication of "Sulak," "Di Grasso," recollections of Maxim Gorky ("Commencement"), and story "The Kiss."

1938   Works in Kiev on the film script based on Nikolay Ostrovsky's *How the Steel Was Tempered*; publishes his story, "The Trial"; finishes a screenplay, now lost, about the civil war hero Grigory Kotovsky.

Suicide of Babel's old friend and associate, Evgeniya Yezhov (Khayutina), after her husband, the NKVD chief Nikolay Yezhov, is denounced and demoted.

Lavrenty Beria takes over the NKVD from Yezhov.

Babel sends a message to Malraux asking to be recalled to France; Signs a contract for an edition of his collected works; collaborates with director Mark Donskoy on the screen version of Gorky's autobiographical trilogy; completes the script for part three, based on Gorky's *My Universities.*

1939   Great Terror subsides.

Babel completes the script of *Old Square* (the Party Central Committee headquarters in Moscow), a topical film about an industrial manager falsely accused of sabotage who successfully clears his name.

Spanish Civil War ends with the victory of the Nationalists.

Yezhov, under arrest, testifies against Babel. Stalin inquires about the progress of Babel's writing.

Babel is arrested on May 15 and subjected to a seventy-two-hour interrogation and beating. He "confesses" and implicates his friends but then repeatedly renounces his testimony.

German-Soviet Non-Aggression pact signed in Moscow; Soviet and German forces occupy Poland; England and France declare war on Germany.

Babel's pleas to have his testimony reexamined remain unanswered.

1940   Babel is number twelve on the NKVD list of three hundred and forty-six "leading members of counter-revolutionary, right-wing Trotskyite, conspiratorial, and foreign intelligence organizations" who are recommended for execution. Stalin signs the list: "I am for it."

On January 26, Babel is tried, pronounced guilty of spying for France and Austria as well as membership in a Trotskyite conspiracy, and sentenced to death. He is shot early the following morning.

False Rumors circulate for years in the Soviet Union and abroad that he is alive in the Gulag.

1953   Stalin's death.

1954   Babel is officially cleared of all charges.

1955   Babel's *Collected Stories,* with an introduction by Lionel Trilling, is published in New York.

1957   *Selected Stories,* with an introduction by Ilya Ehrenburg, is published in Moscow.

1988   First publications of the documents relating to Babel's interrogation and death.

1990   The first uncensored Soviet edition of Isaac Babel's writings, including *1920 Diary,* published in the USSR, edited by Antonina Pirozhkova and annotated by Sergey Povartso.

Selected Bibliography

Scholarship and Criticism in English

Books

Some eighty books deal with Isaac Babel's literary legacy as well as his life, most of them in languages other than Russian and published largely in the United States. With one exception, the selection below is limited to the major and less-specialized monographs in the English language.

Babel, Isaac. *Sochineniya*, 2 vols. Ed. A. N. Pirozhkova. Annot. S. N. Povartsov. Kudozhestvennaya literatura: Moscow, 1990.

Babel, Isaac. *The Complete Works of Isaac Babel*. Edited with an afterword by Nathalie Babel, translated with notes by Peter Constantine, introduction by Cynthia Ozick. New York: Norton, 2002.

———. *You Must Know Everything: Stories, 1915–1937*. Edited, with notes, by Nathalie Babel, translated from the Russian by Max Hayward. New York: Farrar, Straus and Giroux, 1969.

———. *Isaac Babel: The Lonely Years, 1925–1939: Unpublished Stories and Correspondence*. Edited with an introduction by Nathalie Babel, translated from the Russian by Andrew R. MacAndrew and Max Hayward. Boston: Verba Mundi, David R. Godine, Publisher, 1995.

———. *1920 Diary*. Edited by Carol J. Avins; translated by H. T. Willets. New Haven and London: Yale UP, 1995.

Carden, Patricia. *The Art of Isaac Babel*. Ithaca: Cornell University Press, 1972.

Ehre, Milton. *Isaac Babel*. Boston: Twayne Publishers, 1986.

Falen, James. *Isaac Babel: Russian Master of the Short Story*. Knoxville: University of Tennessee Press, 1974.

Luplow, Carol. *Isaac Babel's Red Cavalry*. Ann Arbor, Mich.: Ardis, 1982.

Pirozhkova, Antonina. *At His Side: The Last Years of Isaac Babel*. South Royalton, Vt.: Steerforth Press, 1996.

Rougle, Charles, ed. *Red Cavalry: A Critical Companion*. Evanston, Ill.: Northwestern UP, 1996.

Shentalinsky, Vitaly. *Arrested Voices: Resurrecting the Disappeared Writers of the Soviet Regime*, trans. John Crowfoot, intro. Robert Conquest. New York: Martin Kessler Books, Free Press, 1996. (Babel's interrogation and trial transcripts from 1939–1940.)

Sicher, Efraim. *Style and Structure in the Prose of Isaak Babel*. Columbus, Ohio: Slavica, 1986.

Articles

Over seven hundred articles, critical and scholarly, deal with Babel's oeuvre. The small selection below is representative of the more recent Babel scholarship. Some of these articles have been collected in Harold Bloom, ed., *Modern Critical Views: Isaak Babel*, with an introduction by Harold Bloom (New Haven, Conn.: Chelsea House, 1987).

Avins, Carol. "Kinship and Concealment in *Red Cavalry* and Babel's 1920 Diary." *Slavic Review* 53.3 (1994): 694–710.

Baak, J. J. van. "Story and Cycle: Babel's 'Poceluj' [The Kiss] and *Konarmiia*." *Russian Literature* 15.3 (1984): 321–46.

Borenstein, Eugene. "Isaak Babel: Dead Fathers and Sons." *Men Without Women: Masculinity and Revolution in Russian Fiction, 1917–1929*. Durham, N.C.: Duke University Press, 2000, pp. 73–124.

Brown, Stephen. "The Jew Among the Cossacks: Isaac Babel and the Red Cavalry in the Soviet-Polish War of 1920." *Slavonica* 3.1 (1996–97): 29–43.
Cukierman, W. "The Odessan Myth and Idiom in Some Early Works of Odessa Writers." *Canadian-American Slavic Studies* 14.1 (1980): 36–51.
Davies, Norman. "Izaak Babel's *Konarmiia* Stories and the Polish-Soviet War." *Modern Language Review* 67.4 (1972): 845–57.
Erlich, Victor. "Color and Line: The Art of Isaac Babel." *Modernism and Revolution: Russian Literature in Transition.* Cambridge, Mass.: Harvard UP, 1994, pp. 145–62 (included in Bloom's *Modern Critical Views*).
Freidin, Gregory. "Fat Tuesday in Odessa: Isaak Babel's 'Di Grasso' as Testament and Manifesto." *Russian Review* 40.2 (1981): 101–21 (an abridged version included in Bloom's *Modern Critical Views*).
Freidin, Gregory. "Isaak Babel." *European Writers: The Twentieth Century,* vol. 2, 1885–1914, ed. George Stade. New York: Scribner's, 1989.
Heil, Jerry. "Isaak Babel and his Film-Work." *Russian Literature* 27.3 (1990): 289–416.
Markish, Simon. "The Example of Isaac Babel." *What's Jewish Literature?,* ed. Hana Wirth-Nesher. Philadelphia: Jewish Publication Society of America, 1994, pp. 199–215 (included in Bloom's *Modern Critical Views*).
Rosenthal, Raymond. "The Fate of Isaac Babel: A Child of the Russian Emancipation." *Commentary* 3 (1947): 126–31 (included in Bloom's *Modern Critical Views*).
Safran, Gabriella. "Isaac Babel's El'ia Isaakovich as a New Jewish Type." *Slavic Review* 61.2 (Summer 2002): 253–72.
Sicher, Efraim. "The Three Deaths of Isaac Emmanuilovich Babel." *Enemies of the People: The Destruction of Soviet Literary, Theater, and Film Arts in the 1920s,* ed. Katherine Eaton. Evanston: Northwestern UP, 2002, pp. 179–204.
Siniavsky, Andrei. "Isaac Babel." *Major Soviet Writers,* ed., Edward J. Brown. London, New York: Oxford University Press, 1973, pp. 301–309.
Terras, Victor. "Line and Color: The Structure of I. Babel's Short Stories in *Red Cavalry*." *Studies in Short Fiction* 3, 2 (1966): 141–56 (included in Bloom's *Modern Critical Views*).
Zholkovsky, Alexander. "How a Russian Maupassant Was Made in Odessa and Yasnaya Polyana: Isaak Babel and the Tolstoy Legacy." *Slavic Review* 53.3 (1994): 671–93.